THE
COMMUNITY COLLEGE
STUDENT

THE COMMUNITY COLLEGE STUDENT

Leonard V. Koos

UNIVERSITY OF FLORIDA PRESS
Gainesville / 1970

A University of Florida Press Book

The type for the text of this book
is ten-point Times New Roman.
The display is Goudy Old Style (Ludlow).

COPYRIGHT © 1970 BY THE STATE OF FLORIDA
DEPARTMENT OF GENERAL SERVICES

All rights reserved

Library of Congress
Catalog Card No. 76-630256
ISBN 0-8130-0299-0

MANUFACTURED FOR THE PUBLISHERS BY
LITHO ARTS, INCORPORATED
MIAMI, FLORIDA

To Hazel S. K.

Contents

Foreword by JAMES L. WATTENBARGER / xi

Preface / xiii

Part I
The Later Adolescent

1 Physical Development / 3
Ages of Community College Students / Growth in Height and Weight / Other Physical Changes / Physiological Changes / Growth in Strength and Motor Performance / A Cautionary Word Concerning Measurements / Body Types / Summary / References and Bibliography

2 Mental Development / 39
From Childhood to Youth / Mental Change Through the Life Span / Mental Growth During College Years / Relation of Mental to Physical Growth and to Maturation / Change in Mental Organization with Age / Giftedness and Creativity / Summary / References and Bibliography

3 Personal and Social Development / 69
Explaining Adolescent Behavior / Problems and Interests of Adolescents / Developmental Tasks of Adolescence / The Influence of the Peer Culture / Emancipation from Parents / Assumption of the Social-Sex Role / Attitudes and Values / Religion: Attitudes and Beliefs / Consistency and Change in Personality and Character with Age / Criteria of Maturity / Summary / References and Bibliography

4 Sexual and Dating Behavior / 146
Sexual Behavior / Dating, Including Courtship / Social Policy / Summary / References and Bibliography

5 Occupational Interests / 187

Occupational Preferences and Plans / Vocational Interests as Disclosed by Blanks and Inventories / Summary / References and Bibliography

6 Recreational Interests / 234

Overview of Play and Recreation / Voluntary Reading / Movies, Radio, and Television / Inquiries for Significant Relationships / Summary / References and Bibliography

Part II
Focus on the Student

7 Aptitude, Social Status, and Academic Competence / 269

The Issue of Clientele of the Community College / Comparisons of Aptitude / Comparisons of Socioeconomic Status / Two Comparisons Involving Both Ability and Environmental Factors / Follow-up Inquiries of Junior College Graduates / Academic Deficiencies and Study Habits

8 Personal Characteristics, Attitudes, and Interests / 314

Personal Characteristics / A Comparison on Socioeconomic Values / Interests—Health, Marital, Vocational, and Avocational / Summary (Chapters 7–8) / References and Bibliography (Chapters 7–8)

9 Personal Problems / 350

Identifying the Problems / Other Studies with the Mooney List / Further Studies of Problems / Uses of Data on Student Problems / Summary / References and Bibliography

10 Adult Education and the Adult Student / 385

Growth and Status of Adult Education / The Rationale of Adult Education / Abilities of Adults / Characteristics and Interests of Adult Students / Summary / References and Bibliography

Part III
Implications for the Program

11 Implications for the Curriculum / 433

Purposes of the Community College / General Education / Health and Physical Education / Communications and the Humanities / The Social

Studies, Including History / Instruction in Marriage and Family / Home Economics / Science and Mathematics / Terminal Occupational Education / Transfer Curriculums / Remedial and Developmental Programs / Innovation in Curriculum / Summary / References and Bibliography

12   The Student Personnel Program   /   508

Concept, Need, and Proposals / Admission, Appraisal, and Orientation / Student Services / Student Organizations and Activities / Summary / References and Bibliography

Acknowledgments   /   559

Author Index   /   565

Subject Index   /   570

Foreword

IN EVERY FIELD of inquiry there are certain studies which are recognized as landmark contributions. These studies may be basic to later studies; often they are predictive; at other times, they are normative. Leonard V. Koos in 1924 authored such a study and it has served all these purposes. It was a Research Publication of the University of Minnesota, Education Series No. 5, *The Junior College*. This two-volume publication became the basic contribution to later studies carried out by several generations of researchers in higher education.

Since 1924 the junior college has evolved into the community college and has become the model for institutional development at the post-high-school level. Today more than 2,250,000 students are enrolled in more than 1,000 community junior colleges. All fifty states have now developed these institutions and more and more often they are designed to serve total statewide needs at this post-high-school level. In several "pacesetter" states such as California, Florida, New York, Michigan, Illinois, and Washington, up to two-thirds of the first-time-in-college students are enrolled in community colleges.

During the forty-six years since the publication of Koos' monumental study, a great amount of attention has been given to organizational structure, definition of curriculum, consideration of faculty, and many other specific areas of study. A multitude of individual studies have considered the community college student but there has been no definitive description of these students. Few studies have given attention to the community college student with the scholarly care which is characteristic of Leonard V. Koos. This book represents the research of several years and pulls together a myriad of data about such students. Koos has thoroughly analyzed these data and has included a description of existing research. The result is the most complete profile of the student at this post-high-school level ever published. Undoubtedly it will be basic to many subsequent studies.

FOREWORD

Since the University of Minnesota published the first Koos study, it is fitting and appropriate that this study on the community college student be published by another state university, the University of Florida. As Koos once again makes an outstanding contribution to the literature of the community college field, it is apparent that his professional competence continues to be a model to emulate.

James L. Wattenbarger, Director
Institute of Higher Education
University of Florida

Preface

THE RATIONALE of this book is analogous to that which has made courses in child development a requirement in programs of preparation of elementary school teachers and, similarly, courses on adolescence a requirement for high school teachers in preparation. Over a long period it has been the writer's conviction that teachers, administrators, counselors, and other professional personnel at work with junior college students should have ready access to as nearly a comprehensive understanding of them as is possible with the information available. Relevant researches and writings are widely scattered and no such synthesis has up to this time been at hand.

The scope of the treatment is evident in the part and chapter outline of the book. After first reviewing evidence concerning the ages of full-time junior college students and establishing that they are preponderantly in later adolescence, the chapters of Part I summarize information in print concerning the physical, mental, personal and social development, sexual and dating behavior, and vocational and avocational interests of this age-group. Against this background the chapters of Part II focus on the community college student himself; that is, on his aptitude, socioeconomic status, academic competence, personal characteristics, attitudes, interests, and personal problems. Because adults make up a minority of full-time and a large majority of part-time students, this part includes a chapter on adult education and the adult student. Part III is given over to consideration of the implications of the first two parts for the program of the community college.

Although this synthesis is based on more than three hundred researches in the behavioral sciences bearing more or less directly on later adolescents and/or junior college students, not to mention an extensive body of descriptive and interpretive literature dealing with this population and programs aimed at serving its needs, one can hardly pretend that an all-inclusive understanding is provided. Serious lacunae are left by the reports of researches and other literature drawn upon, and it is a secondary purpose of the treatment, nevertheless an important one, to make these lacunae apparent, with the prospect that readers may be moved themselves to conduct or to encourage others to carry on further research to fill the gaps.

A further word may be in order concerning two of the more serious limitations of published studies that can be drawn upon for a synthesis on later adolescents and community college students. One of these is the relative dearth of longitudinal studies carrying through the full period of later adolescence. This lack is brought on by the fact that in our organization of schools the break between high school and college cuts across this period, and most of the studies either carry up only to the end of the high school or begin with the freshman college year. This obstacle is especially apparent in Part I, where many of the studies drawn upon carry the student only to the threshold of the college and not into early college years. To mitigate to some extent this limitation, the treatment in the chapters of this part must make more use than would be otherwise desirable of evidence from investigations that begin with early adolescence, or even pre-adolescence, so as to project trends that may be expected to continue through the full period of later adolescence. The other limitation is the lack of published studies of characteristics and important aspects of behavior and interest of the community college population itself, which makes it necessary in some areas to report evidence along these lines for other populations at this age-level and to speculate over similarities and differences for such understanding as this may provide.

The writer is under heavy obligation to many persons for encouragement and cooperation while the manuscript was in preparation. Among these are Dr. J. B. White, Dean Emeritus, and Dr. Kimball Wiles, late Dean of the College of Education, at the University of Florida, who approved arrangements for assistance and working space for the project. The following persons, all members of the staff of the Southeastern Junior College Administrative Leadership Program (subsidized by the W. K. Kellogg Foundation), have been helpful through consultation and through permitting try-out of materials for the book in their courses variously concerned with the junior college, college curriculum, college administration, and adult education: Dr. Robert R. Wiegman, formerly Co-director of the Program at the University of Florida (now Dean of the College of Education, Florida Atlantic University); Dr. Raymond E. Schultz, Co-director of the Program and Professor in the Department of Higher Education at Florida State University; Dr. James L. Wattenbarger, currently Co-director of the Program and Director of the Institute of Higher Education, University of Florida; Drs. Willis A. LaVire and Maurice L. Litton, Associate Directors of the Program, respectively, at the University of Florida and Florida State University; Drs. Edwin L. Kurth and Raymond P. Perkins at the University of Florida. In securing access to published materials related to the project the writer has enjoyed the generous cooperation of Professor Hazen E. Nutter, Librarian for the College of Education at the University of Florida, and members of his staff, Miss Linda Sparks and Mrs. Virginia Goodwin. The typescript was prepared by Mrs. Dorothy S. Sappington, who has provided competent and gracious assistance on the project in many other ways.

The cost of publication has been covered in part by the W. C. Kellogg Foundation.

Leonard V. Koos

Part I

The Later Adolescent

1
Physical Development

IN ADVANCE of a canvass of the stage of development and the characteristics of the student body of an institution, like the junior college, it is in point to have in mind the age, or predominant age-group, of the student population. To supply this information, the consideration in this, and the five succeeding chapters, of the physical, mental, and other characteristics and interests of later adolescence is being preceded by presentation of evidence concerning the ages of community college students. As a result, with the more precise knowledge than the reader might otherwise have of the age-group being served by the community college, he should be able to apply the evidence on the development and characteristics reviewed toward a better understanding of the community college student.

Ages of Community College Students

A recent sampling.—One may concede at once that the ages of a large proportion of community college students may be inferred from the fact that it is an institution covering a two-year span following graduation from the high school below. Graduation from high school comes now typically at the age seventeen or eighteen, from which one may readily assume that the typical age of community college students, in view of its two-year span, might be 17 to 20 years. However, there may well be delays at entrance, varying degrees of selection, or other factors at work that influence the distribution of ages in such a student body. In addition, it seems essential to have before one something like a full and precise portrayal of the age distribution in order to interpret better the information on physical, mental, social, and other characteristics in application to the student body.

To this end, evidence is reported here from a recent sampling of community college students, comparisons are made with two earlier studies and a more recent report, and conclusions drawn as to the dominant age-group and the full range of ages.

The recent sampling is of five community colleges in three states, Illinois, Michigan, and Florida. The institutions were conveniently at hand for the writer and the sample, while hardly a large one, is believed to be adequate for the present purpose and for the conclusions drawn. The distributions of ages of these full-time students in the first college year, the second college

TABLE 1.1
DISTRIBUTION BY AGES IN YEARS OF A SAMPLING OF FULL-TIME STUDENTS IN FIVE COMMUNITY COLLEGES

Ages	First Year	Second Year	Both Years
15	1	–	1
16	5	–	5
17	81	9	90
18	147	77	224
19	29	114	143
20	7	30	37
21	7	13	20
22	9	11	20
23	7	10	17
24	3	11	14
25	1	8	9
26	2	3	5
27	3	4	7
28	1	1	2
29	–	3	3
30	2	2	4
31–35	1	4	5
36–40	5	6	11
41–50	1	3	4
51–60	–	2	2
TOTALS	312	311	623
MEDIAN	18	19	18
FIRST QUARTILE	17	18	18
THIRD QUARTILE	19	21	20

year, and in both years are displayed in Table 1.1. It may be noted that the distribution for the first year ranges from 15 years to the 41–50 year interval; for the second year it ranges from 17 to the 51–60 year interval; for both years over the full span from 15 to 51–60 years.

However, a heavy concentration is to be seen for the ages of 17 and 18 in first-year students, for 18 and 19 for second-year students, and for 17, 18, and 19 for both years. These concentrations are reflected in the median and the interquartile ranges reported at the foot of the columns in this table: for the first-year students the median age is 18, and the range in ages of the middle 50 per cent is from 17 to 19; for the second-year students the median is 19, and the range of the middle 50 per cent is 18 to 21; for both years the median is 18, and the range of the middle 50 per cent is 18 to 20.

PHYSICAL DEVELOPMENT

TABLE 1.2
CUMULATIVE PERCENTAGES OF THE AGES OF STUDENTS

Age	First Year	Second Year	Both Years	Age	First Year	Second Year	Both Years
15	0.3	0.0	0.2	25	95.2	91.0	93.1
16	2.0	0.0	0.9	26	95.8	92.0	93.9
17	27.9	2.9	15.4	27	96.8	93.2	95.0
18	75.0	27.7	51.4	28	97.1	93.6	95.3
19	84.3	64.6	74.3	29	–	94.5	95.8
20	86.5	74.0	80.3	30	97.8	95.2	96.5
21	88.8	78.1	83.5	31–35	98.1	96.5	97.3
22	91.7	81.7	86.7	36–40	99.7	98.4	99.0
23	93.9	84.9	89.4	41–50	100.0	99.4	99.7
24	94.9	88.4	91.7	51–60	–	100.0	100.0

SOURCE: Table 1.1.

In interpreting these figures it is well to bear in mind that these ages are reported as of the opening of the school year, almost always in September. From this one may infer that the distribution, if made later on during the school year, would find larger proportions at the 19 and 20 levels, and, therefore, somewhat nearer the end of the "second decade" of life.

The fact of concentration of students in the age groups indicated above

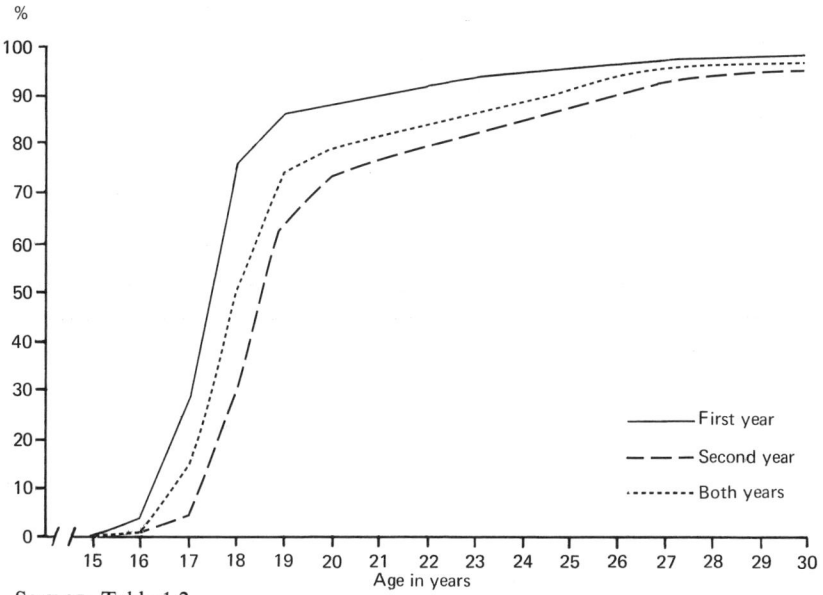

FIG. 1.1
CUMULATIVE PERCENTAGES OF FIRST-YEAR, SECOND-YEAR, AND ALL FULL-TIME STUDENTS IN FIVE LOCAL PUBLIC JUNIOR COLLEGES
(THROUGH 30 YEARS OF AGE)

SOURCE: Table 1.2.

as predominant is underscored by reporting and depicting cumulative percentages, as is done in Table 1.2 and Figure 1.1. In these, the measures, computed from the data in Table 1.1, indicate the percentages of students of and below given ages. For example, one may note that 27.9 per cent of all the first-year students represented were 17 years of age or under. The figure carries the portrayal through only 30 years of age. The impression gained from the rapidly mounting percentages up to 19 or 20 and the slowly rising percentages after these ages is clearly of a student body predominantly in the last few years of the second decade of life. Only a relatively small proportion, roughly an eighth of the first-year students, a fifth of second-year students, and a sixth of students in both years, were reported as older than 20 at the opening of the school term.

TABLE 1.3
MEDIAN AND FIRST AND THIRD QUARTILE AGES IN YEARS AND MONTHS OF FRESHMEN IN SIXTEEN PUBLIC JUNIOR COLLEGES IN 1921–22

Measure	Men	Women	Both
Median	18–6	18–2	18–4
First Quartile	17–9	17–6	17–8
Third Quartile	19–5	18–10	19–2

SOURCE: Drawn from Table LX, p. 170, in Leonard V. Koos, *The Junior College*, vol. 1, Research Publications of the University of Minnesota, 1924.

Comparison with 1921–22.—An impression of the relative stability of the ages of community college students over the years is supplied by comparing the coincidence just reported with computations made by this writer on the ages of freshmen in sixteen public junior colleges for 1921–22. The median and first and third quartile ages as found in this early inquiry are reported in Table 1.3. The earlier inquiry gave tabulations in years and months of age at entrance and this procedure prevents exact comparison with the same measures at the foot of the column for first-year students in Table 1.1. Nevertheless, if the months in the measures for the students of both sexes in Table 1.3 are ignored in the comparison, the ages for the three measures are found to be identical; that is, 18 for the median ages and 17 and 19 as the limits of the interquartile ranges. It may be noted that the measures for women in Table 1.3 are slightly lower by a few to several months than for men, a finding corresponding with a difference that has been reported in studies of the ages of boys and girls at the high school level.

Comparison with Medsker's evidence.—In 1956, Leland Medsker undertook for the Center for the Study of Higher Education at the University of California at Berkeley a large-scale investigation of two-year colleges of various types, a report on which was published in 1960.* Appendix M in this publication lists 78 units in 15 states, which he refers to as "cooperating two-year colleges." Among the types of information secured from ten of these institutions were the ages of "regular day students" and this evidence was compiled and presented in Table 2–6 (p. 43) in his report. For the sake of a comparison with Medsker's evidence, his grouping of ages was followed in a retabulation for the five community colleges represented in the writer's sampling, with results as shown in Table 1.4. Whereas Medsker

TABLE 1.4
NUMBERS AND PERCENTAGES OF STUDENTS BY AGE-GROUPS IN THE AUTHOR'S SAMPLE AND IN MEDSKER'S STUDY

Age	Author's Sample						Medsker's Study	
	Men		Women		All			
	Number	Per Cent	Number	Per Cent	Number	Per Cent	Number	Per Cent
15	1	0.3	–	–	1	0.2	–	–
16–17	49	12.4	46	20.2	95	15.2	270	2
18	132	33.4	92	40.4	224	36.0	3,256	24
19	92	23.3	51	22.4	143	23.0	2,331	17
20–22	69	17.5	8	3.5	77	12.4	1,314	10
Subtotals	343	86.8	197	86.4	540	86.7	7,171	53
23–25	37	9.4	3	1.3	40	6.4	2,506	19
26–29	10	2.5	7	3.1	17	2.7	1,554	12
30 and over	5	1.3	21	9.2	26	4.2	2,073	16
Subtotals	52	13.2	31	13.6	83	13.3	6,133	47
Totals	395	100.0	228	100.0	623	100.0	13,304	100

SOURCE: Leland L. Medsker, *The Junior College: Progress and Prospect* (New York: McGraw-Hill Book Co., 1960), from Table 2–6, p. 43.

found only well over half (53 per cent) of the students (see last column) in the 22-years-and-under groups, with 47 per cent in the groups including students 23 years of age and over, the present writer's figures for a recent period show 86.7 per cent—almost seven-eighths of all—in the 22-and-under groups.

The disparity between the two distributions is so wide as to call for speculation over the causes of the difference. One important factor is the decline during the interval between the two studies in the number and proportion of veterans of the armed forces in the student body. A second

---

*Leland L. Medsker, *The Junior College: Progress and Prospect* (New York: McGraw-Hill Book Co., 1960). *Note:* With a small proportion of exceptions, documentation in this treatise is not, as in this instance, by footnote, but by numbered items in the References and Bibliography at the ends of the chapters. Citation of articles is by the number of item only and reference to books and monographs includes both item number and pages.

important factor may be found in the types of institutions represented. The five institutions represented in the author's sample are all local public institutions with relatively few nonresident students. At least a full third of Medsker's total group of 78 cooperating institutions were private or regional institutions, with larger and considerable proportions of nonresident students. One influence of nonresidence is to delay to some extent for various reasons entrance upon college work. This was seen in a portion of the early investigation of the ages of students already drawn upon above in establishing the stability of ages over the years in the junior college student body. In this portion of the investigation, this writer compared the ages of freshmen in the University of Minnesota (a) whose residences were outside the Twin Cities (Minneapolis and St. Paul) and suburbs and (b) whose residences were within the Twin Cities or suburbs. The median age of the former group was 19 years, and of the latter group 18 years, 3 months—a difference in the medians of 9 months. The interquartile range for the former group was 18 years, 2 months, to 20 years, 3 months; for the latter group, 17 years, 6 months, to 19 years, 1 month. Thus one effect of localization of the student body which is encouraged by the community college is to lower appreciably the age of college attendance.

More recent evidence concerning the ages of junior college students than that from the writer's sample is available in an investigation of characteristics of full-time students in the junior colleges of Minnesota by White.* The procedure in tabulation differs from those followed in the evidence on ages previously reported here, but not so widely as to prevent plausible comparison. The tabulation for this study is that of their years of birth as reported by students in twelve junior colleges (ten public and two private) in this state, this number including all but two such institutions in the state in 1962. A total of 2,831 students (2,360 in public and 471 in private units) is represented in the following percentage distribution of years of birth:

	1944–45	1943	1942	1941	1940	1939 AND EARLIER	NO INFORMATION
Public	0.8	45.7	36.0	6.2	3.0	8.0	0.3
Private	2.1	41.2	46.9	5.7	1.7	2.4	—
All Junior Colleges	1.0	44.9	37.8	6.1	2.8	7.2	0.2

Simple addition of the percentages discloses that 82.5 per cent of students in the public units, 90.2 per cent of those in private units, and 82.7 per cent

---

*Richard E. White, "Patterns of Institutional Press Among Selected Groups of Junior College Students" (Ph.D. thesis, University of Minnesota, 1965), p. 67.

(well over four-fifths) of those in both units were under 20 years of age.

In view of the evidence presented from these several compilations, it seems safe to conclude that typically the ages of no less than two-thirds to four-fifths and even up to nine-tenths or more of the community college student body are within the later years of the second decade of life, meaning by this the ages of 17, 18, 19, and 20. As stated at the opening of the chapter, it is appropriate to bear this important fact in mind while reviewing the evidence on the characteristics and stage of development in the population during this age span.

This is not to say that the nature and characteristics of older students can be ignored. After all, these older students make up at least a significant minority of the full-time student body in every community college. At the same time, these characteristics and stages of development are those mainly of early and later adulthood, into which the nature and characteristics of later adolescents merge. The characteristics of the older group are reviewed in a later chapter of this book (Chapter 10).

Age differences of the sexes.—Any consideration of the ages of community college students should inquire into the similarities and differences in the ages of men and women in attendance. The subtotals in the columns of percentages for men and women in the author's sample in Table 1.4 yield an impression of practically no difference between the two, as the percentage of men 22 and under is 86.8, and that for women is 86.4. Correspondingly, the percentages for men and women 23 and over are, respectively, 13.2 and 13.6. However, examination of the distribution of percentages *above* the subtotals mentioned does disclose a tendency to difference, with a perceptibly larger proportion of women than of men in the 16–17 and 18 year groups and a perceptibly larger proportion of men in the 20–22 year group. Specifically, the percentage of men 16–17 years of age in this sample was 12.4, while that of women was 20.2; and the percentage of men 18 years of age was 33.4, while that of women was 40.4. The percentages at 19 were not far apart, but the percentages for men and women from 20–22 were, respectively, 17.5 and 3.5.

A similar tendency to difference is seen also in the figures compiled by the author for junior colleges in 1921–22, as reported in Table 1.3 above. The man of median age was older by four months than the woman of median age. There were three months difference in the same direction at the first quartile and seven months at the third quartile.

Without going into a lengthy explanation in advance of the consideration of the physical, mental, and other characteristics of youth in the later years of the second decade of life in this and subsequent chapters, one may say that the tendency to difference in ages is in harmony with the somewhat earlier maturity of women than of men.

Growth in Height and Weight

Preview of the treatment.—With the facts at hand concerning the ages, more especially the predominant ages of 17 through 20 years, of students in community colleges, we may proceed to consideration of the growth and characteristics of the population of these ages, in an effort to apply these facts of growth and characteristics to the putative community college student body. In the remaining portions of this chapter, evidence from the realm of the physical and physiological growth and status will be reviewed;

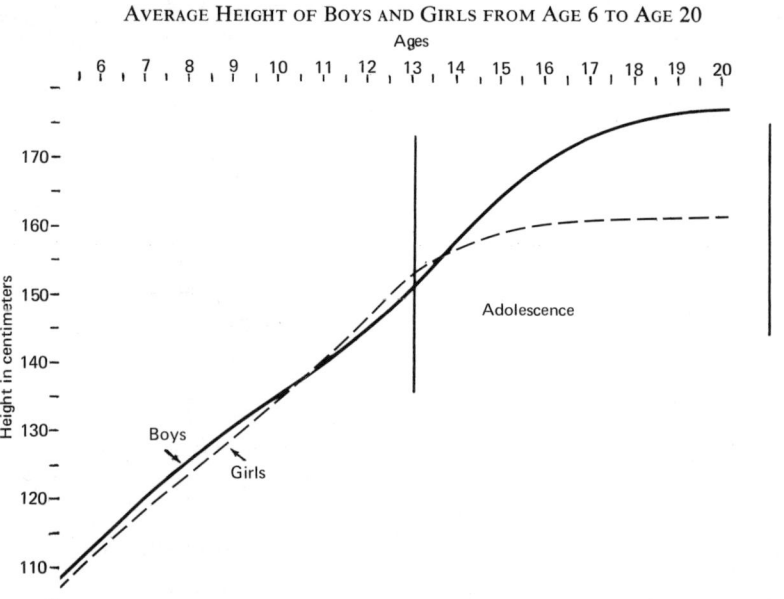

FIG. 1.2
AVERAGE HEIGHT OF BOYS AND GIRLS FROM AGE 6 TO AGE 20

SOURCE: Drawn from Shuttleworth (*28*, 248–49).

evidence on mental, or intellectual, growth and status in Chapter 2; on personality and attitudes in Chapter 3; on sexual and dating behavior in Chapter 4; and on vocational and recreational interests and preferences, respectively, in Chapters 5 and 6.

In order to achieve an effective understanding of the physical characteristics of the predominant community college age-group, it is necessary to keep the group in a setting for comparison with younger and older ages in the population. To this end, evidence concerning younger and older ages will be reviewed so as to identify the stage or stages of growth toward maturity which the community college student may have attained. At many points, the status of the later adolescent may be better understood when the stages out of which he comes and into which he grows are in view. The intent will be to focus on the population of the 17-through-20 years group.

Curves of growth in height and weight.—The description of the later adolescent may well begin with the facts concerning growth in the external characteristics of height and weight. For this purpose, the curves drawn from averages at each age reported by Shuttleworth (*28*) are presented in Figures 1.2 and 1.3. The course of growth in height of the members of both

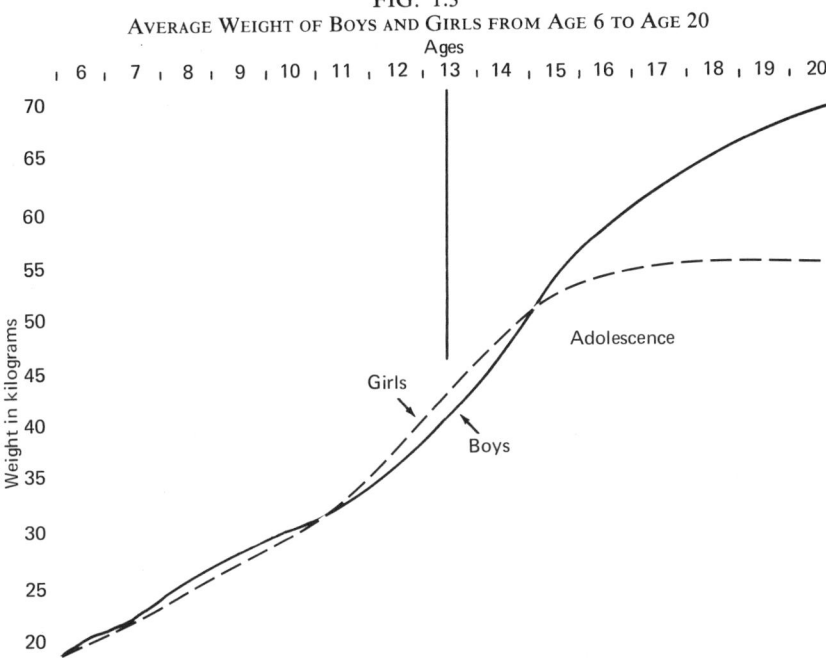

FIG. 1.3
AVERAGE WEIGHT OF BOYS AND GIRLS FROM AGE 6 TO AGE 20

SOURCE: Drawn from Shuttleworth (*28*, 248–49).

sexes describes something approaching a straight line from the age of 6 to 13 or 14 but the curve then flattens rapidly, first for girls and a year or so later for boys. Both curves are almost flat by the end of the period, but that for boys indicates a notably greater stature for them than for girls. Close scrutiny of the curves shows that, on the average, boys are slightly taller than girls up to about 10, when the girls, on the average, slightly surpass the boys until about 13 or 14.

The curves for weight in Figure 1.3 disclose the same approximately straight line growth to 13 or 14 for both sexes, with the average weights slightly less for girls than for boys up to about 10 and averages for boys somewhat less from this point to about 14. There is also the same earlier trend to flattening of the curve for girls from about 13, a trend to increasing flattening for boys a year or so later, and a large difference in weight in favor of boys at the later ages.

Proportion of mature height at successive ages.—Interpretation of Figures 1.2 and 1.3 noted the flattening of the curves of growth for both boys and girls beginning with the thirteenth and fourteenth years, which means a slowing down of growth as adult dimensions are being achieved. How near youth in these later years of the second decade of life are to maturity in respect to height is made apparent in Table 1.5 which is adapted from data reported by Bayer and Bayley (*3*, 46, Table 6).

TABLE 1.5
PMH (PERCENTAGE OF MATURE HEIGHT) ACHIEVED BY BOYS AND GIRLS AT SUCCESSIVE AGES, 10 TO 18 YEARS

Age	Boys	Girls	Age	Boys	Girls
10.0	78.40	84.76	14.5	92.60	98.74
10.5	79.82	86.85	15.0	94.60	99.31
11.0	81.30	88.65	15.5	96.00	99.54
11.5	82.54	90.81	16.0	97.09	99.62
12.0	84.00	92.61	16.5	97.95	99.75
12.5	85.43	94.72	17.0	98.79	99.95
13.0	87.32	95.96	17.5	99.28	99.91
13.5	89.22	97.17	18.0	99.55	99.96
14.0	91.00	98.27			

SOURCE: Adapted from Bayer and Bayley (*3*, 46, Table 6).

It may seem that by the age of 10 girls have achieved a larger proportion of their stature at maturity than boys, and the proportion remains greater than that for boys throughout the period to 18 years of age although the difference decreases with the approach to 18. In point of fact, the average girl has attained almost all her adult stature by the age of 15, and will gain little in height after that age. The average boy does not attain the equivalent percentage reached by the girl at 15 until he is 17½. At 18 he still has some growth to achieve.

As everyone knows, youth vary widely in their rates of growth in stature and in other ways, some growing at a rapid rate, some at a slow rate, and others at rates between. The same authors whose evidence concerning PMH has just been cited have plotted also analogous percentage measures for groups of youth they have designated as "average," "accelerated," and "retarded," these terms applying specifically to stature. The measures they report for boys and girls on these three groups are presented in Table 1.6. One may note that boys in the average group have reached mature stature at 18½ years, the accelerated group a year earlier, and the retarded group not until they are 20. By contrast, the group of average girls has reached mature height at 17, the accelerated group at 16½, and the retarded group at 18.

Growth as related to MG-age.—As one may infer from the evidence just cited from Bayer and Bayley, the curves of rates of growth drawn from studies by Shuttleworth and based on averages of large numbers of subjects at given ages conceal the fact of wide differences among individuals and among groups of individuals in the population represented. As one aspect of the Harvard Growth Study, Shuttleworth analyzed his evidence in such a way as to show the extent of variation, to probe for its rationale, and to make reliable comparisons of the difference in growth rates in the two

TABLE 1.6
PMH (Percentage of Mature Height) of Average, Accelerated, and Retarded Boys and Girls

Age	Boys			Girls		
	Average	Accelerated	Retarded	Average	Accelerated	Retarded
10.0	78.0	79.7	76.4	84.4	87.9	81.0
11.0	81.1	83.4	79.5	88.4	92.9	84.9
12.0	84.2	87.2	82.2	92.9	96.6	88.2
13.0	87.3	91.3	84.6	96.5	98.2	91.1
14.0	91.5	95.8	87.6	98.3	99.1	95.2
15.0	96.1	98.3	91.6	99.1	99.5	97.8
16.0	98.3	99.4	95.7	99.6	99.9	98.9
16.5	–	–	–	–	100.0	–
17.0	99.3	99.9	98.2	100.0	–	99.6
17.5	–	100.0	–	–	–	–
18.0	99.8	–	99.2	–	–	100.0
18.5	100.0	–	–	–	–	–
19.0	–	–	99.8	–	–	–
20.0	–	–	100.0	–	–	–

Source: Bayer and Bayley (*3*, *50*).

sexes. Several investigations have disclosed a striking relationship of rates of growth in the individual girl to the time of the menarche (first menstruation). This is an objective and readily identifiable event in the girl's life. No comparably reliable indication is available for boys. Shuttleworth points out that "since the early and late appearance of the characteristically accelerating and decelerating phases of growth in standing height is undoubtedly under the control of endocrine factors, it follows that classification according to the MG-age [his shorthand for the phrase 'age-at-the-close-of-the-year of maximum growth'] automatically provides an approximate grouping of cases according to the timing of endocrine events. Our ignorance of the details of these events as they apply to human growth is profound, but it is nevertheless not a violent assumption to suppose that age at maximum growth is at least as good an indication of timing of endocrine events as age at the advent of the menarche in girls or of sexual maturity in boys" (*28*, 2). Some of the major significance of use of the procedure is made apparent by Figure 4 which is adapted from Shuttleworth's report from Bayley and Tuddenham (*12, 41*, Fig. 4). In presenting the figure these authors direct the reader to "note the more sudden and pronounced growth spurt in the early maturing individuals, and the later and less spectacular growth period among late-maturing individuals." The findings of greatest importance in the figure for the person seeking information con-

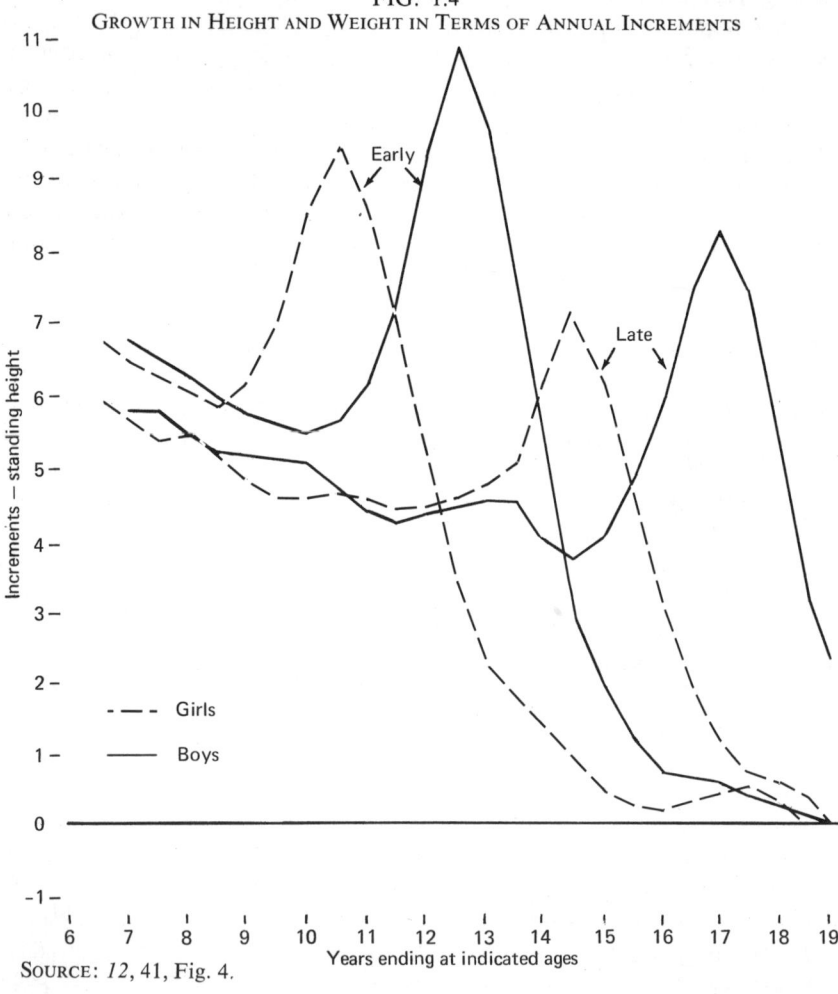

FIG. 1.4
GROWTH IN HEIGHT AND WEIGHT IN TERMS OF ANNUAL INCREMENTS

SOURCE: *12*, 41, Fig. 4.

cerning the physical growth and status of the community college student are to be found in the facts that early maturers among both boys and girls and the late maturers among girls have, on the average, little growth ahead of them to attain their adult statures, and that the only group still due for substantial growth ahead is that including the late-maturing boy.

Rates of growth in relation to menarche.—The facts of rates of growth as influenced by endocrine events are of such significance that it is desirable to cite findings of another investigation. This study is concerned with girls only, and was reported by Simmons and Greulich (*29*). It was made from an analysis of 1,339 examinations at birthdays of 200 girls described, as a group, as "above average socio-economically." The measurements included height, weight, and skeletal ages. The results are reported in annual increments in relation to menarcheal age. The investigators summarized the evidence on growth in height as follows: "The year of maximum increment in standing height is related to menarcheal age; the greatest mean annual height increment occurs between 10 and 11 years for girls with menarches from 10 years to 11 years, 11 months; between 11 and 12 years for girls with menarches from 12 years to 12 years, 11 months; and between 12 and 13 years for girls with menarches from 13 to 15 years. Values of maximum annual increments are negatively related to menarcheal age; girls with early menarches experience the greatest acceleration, followed by the greatest deceleration; girls with late menarches experience the least acceleration followed by the least deceleration. The average girl experiences her greatest height increment during the year preceding the year of menarche; maximum increment does occur during the year of menarche; it does occur during the second year preceding menarche, and some girls with late menarches seem to experience little or no pre-menarcheal acceleration. Maximum increment in standing height, in this series, never occurs after menarche...."

The findings concerning growth in weight and in skeletal ages (extent of ossification of joints in hand, foot, elbow, knee, hip, and shoulder as determined by X-rays) of girls, while not exactly like those of growth in height, are sufficiently similar that brief paraphrase of Simmons and Greulich will suffice for our present purposes. From 7 to 16 years of age the means of weight of girls with early menarches are "invariably" greater than those of girls with late menarches, but the decline in weight increment following the maximum is less marked than the decline in height increment. This decline is most marked for girls with early menarches and least marked for those with late menarches.

In skeletal age assessments, from 7 to 17 years of age, girls in the early menarcheal age group are advanced over the girls in the average menarcheal age group, and girls in this latter group, in turn, are advanced in mean skeletal age over those in the late menarcheal age group. Moreover, skeletal age is more highly correlated with menarcheal age than are standing height, weight, weight-height index, or annual increments in standing height. The curves of plotted increments for this age span among girls show that growth in skeletal age has with minor exceptions practically come to an end by the sixteenth or seventeenth year.

The upshot of the evidence assembled and analyzed by Simmons and Greulich as applied to girls for the predominant age-group in the community college is that almost all of them have attained physical maturity in respect to height, weight, and skeletal age, and that those who have not are very near it.

Height and weight in college years.—With the conclusions at hand from the studies bearing on growth in stature and weight during late adolescence, it should be helpful to an understanding of the student population to know something about the facts of growth and status in these respects concerning men and women in the community college student body. Unfortunately, no

TABLE 1.7
STATURE (IN INCHES) OF STUDENTS AT
ENTRANCE BY AGES, CLASSIFIED TO
THE NEAREST HALF YEAR

Age	Number	Mean Height
16½	159	63.37
17	380	63.35
17½	344	63.35
18	449	63.22
18½	270	63.23
19	179	63.35
19½	91	63.26

SOURCE: Gould (*10*).

published reports in the area are available. Even for student bodies in four-year colleges and universities the number of reports in print on this subject are few, although we may be sure that the files of these institutions contain much of the basic information needed for such an understanding. Moreover, more of the reports in print deal with women in the colleges than with men. On this account, the consideration here begins with women in college and follows with a report on the height and weight of men.

(a) *Height of women.* An early investigation involved women in Newcomb College of Tulane University in New Orleans and was based on records accumulating over a span of twenty years, 1909–1928 (*10*). Measurements were taken every six months from the fall of the freshman year. The modal age at entrance was 18, while the mean age of entrants who remained for the full college course was 17.62 years. Mean ages of students at each half year of age from 16½ to 19½ years are shown in Table 1.7. The means for younger and older ages are omitted because those for smaller numbers of students at the extremes would prove unreliable. It is to be noted that the mean statures for all ages listed are very much alike, with only small fractional differences from age to age and with no apparent trend toward increasing or decreasing height with increase in age at entrance. The investigator noted, in reporting this evidence, that Jackson, at the University of Minnesota (*13*), had found no increase in height with age of male and female students and had suggested that the condition is probably due to a selection of the physically better developed for early college entrance.

However, this finding by Jackson from what may be referred to as single, or "cross-sectional," measurements of a large number of subjects at different ages is not strictly comparable with that from an investigation using successive measurements of the same individuals, in a "longitudinal" study, which were mainly used in the study by Gould (*10*). Measurements made in this way yielded the average increments from year to year of age shown in Table 1.8. The total average increment is not large and it is seen to de-

TABLE 1.8
AVERAGE GROWTH IN STATURE (IN INCHES) DURING
COLLEGE ATTENDANCE BY AGE AT ENTRANCE

Age	Number of Students	Average Increment
16	82	.38
17	315	.32
18	327	.29
19	105	.25

SOURCE: Gould (*10*).

crease with age at entrance. In elaboration of the evidence in this area, the investigator says: "In the group under consideration 678 students increased in height, 89 showed no change, and 100 showed diminution in height. It is quite possible that many cases of apparent loss of stature were due to error of measurement or inconstant posture. . . . One can at least say that 78 per cent of these young women were still growing."

A fact emerging in this study (but not here reported in tabular form) of somewhat special significance for community college students, because the institution they attend is a two-year unit, is that of the entire mean increase of .33 inch over three and a half calendar years, .27 inch—almost all—was attained by the spring of the sophomore year.

The findings just reported concerning growth in height are rather closely paralleled in another investigation reported some years later for women students in Stanford University (*2*). Again, in this investigation, when measurements of independent samples were made at each age from 17 to 21, inclusive, no consistent change in height was found as related to chronological age, but successive measurements of the same individuals disclosed what the authors refer to as "a small significant mean annual increment," the total from 17 to 20 years amounting to approximately .4 inch for the four-year period, which is little different from that reported for the women at Newcomb. The authors say, "the age at which mean growth ceases altogether cannot be stated, but it appears to be at an age beyond twenty years."

The study of Stanford women included consideration of height in relation to the age of menarche. It is desirable to quote the conclusion from this phase of the inquiry (221): "There is a low, positive correlation between menarcheal age and the standing height of Stanford women for the ages 17 to 21. The partial correlation, with age held constant, is $.138 \pm .018$. For each year's difference in menarcheal age there is an average difference in height of .24 inches. This means, for example, that women who reach puberty at 15 years of age are, on the average, almost one inch taller than those who become pubescent at 11 years."

(b) *Weight of women.* In respect to matters of weight the investigations of women at Newcomb and Stanford come to somewhat but not notably different conclusions. Gould reports (*10*) that the mean weight of his subjects "increases but slightly during the four years" and that at no time did his students become as heavy as the freshman women at certain northern and western institutions. He said further that, while there is no significant change in weight alone, the weight-height index (ratio of weight to height) shows a trend toward slenderness, particularly in the last few years of the period covered by his study. It is not unlikely that this trend was brought about by the increasing concern of young women over their weight and their consequent attention to diet.

In the investigation at Stanford (*2*) it was found that the mean annual increment, while small, was "significant" for the ages 17 to 19 and that the total increment for the four-year period was approximately 5.75 pounds. At the age of 17 there was a small negative correlation ($-.233 \pm .034$) between weight and menarcheal age, a relation which decreased progressively with chronological age so that by 20 and 21 years the correlation was entirely absent. The women with relatively late menarcheal ages as girls continued to increase in weight during college years slightly more rapidly than those with early menarcheal ages.

These facts concerning growth in height and weight of college women bear out what we are led to expect from the trends of growth reported in the earlier sections on growth from 10 to 17 or 18—that growth in these respects continues into the college period although the rate is decelerated, the total increment is not large, and the greater growth comes to those with later menarches. Girls have almost, although not quite, reached adult stature and weight by the time of college entrance.

(c) *Height and weight of men.* Evidence on growth in height and weight of college men is even sparser than for college women. Reliance is here placed on a report by Jackson, whose observations on the absence of growth in stature of male and female students at the University of Minnesota was cited above (*13, 14*). The limitation of his successive averages is that they were based on cross-sectional rather than longitudinal measurements, a procedure which operates somewhat to conceal increases, for the reason that younger entrants to college would tend to be precocious, as compared with classmates, in both aptitude and physique (inclusive of stature and weight). Before reporting and considering the measurements of stature and weight of men at Lehigh University and Amherst College, Jackson mentions an investigator at the University of Pennsylvania who stated that "the entire class entering the University of Pennsylvania in 1909 during their four years of college life made an average gain of about one inch in stature, 3 inches in chest girth (expanded), and 7 pounds in weight." The averages reported for men at Lehigh in 1926 were as follows:

AGE IN YEARS	STATURE (INCHES)	WEIGHT (POUNDS)
18.63	68.42	138.43
19.97	68.62	141.26
20.98	68.21	144.55
21.98	68.86	145.01

These figures indicate that the average gain in stature was .44 inch, and in weight between 6 and 7 pounds. The average statures reported for an earlier period for Amherst increased from 67.4 for freshmen to 67.96 for seniors, which means an increase of about a half inch. For the same students the increase in weight was from about 133 to 142 pounds, or an increase of about 9 pounds. These data, Jackson said, are in "substantial agreement" with those at Minnesota.

Thus, the increments in height and weight for men, while far from striking, appear to be appreciably greater for men than for women. This is to be expected, both because of the later maturing of human males than females and their larger mature dimensions. It is likely, also, that, for the same reasons, these slight increments may extend more than for women into the later college years.

Other Physical Changes

More physical changes.—Up to this point, consideration of growth in youth has been focused on stature and weight and, to a lesser extent, on skeletal development. Growth and change have been studied in many other aspects and much evidence is available in print from the investigations. It will be impossible here to summarize the evidence on all significant aspects, and what is presented aims to be illustrative rather than comprehensive. For more complete reviews of these other changes, the reader is referred to excellent treatises on adolescence, and especially to the *Yearbook* of the

National Society for the Study of Education published in 1944 (*12*). Throughout the treatment here attention will be given so far as possible to the later years of adolescence—those nearest the predominant age-group in the community college—although it will be necessary to reach into prior years for backgrounds of growth in this age-group. Evidence on the more obvious physical changes will be followed by some on physiological changes and by some consideration of change in physical abilities and activities.

The further physical changes to be reviewed are often referred to as "primary" and "secondary" sexual characteristics. One of the latter is change in voice. While voice in girls undergoes some change in quality, that of boys undergoes change in pitch to the deeper voice of the adult. This change seldom begins before the appearance of some pubic hair and is in most cases not complete before early adulthood. It is believed that depth of voice and masculinity bear no relationship to each other.

One of the most pronounced changes during adolescence toward difference in the secondary sexual characters of the two sexes is in facial hair. There is no difference prior to puberty. The appearance of the beard in boys results in a change from the downy hair of childhood, to an intermediate stage, followed by coarser and more highly pigmented terminal hairs, at which time shaving becomes necessary. This is at an average age of 16 or 17, although there is considerable variation among individuals, deriving from differences in time of puberty and genetic factors. Mention should be made of the growth of pubic and axillary hair in both sexes during the period of sexual maturing, the axillary hair manifesting little difference as between the sexes and usually appearing after pubic hair.

Greulich (*11*, 27), relying on Stratz, identifies four stages of development of the female mammary gland. The stages that would be characteristic of students of the predominant age-group in the community college would be the "primary" breast, due principally to an increase of fatty tissue underlying the areola, and the "secondary" or "mature" breast. He reports Stratz as indicating that the breasts of some women never attain this final stage throughout life but apparently function as efficiently as those of the "secondary" stage.

Mention has been made above of the menarche in girls. Its time of appearance is influenced not merely by chronological age but by race, inheritance (rather high correlations have been found for menarches of mothers and daughters), economic status, nutrition, emotion, etc. The range in ages of menarche have been reported to be from 11 to 16-plus years, with averages at 12.5–13.5 years. These studies made over a long span of years appear to disclose some trend toward younger ages. It should be apparent that for the predominant age-group in the community college the menarche is an item of personal history and menstruation for practically all will have moved into its cycle of regularity. As a concluding word concerning the relation of menarche to maturity in girls, it may be well to quote once more from Greulich (*11*, 30): "it would seem best to regard

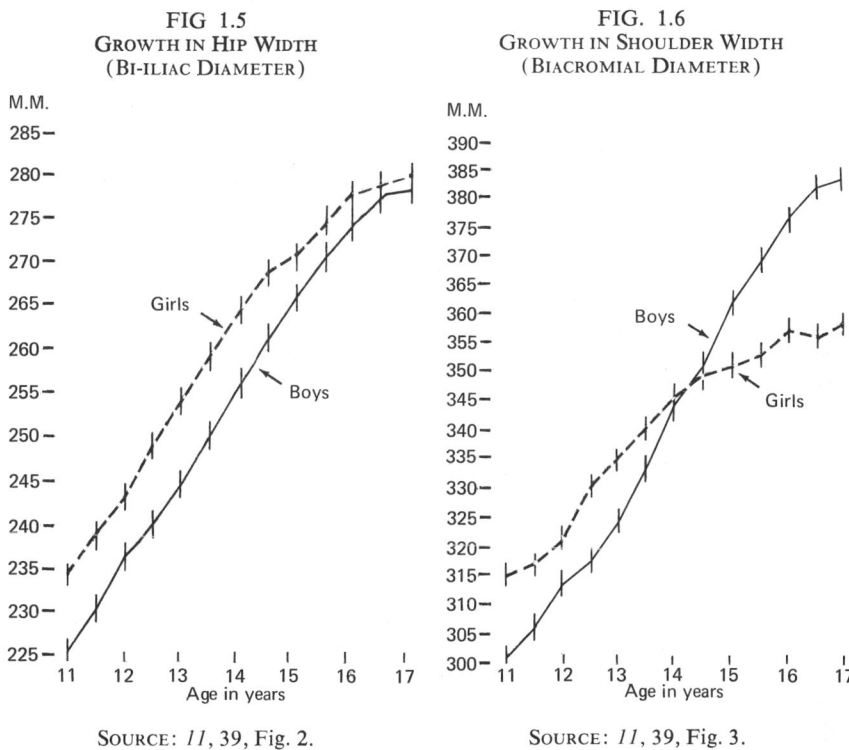

FIG 1.5
GROWTH IN HIP WIDTH
(BI-ILIAC DIAMETER)

SOURCE: *11*, 39, Fig. 2.

FIG. 1.6
GROWTH IN SHOULDER WIDTH
(BIACROMIAL DIAMETER)

SOURCE: *11*, 39, Fig. 3.

the menarche as neither a dependable criterion of maturity nor as necessarily the expression of any narrowly circumscribed stage of sexual maturation. It is rather the reflection of a physiological state which may occur at different times during the puberal period in different individuals and which usually precedes by a considerable interval the attainment of the capacity to reproduce."

Hip and shoulder width.—The two remaining aspects of physical growth toward maturity to be used illustratively here relate to two measures of body build: bi-iliac diameter (hip width) and biacromial diameter (shoulder width). The evidence on these helps toward understanding the extent of growth toward physical maturity and the differences of physique in the two sexes as they approach adulthood. The averages for the two sexes at ages from 11 to 17 years are charted in Figures 1.5 and 1.6. It will be noted in the first of these figures that girls have a greater hip width than boys throughout the age-span for which the curves are drawn, but that the measure for boys is almost that for girls at 17.

The second figure shows the situation to be very different for shoulder width. Whereas for girls this measure is greater than for boys up to 14 years, the growth for them has begun to decelerate by this age, while that for boys is accelerated and by 17 is larger than that for the girls by about a third of the full span of growth represented by the figure. Both measures are decelerating in the later years of the age-span represented and for both sexes.

At the same time, it is to be noted that, as with the curves of increase in height and weight, these figures show that growth in these two aspects will continue for some time after the terminal age in the figures. It also appears that the growth for boys will continue longer than for girls. It should be kept in mind, however, that these curves depict averages, and that there is wide variation from individual to individual. We may assume that it is in the main the late maturing individuals who account for the increments after the seventeenth year of age.

Physiological Changes

Pulse rates, blood pressure, etc.—Certain physiological changes during adolescence, again illustrative rather than comprehensive, are here briefly described. These changes are not so apparent to the eye as are most of the physical changes, many of which are external, but they are no less important and are a part of the whole integrated process of development during the later growing years. As usual, the changes will be noted for their bearing on the characteristics of the two sexes as members of the predominant age-group in the community college. The changes reviewed relate to pulse rate, blood pressure, basal metabolism, oxygen consumption, and breathing capacity. This review will conclude with a brief consideration of the endocrine factors which induce and control the physical and physiological development.

From a part of the Adolescent Growth Study at the University of California, in which measurements were made on the same 50 girls and 50 boys at 6-month intervals between the ages of 11.5 and 17.5 years, the curves drawn from average pulse rates disclose a decrease of 8 to 9 beats per minute for both sexes over the adolescent period. The average rate for girls is from two to six beats faster than for boys and increases somewhat with age (26).

The curves for average systolic blood pressure are in contrast with those for pulse rate as just described, as they rise with age for the same groups of subjects. The measures do not differ significantly before the age of 13.5 years, but after this age the pressure in boys rises more rapidly than for girls, and a significant sex difference becomes established.

The curves for average basal metabolism, in contrast with those for blood pressure, decrease with age (26). They are found to decrease gradually throughout the adolescent period. The rate of fall for girls is so small by the age of 17 that the average rate is close to that for adults, but in boys the rate of decrease continues beyond the age of 18, providing further evidence of the earlier maturing of girls. The investigator points out that

TABLE 1.9
Mean Breathing Capacity in Cubic Inches for Boys and Girls in Successive Age Groups from 8 Years, 6 Months, to 18 Years, 5 Months

Age Group years and months	Boys	Girls
8–6 to 9–5	103.46	94.77
9–6 to 10–5	115.50	105.23
10–6 to 11–5	127.54	119.37
11–6 to 12–5	141.91	134.62
12 6 to 13–5	157.44	151.52
13–6 to 14–5	179.89	166.74
14–6 to 15–5	203.81	172.22
15–6 to 16–5	227.45	177.25
16–6 to 17–5	247.46	179.61
17–6 to 18–5	257.22	178.67

Sources: For boys, 21, 28, Table 14; for girls, 5, 40, Table 22. Although the ages given in the table are at even year points, that is 8, 9, 10, etc., it is explained that they are midpoints for each age-group covering a year, as indicated in the first column.

the curves for these averages, as for other physiological variables, because of wide variations from subject to subject, afford no basis for predicting the pattern of age changes for individual boys and girls.

Illustrative evidence concerning breathing capacity is summarized from two earlier investigations at the University of Iowa on populations of boys by Meredith (21) and of girls by Boynton (5). The investigations are to some extent cross-sectional rather than strictly longitudinal, but the averages for successive ages disclose growth trends analogous to many others in the physical and physiological areas. They are presented in Table 1.9. They show, for boys, increasing increments to the 14–6 to 15–5 age-group, followed by some deceleration with the 15–6 to 16–5 age-group, which is much more rapid during the next year. However, from this evidence one may assume some further growth, although slackened, beyond the eighteenth year, in all probability mainly among the late maturing boys. The increase for girls decelerates earlier, and full maturity in this respect may be assumed for practically all before or by the end of the span of years represented.

In anticipation of the treatment of physical and athletic ability and activity of late adolescents at a later point in the current chapter, it is desirable to report on pulse rate, blood pressure, and oxygen consumption as affected by physical exertion. As summarized by Shock (*12*, 65–67), experimental evidence shows that the pulse rate after exercise was increased more in girls than boys at all ages from 13 through 17, but that for both sexes the increase is less as youth grow older. A sex difference is also apparent for systolic pressure, which "becomes greater with age in the case of boys, and smaller with age in the case of girls—suggesting a possible physiological basis (at least in part) for adolescent sex differences in athletic activity." Oxygen consumption after exercise was found to be higher for boys than girls at all ages from 13 through 17 and the rate of recovery to basic levels showed "conspicuous" differences at different age levels. "While some of the younger adolescents returned to their normal rates within 20 minutes after exercise, college students and adults were found to require as long as three hours to effect the same degree of recovery."

Endocrine factors.—Because they are in such large part causal and regulatory of growth and change during adolescence, there would have been justification for considering endocrine changes and influences in advance of reviewing the physical and physiological changes of this period in the lives of members of both sexes. Certainly, they are too important to any understanding of growth to be left out of account. While the human body houses many glands with numerous effective secretions, attention here will be restricted to the pituitary gland at the base of the brain and the gonads, that is, the testes in the male and the ovaries in the female.

Two hormones produced by the anterior lobe of the pituitary gland are of particular interest in the consideration of development toward maturity. One of these is the growth hormone which induces attainment of adult body size. The second pituitary hormone important to maturation is called the "gonadotrophic," or gonad-stimulating, hormone. Under stimulation of this second hormone, the testes and ovaries begin to produce mature spermatozoa and ova, respectively, and also begin to liberate larger amounts of the appropriate sex hormones, both of which are produced in both sexes. With the gonads developing in response to this second hormone of the pituitary gland, they begin themselves to produce hormones in quantity. The male hormones, the androgens, stimulate the growth of the prostate gland, the seminal vesicles, and the penis, as well as the secondary male characteristics already mentioned above, the beard, pubic and axillary hair, lowering of voice pitch, etc. The female hormones, the estrogens, stimulate the growth of breasts, mammary glands, uterus, Fallopian tubes, and vagina, and bring on development of secondary female sexual characteristics.

Another important function of the gonadal sex hormones is acting on the pituitary gland so as to cause a gradual decrease in influence of that gland's growth hormone and to bring its action to an end. As put by Greulich, "it appears ... that normal growth and development are contingent upon the reciprocal and properly timed action of pituitary and gonadal hormones" (*11*, 16).

Greulich and associates have investigated, by complex laboratory procedure, when, in the life of boys, these endocrine substances are produced (*11*). The procedure involved recovery of androgenic and estrogenic substances and gonadotrophic hormone from the urine. For the investigation of androgens the subjects ranged from 8 to 18 in chronological age and for investigation of estrogens and gonadotrophic hormone from 8 to 17. The evidence was analyzed both by chronological ages and by five "maturity groups" based on skeletal age. Excretion of these substances was found hardly to begin before the age of 12. While it showed increase with chronological age, there was wide variation from boy to boy in the same chronological age-group. The correlation of increase with maturity group was more often statistically significant than with chronological age. In Maturity Group V, that of greatest maturity as indicated by skeletal age, the excretion of gonadotrophin of about half the subjects was found to be below the adult range and for the remainder it was within that range.

Growth in Strength and Motor Performance

Tests of strength.—One of the standard measures of strength used in investigating the development of youth is the strength of grip, and the device used is the dynamometer, which is placed in the hand so that maximum pressure can be applied between the base of the thumb and the second joints of the fingers. This measure, among others, was taken on 93 boys and 90 girls in the schools of Oakland in connection with the Adolescent Growth Study at the University of California (*15*). The first measurements were made when the subjects were in high fifth and low sixth grades and were continued for six and a half years until all members of the study were seniors in high school. The curves based on these measurements are shown in Figure 1.7. These curves indicate an increasing strength of grip for both sexes throughout the age-span represented, and projection of the curves beyond 17 appears to promise some further increase. The measures for boys are seen to be higher than for girls throughout the period, indicating some acceleration at 13 to 14, and these trends, together with the slackening gain for girls at about the same time, make for a striking difference by the end of the period.

Other tests of strength used in this investigation were of pull and thrust, again with dynamometers (*15*). The curves derived from these measurements, not reproduced here, differ from those for grip as follows: the average measurements of pull for boys and girls are much alike from 11 to 13, but those for girls slacken from 13 on, while those for boys increase at a rapid rate until 16. By the end of the period there is a wide disparity of average strength between the sexes. Average measurements of thrust are

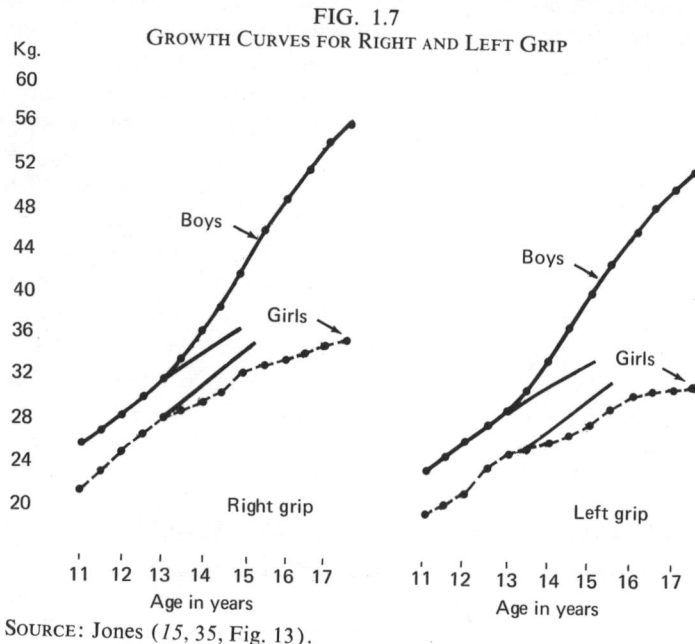

FIG. 1.7
GROWTH CURVES FOR RIGHT AND LEFT GRIP

SOURCE: Jones (*15*, 35, Fig. 13).

high for girls until about 13, when, because of rapid acceleration for boys, there is again a wide difference between boys and girls. Both average measurements for boys show some slight decline from 16 to 17. It should be stated that certain other investigations involving dynamometric procedures disclose no discontinuance of strength in boys, and, in this respect, seem to be in agreement with evidence on other aspects of development for boys which show continuance of growth beyond the age of 17 for this sex.

Motor performance.—Another investigative project in the Adolescent Growth Study at the University of California went extensively into the development of motor performance in boys and girls. This longitudinal study by Espenshade (*9*) utilized measurements made at half-year intervals on 85 boys and 80 girls beginning with the lower half of the eighth grade

(8B) and continuing for boys through four years (through 11B) and for girls through three and a half years (through 11A). It will aid in the interpretation of the evidence from the study to be reported here to recall that the normal age for grade 8 is 13 years and that for the remaining three grades the ages are, respectively, 14, 15, and 16 years. The subjects are characterized in the report as "a fairly representative sampling of California urban school population."

The motor tests administered to these subjects included the 50-yard dash, standing broad jump, jump and reach, target throw, distance throw, and the Brace test involving "stunts like walking in a straight line, heel to toe," "kicking right foot up at least level with the shoulders," etc. The

TABLE 1.10
MEAN MEASURES OF MOTOR PERFORMANCE
FOR BOYS AND GIRLS

Grade Classification	Seconds for 50-Yard Dash		Feet and Inches in Broad Jump		Feet in Distance Throw	
	Boys	Girls	Boys	Girls	Boys	Girls
8B	7.27	7.85	5–11.1	5–6.7	106.0	70.8
8A	7.31	8.03	6–2.8	5–6.2	115.5	72.5
9B	7.13	7.94	6–3.9	5–5.3	124.1	73.5
9A	7.22	8.02	6–8.9	5–6.5	135.8	74.6
10B	7.11	8.24	6–11.2	5–3.7	130.0	74.3
10A	7.22	8.38	7–7.6	5–3.3	140.8	72.8
11B	6.77	–	7–4.5	5–2.8	142.9	74.1
11A	6.34	–	7–0.9	–	149.5	–

SOURCE: Espenshade (9, 63).

mean measures for the successive half grades for three of these tests are reported in Table 1.10. In the 50-yard dash boys at least maintained their average speed during the first three grades and were increasing it thereafter, while girls were losing speed through ninth and tenth grades. In the broad jump boys were making gains almost throughout the grade-span while girls were losing distance, especially during the last three half-grades for which average measures are reported. In these two tests, boys and girls were not far apart in the first half grade represented. For the distance throw boys had much higher averages throughout and made gains for each half grade, while girls made slight gains at first but hardly held their own thereafter. In the jump and reach test and in the Brace test, evidence on which is not reproduced here, the mean scores for girls show some continuing improvement from grade to grade.

It was possible in this investigation to relate performance not only to grade level and chronological age, but also to skeletal and physiological age. The following is quoted from Espenshade's findings in this aspect of the study: "With the exception of the jump and reach . . . mean scores [for girls] tend to decline with skeletal growth. . . . However [for boys] there is a clear increase in performance in each event with skeletal maturity. The most consistent increases and greatest relative changes occur in the distance throw, the broad jump, and the jump and reach. All events for girls except the jump and reach correlate negatively with skeletal maturity. . . . The largest correlations are with the Brace test, −.26, and with the distance throw, −.19. . . . Correlations between skeletal maturity of boys and motor performance are positive. The highest correlation is with the broad jump, +.56" (9, 65).

Espenshade offers three hypotheses in explanation of the low negative correlations found between motor performance and skeletal maturity for girls. First, skeletal maturing in girls from 13 to 16 may be accompanied by increase in weight which is found in girls to be negatively related to motor performance. "Second, skeletal maturing coincides with physiological maturing, resulting in a restriction in the practice of motor activities. Finally, skeletal maturing is accompanied by change in interests and attitudes, usually with a decreasing interest in vigorous physical activity" (9, 66).

The author sums up conclusions from her investigations by saying that growth in ability to perform motor acts reaches its maximum at approximately 14 years of age in girls but continues in boys through the seventeenth year. She points out, however, that there are wide individual differences in both rate of growth and level of ability (9, 118).

The differences in motor abilities thus reviewed have much to do with the differences between the sexes in athletic prowess during later adolescence; in comment on this difference, Espenshade says, "In contemporary society the general approbation accorded physical skill in girls ceases with early adolescence. At this time for boys the role of sports and the prestige surrounding the outstanding athlete assume exaggerated importance. This social attitude cannot but influence the child's interpretation of his personal needs" (9, 119).

An interesting and significant study related to the difference in motivation of boys and girls as related to physical (or motor) activity, in this instance that involved in the "gym" work in the schools' physical fitness program, has been reported by Lund (20). The study is based on "medicals," that is, physicians' excuses of boys and girls from "gym" classes in four (two junior and two senior) high schools in Philadelphia. The classification of grounds indicated for these excuses ranged widely among cardiac, glandular, postoperative, structural, nutritional, respiratory, etc. The percentages of students enrolled for whom excuses were provided were as follows:

JUNIOR HIGH SCHOOL	BOYS	GIRLS
7th	6.7	6.8
8th	7.1	8.2
9th	6.3	10.2
SENIOR HIGH SCHOOL		
10th	6.5	9.3
11th	7.3	16.7
12th	7.6	24.3

The percentage for boys excused changed little from grade to grade, while that for girls increased from grade to grade at both junior and senior high school levels, attaining almost a fourth of all girls enrolled in grade 12.

Three possible interpretations of the larger and increasing proportions of girls with these "medicals" were listed by the author. The first is that the excuses are genuine; the second, "increasing consciousness of existing disabilities"; and, third, "the problem is one of motivation in which the changes incident to adolescence give rise to new interests centering about conditions which make it highly desirable to secure the medical certificate which alone will excuse the pupil from 'gym' work."

Lund quickly discredits the first two of these interpretations. Concerning the first he points out that no competent authority would be inclined to support it or believe that girls are any more subject to disease during their teens than at any other time. It is contended that increasing awareness of existing disabilities, the second interpretation, could not be valid, because such awareness "should be equally in evidence among the boys." The third interpretation, that the problem is one of adolescent motivation, is supported by the considerations (1) that the increase is confined to girls; (2) that the increase occurs during and following adolescence, "a period of transition in which the interests of the girls are given strong social direction with subsequent loss of interest in activities of a purely physical nature"; and (3) that the reports of the teachers of the girls' "gym" classes are "strikingly in accord on certain points: most of the girls are not physically handicapped at all, and that the underlying and real considerations are to be found in (a) physical disinclination; (b) concern lest 'hair-do' and 'make-up' be disturbed; (c) fear of developing big muscles; and (d) unwillingness to make the change in dress required before appearing on the gymnasium floor."

Fine motor and mechanical abilities.—The studies affording evidence concerning development of fine motor and mechanical abilities are so extensive that they cannot be adequately dealt with here. An admirable synthesis of investigations reported up to the time of publication was provided by Jones and Seashore in Chapter 7 of the yearbook on adolescence of the National Society for the Study of Education (*12*, 123–45). In their opinion, "The outstanding fact is that in proceeding outward from the arm to the fingers, and from larger to smaller muscles, the relative maturity (i.e., the proportion of later performance) decreases at any given age. This may be taken as an illustration of the so-called 'law of developmental direction,' emphasizing a sequence in maturing, from proximal muscles (nearer the midline of the body) to those in more peripheral position. Similar age curves were obtained for girls, except that at most ages girls were relatively more mature."

These authors cite illustrative evidence from studies of various abilities, such as reaction time to sound, spatial eye-hand coordination, temporal eye-hand coordination, bi-manual coordination, serial discrimination, and manual steadiness, in some of which boys are superior to girls and others in which girls are equal or superior to boys. However, the authors admonish the reader to bear in mind that even where sex differences are statistically significant, they are considerably smaller than the range of variation within either sex. Also, they point out that the manual functions tested "reach a limit which is definitely earlier than that of intellectual abilities." However, they indicate that "as motor tasks increase in complexity, and as they increase in the demand which they place upon persistent effort and upon flexible adaptation of work methods, we may expect that the age limit for top performance, in unpracticed activities, will move forward to twenty or beyond."

Included in the synthesis on tests of fine motor skills Jones and Seashore considered certain proficiencies in the handling of tools, machines, and other physical materials, which they grouped together roughly as mechanical abilities. They compared the results of two rather well-known tests, one of spatial relations and the other an assembly test, as reported in an investigation made at the University of Minnesota (22). They reported that each of the two tests shows an increase in ability to perform with age throughout the period 12–19 years. However, the course of growth for the two tests is not the same, as the assembly test yields linear gains after 15 years of age while the curve for spatial relations is negatively accelerated from this age on. They noted, further, that each test showed smaller age changes than are ordinarily found for mental ability scales (from which evidence will be reported in Chapter 2). They observed also "that there are relatively few evidences that any such broad unitary abilities as general 'mechanical ability' or 'manual dexterity' exist," or that "the tests are actually measures of aptitude for the prediction of rate or final level of learning complex practical skills such as carpentry, automotive service, or industrial machine operation." This is, of course, a matter of more concern for a treatment of guidance; here our interest is in development of motor ability.

Awkwardness and adolescence.—Brief comment should be made concerning the rather widespread belief that the period of adolescence, because of its rapid rate of physical growth, is one in which awkwardness is unusually manifest. One investigator of boys during adolescence, Dimock, concluded from his inquiries that motor ability or coordination, as measured by the Brace test, increases throughout adolescent years, but less rapidly in the period during which pubescence is reached, in which boys increase in height and weight more rapidly than before and after, but that, even during this period, they experience "substantial improvement" in motor coordination. He concludes from his consideration of this issue of awkwardness in boys that it is "more likely to accompany the rather *sudden beginnings of growth*" in the prepubescent-to-pubescent period than in the later and more rapid growth (*8*, 249). Examination of the evidence reported on the Brace test by Espenshade indicates in the main a straight-line growth for both boys and girls with no marked dip at puberty (*9*). The earlier deceleration for girls in the "stunts" has been previously noted, and stems more from attainment of mature strength at earlier ages and from motivation. It is necessary to mention that we are here again dealing with averages and that there are doubtless individuals whose coordination develops less regularly than that of others in the groups, and this may account for the unsubstantiated popular generalization that adolescence is the "awkward age."

The interest here is for the most part in any marked incidence of lack of coordination as this might be induced by growth in the later years of adolescence, from which the predominant age-group of the community college is drawn. Insofar as Dimock was right, this population is long past the age for such a manifestation, except for variation among individuals. Such variation can continue well into adulthood. The awkward behavior arising out of a consciousness of ineptness in social situations can hardly be counted here, as this in effect should be classified under social behavior, which is not a concern of the current chapter. Awkward behavior induced by embarrassing social situations plagues most of us in adolescence and far into maturity.

A Cautionary Word Concerning Measurements

At several points in this effort at portrayal of physical development of youth, reference has been made to the limited usefulness of averages in affording an adequate understanding of rates of growth in individuals. Variations among members of groups represented in the investigations are so wide as often to obscure or even to misrepresent the growth pattern of individual subjects.

Beyond this inadequacy of measures of central tendency for attaining a reliable understanding of growth in its diverse aspects, there are further limitations it is well to bear in mind in interpreting and applying the evidence available from researches to date—limitations arising from the populations represented and the changes taking place over the years in the populations themselves. Some of these limitations a few decades ago were identified by a competent anthropometrist, Scammon, in a paper reviewing the physical development of later adolescents (23). The first limitation to which Scammon called attention is the nature of the population included in the investigations available; these investigations, after the age of sixteen or so, are often restricted to "very selected groups," such as college students. A second "very important fact is that our base line of reference has been changing for a long period, and particularly in the last generation or two." He cites as illustrations of these changes the fact that the final size of the human body, particularly as measured by the common criteria of stature and weight, has been on the increase, and that the time of puberty in both sexes comes earlier in life than formerly. It is obviously important to remain alert to such changes and the investigations reporting them, and to participate in and encourage research in these areas.

Body Types

Identification of somatotypes.—The final section of this chapter before the summary has to do with the effort to identify and classify body types. The treatment here will be as brief as possible and will be restricted to report on a procedure which has promise but has been applied on a large scale only to young men. Reference is made to a procedure in classifying types of human physique, or somatotyping, by Sheldon and associates (24). The procedure involved analysis by measurement from photographs of about 4,000 Harvard students at the age of 18. As a result three polar types of physique were identified, designated by the authors as endomorph, mesomorph, and ectomorph. The authors have characterized these as follows (24, 5):

"*Endomorphy* means relative prominence or soft roundness throughout the various regions of the body. When endomorphy is dominant the digestive viscera are massive and tend relatively to dominate the bodily economy. The digestive viscera are derived principally from the *endodermal* embryonic layer.

"*Mesomorphy* means relative prominence of muscle, bone, and connective tissue. The mesomorphic physique is normally heavy, hard, and rectangular in outline. Bone and muscle are prominent and the skin is made thick by a heavy underlying connective tissue. The entire bodily economy is dominated, relatively, by tissues derived from the *mesodermal* embryonic layer.

"*Ectomorphy* means relative predominance of linearity and fragility. In proportion to his mass, the ectomorph has the greatest surface area and hence relatively the greatest sensory exposure to the outside world. Relative to his mass he also has the largest brain and nervous system. In a sense, therefore, his bodily economy is relatively dominated by tissues derived from the *ectodermal* embryonic layer."

Sheldon used a seven-point scale of rating to indicate the degree to which an individual manifests each of these three sets of attributes. An individual whose morphological characteristics are almost entirely in the endomorphic classification is rated 7 in endomorphy, 1 in mesomorphy, and 1 in ectomorphy, and the rating would be 711. An extreme ectomorphic would be rated 117, and an extreme mesomorph, 171. An average individual with the three sets of traits found to be present to a median degree and equally apparent would have a rating of 444.

Visualization of the method of rating is aided by assigning each of the three attributes to one angle of an equilateral triangle. For instance, if the rating of 7 for endomorphy is assigned to one of these angles, the two opposite angles would represent ratings of 1 in mesomorphy and 1 in ectomorphy. The point of intersection of the bisectors of the three angles would locate the rating for the individual with the 444 rating. By means of the three axes emanating from the three corners of the triangle it is possible to plot within it the location of the three-point rating of any individual.

The investigation found 343 "theoretical possibilities" in somatotypes. However, the particular procedure used identified only 76 somatotypes in about 4,000 men of the full theoretical series, although it is explained that this is because the investigators elected to use a seven-point scale and to ignore fractional values.

It should be a matter of some importance to persons interested in students at the community college level that the authors believe that their norms for 18 year-old males "may perhaps be regarded as satisfactorily established." They consider the distributions appearing in their book as norms for the age-level 16–20. At the time of writing they were attempting to build up a sufficient collection of data for standardized photographs to publish similar norms for later age-levels; but on the basis of partial evidence they state that, in most somatotypes, the measurements, except for chest and abdomen, vary little at these later ages. They cite as further proof of the stability of somatotype in the individual male adult the fact that the distributions of types found at the later ages were nearly the same as for the college age. Even more to the point as concerns stability of the somatotype is their hypothesis, if found to be true, that it can be accurately measured at age 6, "and that it can be approximately predicted from birth, but both suppositions remain to be tested" (*24*, 224).

Although the procedure used identified 76 somatotypes, the investigators found it necessary to a complete typology to isolate several "second-order" variables to describe all morphological differences among members of the same somatotype. Dysplasia is the aspect of disharmony between different regions of the same physique, when, for example, a body is of one somatotype in the region of the head and neck and of another somatotype in the legs and trunk. Gynandromorphy refers to the bisexuality of a physique, when members of each sex exhibit more or less of the secondary characteristics of the opposite sex. Other second-order variables are texture, referring to the "fineness" or "coarseness" of the structure displayed, and hirsutism, referring to hairiness.

The question arises as to whether or not the same procedure in somatotyping is applicable to women. On this issue, Sheldon and associates report that they had been unable to secure an extensive series of standardized photographs of women. They had, however, been able to classify 2,500 such pictures. They admit that such a predictive distribution is "not sufficiently accurate or valid to be taken at face value," but they report that the same 76 somatotypes as were found among men *seem* to occur among women, but that the distribution of the female population among the somatotypes is different. "Endomorphy, and physiques combining a strong first [endomorphic] and third [ectomorphic] component against the second [mesomorphic] component, are much commoner in women than in men. Mesomorphy, and the strong combination of the first and second components against the third, are commoner among men" (*24*, 66–67).

Although consideration of personality and temperament will be centered in Chapter 3, it may not be out of place to mention at this point that Sheldon and associates included in their investigation a motivation and temperament analysis analogous to their study of somatotypes. They refer to these components, again tri-polar, as *visceratonia, somatatonia*, and *cerebrotonia*: "Visceratonia is roughly identifiable with love of comfort, relaxation, sociability, conviviality, and sometimes with gluttony. . . . Somatatonia is the motivational pattern dominated by the will to exertion, exercise and vigorous self-expression. . . . Cerebrotonia refers to the attentional and inhibitory aspect of temperament. In the economy of the cerebrotonic individual the sensory and central nervous systems appear to play dominant roles . . ." (*24*, 8).

Their investigation found rather high correlations between these analogous ratings and those of somatotypes. These correlations, if valid, could be highly significant. There has been some disposition to question their validity, however, on various grounds, one of these being that both sets of ratings were made by the same investigators, and, because those on temperament are less objectively determined than those on physique and were made after them, a "halo effect" may have crept in to exaggerate the relationship. At the same time, estimable scholars in the field of human measurement, for example Bayley and Tuddenham, believe that "the implications of the results are sufficiently provocative to warrant further careful study by independent workers" (*12*, 53).

Body types in relation to athletics and health.—Areas in which the ratings of somatotype might be expected to prove useful would be those of physical fitness and athletic performance. One writer who has explored this possibility to some extent is Cureton (7). After spotting tripolar ratings like "354, Sprinters," "261, Weight throwers," etc., on a triangular chart resembling that devised by Sheldon and associates, Cureton discusses "Constitutional Type and Health" as follows: "Health is an aggregate term, the composite of all types of physical fitness. It is a valid concept but difficult to measure with objective tests because of their limited and specific nature. If there is any basis upon which a prediction of health over life as a whole may be predicted, it is possibly the constitutional type basis. In general, the types 127, 126, 235, 136, 245, 244, 154, and 163, in other words, those high in ectomorphy and low in endomorphy are the virile, long-lived types with remarkable immunity to most types of fatal diseases. The types low in mesomorphy . . . are usually hypopituitary types with poor posture, weak musculature and are low in endurance and energy for living. These include the numbers 217, 216, 316, 415, 515, 514, 613, 612, 712, and 424. Those types extremely high in endomorphy are susceptible to many of the most serious diseases, are relatively short-lived, and are harmfully overweight as a rule. Persons extremely high in mesomorphy are the energetic, healthy types, although not noted for longevity. They have strength and ruggedness, make good athletes, and are subject to few ailments. . . . Throughout this broad picture, muscular types seem to have a health advantage for active living. They represent good 'selections' for army and navy recruits."

Summary

A recent sampling of full-time community college students finds the predominant age-group to be 17 through 20 years of age, the later years of the "second decade" of the life span, often referred to as "late adolescence." Comparison with older distributions indicates the stability of this predominance. Women students appear to be somewhat, but not notably, younger than men students. The concentration of students in this age-span justifies a focus of attention on their growth and characteristics—physical, mental, social, and other. The fact that community college student bodies usually include a significant minority of older adults warrants some consideration of the characteristics and interests of this age-group also.

As concerns *average* growth in stature, after roughly equal increments approximating a straight line until 13 or 14, the growth for girls decelerates while that for boys continues, so that by 17 or 18, the age of college entrance, there is a notably large average difference in height between the two sexes. The curves of growth are still showing some increase for the later years, but less for girls than for boys. Measures of PMH (per cent of mature height) for boys and girls, when made for groups classified as "average," "accelerated," and "retarded" as concerns their rates of growth, suggest that the increments in the average measures after 16 derive mainly if not entirely from growth in the late maturers, as measured by age of maximum increment, skeletal age, etc.

The curves of growth in weight are similar to those for height except that for girls the decline in weight increment following the period of maximum growth is smaller than the decline in height increment. Facts on growth in height and weight of college women bear out what we are led to expect from the trends of growth approaching 17 or 18, and that is that the growth continues into the college period, but at a greatly decelerated rate and mainly in the late maturers and in the early college years. It was inferred, on the basis of evidence up to 18 to 20, that men, especially the late maturers, add to stature and weight during early college years. Many other changes during adolescence have been noted and measured.

Primary and secondary sexual characteristics of the two sexes are far advanced toward mature status in both boys and girls by 17 or 18, except for the late maturing which affects more boys than girls at these ages. Average bi-iliac diameter of girls is greater for boys from 11 to 17, but at this age the increment is greater for boys and promises to exceed that for girls. Biacromial diameter of girls begins higher at 11, but the curves for the sexes cross between 14 and 15 and the gap between them widens notably with the curve for boys still rising rapidly while that for girls is decelerating.

These physical changes are accompanied by profound physiological changes with many striking differences between the sexes. These changes are induced and controlled by endocrine factors with most of the effects rounded out by 17 or 18, except, again, for late maturers.

On tests of strength, averages for boys are seen to exceed those for girls from 10 or 11 on, with marked acceleration for boys near pubescence and deceleration for girls. Performance by boys on motor tests involving the larger muscles bears out expectations from the tests of strength. The large disparities in this respect are believed to be induced in part by differences in motivation. Performance in fine motor and mechanical activities appears not to be affected by changes during adolescence. The rather widespread belief that adolescence is the "awkward age" seems not well founded. Although there may be some increase in lack of coordination in individuals with rapid spurts of growth, these seem to come in early adolescence, and the manifestation of awkwardness in late adolescence emerges primarily in social settings.

Because of wide variation in rates of growth and change among individuals, there is repeated warning against too great reliance on averages. Beyond this, caution in reliance is advised on grounds of dangers of unrepresentativeness of the populations studied and of significant changes in some measurements over the generations.

A promising procedure yielding a tripolar description of somatotypes, with variations, among young men was described. To date it had not been extensively applied to women nor developed to the point of reliable prediction from childhood to adult men.

References and Bibliography

1. Ausubel, David P. *Theory and Problems of Adolescent Development.* New York: Greene & Stratton, 1954. Chs. 4–5.
2. Barker, Roger G., and Stone, Calvin P. "Physical Development in Relation to Menarcheal Age in University Women." *Human Biology,* 8 (1936), 198–222.
3. Bayer, Leona M., and Bayley, Nancy. *Growth Diagnosis: Selected Methods for Interpreting and Predicting Physical Development from One Year to Maturity.* Chicago: University of Chicago Press, 1959.
4. Bernard, Harold W. *Adolescent Development in American Culture.* Yonkers-on-Hudson, N.Y.: World Book Co., 1957. Ch. 5.
5. Boynton, Bernice. *The Physical Growth of Girls: A Study of the Rhythm of Physical Growth from Anthropometric Measurements on Girls Between Birth and Eighteen Years.* XII (no. 4). Iowa City, Iowa: The University, 1936.
6. Cruze, Wendell W. *Adolescent Psychology and Development.* New York: Ronald Press Co., 1953. Chs. 3–4.
7. Cureton, Thomas K. "Body Build as a Framework of Reference for Interpreting Physical Fitness and Athletic Performance." *Research Quarterly of the American Physical Education Association,* 12 (May, 1941), 301–30.
8. Dimock, Hedley S. *Rediscovering the Adolescent: A Study of Personality Development in Adolescent Boys.* New York: Association Press, 1937.
9. Espenshade, Anna S. *Motor Performance in Adolescence, Including the Study of Relationships with Measures of Physical Growth and Maturity.* Monographs of the Society for Research in Child Development, vol. 5, no. 1. Washington: National Research Council, 1940.
10. Gould, Harley N. "The Physique of Women Students at Newcomb College of Tulane University. I. Stature and Weight." *Research Quarterly of the American Physical Education Association,* 1 (Oct., 1930), 1–17.
11. Greulich, Walter W., et al. *Somatic and Endocrine Studies of Puberal and Adolescent Boys.* Monographs of the Society for Research in Child Development, vol. 7, no. 3. Washington: National Research Council, 1942.
12. Henry, Nelson B., ed. *Adolescence.* Forty-third Yearbook of the National Society for the Study of Education, part 1. Chicago: University of Chicago Press, 1944.
13. Jackson, C. M. "Physical Measurements of Female Students at the University of Minnesota, with Special Reference to Body Build and Vital Capacity." *American Journal of Physical Anthropology,* 6 (1923), 331–53.
14. Jackson, C. M. "The Physique of Male Students at the University of Minnesota:

A Study in Constitutional Anatomy and Physiology." *American Journal of Anatomy,* 40 (Nov., 1927), 59–126.
15. Jones, Harold E. *Motor Performance and Growth: A Developmental Study of Static and Dynamometric Strength.* Berkeley and Los Angeles: University of California Press, 1949.
16. Kodlin, Dankword, and Thompson, Donovan J. *An Appraisal of the Longitudinal Approach to Studies of Growth and Development.* Monographs of the Society for Research in Child Development, vol. 23, no. 1. Lafayette, Ind.: Child Development Publications, 1958.
17. Krogman, Walton M. *The Physical Growth in Children: An Appraisal of Studies.* Monographs of the Society for Research in Child Development, vol. 20, no. 1. Lafayette, Ind.: Child Development Publications, 1956.
18. Kuhlen, Raymond G. *The Psychology of Adolescent Development.* New York: Harper & Brothers, 1952. Ch. 2.
19. Lehman, Harvey C. "Chronological Age *vs.* Proficiency in Physical Skills." *American Journal of Psychology,* 64 (April, 1951), 161–87.
20. Lund, Frederick H. "Adolescent Motivation: Sex Differences." *Journal of Genetic Psychology,* 64 (1944), 99–103.
21. Meredith, Howard V. *The Rhythm of Physical Growth: A Study of Eighteen Anthropometric Measurements on Iowa City White Males Ranging in Age Between Birth and Eighteen Years.* XII (no. 3). Iowa City, Iowa: The University, 1935.
22. Paterson, Donald G. et al. *Minnesota Mechanical Ability Tests.* Minneapolis: University of Minnesota Press, 1930.
23. Scammon, Richard E. "Physical Development from Fifteen to Twenty-two." In *Growth and Development: The Basis for Educational Progress,* pp. 85–93. New York: Progressive Education Association, 1936.
24. Sheldon, W. H.; Stevens, S. S.; and Tucker, W. B. *The Varieties of Human Physique—An Introduction to Constitutional Psychology.* New York: Harper & Brothers, 1940.
25. Shock, Nathan W. "The Effect of Menarche on Basal Physiological Functions in Girls." *American Journal of Physiology,* 139 (June, 1943), 288–92.
26. Shock, Nathan W. "Standard Values for Basal Oxygen Consumption in Adolescents." *American Journal of Diseases in Children,* 64 (1942), 19–32.
27. Shuttleworth, Frank K. *The Adolescent Period: A Graphic Atlas.* Monographs of the Society for Research in Child Development, vol. 14, no. 1. Lafayette, Ind.: Child Development Publications, 1951.
28. Shuttleworth, Frank K. *Physical and Mental Growth of Girls and Boys Six to Nineteen in Relation to Age at Maximum Growth.* Monographs of the Society for Research in Child Development, vol. 4, no. 3. Washington: National Research Council, 1939.
29. Simmons, Katherine, and Greulich, Walter W. "Menarcheal Age and the Height, Weight, and Skeletal Ages of Girls 7 to 17 Years." *Journal of Pediatrics,* 22 (May, 1943), 518–48.
30. Stolz, Herbert R., and Stolz, Lois M. *Somatic Development of Adolescent Boys: A Study of the Growth of Boys during the Second Decade of Life.* New York: The Macmillan Co., 1951.
31. Stone, Calvin P., and Barker, Roger S. "On the Relationship between Menarcheal Age and Certain Measurements of Physique in Girls of the Ages of 9 to 16 Years." *Human Biology,* 9 (Feb., 1937), 1–28.
32. Tanner, James M. *Growth of Adolescence.* Springfield, Ill.: C. C. Thomas, 1955.
33. Tuddenham, Read D., and Snyder, Margaret M. *Physical Growth of California Boys and Girls from Birth to Eighteen Years.* University of California Publications in Child Development, vol. 1, no. 2. Berkeley and Los Angeles: University of California Press, 1954.

2
Mental Development

IN ORDER to provide a setting for the status and development of intelligence in the predominant community college age-group, this chapter will begin, as did Chapter 1 on physical growth, with a brief portrayal of development during the age-span 8 or 9 to 17. This is done in order to provide an understanding of growth trends up to college age. The portrayal will include a comparison of intelligence of boys and girls. The growth in this earlier age-span will next be placed in the setting of changes in intelligence from childhood to old age. Evidence from studies of mental growth during college years will be reviewed. Note will be taken of the relationships of mental to physical growth and of physiological maturing to intelligence. The two remaining sections of the chapter prior to the summary will deal with the organization of intelligence and the nature of giftedness.

From Childhood to Youth

Mental growth from 8 to 17.—As in the case of physical growth, longitudinal studies, that is, studies involving successive measures of the same individuals over a span of years, can provide a more usable picture of growth of intelligence than "cross-sectional" studies based on single measures of a large population at different ages. Illustrative evidence comes from an early investigation employing this procedure, Freeman and Flory (*12*), one from which evidence has been quoted over the years. A total of 469 different individuals were tested, 219 boys and 250 girls. A limitation of this investigation sometimes mentioned is that the subjects were students in a rather selective laboratory school of a university, although it must be said that they included some boys and girls of average and less than average ability. The evidence on mental growth used was obtained from administering an intelligence test referred to as VACO, the spelling signifying the four parts of the test, vocabulary, analogies, completion, and opposites. The investigation made use of the scores on separate parts and total scores.

The composite curves described by lines joining the mean measures from 8 to 17 years of age for boys and girls in the Freeman and Flory investigation are shown in Figure 2.1. The lines are not far from straight. There is, however, a noticeable flattening of the curves in the later years. The authors explain this by the fact that the full complement of scores was not available for some students who were represented at earlier ages but had left the school before their sixteenth or seventeenth years, mainly by graduation, and these were among the brightest. Even with this disappearance of some superior subjects, the curves are still steep at 17, affording assurance of further rises in scores "well beyond," as the writers say, the ages of 17 and 18.

FIG. 2.1
COMPOSITE CURVES FOR THE MEAN SCORES ON VACO OF BOYS AND GIRLS

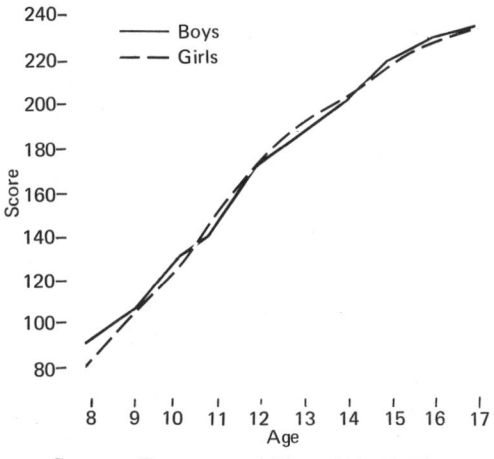

SOURCE: Freeman and Flory (*12*, 44, Fig. 13).

Variation among individuals.—As with average rates of physical growth, average rates of mental growth cannot disclose variations in growth from individual to individual. This may be illustrated by reproducing a pair of figures, one showing the records of five boys and the other of five girls. This is done in Figure 2.2. These individual growth curves show considerable fluctuation, especially well illustrated by curve E in the portion of the figure for boys. This is a slowly developing boy whose growth rate "may seem to support the view that duller children develop at a slower pace than bright ones, but he also helps to increase the variability of the growth with advancing age." One may note that his rate of growth has not decreased at age 18. There is less variation in the slope of the curves for the five girls represented.

MENTAL DEVELOPMENT 41

The ten curves show irregularities in rate of advancement at one or more ages. The authors say that the irregularities may be due to accidental or trivial causes, such as "transitory emotional attitudes," "temporal physical condition," "variations in testing procedure or in rapport between the examiner and the child." They point out that, nevertheless, the developmental picture of the majority of subjects "fits into a regular developmental trend rather than a growth pattern characterized by periods of spurts and retardations" (12, 57).

Comparison of the sexes.—The issue of similarity or difference in mental ability of the two sexes can be resolved by referring again to the results of the investigation by Freeman and Flory. It has already been noted

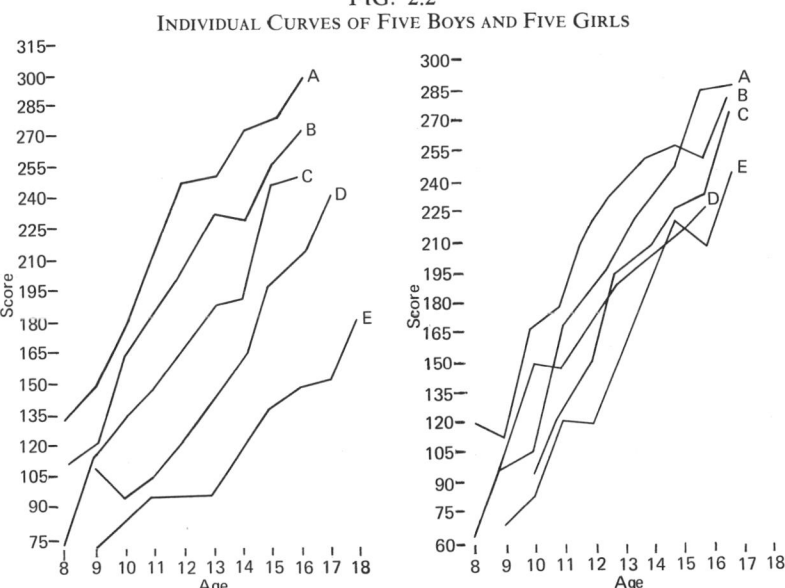

FIG. 2.2
INDIVIDUAL CURVES OF FIVE BOYS AND FIVE GIRLS

SOURCE: Freeman and Flory (12, 56–57, Figs. 26–27).

that the curves for boys and girls in Figure 2.1 follow each other very closely. We are assured that there is no statistically significant difference between the sexes at any point in this age-span and no trend toward difference toward the end of the period, which is the beginning point of the age-group of most interest to persons concerned with community college students. Comparisons of scores on intelligence have uniformly indicated equality of the sexes in the ability they measure.

Because the VACO test used by these investigators was actually made up of four subtests as described above, it was possible for Freeman and Flory to inquire into sex differences in ability as indicated in vocabulary, analogies, completion, and opposites. No one of the differences shown does more than approach statistical significance. In mean measures of vocabulary, boys were found to be slightly superior to girls throughout the age-span measured, which disagrees with the conclusions from inquiries that have found girls somewhat superior in abilities involving language. This difference is compensated for by a slight difference in the completion test which is in favor of the girls.

As it may seem desirable not to rely on a single investigation to support the now rather generally held belief of the essential equality of youth of the two sexes in rates of growth and status in mental ability, conclusions are cited from other inquiries, one by Thorndike and the other a synthesis of the findings of a number of reputable investigations in this area. The report by Thorndike dates back to 1926 (47) and involved 5,300 boys and 6,300 girls ranging in age from 13 to 18 in high schools in three cities. He found the scores for boys exceeding those for girls at all ages but by small amounts, and gave as the explanation the elimination of larger proportions of boys than girls from school, resulting in a higher degree of selection for boys than girls. It is well to remember in this connection that in the period represented enrollment of girls in high school exceeded that of boys, especially in upper grades. Thorndike appropriately concluded that "After reasonable allowance is made for differential selection, the inherent male superiority at ages 15 to 19, if it exists at all, is very small in comparison with the variation within either sex."

The synthesis is by Kuznets and McNemar (26). Referring to consistent differences found in the studies they reviewed, sometimes for boys and more often for girls, these writers conclude that the survey "has yielded largely negative conclusions. When large unselected groups were used, when age is taken into account, when possibilities of bias in test content are allowed for, startling differences between the sexes either in average tendency or in variation fail to emerge." However, they note that the conclusion is restricted to overall measurements of mental status and that "comparisons on more specific types of performance may, and in fact do, reveal systematic differences between the sexes."

The nature of the mental growth curve.—The average mental growth curves for boys and girls in Figure 2.1 were seen to be roughly straight lines with some deceleration in the later years. It is doubtful that growth of intelligence in these years is thus correctly represented. The source of the doubt lies in awareness that uniform units of measurement like those used in making the curves for growth in height, weight, etc., are not available for mental growth. Raw score differences at different age levels may actually be far from equal. Jones and Conrad, in the yearbook on adolescence (22, 149–54), addressed themselves to this problem and applied a method that had been used by Thurstone, which was to transform raw scores into absolute scores computing percentages of adult performance. The outcome of this procedure, applied to three studies of mental growth, is displayed in Figure 2.3. Jones and Conrad's

FIG. 2.3
MENTAL GROWTH CURVES IN PERCENTAGE OF MATURE STATUS

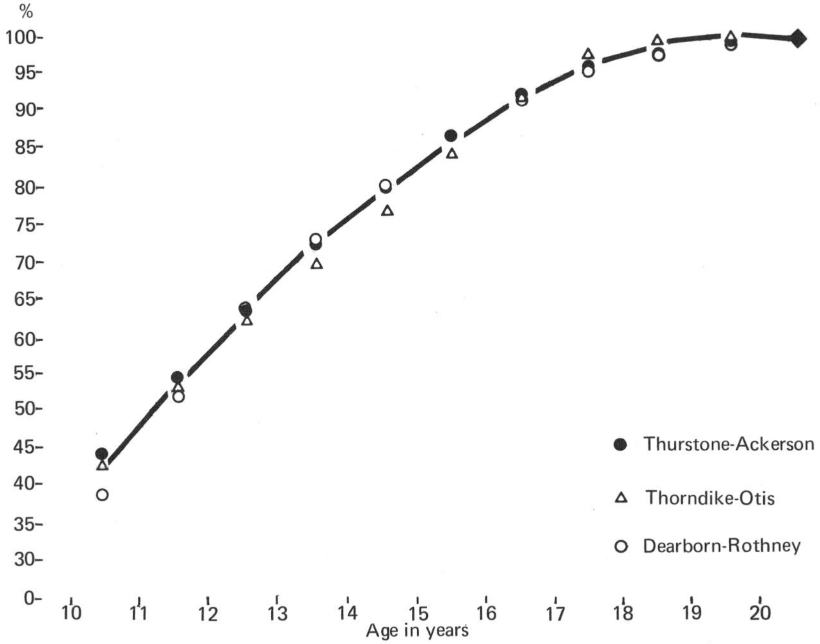

● Thurstone-Ackerson
△ Thorndike-Otis
○ Dearborn-Rothney

SOURCE: 22, 153, Fig. 3.

interpretation calls attention to the fact that the "points for the three studies lie so close together that it is not possible to show three curves; the curve that is drawn represents, rather, an average of the three." It may be seen that half the adult's mental growth is reached shortly after 11 years and that the remaining half occurs during adolescence and early postadolescence. The reader may wish to compare this curve with those of physical growth reproduced in Chapter 1. He would note, for instance, by looking at Figure 1.2, that the reconstructed curve for mental growth is much more nearly parabolic than that for growth in height.

Mental Change Through the Life Span

To add to the background for an understanding of mental growth trends in the predominant age-group in the community college it should be helpful also to have in mind the picture of mental growth and other mental changes through most of the life span. This is made possible by evidence from certain investigations which have undertaken to ascertain trends of growth in representative populations.

TABLE 2.1
Distribution by Age of Army Alpha Scores of the
Population 10 to 60 Years of Age in Certain
Rural New England Communities

Score	Age												
	10	12	14	16	18	19–21	22–24	25–29	30–34	35–39	40–44	45–49	50–54	55–59
200–210						2								
190–199							1	1	1					
180–189					1	2				1				
170–179					2	6		2	3	3			1	1
160–169				1	2	2	1	2	2		3	2	2	
150–159				5	2	4	3	4	2	1	4	1	2	2
140–149				4	1	5		4	5	4	6	5	1	1
130–139			2	6	3	1	3	1	9	7	7	3	2	1
120–129			1	6	1	6	4	1	7	8	5	1	7	
110–119		2	4	8	6	6	4	8	7	6	6	5	3	1
100–109		1	4	3	1	3	3	6	5	5	5	3	3	2
90–99	3	2	5	5	5	9	3	12	2	7	9	4	3	2
80–89		8	13	10	3	5	2	10	11	11	10	7	2	5
70–79	1	7	1	5	3	10	6	12	12	5	5	5	4	2
60–69	5	5	9	5	8	7	3	6	8	5	7	8	5	5
50–59	2	10	7	5	1	11	2	9	8	9	8	11	6	2
40–49	8	9	4	4	5	1	4	3	7	6	5	3	6	2
30–39	4	16	3	4	1	6	3	3	6	8	3	4	7	6
20–29	7	4	2	3	1	1	1	1	5	7	3	2	3	
10–19	2	1					1	2	5	3	6	4	2	
0–9	2		1	1				1	1		1			1
Total	34	65	56	75	46	87	44	88	106	96	97	68	59	33
Mean	44	57	76	93	97	101	92	90	87	85	92	81	81	79

Source: Jones and Conrad (24, 240).

The procedure in one of these, Miles and Miles (31), was to obtain scores on a 15-minute self-administered test of intelligence for samples of age-group by half decades in two cities in California, one of about 12,000 and the other of about 15,000 population. The procedure in this investigation relied mainly on computing coefficients of correlation between mental age on the test and chronological age. As might be expected, from what we know about rates of mental growth in childhood and youth, the relationship found for ages 7 to 17 was high and positive, namely, +0.80. From about 18 years of age on, the trend of mental age was, at first, found to be almost level, but dropped 15 or 16 mental age months by the chronological age of 50 years. During the period covered by the fourth and fifth decades (from age 30 to 50), the coefficient indicating the relation of score to chronological age was found to be -0.283 for men and women combined, reflecting appreciable decline.

Another study from about the same period aimed at ascertaining the trends in mental growth from age 10 to age 60 was by Jones and Conrad (24). It involved a sampling of the total population in certain New England communities and made use of the Army Alpha intelligence examination. The distribution of scores by chronological age is shown in Table 2.1. The bold-faced type in the columns identifies the score-span in which the means for the different age-groups are located. The mean score for the 10-year-olds is in the 40–49 score category. The mean score is seen to rise rather steadily and rapidly from 10 to 16 and to continue to increase with some deceleration in the 18 and 19–21 age-groups. The mean from this point on tends to drop with some approach to consistency to the last age column in the table. One may note that the mean score for the 55–59 age-group is in the same score-span as that for age 14. The drop during adulthood is seen to be much slower than the rise during the growth years.

One of the most striking impressions afforded by Table 2.1 is in the widespread distribution of scores for every age-group from youngest to oldest. The range for 10-year-olds extends from 0–9 on the test to the 90–99 score category, in which the mean score for 16-year-olds is located. The spread of scores increases to the 18 and 19–21 age-groups, after which it is somewhat restricted but, nevertheless, remains very wide. Even the oldest age-group contains scores up with the highest for earlier ages.

In comment on the distribution of low scores in later adulthood it may be said that some of these and, therefore, some of the decline in averages may be explained by the fact of less experience of the older population with tests than the younger, less motivation of the older population in taking the tests, or slower work habits of older people on a test with a time limit.

In another use made of the data gathered in the investigation just drawn upon, comparison was made of the scores for the two sexes through the same total age-span (9). Illustrative of the evidence are the mean scores in Table 2.2. These are reported as scores on "Abbreviated Alpha," which means the omission of two of the eight subtests, one of which measures vocabulary through an opposites test while the other measures information. This was done because the authors believed that accumulated experience "tends unduly to weight" these tests. Except for two of the means in Table 2.2, those for girls and women exceed those for boys and men, but in most cases by small margins only. The authors point out that the sex differences found on the individual subtests are by no means uniform. "In four strongly verbal tests (common sense, opposites, disarranged sentences, and

TABLE 2.2
MEAN SCORES FOR AGE-GROUPS FROM 10 TO 55–59 FOR THE TWO SEXES ON THE "ABBREVIATED" ARMY ALPHA TEST

Age-Group	M	F	Age-Group	M	F
10	31.3	34.7	19–21	59.6	71.3
11	30.9	35.2	22–24	54.0	68.7
12	38.4	42.2	25–29	60.1	52.1
13	38.2	49.8	30–34	53.9	55.7
14	50.8	55.3	35–39	47.1	55.6
15	51.4	69.5	40–44	54.7	53.7
16	63.7	64.5	45–49	46.6	50.7
17	65.3	67.0	50–54	38.9	57.1
18	61.4	66.7	55–59	43.8	47.2

SOURCE: Conrad, Jones, and Hsaio (9).

analogies), the males are rather consistently inferior; in two tests (numerical completions and general information), the sex differences are relatively slight . . . in one test (arithmetic problems), the males are quite definitely superior." The authors conclude that the direction and extent of difference between the sexes in a composite mental test like the one used in their investigation are dependent on the make-up of the test and the weighting of its parts and that, in the range of ages from 10 to 60, "the impressive fact is not the degree of sex difference, but rather the similarity of the developmental curves for the two sexes."

FIG. 2.4
CHANGES IN FULL-SCALE SCORES OF THE WECHSLER-BELLEVUE FORM I, AGES 7 TO 65

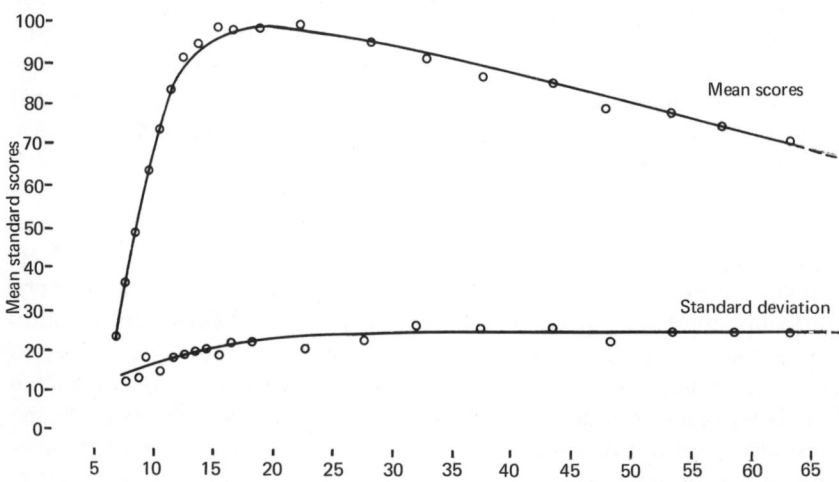

SOURCE: Wechsler (52, 31, Fig. 1).

The third effort to study mental growth and change over the life-span to be drawn upon here is one by Wechsler using what he called the Wechsler-Bellevue Form I. The curve showing the changes in full-scale scores of this test as reported by him is reproduced in Figure 2.4. This curve is as presented in the latest revision of his report (52, 31, Fig. 1) and reflects the results of numerous refinements in research procedure over those he had previously applied. He refers to the curve as a "logistic growth curve" and says that it "shows that intellectual growth is not linear, that is, that it does not proceed by equal amounts throughout its development" (31).

In citing these projects undertaking portrayal of the evidence of change in mental ability over the life-span from childhood to old age, the purpose here is not to regard as closed the issue of the decline during adulthood. The references are brought in primarily to afford some background for portrayal of the growth of intelligence in childhood and youth. The proper place for consideration of the issue of growth and decline in adult life is Chapter 10 which is concerned with the adult student. However, it is appropriate at this point to intimate that the conclusion of a marked decline during adulthood is currently suspect, and that the present belief among the scholars in this field is that the individual's primary intelligence is maintained through most of the life-span.

Mental Growth During College Years

The expectation.—The controversy over what is the age ceiling for mental growth is certainly not as violent now as it was a half century ago, and discussion at present centers more about the factors that raise or lower that ceiling. Time was when some psychologists contended that mental growth ceased at 14 or 15. Experience with tests has had major influence in changing opinions on the placement of the ceiling. An instance of a study that influenced these opinions is one reported by Thorndike in 1926 (47). The population investigated was the same as he used in inquiring into sex differences in intelligence, cited earlier in this chapter, and involving 5,300 boys and 6,300 girls in high schools in three cities. The procedure included testing the subjects and retesting them a year later. The procedure included also (a) the use of alternative forms so as to avoid the defect of computing gains from repeating an identical test by individual subjects and (b) subtractions for gains for "practice effect." Thorndike concluded that "the doctrine that the ability to improve one's score in a measure of intelligence necessarily ceases at 14 or 16 . . . should be abandoned" and that there "seems to be evidence that this ability improves, at least in the case of those who are subject to intellectual education, beyond 18."

The expectation of mental growth during the college age-span is encouraged also by the increase in scores reported for the age-groups 18 and 19-21 in the studies just cited on mental growth during the life-span. While the rate of growth is seen to be decelerating in these age groups, appreciable increments in the averages are, nevertheless, to be noted.

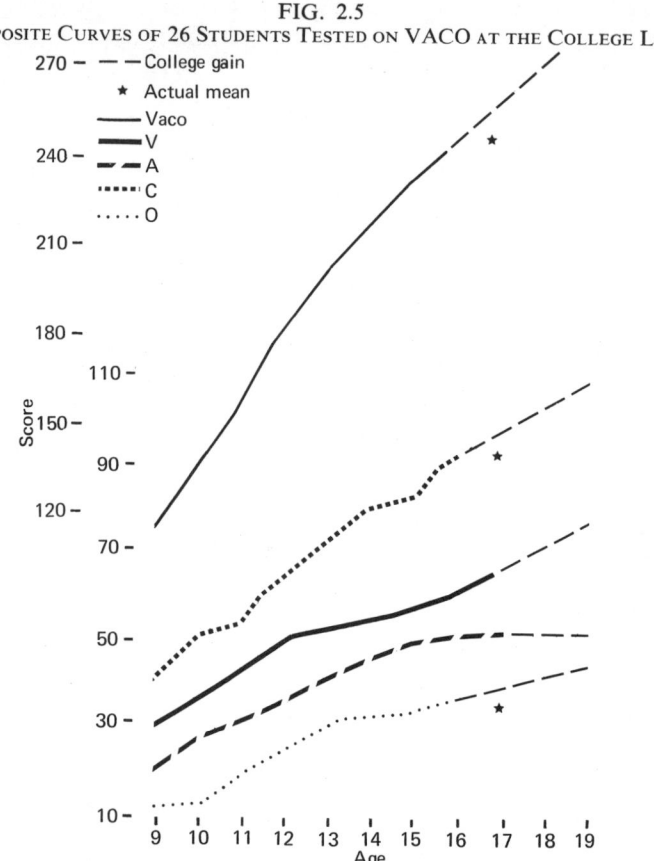

FIG. 2.5
COMPOSITE CURVES OF 26 STUDENTS TESTED ON VACO AT THE COLLEGE LEVEL

SOURCE: Freeman and Flory (*12*, 82, Fig. 49).

Investigations of college students.—An oft-quoted investigation of mental growth at the college level is one by Freeman and Flory cited early in this chapter in describing the growth of intelligence from 8 to 17. During the period represented about a third of these laboratory school graduates continued their schooling at the University of Chicago. A list of all such individuals was compiled and, through college authorities, about thirty were found available and invited to submit to retest. A total of 26 students, 15 men and 11 women, were retested. Attendance in college ranged from six months to three years. The test scores showed that all individual subjects, except one man who admitted that he was physically in no condition to take the test, continued to advance in mental ability.

The composite curves on the VACO tests for all 26 subjects are displayed in Figure 2.5, which is devised to show the means of the test records through the laboratory school and in college, both as to total score and for the four parts of the test, vocabulary, analogies, completion, and opposites. Interpretative comment of the investigators is as follows (*12*, 82): "It is indeed striking that the curve continues to advance with little decrease in rate at the college level. The period of most rapid growth seems to come early, but there is no indication that these twenty-six students are nearing their maximum development. . . . The evidence is so clear with reference to the mental development of these subjects that one must conclude that intellectual growth continues well beyond the high school years, at least for individuals who attend college."

An issue forced upon those who consider these increments of mental growth, especially during adolescence and beyond, is whether they are mainly the results of maturing or of schooling and experience. The investigators' observation on this issue was that "it seems unlikely that the intellectual growth beyond middle adolescence is due in large measure to maturation. . . . That is, intellectual growth throughout childhood and early youth as well as during later youth and adulthood is to be attributed in large measure to education and training, both informal and formal" (*12*, 86).

Four other investigations into the question of mental growth in college years will be capsulized, with emphasis on procedures and findings. These are by Rogers (*34*), Livesay (*27*), McConnell (*28*), and Hartson (*21*). The Rogers study involved a comparison of scores on the Thorndike Intelligence Examination of students in Bryn Mawr, a highly selective college for women, with scores obtained by these same students as freshmen. Their average age as freshmen was 18½ years, although the range was from 16 to 20. The number of seniors who volunteered for the retest was 56. The classification of these students on the repeated tests was such that some were retested after an interval of one year, some after two years, and some after three years. The average gains made for these three groups were, respectively, 2.6 points, 3.86 points, and 5.6 points, thus showing some increase in gain for each additional year in school. Rogers concludes from this aspect of the investigation that "there is for college women significant improvement in general intelligence . . . after the age of 18. The gain in intellectual power in college years, though slight, is significant."

Scores on the subtests of the Thorndike Intelligence Examination made possible inquiry into growth in a number of special abilities, namely, linguistic, language completion, reading, mathematical, mechanical aptitude, information, reasoning, and visual perception. No significant gain was made in linguistic ability. This is "probably explained by the fact that the tests need to be lengthened by the addition of more difficult items to measure Bryn Mawr students adequately." Retest of language completion yielded a significant increase. The retest of reading ability showed the largest gain of all, which is explained by the fact that much academic work is concerned with getting thought from the printed page. The gain in mathematical ability varied with the amount of work students had taken in the subject, with students taking none showing a small loss. The test on information showed an "insignificant" average loss. Rogers concludes that the evidence submitted by Thorndike of improvement in intelligence scores beyond 14 years is in this investigation supplemented for a "group of superior women" beyond the ages of 18 and 19.

The study by McConnell involved 70 men and women seniors in Cornell College (in Iowa) who, as freshmen, had been tested on the 1927 edition of the Psychological Examination of the American Council on Education, and, after volunteering on invitation, were retested on the 1928 edition of the same test. For the comparison the 1927 scores were transmuted into 1928 equivalents. The mean score of the seniors was 185.2, whereas the mean for the group as freshmen had been 144.78, representing a substantial difference of 40.42. The mean gain of the women was 11.85 points more than that made by the men, but McConnell found it not to be statistically significant. Seniors who had been in the upper half of the distribution as freshmen made an average gain of 37 and those in the lower half did no less well, scoring an average increase of 43.28.

McConnell admitted the impossibility of indicating the relative influence of various factors on the increase in scores, but nevertheless listed and considered them. He mentioned four in particular: (1) "growth in underlying capacity," which would be the result of maturation; (2) "growth in effective use of endowment," as when the score on the test of artificial language "might be bettered by acquisition of more effective modes of attack on language learning situations"; (3) specific training, as when course instruction received by the student may directly affect his performance; and (4) "varying sets, emotional states, motivation and other like factors." Concerning the factor last named, he says, "It is probably true that the emotional state of many freshmen confronted with an intelligence examination is not conducive to best performance. That better poise on the part of the senior examinees could have been responsible for a large share of the average increase, however, is doubtful. As a matter of fact, it is probable that these students as freshmen were more concerned with making good scores than they were as seniors. The seniors realized that their score on the test was not a crucial matter. It is possible, therefore, that the depressing factor of emotional tension in the original test situation was offset by the stimulus of strong motivation; and that the emotional ease of the later situation was offset by reduced initiative."

The investigation by Livesay, like that by McConnell, used the Psychological Examination of the American Council on Education and involved fifty seniors at the University of Hawaii who took the test voluntarily, after having been subjected to the same test as freshmen. They had had no experience with the test during intervening years. Every individual gained on the test. However, except for the completion test, the picture was different on the subtest scores as comparison of the scores disclosed losses for varying numbers of subjects in artificial language, analogies, or arithmetic. When the subjects were divided into ability groups, by fourths of the total group, the largest gains in every instance were made by the two middle groups. The lowest group made greater gains than the highest group in all subtests but arithmetic, but it was evident that the highest group had less chance for increase because of higher initial scores.

The most extensive investigation of improvement of intelligence test scores to be drawn upon here is one by Hartson (21) made on seniors at Oberlin College. These seniors were all retested on a different form of the Ohio State University Psychological Examination than they had taken as freshmen, and the author observed from a controlled comparison of the two forms that "the learning of specific items of the freshman test constitutes but a small portion of the gain made." The examination consisted of five tests: 1, Arithmetic; 2, Synonyms-Antonyms Vocabulary; 3, Verbal Analogies; 4, Number Series; 5, Reading Comprehension. Scores were transmuted into centiles, using the state freshman norms, in order to equate the scales for variations in difficulty.

The findings of this investigation that concern us most relate to (a) the overall gains made on the retest and (b) the gains (or losses) on different parts of the examination with respect to the subjects in which the students had specialized. Hartson found that there was significant improvement in the total scores—improvement which could not be a factor of selection inasmuch as the students making up the two groups were identical. Students who had fallen behind or had transferred to other institutions were not included in the comparisons. No significant differences were found between the total scores of men and women, although there were differences on the separate parts of the examination: men surpassed the women in parts employing numbers and were somewhat superior in Reading Comprehension, whereas women had the better record in the parts involving vocabulary. Another general finding of importance is that students in the lower deciles of ability as freshmen made on the average greater gains than those in the higher deciles, although this may be partly explained by limitations of the test. Hartson observed, "Even the least capable freshmen were not so intellectually mature as to be incapable of making remarkable improvement in test intelligence after the age of eighteen."

Following are excerpts from Hartson's interpretation of his evidence bearing on the relationships of the students' specializations to the changes in test scores: "One wonders whether scores in the different varieties of test reflect the training associated with one's field of specialization. The examination includes but two contrasting forms of material. Tests 1 and 4 require computations in numerical symbols; 2 and 3 test verbal relationships. Inspection of the tabulated data shows that it is the students who majored in the Mathematics-Science division who proved the most apt in the numerical computations, and it is those who majored in the Language-Literature groups who showed greatest ability in handling verbal relationships. These are the only major groups in which test scores appear to be related definitely to the subject-matter of their courses. . . . More striking than good freshman showing of students who later chose to major in Mathematics or Science is their improved status, after three years' training, in the tests employing the numerical symbols. These students proved to be the most capable in Arithmetic, whereas the students in the English and Language groups were less intelligent in this field as seniors than when they entered college. . . . In both vocabulary tests the highest scores, initial and final, were made by the majors in the foreign languages, although they were but ninth in arithmetic and sixth in number series. . . ."

In the summary of his study, Hartson expresses his belief that the discovery of a definite relationship between the nature of the tests and the character of the courses in which one has specialized is of greater significance than the increase in the total score. "Continued maturation," he concluded, "is not a general process of unfoldment of inner capacities, which occurs independently of particular training."

The general inference from the several studies involving repeated application of intelligence tests at the college level is that test intelligence improves with college attendance. The improvement is reflected in the increase of total scores and is shown in about equal extent in the two sexes. The increments on subtests are significantly related to areas in which the students have continued their education, from which there is an approach to consensus that the gains are less dependent on a general maturing of inner capacities than on development of special aspects of mentality conduced to by the various areas of instruction.

All the five investigations that have been abstracted in order to ascertain the trend of mental changes at the collegiate level have had to do with students in four-year colleges or universities. Unfortunately, no report of inquiry concerning this question in the community college, if any has been made, has found its way into print. This question as it relates to this institution can only be answered inferentially. In Chapter 7 it will be seen that, while the community college enrolls some students no less competent on measures of intelligence than those in highly selective colleges, this new institution customarily admits students of a wider range of ability and, therefore, larger proportions of students with somewhat lower performance on tests of aptitude. However, certain of the studies that have been reviewed have found greater increments of growth for those with lower initial scores than for those in the higher ranges, although the qualification has been made that this is in part owing to limitations of the tests used. There would seem to be no reason to believe that total test scores or scores on subtests would not be influenced in the same directions in community colleges as in four-year institutions.

Relation of Mental to Physical Growth and to Maturation

Mental and physical growth.—Studies of the relationships between different physical measurements of children and measurements of chronological age have found rather high positive coefficients of correlation. The coefficients, however, resulting from calculations of the relationships between measures of intelligence and of physique, such as height, weight, etc., are much lower. Abernethy (*1*) found the closest relationship for both boys and girls to be with standing height, with a median coefficient of .30 in the case of boys. She found sitting height and weight next in correlation, while measures of girth for boys and of ossification ratio for both sexes correlated less consistently than did measures of other physical traits. Considering the data in general, Abernethy observed that the coefficients for boys tend to be slightly higher than for girls. These correlations are, nevertheless, low.

We may judge from the findings of an investigation involving 490 freshmen made by Middleton and Moffett (*29*) that the relations of measurements of height and weight to intelligence are even lower, although still positive, at the collegiate level. The correlation for intelligence and height was .22, while that for intelligence and weight was .15. Abernethy's calculations for adults found "zero or negligible" coefficients of correlation between mental test scores and measures of height and weight, which she indicated had been found in previous investigations.

Mental growth and puberty.—In the consideration of the relationships between intelligence and physique, it remains to inquire into the often claimed acceleration of mental growth at adolescence. To investigate this question as it applies to girls, Stone and Barker (*40*) compared Otis group intelligence test scores of 175 postmenarcheal and 175 premenarcheal girls paired for chronological ages. They found that the postmenarcheal girls obtained a mean score 2.25 points higher than the premenarcheal group. This difference is 2.47 times its standard error and may be said to indicate a difference approaching statistical significance.

For light on this issue as it applies to boys as well as girls, we may refer again to Shuttleworth's monograph (*38*, ch. viii, 196–202) drawn upon near the opening of the treatment of physical growth in Chapter 1. The reader will recall that Shuttleworth relied on the MG age (age at maximum growth) for his age of the timing of endocrine events conducing to sexual maturity. By using this MG-age, which correlated highly with menarcheal age for girls and which would have a similar correlation with corresponding changes in boys, he could readily study and compare the growth of boys and girls as influenced by endocrine events. In advance of drawing conclusions from his own inquiry, he summarizes the findings of earlier investigations in this area by inducing that early maturing girls and boys have very slightly higher average IQs, but that in no instance have the differences proved statistically reliable. From his own investigation he concludes: "At every age and at every one of a long series of intelligence tests both boys and girls with early MG-ages tend to be brighter than those with late MG-ages. The differences, however, are such that only a minority of the comparisons are statistically reliable. The data establish the existence of some relation between intelligence and MG-age, but the relationship is tenuous and the nature of the underlying forces is unknown. . . ."

With the knowledge that the processes of sexual maturing take place in girls on the average a year and a half to two years before those in boys, we are made aware that the acceleration in intelligence accompanying them, statistically or educationally significant or not, must, on the average, affect girls before boys. Except for this difference, the growth curves of intelligence of the two sexes, as has previously been noted, are very nearly alike.

The relationships and trends just canvassed, with whatever statistical or educational significance they may have, are, because of their age-incidence, exclusively in the precollege age-group. In view of the primary concern of this treatise with the population of college age, the question here turns on whether or not, or in what degree, the intelligence of the college student is affected by the changes noted in early adolescent years. As long as a third of a century ago Viteles (*51*) gave an answer to this question, as concerns freshman women. These women were asked to supply their ages at menarche. These ages were classified in six groups as follows: 9.0–12.5, 12.6–13.0, 13.1–13.8, 13.9–14.2, and 14.3–17.6. Because the Brown Psychological Examination had been administered to all these students, it was possible to compute the average score on this examination for each of these groups. These averages, in the order of the groups as listed, were 47.4, 46.2, 44.5, 45.9, and 47.8. They disclose no influence of age at menarche. Another investigation reported a few years later by Stone and Barker (*41*), involving women, mainly freshmen, at San Jose State College and Stanford University, found no significant relationships between intelligence scores and reported age at menarche.

The literature on growth seems not to contain substantial studies on college men analogous to those by Viteles and by Stone and Barker, that is, that would inquire into the relationship of measures of intelligence in college years of men with their ages of pubescence as boys. However, the presence of little if any significant relationship may be inferred from the near identity of growth curves as shown by total scores on intelligence tests of the two sexes through later adolescence. Differences in subtests have been reported, such as differences in favor of men in numerical aspects and of women in linguistic portions, but these differences have tended to offset each other toward equivalence of total scores. If there is any surviving difference, it would be likely to be inconsiderable and would be occasioned by the few boys of very late pubescence.

Change in Mental Organization with Age

Change at younger ages.—Up to this point in this chapter attention has been directed to mental growth in general rather than to intelligence in special aspects. Differentiation has been touched on only as it concerns variability in general intelligence, which was reported to increase with age, and as it emerges in tendencies of divergence of performance of the two sexes on subtests of intelligence examinations. Survey here of mental growth has not yet considered the evidence on change in organization or patterns of intelligence from childhood into adulthood or on the variation in pattern in college years.

Intensive interest in the question of mental organization must have begun with the rapid spread of development and application of mental tests during which it became apparent that the same individuals often do not perform equally well on different kinds of items or subtests in an intelligence examination. For three decades or more psychologists have been trying to ascertain the degree and the meaning of this divergence. The following effort at illustrating the trend of evidence and discussion of the findings and problems in the area will identify some of the persons who have done much in it.

Consideration of changes in mental organization may well begin with a report of principal results of investigations analyzing test results for children of different age-groups. One of these investigations was made by Garrett, Bryan, and Perl (15) and involved three groups, composed of 9-, 12-, and 15-year-olds, of about 250 boys and girls in equal proportions. They were reported to be, to a greater extent than is usual in such groups, representative of their populations. A battery of ten mental tests was administered to these children, consisting of six tests designated as "memory" tests and four as "non-memory" tests (tests of verbal and number ability).

The authors reported from this investigation that the memory tests taken alone exhibited reliable increases from 9 years to 12, but no significant increase from 12 to 15. The tests of verbal ability (vocabulary) and number ability (arithmetic) showed increase up to 15 years, the increase for boys being relatively greater than for girls. The correlations between verbal and number scores decreased rather consistently from 9 to 15. The authors concluded that the abilities measured by their tests tend to become more and more specific and their "tentative" explanation of the drop in correlations signifies that "intelligence in younger children is amorphous to a greater degree than during later growth periods."

Clark (8) administered the Chicago Tests of Primary Abilities to something more than a hundred boys of each of the ages 11, 13, and 15. These tests were designed to measure six mental abilities or components: number, verbal understanding, space, word-fluency, reasoning, and memory. The three groups were approximately equivalent in the distribution of their intelligence test scores as determined by group tests (Henmon, Otis, etc.). Statistically significant increases with age in the mean scores were found for all the six components. There was also a consistent tendency for increase in variability with age of scores for each component. Analysis of the intercorrelations led to several important findings. The memory factor was found to have very little relationship to the other factors at any age from 11 to 15 and showed no consistent change in this respect within the age range. With this single exception there was a consistent decrease in the intercorrelations among the six abilities as age increased. "The correlations of each one of the mental components with the other five combined showed the same decrease in correlation with age. When all of the intercorrelations were averaged, the decrease with age was quite clear-cut." It was found further that with the exception of the memory component, changes with age in the primary mental abilities were not noticeably influenced by the general intelligence level as indicated by intelligence tests.

In the face of this kind of evidence Garrett undertook to formulate a "developmental theory of intelligence" (*13*) which is presented here in part by quotation and in part by paraphrase. The term "intelligence" (omitting the qualification "general") includes "at least the abilities demanded in the solution of problems which require the comprehension and use of symbols," meaning words, numbers, diagrams, equations, formulas, which represent ideas and relationships ranging from the fairly simple to the very complex. The ability to deal with such stimuli may be called *symbol* or *abstract intelligence.* "Abstract or symbol intelligence changes its organization as age increases from a fairly unified and general ability to a loosely organized group of abilities or factors. If this hypothesis is true, the measurement of intelligence must perforce change its methods and objectives with increase in age."

After citing evidence from additional investigations, Garrett said, "From these various studies I believe we can predict a steady drop in correlation among tests involving verbal, numerical, and spatial concepts from about age 8 to age 18. With increasing age there appears to be a gradual breakdown of an amorphous general ability in a group of fairly distinct aptitudes. It seems highly probable that maturation has much to do with this differentiating process, but increasing experience and diverging interests must also contribute heavily. . . . Over the elementary school years we find a functional generality among tests at the symbol level. Later on this general or 'g' breaks down into the quasi-independent factors reported by many investigations."

The college age and beyond.—Unfortunately for our purposes most of the investigations looking into change with age are restricted to younger ages than those that are our present concern, the early college years. However, some have been made at the college age and beyond from which comparisons may be made with findings of those at earlier ages, and inferences drawn as to whether or not the trends shown at the lower ages persist. Schneck (*35*) administered nine group tests, five of them verbal and the rest numerical, to 210 men enrolled in a course in psychology in the College of the City of New York. The men were 18 to 21 years of age representing "a minimum of diversity with respect to education, ancestry, economic and social status, and age." General factors for verbal ability (V) and for numerical ability (N) were found. These two abilities were found to have little in common, the correlation between V and N being .26. "It was established that either V or N contains something which is not present in the other."

At about the same time, Garrett (*14*) had administered Thorndike's CAVD test to 338 freshmen women in the Brooklyn branch of Hunter College, almost all of whom were graduates of New York City high schools. The test was of four parts: C, sentence completion; A, arithmetic problems; V, vocabulary; and D, directions (requiring the reading and comprehension of sentences). Intercorrelations were computed for the four parts. The average intercorrelation of C, V, and D was .54, while the average intercorrelation of A with C, V, and D was .27. The interpretation concludes that "these results are consistent with those reported by Schneck to the effect that verbal ability (defined loosely as the ability to use words and manipulate language relations) and number ability (aptitude in handling quantitative concepts) are really independently varying traits."

To round out the picture of differential aptitude over the life-span, we may quote from Anastasia and Foley's (*3, 525*) citation of findings of the standardization data of the Wechsler-Bellevue Intelligence Scale. These data, say the writers, "provide some information regarding age changes in factor patterns among adults. The average intercorrelation of the subtests dropped steadily from the 9-year-old group to the 25–29-year-old group, thus corroborating the results of other studies. In the 35–44-year group, however, it rose to .31, and in the 50–59-year group it rose again to .43 . . . thus, in this study, specialization seemed to reach a peak during the middle age levels; in both the younger and the older groups, generalization of ability seemed to be the rule."

The controversy of general intelligence vs. differential aptitudes.—In the foregoing report of the evidence bearing on the change in mental organization more might have been said about the controversy over the relative prominence and importance from childhood through adolescence of general intelligence and of specialized aptitudes. This controversy, as persons conversant with the area well know, has resulted in a considerable body of investigative and discussional literature. This is hardly the place to undertake to resolve the controversy, but we can do no less than illustrate the diverging points of view and await the results of further inquiry and a nearer approach to consensus on the issue.

The finding by Clark (*8*), in an investigation with the Chicago Test of Primary Abilities involving boys of 11, 13, and 15, that there was a consistent decrease in correlations between the scores on six tests of abilities has already been cited. The Thurstones, of the University of Chicago, a few years previously had reported on their extensive factorial investigation into "primary mental abilities" with eighth-grade pupils in the Chicago public schools (*50*). The procedure had involved administering, first, 63 tests, and later, after eliminating a number of tests with low correlations, 21 tests. From these were selected three sets of tests for seven abilities as follows: P, Perception; M, Memory; V, Vocabulary; W, Word Comprehension; S, Spatial; N, Numbers; and R, Reasoning. They reported, after analysis of the results from administering these tests, that they were unable to find a general factor distinct from the primary factors, but had found a second-order general factor which "should be of as much psychological interest as the more frequently postulated independent general factor of Spearman." They contended that the factorial methods they used were adequate for finding such a general intellective factor, either as a factor independent of the primaries or as a factor operating through correlated primaries. In connection with a review of their evidence, they said (*50*, 8), "It seems strange that, with all this experience in differential psychology, we have clung so long to the practice of summarizing a child's mental endowment by a single index, such as the mental age, the intelligence quotient, the percentile rank in general intelligence, and other single average measures. . . . The error that is frequently made is that the intelligence quotient is sanctified by the assumption that it measures some basic functional unity, when it is known to be nothing more than a composite of functional unities."

Another investigator at the University of Chicago, Swineford (*43*), applied factorial procedures to scores on tests administered to children in grades 7 and 9 and found "No evidence . . . to support the view that with increasing maturity the general factor plays a less important role as special abilities are developed. Moreover, there appears no shift to the verbal factor in the correlations of the general factor scores at the lower grade with the verbal-factor scores at the higher grade."

Subsequently, she reported from a further investigation involving the administration of the same battery of nine tests in grade 9 to children who had taken them three years before in grade 6 (*42*). This was, thus, a longitudinal instead of a cross-sectional study. She summarizes, "The three-year growth in factor scores, indicated by means of factor estimates, confirms the findings of an earlier cross-section study. In terms of the variability of the group, the general factor shows the greatest increase. The verbal factor, likewise, increases, but by a much smaller amount. No increase during this period is apparent for the spatial factor estimates."

More recently, the British psychologist Burt (*7*), while carefully reviewing all the investigations that had been made in this controversial area, commented that a conclusion from Swineford's study that there is no indication that the general factor tends to disappear with increasing maturity can hardly be drawn from this investigation. He admitted that Swineford's figures show no signs of mental-differentiation with increasing *grade*; and implied that the conclusion could not be applied to increasing *age* because each grade included children of very mixed ages, ranging over four or five years. Quotation is made here from Burt's "Summary and Conclusions" from his critique of all the studies: "1. Biological, neurological, and statistical evidence all appears strongly to support the view that with increasing age intellectual ability tends to become more and more specialized. Thus, the general factor accounts for a distinctly smaller proportion of the total amount of individual variation, while group factors play an increasingly predominant part. 2. Changes of this kind are shown most clearly in tests of scholastic attainments, but may be here due in some degree to environmental influences and to a specialization of interest rather than of ability. Similar changes, however, are also found with tests of mental capacities such as are less likely to be affected by extraneous conditions, and must, therefore, at least in part, be the result of intrinsic processes of maturation."

For the time being, because of the apparent conflict in the interpretation of the evidence and discussion, this issue of whether and to what extent the general factor is being displaced in mental development from childhood to adulthood must in some degree be left hanging. The disagreement has not prevented efforts at utilization and development of tests of differential aptitude. For example, Segel (37) made experimental use in high schools of War Department aptitude tests of mechanical aptitude, spatial relationships, speed of perception, code learning, word fluency, language usage, and mathematical reasoning. He concluded that this type of material can be used in grades 9 through 12. He observed that the reliability of these particular tests could be improved if they were lengthened, and that the evidence in his study supports the hypothesis that a multiple-aptitude test of the type is of value for individual diagnosis and prognostic work. Further instances of confidence in the usefulness of such tests are to be found in their multiplication in recent years. One such test is that published by the Psychological Corporation, which is made up of a battery of Differential Aptitude Tests (5) with subtests of verbal reasoning, numerical ability, abstract reasoning, space relations, mechanical reasoning, clerical speed and accuracy, and language usage (spelling and sentences).

Giftedness and Creativity

Gifted young people.—Because the community college will enroll a share of gifted youth, it is desirable to review, of necessity concisely, the characteristics and the trends of development of this promising segment of the school population. The study of gifted children and youth has been so well done and carried on over such a long period by investigators like Terman (45, 46), Miles (30), Hollingsworth (23), and Witty (53), to name a few, that much of the information is common knowledge to educators and psychologists. On this account illustrative conclusions will be summarized without documentation in detail. This brief portrayal will be followed by a partial résumé of a recent inquiry into creativity in youth, which has opened the way to an improved understanding of giftedness.

Screening for the gifted in school populations received a powerful impetus with the advent of group and individual intelligence testing and with the invention of the concepts of mental age and intelligence quotient (IQ). The screening point for giftedness was somewhat arbitrarily set at IQ 130 and above, a range on the distribution of ability as measured by intelligence tests that includes something like 1 per cent of the population. It is well known that, owing to the process of selection, the proportion in this range of IQ 130 and above increases with grade level, from elementary school through secondary school to college.

Researches have shown that high intellectual ability and achievement of these gifted youth persist with their progress through the school system. Superior physique and health, as well as desirable personal and social traits, much more often than not are characteristic of children in this high-intelligence group. Sexual maturity, as indicated by pubescence, comes sooner for most members of this group.

The fathers of these children with high intelligence have been found to be employed in a wide variety of occupations, ranging from the professions down through unskilled labor, but the proportionate representation is much greater for the higher than the lower socioeconomic groups as indicated by occupation. The proportion runs high for those from homes where the heads of the household are in professional, financial, political, religious, or executive positions.

Early investigations identified more boys than girls in the gifted range, but later studies, probably because the populations have been more representative, have found the proportion of the sexes more nearly equal.

Children in the gifted range have been found to begin school earlier and to progress through the grades more rapidly. Their work in school is notably superior in subjects involving verbal comprehension, but less so, with exceptions for some children, in those involving manual performance. Being successful in it, they like school, and are regular in attendance. Achievement profiles are like those of average children, except that their ratings run higher. The favorite recreation of gifted children is reading, and their play interests, more often than for average children, involve reading. Among their hobbies, collections are more numerous.

Follow-up studies of these gifted children in college have found them to maintain their high status in intellectual, academic, and social relationships. Extensions of the follow-ups into adult life have found them to be at work in higher occupational levels and with higher economic return than for those of average mental endowment.

The differences reviewed are not, to be sure, universal for this range, but they are nevertheless notable.

Intelligence vs. *creativity*.—While all these manifestations of superiority of the gifted as measured by intelligence tests have been known and admitted over a long period, many persons, both in print and discussion, have expressed doubts as to the efficacy of the usual intelligence test to identify all the gifted in a population. These doubts are lodged in considerable part in the adequacy for this purpose of instruments weighted as heavily as these mental examinations are with verbal components. The skepticism has recently been substantiated by an investigative effort to identify creativity in students as contrasted with high performance on the conventional tests of intelligence. The research is that of Getzels and Jackson (*19*) of the University of Chicago, and an attempt to abstract their report will make up the final paragraphs of this chapter before the summary. Abridging the report of the research will be done by paraphrasing and quotation, more of the latter because the report on which reliance is placed is already estimably succinct and well written.

The total population of 449 in a "midwestern private secondary school" supplied the subjects for the experiment. The two groups compared were selected from this population on the basis of performance on the following tests assembled, developed, and adapted for the purpose of the experiment (*19, 7*): standard IQ tests (the scores all converted by regression equation to comparable Stanford-Binet IQs), and five creativity tests—(1) Word Association; (2) Uses for Things; (3) Hidden Shapes; (4) Fables (to compose endings); (5) Make-up Problems (mathematical).

The two experimental groups were formed on the basis of the IQ measure and the mean of the five creative measures. The high-creativity group, made up of 26 students (15 boys and 11 girls), consisted of the top 20 per cent in creativity, compared to students of the same age and sex, but *not* in the top 20 per cent in IQ. The high-intelligence group of 28 students (17 boys and 11 girls) consisted of the top 20 per cent in IQ, but *not* in the top 20 per cent in creativity.

The two groups were then compared with each other and with the total population of the school on the following variables: (1) school performance as measured by standardized verbal and numerical tests appropriate to each grade level; (2) teacher preferences on having them in class; and (3) "need-achievement" as measured by conventional scoring of responses to six McClelland's stimulus pictures about which, following projection on a movie screen, students are asked to write short stories.

Results of the comparison appear in Table 2.3. It may be seen that, notwithstanding the striking differences in mean IQ, the groups were equally superior in school achievement; "the intelligent subjects rather than the creative ones were preferred by teachers"; and there was no essential difference in the need-for-achievement measures.

Results of the investigators' inquiry for occupational choices of the two groups are summarized as follows (*19*, 11, 14): "Differences between the two groups appeared in both the *quantity* and the *quality* of occupational goals. The *quantity* of occupational possibilities mentioned is significantly greater for the high creatives than for the high IQs. ... The *quality* of the different occupations mentioned is also significantly different for the two groups. ... With respect to the *quantity* of occupations considered, depending on one's point of view, one might say that the high-creativity adolescents are more 'diffuse' in occupational goals than the high-IQ adolescents, or that they are more able and willing to deal with a greater range of career possibilities. As for the *quality* of occupations considered, again depending

TABLE 2.3
MEANS OF HIGHLY CREATIVE AND HIGHLY INTELLIGENT GROUPS ON EXPERIMENTAL VARIABLES*

Variables	Total Population (449)	High IQ (28)	High Creative (24)
IQ	132.00	150.00	127.00
School achievement	49.91	55.00	56.27
Teacher-preference ratings	10.23	11.20	10.54
Need-for-achievement (T-scores)	49.81	49.00	50.04

SOURCE: Adapted from Getzels and Jackson (*19*, Table 1).
*Omitting standard deviations.

on one's point of view, one might say that the high-creativity adolescents are either more 'eccentric' in their occupational goals or more able and willing to deal with career risks; that is, to take liberties with accepted standards of adult success."

In the minds of the investigators the "most relevant and striking differences ... between the two groups in the context of the present inquiry are observed in the relationship of qualities they want for themselves, the qualities they believe lead to adult success, and the qualities they believe teachers favor." The subjects had been asked to rank eight personal traits in the orders (a) in which they would like to be outstanding, (b) in which these traits were predictive of success, and (c) in which they were preferred by teachers (*19*, 15): "The high-IQs ranked the qualities in which they would like to be outstanding in the following order: (1) character; (2) emotional stability; (3) goal-directedness; (4) creativity; (5) wide range of interests; (6) high marks; (7) IQ; and (8) sense of humor. The high-creatives ranked the qualities in the following order: (1) emotional stability; (2) sense of humor; (3) character; (4.5) wide range of interests; (4.5) goal-directedness; (6) creativity; (7) high marks; (8) IQ. Most noteworthy here was the extraordinarily high ranking given by the high-creativity group to 'sense of humor,' a ranking which not only distinguishes them from the high-IQ group (who ranked it last) but from all groups to which the test had been given."

The rank-order correlations reproduced in Table 2.4 bring the differences in the three rankings more clearly into focus. The relationship of the rankings by the two groups of traits believed predictive of success and favored by teachers are not far from identical. The pairs of correlations for the two remaining rankings differ remarkably. For the high-IQ group the correlation for the second ranking in the table is high, at 0.81; for the

TABLE 2.4
RANK-ORDER CORRELATIONS AMONG SUBSECTIONS OF THE OUTSTANDING TRAITS TEST, FOR HIGH-IQ AND HIGH-CREATIVE STUDENTS

Components of Correlation	Students	
	High-IQ (28)	High-Creative (26)
Personal traits believed "predictive of success" and "favored by teachers"	0.62	0.59
Personal traits "preferred for oneself" and "believed predictive of adult success"	0.81	0.10
Personal traits "preferred for oneself" and "believed favored by teachers"	0.67	−0.25

SOURCE: Getzels and Jackson (*19*, 15, Table 5).

high-creativity group it is low, at 0.10. For the high-IQ group the correlation for the third ranking is 0.67, while for the high creatives it is even in the opposite direction, at −0.25.

Some of the Getzels and Jackson observations in interpretation of these differences are (*19*, 15–16): "In effect, the high-IQ adolescent wants the qualities he believes make for adult success and qualities similar to those he believes teachers like; the high-creative adolescent favors personal qualities which have no relationship to those he believes make for adult success and are in some ways the reverse of those he believes his teachers favor. The high-creativity adolescents are thus more 'rebellious' or more 'autonomous' than the high-IQ adolescents with respect to adult standards of success, depending on one's point of view, and the high-IQ adolescents are more 'compliant' or more 'realistic'. . . . The high-IQs and the high creativity groups are characterized by differences in their career aspirations: differences all the more basic since the school achievement of the two groups as measured by standardized verbal and numerical subject-matter tests was the same."

In bringing the interpretation of their findings to a close, these writers refer to Guilford's designation of "convergent" and "divergent" modes of problem-solving (*20*), and go on to say (*19*, 17–18): "In this sense, the high-IQ adolescents tend to favor 'convergent' modes of problem-solving, and the high-creative adolescents tend to favor 'divergent' modes of problem-solving, whether in the cognitive function represented by performance on intelligence and creativity measures, or in the personal-social function represented by occupational or career choice. . . . Failure to distinguish between convergent and divergent talent in our schools may have serious consequences for the future of our society. Both kinds of talent are sufficiently important to warrant attention in educational theory and practice, and it is unwise to think of divergent fantasy as simply rebellious, rather than germinal, or unconventional career choice as invariably unrealistic rather than courageous."

This investigation by Getzels and Jackson stands as a sizable contribution toward the rounding out of our understanding of giftedness in youth. While the population investigated was of high school age, the conclusions cannot fail to have meaning for the educational worker at the collegiate level. However, a follow-up study, when these youth have entered college and/or when they have become adults, could be even more enlightening.

Summary

The curve of mental development rises rapidly during the growth years from 8 to 17. It shows some deceleration in the later years of this span, although it is still rising, giving promise of further increase in late and post-adolescence which is the predominant community college age-span. The rate and total growth are essentially identical for the two sexes, although there are tendencies to differences in performance on subtests for the two sexes, as in numerical subtests in favor of boys and in linguistic subtests for girls. The average curves, to be sure, conceal wide differences in records of mental growth in individuals.

Application of appropriate statistical procedures to compensate for the fact that units of measurement of mental growth are not comparable to those in physical measurements (which are of assured equal length) suggests that the curve of mental growth is more nearly parabolic than the virtually straight lines for stature and other aspects of physical growth.

Earlier investigations of mental change in total populations ranging in age from 8 or 9 through most of the life span supported the conclusions of rapid development during the growth years, some continuation of growth to 21 or thereabouts, and, following this, a slow decline to age 60. Subsequent inquiry, to be reviewed in a later chapter on adults, casts doubt on this decline with age. Investigations of high school graduates continuing their education have found continued increase in test intelligence in college. Discussion of the factors of this growth emphasize maturation in the earlier portions of the period with a shift to environmental or educational factors in later portions. This is reflected in large increments in those subtests related to the several disciplines.

Advent of puberty is accompanied by appreciable acceleration in mental growth, resulting in intelligence scores slightly higher for boys and girls maturing earlier than for others. Such differences have disappeared by late adolescence and college age.

Some investigations have reported a change in mental organization from 8 or 9 to 15 or 16 and beyond, from an intelligence dominated by a general factor toward special abilities, or aptitudes. Others have purported to find no such trend, with the general factor prevailing. Although the issue is still somewhat in controversy, development and application of tests for high school and college levels seem increasingly to rely on the belief that mental growth proceeds from general ability to special abilities.

From the long-time earlier dependence on intelligence tests and the IQ to identify the gifted in the school population, the concept of giftedness has of recent years been rounded out by measuring also for what is referred to as creativity.

References and Bibliography

1. Abernethy, Ethel M. *Relationships between Mental and Physical Growth.* Monographs of the Society for Research in Child Development, vol. 1, no. 7. Washington: National Research Council, 1936.
2. Anastasia, Anne. *The Influence of Specific Experience upon Mental Organization.* Genetic Psychology Monographs, 18, no. 4 (1936), 245–355.
3. Anastasia, Anne, and Foley, John P., Jr. *Differential Psychology; Individual and Group Differences in Behavior.* Rev. ed. New York: The Macmillan Co., 1949.
4. Balensky, B. *An Analysis of the Mental Factors of Various Age Groups from Nine to Sixty.* Genetic Psychology Monographs, 23 (1941), 191–234.
5. Bennett, George K.; Seashore, Harold; and Wesman, Alexander G. *A Manual for Differential Aptitude Tests.* New York: The Psychological Corporation, 1952.
6. Bernard, Harold W. *Adolescent Development in the American Culture.* Yonkers-on-Hudson, N.Y.: World Book Co., 1957.
7. Burt, Cyril. "The Differentiation of Intellectual Ability." *British Journal of Educational Psychology,* 24 (June, 1954), 76–90.
8. Clark, Mamie P. *Changes in Primary Mental Abilities with Age.* Archives of Psychology, no. 291 (May, 1944).
9. Conrad, Herbert S.; Jones, Harold E.; and Hsaio, H. H. "Sex Differences in Mental Growth and Decline." *Journal of Educational Psychology,* 24 (March, 1933), 161–69.
10. Cruze, Wendell W. *Adolescent Psychology and Development.* New York: Ronald Press Co., 1953.
11. Eckert, Ruth E. "Intellectual Maturity." *Journal of Higher Education,* 5 (Dec., 1934), 478–84.
12. Freeman, Frank N., and Flory, Charles D. *Growth in Intellectual Ability as Measured by Repeated Tests.* Monographs of the Society for Research in Child Development, vol. 2, no. 2. Washington: National Research Council, 1937.
13. Garrett, H. E. "A Developmental Theory of Intelligence." *American Psychologist,* 1 (1946), 372–78.

14. Garrett, H. E. "A Study of the CAVD Intelligence Examination." *Journal of Educational Research*, 21 (Feb., 1930), 103–8.
15. Garrett, H. E.; Bryan, A. I.; and Perl, R. *The Age Factor in Mental Organization*. Archives of Psychology, no. 176 (1935).
16. Garrett, H. E., and Kellog, N. N. "The Relation of Physical Constitution to General Intelligence, Sound Intelligence, and Emotional Stability." *Journal of Experimental Psychology*, 11 (April, 1927), 113–29.
17. Getzels, Jacob W., and Jackson, P. N. *Creativity and Intelligence: Explorations with Gifted Students*. New York: John Wiley & Sons, Inc., 1962.
18. Getzels, J. W., and Jackson, P. N. "The Meaning of 'Giftedness'—An Examination of an Expanding Concept." *Phi Delta Kappan*, 40 (Nov., 1958), 75–77.
19. Getzels, J. W., and Jackson, P. N. "The Study of Giftedness: A Multidimensional Approach." In *The Gifted Student*, pp. 1–18. Cooperative Research Monograph no. 2. U.S. Department of Health, Education, and Welfare. Washington: Government Printing Office, 1960.
20. Guilford, J. P., et al. *A Factor-Analytic Study of Creative Thinking II: Administration of Tests and Analyses of Results*. Reports from the Psychology Laboratory, no. 8. Los Angeles: University of Southern California, 1952.
21. Hartson, L. "Does College Training Influence Test Intelligence?" *Journal of Educational Psychology*, 27 (Oct., 1936), 481–91.
22. Henry, Nelson B., ed. *Adolescence*. Forty-third Yearbook of the National Society for the Study of Education, part 1. Chicago: University of Chicago Press, 1944.
23. Hollingsworth, Leta S. *Gifted Children: Their Nature and Nurture*. New York: The Macmillan Co., 1926.
24. Jones, Harold E., and Conrad, Herbert S. *The Growth and Decline of Intelligence: A Study of a Homogeneous Group Between Ages of Ten and Sixty*. Genetic Psychology Monograph, 13 (1933), 227–98.
25. Kuhlen, Raymond G. *The Psychology of Adolescent Development*. New York: Harper & Bros., 1952.
26. Kuznets, G. M., and McNemar, Olga. "Sex Differences in Intelligence Test Scores." In *Intelligence: Its Nature and Nurture*. Thirty-ninth Yearbook of the National Society for the Study of Education, part 1, ch. 6 (1940). Bloomington, Ill.: Public School Publishing Co., 1941.
27. Livesay, T. M. "Does Test Intelligence Increase at the College Level?" *Journal of Educational Psychology*, 30 (Jan., 1939), 63–68.
28. McConnell, T. R. "Change in Scores on the Psychological Examination of the American Council on Education from Freshman to Senior Year." *Journal of Educational Psychology*, 25 (Jan., 1934), 66–69.
29. Middleton, Warren C., and Moffett, D. C. "The Relation of Height and Weight Measurements to Intelligence and Dominance-Submission Among a Group of College Freshmen." *Research Quarterly of the American Association for Health, Physical Education, and Recreation*, 11 (Dec., 1940), 53–59.
30. Miles, Catherine C. "Gifted Children." In *Manual of Child Psychology* by L. Carmichael, pp. 886–963. New York: John Wiley & Sons, 1946.
31. Miles, Catherine C., and Miles, Walter R. "The Correlation of Intelligence Scores and Chronological Age from Early Childhood to Late Maturity." *American Journal of Psychology*, 44 (1932), 44–78.
32. Pressey, Sidney L., and Kuhlen, Raymond G. *Psychological Development through the Life Span*. New York: Harper & Bros., 1957.
33. Reichard, Suzanne. *Mental Organization and Age Level*. Archives of Psychology, no. 295 (1944).
34. Rogers, A. L. "The Growth of Intelligence at the College Level." *School and Society*, 31 (May 24, 1930), 693–99.
35. Schneck, M. R. *The Measurement of Verbal and Numerical Abilities*. Archives of Psychology, no. 107 (1929).

36. Segel, David. *Intellectual Abilities in the Adolescent Period.* U.S. Office of Education Bulletin no. 6. Washington: Government Printing Office, 1948.
37. Segel, David. "The Validity of a Multiple Aptitude Test at the Secondary School Level." *Educational and Psychological Measurement,* 7 (1947), 695–705.
38. Shuttleworth, Frank K. *The Physical and Mental Growth of Girls and Boys Age Six to Nineteen in Relation to Age at Maximum Growth.* Monographs of the Society for Research in Child Development, vol. 4, no. 3. Washington: National Research Council, 1939.
39. Staff, Division of Occupational Analysis, War Manpower Commission. "Factor Analysis of Occupational Aptitude Tests." *Educational and Psychological Measurement,* 5, no. 2 (1945), 147–55.
40. Stone, Calvin P., and Barker, R. G. "Aspects of Personality and Intelligence in Post-menarcheal and Pre-menarcheal Girls of the Same Chronological Age." *Journal of Comparative Psychology,* 23 (1937), 439–55.
41. Stone, Calvin P., and Barker, Roger G. "On the Relationships Between Menarcheal Age and Certain Aspects of Personality, Intelligence, and Physique of College Women." *Journal of Genetic Psychology,* 45 (1934), 121–35.
42. Swineford, Frances. "General, Verbal, and Spatial Bifactors after Three Years." *Journal of Educational Psychology,* 40 (Oct., 1949), 353–60.
43. Swineford, Frances. "Growth in the General and Verbal Bifactors from Grade VII to Grade IX." *Journal of Educational Psychology,* 38 (May, 1947), 257–72.
44. Tanner, James M. *Growth at Adolescence.* Springfield, Ill.: C. C. Thomas, 1955.
45. Terman, L. M.; Oden, Meleta H.; et al. *The Gifted Child Grows Up: Twenty-five Years Follow-up of a Superior Group.* Genetic Studies of Genius, vol. 4. Stanford, Cal.: Stanford University Press, 1947.
46. Terman, Lewis M., et al. *Mental and Physical Traits of a Thousand Gifted Children.* Genetic Studies of Genius, vol. 1. Stanford, Cal.: Stanford University Press, 1925.
47. Thorndike, Edward L. "On the Improvement of Intelligence Scores from Thirteen to Nineteen." *Journal of Educational Psychology,* 17 (1926), 73–76.
48. Thorndike, Edward L. "Sex Differences in Status and Gain in Intelligence Scores from Thirteen to Eighteen." *Pedagogical Seminary,* 33 (1926), 167–81.
49. Thorndike, R. L. "Growth of Intelligence during Adolescence." *Journal of Genetic Psychology,* 72 (March, 1948), 11–15.
50. Thurstone, L. L., and Thurstone, T. C. *Factorial Studies of Intelligence.* Psychometric Monograph, no. 2. Chicago: University of Chicago Press, 1941.
51. Viteles, Morris S. "The Influence of Age of Pubescence upon Physical and Mental Status of Normal School Students." *Journal of Educational Psychology,* 20 (1929), 360–68.
52. Wechsler, David. *Measurement and Appraisal of Adult Intelligence.* 4th ed. Baltimore: Williams and Wilkins Co., 1958.
53. Witty, Paul, ed. *The Gifted Child.* Boston: D. C. Heath & Co., 1949.
54. Wright, Melvin B. "The Development of Mental Ability at the College-Adult Level." *Journal of Educational Psychology,* 22 (Nov., 1931), 610–28.
55. Wright, Ruth E. "A Factor Analysis of the Original Stanford-Binet Scale." *Psychometrica,* 4 (Sept., 1939), 209–20.

3
Personal and Social Development

As COMPARED with the portrayal of physical and mental growth during adolescence to maturity, the problem of reporting the trends of personal and social development to which attention is directed in this chapter is more complex and difficult. This is so because we are dealing, much more than in the realms of physique and mentality, with intangibles, because we are concerned with both psychological and sociological factors, and also because of the even greater dearth of reliable evidence concerning personality and socialization relating particularly to late adolescence. Even more than in matters of physique and mentality, in this area the treatment is hampered by the lack of longitudinal or even cross-sectional studies that bridge the institutional gap between high school and college.

Explaining Adolescent Behavior

The stereotype of adolescence.—Our problem is further complicated by general acceptance in the popular mind of the stereotype of adolescence as a period of "storm and stress," traditionally believed to be induced solely by the physical and physiological changes of the kind we have reviewed and illustrated in Chapter 1. It is not so much that the adolescent does not have problems in his efforts to attain maturity: we shall shortly find that he faces these in disturbing numbers. The issue is rather concerning the contention that they originate as an inevitable psychological accompaniment of the biological changes.

A demurrer to "storm and stress."—We should not overlook the fact that some writers have gone so far as to deny that the adolescent faces serious problems of adjustment. Among these are Elkin and Westley (33) who investigated, by interviews with both the children and their parents, twenty youths 14 and 15 years old in a suburb of Montreal, which they call "Suburb Town." The suburb is clearly middle class, referred to as "well-to-do," with about seven-tenths of the labor force in executive, managerial, and professional roles. The data of the study were drawn from four or more interviews per family. Following are excerpts from these investigators' interpretation of their evidence: "The activities of the adolescent take place almost completely within the suburban community and in view of the adult figures. The adolescent, in effect, has little unstructured time. Typically, on school days, he spends his time out of school doing two hours of homework, helping in the household activities, and particularly in school organizations, directed sports, or church and 'Y' activities. On weekends, he participates in some family projects, has certain allotted household tasks, and often attends gatherings at which adults are present. . . . Family ties are close and the degree of family consensus is high. The parents are interested in all the activities of their children and the adolescents, except for the area of sex, discuss their own behavior and problems with them. In many areas of life, there is joint participation between parents and children. . . . In many respects, for this given sample of adolescents, the continuity of socialization is far more striking than the discontinuity. . . ." The authors go on to say that other investigators have found similar conditions, especially in upper-middle-class and "upwardly mobile" groups. They name, in particular, Hollingshead's comparable findings in "Elmtown." The observations concerning peer-groups in Suburb Town will be touched on in dealing with this subject later in the chapter.

The cultural explanation.—Many students of this area are inclined to concede some degree of maladjustment during adolescence, but enter denials concerning its magnitude and refuse in particular to ascribe it directly to the biological changes. Reuter (*96*) has contended, while admitting that "some degree of disorganization in adolescent years is to be expected and seems to be everywhere present," that "the amount of personal and social disorder erupted in the second decade of life is apparently somewhat grossly exaggerated." He argues that the "disordered behavior" cannot be explained exclusively in biological terms, for, if such dependent relation obtains, three things would be found: (1) the mental disorder would appear in all children; (2) the physical and social maladjustments would "coincide or follow a uniform time sequence"; and (3) "the same characteristics will mark the age period in all civilizations." He points out that this is not the case.

The explanation of the maladjustments Reuter put forward resides, instead, in the prevailing culture. In the American society there is a "lengthened period of preparation for the activities of adult life and this has worked out as a prolongation of social adolescence." The changing nature of our economic order operates to the same end. Our industrialized society has little or no place for the boy in his teens. "In the modern world, the lack of any real place or vital function leaves the adolescents in a position of tolerated parasitism. In the absence of opportunity for serviceable activity, youth turns to sport and other forms of restless and disorganizing behavior."

It was the anthropologist Benedict who elaborated the concept of continuities and discontinuities with which one may explain aberrations in behavior of adolescents in our society. In one discussion of the issue (6), she illustrated the differences between societies in their customs respecting three roles in which our society manifests striking contrasts between children and adults. These are (1) "responsible–non-responsible status role," which in our society requires responsibility of the adult but proscribes it to the child, whereas in certain other societies children are early inducted into responsibilities in accordance with their abilities; (2) "dominance-submission," in which in our society the adult commands and the child obeys, whereas in certain societies children behave without "respect" to elders; and (3) the "contrasted sexual role," in which in some societies the belief appears to be that the child is "anything but sexless," whereas in our society we hold to the opposite dogma. The discontinuities engender strain from which the aberrations in behavior emanate. However, the major inferences from this exposition are that the discontinuities have a cultural origin, and not the biological origin assumed by those who still accept the adolescent stereotype.

A variant interpretation.—Although this opinion of the origins of the aberrations of the adolescent period in our culture rather than in biological change in the second decade of life appears now to be in the ascendancy, it is desirable, before dropping consideration of the subject, to report on some aspects of the position of a psychologist. Luchins (74), while reviewing the field of controversy, put forward a somewhat divergent point of view. He begins his discussion by citing the opinion of Kuhlen (68, 180) concerning the point at which adolescence terminates and adulthood arrives. This is to the effect that, regardless of chronological age or state of biological equipment, an individual is adolescent to the extent that he is engaged in the process of making sexual-social adjustments, ideological adjustments, vocational adjustments, and adjustments relating to achievement of freedom from parents. Said Luchins, "One is preadolescent in the years before he is concerned with such problems, and he is adult to the extent that he has successfully solved these difficulties and eliminated them as problems."

Luchins also re-examined the "characteristics of adolescence" and questioned the theory of the biological origin of adolescent behavior by citing the evidence from cross-cultural comparisons in the reports of anthropologists and pointing out that adolescent "disturbances" were not apparent in our earlier society with its differing socioeconomic conditions.

An important part of Luchins' exposition is a description of three boys in a group he studied, and from which the following is the concluding paragraph: "What can be inferred from these three cases? Firstly, it would seem that youths living in the same locality and having similar socio-economic backgrounds may manifest strikingly different behavior patterns. Secondly, similar physiological changes may be accompanied by different behavior patterns. Also, individuals who are far apart with regard to physical maturity may display similar behavior patterns.... Thirdly, the kind of emotional storm and stress which is sometimes considered as characteristic of adolescence may not be manifested at all, may occur long before or only long after puberal changes, may be momentary or of rather limited duration, or may be generally characteristic of the individual."

From this illustration of the wide variation in behavior during adolescence it is a logical step for Luchins to the formulation of his hypothesis, for future research, that "emotional instability may tend to be manifested at any chronological age when the individual lacks a clear frame of reference with which to meet reality, when his behavioral world is not clearly structured, and when there are marked discrepancies between his aspiration and his achievements."

Another logical corollary of Luchins' position is his advocacy of the study of individual cases and his contention that, while correlations may portray trends, the individual may be lost in them. One may agree with this observation as concerns diagnosis of and remedial action for the individual, and still hold to the belief that the disclosures of trends may be a help in understanding the individual. Besides, a substantial piling up of cases may help in arriving at reliable trends.

Problems and Interests of Adolescents

The studies available.—The tendencies to behavior, whether regarded as commendable or untoward, and their accompanying emotions, which are implied in the treatment of adolescence in the foregoing section, should in substantial degree be reflected in the problems, or needs, and interests of this age-group. The reports of a number of investigations of these problems and interests are available in print and one can resort readily to their findings. Among the reports are several surveying problems of high school students, of some significance for purposes here because they portray the problems of youth on the threshold of later adolescence. Here would be included reports of inquiries by Pope (*87*) on problems of students in the Cleveland High School of St. Louis, and by Williams (*134*) on problems of and further data concerning youth in high schools in widely distributed states. Fortunately, for purposes here, reports are available from a cluster of studies made by the late Professor Symonds, who administered an identical instrument requesting the ranking of problems and interests by high school students (he called them "adolescents"), college students ("older adolescents"), and graduate students ("adults") (*120, 118, 121*). Although these studies were reported a quarter century ago, the value of their results is enhanced for us by reapplication of the instrument to high school students two decades later (*54*) and recently enough to help in understanding the adolescent today. The fact that this battery of studies by Symonds includes one with data from later adolescents is especially to the point. In introducing the evidence from it, Symonds made this observation (*118*): "The later years of adolescence are a sort of no-man's-land in psychology, an unexplored area concerning which there is little accurate information, but mostly surmise and conjecture. The facts relating to maturity of physical growth are, to be sure, well known. Strangely enough, we are only at this late date through the work of Freeman and others, obtaining accurate information concerning the nature of mental growth. . . . We know even less about emotional development of later adolesence."

Categories in the checklist.—The "items," or areas, of problems and interests included in the checklist submitted by Symonds in all his cluster of studies, and applied again by Harris, were obtained from interviews with young people. He also followed their usage in the words by which these items were described. These items, as appearing in the checklist, were:

Health—eating, drinking, exercise, posture, sleep and rest, air and temperature, sunlight, clothing, bathing, care of special parts, cleanliness and prevention of disease, excretion and elimination, use of drugs.
Sex adjustments—love, petting, courtship, marriage.
Safety—avoiding accidents and injuries.
Money—earning, spending, saving.
Mental hygiene—fears, worries, inhibitions, compulsions, feelings of inferiority, fantasies.
Study habits—skills used in study, methods of work, problem-solving.
Recreation—sports and games, reading, arts and crafts, fellowship and social activities, hobbies.
Personal and moral qualities—qualities leading to success, qualities of good citizenship.
Home and family relationships—living harmoniously with members of the family.
Manners and courtesy—etiquette.
Personal attractiveness—personal appearance, voice, clothing.
Daily schedule—planning twenty-four hours in a day.
Civic interests, attitudes, and responsibilities.
Getting along with people.
Philosophy of life—personal values, ambitions, ideals, religion.

Directions to the students in administering the checklists were simple indeed: "First ... indicate the order in which they are *personal problems* to you ... and second, the order of *interest* to you."

Comparing rankings by high school students in 1935 and 1957.—The means of the ranks assigned by high school students to the items as problems and as interests in 1935 and 1957 together with the resulting rankings of these means are reported in Tables 3.1 and 3.2. The raw data from which these tables were compiled were obtained in 1935 from students in the high schools of Tulsa, Oklahoma, and the Grover Cleveland High School in New York City. Those for 1957 were obtained from high school

TABLE 3.1
MEAN RANKS GIVEN ITEMS CONSIDERED AS PROBLEMS BY HIGH SCHOOL STUDENTS IN 1935 AND IN 1957

Items	1935		1957	
	Mean Rank	Rank of Mean	Mean Rank	Rank of Mean
Money	6.5	1	6.4	2
Health	6.6	2	8.9*	12.5
Personal attractiveness	7.0	3	7.3	4
Study habits	7.1	4	5.7*	1
Personal and moral qualities	7.2	5	6.9	3
Philosophy of life	7.5	6	7.6	5.25
Manners and courtesy	8.2	7	8.1	8
Home and family relationships	8.2	8.5	8.0	7
Getting along with other people	8.2	8.5	8.3	10
Recreation	8.3	10	10.1*	15
Mental hygiene	8.5	11	7.6*	5.5
Safety	8.6	12	9.6*	14
Civic interests, attitudes, and responsibilities	8.7	13	8.2*	9
Daily schedule	9.2	14	8.5*	11
Sex adjustments	10.0	15	8.9*	12.5

SOURCE: Harris (*54*, 336, Table 1).
*Change from 1935 significant at the 1 per cent level.

students in Minnesota. Thus, the populations represented were distinct not only in time, but also geographically. The latter difference presents a hazard in interpretation, but one of which Harris is aware and of which he strives to take account. No information is supplied concerning the socioeconomic comparability of the two populations.

Explication here of the evidence in the tables will depend mainly on Harris' comments on Symonds' interpretations and on observations of his own, but in advance of paraphrasing and quoting them it seems desirable to call attention to a fact of considerable significance not played up with enough prominence by either author: this is the rather *limited range of average ranks* of the items both as problems and as interests. For instance, the range of average ranks of the items as problems in Table 3.1 is only from 6.5 (for "Money") to 10.0 (for "Sex adjustments"). This means that the average ranks in this column range only over less than a third of the full range from 1 to 15, which the students were directed to assign to the fifteen different items. Similarly, the range of average ranks in 1957 was only from 5.7 (for "Study habits") to 10.1 (for "Recreation"). The ranges for the items as interests in Table 3.2 are only from 5.2 (for "Recreation") to 10.4 (for "Daily schedule") in 1935 and from 6.7 (for "Health") to 11.2 (again for "Daily schedule") in 1957. These narrow ranges could not emerge from these studies without high rankings assigned

TABLE 3.2
MEAN RANKS GIVEN 15 ITEMS CONSIDERED AS INTERESTS BY HIGH SCHOOL STUDENTS IN 1935 AND IN 1957

Items	1935 Mean Rank	1935 Rank of Mean	1957 Mean Rank	1957 Rank of Mean
Recreation	5.2	1	6.8*	3
Health	6.1	2	6.7*	1
Personal attractiveness	6.8	3	7.0	6
Manners and courtesy	6.9	4	8.6*	10
Philosophy of life	7.5	5	6.9*	5
Getting along with other people	7.6	7	6.8*	3
Personal and moral qualities	7.6	7	7.2*	8
Money	7.6	7	7.4	9
Home and family relationships	8.4	9	6.8*	3
Safety	8.5	10	9.5*	12
Study habits	9.0	11	9.6*	13
Mental hygiene	9.2	12	8.8*	11
Sex adjustments	9.3	13	7.1*	7
Civic interests, attitudes, and responsibilities	9.4	14	9.8*	14
Daily schedule	10.4	15	11.2*	15

SOURCE: Harris (*54*, 337, Table 2).
*Change from 1935 significant at the 1 per cent level.

on all items by substantial numbers of individual students. This is to say that *all* the areas are of relatively high importance as problems and as interests to *some* students. The *re*-ranking of the items from 1 to 15 on the basis of the average ranks as done in the tables tends to exaggerate the relative importance of the problems and interests to these student groups as wholes, although they may not do so for individuals in the groups.

Harris inquires as to how these young people, "separated by almost a generation," compare in the order they assigned the items as problems and as interests. He reports that the two groups showed "considerable similarity" (coefficient of correlation, +.60) in ranking the items as problems and "slightly greater similarity" (coefficient of correlation, +.73) in ranking the items as interests. There were more instances of significant changes in items as interests (13) than as problems (8).

Money was rated high as a problem in both periods: it had first place in 1935 and second in 1957. Physical health was much less of a problem in the 1957 study. Mental hygiene rose to an appreciably higher rank—from 11 in 1935 to 5.5 in 1957. Recreation dropped from tenth place to be the bottom item. Daily schedule and civic interests, attitudes, and responsibilities, though still low in 1957, "rose appreciably." Study habits, seen as a serious problem in 1935 (fourth), had an even more prominent position in 1957 (first).

TABLE 3.3
RANKS OF THE MEAN RANKINGS GIVEN 15 ITEMS CONSIDERED AS PROBLEMS AND INTERESTS OF MEN AND WOMEN COLLEGE STUDENTS

Items	Men		Women	
	Problems	Interests	Problems	Interests
Money	1	5	2	13
Study habits	2	12	1	12
Health	3	1	8	8.5
Philosophy of life	4	2	3	1
Personal and moral qualities	5	4	6	3
Personal attractiveness	6	10	4	2
Mental hygiene	7	8	5	8.5
Daily schedule	8	15	7	14
Sex adjustments	9	3	14	6
Civic interests, attitudes, and responsibilities	10	11	9	10
Getting along with others	11	9	11	5
Manners and courtesy	12	7	10	4
Recreation	13	6	13	7
Home and family relationships	14	13	12	11
Safety	15	14	15	15

SOURCE: Adapted from Symonds (*118*, 84, Table 2).

"In ranking the 15 items as interests, students in 1957 gave sex adjustments a much higher place than students in 1935 did. Home and family relationships and getting along with people were also placed higher in 1957. Interest in manners and courtesy showed a sharp drop.... Interest in recreation and health was high in 1935 and continued so in 1957. Though daily schedule and study habits were rated as significant problems in 1957, interest in these items was low. Civic interests, attitudes, and responsibilities had a low place on the list of interests, lower than the place assigned to the item as a problem."

Rankings by older adolescents.—The rankings of the items as problems and interests secured by Symonds from what he called "older adolescents" were by students in two institutions in the Midwest, Purdue University and

Kansas State Teachers College. The mean ranks computed are not reported in Table 3.3. Instead, only the re-rankings on the basis of the mean ranks as computed are reported, as scrutinizing these provides about as much of significance as would examination of both mean ranks and rankings of the means. It may be noted that the rankings are here reported separately for the sexes, and the items are listed in the order of the men's ranking of the items as problems.

Among what seem to be justifiable interpretations, one may note that money and study habits rank high as problems with both sexes, although they are less important as interests. It is difficult to understand why health should be a matter of greater concern and interest with men than with women. Philosophy of life stands high with both sexes both as problem and as interest, while personal and moral qualities rate slightly lower, although well above the median. Personal attractiveness is rated higher by women than men both as problem and interest. For both sexes the daily schedule is near median position as a problem but of somewhat less interest. Sex adjustments rate lower as problems with both sexes, but appreciably higher as interests. The lower ratings of this item by women are compensated by the higher ratings of personal attractiveness by women. Some readers may be inclined to comment on the rather low rating of civic concerns by both sexes both as problem and as interest. Getting along with others, manners and courtesy, and recreation appear to be somewhat less significant as problems than as interests. The low rank of home and family relationships may be explained by the advance toward emancipation from parents frequently ascribed to later adolescence.

This particular one of the cluster of Symonds' studies makes possible not only the assessment of problems and interests by older adolescents but, by comparison of results of assessment by adolescents at the high school level, the identification of trends of attitude with approach to maturity. It would seem that the purpose will be better served by comparing the rankings in Table 3.3 with those for 1935 in Tables 3.1 and 3.2. The difference in organization of the tables for the two age-levels is something of a hindrance to the comparison, but conclusions of some significance may nevertheless be drawn from the effort.

Money remains high as a problem throughout adolescence, although it drops somewhat in interest, more with girls than with boys. The attitude toward study habits does not change much, ranking high continuously as a problem, but relatively low as an interest. Health remains high in rank except for girls as both problem and interest. Further approach to maturity raises the rank assigned to philosophy of life, both as problem and as interest. The ranking of personal and moral qualities goes up appreciably, as might be expected from the elevation of philosophy of life. Personal attractiveness retains its high rank with girls, but seems to suffer some loss in rank with boys, both as problem and interest. Mental hygiene moves up in rank as both problem and interest, and especially as a problem with girls. For both sexes daily schedule moves up as problem but remains low as an interest. Sex adjustments rise in rank as an interest with both sexes, but less so as a problem, especially with girls, for whom the maintenance of high rank of personal attractiveness, previously mentioned, may be compensatory. The moderate rise in rank of civic interests, attitudes, and responsibilities, both as problem and interest, may not satisfy the critics of youth. Manners and courtesy falls to some degree as a problem with both sexes. Recreation falls both as problem and interest, but more sharply as problem, presumably because needs in these areas may be better served now than formerly. Home and family relationships, both as problem and interest, show the shift to lower ranking which may be expected from progress toward maturity. The ranking of safety remains low both as problem and interest. For the most part, the changes and shifts in rank with age from mid to late adolescence as disclosed by the comparison appear to be in the direction of achieving maturity.

Problems and interests in relation to happiness.—In still another in his cluster of studies Symonds inquired into the relationship of certain self-ratings of his subjects on happiness to their rankings of his items as problems and interests (*119*). At the time of administering his checklist he asked the students to rate themselves on a seven-level scale of happiness ranging from "full of deep joy, excitedly happy, enthusiastic, thrilled" as the highest level down to "gloomy, miserable, a failure, no pleasure in anything" as the lowest. The intervening levels were correspondingly described. Subjects were again grouped as high school, college, and graduate students, and designated "adolescent," "older adolescent," and "adult." The concern here is mainly with the first two groups.

The modal self-rating in all three groups is 4, which is phrased "contented at times and at other times discontented, life has both favorable and unfavorable features." However, the proportion at this rating for high school students is smaller than for college students, while the proportion at 5, "satisfied, comfortable, life goes smoothly, peaceful," is somewhat larger. This contrast means that there is some drop in rating through the period of adolescence.

However, it is not for these ratings on happiness themselves that Symonds made the study, but rather to discover their relationship to the rankings by the subjects of his list of problems and interests. Concerning this relationship his conclusion is that "Happy and unhappy are remarkably alike in their problems and interests. The unhappy do not have peculiar problems but make less satisfactory adjustments to their problems.... The happy are more concerned with affairs outside themselves. The unhappy are more concerned with themselves and with their relations to others. . . . The happy tend to find philosophy of life (ideals, ambitions, religion) more of an interest and less of a personal problem than the unhappy."

Developmental Tasks of Adolescence

Origin of the concept.—To thoughtful persons who contemplate the results of studies of compilations of youth's problems, like those by Symonds and others, the results seem to bear an important relationship by having much in common with what are called "developmental tasks of adolescence." The origin and elaboration of the concept of developmental tasks is usually credited to Havighurst, who identified and described these tasks for the major age-levels from infancy through maturity (56, 1–2). According to him, "A developmental task is a task which arises at or about a certain period in the life of an individual, successful achievement of which leads to his happiness and to success with later tasks, while failure leads to unhappiness in the individual, disapproval by society, and difficulty with later tasks." Some of these tasks, Havighurst goes on to say, "arise mainly from physical maturation," others "primarily from the cultural pressures of society," and still others from the "personal values and aspirations of the individual." In most cases they arise "from combinations of these factors acting together."

An early formulation of the tasks as they concern the adolescent was presented by Corey (*21*, ch. 5, 70–99) in 1946 in a yearbook of the John Dewey Society. In presenting this formulation, he indicated his indebtedness to Havighurst and Daniel A. Prescott for the concept. The tasks presented by Corey were only three in number and were stated as follows: "Achieving independence of parents," "achieving adult social and economic status," and "acquiring self-confidence and a system of values." In his exposition, Corey identifies the ways of finding out what the tasks, "the required learnings of boys and girls," are. One of these is for adults to try to remember what their experiences were when they were 13 to 18 years of age, a second is to ask the subject questions, and the third is to observe adolescents. Symonds' procedure, as reported above, will be recognized as a variant of the second method, although he was doubtless conversant with the outcomes of investigations following the third method when organizing the items in his checklist.

Havighurst's and others' formulations.—The list of developmental tasks of adolescence as identified by Havighurst is as follows (*56,* ch. IX, 111–19):

1. Achieving new and more mature relations with age-mates of both sexes.

2. Achieving a masculine or feminine social role.
3. Accepting one's physique and using the body effectively.
4. Achieving emotional independence of parents and other adults.
5. Achieving assurance of economic independence.
6. Selecting and preparing for an occupation.
7. Preparing for marriage and family life.
8. Developing intellectual skills and concepts necessary for civic competence.
9. Desiring and achieving socially responsible behavior.
10. Acquiring a set of values and an ethical system as a guide to behavior.

Examination of the literature of psychology and education will find a number of other formulations, especially in material published in the early 1950s, and this is evidence of a rather general acceptance of the concept. The formulations vary from author to author, both in manner of statement and in number of tasks identified, the variation in number being somewhat dependent on the degree of particularization. The list by Havighurst is seen to contain ten tasks, whereas no other formulation examined exceeds seven and others contain four or five, although some of the tasks as defined seem to be composites of two or more as stated by Havighurst.

The diversity in manner of statement may be illustrated by quoting several variants. The reader should be readily able to identify the specific tasks as phrased by Havighurst with which the following variants most nearly coincide: "getting along with age-mates"; trying to "clarify and accept the feminine role and select a version of that role she will try to play, and decide what she will do with her sexuality"; "effecting emancipation from his parents and family"; "achieving emotional independence of parents and other adults"; "deciding upon a vocation and doing some work in preparation for it"; "developing intellectual skills"; "acquiring a philosophy of life"; "developing conscience, morality, and a set of values."

Relations of problems to developmental tasks.—It could hardly be expected that the classification emerging from the approaches used in a project like that of Symonds, dependent primarily on interviews with youth, would coincide with that arising from the more inclusive procedures followed by Havighurst. Nevertheless, as may be noted by direct comparison, the categories of problems and the definitions of task, while being far from identical, reveal a significant degree of correspondence. For instance, "home and family relationships" in Symonds' problems would fall in the area of "achieving emotional independence of parents and other adults"; "philosophy of life" would practically coincide with "acquiring a set of values and an ethical system as a guide to behavior." Other near-equivalences may easily be identified. At the same time, it would involve rather complex ratiocination to fit all problems with all tasks. However, this judgment may be ventured concerning the overlap: that solving the problems would go far toward achieving the developmental tasks and, conversely, achieving the tasks would go far toward solving the problems.

The Influence of the Peer Culture

Derivation of the peer group.—The derivation, or origin, of peer groups is the same as that of Benedict's "discontinuities" that make for the aberrations of behavior usually observed in or ascribed to adolescence. It will be recalled that, in citing her analysis, three areas of behavior were identified as those in which the untoward behavior might be manifested: the area in which responsibility is proscribed to youth; the dominance-submission area in which the adult commands and the child obeys; and the "contrasted sex role." Encountering frustration in these and other areas represented by the developmental tasks, youth tend to set up their own social groups ("crowds," "cliques," "gangs," etc.) and to follow their own purposes. In considering the origins of peer culture, we should not leave out of the account that suggested by psychoanalytic theory. This and the major portions of the adolescent's preoccupation with group experience, according to Ausubel (5, 349), "are simple derivatives of the mechanism of sublimation. It is assumed that the energy of the culturally frustrated sex drive is directly channeled into group activities and, as a result, sex needs are vicariously satisfied." The question may be asked whether all the voluntary manifestations of group life of youth should be explained by a single drive and whether there are not other drives which are implied in additional developmental tasks and which contribute to the origin and growth of these juvenile subcultures.

An objector to the concept.—Although the existence of the peer culture is admitted by most students of adolescent youth, one may encounter an occasional demurrer in psychological or sociological literature. Among these are Elkin and Westley (33) whose study by interviews with the children and their parents of twenty youths 14 and 15 years old in a suburb of Montreal yielded their conclusion to the effect that little evidence of discontinuities was apparent in the lives of these young people. In reporting this study they refer to the second assumption "that a youth culture exists and is a widespread and dominant pattern among adolescents in American life." Their conclusion in this respect is a logical accompaniment of the one just quoted. They concede that in Suburb Town and other communities the elements of a youth culture exist, but they are "less dominant than are accepted family and authority guidance patterns. . . . The adolescents in their peer groups are not compulsively independent and rejecting of adult values; they are not concerned solely with immediate pleasurable gratifications. Furthermore, in regard to those aspects of their lives which might be regarded as youth culture, they are remarkably sophisticated, they themselves pointing out that their dating patterns and their 'kidding around' are passing temporary phenomena. . . . This contradiction between current sociological characterization of adolescence and the reported data for a middle-class group suggests that 'adolescent culture' has a somewhat mythical character."

The society of Suburb Town has been described as middle class and well-to-do, with most of the labor force in executive, managerial, and professional roles. It may be assumed that the degree of dominance of the peer culture in a community may vary in some degree with social class, as well as other factors. The tendency to variation will be illustrated again in one of the investigations of youth cultures which will be reviewed next.

The peer culture in early adolescence.—Illustrative explication here of changes in attitudes and behavior of juveniles as influenced by the peer culture will be accomplished in the main by describing the procedures followed and conclusions drawn from two investigations, one of them at the junior high school and the other at the four-year high school level. The procedures used in both investigations are sociometric, but differ in detail, so that the findings are not strictly comparable. The study at the junior high level carries youth from preadolescence into early adolescence, that is from 12 to 15 years of age, and may be regarded, because more than three-fourths of the subjects at the older age were represented also at the lower age, as in essence longitudinal. The study at the high school level is, instead, cross-sectional. Evidence from a longitudinal investigation comprehending the full period from pre-adolescence through adolescence would be greatly to be preferred. Nevertheless, a review of the two investigations, with sidelights from a few others, should lead to at least a partial understanding of the nature and degree of the dominance of the peer culture.

The investigation at the lower level, by Tryon (*129, 130, 131*), was a pioneering effort in the field and has attracted widespread attention. It involved boys and girls in roughly equal numbers at two grade levels: 170 boys and 169 girls enrolled in about equal numbers in half-grades 6A and 7B, a half year apart, and 169 boys and 181 girls, three years later, in grade 9. The mean ages at the two levels were, respectively, 12.1 and 14.9. It may be assumed from these ages that comparison is being made chiefly of preadolescents with early adolescents, although girls on the whole would be somewhat further along in pubescence than boys. It is also well to keep in mind that the school organization was different at the two levels. This is described by Tryon as follows (*131*, 545–46): "[The pupils at the time of the first testing in Grades 6 and 7 B] were in nine different classrooms which ranged between 35 and 45 in population. At this time a child spent all the school hours with this one group, his class. There was a marked tendency for a class group to be together on the playground, too, though there was definite voluntary segregation by sex. At the time of the second testing the children were finishing the ninth grade.... They had entered a departmentalized school program and the day's class periods were spent by each child with different class groups. During recreation periods the children tended to seek out their friends; there was some voluntary mingling of the sexes."

The method of testing was a variant of the "Guess Who" technique in which the respondent matches a personal quality with the name of an associate, in this case the name of a classmate. The instrument, or "test," used listed forty traits, that is, twenty traits stated in their extremes: for example, *Restless* ("1. Here is someone who finds it hard to sit still in class; he (or she) moves around in his (or her) seat or gets up and walks around"); *Quiet* ("2. Here is someone who can work quietly without moving around in his (or her) seat"). The remaining nineteen contrasts were as follows. *Talkative–Silent*; *Active* in games–*Sedentary*; *Humor* about jokes–*Humorless*; *Friendly–Unfriendly*; *Fights–Avoids fights*; *Grown-up–Childish*; *Shy* in class; *Daring–Afraid*; *Unkempt–Tidy*; *Older friends–Younger friends*; *Humor about self–Humorless*; *Attention-getting–Non-attention-getting*; *Assured* with adults–*Shy* with adults; *Popular* (likeable)–*Unpopular*; *Happy–Unhappy*; *Good-looking–Non-good-looking*; *Enthusiastic–Listless*; *Bossy–Submissive*. Each trait was followed by a blank space in which the children were directed to write the names of classmates whom they thought to be like the description, and they were reminded that several people might fit one picture, that the same person might be named for more than one word picture, or that any word picture could be skipped if there was no one in the class to fit it. Each subject was supplied with an alphabetical list of his classmates.

The method of scoring assigned pluses for being named on positive traits and minuses for negative traits and arrived algebraically at a total score for each student. Statistical treatment included an adaptation of the factorial method to arrive at "clusters" or "constellations" of traits.

Tryon's findings concerning the traits approved at each of the two age-levels are important, but citation here will be restricted to her summary of trends from age 12 to age 15 for the two sexes (*130*, 77–79): "During the period between twelve and fifteen, values for girls have undergone some revolutionary changes; values for boys have undergone relatively minor changes, mainly in terms of slightly shifted emphases. For the twelve-year-old girl, quiet, sedate, non-aggressive qualities are associated with friendliness, likableness, good humor and attractive appearance. Behavior which conforms to the demands and regulations of the adult world is admired. Tomboyishness is tolerated. At the fifteen-year-old level admiration for the demure, docile, rather prim lady-like prototype has ceased. Instead, many of the criteria for the idealized boy, such as extroversion, activity and good sportsmanship, are highly acceptable to the girl. The ability to organize games for parties involving both sexes and the capacity to keep such activities lively and entertaining is admired. In addition the quality of being fascinated or glamorous to the other sex has become important but is looked upon as relatively specific or unrelated to other desirable qualities. At the twelve-year-old level the idealized boy is skillful and a leader in games; his daring and fearlessness extends beyond his social group to defiance of adult demands and regulations. Any characteristic which might be construed as feminine by one's peers such as extreme tidiness or marked conformity in the classroom is regarded as a weakness. However, some personableness and certain kindly, likable qualities tend to be associated with the more highly prized masculine qualities. At fifteen years, prestige for the boy is still in a large measure determined by physical skill, aggressiveness and fearlessness. Defiance of adult standards has lost emphasis; though still acceptable and rather amusing to them, it tends to be associated with immaturity. In addition, much greater emphasis is placed on personal acceptability, suggesting the effectiveness of risking heterosexual interests. In fact, Unkempt–Tidy, related to this constellation is the only trait among the twenty on which the boys completely reversed their evaluation."

Tyron's concluding remark on the findings from the whole study concerns an impression of the "lack of steadfastness" to values revealed by the girls as compared with the boys over this relatively short period of three years.

The peer culture through high school years.—The investigation into the peer culture at the high school level to be drawn upon here is a large-scale inquiry by Coleman (*19*). By sociometric and what he refers to as "semi-projective" methods, through elaborate questionnaires, he obtained information concerning the attitudes of more than 8,000 students in ten high schools in northern Illinois. The questionnaires were administered in such a way as to assure the respondents of complete anonymity. The report of the investigation is so extensive that only a few aspects of it are selected, and these for illustration.

The ten high schools from which Coleman obtained his basic data were selected so as to represent a wide variety of communities, ranging from rural-farm to large city including suburban. Fictitious names were assigned as in the following list, which includes also the enrollment of each school and the characterization of the community or location:

TYPE OF COMMUNITY	NAME ASSIGNED	POPULATION	ENROLLMENT
Small town	0. Farmdale	1,000	169
	1. Marketville	4,000	364
	2. Elmtown	7,000	513
	3. Maple Grove	6,000	421
	4. Green Junction	5,000	538
Large city, parochial	5. St. John's High (boys)	3,600,000	733
Suburb	6. Newlawn	9,000	1,053
Small city	7. Millburg	25,000	1,383
	8. Midcity	10,000	1,935
Suburb	9. Executive Heights	17,000	1,862

While not strictly within the region of the peer culture, but nonetheless somewhat germane to it, are the facts concerning smoking and drinking of the adolescent population. Coleman reports these facts as percentages of the two sexes who smoke, drink beer, and drink liquor regularly, occasionally, or not at all. These percentages are presented in Table 3.4.

TABLE 3.4
PERCENTAGE OF HIGH SCHOOL BOYS AND GIRLS INDICATING CERTAIN ANSWERS TO QUESTIONS CONCERNING SMOKING AND CONCERNING DRINKING BEER AND LIQUOR

Question	Boys	Girls
Do you smoke?		
Yes, regularly	15.2	7.6
Yes, occasionally	17.0	15.5
No	67.7	76.9
Do you drink beer?		
Yes, regularly	3.4	0.5
Yes, occasionally	26.8	12.6
No	69.6	86.9
Do you drink liquor?		
Yes, regularly	1.9	0.4
Yes, occasionally	17.0	11.8
No	81.0	87.8

SOURCE: Adapted from Coleman (*19*, 16).

The percentages would have been more meaningful if they had been reported by successive high school classes, from freshmen to seniors. Nevertheless, to persons who have been told that "all high school youth smoke and drink," the figures will come as a surprise, as more than two-thirds of the boys and more than three-fourths of the girls report that they do not smoke. The proportion not drinking beer is larger, and those for not drinking liquor rises with boys to four-fifths and with girls to almost nine-tenths. The percentage of boys smoking habitually is less than a sixth of all, with the proportion of girls a half of this.

A question, answers to which fall indubitably in the area of the peer culture, is, "Which one of these things would be hardest for you to take—your parents' disapproval, your teacher's disapproval, or breaking with your friend?" The percentage distributions of responses for the two sexes are given in Table 3.5. Coleman's comment on the figures is: "The responses indicate a rather even split between friend and parent, while the teacher's disapproval counts most for only a tiny minority. The balance between parents and friends indicates the extent of the state of transition. The adolescents experience—leaving one family, but not yet in another, they consequently look both forward to their peers and backward to their parents" (*19*, 5).

TABLE 3.5
PERCENTAGE OF ANSWERS TO TWO QUESTIONS ASKED OF HIGH SCHOOL STUDENTS

Question	Boys	Girls
*Hardest thing to take		
Parents' disapproval	53.8	52.9
Teachers' disapproval	3.5	2.7
Breaking with friend	42.7	43.4
†Prefer to be remembered as		
Brilliant student	31.5	27.9
Athletic star (boys)	45.1	37.8
Leader in activities (girls)	23.4	34.2

SOURCE: Adapted from Coleman (*19*, 5, Table 1, and 30, Table 11).
*Numbers answering: boys, 3,621; girls, 3,894.
†Numbers answering: boys, 3,690; girls, 3,876.

The lower part of Table 3.5 presents the distribution of responses to the question of how they would want to be remembered in school—as brilliant student, athletic star, or leader in activities. The low esteem in the value system of students in which scholarship is held, in comparison with athletics by boys and with leadership in activities by girls, is apparent.

It is likely that the range of values exhibited in these three categories in the lower part of Table 3.5 does not present a field of choice wide enough to do justice to the value systems of high school youth. Some answer to this question may be provided in Table 3.6, which reports the proportions of the two sexes who identify which among nine attributes they believe to be important for membership in the school's leading crowds. What is called "personality" stands high in the opinion of both boys and girls, but highest of all categories with girls. Cole intimates it may be almost the equivalent of "being friendly" or "being nice with other kids." Among other categories standing high with boys are "good reputation," "be an athlete," and "good looks." Girls also emphasize "good reputation," "be friendly," "good looks," "be neat, dress neatly," "have money," and "good clothes." Again, "good grades" takes a relatively inferior position, although some others are as low or lower.

The occasion for listing the pseudonyms of the schools near the outset of this treatment of Coleman's investigation is to facilitate mention of variations in value systems from school to school, although the relative prominence of the categories for individual schools is not reported here. Apropos of the presumed variation, the author says that "these schools are more alike than they are different" and that "the relative positions of the various dimensions by which status is gained is somewhat similar in all of them" (*19*, 92–93). However, we may at least illustrate such variation as exists, mostly in the author's words.

TABLE 3.6
PERCENTAGES OF BOYS AND GIRLS IDENTIFYING CERTAIN ATTRIBUTES AS BEING IMPORTANT FOR A BOY'S OR GIRL'S MEMBERSHIP IN THE LEADING CROWD*

Attributes	Boys	Girls
Personality	23	40
Good reputation	17	24
Be an athlete (boys)	16	–
Be friendly (girls)	–	16
Good grades	12	11
Good looks	15	29
Have a car (boys)	10	–
Be neat, dress neatly (girls)	–	17
Have money	6	16
Come from right neighborhood	3	3
Good clothes	10	27

SOURCE: Adapted from Coleman (*19*, 40, Fig. 29).
*The percentages are estimated from the height of the bars in Coleman's figure, as he does not present the numerical data anywhere in his monograph.

The one item mentioned more frequently by the boys in Farmdale is cars. "Cars, having a car, fixing it up, riding around, are of extreme importance to them." For girls, "the only dimension on which this status system was not low is good looks and popularity with boys." The boys in Marketville have one of the two status systems "most orientated to scholastic success," but athletic success is still more important than good grades. In this school, the girls' status system emphasizes good grades even more than that of boys. In Green Junction, "the boys' system is distinctive in the emphasis it places on athletic success." The girls' pattern complements that of the boys: low in importance it attaches to grades and high on the cheerleader-popularity dimension.

In Executive Heights, the combination for boys is different from the others. Although neighborhood is important, scholastic success is not.

The system is high, although not highest, in the status it gives scholastic achievement.

The most conspicuous and persistent conclusion from this investigation concerns the lowly place "good grades" (scholarship, success in course) hold in most of this adolescent subculture. Coleman appears to be concerned about it, as well he might, in view of our purpose in maintaining schools. During the discussion in the later portions of his book, he identifies two alternative ways of establishing values that will give scholarship a more prominent place. While it is outside the province of this treatise to consider at length ways in which our high schools may be made more effective, it is hardly out of place to mention these ways and speculate briefly on their usefulness for the purpose.

The first of these ways is to reorganize our manner of living so that youth will have more time and activities in their homes and with their parents and others in the family. This is in effect the condition in Suburb Town which led Elkin and Westley to the conclusion that there is much less substance to the adolescent subculture than is ordinarily believed. Coleman inclines to the opinion that re-establishment of the former manner of family life, while desirable, is out of the question. His alternative is to set up a competitive system within and between schools, through marks, academic contests, and the like, that will conduce to giving priority to good scholarship. Many persons considering this question will not see these as mutually exclusive alternatives; rather, they would urge that both approaches be used simultaneously and generously to offset to some extent such deleterious effects as the peer culture may have.

More recent opinions on the subculture.—During the last few years the literature concerning adolescence has been reflecting some recession from belief in the high degree of influence on behavior and attitudes of the peer culture inferred by Coleman—a recession that would rate the influence somewhere between that seen for Suburb Town by Elkin and Westley near the opening of this chapter and that just generalized from the Coleman project. To illustrate the trend reference will be made to an investigative project by Epperson (37) and to observations by the coauthors of *The Adolescent Experience* (29).

The Epperson project bears directly on Coleman's investigation and is critical of the manner of putting questions to the high school youth. Coleman used the word "disapproved" in inquiry in relation to parent and teacher, whereas the expression was "break with" in relation to the youth's closest friend. Epperson challenged the equivalence of "disapproved" and "break with." To overcome the apparent weakness, he constructed the question as follows: "Which one of these things would make you most unhappy?: (a) If my parents did not like what I did; (b) If my favorite teacher did not like what I did." Over 80 per cent of Epperson's sample of students in grades 10, 11, and 12 indicated that it would make them most unhappy if their parents did not like what they did, and the percentages for "best friend" dropped correspondingly. The percentages were very much alike for boys and girls.

Epperson supports further his opinion of the overestimation of the influence of the subculture by comparing the answers made by a sample of preadolescents (pupils in grades 3–6 in elementary schools) with those of his adolescent sample and found the percentage distribution not strikingly different for the two age-groups, although the percentages favorable to parents were even a little *larger* for adolescents.

The observations by Douvan and Adelson in *The Adolescent Experience* are based on investigations by interview, done by the University of Michigan Survey Research Center and involving national samples of boys aged 14 through 16 and girls in grades 6–12. The authors are frank to admit (29, 197–202) that the interview is not the method of choice for studying the operation of the peer group. They "feel, nevertheless, that many recent writings on adolescence have gone too far to estimate the actual power of peer influence," and they state their reasons for the feeling. However, they are far from negating its importance and affirm that during the period the youth "is in process of abandoning his dependence and parental standards and is trying to find his own," and that "he looks to his peers for support and guidance." It is these authors' observation, also, that the peer group "looms larger in the boy's experience" than in the girl's.

The peer culture and the developmental tasks.—What has just been said should help to disabuse those who may have come to believe that there is nearly a consensus that the influence of the peer cultures is mainly or uniformly bad. Some of Coleman's findings do bear witness to untoward manifestations of behavior and attitudes. However, the position increasingly accepted is that, in the absence of more participation in the life and affairs of adult society, the peer group affords youth an avenue of accomplishing certain essential developmental tasks. This service should become more apparent in subsequent sections of the chapter which deal directly with two of the tasks.

This constructive service of the peer culture has been well expressed by Ausubel (5, 344): "It is clear that the social goals of adolescents are basically oriented toward the adult world, and that the chief function of the adolescent peer group is to provide a substitutive status, from the fact that it dissolves as soon as adolescents achieve anchorage and status roles in the wider community. This basic orientation can also be inferred from the fact that the social experience of the peer group is hardly discontinuous with the types of social skills and attitudes necessary for adult socialization.

In fact, one of the chief functions that both adolescents and their culture attribute to the peer group is the apprenticeship it provides for adult living."

Regrettably, we are without adequate investigation of the extent of the survival and of the influence of the peer culture at the level of the predominant community college age-group. It will be helpful to workers in these new institutions when definitive inquiries in this area are reported. We do know that by or during this age-span all youth attain their physical and mental maturities. How closely attainment of social maturity is coordinated with these we do not know. Doubtless it varies from community to community and from individual to individual. The hope would be that large proportions would have their anchorages in social adulthood by the end of the span.

Emancipation from Parents

Consideration of two tasks.—Attention will next be given directly to the question of the progress of youth toward accomplishing two of the developmental tasks of adolescence listed in an earlier section of the chapter. The two tasks that will be addressed are, as phrased by Havighurst, "achieving emotional independence of parents and other adults" and "achieving a masculine or feminine social role." These are not singled out because they are more important than others, but mainly because some evidence bearing directly on them is at hand and can be readily reviewed. Other developmental tasks are somewhat less directly addressed in the remaining sections of the current chapter, and in Chapters 4, 5, and 6 dealing, respectively, with sex behavior and interests and the development of vocational and recreational interests, but they are nonetheless kept in mind so as to make it possible to observe what progress is made by or during later adolescence toward accomplishing them.

Boys, by late puberty.—Dimock, in a study applying to boys at ages somewhat younger than predominant community college age, investigated the degree of emancipation from parents and some of the factors affecting it (27, Ch. VII). Scores on an EFP (emancipation from parents) scale were derived from the boys' positive and negative reactions to statements like "Decide things for myself," "Depend on my parents to buy all my things for me," "Spend my allowance as I choose." Computation of the relation between these scores and chronological ages from 13 to 16 yielded a coefficient of only $+.14$, which "confirms the conclusion that age, although a factor, is not a substantial or decisive one in its effect upon the adolescent's emancipation status." The coefficient for these EFP scores as related to intelligence test scores is even slightly smaller. Coefficients were largest for three physical measures: physical strength, $+.24$; weight, $+.24$; and height, $+.22$. Because of the known close relationship between pubescent growth and increase in height, weight, and strength (see Chapter 1), Dimock infers that pubescence, or sexual maturing, "may tend to accelerate the emancipation process insofar as physical growth has any bearing upon it."

Criticisms of parents by adolescents.—Among studies disclosing a basis of discontent from which the urge for emancipation derives are those inquiring about criticisms of their parents by adolescent boys and girls. One such investigation is that by Stott (*115*). In it, the "types of criticism" were classified by the investigator under categories like "Matters related to discipline and control," "Temperamental traits and behavior," "Per-

TABLE 3.7
PERCENTAGE CLASSIFICATION BY AREAS OF QUARRELS OF BOYS AND GIRLS WITH FATHERS AND MOTHERS

Areas of Conflict	With Father		With Mother	
	Boys	Girls	Boys	Girls
Social life and friends	40.2	50.6	36.1	41.7
Economic factors relating to work and spending money	34.7	25.1	30.5	23.2
Clothes	1.0	4.8	5.8	17.5
Education and vocation	6.6	4.7	7.9	2.9
Other members of family	2.3	3.7	4.8	5.4
Other matters	15.2	11.1	14.9	9.3

SOURCE: After Punké (*93*).

sonal habits and conduct," "Educational adjustment and control," "Ideas, attitudes, and beliefs," "Work, self-sacrifice," and "Social adjustments and behavior." The total number of criticisms by both boys and girls of both mother and father is large. A distinction between parents is found in the much more frequent criticisms of fathers than mothers, by both boys and girls, because of personal habits and conduct.

Quarrels of youth with fathers and mothers.—Another approach, not unrelated to the one used by Stott, is through inquiry about quarrels between adolescents and their parents. This approach was followed by Punké (*93*) who asked high school boys and girls to report on quarrels they had had with fathers and mothers. Reports were made in such a way as to permit classification of the areas of conflict. Punké found about a third of the youth reporting quarrels. His classification of these quarrels and the percentage distribution of all quarrels as reported according to the sexes of parents and of youth are shown in Table 3.7. A half of all girls' quarrels with their fathers are seen to be over social life and friends. This category of conflict accounts for about two-fifths of all quarrels between boys and their fathers, and between boys and their mothers. Economic matters account for the next largest proportion of quarrels, ranging from about a fourth to a third of all, in the four relationships. Beyond these areas, quarrels of girls with mothers over clothes is the only additional category accounting for more than a sixth of all quarrels. Punké remarked about the relatively small proportion owing to conflicts over education and vocation. It is likely that this proportion would have been larger for seniors only, as the problem of making plans in this area grows more acute near high school graduation.

Emancipation at the college level.—These inquiries into aspects of the emancipation problems of youth at the high school level are somewhat helpful to our purpose of understanding youth of community college age, since they bring us up to this age, even if it is not covered completely. Report of a study by Sherman (*109*) in this area, because it applies to college level students, should add something to this understanding, although the age-group involved and the situation represented do not correspond with those in the community college. In this study an emancipation questionnaire suitable for both sexes was devised which consisted of sixty items, of which the following are illustrative: "I plan my daily schedule without assistance from my parents" (yes); "I decide what courses I shall pursue without assistance from my parents" (yes); "I tell my parents about every date I have" (no); "I often daydream about my mother and father" (no). Scores were obtained from administering the questionnaire to upwards of four hundred students with roughly equal representation of the sexes. All subjects included were unmarried, not living with parents while attending college, and raised to maturity in a home which included presence of both parents. The method of scoring was to count each item answered correctly +1 (indicating emancipation on the item) and 0 if answered incorrectly. Thus, theoretically, the score range was from 0 to 60. In manipulating his data Sherman compared the top 106 cases, as indicated by their scores, with the bottom 104, with about a fourth of all cases in each group.

The greatest difference between the groups was in respect to sex: the "most emancipated" group included 72 per cent men and 28 per cent women; the "least emancipated" group included 32 per cent men and 68 per cent women. The most emancipated were somewhat superior in intelligence. They also averaged seven months older in age and had been away from home somewhat longer. Inquiry into socioeconomic status disclosed no significant differences. In appraising his study, the investigator himself indicated the inadequacy of looking only at the emancipation process and the need for including consideration of the "interacting personalities of both parents and the child in order to understand the process of psychological weaning and the achievement of emancipation from the parent by the young adult."

As in many other areas, it is apparent that we are in need on behalf of the community college movement of a comprehensive inquiry into emancipation from parents of the population of this age-group in attendance. Available evidence does not apply fully to the age-group that is our chief concern, and where it applies to the college level, it cannot be representative of the situation in an institution in which most students are living at home and attend by commuting—a situation less obviously conducive to emancipation than in colleges primarily residential.

In the absence of findings from such an investigation, inferences from such as have been summarized may be assumed to be applicable in part. The areas of conflict between youth and parents through which emancipation is to be achieved are known; we also know something of the relative proportions they assume. Besides, some factors of emancipation have, in part, been revealed as, with boys, physical measures like height, weight, and strength, rapid increments of which are associated with pubescence. We know, too, that boys and men are on average farther along toward emancipation than girls and women. Intelligence is also at least a partial factor.

Assumption of the Social-Sex Role

Roles from childhood into adolescence.—In speaking of the social-sex role, writers on adolescence or on other periods of life are not thinking particularly of sexual behavior and attitudes. These, with a focus on later adolescence, are reserved for special consideration in the next chapter. Instead, they have in mind patterns of social behavior of the two sexes toward each other, as differentiated in our cultural structure. These roles change from age to age beginning with early childhood, and continuing through middle childhood, adolescence, adulthood, and into the decline of life. One investigator, Campbell (*13*, 545), in referring to "social-sex development," defines it as "the child's social relationships with the opposite sex, leading toward heterosexual adjustment in adolescence." To better understand the roles at adolescence, one needs a glimpse of them during earlier years.

Following is a summary by running description of the social-sex roles as observed by Campbell "in recreational groups with a membership of 112 former nursery school children, 53 girls and 59 boys, aged 5 to 17, above average intelligence and socioeconomic status, where the program was free enough to allow the boys and girls to form activity groups of whatever sex composition was preferred . . ." (*13*, 527–28): "At six, both boys and girls are in a non-sexual or undifferentiated phase of social-sex development. They play with companions of either sex. They are not self-conscious about their bodies and are not embarrassed by physical affection from adults or physical contact with the opposite sex. Boys fight girls and have no special courtesy toward women. They care nothing about their personal appearance. They do not regard any particular work or play as more suitable for one sex than the other. This period lasts until about 8½ years in both sexes. At this time they enter into a unisexual phase characterized by strong attachment to their own sex, and lasting for a shorter period in girls than in boys. Toward the end of this period (11 years) girls are showing self-consciousness at touching boys, except under conventional conditions; boys reach this stage at 12. In this period girls classify games according to sex. At 13 a girl is sufficiently self-conscious to feel shy in a group of boys. . . . At 13½ she will not admit that any boy could be attractive to her, but from her behavior one knows she is interested. Boys do not reach this stage until a year later. Sex modesty appears in both sexes at 14. At 14, the girl is definitely beginning the heterosexual phase by primping, being enthusiastic about dancing, admiring the clothes of women, and seeming interested in the attentions of boys. The boy of this age is more careful of his appearance and self-conscious about the attention of girls, but he is not interested in dancing until a year later. . . . Girls assume the external manners of an adult at 15½, boys at 16. The patterns are similar for boys and girls, with girls from six months to a year in advance of boys." Campbell admits that the time differences between the sexes as here reported are not as great as some of the literature on the subject leads one to expect and that some writers suggest an advance of as much as two years in the girl over the boy.

As seen by a sociologist.—While the running description by Campbell carries from childhood through early adolescence, the picture here of social-sex roles should be rounded out by being carried through adolescence to early adulthood. This is made possible by reproducing by quotation and paraphrase portions of a description of these roles as seen by Talcott Parsons (*84*). His portrayal covers these roles over the full life-span, but, as interest here is mainly in adolescence and later adolescence, only the portions that relate to this period are paraphrased. Parsons concentrated in his description on the urban middle and upper middle class, which, because Campbell made her analysis for a similar cultural level, should make for something like continuity. The social-sex roles for classes below would be expected to differ in some degree and kind.

After describing the equality of treatment accorded the two sexes during childhood, Parsons speaks of new features appearing at the transition from childhood to adolescence which "disturb the symmetry of sex roles," while "still a second set of factors appears with marriage and the acquisition of full adult status and responsibilities." One indication of change is the practice of chaperonage, through which girls are given a kind of protection by adults. Boys of the same age are not similarly chaperoned, except in their relations with girls of their own class. The supervision has been extended to girls in boarding schools and colleges, although there has been some decline in this regard. "It is at the point of emergence into adolescence that there first begins to develop a set of patterns and behavior phenomena which involve a highly complex combination of age grading and sex-role elements. These may be referred to together as the phenomena of the 'youth culture.' Certain of its elements are present in preadolescence and others in the adult culture. But the peculiar combination in connection with this particular age level is unique and highly distinctive of American society."

Parsons thinks the best single point of reference for characterizing this youth culture lies in its contrast with the dominant pattern of adult male role. By contrast with this role and its emphasis on responsibility, the youth culture, as concerns the male, is "more or less specifically irresponsible." It aims at "having a good time," especially with the opposite sex. It gives prominence to athletics and implies the personal qualities associated with the "swell guy." "On the feminine side, there is correspondingly a strong tendency to accentuate sexual attractiveness in terms of various versions of what may be called the 'glamour girl' pattern. Although these patterns defining roles tend to polarize sexually—for instance, as between the star athlete and the socially popular girl—yet on a certain level they are complementary...."

A further feature of this culture and the roles of the two sexes in it is "the extent to which it is crystallized about a system of formal education." The principal centers for the dissemination of prestige are the colleges, but, as we know from Coleman's investigation, most of the distinctive phenomena are to be found also in high schools. "In both sexes the transition to full adulthood means loss of a certain 'glamorous' element. From being the athletic hero or the lion of college dances, the young man becomes a prosaic business executive or lawyer. The more successful adults participate in an important order of prestige symbols, but these are of a very different order from those of the youth culture. The contrast in the case of the feminine role is perhaps equally sharp, with at least a strong tendency to take on a 'domestic' pattern with marriage and the arrival of children."

Attitudes and Values

Scope of the section.—A chapter on personal and social development of later adolescents could hardly leave out of account consideration of the status and/or changes in attitudes and values during the age-span which extends through the later years of the second decade of life and reaches into the earliest years of the third. "Attitude" and "value" are terms used here in the broad sense of what Thompson refers to as "mediational states within the individual that *predispose* him toward certain courses of action and toward certain beliefs and evaluations" (*125*, 514). These attitudes are rather clearly distinguishable from reflexes and purely innate tendencies and are, therefore, presumably relatively modifiable by education and the culture. They are manifested in wide variety, as suggested by the diversity of terms applied to them, as likes and dislikes, prejudices, fears, superstitions, opinions, convictions, conceived notions, and the like.

Although there is a rather extensive literature reporting studies of attitudes and values held by various elements of the total population, we are once again embarrassed by a scarcity of investigations covering the age-span of the predominant age-group in the community college, the 17- to 21-year-olds. There are numerous inquiries that carry through high school years, that is, up to the first college year, and there are also numerous investigations applying to students in four-year colleges and in universities; but few are in print that extend from mid-adolescence into early adulthood, so that trends or stability in attitudes during the age-span with which we are particularly concerned cannot be unequivocally established. However, certain of the studies have made use of the same instrument or procedures with populations at both high school and college levels, which makes possible some conclusions concerning changes with age. At the same time, the studies restricted to populations at the high school level do carry inferences into the lower limits of our age-group, and those applying to college and university students also overlap on this age-group, so that some applicable inferences can be drawn that advance our understanding of the later adolescent and young adult.

Another source of weakness of some of the investigations digested in this section on attitudes and values, one which will emerge in the interpretations, is their partial lack of timeliness. Some of them were made so long ago that some of the issues they raise now seem outdated, or at least of less consequence than when the studies were made. One may judge from the descriptions of certain projects listed by Heckman and Martin in the *Inventory of Current Research in Higher Education* (1968) of the Carnegie Commission on Higher Education that a considerable amount of research into the attitudes and value systems of college students is presently underway, but, until the results are made available, dependence for understandings in this area will need to depend in some degree on the older inquiries.

A wide array of procedures has been and is being used to ascertain attitudes and values. Among the methods most often used in the past are questionnaires (with check list as variant) and interview (with the poll as a variant), and observation. Latterly, specially devised scales of opinion have been extensively applied. Sociometric instruments and projective techniques (aimed at catching respondents off-guard) have been more recent developments in attitude measurement, although studies involving these procedures are not represented in the digests to follow, mainly because none falls directly in the fields of our concern.

Repeated investigations of wrongs, likes, and worries.—A cluster of investigations rather unusually informative in the area of attitudes involved the use of the Pressey X-0 Test (Form B). This test had been administered to public school students in grades 8, 10, and 12 and to university students in all four college classes in 1923, to university students again in 1933, and to public school students and university students of the same classifications in 1943 (*89*). Evidence is available for both sexes. The public school students were in Ohio communities and the students at the college level were in the Ohio State University, making for comparability of the populations at the two main levels. Large numbers of students were tested in each of the three investigations. Comparisons of the evidence from these several investigations thus make possible ascertaining trends in certain attitudes (a) over a span of twenty years, from 1923 to 1943 and, what is more important to our purpose, (b) through the spans of high school and college years.

The digest and interpretation here will rely largely on the report by Pressey based on his data for 1943, which he compares with evidence collected and interpreted in the studies of 1923 and 1933.

The X-0 Test is made up of three parts, or subtests. Test 1 consists of 125 items in the nature of "wrongs" or "disapprovals," described by the author of the test as "borderline issues of morals and manners" (begging, smoking, flirting, spitting, giggling, etc.). The testee merely crosses off the items he thinks wrong. Test 2 consists of a list of 125 "worries" or "anxieties" (loneliness, work, forgetfulness, school, blues, etc.). In Test 3, with an equal number of items, the testee is requested to mark those things he "likes" or is "interested in" (fortune-telling, boating, beaches, mountains, vaudeville, etc.). Pressey says of the test that it was developed in 1920, that it contains certain items which "seem nostalgic of that earlier period but now out of date," some which now seem "silly or petty" but were included for use with children, and some items which are irrelevant or "jokers" to check on careless marking.

Pressey's handling of his data falls naturally into three parts. First is the question as to changes over the 20-year period in what may be called total scores, or total number of items marked as disapproved, worried about, or liked. Next is the problem of gross trends as shown by item analysis. The third task is the identification of some of the more significant individual items in the test and the changes regarding them, although, on account of the lack of timeliness for the current social scene, less use will be made here of this portion than others. Recourse to this investigation will be concluded by citing two "general trends" which he noted as "of great and pervasive importance." In advance of drawing on the evidence and conclusions from the study, we may note that the investigation is set up to disclose two types of trends, first, shifts in attitude over a period of time (1923 to 1943), and, second, shifts with advance in age and school classification, that is, from public school grades through college years. While trends over the 20-year time-span are of some concern to us as background, chief focus of our interest is on trends during the age-span from school through college.

TABLE 3.8
AVERAGE CHANGE IN MEANS FOR DISAPPROVALS, WORRIES, AND DISLIKES
OF PUBLIC SCHOOL AND COLLEGE CLASSES FROM 1923 TO 1943*

Subtests	Grades 8, 10, 12		Four College Years		All Groups	
	Boys	Girls	Men	Women	M	F
Disapprovals	−2.0	−5.0	−10.2	−15.0	−6.1	−10.0
Worries	0.7	0.0	− 1.2	0.0	−0.2	0.0
Likes	−7.0	2.3	3.2	11.0	−1.9	6.0
Total Change†	9.7	7.3	14.6	26.0	8.2	16.0

SOURCE: Pressey (89, Table 1).
*Minus signs show a decrease in 1943 as compared to 1923.
†These totals in disregard of sign.

1. Main changes in gross scores as reported by Pressey are shown in Table 3.8. Minus signs indicate decreases in scores from 1923 to 1943, which, for example concerning disapprovals, signify decreases in them. Pressey identifies the most significant changes in the table as the decreases in disapprovals: while small in the school grades, these decreases were substantial in college years and notably larger for women than for men. Average changes in scores for worries seem negligible. For college women there appears to have been a marked increase in likes.

2. Gross trends as shown by item analysis must be sought in Tables 3.9 and 3.10. The reader will recognize these tables as resulting from compilation, referred to by Pressey as "tedious," for each of the 375 items in the three subtests, for 1923 and 1943, for each school grade and college class, and separately for the sexes. Following is Pressy's interpretation of the first of these tables: "The first part of Table [3.9] shows average differences in percentages marking each item in '23 and '43, these differences being added without regard to sign. Again the disapprovals show the greatest differences, which increase consistently from high school through college, and are consistently greater for girls. Changes in likes show up more than in Table [3.10] where the net total score changes... were kept down by more items of the opposite sign; in fact changes are greater in likes

TABLE 3.9
CHANGES FROM GRADES 10 AND 12 TO COLLEGE JUNIORS AND SENIORS IN PERCENTAGES MARKING EACH ITEM

Subtest	Male			Female		
	Grades 10, 12	College Freshmen, Sophomores	College Juniors, Seniors	Grades 10, 12	College Freshmen, Sophomores	College Juniors, Seniors
	(Average Difference in Percentages)					
Disapprovals	7.6	11.5	12.2	10.0	12.9	15.9
Worries	6.0	5.2	10.4	7.0	5.7	7.3
Likes	9.8	9.5	10.1	11.9	12.0	13.6
Total	23.4	26.2	32.7	28.9	30.6	36.8
	Number of Items with 20 Per Cent or More Difference					
Disapprovals	5	22	24	16	28	43
Worries	3	1	12	5	1	6
Likes	20	11	16	26	22	24
Total	28	34	52	47	51	73

SOURCE: After Pressey (89, Table 3).

than disapprovals in high school for both sexes. Worries show least change, and no consistent age or sex differences. The totals emphasize the greater aggregate changes for girls. The lower part of Table [3.9] shows numbers of words with 20 per cent or more differences. The consistent increase in scores for disapprovals [meaning decrease in disapprovals] from high school through college, and larger numbers for girls, are especially to be noted...."

Table 3.10 is the third and last to be reproduced from the report of Pressey's investigation and, because it bears directly on changes in attitudes with age through adolescence toward maturity, it has most signifi-

TABLE 3.10
AVERAGE DIFFERENCES IN PERCENTAGES MARKING ITEMS IN 1923 AND 1943, AND NUMBER OF WORDS HAVING DIFFERENCES OF 20 PER CENT OR MORE

Subtest	Male		Female	
	1923	1943	1923	1943
	(Average Difference in Percentages)			
Disapprovals	11.2	18.8	18.4	24.8
Worries	7.0	8.9	7.6	7.8
Likes	13.2	14.0	12.1	13.4
Total	31.4	41.7	38.1	46.0
	Number of Items Showing Differences of 20 Per Cent or More			
Disapprovals	14	56	54	82
Worries	6	6	7	7
Likes	29	39	26	26
Total	49	101	87	115

SOURCE: Pressey (89, Table 5).

cance for our purpose. This table reports in its upper half the changes from grades 10 and 12 (as a single group) to college juniors and seniors (also as a single group) for each of the two years 1923 and 1943. Thus it makes possible comparison of changes for each of these two years in disapprovals, worries, and likes from high school to later college years. It will be noted that the scores on disapprovals (signifying decreases in them) rose more for this age-span in 1943 than in 1923, and rose considerably more for girls than for boys. The scores for worries and for likes rose only slightly. The evidence in the lower half of the table, giving the number of disapprovals, worries, and likes showing differences of 20 per cent or more, is in the main in harmony with the observation just made.

Pressey's interpretation of the table points out what has been noted, that the total change was decidedly greater in 1943 than in 1923, saying that in both years the girls showed about 10 per cent more total change than the boys, almost all of this in the last four years. "It would seem that while at home the girls were held closer to the conventions of their parents, but upon going to college reacted away from home restraint even more than the boys, at least in their declared attitudes."

3. To illustrate the shifts on individual items in the tests we quote a brief paragraph from Pressey's interpretation: "Twelve wrongs showed decreases of 25 per cent or more in 1943 from 1923. Four items might be roughly classified as having to do with sex-social conduct: *flirting* was marked as wrong by 23 per cent fewer men in '43 and 41 per cent fewer women, *toughness* by 31 per cent and 39 per cent fewer, *disgrace* 15 per cent and 32 per cent, and *sportiness* 21 per cent and 31 per cent. Five items might be classified as minor vices: *smoking* (17 per cent and 26 per cent), *overeating* (33 per cent and 30 per cent), *extravagance* (28 per cent and 25 per cent), *betting* (21 per cent and 26 per cent), *craps* (26 per cent and 29 per cent). A third group might be considered to deal with borderline issues of manners and good taste: *slang* (23 per cent and 28 per cent), *chewing gum* (12 per cent and 30 per cent), and *talking back* (9 per cent and 25 per cent). Most of these changes seem unimportant but as bearing on everyday adolescent conduct, might be more significant than serious issues."

Pressey's answer to the question of whether "any significantly larger generalizations" are possible from the evidence of this battery of investigations is that two general trends are discernible. The first is the general freeing of young people from a great variety of borderland social taboos, inhibitions, and restrictions, and from anxieties connected with these or with natural phenomena. "That the changes are greatest as to wrongs, which most explicitly involve the mores, and least as to the more personal anxieties, emphasized the fact of change in the culture." The second is the growth of social interests, freedoms, and also sensitivities. More succinctly, Pressey calls these findings "two major cultural trends," "a gradual escape from old social taboos, inhibitions, and fears"; and "increased socialization."

Unfounded beliefs or misconceptions.—Another area of attitude it seems desirable to explore for light it may throw on personal and social development during later adolescence is what are referred to variously as "unfounded beliefs," "popular misconceptions," or simply "superstitions." Reports of very recent studies in this area are not available, but a spate of them found their way into print during the third and fourth decades of this century. Those relied on here for evidence were published during this period (*43, 75, 132*) except that the last one to be referred to dates back to 1919 (*20*). As will be noted, the studies as a group will make possible comparisons of high school seniors, who may be regarded as on the threshold of college attendance, and college students of varying classification, as well as adults. The comparisons justify speculation on the trends with age through adolescence with respect to these unfounded beliefs.

In the investigation involving high school seniors, Garrett and Fisher (*43*) took a list of thirty false statements that had previously been used with adults by Nixon (*81*), added to it ten more, and submitted the list to senior girls in the Washington Irving High School and to senior boys in the DeWitt Clinton High School in New York City. The average age of these seniors was seventeen. The subjects merely marked each statement T or F. All the statements were false. The authors, for convenience, utilized the evidence for just a hundred students of each sex for whom records were complete and for whom they also had intelligence quotients. The average number of statements marked true was 17.6 for boys and 19.9 for girls. The difference of 2.3 between the averages of boys and girls was found to be statistically reliable. Although the average numbers were somewhat larger for girls than for boys, suggesting a somewhat higher degree of credulity for the girls, the coefficient of the rank orders assigned to the statements, on the basis of frequency of marking them as correct, was .92, indicating a high measure of concurrence for the two sexes.

One of the most surprising outcomes of the Garrett-Fisher investigation—in the minds of the authors, the most significant—was in the low coefficient of correlation found between misconception scores and IQs. For boys and girls, disregarding age, these coefficients were, respectively, -0.02 and -0.11. For the same pair of variables, with chronological age held constant, the coefficients were even smaller, being respectively 0.00 and 0.01, that is, indicating no relationship.

In their study, Garrett and Fisher compared the results for their high school seniors with those obtained earlier for adults by Nixon (*81*). For

102 THE LATER ADOLESCENT

illustrative purposes here it will be preferable to compare them with results obtained later by Valentine on the statements common to Garrett and Fisher's and Nixon's lists, and also used by Valentine, although the investigator last named, as will be noted below, used a much longer list on all his subjects. This list is reproduced in Table 3.11, and includes 29

TABLE 3.11
PERCENTAGES OF POPULATIONS IN TWO STUDIES WHO HOLD THE MISCONCEPTIONS INDICATED

Belief	Garrett and Fisher		Valentine	
	Boys (100)	Girls (100)	Men (773)	Women (665)
Concentration developed by chess and checkers	93	96	81	75
Mathematics gives a logical mind	92	93	70	73
Man's senses five	69	80	57	59
Silent men deep thinkers	66	87	24	25
Overstudy causes feeblemindedness	65	56	39	36
Artistic nature indicated by hands and fingers	55	61	38	37
Telepathic influence in staring	35	60	23	29
Face shows intelligence	51	72	23	29
Women purer in nature than men	50	63	18	29
Shifty eye indicates dishonesty	50	69	23	36
Prenatal influence	48	43	29	34
Slow learners good retainers	45	59	32	41
Some animals as intelligent as humans	43	66	20	23
Bright children physically retarded	43	29	33	32
Brains and beauty rarely go together	37	53	18	19
Fat people good natured	36	19	13	16
Thinking may cause disease	36	36	16	21
Faith can heal a broken limb	34	23	5	8
Instinctive knowledge of good	34	38	15	21
Marriage of cousins	32	32	20	25
Lines on hand foretell future	24	51	13	19
Influence of stars on character	21	40	20	21
Women inferior to men in intelligence	20	7	11	10
Cold hands, warm heart	18	15	4	8
Burning ears	15	9	2	6
Blonds less trustworthy	13	3	14	8
Thirteen unlucky	5	3	0	1
Green-eyed people untrustworthy	4	2	6	4
Friday unlucky	3	6	0	0

SOURCE: Valentine (*132*, Table 1).

statements which are given in rank order, from highest to lowest, as found for boys in the Garrett and Fisher study. In this table, the statements, for the sake of convenience, are put in shortened form, although readers, from their general knowledge, will be able to make good conjectures on the complete statements. For example, "Burning ears," near the bottom of the table, was stated in the test used as "If your ears burn, it is a sign that someone is talking about you," and "Friday unlucky," the last one on the list, reads in full as "Beginning an undertaking on Friday is almost certain to bring bad luck."

As already indicated, the percentages in the first two columns of the table are those for high school seniors in New York City reported by Garrett and Fisher. The percentages credited to Valentine are those for students in the Ohio State University who took the tests at the outset of a beginning course in psychology, before having been exposed to the course. They are reported by Valentine to have been mainly freshmen, although mixed with some sophomores or others.* Computation of the means of the percentages in the table yields the following results: high school seniors —boys, 39.2; girls, 43.9; college students—men, 23.0; women, 25.7. These figures reflect the differences previously reported between the sexes. They are not large, and, while they are statistically significant, Valentine expressed the belief that they could be eliminated by selection of items. The differences, however, between the means for high school seniors and for college students are so large as to bespeak decrease in credulity through later adolescence even after allowance is made for selection between high school and college and for some difference owing to geographic location of residence. At least, a substantial decrease with age may be assumed until either longitudinal or cross-sectional studies are made in the same or socioeconomically similar populations in a single geographic area. This conclusion has the support also of some decline in the percentages for students who began the courses in psychology in the winter and spring quarters, as compared with those who began it in the autumn quarter, that is, the first quarter in the school year, although some of this decline, too, could be attributable to selection and elimination during the school year.

A study by Lundeen and Caldwell (75) involved seniors in high school distributed over a number of states and in smaller and larger cities. College students represented in the study were not as widely distributed as the high school seniors and were referred to as "adults," as the men averaged 23 and the women 26 years of age. The procedure in response differed from the studies previously reviewed here in that respondents were asked which of a long list of unfounded beliefs they had "heard," "believed," and were "influenced by." Seniors on the average had heard of approximately half the total of ideas and on the average reported "belief" in and 'influence" by an approximate fifth of them. College students reported belief in and influence by a smaller proportion, indicating, as in the other studies, some decrease with age. Again in this study the percentages of girls and college women who indicated belief in and influence by these ideas were higher than those of their peers in the other sex.

*Valentine's words: "Freshmen composed in all cases the majority of the group."

An older study (*20*), made at the University of Oregon, asked students in classes in psychology to "state briefly any superstitions which you believe or which influence your conduct." The investigator had evidence on the ages of his respondents, which ranged from 16 to 25 years but, regrettably for our purpose of noting change with age, made no inquiry into this relationship. However, two-fifths of the males and two-thirds of the females reported belief and influence, among the more common superstitions being knocking on wood, finding four-leaf clovers, dreams prophetic, number 13, sleep on wedding cake, black cats, etc. Chief inference from this study is that students of college age *admitted* believing in and being influenced by superstitions.

Before leaving this illustrative abstract of investigations of unfounded beliefs held by youth and adults, it seems desirable to touch again on the relationship of scores on them to intelligence. It was reported above that Garrett and Fisher found the relationship between these scores and IQ as negligible or nonexistent. Other investigators mentioned have found more relationship, but never a high correlation. It does appear that the coefficients between measures of intelligence and of misconceptions held increase (in a negative direction) when these misconceptions have specific confrontation in courses in psychology, within which it is obvious many of the misconceptions would logically fall. This finding led Valentine to conclude that "instruction in college is too general. Too much is expected in the way of transfer from broad general scientific principles to specific items of everyday experience. Only a few students are capable of incorporating scientific principles into their everyday lives unaided by an instructor." The implication is that attitudes of the sort here described can be weeded out by direct attention to them at appropriate points in instructional programs.

Conversational interests of college students.—Conversation belongs under the heading of behavior rather than of attitudes and values. However, topics of conversation can supply clues to values and, on this account, recourse is taken here to conclusions from systematic observation and analysis of conversational behavior of students as reported by Stoke and West (*113*). The study was made "in a state university of between 2,000 and 2,500 students," the location of which is in a town of about 7,000 population. A majority of the students came from rural communities, although a considerable number came from urban environments. The conversations studied took place in 26 different groups of students in fraternity houses, sororities, and dormitories. Recording was done secretly by 36 students against a checklist and extended over almost the full cycle of a college year. Some impression of the bulk of the evidence compiled for the analysis may be gained from the following facts: 498 sessions of "just talk" were reported, 259 by men and 239 by women; there was a total of 2,230 topics, 1,353 by men and 877 by women. No reporter was used on the investigation who was unwilling to report any topic of conversation regardless of whether or not it might be taboo in mixed company.

The report of this study includes a long table with many topics presented in declining order of frequency from high to low for men, and a second column for women for direct comparison. It included 58 categories for men and 66 for women, but it is unnecessary to reproduce the table here as major inferences from the study may be made from the grouping of topics into larger areas. The following quotations disclose the four major findings by the authors, centering around four main areas of topics, namely, sex interests, personalities, intellectual and artistic interests, and problems of a personal or a social nature:

[1] "The general topic of greatest interest is that of sex. The total of all items dealing with this subject for men is 22 per cent of all topics mentioned; for women the total is 25.55 per cent. Evidently between a fourth and a fifth of the conversational interests center around this subject. This is not at all excessive. . . . The proportion devoted to sex interests outside of college circles is much greater than inside. . . .

[2] "If topics dealing largely with personalities are abstracted from the general list, we find that women are discussing them far more frequently than men. The total percentage for women is 19.6, while for men it was 12.7. . . . The finding is in general agreement with the belief that women are more interested in people while men are more interested in things.

[3] "A total of 21 topics might be classified as entirely, or partially, of an intellectual or artistic nature. Many of them are mentioned only infrequently and therefore the percentage they formed of the total number of topics is disappointing. The percentage for men was 16.1, while for women it was 15.3. 'Studies' head the list for both men and women.

[4] "Social problems of a personal nature are much more provocative of discussion than social problems of an impersonal sort. Men discuss such problems as drinking, smoking, sex problems, etc., a total of 11.1 per cent of all things mentioned, while they discuss such things as communism, world peace, government ownership of utilities, etc., only seven-tenths of one per cent. The contrast is even greater with women, who discuss social problems of a personal nature 12.1 per cent. The college youth is evidently little interested in the colossal social experiments of the day. His world is a narrow one in which his own affairs are paramount."

The findings of this observational investigation are certainly informative of attitudes and values of college students. The lack of complete *timeliness* because the study was made a generation ago is in considerable part offset by the *timelessness* of the categories under which the conversations were classified. At the same time, it is desirable to call attention to its strictures in application to a community college student body. It was made of a population including students in all four college years and, therefore, many who were beyond predominant community college age. The findings apply to a student body largely residential and living in fraternities, sororities, and dormitories, whereas almost all community college students live at home. It is lacking also in that it was not set up to disclose trends with age, which is a matter of concern in the community college which typically carries the student body from late adolescence into early adulthood. Workers in community colleges must make or await the making of studies which compensate for these strictures and, in the meantime, apply with caution the conclusions that have been drawn.

The fourth conclusion extracted above from the study by Stoke and West, to the effect that problems of a personal nature are more provocative of discussion than social problems of an impersonal sort, is in large part corroborated as applicable to a larger college population in an investigation by Gillespie and Allport (46). The source of the corroboratory conclusion in this instance is not in an analysis of conversations, but from autobiographies and responses to questionnaires with 50 questions and subinquiries on various attitudes by students in liberal arts programs in colleges in the United States and in nine foreign countries. The investigation is referred to by the authors as a sort of "fishing expedition" or "pilot study," and they did not resort to statistical procedures. In endeavoring to identify the predominant value-orientation of the American student (in comparison with the student in the foreign countries), the authors say that the best way to generalize his goals seems to be "in terms of a search for a rich, full life." However, they report "another prominent American characteristic" in "the relatively low interest in social problems." Poverty, delinquency, politics, and race relations are less frequently mentioned by American students than by those in most foreign countries represented. The prevailing attitude "reflects . . . relatively small interest in the life of the group or nation, and little awareness of the political and social context of the American student's existence." The phrase "a strong flavor of privatism" is used to characterize his prevailing attitude.

Personal attitudes and social values.—So far in this section evidence has been presented from studies revealing a wide variety of attitudes, such as disapprovals, anxieties, unfounded beliefs, and conversational interests. Because the approach in some of these has been essentially negative, in that attitudes have been sought toward what has been typically regarded as questionable behavior, attention will next be directed to investigations involving positive or favorable personal attitudes and social values. However, in order to make the differing approaches apparent by contrast, brief reference will first be made to one more investigation with the negative approach, made by Slavens and Brogan (*111*), involving a comparison of attitudes of representative groups of students in two high schools in two different cities in Texas and at the University of Texas. The students were asked to rank 15 practices from 1 to 15 as to "worseness" and as to frequency. Because at this point our interest is in attitudes rather than behavior, findings reported here will emphasize the rankings on worseness. Among the practices ranked were the following: stealing, cheating, lying, drinking, gambling, swearing, vulgar talk, Sabbath-breaking, etc. The outstanding conclusion from the comparison of the rankings of the different groupings by sex and in school or university is their similarity. Coefficients of correlation were computed between the various rankings and all were found high. For example, the coefficient for the sets of rankings by boys in the two high schools was .98; between boys in one high school and girls in the other was .98; between the boys in one high school and university men was .96, and so on. No coefficient reported was below .89. If one concedes the merit of procedures in such a study, the conclusion of similarity of attitudes concerning these practices held by boys and girls in high school, by men and women in college, and by students at the two levels is inevitable. There is greater variation in the rankings on frequency than on worseness, but not enough to prevent the conclusion "that the moral ideas and conduct of high-school students are very similar to the moral ideas and conduct of university students." It should be mentioned that, out of respect for the wishes of the high school authorities, one of the practices rated by university students, "sex irregularity," was omitted from the high school portion of the study. The conclusion of similarity of attitudes at high school and college levels suggests that stability in these attitudes is attained even before high school years.

An investigation into age trends in social values with a more positive approach is one by Thompson (*124*), who executed it in two steps. The first step involved asking 80 students of each sex in grades 6 through 12 (more than a thousand students in all) "to list things they could be doing for which other boys and girls would praise them." In the second step the ten most frequent activities, which are listed in Table 3.12, were presented in paired-comparison form to a new population sample of the same size and age-range. The ranks assigned to the ten activities by boys and girls in grades 6 and 12 are indicated in the table. A strong impression yielded by examination of the table is of the rather high degree of concurrence of these rankings, both as between the sexes and also as between grades 6 and 12. This impression is emphatically reinforced by examination of Thompson's figure, not reproduced here, depicting the rankings in each grade by each sex and reporting the coefficients of correlation between these rankings from one grade to the next from grade 6 to grade 12. In no instance does the coefficient fall below .94 for either boys or girls, and the correlations of the rankings grade by grade between the sexes are equally high. These correlations lead to the conclusion of stability of the values throughout the age-span. There is also the inference that, since these values seem stabilized by grade 6, the stabilization must take place some time previous to this grade.

Attitudes toward property.—Among attitudes of major importance in personal and social relationships are those toward property. The interest here again is the same as that throughout this section on attitudes and

TABLE 3.12
RANK ORDER OF SOCIAL VALUES AS APPRAISED BY
BOYS AND GIRLS IN GRADES 6 AND 12

Personal-Social Values	Rank Order			
	Grade 6		Grade 12	
	Boys	Girls	Boys	Girls
Be honest	1	1	2	1
Be polite	2	2	1	2
Be kind	3	3	6	5
Be cooperative	4	4	3	3
Don't brag	5	6	7	6
Be friendly	6	5	4	4
Be generous	7	8	9	9
Be clean	8	7	8	7
Have social skills	9	9	5	8
Be proficient in sports	10	10	10	10

SOURCE: After Thompson (*124*, 534–35).

values, that is, in "mediational states within the individual," to use again Thompson's definition, "that predispose . . . toward certain courses of action and toward certain beliefs and evaluations." Admittedly, it is not the equivalent of investigations of actual behavior, as reported in *Studies in Deceit* by Hartshorne and Mays (*55*) or in the extent of cheating in taking tests as reported by Howells (*60*), however important direct measurement of behavior may be.

An illustrative study is one by Eberhart (*31*) involving 836 boys from grade 1 through grade 12 in three schools—two elementary schools and a high school—in one neighborhood in the "near west side" of Chicago. The boys ranged in age from 6 to 21, with the number beyond 18 being small except that a group of 32 adult males was included. The procedure was one of paired-comparisons, similar to that used by Thompson in his study of values reported above, of 20 offenses against property rights which had been recurrently found in the schools. To obtain supplementary information interviews were also held with about 10 per cent of the boys.

Among the findings of this investigation were (1) some stability in attitudes toward property as early as the first-grade level; (2) steadily increasing discrimination with age among the various offenses with regard to seriousness; and (3) progressively closer approximation to an adult norm with increase in age and grades. In addition, the younger boys tended to judge the seriousness of an offense on the basis of fear of punishment, while the older boys more often mentioned unwillingness to injure others, a finding which the investigator believes "indicates an important qualitative shift in values that probably parallel the perceptual-social growth of children."

The rate of progress in evaluating the seriousness of offenses is rapid between the first and third grades. Above the third grade changes in this direction continue at a slower rate, although they are "regular and orderly." The overall steadiness of the change is suggested by the average correlation of $+.97$ between the ranks of adjacent grades, although, to be sure, more widely separated grades yielded lower coefficients.

Concreteness can be added to conclusions from this investigation by reporting illustratively the ranks assigned to specific wrongs presented to the subjects. Ranked 1 for all ages from 10 to (and including) adult was "To swipe your mother's wrist watch and pawn it." Ranked either 2 or 3 for all ages and 4 by adults was "To swipe a dollar from your boss's desk." Ranked 18, 19, or 20 (most often 20) at all ages and 20 by adults was "To borrow your brother's baseball without asking." Ranked 7, 8, 9, 9.5, and 10 by different age groups and 9 by adults (that is, about midway as to seriousness) was "To swipe and sell lead pipes from an old warehouse."

Judgments of the seriousness of the property offenses seem, according to Eberhart, to be based principally upon the relationship of the owner to the offender, the likelihood of real injury to the owner, the possibility of punishment of the offender, the kind of property involved, the value of the property, and, particularly with older subjects, the offender's motive.

Single special studies like this one by Eberhart afford a slender basis for generalizations concerning the development of value systems in the youth of the land. If attitudes in areas other than property rights develop similarly, one may conclude that considerable progress toward stabilization has been made as early as the first grade in school, that the change in values is steady rather than irregular or saltatory at any particular part of the age-span investigated, and that, by the end of the high school period, that is, by the age of 17 or 18, the values approximate those of adulthood. The evidence reported by Thompson, as reviewed above, suggests that the values differ little as between the sexes.

Concerning ascription of social idealism.—Before leaving consideration of attitudes and values among later adolescents, attention will be directed to a query that must have emerged in the minds of many readers during the consideration of the results of the studies that have been reviewed in this section. The query concerns the attitude of social idealism that is often ascribed to youth, and asserted to be characteristic of them in the late teens and early twenties. As evidence of this attitude those putting the query can cite the current interest of college youth in volunteering for service in the Peace Corps and Vista, and they could cite analogous enthusiasms in earlier student generations.

It is true that an attitude of social idealism as typical does not protrude from the results of the studies summarized. The nearest approach to it would be found in the high rankings of certain personal-social values in the investigation by Thompson and in the small proportion of "social problems of an impersonal sort" represented in the conversations analyzed in the investigation by Stoke and West. Less reassuring is the conclusion by Gillespie and Allport of the "relatively low interest in social problems" of the American student, although this characteristic may in part be qualified by the observation of the authors that the best way to generalize his goals seems to be "in terms of a search for a rich, full life," since such a life might well call for an element of social idealism.

An inquiry, mainly with youth from 8 to 18, one finding of which is partially congruous with the observation that social idealism is characteristic of a minority and not a majority of adolescents, is one by Havighurst, Robinson, and Dorr (57). This was an investigation bearing on the Freudian concept of the ego-ideal, or ideal self; it inquired into the kinds of persons with whom the subjects were inclined to identify. The young people represented complied with directions to "Describe in a page or less the person you would most like to be like when you grow up." Further details in the directions suggested that this person might be a real person, or an imaginary one, or a combination of people, and that the subjects should "tell something about this person's age, character, appearance, occupation, and recreations." The responses were classified under eight categories, as follows: (1) Parents (and other relatives of the parental or grandparental generation); (2) Parent-surrogates (teachers, neighbors); (3) Glamorous adults (movie stars, military heroes, athletes); (4) Heroes, "people with a substantial claim to fame, e.g., Florence Nightingale, Abraham Lincoln"; (5) Attractive and successful young adults within the individual's range of observations; (6) Composite or imaginary characters; (7) Age-mates or youths only two or three years older than the respondents; (8) Miscellaneous responses.

Among the conclusions drawn from the evidence portrayed are two of most concern at this point. One is that the responses fall mainly into four categories, namely, parents, glamorous adults, attractive and visible young adults, and composite imaginary characters. Parent-surrogates such as teachers and older adults are seldom named, and heroes even less often. The other conclusion is that an age-sequence exists, "moving outward from the family circle, becoming more abstract, and culminating in the composite, imaginary person." The proportion of "heroes," less than 10 per cent, was much smaller than in studies made 10 to 50 years earlier.

What deliberation over such evidence as is available to bear on this ascription of social idealism to adolescents adds up to is that the attitude is not a prevailing characteristic in the sense that it is to be found in all or even in most youth. It can hardly be denied, however, that it is a trait of at least a *minority* of young people. It is well to remember in considering the evidence from the studies reviewed that the investigators were seeking generalizations applying to majorities rather than to minorities, and it is well to bear in mind also that an attitude like social idealism in a minority can be highly significant for a society even if the minority is numerically not too impressive.

A word should be said concerning the ascription of social idealism to youth in relation to the student protests that have in recent years been occuring on college and university campuses. While some critics see in these outbreaks only wanton destructiveness egged on by a mob spirit, other observers have noted the frequent references among the protesters to wrongs they believe need correction in our society, such as prosecution of the war in Southeast Asia and militarism in general, wide-spread violation of civil and human rights, and increasing pollution of the environment. To the extent that the protesters are motivated by these wrongs, the ascription of some social idealism to them is warranted. At the same time, it is well to bear in mind, in judging the extent of this idealism, that the protesters never exceed a minority of the total student bodies represented.

Relationship of morality and intelligence.—While considering mental growth in Chapter 2, some attention was given to the relationship between growth in physique and mentality. It is appropriate at this point to give at least brief consideration to the question of the relationship between intelligence and personal and social characteristics, preferably to *growth* of intelligence and of these characteristics. While the problems of investigating the relationship between physical and mental growth is far from easy, it is much less difficult than those between intelligence and personality. At least we have objective measures of physique, and the tests of intelligence, while still not fully satisfactory, yield a measure of considerable reliability for inquiry into correlation in these areas. Traits of personality and attitudes are acknowledged to be even more complex and intangible than is intelligence.

What is needed to serve our purpose is a longitudinal study of the relationship between available measures of intelligence and reliable measures of traits or attitudes, extending from early to later adolescence and on into adulthood. Evidence from such a study seems not to be available in the literature, so we must rely for any conclusion on studies mainly cross-sectional at different ages and on a variety of aspects of behavior, traits, and attitudes. Whatever is purported to be measured in the area of personality in these studies, whether designated as types of behavior, traits, character, or attitudes, the focus of interpretation here is on morality.

A large-scale inquiry, the findings of which bear on our question, is the widely known one by Hartshorne and Mays (55), especially the portion reported in the volume of *Studies in Deceit,* which deals with investigation into the incidence of cheating, lying, and stealing in children of the ages of 8 to 16. One conclusion from the inquiry is that honesty is positively related to intelligence: "In almost any group of children of approximately the same age, those of higher levels of intelligence deceive definitely less than those of lower levels...." The conclusions call attention to other factors which increase the incidence of deceit, including emotional instability and socioeconomic and cultural backgrounds, whereas sex and physical condition were found to be unrelated (408–9). An investigation by Dimock (27, 154) of adolescent boys found intelligence and socioeconomic background of greater influence than other factors in determining moral knowledge. In an investigation of 16-year-olds which arrived at measures of "character reputation" derived from ratings on friendliness, honesty, loyalty, moral courage, and responsibility by adults well acquainted with the subjects, Havighurst and Taba (58, 179) found a coefficient of correlation of .49 between these measures and Stanford-Binet IQ. In an investigation to be summarized below in the section on criteria of maturity, and involving use of a Social Maturity Scale, Sargent (28, 483 ff.) computed the coefficients of correlation between IQ and SQ (Social Quotient). The scale is set up to measure social competence, which can be assumed to be heavily dependent on personal responsibility. He reports the coefficients to be "low and unreliable" (.20 for high school seniors and .00 for college freshmen). However, the author explains that the scores were in narrow range and the number of subjects small. It is possible that, with a wider range of scores and larger population, the coefficients might have been larger.

Still another investigator, Chassell (*16*), some years after having completed a special project inquiring into the relationship of morality and intellect, undertook a synthesis of the findings of all reported investigations bearing on the question. Her "final conclusion" was formulated as follows (470): ."The relation between morality and intellect in restricted groups is clearly direct. The obtained relationship is extremely variable, but tends to be low. It is dependent upon the type of evidence, the type of the group, the type of coefficient, and possibly even the country represented. The true relation is undoubtedly higher than the obtained relation, but apparently at best it tends to be only marked. . . ." At a later point (411) Chassell presents a table of classification of coefficients in which the category "marked" ranges from .40 to .69. Also, in her summation she admits the influence of factors other than intelligence by asserting that the research "does not answer the question as to the relative importance of heredity and environment in determining the degree of relationship found" (489).

The conclusion from the evidence available is that, while the relation between intellect and morality is not high, it is apparently greater than that between intelligence and physique. Ausubel (5, 249) has provided the rationale for a positive relationship between intellect and morality where he says, "Growth in cognitive capacity alone accounts for several significant changes in character organization during adolescence. For one thing, moral concepts, like all other concepts, become more abstract. This enables moral behavior to acquire greater generality and consistency from situation to situation, since abstraction presupposes the identification of essential common elements."

Religion: Attitudes and Beliefs

The age-incidence of religious conversion.—An opinion more frequently held by observers of youth some decades ago than at present is that adolescence is notably a period of religious awakening, in particular of religious conversion. The opinion was based on the evidence concerning the ages at which conversions took place. Compilations of these ages around the turn of the century found the typical ages for conversion to be mainly between 15 and 20—just prior to or within the age-group that is the major concern here. The assumption was that this incidence is an accompaniment of and originates in the signal biological changes of adolescence. Compilations made a few decades later found an earlier incidence, with the typical age around 12 and before the advent of adolescence for most youth. The downward shift in typical age was one of the considerations that lead to discrediting of the belief in adolescence as a period of the "flowering" of a religious impulse. The current belief is that the pile-up of conversions was primarily the result of pressure of evangelism characteristic of religious denominations that was placed on this particular age-span. It was thus an outcome of one aspect of the culture of the period. The subsequent lowering of the age-incidence was similarly a result of this influence on a younger age-group. Students of the problem have noted that the manifestation persists in those groups in our culture with whom the pressure of evangelism on youth of these ages persists.

Dimock's study of boys.—One of the investigations, conclusions from which did much to discredit the belief in a saltatory acceleration of religious interest at adolescence paralleling the striking biological changes, was made by Dimock (26). This study was restricted to boys ranging in age from 12 to 16. The results are based on performance on a test of sixty items classified under six sections or topics: ideas of God; ideas of Jesus; ideas of prayer; ideas of the Church and Kingdom; ideas of other religions; and ideas of life purpose. The kinds of questions used were designed to reveal opinions, judgments, and attitudes rather than factual knowledge. Dimock says of his instrument that "it might be stretching things a bit to call it a test of maturity in religious thinking."

TABLE 3.13
AMOUNT OF GROWTH OVER A TWO-YEAR PERIOD IN RELIGIOUS THINKING OF BOYS WITH DIFFERENT RELIGIOUS AFFILIATIONS

Religious Group	Number Boys	Average Age (months)	Average IQ	Socio-economic Status	Religious Thinking Score		
					First Test	Second Test	Change
Jewish	9	156	111	20	126	140	14
Protestant (Conservative)	28	160	102	20	123	135	12
Protestant (Liberal)	31	152	111	22	123	135	12
Lutheran	31	158	102	17	118	129	9
Catholic	38	160	96	15	111	119	8

SOURCE: After Dimock (26).

The average scores on the test by Dimock's boys at each age were as follows: 12 years, 115; 13 years, 125; 14 years, 127; 15 years, 125; 16 years, 125. In light of this evidence Dimock's answer to the question of what happens in religious thinking during adolescence is "nothing."

The test was administered twice to the same boys at an interval of a year and the average increases in scores computed for boys in six groups defined in relation to stages of pubescent growth as follows: (1) boys who changed from prepuberty to pubescence during the year; (2) boys who were and remained postpubescent; (3) boys who changed from prepuberty to postpubescence; (4) boys who changed from puberty to postpubescence; (5) boys who were and remained pubescent; and (6) boys who were and remained prepubescent. Dimock reports being "almost startled" by comparison of the average increases in scores. For instance, he points out that the boys who remained prepubescent gained almost three times as much on their religious thinking scores in one year (10.7 points) as did the boys who changed from prepuberty to postpubescence during that year (4.2 points). The inference of a lack of relationship of growth in religious thinking to sexual maturation appeared to Dimock as inescapable.

Dimock deemed it necessary to look beyond the stage of physical maturity for the explanation of differences in growth in religious thinking. Certain results of his inquiry are reported in Table 3.13 in which the classification of subjects is by denominational affiliation. In addition, for the boys in each religious group Dimock reported, among other data, the average IQ, the average measure of socioeconomic status, and the average Religious Thinking Scores on the first and second tests, together with the average change from the first test to the second. He concluded that his data "suggest a combination of closely associated factors as the explanation of the differences in the scores: socioeconomic status, religious background, and mental ability. There is a definite correlation between religious thinking and the socioeconomic background and intelligence." Dimock's conclusions leave little basis for a belief in religious change closely coextensive with physical change in the adolescent period.

Kuhlen and Arnold's study of boys and girls.—Following Dimock's study by several years was Kuhlen and Arnold's involving both boys and girls (*69*). This investigation differed from Dimock's also in extending over a much longer age-span, as it included populations in grades 6, 9, and 12, with mean ages, respectively, at approximately 12, 15, and 18 years. The authors point out that the significance of these grade groups in the study of adolescence "lies in the fact that the sixth-grade group is largely prepubescent, the ninth-grade group is largely pubescent (at least for boys, girls maturing somewhat earlier), and the twelfth-grade group postpubescent." The study was, however, cross-sectional rather than, as was Dimock's in some aspects, longitudinal.

The project involved the use of a questionnaire which listed fifty-two statements representing various religious beliefs which were to be marked according to whether the subject "believed" the statement, did "not believe" the statement, or did not know whether he believed it or not but had "wondered about" it. A second part of the questionnaire listed eighteen problems of a religious sort, from the Mooney Problem Check List (Junior and Senior High School Forms), with directions asking the subject to circle an N, S, or an O depending on whether he felt that a particular problem troubled or bothered him "never," "sometimes," or "often."

In disagreement with Dimock's conclusion of little change in beliefs, these investigators say that an examination of their findings indicates that "a number of rather significant changes" have occurred. They note a fairly marked discarding of such beliefs as "Every word in the Bible is true" and "It is sinful to doubt the Bible." About two-thirds of the 12-year-olds believed these statements to be true, whereas only a third or fewer of the 18-year-olds would agree. Other statements notably less often believed by 18-year-olds than 12-year-olds were "Only good people go to heaven" and

"Prayers are to make up for something wrong you have done." The authors observe that many rather specific beliefs taught to, or picked up by, children are no longer held by most of those in their late teens.

Another observation of the authors is an increase in tolerance with increase in age, as seen in the fact that many more 18-year-olds than 12-year-olds agree that "Catholics, Jews, and Protestants are equally good" and that "It is not necessary to attend church to be a Christian."

Still another observation related to the fact that drops in the proportion "believing" a statement are not necessarily compensated by increases in the proportion "not believing" it. Many beliefs are far from settled even by 18 years of age, as reflected in the proportions "wondered about." Among these are beliefs involving the hereafter (death, heaven, and hell), certain concepts of God, certain beliefs with respect to prayer, and belief in the Bible.

Kuhlen and Arnold call attention to the fact that they found significant changes in religious beliefs, whereas Dimock's conclusion denied such changes. They do not say so, but it seems more than likely that this is because of the longer age-span involved in their population. Their discussion of the causes of the change is in part as follows: "It is not implied by the selection of age groups of varying statuses with respect to pubescence, that the differences shown are a function of pubescence. Rather, it would seem more reasonable to assume that they are the result of accumulated experience in combination with increasing intellectual maturity which makes the adolescent more capable of interpreting the environment of ideas and facts in which he is becoming increasingly immersed. Greater intellectual maturity might be expected to increase sensitivity to inconsistencies either among the beliefs and views or between his already established beliefs and new learnings. Also with greater maturity the adolescent is more capable of abstract generalizations which might result in discarding some specific beliefs in favor of more general ones."

In the second part of the study relating to problems, a "problem score" was computed for each subject by assigning weights of zero, one, and two, respectively, to responses of "never," "sometimes," and "often" and summating the eighteen responses. The average scores for the three age-groups were: 12 years, 9.7; 15 years, 9.9; 18 years, 9.9. These figures discredit the hypothesis that adolescence is a period of *generally* increased religious doubts and problems.

Beliefs at the college level.—Evidence reported up to this point concerning religious attitudes and beliefs has carried to the end of the high school age and up to the point of entrance to college. From it may be obtained some understanding of the trends of religious beliefs and rate of change in these beliefs of youth who are reaching or are soon to arrive at the stage of later adolescence. Attention will now be directed to these beliefs as held at the level beyond high school and at the collegiate level, with the aim of throwing light on this aspect of the character of the community college student. Unfortunately for this purpose, there is little or no published evidence from studies with a focus on students in this institution. The evidence available along these lines concerns students in four-year colleges and universities, and one is obliged to do what he can by way of interpreting it in application to the community college student body. While community college students doubtless have characteristics in common with students in institutions of the other types, especially with those at the level of the first two years, it would be unwise to assume that they are identical.

The investigations drawn upon resort mainly to two types of procedure. The earlier studies relied on questionnaires and asked the subjects to rate certain religious beliefs, whereas the later ones applied scales containing statements making up a continuum on which the subjects were asked to identify the statement most nearly coinciding with their beliefs.

Beliefs as found by questionnaire.—The recount of studies at the collegiate level will begin by brief reference to one reported almost a half century ago by Leuba (72) concerning two religious concepts, belief in a personal God and belief in immortality, as held by students. Inquiry summated for a number of colleges found 56 per cent of men and 82 per cent of women students holding a belief in a personal God, with the remaining students holding a belief in an "impersonal God" or being "doubters." The investigator called attention to the notably larger proportion of believers in a personal God among women students.

Investigation of the belief in immortality was restricted to one college for women described as "of high rank" in which "the spirit . . . is assuredly as religious as that of the average American college." The percentages of believers in immortality for the four college classes were as follows: freshmen, 80.3; sophomores, 76.2; juniors, 60.0; seniors, 70.1. Leuba referred to the high percentage of believers in the lower classes and the relatively high percentage of disbelievers in the upper classes "as the most striking result of the inquiry." He did not undertake to explain the rise in percentage from juniors to seniors. A justifiable comment is that, although there was some decline during the college years, the belief in immortality was still a prevailing one in the later college years.

An investigation by questionnaire by Dudycha (30) completed in the early 1930s was much more extensive in that it involved more students in more colleges and a longer list of beliefs. The colleges were all in the Midwest and were institutions with denominational affiliations. The subjects involved were freshmen in seven colleges and seniors in six, most of these institutions being represented by students at both freshman and senior levels. The freshmen made their responses to the propositions during the first week of instruction, and it may be assumed that their judgments had not been influenced by the college but were made in accord with the beliefs the students brought with them from their home communities. The seniors were confronted with the same list of proposi-

TABLE 3.14
PERCENTAGES OF CERTAIN RELIGIOUS PROPOSITIONS
BELIEVED BY COLLEGE FRESHMEN

Proposition	Percentage Believing
1. Ten Commandments should be obeyed	92
2. Existence of God	88
3. Existence of the soul	81
4. Divinity of Jesus Christ	82
5. Christ died to save sinners	81
6. Power of prayer	75
7. Forgiveness of sin	77
8. Reality of sin	73
9. Sunday is a holy day	77
10. Virgin birth of Christ	72
11. Fatherhood of God	68
12. Genuineness of Christ's miracles	69
13. Bible is the word of God	69
14. Holy Spirit	69
15. Existence of heaven	66
16. Sacrament of baptism	59
17. Immortality	56
18. Man is saved by faith, not by works	56
19. A day of final judgment	55
20. Resurrection of the body	53
21. Existence of angels	43
22. Existence of hell	44
23. Existence of the devil	39
24. World was created in six solar days	38
25. Present-day miracles	30

SOURCE: Adapted from Dudycha (*30*, 587, Table 1).

tions in the spring of the year and thus almost at the close of their college course. The investigator assumes that their judgments were influenced to a certain extent by their four years of college instruction.

In the questionnaire each proposition was stated briefly, clearly, and affirmatively. To the right of each proposition were five groups of parentheses labeled from left to right A, B, C, D, and E. The student was requested to make a cross (X) in one of the five columns to indicate his belief: "Under A if you implicitly believe, Under B if you are inclined to believe but doubt," etc., to "Under E if you absolutely do not believe." Percentages were computed for the numbers of students indicating belief at each level for each proposition.

The percentages of freshmen indicating belief (placing crosses under A) for each of the propositions are reported in Table 3.14. The propositions are placed roughly in the order of the size of the percentage and are seen to range from 92 down to 30. One is impressed by the large proportion of freshmen who indicated implicit belief in most of the propositions: only five propositions failed to get a half or more indications of belief at this level.

The evidence as reported by Dudycha makes possible observations along two additional lines important to an understanding of the beliefs of col-

TABLE 3.15
PERCENTAGES OF COLLEGE FRESHMEN AND COLLEGE SENIORS FIRMLY BELIEVING OR INCLINING TO BELIEVE CERTAIN RELIGIOUS PROPOSITIONS

Denomination	Percentages	
	Freshmen	Seniors
All denominations	65	49
United Presbyterian	79	56
Lutheran	78	64
Roman Catholic	79	–
Baptist	69	38
Presbyterian	67	56
Methodist	62	46
Miscellaneous	59	51
Congregational	50	41
No Denomination	39	38

SOURCE: Adapted from Dudycha (*30*, 588, Table II; 597, Table IV).

lege students: (1) the variation by denominational affiliations and (2) the change in extent of belief between entrance to college and graduation. Data providing information along these lines have been assembled in Table 3.15, in which are shown the proportions of students placing crosses in the A or B columns of parentheses, the two columns which indicated, respectively, acceptance and favorable inclination toward the propositions. The data show about two-thirds of freshmen of all denominations with these attitudes with only about two-fifths indicating no denominational affiliation making these favorable answers in their questionnaires. United Presbyterians, Lutherans, and Catholics were found to be almost four-fifths favorable, with proportions appreciably smaller for all other groups with no denomination falling below a half.

A glance at the column for seniors shows the proportion for "all denominations" with these attitudes had dropped to just under half and the proportions for the different denominational groups by differing amounts, but with only three specific denominational groups still above a half. No figure was reported for Catholic seniors, presumably because of the small number represented. The group identified as being of no denominational affiliation showed least change but the percentage of believers among freshmen was also the lowest. Dudycha's main conclusions are that there is a "marked drop off" in belief from admission to graduation but that for both levels "belief is much greater than disbelief."

TABLE 3.16
DISTRIBUTION OF UNIVERSITY FRESHMEN ACCORDING TO VALUES INDICATED ON THE THURSTONE-CHAVE SCALE OF ATTITUDES TOWARD GOD AS INFLUENCE ON CONDUCT

Scale Value	Per Cent	Scale Value	Per Cent
10.0–10.9	3.4	4.0–4.9	2.8
9.0– 9.9	25.7	3.0–3.9	3.4
8.0– 8.9	25.5	2.0–2.9	1.9
7.0– 7.9	10.8	1.0–1.9	0.6
6.0– 6.9	10.4	0.0–0.9	0.2
5.0– 5.9	9.3	–	–

SOURCE: Adapted from Nelson (*80*, 390, Table 28).

Beliefs as found by scales.—The studies of religious beliefs of college students by means of scales used instruments constructed according to a procedure devised by Thurstone that involves the grouping (with elements akin to ranking) of a large number of different statements of attitude on some issue and then by statistical procedure arriving at a numerical value for each statement used in the scale. The statements provide a continuum of attitude from very negative, through a neutral position, to a highly favorable or positive attitude.

One of the most extensive of these studies, from the standpoint of types of higher institutions represented, was made by Nelson (*80*) who administered four scales of attitudes bearing on religion, devised by Thurstone and Chave, in four universities (one in the south, others in the Midwest), six Lutheran colleges (one in the South), three Friends' colleges, one Methodist university, and one college each for United Brethren, Adventists, and Catholic (women only). The four scales measured attitudes toward Sunday observance, attitudes toward the church, attitudes toward God (the reality of God), and attitudes toward God as influence on conduct.

Emphasis of interpretation here will be mainly on the scale last named, which contains 22 statements with the lowest scale value, .10, assigned to "Only fools and hypocrites talk about God influencing them"; a statement near the midpoint reading, "The idea of God neither helps nor hinders my endeavor to lead a decent life"; and the highest score, 10.8, being assigned to "I have completely surrendered my life to God." The mean scale values for the four classes in the state universities were found to be: freshmen, 7.65; sophomores, 7.08; juniors, 7.25; seniors, 7.17, indicating a slight decline during the college career. The mean for all students in these universities was 7.40 (390, Table 28). The significance of this measure for all students may be better appreciated by quoting two statements, one slightly above and one slightly below this scale value: "I believe that one has to be faithful to God in order to prosper in life and act accordingly" and "I love God but I am too selfish to love my neighbor as myself."

Because among the institutions represented in Nelson's investigation, the scale values of freshmen in state universities will probably be most nearly like those in community colleges, the distribution for them is reproduced in Table 3.16. It will be noted that these values accumulated mainly between 6.0 and 9.9, with concentration (over half of all) between 8.0 and 9.9. Relatively few are to be found in the lower ranges from 0.0 to 4.9.

Variations of mean scale values for different types and locations of institutions are interesting. When four different state universities are compared, the one in the South yields the highest of the four means. When Lutheran colleges are compared, the college in the South yields the highest mean. The highest mean for all institutions is the one for the Catholic college for women and the next highest that for the Adventist colleges. Nelson's final inference from examination of the values on this particular scale is, "With due recognition to institutional, class, sex, and individual differences . . . we may conclude that for this group as a whole these data indicate a definite recognition of God as influencing conduct" (*80*, 405).

At the end of his summary chapter and in relation to evidence from all scales used, he says (421): "In conclusion, these college and university students seem to be strongly favorable toward the church, they believe in the reality of God, they are even stronger in their attitude toward God as an influence on conduct, and they are neutral or slightly favorable toward Sunday observance. . . . Yet the differences found are of interest and of practical significance. In general, students at denominational colleges are more religious than in state universities, institutions located in the South are more religious than those in the North. Women are more religious than men in each one of the religious areas, and freshmen show higher religious scores than seniors. The more conservative (politically) students and those showing stronger approval of the college attended are also the more religious."

Because the Nelson study using scales is based on data collected in the 1930s, there may be some question as to the applicability of his conclusions to present-day students. On this account, recourse is taken here to an investigation by Gilliland, who administered scales of religious attitude to students in the same institution, Northwestern University, over a period of several years (48). The students were those in classes in beginning psychology who were mainly freshmen and sophomores, although the classes included some upperclassmen. Gilliland said there was no reason to believe that the students were not a true sample of Northwestern undergraduates. Three scales were administered: (1) attitude toward God (reality of God); (2) attitude toward God (influence on conduct); and (3) attitude toward church. Mean score values obtained for the different years are shown in Table 3.17. In interpreting the measures reported it is impor-

TABLE 3.17
MEAN SCORES OF STUDENTS AT NORTHWESTERN UNIVERSITY ON THREE SCALES OF RELIGIOUS ATTITUDE

Year	Scales		
	Reality of God	Influence on Conduct	The Church
1933	6.60	*	*
1937	6.52	4.69	4.51
1943	7.23	4.11	3.14
1944	7.07	3.75	3.40
1946	7.28	3.62	3.39
1948	7.41	3.62	3.23
1949	7.77	3.28	2.94

SOURCE: Adapted from Gilliland (48).
*Not administered in 1933.

tant to bear in mind that an increasingly favorable attitude on the reality of God scale brings a higher numerical score, while the reverse is true for the other two scales. It may be noted that all three attitudes became more favorable over the span of years represented. One gathers from Gilliland's discussion that the change cannot be accounted for by changes in religious influences on campus or by change in proportion of men and women (since he found no difference in attitudes between the sexes), but seemed to him consistent with the increase in church membership generally during the period.

As in other studies here reviewed, Gilliland found the attitudes of younger classes more religiously favorable than those of upperclassmen, but not strikingly so. He observes that the "typical student's attitudes are not to be interpreted as strongly religious, but for the large majority of students there is a very definite respect for and belief in God and the Church."

Allport on religion in adolescence and among college students.—One of the most perceptive treatments of religion in youth is provided by Allport in *The Individual and His Religion: A Psychological Interpretation (1).* In early portions of this monograph he sums up the evidence on religious attitudes during adolescence and, in later portions, during the college period in particular. Among his observations concerning religious attitudes during adolescence Allport directs attention to the reaction of about two-thirds of children against parental teaching, with half the rebellions taking place before sixteen and half later, and with those for girls averaging earlier than for boys. In harmony with what we have reported above, he asserts that the earlier evidence concerning prevalent traumatic or semi-traumatic conversions with the peak of incidence around 16 years of age no longer applies: 71 per cent of his cases reported "a gradual wakening, with no specifiable occasion being decisive" (34).

Allport's study involving college students included men at Harvard, two-thirds of whom were veterans of World War II, all undergraduates, and women at Radcliffe, likewise undergraduates. It was made by a questionnaire in which the pivotal question was: "Do you feel that you require some form of religious orientation or belief in order to achieve a fully mature philosophy of life?" Allport reports that to this question seven out of every ten students gave an affirmative reply. He goes on to say that "it would be incorrect to assume that seven in ten are theists, or church goers, or traditionalists. We can only say that, given an opportunity to define religion in any way at all, seven out of ten regard themselves as actually or potentially religious" (37).

Only several of the more important findings of Allport's investigation follow, as it is hardly necessary to review them all. More women than men expressed a need for religious orientation, although the difference was not striking, seldom exceeding 20 per cent in subgroups and usually being much smaller. The age factor was important, young men of 20 and under more often feeling the need than fellow students 21 or over (37). Students who report religion to have been a marked or even moderate influence in the home were much more likely than others to express the need for a religious orientation, although Allport refers to "striking exceptions." Denominational differences in parental backgrounds were highly influential: nearly all who were reared in the Catholic faith report a need for some religious orientation; at the other extreme, 40 per cent of those brought up in some form of Judaism or in liberalized Protestantism (defined as including Unitarianism or Universalism) "fail to regard the religious sentiment as a necessary component of their personalities" (38). Asked to name the influences underlying this sense of need, the students named them in great variety, among them, in declining order of frequency, parents, other human beings, fear, the church, gratitude, aesthetic appeals, reading, sorrow or bereavement, and sex turmoil.

The students who had expressed a need for some religious orientation were asked which of the great religious systems seemed to meet their need: Roman Catholicism, Anglo-Catholicism or Eastern Orthodoxy, Protestant Christianity, liberalized Christianity (Unitarianism, Universalism), an ethical but not a theological Christianity (humanism, ethical culture), some form of Judaism, or some other they might specify. They were also asked to indicate the character of the religious influence in their own upbringing, the same classification being used. Comparison of the two responses made it possible to "characterize the shifts of allegiance" that had occurred. Only about 60 per cent reported the system in which they were reared as satisfactory. However, 85 per cent of Roman Catholic students expressed themselves as satisfied with this faith. The drift throughout seemed to be from a theological to an ethical emphasis (41).

Among these students orthodox faith in theological dogma seemed to be more rapidly on the wane than religious *practices* such as prayer and church attendance. Large proportions, but more women than men, were continuing to pray and to attend church. Thus, practice tended to be more conservative than belief.

Allport warns against inferring that such findings are peculiar to the college generation represented. He mentions earlier studies that show the same trends and refers to the problem as "perennial" (45).

Without evidence along analogous lines concerning community college students, we can only speculate on the applicability of Allport's findings to them. He was of the opinion that his sample of students was "probably not seriously out of line with the large population of ambitious and intelligent young men and women now crowding our institutions of higher learning" (36). However, from evidence presented in Chapter 7, we know that, although many community college students are on a par in intelligence and socioeconomic status with those in Allport's colleges, there is a *typical* difference in such measures and these might well be associated with some difference in religious attitudes. Another factor of difference would be the greater maturity of Allport's subjects, since his men included many veterans and he disregarded classification, whereas community college students include only freshmen and sophomores. We have seen from other studies that traditional beliefs decline from freshman to senior years. The most we can say is that the attitudes he found apply to a degree to community college students, but we can only guess at this degree.

Consistency and Change in Personality and Character with Age

Obstacles to generalization.—Up to this point in this long chapter a considerable body of evidence has been reviewed pertaining to personal and social development of young people. Rather than merely to present a summary at the end of the chapter, which will also be done, it would be highly desirable if the meaning of this evidence, which is in far-ranging variety, could be woven together by reference to a generally acceptable theory of personality. The difficulty here is what Hall and Lindzey (*53, 554*) refer to as the "diversities and disagreements" among current theories of personality. In the last chapter of their review and analysis of theories by Freud, Jung, Murray, Allport, Sheldon, and others, they conclude, "In spite of the clustering about certain modal theoretical positions there has been, as yet, little progress in the direction of developing a single widely accepted theoretical position." And, although they take the pains to point out such common elements as exist, they do not venture a synthesized theory based on those they analyzed, nor a theory of their own.

Generalization concerning development of personality in youth is further hampered by a lack of definitiveness in methods of measurement, a condition which may well be expected in some part to follow from disagreement on personality theory. The methods and instruments often used for personality appraisal are personality questionnaires or inventories, known also as self-report instruments. After some years of experience with them in many places, critics are still doubtful of their usefulness. This skepticism may be illustrated by drawing on the conclusions of Ellis (*35*), who has recurrently reviewed the researches making use of these instruments, from an examination of researches in this area published during the years 1946 to 1951, inclusive. In part, he says, "It was found that in most instances the inventories are not measuring the independent traits they are supposed to be measuring; they do not agree too well with each other nor with the results of Rorschach and projective tests; they are easily faked; and they usually do not give group discriminations when used with vocational, academic, socioeconomic, and disabled and ill groups. It was especially found that, in none of the areas in which they are commonly employed, do personality inventories show significant group discriminations. . . ."

While not so drastic in unfavorable appraisal of the instruments, Thorpe and Schmuller (*126*), at the close of their chapter on the "Evaluation of Personality" in their treatise on personality, indicate serious doubt concerning the adequacy of current efforts at measurement of personality (344): "Being a product of both heredity and environment, and cutting across every aspect of human affairs, personality cannot, in the light of present knowledge, be assessed with the kind of quantitative measuring units commonly utilized in the province of the physical sciences. Since testing is a human contrivance liable to all the subjectivity which this implies, there is . . . no magic in testing per se. This is not to say that scientific measurement is not applicable in the assessment of personality. However, such an approach needs to be flexible and varied and to keep in view that the human personality is 'something more' than the sum of all the measurements which can be made regarding it. This something more, for the present at least, calls for caution in the appraisal of personality by means of rating scales, inventories, and projective instruments."

An unfavorable opinion toward the self-report instruments is also expressed by Bloom in his *Stability and Change in Human Characteristics* (*8*) which is his discerning effort at comprehensive synthesis of all longitudinal (and many cross-sectional) inquiries into human characteristics in respect to physique, intelligence, achievement, interests, attitudes, and personality. He noted that he was "struck by the susceptibility of these instruments to conscious as well as unconscious distortion by the examinee." He says he was "led to the conclusion that it is unlikely that the stability of personality can be determined with any degree of precision by these instruments" (173). He goes on to say that he had hoped to secure a large number of longitudinal studies utilizing projective techniques, but that few such studies were found, as most of them using Rorschach, TAT, and sentence completion tests applied them "for case studies and normative purposes rather than for the determination of stability and change." In actuality he relied more in his treatment of personality on studies of "characteristics observed by others" than by the other procedures, although his stricture on these is that observations are "indications of outward manifestations of personality rather than more deep-seated characteristics" (157). It may be gratuitous to point out that inquiries by observations by others can often be made in such a way that they fail to disclose such stability of personality as may exist.

In view of the dilemma presented by the absence of consensus on personality theory and the paucity of longitudinal investigations applying approvable procedures and instruments, consideration of the question of the consistency and change in personality and character with age, with the aim at arriving at a tentative conclusion, will proceed here by reviewing several investigations that have been made with more care than others and that, with overlapping age-spans, extend from early childhood into adulthood. Three of these investigations followed plans combining observation with rating, one applied a test for value patterns, and the remaining study resorted to a projective technique.

From early childhood to adolescence.—A comparison of personalities in early childhood and in adolescence that has attracted the interest of psychologists is one by Neilen (*78*). Personality sketches had been written of 19 children on the basis of observations during the first two years of life and the procedure involved matching these descriptions with those on the same individuals based on test and rating material made 15 years later when the subjects were 17 years old. Five judges matched ten sketches of adolescent boys and ten judges matched five sketches of adolescent girls. The later sketches were prepared without acquaintance with the earlier ones and the judgments made by persons who read the descriptions but had seen the subjects neither as babies nor as adolescents. Statistical computation of the results of the individual judges and of the mean scores of all judges in matching found them to be "significant as to chance." The two conclusions of main importance to the concern here were that (1) "personality similarities in an individual persist over a period of time" and (2) "some individuals are more readily identifiable after a period of time, presumably due to greater uniqueness of personality pattern."

Character development from age 10 through 16.—A second study, Peck and Havighurst (*86*), referred to by the authors as "exploratory" rather than "definitive," was based on ratings made by judges on 34 children in "Prairie City" at ages 10, 13, and 16. The ratings were in reference to certain qualities of character. "Character," in the minds of these authors, "can be regarded as a special aspect of personality; or, otherwise stated, as a function of certain personality characteristics" (166). The coefficient of correlation between the ratings on "conscience and moral values" for the subjects at 10 and 13 years was .80; at 13 and 16 years, .98; and at 10 and 16 years, that is, over the entire span of years, .78. All three coefficients are high, indicating considerable consistency of character—greater, as might be expected, for the two three-year spans than for the six-year span. Coefficients for ratings in reference to other developmental tasks, namely, emotional independence, sex role, relations with age-mates, and intellectual skills, were almost all correspondingly large.

Value patterns from high school to college.—In a third study, Todd (*128*) inquires into the value patterns of high school seniors and the changes in these patterns by the time the students have completed the freshman year in college. The subjects were more than 3,000 boys in about a hundred high schools in the New England and Middle Atlantic states. The information secured included both objective and subjective data from the subject and from the schools and colleges, and, for 137 of the total group, involved the use of interview and the administration at both high school and college levels of a Study of Values Test. On the basis of the evidence collected the subjects were classified according to a typology postulated by Spranger (*112*). This categorization included: 1. Theoretical; 2. Economic; 3. Aesthetic; 4. Social; 5. Political; 6. Religious. The adjectives used for the grouping are clues to the values dominant for the different types.

Section headings in Chapter 2 of Todd's monograph indicate the order of prominence of the six types. These headings read: "Economic Values are Dominant," "Political Values are Second," "Theoretical Values Come

Next," "Social Values are Low," "Religious Values are Even Less Important," and "Aesthetic Values are Lowest." He says, by way of reiteration in the summary to the chapter, "The emphasis on securing tangible wealth, gaining renown and power, and the utility of scientific knowledge greatly outweighs the considerations of improved social conditions, the unity of religious experience, and the aesthetic satisfactions of life" (40).

Comparison based on performance on the Study of Values Test found the rank order of prominence of the six values to be the same for students after a year of college as it had been for them as high school seniors. However, Todd reports that within this order there were changes in four areas: political and religious values had declined significantly, while appreciation of the beautiful and concern for economic values had risen (95).

From adolescence to adulthood.—An investigation carrying the same individuals from adolescence into adulthood was made by Symonds and is the only one drawn upon in this section that relied mainly on projective techniques. It was made by Symonds but was completed posthumously with cooperation by Jensen (*117* and *123*). It began with 40 children (20 boys and 20 girls) ranging in ages from 12 to 18 and distributed from grade 7 through grade 12 in "Suburban City." The procedure involved having the subjects narrate stories about 40 pictures drawn especially for the investigation and providing the basis for studying the subjects' fantasies. Much additional information was at hand concerning the subjects. In the follow-up, thirteen years later, the same procedure was used, with the addition of the Rorschach Test, on 28, or 70 per cent, of the original subjects. In their interpretation of the evidence, the authors refer to "the remarkable similarity in fantasy over the thirteen-year interval between the two studies. In instance after instance it was found that the subjects told stories with identical themes to the same pictures." Judges were able to match the sets of stories of subjects told thirteen years apart even when interspersed with the stories of other subjects (*117*, 188.). Nevertheless, despite the tendencies toward stability of fantasy, some changes were noted both for the group as a whole and in individuals, the most striking being a general increase in depression and a decrease in happy endings, "signifying that adolescent exuberance has given way to discouragement" (189). In a summarizing conclusion it is stated (210), "There is a high degree of consistency in overt personality over the thirteen-year interval in (a) physical characteristics, (b) general personality characteristics, including aggressiveness, in response to the interview situation and to the tests; (c) nervous signs, (d) hobbies, and (e) attitudes."

From precollege, through college, to postcollege years.—The last of the five studies from which findings are drawn to throw light on the issue of consistency of personality in the growth process is one by Roberts and

Fleming (97) concerning twenty-five women on whom evidence was available at three periods in their lives referred to as precollege, college, and postcollege. The subjects were all "on the whole, well-adjusted, American-born, college graduates of Protestant faith, who represent the higher socio-economic levels" (32). Twenty of the women were married and fifteen had children. The study was made by a combination of the case method, with an average of more than 90,000 words per case, and statistical procedures, with evidence on "traits" and "attitudes" gathered at all three of the age levels.

From the investigation of traits it was found that "in about two-thirds of these twenty-five life histories a tendency for personality patterns to persist occurs" (37). In the remaining third, persistence and change are about equal in some cases, and in a smaller number of cases "more change than persistence is apparent." The persistence of particular traits was also studied and for these also "more persistence than fluctuation was the rule" (38). The main inference from the study of traits is that "while persistence of personality pattern is more likely than not to be the rule, a great deal of modification is possible. Less persistence in attitudes than in traits was found, and in the degree of flexibility of both." The authors see "great promise for the fruitful functioning of education, whether the education be carried on by parents, school, church, associates, or the person himself" (136).

Generalization concerning consistency.—The recurrent inference from all these inquiries into change and consistency of personality with age is that there is more of consistency than of change. This is true for both sexes and at all ages from early childhood into adulthood. The evidence discredits a belief formerly often held that personality undergoes rather marked change at adolescence at rates comparable to those in physical growth during this period. At the same time, although some of the studies appear to show more change or flexibility than others, none seems entirely to preclude it. The flexibility provides leeway for the influences of education. The inference of a considerable degree of consistency has the corroboration of Bloom's conclusion: "There is strong evidence of levels of stability which are as high or higher than those reported . . . on physical characteristics, intelligence, aptitudes, and school achievement" (8, 176).

College impact on personality.—Although no conclusive answer to the question of what the influence of attending college is on the personalities of students, it seems desirable to speculate on the problem, at least as briefly as may be done. It should help in this consideration to do so against the background of other changes that may be expected as results of the college experience. Freedman (40) in 1960 reviewed the researches concerned with this impact and reported his summation under a three-part classification, namely, (a) changes in mental ability, skills, and knowledge; (b) changes in attitudes and values; and (c) changes in personality. As expected, he found in the literature a considerable body of evidence of gains derivable from college attendance for learning under the first of these headings. In discussing the changes in attitudes and values he drew on the general findings of Jacob's controversial project of the later 1950s. Instead of listing these relatively particularized findings, quotation is made here of the final paragraph of Jacob's summary as it appears in *Changing Values in College* (*61*, 11): "This study has discovered no specific curricular pattern of general education, no model syllabus for a basic social science course, no pedigree of instructor and no wizardry of instructional method which should be patented for its impact on the values of students. Student values do change to some extent in college. With some students, the change is substantial. But the impetus to change does not come primarily from the formal educational process. Potency to affect student values is found in the distinctive climate of a few institutions, the individual and personal magnetism of a sensitive teacher with strong value-commitments of his own, or value-laden personal experiences of students imaginatively integrated with their intellectual development." This is a conclusion of limited impact, and one can readily understand the shock of friends of college education who had been assuming a much greater and more prevalent alteration of values and attitudes. Freedman drew also on the findings of the project by Gillespie and Allport which were summarized above (*46*) while reviewing the values and attitudes of the college population.

Under the heading of his third classification, Freedman says, "Change in personality during the college years is an area in which research has hardly begun to scratch the surface," at the same time that he admits that the number of studies is not small (*40*, 17). He emphasizes the researches carried out by the Mellon Foundation at Vassar College and of the writings of Sanford and R. H. White. Instead of quoting Freedman's summary, resort will be taken to capsulizing Sanford's position as presented in the chapter on "Personality Development in College" in his recent book *Self and Society* (*101*, 274–91). In this chapter Sanford considers the possibility of change after having reviewed in earlier portions of the book the "relative fixity or persistence of tendencies established early in the individual life," which is not out of accord with the predominating consistency generalized from the researches reviewed earlier in this section.

After emphasizing the "pressing need . . . for theory concerning the nature and conditions of personality development during the years seventeen to twenty-two, under the impact of those rather complicated social and cultural processes which constitute the college student's world," Sanford adopts for consideration four major psychological "growth trends" identified by White, and adds to them another concept of his own formulation. The four by White are the stabilizing of ego identity (borrowed from Erikson), deepening of interests, freedom in personal relationships, and the humanizing of values. Sanford's complementary growth trend is general development and strengthening of the ego. He seems confident that with the clarified theory and the methods and techniques at hand, research on personality change in college has great promise. In the meantime the outcomes on which to lean are slender and apply only to the four-year colleges. Research on the impact on personality of the community college is all prospective and, because of the two-year span of the institution, will present unusual difficulties.

Criteria of Maturity

A scale of social competence.—Before turning to a summary of the treatment of personal and social development of youth in this chapter, it seems desirable to take a brief look at the approach to maturity that is always in the background and often in the foreground while considering growth. What is maturity and how is its degree of attainment to be measured? Some efforts have been made to measure social maturity empirically and with an approach to comprehensiveness, and many formulations of less objective criteria of maturity are to be found in the literature of psychology and personality. One of the better efforts at a scale for measurement will now be briefly described, and illustrative application of the instrument cited. The section will be closed with an abstraction of a set of criteria of maturity formulated by one of our leading students of personality development.

The scale is one for the measurement of "Social Competence" by Doll (*28*). It consists of "items" which are essentially abilities in behavior classified under categories like "Self-Help General," "Self-Help Dressing," "Locomotion," "Occupation," "Communication," "Self-Direction," and "Socialization." Quoted here are items in numerical sequence in the order of difficulty "in terms of mean-age calibration" (*49*). The items are those in the scale for ages 10 to 11 and beyond to adulthood (the grouping by ages indicated by Roman numerals) (*53*).

X-XI
78. Writes occasional short letters
79. Makes telephone calls
80. Does small remunerative work
81. Answers ads; purchases by mail

XI-XII
82. Does simple creative work
83. Is left to care for self or others
84. Enjoys books, newspapers, magazines

XII–XV
85. Plays difficult games
86. Exercises complete care of dress
87. Buys own clothing accessories
88. Engages in adolescent group activities
89. Performs responsible routine chores

XV–XVIII
90. Communicates by letter
91. Follows current events
92. Goes to nearby places alone
93. Goes out unsupervised daytime
94. Has own spending money
95. Buys all own clothing

XVIII–XX
96. Goes to distant places alone
97. Looks after own health
98. Has job or continues schooling
99. Goes out nights unrestricted
100. Controls own major expenditures
101. Assumes personal responsibility

XX–XXV
102. Uses money providently
103. Assumes responsibility beyond own needs
104. Contributes to social welfare
105. Provides for future

XXV+
106. Performs skilled work
107. Engages in beneficial recreation
108. Systematizes own work
109. Inspires confidence
110. Promotes civic progress
111. Supervises occupational pursuits
112. Purchases for others
113. Directs or manages affairs
114. Performs expert or professional work
115. Shares community responsibility
116. Creates own opportunities
117. Advances general welfare

In further explanation of the construction the author says, "The numerical progression considered cumulatively is reduced to total point scores, and these are further reduced to age-level groups by progressive interpolation. The SA (Social Age) item values are then taken as proportional to the number of items per year-group." The scale may be used to ascertain SQ (Social Quotient), which is arrived at by a procedure analogous to computation of the IQ from chronological age and mental age: by dividing the SA by the LA (Living Age).

Some appreciation of the possible usefulness of the scale may be obtained from abstracts of what are referred to as "exploratory" applications. In one of these, credited to Sargent, fifty high school seniors and fifty college freshmen were the subjects, all in their eighteenth year. The investigator said of these subjects that their selection was "otherwise uncontrolled"; some were passing and some were failing in both groups. Forty-two of the college subjects as against twenty-one of the high school subjects came from homes where the parents' occupations were above skilled labor, while no college subject against eighteen high school subjects came from homes where the parents' occupations were from common labor. The procedure employed is referred to as "self-informing" with certain safe-

TABLE 3.18
LA (LIVING AGE), SA (SOCIAL AGE), AND SQ
(SOCIAL QUOTIENT) MEASURED FOR 50 HIGH
SCHOOL SENIORS AND 50 COLLEGE
FRESHMEN

Measure	High School Seniors	College Freshmen
Mean LA	17.5	17.6
Lowest SA	15.8	16.7
Highest SA	20.0	22.3
Mean SA	17.9	18.4
Lowest SQ	90	97
Highest SQ	111	127
Mean SQ	102	106

SOURCE: After Sargent (28, 483).

guards of specific and elaborative questions. Measures from the comparison are reported in Table 3.18, in which one may note a moderate if not striking tendency toward higher measures for college freshmen than for high school seniors. The investigator also reports "low and unreliable" coefficients of correlation between IQ and SQ (.20 for the high school subjects and .00 for the college subjects). While commenting on his results the investigator points out the significance of social maturity for college entrance and high school guidance and urges that measurement of intelligence and scholastic attainment be supplemented by measurement of social competence. His report, however, contains no description of actual use in this way of the scale used in testing.

In another investigation in which the Social Maturity Scale was used by Powell and Laslett (88), a hundred students in grades 10, 11, and 12 in a small high school were scored on it by pooled judgments of three persons familiar with the students for several years. The LA range was found to be from 15 to 20 years. The mean SQ was 98.75 for all students and the means for the two sexes differed only slightly. It was noted that students with low scores came "almost uniformly" from poor home environments. The following excerpt indicates the investigators' observation on the effects of use of the scale: "[It] caused the adults working with these pupils to be more objective and analytical in their counseling work. . . . When pupils found that they were being measured on scales, they paid more attention to their behavior as the expression of their personalities. . . . A few of the pupils with the lowest scores were shown the ratings which they had received. In all these cases this had a valuable stimulating influence because the pupils were somewhat shocked to find the ways in which they appeared to others whose good opinion they desired. . . . The writers believe that, if all of these pupils were rescored today, they would score considerably higher than they did on the first measurement."

A formulation of criteria of maturity.—The criteria of maturity will be presented here as recently summarized by Allport at the end of his chapter on "The Mature Personality" (2, Ch. 12), in which he reviews formulations of such criteria by various authors. The formulation may be thought of as a sort of synthesis of, or consensus on, such criteria. The summary is so succinct that it seems desirable to amplify the criteria mainly by additional brief quotations of sentences or phrases from preceding portions of the chapter and less often by paraphrase. The criteria have not been quantified by scale or test, as has been done for the items in his Social Maturity Scale by Doll. Because of the relatively much greater intangibility and complexity of the traits represented, quantification is something for the future rather than for the present. The criteria can, nevertheless, prove useful, even if exact locations on scales cannot be found, in passing qualitative judgment on personalities, for keeping in mind as goals for one's own personal development, or as sources of hypotheses in efforts at objective measurement of personality.

Following is the summary (2, 307): "Surveying some of the vast literature on the subject, we find considerable agreement, at least so far as the value-conceptions of Western culture are concerned. In particular we find six criteria that sum up the area of agreement. The mature personality will (1) have a widely extended sense of self; (2) be able to relate himself warmly to others in both intimate and nonintimate contacts; (3) possess a fundamental emotional security and accept himself; (4) perceive, think, and act with zest in accordance with outer reality; (5) be capable of self-objectivication, of insight and humor; (6) live in harmony with a unifying philosophy of life."

Meeting the first criterion, according to Allport, requires that "new ambitions, new memberships, new ideas, new friends, new recreations and hobbies, and, above all, one's vocation become incorporated into the sense of self" (2, 285), but as autonomous interests rather than as opportunistic or peripheral functions. The second criterion requires a "respect for persons as persons," which is "achieved through an imaginative extension of one's own rougher experiences in life." It fosters "tolerance" and the "democratic character structure so often advanced as earmarks of maturity" (285–86). Emotional security, or self-acceptance, "includes the ability to avoid over-reaction to matters pertaining to segmental drives." "The mature person puts up with frustration, takes the blame on himself, if it is appropriate to do so" (287–88). In one restatement of the fourth criterion, Allport insists that "a mature person will be in close touch with what we call 'the real world.'" He will "see objects, people, and situations for what they are. And he will have important work to do" (290). Concerning the fifth criterion: "Perhaps the most striking correlate of insight is the sense of humor," which "must be distinguished from the cruder sense of the comic" (292). The latter consists for the most part "in the degradation of some imagined opponent" (293). And concerning the sixth and last criterion Allport says, "Maturity requires, in addition to humor, a clear comprehension of life's purpose in terms of an intelligible theory," which gives to one's life what he refers to as *directedness* (294).

Summary

This long chapter has drawn upon more than a half hundred investigations as well as numerous theoretical discussions of behavior, traits, and attitudes ranging mainly from early to late adolescence and into adulthood, but, for background, occasionally dipping back into childhood. It could be more easily summarized if only (1) a larger proportion of the studies were longitudinal through the adolescent-to-adult age-span and (2) their interpretation could be in greater degree integrated by reference to a generally acceptable theory of personality. As has been pointed out, the making of longitudinal studies for the age-group that is the main concern here is obstructed by an institutional organization, high school and college, that discourages continuity in populations investigated, and the theories of personality are so diverse and the investigations have been made on such a diversity of hypotheses that it is quite out of the question in a summary to weld the evidence into anything approaching a unified whole. The evidence is, nevertheless, even if rather piecemeal, in the main significant and helpful to an understanding of personal and social development in later adolescence. It is here briefly summarized, although, because of the obstacles mentioned and the great diversity of testimony and procedures, the recapitulation must be incomplete and at some points be restricted to inadequate illustration.

The present trend of thought concerning adolescence is notably away from the traditional conception of it as a period of "storm and stress" induced solely by the rapid biological changes during this period of life. It is more toward a belief that, while it concedes some degree of maladjustment during the period but less than formerly assumed, the explanation is chiefly cultural rather than biological.

The range of their problems and interests as reported by younger and older adolescents is so wide as to preclude relisting them in summary. Comparison of the rankings of problems recently with them two decades earlier shows considerable similarity. Comparison of these problems and interests for earlier and for later adolescents yields, among others, the following observations. Money as a problem remains high throughout adolescence. Rank assigned to philosophy of life, both as problem and interest, rises, and the ranking of personal and moral qualities also rises. Sex adjustment rises in rank as an interest, but less so as a problem. Rise in rank of civic interest, attitudes, and responsibilities is only moderate. Home and family relationships shift to lower ranking. For the most part, the changes in rank appear to be in the direction of achieving maturity.

The problems of adolescents as thus identified have much in common with the developmental tasks of adolescence, formulations of which include such categories as "achieving a masculine or feminine social role," "achieving emotional independence of parents and other adults," and "acquiring a set of values and an ethical system as a guide to behavior." One may say that solving the problems would go far toward achieving the developmental tasks and, conversely, achieving the tasks would go far toward solving the problems.

A concept having wide currency in present-day discussions of adolescence is the peer group, which is asserted to have its origins in the discontinuities applying to youth in our culture. Frustrations originating in the discontinuities impel youth to set up their own "crowds," "gangs," etc., and to follow their own purposes. Certain writers demur to the concept and report evidence to discredit it, but large-scale investigations among early and later adolescents substantiate it, albeit the pervasion of influence of the peer group must vary from community to community.

One extensive investigation in ten high schools in diverse communities of northern Illinois found a rather even split among students between indicating "parents' disapproval" and "breaking with friend" as the "hardest thing to take," with "teachers' disapproval" indicated by only a small minority. Fewer than a third of these students "prefer to be remembered" as "brilliant student" in comparison with almost half the boys' preferences being "athletic star" and more than a third of the girls "leader in activities." These preferences signify values differing from those entertained by adults. A high choice of both boys and girls from a list of nine attributes is "personality," which the investigator intimates may be almost the equivalent of "being friendly" or "being nice with other kids," while "good grades" takes a relatively inferior position.

The more common position of students of adolescence is not so much that the influence of these subcultures is harmful, although the effect is oftimes detrimental, but rather that, in the absence of more direct participation of youth in the life and affairs of adult society, they offer youth an avenue of accomplishing certain essential developmental tasks.

As part of the treatment accorded the first of two developmental tasks, emancipation from parents, evidence was reported concerning the quarrels of adolescents with parents. A third of the youth reported having quarrels; a third to a half of the quarrels concerned social life and friends, with economic matters ranking next in frequency. Summing up on the assumption of the social sex role, the second of the tasks discussed, is here focused on later adolescence. For the middle class, by contrast with the dominant pattern of the adult male role with its emphasis on responsibility, the role of the younger male is "more or less specifically irresponsible," and aims at "having a good time," especially with the opposite sex, and gives prominence to athletics and to personal qualities associated with the "swell guy." "On the feminine side," as put by Parsons, there is correspondingly a strong tendency to accentuate sexual attractiveness in terms of various versions of what may be called the "glamour girl" pattern.

Summation of the evidence from studies of attitudes and values held by youth is rather difficult, for reasons previously indicated, and because, in some respects, the evidence may be in conflict. A cluster of studies of "disapprovals" or "wrongs" on the X-O test devised by Pressey and administered to high school and college students found a decline in disapprovals for both sexes over a span of two decades. Another finding nearer to our special concern is that the change was greater from lower to upper college years than during precollege years or from later high school into early college years. The changes for women in college years was consistently greater than for men. An explanation of this difference is that while at home the girls are held closer to the conventions of their parents, but upon going to college react away from home restraint even more than the boys. The areas in which the items showing greatest change fell were designated as sex-social conduct, minor vices, and borderline issues of manners and good taste. Another investigator asking high school seniors and university freshmen to rank certain practices in the order of their "worseness" found a very high coefficient of correlation for the average rank orders at the two levels and by the two sexes. Still another investigation, following a procedure of paired comparison of personal-social values with students ranging from grade 6 through grade 12, found very high coefficients of correlation for the rank orders assigned by pupils in each grade with those assigned in the next higher grade throughout the six-year span, thus indicating a relative stability of the values as early as grade 6 with no notable shift by the end of the period. The coefficients for rank orders assigned to values by the two sexes are equally high.

Some decades ago unfounded beliefs, popular misconceptions, or "superstitions" held by high school seniors and by college students, mainly freshmen, were rather extensively investigated. Large proportions of students were found to give credence to them, and the proportion was somewhat larger for the high school than for the college students. Girls were found to be more credulous than boys, although the relationship between the rank orders of the beliefs for the two sexes was high. Little or no relationship was found between extent of belief and measures of intelligence.

Inquiries into the areas of conversation engaged in by college students found the order of interest to be, from greatest downward, as follows: sex (but judged "not excessive" as compared with outside-of-college circles); personalities; interests of an intellectual or artistic nature; and social problems, with those of a personal nature, like smoking and drinking, being more provocative of discussion than those of an impersonal sort, like communism or world peace. The most notable difference between men and women was in the area of interest in personalities in which the proportion for women was markedly larger. The finding of a small proportion in the category of important social issues is corroborated by another study involving autobiographies of and interviews with college students across the country, which pointed to a relatively low interest in social problems. Such findings tend to belie a rather prevalent ascription of social idealism to young people. An appropriate observation here seems to be that the conclusions drawn from most studies concerning attitudes and values of students pertain to majorities and tend, therefore, to overlook those of a minority which could be characterized by social idealism and which are vital to social welfare and progress.

The measured relationship between morality and intelligence, while not high, has been found to be somewhat higher than that between physique and intelligence. Statistical description of the degree of relationship is indicated as "marked," whereas that between physical development and intelligence is designated as "low." The rationale of the relationship, between intelligence and morality, as indicated by Ausubel, is that moral concepts, like others, become more abstract with growth in cognitive capacity, enabling moral behavior to acquire greater generality.

Until recent years much was made of the notable incidence of religious conversion during the period of adolescence, with the assumption that religious awakening is the accompaniment of and originates in the signal biological changes of the period. This was a prevalent belief around the turn of the century. As time passed, however, the incidence fell to lower ages, with the peak nearer twelve years of age and before the advent of puberty for most youth. Besides, the high incidence dropped in considerable degree. The current opinion is that the pile-up of conversions was primarily the outcome of pressures on youth of the adolescent age-span by evangelistic denominations, with the meaning that the incidence was much more a reflection of the culture than of physical change. Discrediting of the belief of adolescence as the period of the "flowering of the religious impulse" has been accelerated by investigations of religious knowledge and attitudes at the precollege level that find the changes to be gradual rather than saltatory. Allport associates the gradual awakening with the reaction of children against parental teaching, which, in line with one of the developmental tasks, could reflect in some degree effort at emancipation.

The literature on religious attitudes at the college level is extensive, with conclusions at times in disagreement, although the main significance may be concisely generalized. The earlier studies at the college level were mainly by questionnaire, inquiring into acceptance of a considerable number of statements on religious issues, the later studies mostly by scales consisting of statements making up a continuum on a single issue on which the subject is asked to identify the statement most nearly coinciding with his own attitude. As is to be expected, the changes in attitude *during* college are much greater than between high school and college, and almost all the studies, whether made by questionnaire or by scale, found some decline in religious beliefs and attitudes between freshman and senior years. The two statements on the Scale of Attitude toward God as Influence on Conduct just above and just below the mean scale value of 7.40 found for all students in four state universities were, "I believe that one has to be faithful to God in order to prosper in life and act accordingly" and "I love God but I am too selfish to love my neighbor as myself." The distribution of freshmen in these institutions showed more than half at scale values higher than the statements just quoted.

Certain other findings of these studies are deserving of mention. Religious attitudes vary rather widely by type of institution, with higher religious orientation in colleges with denominational affiliations than in state universities, in colleges with traditional than with liberal denominational affiliations, and in southern than in midwestern institutions. Except in one study, in which no difference was found in the religious attitudes of the two sexes, women were found to be more religiously oriented than men. One investigator, from inquiries repeated in the same institution over a rather long period of years, found an increase in religious attitude—a change which he was inclined to attribute to a general trend toward church membership rather than to any special religious influences on campus.

Several studies, all longitudinal, with differing definitions of personality or character, on different hypotheses, and using diverse procedures of investigation, including observation, rating, case study, and projective techniques, have been made at various age levels from early childhood to adulthood, with the purpose of ascertaining the degree of consistency and change. Although some of the studies appear to point to more change and flexibility than others, the recurrent inference is that consistency is greater than change. The extent of change or flexibility found may be assumed to allow leeway for the influence of education on personality.

Personality measurement would be greatly advantaged if there were available reliable instruments by use of which the degrees of maturity reached by youth in a variety of attitudes and traits might be readily obtained. The instruments available are still very much in the experimental stage or involve projective procedures out of popular reach. In the absence of such instruments reliance must be placed on subjective and unquantified criteria of maturity. A summary synthesis of such criteria was presented in the main text of the present chapter, and such a formulation can prove useful in passing qualitative judgment on personalities, for keeping in mind as goals for one's own personal development, or as sources of hypotheses in efforts at objective measurement of personality.

The final observation to be made in this summary of the literature on personal and social development in adolescence is that nowhere in the behavior and attitudes under review do sudden or saltatory changes take place to accord with the stereotype of this period of life. The changes taking place appear almost exclusively to be gradual, as concerns the generality of the adolescent population, although individuals may manifest accelerated modification. The nearest the changes approach the stereotype is in adjustments in achieving developmental tasks, and these are currently explained pre-eminently by cultural rather than biological factors.

References and Bibliography

1. Allport, Gordon W. *The Individual and His Religion: A Psychological Interpretation.* New York: The Macmillan Co., 1953.
2. Allport, Gordon W. *Pattern and Growth in Personality.* New York: Holt, Rinehart, and Winston, 1961.
3. Allport, Gordon W.; Gillespie, James W.; and Young, Jacqueline. "The Religion of the Post-war College Student." *Journal of Psychology,* 25 (1948), 3–33.
4. Ausubel, David P. "Problems of Adolescent Adjustment." *Bulletin,* National Association of Secondary School Principals, 34 (1950), 1–84.
5. Ausubel, David P. *Theory and Problems of Adolescent Development.* New York: Greene & Stratton, 1954.
6. Benedict, Ruth. "Continuities and Discontinuities in Cultural Conditioning." *Psychiatry,* 1 (May, 1938), 161–67.

7. Bernard, Harold W. *Adolescent Development in American Culture.* Chs. 10, 12, 14. Yonkers-on-Hudson, N.Y.: World Book Co., 1957.
8. Bloom, Benjamin S. *Stability and Change in Human Characteristics.* New York: John Wiley & Sons, 1964.
9. Blos, Peter. *On Adolescence—A Psychoanalytic Interpretation.* Glencoe, Ill.: Free Press, 1961.
10. Brogdon, Hubert E. *The Primary Personal Values Measured by the Allport-Vernon Test, A Study of Values.* Psychological Monograph, 66, no. 16 (whole no. 348). Washington, 1952.
11. Buck, Walter. "A Measurement of Changes in Attitudes and Interests of University Students over a Ten-Year Period." *Journal of Abnormal and Social Psychology,* 31 (April-June, 1936), 12–19.
12. Burks, F. W. "Some Factors Related to Social Success in College." *Journal of Social Psychology,* 9 (May, 1938), 125–40.
13. Campbell, Elise H. *The Social-Sex Development of Children.* Genetic Psychology Monographs, 21, no. 4. Provincetown, Mass.: Journal Press, 1939.
14. Cattell, R. B. "The Principal Trait Clusters for Describing Personality." *Psychological Bulletin,* 42 (1945), 129–61.
15. Chambers, Othaniel R. "A Method of Measuring the Emotional Maturity of Children." *Pedagogical Seminary,* 32 (Dec., 1925), 637–47.
16. Chassell, Clara F. *The Relation between Morality and Intellect.* Teachers College Bureau of Publications, no. 607. New York, 1935.
17. Clark, E. T. *The Psychology of Religious Awakening.* New York: The Macmillan Co., 1929.
18. Cole, Luella. *Attaining Maturity.* New York: Farrar & Rinehart, 1944.
19. Coleman, James S. *The Adolescent Society: The Social Life of the Teenager and Its Impact on Education.* Glencoe, Ill.: Free Press of Glencoe, 1961.
20. Conklin, E. S. "Superstitious Beliefs and Practices among College Students." *American Journal of Psychology,* 30 (1919), 83–102.
21. Corey, Stephen M. "Developmental Tasks of Youth." In *The American High School: Its Responsibility and Opportunity,* ch. 5. Eighth Yearbook of the John Dewey Society. New York: Harper & Bros., 1946.
22. Cruze, Wendell W. *Adolescent Psychology and Development.* Chs. 7–9. New York: Ronald Press Co., 1953.
23. Davis, Allison. "Socialization and Adolescent Personality." In *Adolescence,* ch. 11. Forty-third Yearbook of the National Society for the Study of Education, part 1. Chicago: University of Chicago Press, 1944.
24. Davis, Kingsley. "The Sociology of Parent-Youth Conflict." *American Sociological Review,* 5 (1940), 513–35.
25. Diamond, Solomon. *Personality and Temperament.* New York: Harper & Bros., 1957.
26. Dimock, Hedley S. "New Light on Adolescent Religion." *Religious Education,* 31 (Oct., 1936), 273–79.
27. Dimock, Hedley S. *Rediscovering the Adolescent: A Study of Personality Development in Adolescent Boys.* New York: Association Press, 1937.
28. Doll, Edgar A. *The Measurement of Social Competence: A Manual for the Vineland Social Maturity Scale.* Circle Pines, Minn.: American Guidance Service, Inc., 1953.
29. Douvan, Elizabeth, and Adelson, Joseph. *The Adolescent Experience.* New York: John Wiley and Sons, 1966.
30. Dudycha, G. J. "Religious Beliefs of College Students." *Journal of Applied Psychology,* 17 (1933), 585–603.
31. Eberhart, J. C. "Attitudes toward Property: A Genetic Study by Paired-Comparisons Rating of Offenses." *Journal of Genetic Psychology,* 60 (1942), 3–35.
32. Eckert, Ruth E. "Intellectual Maturity." *Journal of Higher Education,* 5 (Dec., 1934), 478–84.

33. Elkin, Frederick, and Westley, William A. "The Myth of Adolescent Culture." *American Sociological Review,* 20 (Dec., 1955), 680–84.
34. Ellis, Albert. "Love and Family Relationships of American College Girls." *American Journal of Sociology,* 55 (May, 1950), 550–58.
35. Ellis, Albert. "Recent Research with Personality Inventories." *Journal of Consulting Psychology,* 17 (Feb., 1953), 45–49.
36. Ellis, Albert. "The Validity of Personality Questionnaires." *Psychological Bulletin,* 43 (Sept., 1946), 385–440.
37. Epperson, David C. "A Reassessment of Indices of Parental Influence in *The Adolescent Society.*" *American Sociological Review,* 29 (Feb., 1964), 93–96.
38. Fleege, Urban H. *Self-Revelation of the Adolescent Boy. A Key to the Understanding of the Modern Adolescent.* Milwaukee, Wis.: Bruce Publishing Co., 1945.
39. Frank, Lawrence K., et al. *Personality Development in Adolescent Girls.* Monographs of the Society for Research in Child Development, vol. 16, serial no. 53–1951. Lafayette, Ind.: Child Development Publication, 1953.
40. Freedman, Mervin B. *Impact of College.* New Dimensions in Higher Education, no. 4. Washington: U.S. Department of Health, Education, and Welfare, 1960.
41. Furfey, Paul H. "The Group Life of the Adolescent." *Journal of Educational Psychology,* 14 (Dec., 1940), 195–204.
42. Furfey, Paul H. "A Revised Scale for Measuring Developmental Age in Boys." *Mental Hygiene,* 14 (1930), 129–36.
43. Garrett, H. E., and Fisher, T. R. "The Prevalence of Certain Popular Misconceptions." *Journal of Applied Psychology,* 10 (1926), 411–20.
44. Garrison, Karl C. "A Comparative Study of the Attitudes of College Students toward Certain Domestic and World Problems." *Journal of Social Psychology,* 34 (1951), 47–54.
45. Garrison, Karl C. *Psychology of Adolescence.* 5th ed. Part III. Englewood Cliffs, N.J.: Prentice-Hall, 1956.
46. Gillespie, James M., and Allport, Gordon W. *Youth's Outlook on the Future: A Cross-National Study.* New York: Doubleday & Co., 1955.
47. Gilliland, Adam R. "The Attitudes of College Students Toward God and the Church." *Journal of Social Psychology,* 11 (1940), 11–18.
48. Gilliland, Adam R. "Changes in Religious Beliefs of College Students." *Journal of Social Psychology,* 37 (Feb., 1953), 113–16.
49. Ginzberg, Eli, ed. *Values and Ideals of American Youth.* New York: Columbia University Press, 1961.
50. Gordon, Wayne C. *The Social System of the High School: A Study in the Sociology of Adolescence.* Glencoe, Ill.: Free Press, 1957.
51. Grant, Bruce. "Survey of Studies on Problems of Adolescents." *California Journal of Secondary Education,* 28 (May, 1953), 293–97.
52. Gustad, John W. "A Longitudinal Study of Behavior Variables of College Students." *Educational and Psychological Measurements,* 12 (1952), 226–35.
53. Hall, Calvin S., and Lindzey, Gardner. *Theories of Personality.* New York: John Wiley and Sons, 1957.
54. Harris, Dale B. "Life Problems and Interests of Adolescents in 1935 and 1957." *School Review,* 67, 3 (Autumn, 1959), 335–49.
55. Hartshorne, Hugh, and Mays, Mark A. *Studies in the Nature of Character.* Studies in Deceit, vol. 1. New York: The Macmillan Co., 1928.
56. Havighurst, Robert J. *Human Development and Education.* New York: David McKay, Inc., 1953.
57. Havighurst, Robert J.; Robinson, Myra Z.; and Dorr, Mildred. "The Development of the Ideal Self in Childhood and Adolescence." *Journal of Educational Research,* 40 (Dec., 1940), 241–57.
58. Havighurst, Robert J., and Taba, Hilda. *Adolescent Character and Personality.* New York: John Wiley & Sons, 1949.
59. Henry, Nelson B., ed. *Adolescence.* Forty-third Yearbook of the National Society

for the Study of Education, part 1, chs. 11–13. Chicago: University of Chicago Press, 1944.
60. Howells, T. H. "Factors Influencing Honesty." *Journal of Social Psychology,* 9 (1938), 97–102.
61. Jacob, Philip E. *Changing Values in College.* New York: Harper & Bros., 1957.
62. Jersild, Arthur T. *The Psychology of Adolescence.* 2d ed. New York: The Macmillan Co., 1963.
63. Jones, Harold E. *Development in Adolescence: Approaches to the Study of the Individual.* New York: Appleton-Century-Crofts, 1943.
64. Jones, Mary C., and Bagley, Nancy. "Physical Maturing Among Boys as Related to Behavior." *Journal of Educational Psychology,* 41 (March, 1950), 129–48.
65. Jurovsky, Anton. "Relations of Older Children to Their Parents." *Pedagogical Seminary and Journal of Genetic Psychology,* 72 (March, 1948), 85–100.
66. Katz, Daniel, and Allport, Floyd H. *Student Attitudes: A Report of the Syracuse Reaction Study.* Syracuse, N.Y.: Craftsman Press, 1931.
67. Kluckhohn, C., and Murray, H., eds. *Personality in Nature, Society, and Culture.* Revised and enlarged. New York: A. A. Knopf, 1953.
68. Kuhlen, Raymond G. *The Psychology of Adolescent Development.* New York: Harper & Bros., 1952.
69. Kuhlen, Raymond G., and Arnold, Martha. "Age Differences in Religious Beliefs and Problems during Adolescence." *Journal of Genetic Psychology,* 65 (1944), 291–300.
70. Kuhlen, Raymond G., and Lee, Beatrice J. "Personality Characteristics and Social Acceptability in Adolescence." *Journal of Educational Psychology,* 34 (Sept., 1943), 321–40.
71. Lehman, Irvin J., and Payne, Isabelle K. "An Exploration of Attitudes and Value Changes of College Freshmen." *Personnel and Guidance Journal,* 41 (Jan., 1962), 403–8.
72. Leuba, James H. *The Belief in God and Immortality.* Boston: Sherman, French and Co., 1916.
73. Linton, Ralph. "Age and Sex Categories." *American Sociological Review,* 7 (Oct., 1942), 589–603.
74. Luchins, A. S. "On the Theories and Problems of Adolescence." *Journal of Genetic Psychology,* 85 (1954), 47–63.
75. Lundeen, Gerhard E., and Caldwell, Otis W. "A Study of Unfounded Beliefs among High School Seniors." *Journal of Educational Research,* 22 (Nov., 1930), 257–73.
76. Moore, Harry H. "The Social Impulses of Youth." *School and Society,* 42 (Nov. 16, 1935), 657–64.
77. Murphy, Gardner. *Personality: A Biosocial Approach to Origins and Structure.* New York: Harper & Bros., 1947.
78. Neilen, Patricia. "Shirley's Babies after Fifteen Years." *Journal of Genetic Psychology,* 73 (1948), 175–86.
79. Nelson, Erland. "Attitudes: I. Their Nature and Development; II. Social Attitudes; III. Their Measurement." *Journal of Genetic Psychology,* 21 (1939), 367–436.
80. Nelson, Erland. *Student Attitudes toward Religion.* Genetic Psychology Monographs, no. 22 (1940), 324–423. Provincetown, Mass.: Journal Press, 1940.
81. Nixon, H. K. "Popular Answers to Some Psychological Questions." *American Journal of Psychology,* 36 (1925), 418–23.
82. Overstreet, Harry A. *The Mature Mind.* New York: W. W. Norton & Co., 1949.
83. Paisios, John P., and Remmers, H. H. "A Factor Analysis of the SRA Youth Inventory." *Journal of Educational Psychology,* 46 (Jan., 1955), 25–30.
84. Parsons, Talcott. "Age and Sex in the Social Structure of the United States." *American Sociological Review,* 7 (Oct., 1942), 604–16.

85. Pawley, Berthold G. "Relationship between SRA Youth Inventory Scores and School Citizenship." *Personnel and Guidance Journal,* 37 (Nov., 1958), 207–11.
86. Peck, Robert F., and Havighurst, Robert J. *The Psychology of Character Development.* New York: John Wiley & Sons, 1960.
87. Pope, Charlotte. "Personal Problems of High School Pupils." *School and Society,* 57 (April 17, 1943), 443–48.
88. Powell, Lee, and Laslett, H. R. "A Survey of the Social Development of the 10th, 11th, and 12th Grade Pupils in a Small High School." *Journal of Experimental Education,* 9 (June, 1941), 361–63.
89. Pressey, Sidney L. "Changes from 1923 to 1943 in the Attitudes of Public School and University Students." *Journal of Psychology,* 21 (1946), 173–88.
90. Pressey, Sidney L.; Janney, J. Elliott; and Kuhlen, Raymond G. *Life: A Psychological Survey.* New York: Harper & Bros., 1939.
91. Pressey, Sidney L., and Kuhlen, Raymond G. *Psychological Development through the Life Span.* New York: Harper & Bros., 1957.
92. Pressey, Sidney L., and Pressey, Luella C. "Development of Interest-Attitude Tests." *Journal of Applied Psychology,* 17 (1933), 1–16.
93. Punké, H. H. "High School Youth and Family Quarrels." *School and Society,* 58 (Dec. 25, 1943), 507–11.
94. Remmers, H. H., and Radler, D. H. *The American Teenager.* Indianapolis, Ind.: Bobbs Merrill Co., 1957.
95. Remmers, H. H.; Whisler, Lawrence; and Durwald, Vector F. "Neurotic Indicators at the Adolescent Level." *Journal of Social Psychology,* 9 (1938), 17–24.
96. Reuter, E. B. "The Sociology of Adolescence." *American Journal of Sociology,* 43 (Nov., 1937), 414–27.
97. Roberts, Katherine E., and Fleming, Virginia V. *Persistence and Change in Personality Patterns.* Monograph of Social Science Research Council in Child Development, 8, no. 3. Washington: National Research Council, 1943.
98. Rosander, A. C. "Age and Sex Patterns of Social Attitudes." *Journal of Educational Psychology,* 30 (Oct., 1939), 481–96.
99. Rosen, Bernard C. "Conflicting Group Membership: A Study of Parent-Peer Group Cross Pressures." *American Sociological Review,* 20 (April, 1955), 155–61.
100. Ross, Murray G. *Religious Beliefs of Youth.* New York: Association Press, 1950.
101. Sanford, Nevitt. *Self and Society: Social Change and Individual Development.* New York: Atherton Press, 1966.
102. Saul, Leon J. *Emotional Maturity.* Philadelphia: J. B. Lippincott Co., 1947.
103. Schoeppe, Aileen. "Sex Differences in Adolescent Socialization." *Journal of Social Psychology,* 38 (Nov., 1953), 175–85.
104. Sears, R. R. *Survey of Objective Studies of Psychoanalytic Concepts.* Social Science Research Council Bulletin. Washington, 1943.
105. Seidman, Jerome M. *The Adolescent—A Book of Readings.* Rev. ed. Chs. v–ix. New York: Holt, Rinehart, and Winston, 1960.
106. Sheldon, W. H., and Stevens, S. S. *The Varieties of Temperament: A Psychology of Constitutional Differences.* New York: Harper & Bros., 1942.
107. Sheldon, W. H.; Stevens, S. S.; and Tucher, W. B. *The Varieties of Human Physique—An Introduction to Constitutional Psychology.* New York: Harper & Bros., 1940.
108. Sherif, M., and Cantril, H. *The Psychology of Ego-Involvements.* New York: John Wiley & Sons, 1947.
109. Sherman, A. W., Jr. "Emancipation Status of College Students." *Journal of Genetic Psychology,* 68 (1946), 171–80.
110. Shimberg, B. "Information and Attitudes toward World Affairs." *Journal of Educational Psychology,* 40 (April, 1949), 206–22.
111. Slavens, G. S., and Brogan, A. P. "Moral Judgments of High School Students." *International Journal of Ethics,* 38 (Oct., 1927), 57–69.

112. Spranger, Edward. *Types of Men.* Trans. New York: G. E. Steckert & Co., 1928.
113. Stoke, Stuart M., and West, Elmer D. "Sex Differences in Conversational Interests." *Journal of Social Psychology,* 2 (1931), 120–26.
114. Stone, Calvin P., and Barker, Roger R. "On the Relationships between Menarcheal Age and Certain Aspects of Personality, Intelligence, and Physique in College Women." *Journal of Genetic Psychology,* 45 (1934), 121–35.
115. Stott, L. H. "Adolescent Dislikes Regarding Parental Behavior and their Significance." *Journal of Genetic Psychology,* 57 (1940), 393–414.
116. Strang, Ruth. "Manifestations of Maturity in Adolescents." *Mental Hygiene,* 33 (1949), 563–69.
117. Symonds, Percival M. *Adolescent Fantasy; An Investigation of the Picture-Story Method of Personality Study.* New York: Columbia University Press, 1949.
118. Symonds, Percival M. "Changes in Sex Differences in Problems and Interests of Adolescents with Increasing Age." *Journal of Genetic Psychology,* 50 (1937), 83–89.
119. Symonds, Percival M. "Happiness as Related to Problems and Interests." *Journal of Educational Psychology,* 28 (April, 1937), 290–94.
120. Symonds, Percival M. "Life Problems and Interests of Adolescents." *School Review,* 44 (Sept., 1936), 506–18.
121. Symonds, Percival M. "Life Problems and Interests of Adults." *Teachers College Record,* 38 (Nov., 1936), 144–51.
122. Symonds, Percival M. "Sex Differences in Life Problems and Interests of Adolescents." *School and Society,* 43 (May 30, 1936), 751–52.
123. Symonds, Percival M. (with Arthur R. Jensen). *From Adolescent to Adult.* New York: Columbia University Press, 1961.
124. Thompson, George G. "Age Trends in Social Values during the Adolescent Years." *American Psychologist,* 4 (July, 1949), 250.
125. Thompson, George G. *Child Psychology: Growth Trends in Psychological Adjustment.* 2d ed. Boston: Houghton Mifflin Co., 1962.
126. Thorpe, Louis P., and Schmuller, Allen M. *Personality: An Interdisciplinary Approach.* Princeton, N.J.: D. Van Nostrand Co., 1958.
127. Thurstone, Louis L., and Chave, E. J. *The Measurement of Attitude: A Psychological Method and Some Experiments with a Scale for Measuring Attitude Toward Church.* Chicago: University of Chicago Press, 1929.
128. Todd, John Edward. *Social Norms and the Behavior of College Students.* T. C. Contributions, no. 833. New York: Bureau of Publications, Teachers College, Columbia University, 1941.
129. Tryon, Caroline M. "The Adolescent Peer Culture." In *Adolescence,* Forty-third Yearbook of the National Society for the Study of Education, part 1, ch. 12. Chicago: University of Chicago Press, 1944.
130. Tryon, Caroline M. *Evaluation of Adolescent Personality by Adolescents.* Monographs of the Society for Research in Child Development, vol. 4, no. 4. Washington: National Research Council, 1938.
131. Tryon, Caroline M. "Evaluations of Adolescent Personality by Adolescents." In *Child Behavior and Development* by K. G. Barker, J. S. Kouning, and H. F. Wright, ch. 31. New York: McGraw-Hill, 1942.
132. Valentine, W. L. "Common Misconceptions of College Students." *Journal of Applied Psychology,* 20 (1936), 633–58.
133. Wattenberg, William W. *The Adolescent Years.* Chs. 11, 15, 16. New York: Harcourt, Brace, and World, 1955.
134. Williams, Lucile H. "Their Problems Come with Them." *California Journal of Secondary Education,* 24 (Nov., 1949), 422–27.

4
Sexual and Dating Behavior

THE FIELD of sexual and dating behavior has obvious relationships with certain matters of concern that have been dealt with in the three foregoing chapters and might have been considered there, but doing so would have provided a less coordinated treatment and would have expanded one or more of the chapters to unwieldy proportions. It seems desirable also to review the field in a separate chapter because, as the evidence to be reported indicates, manifestations of sex in behavior and attitudes are at their maximum during later adolescence and early adulthood, and thus deserve the prominence accorded by concentrated consideration.

The chapter will begin with report on sexual behavior of males and females as reported in objective investigations. While the focus will be on behavior in the age-group predominant in community colleges, it will be necessary, for best understanding, to relate it to some extent to age-groups below and above. This section will be followed by a report of practices and attitudes in dating, including courtship, which in turn will be succeeded by brief consideration of social policy in respect to sexual behavior and attitudes, and by the chapter summary.

Sexual Behavior

Evidence from the Kinsey reports.—The first evidence concerning sex behavior will be drawn from the monumental investigations by Kinsey and associates (*34, 35*). While the reports from these investigations were highly controversial when first published, and still are in considerable degree, they afford the most comprehensive and reliable evidence extant in this area of human behavior. The investigations were made under the sponsorship of the Committee for Research on Problems of Sex of the National Research Council, a committee consisting of eminent scholarly representatives of such related disciplines as zoology, genetics, embryology, anthropology, and psychology. The vast total body of information analyzed for the two reports was obtained from extended interviews with about 5,300 white males (34, 6) and 5,940 white females (35, 43) of widely ranging ages and characteristics. Data on other groups were being collected but were not reported in the first two major publications from the total project.

The first measures of sexual behavior reported here from the Kinsey projects concern the total outlet in median numbers of orgasms per week of the two sexes for four age-groups: beginning of adolescence to 15, inclusive; 16–20; 21–25; and 26–30. The evidence for these groups is presented because, besides including the predominant age-span for the

TABLE 4.1
MEDIAN TOTAL NUMBERS OF OUTLETS PER WEEK FOR MALES AND FEMALES IN CERTAIN AGE GROUPS FOR THE TOTAL SAMPLE AND FOR THE SAME AGE GROUPS OF MALES OF THE 13+ EDUCATIONAL LEVEL AND FEMALES OF THE 13–16 EDUCATIONAL LEVEL

Age-Group	Males		Females	
	Total Population	13+	Total Sample	13–16
Adolescent–15	2.18	2.3	0.0	0.5
16–20	2.19	2.1	0.0	0.3
21–25	1.95	1.9	0.1	0.4
26–30	1.90	1.8	0.2	0.4

SOURCES: males—evidence from Alfred C. Kinsey, Wardell B. Pomeroy, and Clyde E. Martin, *Sexual Behavior in the Human Male* (Philadelphia: W. B. Saunders Co., 1948), 226, Table 45 (single males), 686ff., Table 152 (single white males); females—Alfred C. Kinsey, Wardell B. Pomeroy, Clyde E. Martin, and Paul H. Gebhard, *Sexual Behavior in the Human Female* (Philadelphia: W. B. Saunders Co., 1953), 549, Table 154 (single females), 550, Table 155 (single females).

community college, it extends both below and above so that trends may be noted. These measures are presented in Table 4.1. By looking at the columns for the total samples, it may be seen that the total outlet for males far exceeds that for females. Examination of the measures in the columns of Table 4.1 for the total samples of the two sexes warrants the assertion that the average adolescent girl was getting along with a fraction only of as much sexual activity as the adolescent boy, and the frequency for the adult female in her twenties was still far below that of the adolescent male.

The two remaining columns of Table 4.1 report the median total outlets for interviewees who had attended or completed college before discontinuing their schooling. The lower classifications as measures of educational level used in the project were 0–8 and 9–12, which signify, respectively, having attended or completed elementary school and having attended or completed high school. Measures for the 13+ classification (indicated in the Kinsey tables for females as "13–16") are quoted because this level seems most nearly appropriate for the community college population. One may correctly assume that this educational level also represents in some degree a social, or socioeconomic, selection. In the main, the median outlet for this educational level seems to be only slightly lower for males than for

TABLE 4.2
ACCUMULATIVE INCIDENCE IN PERCENTAGES OF CERTAIN SEXUAL EXPERIENCES OF MALES AND FEMALES

Experience and Population	Age		
	15	20	25
Masturbation			
Males:			
Total Population	82.2	92.1	93.4
Educational Level 13+	80.2	91.1	93.9
Females:			
Total Sample	20	33	44
Educational Level 13–16	18	32	45
Nocturnal Emission (or Dreams to Orgasm)			
Males:			
Total Population	39.6	77.0	81.5
Educational Level 13+	68.9	93.6	96.2
Females:			
Total Sample	2	8	16
Educational Level 13–16	2	8	14
Petting to Climax			
Males:			
Total Population	8.4	23.6	27.9
Educational Level 13+	7.6	46.0	58.2
Females:			
Total Sample	3	23	31
Educational Level 13–16	2	24	30
Premarital Coitus to Orgasm			
Males:			
Total Population	38.8	73.1	83.3
Educational Level 13+	9.5	44.4	64.4
Females:			
Total Sample	3	20	33
Educational Level 13–16	2	20	39
Homosexual Outlet			
Males:			
Total Population	27.7	36.7	35.4
Educational Level 13+	21.1	27.6	33.0
Females:			
Total Sample	2	4	7
Educational Level 13–16	1	3	7

SOURCES: Kinsey, Pomeroy, and Martin, *Sexual Behavior in the Human Male*. On masturbation, 500, Table 132; nocturnal emissions, 520, Table 133; petting to orgasm, 536, Table 135; coitus to orgasm, 550, Table 136; homosexual outlet, 624, Table 139. Kinsey, Pomeroy, Martin, and Gebhard, *Sexual Behavior in the Human Female*. On masturbation, 180, Table 25; nocturnal dreams, 216, Table 42; petting to climax, premarital, 270, Table 56; coitus to orgasm, premarital, 333, Table 75; homosexual outlet to orgasm, 493, Table 131.

the total sample, and noticeably higher for females but still little more than one-fifth as much as for males in any age-group.

Further illustration of numerical evidence from the Kinsey project concerns the accumulative incidence of certain sexual experiences. "Accumulative incidence" may be defined as the percentages of persons who have ever engaged in the given type of activity by a given age (35, 46). The evidence presented in Table 4.2 includes these incidences for five classifications of experience by the ages of 15, 20, and 25.

A glance down the columns of percentages bears out the expectation, from the figures on total outlet in Table 4.1, that almost all the measures for males are higher than for females. In fact, they are higher at all three ages listed for almost all types of experiences. For instance, the percentages of males in the total population who have masturbated by 15 was 82.2, and rose to 93.4 by 25, whereas for females it was only 20 (an approximate fourth of the male percentage) by 15 and rose to 44 (or less than half the male percentage) by 25. When attention is directed to accumulated incidences by age for the educational level 13+, as compared with the total sample, the experiences showing appreciable to notable increments for males are nocturnal emission and petting to climax, while the data for coitus to climax show a lower accumulative incidence.

Many other analyses of the responses of the interviewees are reported in the two volumes drawn upon for the brief exposition undertaken here. Because of the current rather widespread acquaintance with findings of the Kinsey reports, extensive statistical presentation here is hardly necessary. Among the more significant of additional lines of evidence for purpose of illustration here might be the percentages of total outlet experienced by males and females through each of the several practices (masturbation, petting to orgasm, coitus, etc.) by males and females of successive age-groups (34, 240–60, 686–708; 35, 562–63). For example, there are notable shifts downward for masturbation in these proportions for the total samples and the 13+ educational level from the adolescence–15, table shifts upward for coitus for the same age-groups of both sexes. It through the 16–20, and into the 24–25 age-groups of both sexes, and no- deserves noting that, from the standpoint of our interest in understanding the predominant age-span of community college students, the shifts tend to be greater through these age-groups than in any other cluster of successive age-groups represented in the projects.

Before proceeding with consideration of the Kinsey reports it is appropriate to say a word concerning their earlier reception. It is a matter of rather common knowledge among persons conversant with the literature on personal and social behavior that the reports became highly controversial promptly following their publication. This was largely because questions of sexuality are a highly emotional area of concern and because this incidence of sexual practices of the several sorts, especially in view of the dearth previously of reliable evidence concerning them, was much greater than had been assumed under our generally professed puritanical mores. The controversy must have been accentuated also by society's traditional concern for the welfare of youth who were reported in these investigations to be experiencing shifting and increasing sexual outlets with advancing age toward adulthood.

Individual variation.—Up to this point in the description and analysis of sexual behavior, presentation has involved only measures of central tendency or of percentage of incidence. Nothing has been said of individual variation in sex activity, which is extremely wide in both sexes. This variation extends to both total outlet and patterns of sources. The Kinsey report on males reminds the reader that "behavior characters vary even more than physiologic characters, and these in turn vary more than morphologic characters" (*34*, 89). The total outlet for the sample population of males from adolescence to 30 years of age ranged as widely as from none to 29+ per week (*34*, 198, Table 40). The patterns of combinations of sources of outlet are no less diversified. A figure in the volume on males from the Kinsey project (*34*, 196, Fig. 31) displays patterns for individual cases that range, for example, from complete dependence on masturbation to complete dependence on coitus, or from complete dependence on petting to climax to complete dependence on homosexual activity, with diverse combinations of outlet between such extremes. The volume on female behavior generalizes that "the range of variation in the female far exceeds the range of variation in the male" and comments that "the record will have misled the reader if he fails to note this emphasis on the range of variation" (*35*, 537–38). The actual range in the measures of total outlet per week for the 16–20 age-group of single females is reported to be from none to 29 (*35*, 540, Fig. 116), the same range as for a much longer age-span for males just cited. The range of variation in combinations of outlets is not illustrated here. Instead, quotation is made from the generalization on combination of variables (*35*, 543): "The sexual history of each individual represents a unique combination of these variables. There is little chance that such a combination has ever existed before, or ever will exist again. We have never found any individual who was a composite of all the averages on all of the aspects of sexual response and overt activity which we have analyzed. . . ."

Influences on sexuality.—In addition to reporting on the incidence of sexual practices as related to age and educational level as illustrated in Tables 4.1 and 4.2, the Kinsey projects inquired into other hypothetical influences both on total sexual outlet and the several specific outlets.

Report on one group of these influences was made separately in the two volumes so that the measures must be assembled for comparison. This group includes age at adolescence, parental occupation, rural or urban residence, religious background, and generation or decade of birth, of which all but the first may be thought of as environmental. The second group is referred to as "psychological factors" and the comparisons of the sexes in respect to them are accomplished directly in the volume reporting behavior of females. Evidence depended on for inferences here is for the age-group 16–20, the one most nearly coinciding with later adolescence.

The median total outlet for males declines appreciably with advance in age of arrival at adolescence (*34*, 302, Table 69). By comparison, it declines relatively little for females (*35*, 554, Table 161). The trend for males with level of parental occupation from lower (unskilled) to higher (professional) seems unclear (*34*, 420–21, Table 107), perhaps because of the small populations represented. For females there is at most only a small downward trend (*35*, 551, Table 156). One notes a somewhat but hardly markedly greater total outlet for males of rural as compared with urban residence (*34*, 448, Table 116), but little or no difference on this account for females (*35*, 555, Table 163).

Religious background as defined in the Kinsey reports is a significant influence. Comparisons were made for Protestants, Catholics, and Jews. For males, the designations for the comparisons were Protestant active and Protestant inactive; Catholic active and Catholic inactive; and Jewish Orthodox and Jewish inactive. The median total outlets for the inactive were substantially larger than for the active groups (*34*, 466, Table 125). For instance, the medians for Protestant active and inactive were, respectively, 1.83 and 2.36. For the females, the reports identified three degrees of religious background, "devout," "moderate," and "inactive," and for all three denominations there was a larger median outlet for the inactive than for the devout (*35*, 556–57, Table 165).

A not uncommon current belief has it that, over a considerable period, sex activity has increased, especially among young people, and that traditional sex mores have tended to break down. The Kinsey project presented evidence bearing on this belief. The approach differs for the reports for the two sexes. For males, the interviewees were divided into two groups designated as the "Older Generation" and the "Younger Generation," the former averaging 22 years older than the latter (*34*, 150). For females, the grouping was by decades of birth: before 1900, 1900–1909, 1910–19, and 1920–29 (*35*, 55). For single males of the 13+ educational level of the 16–20 age-group the mean frequencies of total outlet are 2.69 and 2.70 and are practically equal (*34*, 410, Table 104), although the means are greater for the younger generation than for the older for the 0–8 and 9–12 educational levels. The median frequencies per week reported for females of the successive decades disclose little or no increment (*35*, 553, Table 160). If rapid changes have taken place for either sex, this must have been since completion of the interviews for the Kinsey reports or in areas or populations unrepresented.

Under the heading of "Psychologic Factors in Sexual Response" (*35*, Ch. 16) report on the Kinsey project lists 33 different experiences to which the interviewers requested their subjects to indicate the degree of their erotic response: "definite and/or frequent," "some response," and "never." Illustrative experiences in the list are observing the opposite sex, observing portrayals of nude figures, observing commercial moving pictures, observing burlesque and floor shows, observing sexual action, fantasies

TABLE 4.3
PERCENTAGES OF SINGLE COLLEGE MALES REPORTING THE SEXUAL BEHAVIOR INDICATED

Investigator	Mean Age	N	Reporting Masturbation	Reporting Homosexuality	Reporting Intercourse
Ross	21.3	95	94.8	26.3	50.5
Kinsey	21	1980	92.0	28.5	49.1
Finger	19.4	111	92.8	27.0	45.0
Kinsey	19	2565	90.0	26.6	38.0
Ross	21.3	95	90.0–95.0	25.0–30.0	48.0–53.0
Finger	19.4	111	92.8	27.0	45.0
Ross	20.8	79	94.5	25.3	44.3
Kinsey	20.5	2337	91.1	27.4	44.4
Finger	20.0	111	92.8	27.0	45.0

SOURCES: Ross (*51*, Table 1); Finger (*22*).

concerning opposite sex, stimulation by literary materials, and responses to being bitten. The authors report that for all but three in the total list the percentages of males affected were larger than for females; for twelve of the items the percentages of females who were erotically aroused were less than half those for males, and for only three items (moving pictures, reading romantic literature, and being bitten) were the percentages of females larger than for males (*35*, 687).

Corroboration by questionnaire.—A frequent comment by many persons who see the measures on the incidence of sexual activity from the Kinsey project for the first time is that they must be exaggerated. Results of other studies by a different procedure have made it possible to check on the reliability of the Kinsey measures and, because of the populations represented, their relevance to students of typical ages in junior college years. Two such studies will be cited, one by Ross (*51*) using junior college students, the other by Finger (*22*) using college students. Both studies were made by anonymous questionnaire administered to students in classes in psychology. Details of administration included use by the students of a slip of paper containing nothing but 25 numbers. Students were asked to put either an M or an F at the top of the paper to indicate sex, to indicate marital status with *m* or *s,* to give age in years and months, and to answer each question which was read by the instructor with a plus sign if the answer was affirmative and with a zero if it was negative. The twenty-fifth question in the Ross study was, "Are your answers to this questionnaire sufficiently valid that they may be used for scientific research?" Five single males answered this question in the negative and their papers were removed from the basic tabulations. The Ross respondents included 35 females, but he reports no evidence from their replies, presumably because of unreliability for such a small number.

Results of the Ross and Finger measures in comparison with those from the Kinsey project are reported in Table 4.3, which also includes the mean ages of the populations and the numbers of respondents represented.

The mean age of the 95 single males in the Ross study was 21 years and 4 months. The ages ranged from 18 to 29 years, with 69 per cent of the cases between 19–0 and 22–11, inclusive. At the time the questionnaire was administered the junior college registration included a large number of veterans, and this explains the presence of a considerable number of older men in junior college years.

As the author indicates, the most striking characteristic of the table is the consistency of all the percentages compared. He reports that no difference between them is significant at the 5 per cent level. The first two lines labeled "Ross" and "Kinsey" compare the percentages obtained in Ross' study with those from the Kinsey project for a group of 21-year-old males. The percentages are practically identical, even though two different methods of obtaining the data were used. The Finger-Kinsey comparison yields results equally consistent for a group of 19-year-old single college males. The Finger-Kinsey comparison for a group of 19-year-olds finds equally consistent results, except that Finger reports a 7 per cent greater frequency of premarital intercourse than does the Kinsey project, a difference not statistically significant. The only comparison in the table requiring special comment is the third one, the Ross-Finger pairing. Ross says that this comparison makes possible ascertaining the limits of error in the present study due to ruling out the responses of the five men who disqualified themselves. If they had all answered "no" to the questions, the percentages would be at the lower extremes reported in the upper row of this particular comparison; if they all had answered "yes," the percentages would be at the upper extremes. As Ross indicated, these data may cast some light on the magnitude of errors in the Kinsey data owing to the refusal of some subjects to be interviewed.

One other comparison emphasizes the close similarity of the Finger and Ross data. Each investigator asked how many of his subjects had masturbated during the last 12 months. The respective percentages of affirmative response were 92.8 and 90–95.

Other studies and writings.—In order in part to check on the acceptability of evidence and interpretations from the Kinsey reports and in part to supplement the understandings they afford, brief treatment will be accorded several other reports of studies of and writings on sex behavior. Most of these antedate Kinsey and fewer are contemporary or later writings. Most of them concern either males alone or both sexes, but none on females alone, which may reflect a traditional reluctance, because of our "double standard," to permit discussion of problems in this area with females.

A useful pre-Kinsey digest of factual information about sexual behavior was made by Willoughby for the Society for Research in Child Development and published under the title *Sexuality in the Second Decade* (60). This summary reports, among other things, that masturbation is all but universal with boys and that the practice among girls represents "a considerable reduction from that of boys." Willoughby expressed the opinion that, even when the questioning is done anonymously, the resulting figures must be taken as minimas. He believes that the sex difference in this respect is cultural rather than biological, what sociologists call "sociosexual acculturation," and "represents a more effective banishment of sexuality from the consciousness of girls than of boys." There is also an assertion concerning any deleterious effect of self-gratification which will be cited below while referring to the study by Pullias. After reporting the percentages of females without homosexual experience, which were found to be smaller for graduates of women's than of coeducational colleges, the author observes that the incidence of homosexuality is "rather larger than would ordinarily be supposed" (60, 34). In concluding on the incidence of coitus he observes that habitual sexual contacts are a phenomenon of the later years of the second decade.

An extensive investigation of sexual behavior of boys, contemporary with the Kinsey project, and, like it, made out of Indiana University, was reported by Ramsey (48). The interviewees were 291 boys ranging in age from 10 to 20 years in a midwestern city of over 100,000 population. The boys were primarily from the middle and upper-middle socioeconomic classes in the population. The varieties of evidence are too extensive to be reported here, but it may be said that the main findings concerning proportions with the types of outlet differ in no important respects from those presented in the Kinsey reports.

An investigation by Hohman and Schaffner (30) had as interviewees

4,600 unmarried men, mainly from New York and Maryland, being examined for induction into the United States Army in accordance with the Selective Service Act, but before we had entered the war and before the war psychology could have markedly changed sex mores. Over 95 per cent of these men were between 21 and 28, so were mainly beyond the age-group of our predominant concern. However, the manner of reporting the evidence makes some of it comparable to that in the Kinsey project. The percentages of these men who had not had heterosexual relations, according to the level of education completed, were: grades 1–8, 12.3; high school, 1–4 years, 19.1; attended or finished college, 31.7. Family income showed a somewhat analogous relationship, with higher incomes associated

TABLE 4.4
PERCENTAGES OF 75 YOUNG MEN HAVING CERTAIN BELIEFS CONCERNING THE EFFECTS OF MASTURBATION

Belief	Per Cent
Some type of serious damage	82.7
Serious physical damage	44.0
Serious mental damage	37.3
Serious moral damage	24.0
Serious social damage	12.0
Harmful (unspecified)	8.0
Direct cause of insanity	16.0
Not seriously harmful	6.7
No response	10.7

SOURCE: Pullias (45, Table III).

with higher percentages of virginity. The percentages by age of those who had had heterosexual experience increased from 21.3 at 15 to 63.0 at 18 and 86.3 by 20. The percentages of both virgins and nonvirgins admitting masturbation at some time were almost equal, being, respectively, 89.7 and 87.3. Of the nonvirgins, 52.4 per cent admitted continuing it up to the time of the examination. Only the percentage of homosexuality deviated notably from proportions reported from the Kinsey project, and involved less than 1 per cent. The authors say that this is the more significant because they "were specifically instructed by mobilization medical standards to exclude homosexuals."

The study by Pullias (45) which was mentioned above, pre-Kinsey as to date of publication, was concerned with the beliefs of college freshmen on the effects of masturbation. It was the opinion of the author that the students who served as subjects in his investigation were fairly representative of college men in general in respect to the problem studied. The beliefs they held are reported in Table 4.4, from which it is clear that the overwhelming majority believe that the practice is seriously harmful. Informed opinion is that masturbation is not physically damaging. Willoughby, whose résumé of the literature was drawn upon above, expressed the opinion that there is no "deleterious [physical] effect of autosexuality in adolescence or elsewhere" (*60*, 28). However, Pullias asserts that these beliefs of college freshmen produce feelings of both guilt and fear, which must conduce to problems in adjustment: "One is not likely to be happy or wholesome in his adjustment to life who believes that by his own action he has irretrievably and seriously damaged himself physically, morally, or mentally." In a similar vein, Willoughby said there is "some evidence for autosexuality to become a symptom of the withdrawing type of personality maladjustment. . . ."

In a review of more recent inquiries into the sex behavior among young people, Rubin (*52*) adheres to an inference from the Kinsey project that "despite the changes that have taken place since the turn of the century, primarily in females, the tempo of change in sex behavior and mores is not a rapid one." He mentions that the often quoted prediction of Terman of the disappearance of the female unmarried virgin by 1960 is far from realized and that the Kinsey interpretation of no "major revolution in overt sexual behavior in our society over the last sixty years is more convincing." Rubin's opinion that there has nevertheless been an "interregnum of values" will be touched on below in a discussion of social policy.

Dating, Including Courtship

The concept and functions of dating.—The term dating has come to be applied to all premarital paired association of the sexes. It is more comprehensive than courtship, which is assumed to be that aspect of dating which is aimed in particular at finding a mate for marriage. Time was when the only premarital association of the sexes condoned was courtship. For a half century or more, the folkways of young people have expanded the associations of the sexes to go far beyond the narrower function of courtship. The expansion has been made possible by the automobile, which has brought freer movement of the population, and by other inventions like the movie, radio, and television.

The literature descriptive of the phenomenon of dating enumerates a variety of functions for it in addition to courtship. For instance, Lowrie (*41*) identifies, among others, the following "interrelated yet distinguishable ends": "(1) broader experience, (2) greater poise and balance, (3) experience in adjusting to others, and (4) reduced emotional excitement on meeting and associating with a stranger of the opposite sex." To these he adds (5) enrichment and development of personality, (6) bestowal of prestige, and (7) provisions of the means of having a good time and mixing socially. And (8) "Somewhat more debatable yet apparently real, dating, together with the normal interaction and stimulation that accompany it, seems to give a kind of sexual release, a reduction in sexual tension." In consequence of these functions, Lowrie continues, dating (9) "tends to provide a wider acquaintance from which a mate may be selected, [and] (10) its continuation over a period of time normally enhances an individual's ability to judge members of the opposite sex sensibly and objectively."

Dating in early and middle adolescence.—It should help to an understanding of dating behavior in early college years to know something about when it is begun by boys and girls and about its proportions in high school years. Evidence from studies by Punké and by Lowrie make this possible. Punké (47) reported on frequencies of dating by the two sexes for high

TABLE 4.5
FREQUENCY OF DATING OF HIGH SCHOOL STUDENTS AND PERCENTAGES ENGAGING IN DOUBLE DATING

Grade and Sex	Number of Dates Per Month				Per Cent with Double Dating
	None	1–4	5–10	Over 10	
Freshman boys	53.8	20.6	16.0	9.6	45.5
Freshman girls	53.0	21.3	17.0	8.7	81.0
Senior boys	21.6	29.5	28.9	20.0	55.6
Senior girls	13.6	19.4	33.1	33.9	80.6

SOURCE: Punké (47, Table 1).

school freshmen and seniors in nine widely scattered states. Some of his data are presented in Table 4.5. It may be seen that the percentage distributions of freshman boys and girls by numbers of dates per month are nearly alike, with something over a half of each sex reporting no dates, with about a fifth of both sexes reporting 1 to 4 dates per month; about a sixth, 5 to 10; and fewer than a tenth, over 10 dates. As is to be expected, the proportion of seniors not dating is much smaller than of freshmen, and larger proportions than for freshmen are found in the second, third, and fourth numerical columns of the table. However, for senior girls, the percentage with no dates is appreciably smaller than for senior boys, while the percentages for these girls in the two columns of higher frequencies are considerably larger. Punké ventures no explanation of this tendency to difference for seniors, and one wonders whether it is not owing to the inhibiting factors of the availability of transportation, say by automobile, and pocket money, for a considerable proportion of the boys. In view of the similarity of the percentages for the two sexes as freshmen, the difference for seniors can hardly be ascribed only to the known differences in ages of sexual maturation of the two sexes.

In another phase of his investigation Punke inquired into the frequency of chaperonage for the same boys and girls, as "always," "usually," "half the time," "seldom," or "never." The overwhelming majority at both levels reported "seldom" or "never," indicating that chaperonage was an infrequent practice. The percentages reporting chaperonage were somewhat, although not greatly, higher for freshmen than for seniors, and for girls than for boys. The last column of Table 4.5 contains the percentages with double dating, which may be regarded in some part as a substitute for chaperonage. It is seen to be a much more frequent practice at both class levels with girls than with boys.

An investigation by Lowrie (*42*) probed further into the acceptability of a belief frequently held that beginning of dating is closely related to the arrival of sex maturity and therefore begins with girls at younger ages than for boys. He obtained from juniors and seniors in four high schools and from single undergraduates in a state university their ages of first dating, from which he computed the medians and arithmetic means of these ages for high school students grouped by "present ages" at 16, 17, and 18, and for university undergraduates grouped by "present ages" at 18, 19, 20, and 21. The mean ages, for example, for first dates for university men with "present ages" of 18, 19, 20, and 21 were 15.24, 15.25, 15.44, and 15.63, and for university women of the same age-groups, 15.02, 15.21, 15.35, and 15.49. Peculiarly, the age of first dating advances to some extent from one age-group to the next, but, what concerns us more, there is very little difference between the means for the individual age-groups. In his interpretation the author says that in the college samples the mean difference is less than two months and the median slightly more than three months, and his observation is that, "by no stretch of the imagination can such difference be made to resemble the commonly assumed year or two-year difference between boys and girls in the age of sex maturation." He found the same lack of large difference between the sexes for ages of first "going steady." To him the biological emphasis in accounting for dating behavior not only seems unsubstantiated; it appears to be unnecessary, and he is of the opinion that, instead, dating and the accompanying forms of behavior are in large part products of the culture.

Another inquiry into dating bearing mainly on the early and middle adolescent population, in this instance of girls only, was included in an investigation made for the Girl Scouts of America. The behavior and attitudes on which report is made here are only a small part of the total investigation made by the Institute for Social Research at the University of Michigan (*1*). The subjects interviewed were not merely a sample of Girl Scouts but of the total population of girls of ages 11 to 18. In response to the questions "Do you date? About how often?" the answer "no" was given by the following proportions of girls: under 14, 81 per cent; 14–16, 27 per cent; over 16, 5 per cent (*1*, 107, Table 66). All others reported various frequencies, such as "every weekend," "more than on weekends," etc. Asked for their attitudes toward going steady, the same three age-groups gave negative responses as follows: under 14, 25 per cent; 14–16, 55 per cent; over 16, 66 per cent. The reaction was reported as "generally positive" for 14, 19, and 23 per cent, respectively, of these three age-groups. The figures imply a rising proportion in both directions from a neutral position, from which one may conclude that the subject is controversial.

Behavior at the college level.—In the first description here of dating behavior at the college level, dependence will be placed on evidence from a project by Ehrmann (*17*) collected by schedule from students in a public university in a southern state. The report of this project had been preceded by other investigations of sexual behavior by college students, but they were not made with as carefully controlled procedures or with the comprehensiveness of inquiry into the stages of dating behavior. A shortcoming of this investigation sometimes mentioned, even by the investigator himself, is the high ratio of men to women in the college population (16 to 1), which arose from the fact that the institution had only recently been made coeducational, a fact which resulted in the males having dates only or principally with girls in their home towns or in the towns in the adjacent region and then only on weekends. Even this shortcoming could be turned to advantage by adding to the feasibility of inquiry into the influence of differences in social classes on dating behavior.

The information for the project was collected on a "schedule," which may be regarded as a form of questionnaire, filled out by all students represented in the tabulations. In addition, interviews were held with a hundred of the same students. The procedure by schedule is probably not as useful as the interview, which was the exclusive method of collecting data for the Kinsey project, but has the advantage of permitting the gathering of a limited number of items from a larger population within a shorter period of time. Usable schedules were filled out by a total of 841 students, of whom 576 were men and 265 were women. The men included 302 veterans and 274 nonveterans, and the proportion of veterans might lead to doubt of the acceptability of the findings as applicable to males in a community college. The absence of statistically significant differences between veterans and nonveterans in the particular measures cited here affords justification for considering them in some part relevant to our purpose. The ages of veterans raises the average age of men among Ehrmann's subjects, but it is fair to say that the ages of a large proportion of all his men and most of his women fall within the dominant age-span of the community college student body.

The schedule used in the project listed the "stages" to which the respondents reporting went in the "current behavior," that is, the stages to which they were going at the time of the study. On the basis of experience with the first draft, referred to as Schedule A, and at the suggestion of the students, it was revised to some extent midway in the collection of the data, and Ehrmann's tables are made up to take account of the revision. The stages as described in the revised form, Schedule B, are as follows:

STAGE	DESCRIPTION
A	No dates within specified period.
B	No physical contact or only holding of hands.
C_1	Kissing and hugging.
C_2	Boy fondling the girl's breast with his hands outside of her clothes, as well as any activity in C_1.
D	Boy fondling girl's naked breasts, as well as any activity in C_1 or C_2.
E	Boy fondling girl's genitals or naked area around genitals as well as any activity in C_1, C_2, or D.
F	Sexual intercourse, as well as any activity in C_1, C_2, D, or E. (Stages B and C_1, C_2, D, E, and F are mutually exclusive. The same classification of stages is used for Schedule A as for B except that Stages C_1 and C_2 in Schedule B appear together as Stage C in Schedule A as kissing and hugging, or boy fondling the girl's breast with his hand outside her clothes, or both.)

The percentage distributions of most advanced stages to which the respondents reported they were going in their current behavior are reported in Table 4.6. The results of the calculations are given both for males and females of the entire group and for the second group answering on Schedule B only. It may be seen that larger proportions of males than females for both calculations carry the behavior into the further stages, with more than a third to Stage F. By contrast, about two-thirds of the entire group of females stop at or before Stage C and of the second group at or before C_2. The difference in distributions is so marked as to prompt some attempt at explanation. In considerable part this has already been provided in mentioning that a large proportion of these men were having their dates only or principally with girls in their home towns or in the towns of the adjacent region. It is also provided in a related finding of the investigation that males tend to "go further" in the dating in which they cross class lines and date females of lower social classifications.

The schedules used by Ehrmann inquired also into the pattern of control for all the dates represented in his investigation. Specifically, he asked which, the boy or the girl, initiated the behavior and the reason why the behavior went no further than as reported. Compilation of the responses resulted in Table 4.7. Responses by both sexes indicate that in three-fourths or more of the dates the initiative is that of the male. The representatives of the two sexes are not far from agreement that the most frequent reason is that "neither tried" and the reason next in frequency is that the "girl would not." "No opportunity" and "boy would not" account for the remaining explanations, with the last reason seldom offered.

Ehrmann later elaborated the study from which the above excerpts are taken into book form (16) and, for the purpose of adding to understanding in this area of dating behavior, it is desirable to draw on a few of his

TABLE 4.6
THE MOST ADVANCED STAGE TO WHICH INDIVIDUAL GOES IN HIS CURRENT BEHAVIOR

	The Entire Group (Schedule A and B groups)						
	A	B	C	D	E	F	Total
Males	3.9	10.6	30.6	5.4	16.6	38.8	100.0
Females	0.7	4.5	59.7	8.3	17.7	9.1	100.0
	The Second Group (Schedule B group only)						
	A	B	C_1	C_2	D	E	F	Total
Males	4.4	4.2	22.8	11.0	5.0	16.2	36.4	100.0
Females	1.0	3.0	45.5	17.0	5.0	18.0	10.5	100.0

SOURCE: Ehrmann (17, Table 11a, b).

TABLE 4.7
PATTERN OF CONTROL FOR ALL DATES

P.* Percentage of dates on which behavior initiated by	As reported by	
	Males	Females
P_1 Boy	75.3	78.9
P_2 Girl	24.7	21.1
	100.0	100.0

N.† Percentage of dates on which behavior went no further because	As reported by	
	Males	Females
N_1 No opportunity	23.9	13.0
N_2 Girl would not	29.6	30.0
N_3 Boy would not	4.9	2.3
N_4 Neither tried	42.6	54.7

SOURCE: Ehrmann (17, Table 1).
*Positive control ("Who initiates behavior").
†Negative control ("Who or what stops behavior").

conclusions in this more extensive report. This is done without reproducing his supporting evidence. He observes that the limitation of premarital sexual behavior is primarily determined by the female and that the male is restrained either because of his conception of the girl—he "respects her"—or because of her overt refusal to go further, "and to a lesser extent because of morals." Among the conclusions are (269–70):

"Female sexual expression is primarily and profoundly related to being in love and to going steady. (*This is probably the single most important empirical finding of the research.*) Male sexuality is more indirectly and less exclusively associated with romanticism and intimacy relationships.... There is virtual coincidence between the personal code of sex conduct and sexual behavior among females, but not males. Females rarely go beyond the limits set by their codes, whereas males are often not able to go as far sexually as their codes permit.... The findings ... strongly indicate that the difference between males and females in the youth culture with respect to sex and love is so marked that there are distinct male and female subcultures."

Ehrmann's observations concerning the changes that have taken place in sexual behavior during the more recent period are summarized in the treatment of standards of premarital behavior in the section on social policy below.

Diverse investigations relative to dating.—In the investigative literature bearing on dating and/or other social-sexual relations are several writings that at least supplement, even if they do not greatly modify, our understandings in this area of behavior as reported and interpreted by Ehrmann. These are concerned with the sentimental attitudes of girls, the reasons they give for engaging in petting, the aggressions of the male, and a refinement in classification of types of dating. The information on sentimental attitudes was reported by Ellis (*19*), who had received answers to an anonymous questionnaire making inquiry concerning a number of items toward which respondents were requested to indicate their reactions. One of these items read, "When I am in love, being loved by the man or boy I love is to me...." The degrees of importance and the percentage frequencies with which they were checked by 500 girls attending 19 different colleges widely scattered in the United States were: the most important thing in the world, 56; very important, 37; fairly important, 5; hardly important, 1; not important at all, less than 1 per cent; no answer, 1. The majority of the girls stated that at the time of answering they were definitely in love, while only 11 per cent reported that they were definitely not in love. The degrees of high importance for such overwhelming proportions of these respondents could go a long way in explaining the incidence for some of the more advanced stages of dating as reviewed above.

An anonymous questionnaire investigation made as long as four decades ago (*55*) inquired of college women whether or not they had engaged in "petting" (not defined) and asked for their reasons for doing so. The percentages reporting having and not having indulged were, respectively, 92 and 8. The percentages reporting the various reasons were: infatuation, 52; curiosity, 40; because others did it, 30; lack of courage to resist, 12; fear of being unpopular, 11. The total of the percentages far exceeds 100, which is explained by the fact that many women gave more than a single reason. It may be noted that the motives behind some of these reasons are hardly discrete and that "infatuation" and being in love may be overlapping, although far from equivalent, designations.

Description of dating behavior would be incomplete without some reference to the incidence of male aggression in connection with these heterosexual associations. Evidence will be cited from two studies involving girls in the same midwestern university, one of them concerning dating during college years (*33*) and the other concerning dating behavior reported by freshman girls as having taken place during their senior year in high school and the following summer before entering college (*38*). Data for both were supplied on schedules anonymously filled out. In the first study, more than half of the female sample reported themselves offended at least once during the academic year, with 162 offended girls reporting a total of 1,022 offensive episodes. In the second study the incidence of "offensive episodes" was also high. Concerning "situational factors" it is reported that as many as 16 per cent of the episodes took place while the male was "under the influence of alcohol," and 69 per cent were experienced in automobiles. A full four-fifths of the episodes took place after some prior sex play and a majority with regular dates or engaged mates. Explanations of these episodes and their relatively high incidence usually include the greater sex drive of the male and his inclination toward exploitation of the female. It must also be influenced by the definition of "offensive" by the female, which must vary according to her code which we know tends to be more conservative than that of the male.

The investigation reporting a refinement in classification of dating is one by Smith (*54*) concerning practices in "Pioneer College," a refinement that is probably applicable in varying degrees to many campuses. The classification includes the usually predominant "competitive" and "steady," with the competitive found to include 66 per cent of all dates. Steady datings, including the remainder, are divided in turn into two classes, the "noncommitment" steadies and the "commitment" steadies. The proportions of the two within the steadies are two-thirds for commitment and one-third for noncommitment steadies. The commitment steadies have plans for marriage, whereas the noncommitment steadies do not contemplate marriage but are only for convenience in college life. The evidence in the study finds that a larger proportion of men than women (75 against 56 per cent) report competitive dating, that steady dating is more characteristic of the coeds than of the men, and that within the steady-dating group these coeds "are more seriously oriented toward courtship."

An intercultural comparison of attitudes and behavior.—A useful aid to understanding behavior in some area in one's own culture is to compare attitudes and behavior in that area in other cultures. Anthropologists and sociologists often resort to such comparisons. The method makes possible the study of the influences of cultural norms on individual behavior. Such a comparison of attitudes and behavior in sex matters has been reported by Christensen (*11*). The population samples were men and women students in three universities, in (1) Denmark, to represent Scandinavian culture, which is known to be more permissive in sexual behavior than is the United States, (2) a midwestern university, and (3) a university in "considerably restrictive Mormondom in the Inter-mountain region of the United States."

(a) *Attitudes.* The findings of the investigation will be illustrated rather than reported at length. Of the three groups, the Danish student approved the earliest intimacy in the courtship process, the midwestern students next, and the intermountain students latest. More Danish students gave approval to premarital coitus than did midwestern students, and more of the latter than did the intermountain students. For "random or casual dates assuming mutual desire," male approval percentages were 43, 17, and 6, respectively; and female approval percentages were 34, 3, and 1, respectively. In all three cultures approval percentages increased as assumptions of greater courtship commitment were made. The percentages of preference for marrying virgins for males in the three cultures were 39, 86, and 95, respectively; and for females 26, 77, and 89, respectively. In explanation of these smaller percentages for females, the author suggests (a) that the females are "sufficiently realistic to know that chances of getting a virgin male are not high" and (b) "some others feel personally inadequate in the sexual realm and so tend to prefer a male with experience who might show them the way."

(b) *Standards* versus *behavior.* Petting as the terminal stage of activity, Christensen observes, presents a picture opposite to what might be expected, especially with females. The percentages who said they had petted but stopped there (no coitus) were, respectively, for males, 33, 40, and 38, and for females, 34, 56, and 65. The explanations of the higher percentages of petting for the more conservative cultures with greater restrictiveness regarding premarital coitus is the more frequent resort to petting as a coital substitute. Experience with premarital coitus differed in the expected directions: for males, the percentages were 64, 51, and 39, and for females, 60, 29, and 9, respectively. A discovery of the study was that more Danish students approved premarital coitus than had experienced it, whereas the reverse was true for the American samples. As concerns the incidence of feelings of guilt surrounding the first occasion, the percentages were in the order of 2 for Denmark, 13 for the midwestern, and 26 for the intermountain samples.

Characteristics preferred and objectionable in mates.—The account and interpretation at this point of studies pertaining to dating head more directly toward courtship, first, by drawing on those concerned with conduct and characteristics preferred or objectionable in companions in dating or courtship and, second, by digest of a substantial inquiry into courtship in a number of relationships. Three of the studies depended upon are by the same investigator (8, 9, 10), one at the high school and two at the collegiate level. Although the procedures in reporting outcomes for the two levels are not alike, comparison permits one to note similarities and differences. The investigation at the lower level (9) is on a stratified sample of 2,500 representative of the nation's high school population. These students were first asked to rank a list of twenty items from the standpoint of their importance in making or accepting a date. The first six items which emerged highest in ranking, from the highest downward were: (1) Is physically and mentally fit; (2) Is dependable, can be trusted; (3) Takes pride in personal appearance and manners; (4) Has pleasant disposition and sense of humor; (5) Is considerate of me and others; (6) Acts own age, is not childish. The rank order correlation between the rankings for the two sexes was .73, suggesting similarity, but there were some differences. Boys followed expectations by wanting a good cook and housekeeper, and girls by "stressing the importance of a good financial prospect." Boys also placed greater stress on physical attractiveness and nonuse of tobacco. Girls considered the following relatively more desirable: moderation regarding intimacy, parental approval, and consideration toward others.

The patterns of objectionability in dating of high school boys and girls differed significantly. In this aspect boys were characterized as being "less inhibited and more careless, thoughtless, disrespectful, sex-driven, and louder than their partners in dating." Girls were characterized as being "less natural and more touchy, money-minded, unresponsive, childish, and flighty."

Results of rating characteristics preferred in mates in dating by 674 students (332 men and 342 women) at Purdue University (10) who were neither engaged nor married are presented in Table 4.8. The items are listed in the order of ranking by the men for characteristics preferred in women. A glance down the columns reveals that the rankings by the sexes are rather similar, with all but a few of the ranks not more than two steps apart. The only characteristic that men rate notably higher than women is "health and vitality," and the two characteristics rated higher by women are "affectionate" and "conventional sex standards."

Because of the somewhat simpler manner of statistical presentation than Christensen used in the Purdue study, the ratings on objectionability of traits and practices are quoted in Table 4.9 from another study of attitudes by him (8)—one based on ratings by students at Brigham Young University. Christensen expressed the opinion that, except as to drinking and smoking, attitudes in Mormon culture are not much different from those on other campuses. Comparison of the rankings on objectionability by the two sexes of the traits listed are again for the most part rather similar, although differing more widely than for preferred characteristics: differences of four steps or more appear for seven of the twenty items. For three of these the rankings are higher by men. These concern flirting with others,

TABLE 4.8
RANK OF CERTAIN CHARACTERISTICS PREFERRED IN MATES BY COLLEGE MEN AND WOMEN*

Characteristic	Rank by	
	Men	Women
Pleasant disposition	1	2
Well groomed and mannered	2	3
Sociability	3	1
Emotional maturity	4	6
Physical attractiveness	5	5
Considerateness	6	4
Traditional "M" and "F" role	7	9
Health and vitality	8	14
Stable and dependable	9	11
Rates socially	10	10
Affectionate	11½	7
Intellectual stimulation	11½	12
Poised and confident	13	13
Conventional sex standards	14	8
Ambitious and industrious	15	16
Romantic appeal	16	15
Similarity of backgrounds	17	17
Religious nature	18½	18
Normal heredity	18½	20
Family-mindedness	20	21
Does not drink	21	22
Good financial prospect	22	19
Good homemaker	23	23
Does not smoke	24	24

SOURCE: Christensen (*10*).
*Ranking based on weighted values reported.

wanting expensive things, and never thinking to compliment. For the remaining four, the ranking by women is higher: wanting too much necking and petting, preferring to date only popular "numbers," staying too late, and being indefinite about dates.

An older investigation by Mather (*43*) made a direct comparison of the anonymous rankings of traits by high school and by college students. Students at the high school level were sophomores, juniors, and seniors in Ithaca, New York, and those in college were all above freshman level in Cornell University. Little would be added concerning the understanding of preferred traits in courtship to that provided by the materials previously cited by reporting the list of traits with the rankings reported, but one inference from the investigation is important. This bears on the relative stability of the rankings at the two levels. At the high school level there was extensive variability and overlapping in the rankings and this condition persisted through all three years. At the college level there was a much nearer approach to consensus in the rankings. This was reflected in the interquartile range of the rankings, which was much smaller for college than for

TABLE 4.9
RANKING OF TRAITS AND PRACTICES BY DEGREE OF OBJECTIONABILITY BY MALES AND FEMALES

Traits and Practices	Degree of Objectionability by	
	Males	Females
1. Uses profanity or vulgarity in speech	1	3
2. Indulges in drinking and smoking	2	2
3. Wants too much necking and petting	8	1
4. Lacks etiquette or is crude and unrefined	5	4
5. Has bad disposition—argues, complains, finds fault	3	5
6. Is a poor sport—lacks sense of humor, gets mad easily	4	6
7. Flirts with others or brags about other dates	6	12
8. Prefers to date only popular "numbers" or acts as if doing partner a favor	12	7
9. Is too talkative and loud around others	7	10
10. Is a poor conversationalist—lacks interesting ideas	9	8
11. Is too serious, jealous, possessive, and monopolistic	11	11
12. Stays too late—doesn't know when to say goodnight	15	9
13. Indulges in dishonest flattery	16	13
14. Wants always to do expensive things	10	16
15. Is prone to worry excessively and to get moody	13	14
16. Never thinks to offer compliments or say thanks	14	18
17. Is indefinite about a date—just drops in	19	15
18. Is too quiet, self-conscious, shy, or backward	17	19
19. Is late in calling or in being ready for a date	18	17
20. Is a poor dancer	20	20

SOURCE: Christensen (8).

high school students. A manifest conclusion is that the vicinity of the early college years is the period of rapid movement toward stabilization of these preferences.

Courtship among college students.—The investigation of courtship was made by Kirkpatrick and Caplow (37) at the University of Minnesota. It was made by questionnaire and the respondents were mainly students in first and middle-level courses in sociology. The average age was 22 years, which is more than that of community college students, although the distributions of the ages of these students and of community college students would overlap in considerable degree. The total number of students responding was 399, including 141 men and 258 women. The total number of affairs reported on was 896, with 314 for men and 582 for women. Of the total of 896 love affairs, 386 were first affairs, and 300, 162, and 48 were second, third, and fourth affairs, respectively.

The percentages of the affairs were endogamous by religious affiliation for men as follows: Protestant, 79.5; Catholic, 58.5; Jewish, 72.4. For women, the percentages were: Protestant, 80.8; Catholic, 38.0; Jewish, 84.9. The percentages are all high, except for Catholics, especially Catholic

TABLE 4.10
PERCENTAGES OF MALES AND FEMALES REPORTING CERTAIN REASONS FOR INADEQUACY OF PRESENT OPPORTUNITIES TO MEET MEMBERS OF OPPOSITE SEX

Response	Male	Female
No time	42.9	36.9
No money	61.2	11.7
Meet wrong kind	72.2	13.6
Personality limitations	10.2	11.7
Lack social contacts	21.8	48.5
No fraternity (sorority)	18.4	19.4
Other reasons	12.2	14.6

SOURCE: Kirkpatrick and Caplow (37, Table 8).

TABLE 4.11
PERCENTAGE DISTRIBUTION OF RESPONSES OF MALES AND FEMALES TO THE QUESTION "DID THE GIRL TAKE THE INITIATIVE IN TELEPHONING, VISITING, ETC.?"

Responses	Males	Females
Never	29.4	56.5
Occasionally	54.8	39.5
Often	11.3	3.6
Very often	4.5	0.4
Always	0.0	0.0
Totals	100.0	100.0

SOURCE: Kirkpatrick and Caplow (37, Table 13).

women. The authors speculate that the exception may be owing to a greater tolerance by this denominational group in premarital courtship relationships, but think it more probable that Catholics, particularly Catholic girls, "are handicapped as a minority group on the courtship market and, rather than be left out, seek or accept relationships with persons of another religion."

The students reported on a checklist the reasons for inadequacy of opportunities to meet members of the opposite sex. The reasons, with percentages of response, are shown in Table 4.10. It should be mentioned that some students checked more than one reason, so that the totals of the percentages in both columns exceed 100. The categories of reasons are largely self-explanatory and the differences between the sexes in the main plausible.

Inquiry into the proportion of dating expenses paid for by the male found nearly all students of both sexes reporting "all" or "most." The percentage in these two classifications for males totaled 96, and for females 97.5. With minor exceptions the practice in this respect followed what is regarded as convention.

TABLE 4.12
STATUS OF COURTSHIP AFFAIRS AS REPORTED BY MALES AND FEMALES

Response	Males	Females
Married	2.9	1.6
Engaged	2.9	4.8
Continued, but not married or engaged	21.2	22.6
Broken off	73.0	71.0
Totals	100.0	100.0

SOURCE: Kirkpatrick and Caplow (37, Table 17).

TABLE 4.13
CAUSES OF BREAKOFF OF COURTSHIP AS REPORTED BY MALES AND FEMALES

Cause	Males	Females
Parents	5.2	8.6
Friends	3.1	5.8
Subject's interest in another person	15.1	32.2
Partner's interest in another person	29.7	15.3
Mutual loss of interest	46.9	38.1
Totals	100.0	100.0

SOURCE: Kirkpatrick and Caplow (37, Table 21).

Responses to the question "Did the girl take the initiative in telephoning, visiting, etc." yielded the percentage distributions reported in Table 4.11. Very predominantly the percentage distributions follow the conventions. The authors' comment is, "One feels that the women in the sample like to present themselves in a conventional, respectable, and sought-after role."

The large number of second, third, and fourth courtships reported above means that large proportions were broken off. The expectation is affirmed by the percentages for the last response listed in Table 4.12, as the proportions approach three-fourths of all. Small percentages only had resulted in either marriage or engagement, while a full fifth were still in process without having resulted in marriage or engagement.

The distributions of causes of breakoffs are presented in Table 4.13. Small proportions only are accounted for by discouragement or interferences of parents and friends. Shift of the subject's or the partner's interest to another person together account for approximately equal proportions (44.8 and 47.5 per cent for males and females, respectively), although more females than males attributed the change of interest to themselves, while more males attributed it to their partners. About as many responses attributed the breakoffs to mutual loss of interest.

Emotional reactions on account of breakoffs are reported in Table 4.14. No remarkable differences between the sexes emerge for any single reaction. When the bitter-to-crushed reactions are added, the subtotals are 28.0 per cent for males and 33.9 per cent for females. When the indifferent-

TABLE 4.14
PERCENTAGE DISTRIBUTION OF EMOTIONAL STATES FROM BREAKOFF AS REPORTED BY MALES AND FEMALES

Reaction	Males	Females
Bitter	5.9	4.4
Hurt	10.4	14.3
Angry	3.3	3.5
Remorseful	6.6	6.7
Crushed	1.8	5.0
Indifferent	19.4	16.2
Relieved	15.2	16.8
Satisfied	11.5	8.5
Happy	4.4	3.5
Mixed regret and relief	21.9	21.1
Totals	100.0	100.0

SOURCE: Kirkpatrick and Caplow (37, Table 22).

TABLE 4.15
ESTIMATES OF THE DURATION OF PERIODS OF ADJUSTMENT FOLLOWING BREAKOFFS IN COURTSHIP

Estimate	Males	Females
None	51.4	49.4
Several weeks	33.6	19.5
Several months	7.7	19.5
A year	5.0	6.3
Several years	2.3	5.3
Total	100.0	100.0

SOURCE: Kirkpatrick and Caplow (37, Table 25).

to-happy reactions are similarly added, the subtotals are 50.5 and 45.0 per cent, respectively. This comparison yields an appreciable preponderance of disturbed reaction for females, reflecting in some degree the greater sentimentality in affairs ascribed to them. Almost equal proportions of the two sexes report feelings of mixed regret and relief.

As may be seen in Table 4.15, about half of both sexes reported that no time was required for readjustment following the breakoffs. The distributions for the remaining breakoffs disclose a tendency toward longer periods for adjustment for females, which is in accord with the preponderance of bitter-to-crushed reactions found in Table 4.14 for this sex.

Social Policy

A controversial area.—The foregoing sections of the chapter have reviewed available evidence concerning sexual and dating behavior and attitudes with emphasis on what this behavior and these attitudes are during later high school and early college years. To some extent, the portrayal has reached down into years of early adolescence as well as beyond the early college years, but this has been in part because of the dearth of studies bearing directly on the age-group that is the concern of this book and in part to obtain a better understanding than otherwise of the trends during this particular age-span. Our treatment turns now to what may be referred to as social policy touching these aspects of the behavior of youth. This area of policy, because it is concerned with control or direction of behavior in response to one of the human's most potent drives, is highly emotional and controversial. The purpose here is not to crusade, but rather to review the various positions, so that the reader may note what they are and compare them with whatever may be his personal formulation of values.

The positions in treatises on adolescence.—The general positions reviewed here are those presented in or derived by interpretation from treatises on adolescence published to serve as textbooks. These textbooks are eight in number with recent dates of copyright ranging from 1952 to 1963. In two instances the books are revisions, with new copyrights. The books were among those conveniently available on the subject of adolescence and were selected without bias as to position, the chief criterion being that they are intended and used for instructional purposes in higher institutions. A limitation on complete applicability to our purpose is that they are primarily intended for use in courses for secondary school teachers-in-training and focus on early and middle rather than on later adolescence when sex drive is at its maximum, although most of them comprehend the full period of adolescence. In preliminary description of these books it is significant to indicate that they vary widely in their extent of treatment of sexual behavior and attitudes. This is suggested by the fact that one of them has three entries only under "sex" in its index, while in one at the other extreme these entries, under "sex," "sexual," and "sexuality," extend through almost three pages.

In their treatment of sexual behavior two of the eight books may be characterized as advocating conformity to the conventional code which favors continence. One of these declares, at the point of addressing the subjects of dating, petting, and premarital sex relations, "It is assumed ... that it is important to the adolescent to observe the verbally expressed mores of our society and that this can be successfully done by building attitudes that point to the control and delay of sexual appetites" (*3*, 454).

Four of the books appear to make no direct statement of position, but it may be inferred from the manner of treatment that they assume the social preferability of conformity to the code. Still another book seems slanted neither toward conformity nor toward permissiveness, but reports evidence concerning behavior with objectivity and, insofar as it takes a position, is concerned mainly with the individual's achieving an adjusted personality.

The position of the remaining book (2) can not be so briefly and easily generalized. It lays emphasis on necessity of sex education and counseling (428–33). This is also done by most of the others, but Ausubel would carry this education beyond the merely factual and descriptive, where it customarily stops, and would emphasize the psychoaffectional aspects of sex behavior. He is of the opinion that we "must not presume to tell an individual how to behave in an activity that is primarily personal rather than social in nature" and that "the individual still retains his right of self-determination by being free to accept or reject the goals and standards offered him, providing that his behavior does not infringe upon the rights and interests of others" (430). At a later point in his discussion Ausubel says that this psychoaffectional concept of sexuality presumes a "high degree of ego-involvement which disallows a casual attitude toward sex activity" and the "goal toward which it strives is the monogamous type of marital relationship which we have already adopted in our society" (431). His further observation is (432), "If our culture would adopt and teach this point of view, psychosexual development would proceed accordingly, and adolescent boys and girls would really feel this way about sex. The problems of psychophysical sex needs would for the most part vanish. And if marriage could occur at a reasonably early age, the sex turmoil which now characterizes adolescent development would be a thing of the past."

The decreasing age of marriage.—The last sentence quoted from Ausubel suggests the question of what is taking place with us in respect to ages of marriage. Assertions are often made that the age of marriage is lowering and figures are sometimes cited in support. Table 4.16 reports the percentages of males and females of certain age-groups reported as married for census years from 1890 through 1960. The age-groups included are the younger ones in the married population, since they are nearest those attending college. It may be noted that the percentages for all three age-groups for both sexes increased during the 70-year span, although not at uniform rates. Facts of importance to our point of interest is that the most rapid increases took place in the more recent period (1940–60), that the proportion of women under 20 who were married in 1960 was about four times that for men, although it only rose to about a sixth of all, and that for the 20–24 group the percentages married had risen to 45.9 and 69.5 per cent, respectively, for men and women. It is known that the trend is reflected in the colleges, and some estimates have placed the percentage in some coeducational institutions at 20, or even higher. The trend reflects a rather marked shift in practice and, presumably, in social policy.

Pros and cons of steady dating.—A subject of controversy in the area of sexual and dating behavior is "going steady," or steady dating. Report earlier in the chapter* on the attitudes of girls toward this practice found both positive and negative opinions concerning it gaining with age from early to later adolescence, indicating that young people see both advantages and disadvantages. Advantages mentioned by youth include thorough

TABLE 4.16
PERCENTAGES OF MALES AND FEMALES UNDER 20 YEARS OF AGE, 20 TO 24 INCLUSIVE, AND UNDER 25 REPORTED AS MARRIED AT SUCCESSIVE CENSUS YEARS, 1890–1960

Census Year	Males			Females		
	All Under 20	20–24	All Under 25	All Under 20	20–24	All Under 25
1890	0.5	18.9	19.4	9.7	46.7	56.4
1900	1.1	21.6	22.7	11.4	46.5	57.9
1910	1.2	24.0	25.2	11.7	49.7	61.4
1920	2.4	28.3	30.7	13.0	52.3	65.3
1930	1.8	28.1	29.9	13.0	51.6	64.6
1940	1.8	27.4	29.2	11.9	51.3	63.2
1950	4.7	39.9	44.6	17.4	65.5	83.0
1960	4.4	45.9	50.3	16.8	69.5	86.3

SOURCE: United States Census of Population, *Summary: Detailed Characteristics*. Adapted from Table 177, pp. 436–38.

acquaintance with another person, assurance of a companion of the other sex at social functions, and making it possible to act oneself instead of trying to make a good first impression. Psychologists have translated such advantages into attainment of "prestige" and "feelings of security." Disadvantages mentioned by youth include being without a partner for events if the "steady" happens to be away and preventing the development of interests that are derived from variety in associates—in other words, the curtailment of social experience.

Society's concern, while including limitation of social experience imposed by steady dating, goes much further. Although it sees the dependence of successful courtship on "going steady," it is inclined to deplore the practice in early and middle adolescence and prior to marriageable age. The concern is over intimacies encouraged by recurrent and continued companionship which can lead to pregnancies and/or early marriages, sometimes during high school years. One study (5) reported 40 per cent of the girls in high school marriages premaritally pregnant. The seriousness of such evidence

*See p. 159.

is increased by the relatively high rate of divorces for marriages of those under 20 when compared with those of older persons, as reported some years ago by the Bureau of the Census. Ausubel, in the passage quoted above, does not tell us what the "reasonably early age" for marriage to which he refers is, but for most persons conversant with the attendant problems it would not often fall within the high school period. One writer on steady dating at the high school level, Hutson (*31*), makes the proposal to offset its hazards, for a "limited contract" for going steady for a month, to be followed by a "no-contract" month. He identifies the advantages and disadvantages of the plan, and clearly seems to favor it, but no school at the time of writing, to his knowledge, had such a plan in operation.

Concerning masturbation and homosexuality.—In the review of positions on social policy as presented in the textbooks on adolescence and summarized in the opening paragraphs of this section, the sexual outlets in focus are petting and premarital intercourse. These are also the preoccupation in the consideration of existing and proposed codes to be canvassed below. Summation of positions bearing on the two other main manifestations of sexual behavior, masturbation and homosexuality, is in order at this point.

Most of the textbooks on adolescence that were examined acknowledge the high percentages of autoeroticism in youth, with almost all boys and a smaller proportion of girls indulging in it at some time in their lives. They also accept the medical opinion that the practice does not result in physical or mental damage and are concerned primarily with excessive indulgence, accompanied by fantasies, and with feelings of guilt and inclinations for withdrawal from normal and wholesome associations. It is believed that a program that includes ample and engrossing physical and other recreational activities with congenial companions will operate to reduce the urge toward autoeroticism.

Discussions of homosexuality in the treatises on adolescence are mainly very brief to nonexistent. Those dealing with it mention that interest in it is transitory with most boys who engage in it and that girls less frequently engage in it, although there is some increase with age among college women. Homosexuality is held to have deep roots and to emerge from complex causes, some going back to infancy, and the reader is admonished that only "highly trained experts" should undertake remediation of what is accepted as a pathological condition. Recommendations for prevention of homosexuality speak of multiplying wholesome opportunities for heterosexual social activities.

Concerning standards of premarital conduct.—At the close of the first section of this chapter, dealing with sexual behavior, reference was made to Rubin's assertion that, despite the changes that have taken place since the turn of the century, primarily in females, "the tempo of change in sex behavior and mores is not a rapid one." It may be judged from the nature and the frequency of discussion of sex behavior in the current news media and in popular magazines, especially concerning this behavior in colleges and universities, that many persons would not accept this generalization. Against the acceptability of the currently prevalent opinion of sexual permissiveness there is always the likelihood that it may be based on a few individual instances sensationally reported rather than on large-scale objective inquiries like those by Kinsey and Ehrmann.

However, when a person of the reputability of Ehrmann himself expresses such an opinion, it is deserving of consideration. Ehrmann has recently referred to the changes as "the sexual revolution since World War I" (*18*). He proceeds to explain the change as being primarily in the behavior of females and relatively much less in that of males. In discussing this main component of change he expresses the opinion that perhaps its socially most significant aspect is that premarital expression has become "democratized." The shift toward equalization has affected the female chiefly, but has spread also to "young people from all social strata and from all geographical areas, both rural and urban." He also indicates that the patterns and attitudes of males and females are becoming similar and that these patterns of equality are even more characteristic of the college educated than of those who never went beyond elementary and high school.

In considering the problem of standards, or codes, of premarital sexual behavior for youth, it may be well to note again in what degree restraints were in effect on the dating behavior represented in Ehrmann's original project. At the expense of repetition, it may be pointed out that, in Table 4.6, about two-thirds of the entire group of males were reported as stopping before Stage D and two-fifths of the second group before this stage in their current dating. It should be recalled that for these males a large proportion of these dates were with off-campus girls, many of them with girls of lower social class. The proportions of the entire group of girls who reported not going as far as Stage D were fully as large as for boys, and of the second group was much larger than for boys. While the proportion of boys who advanced to Stage F was in excess of a third of all, that for girls was only about a tenth of all. Table 4.7, reporting on patterns of control, indicates that, although the proportion of boys who would not go further than the stages reported was small, the proportion of girls who would not approached a third of all and the proportion reporting that "neither tried" was around a half for both sexes. Even though these data allow for widely varying degrees of permissiveness among individuals, they are very far from signifying sexual anarchy, sometimes currently charged against most of the college population. Certainly for most of the population represented and for the time in which they apply, which was in the vicinity of the 1950s, they establish the existence and operation among youth of standards of sex behavior, albeit at the same time they confirm the presence of intimacies for a considerable proportion of the daters.

It is in place here at least to mention a more recent publication purporting to ascertain the trends of change in sex behavior. A book of recent publication which undertakes to review these trends, including some special attention to premarital intimacy, is Packard's *The Sexual Wilderness* (*44*, Ch. 9). Despite the intimation in this title of widespread relaxation of traditional mores in this area, no firm conclusion of marked changes in *behavior* is established, in large part because populations and procedures in the later inquiries differ from those in earlier investigations. However, there appeared to be justification for an inference of some change in *attitudes*, as, for example, away from separate standards for the two sexes and from extreme concern for virginity in the female. In the absence of further evidence, one can only conjecture on the extent of correlation of change in behavior and attitudes. Whether the changes have been revolutionary or only moderate during the last decade or so we cannot know without further objective studies comparable to those previously made; but whichever of these rates is found to be the true one, the following recent observations by Ehrmann are highly relevant (*18*): "The crux of the dilemma has always been and still is, that youth themselves are expected to mix freely males with females in enjoyable social situations and at the same time exercise sexual restraint. This pleasurable and profitable association was expected to solve the contending cultural values of the sinfulness of sex and the delights of romanticism. The effective control of sexual expression primarily by way of personal restraints of young people is virtually a unique expectation in the history of culture. Other cultures have either permitted premarital sexual activities under rigorous social controls, which has been a solution for the majority, or prohibited sexual activities through the segregation of the sexes by the isolation of the females or by a system of chaperonage. Our own current American youth culture, with almost no help from successive parental generations, developed, or 'invented,' new social devices for coping with this complex situation, and they have met with an amazing degree of success. These new adjustments are dating, petting, going steady, and an elaborate code of sex conduct. . . . In our examination of what young people are doing, we may find some things which are disconcerting. But, before becoming too alarmed, we should remember . . . that young people are not drifting willy-nilly through their sexual problems, but that with and without the help of concerned adults they have already reached a partial solution to a new way of life. . . ."

It should be added that at the point of naming the detailed adjustments youth is making, Ehrmann said parenthetically that in the list should be included early marriage. The fact that it is being so used is confirmed by evidence previously presented in this section.

This discussion of premarital standards may well be brought to a close by reporting two recent classifications of standards, one by Reiss in his book *Premarital Sex Standards in America* (50) and the other presented by Rubin at a Work Conference on Current Sex Mores participated in by fifty men and women deans and counselors. Reiss lists four main sexual standards as operative in America, namely, (a) abstinence, (b) double standard, (c) permissiveness without affection, and (d) permissiveness with affection. He believes that a and b are declining, that c will never have many adherents, and that d is probably the emerging standard. This distribution he ascribed to "the higher educational and occupational segments of our population, since it is predominantly those segments which are known through research." He refers to the emerging standard as only the "dominant" standard, because "there will always be groups who accept other standards" (50, 249–51).

The formulation by Rubin* "categorized six value systems which now exist side by side in the present transitional period in morality":

(1) "Traditional repressive asceticism" which maintains that sex is essentially bad and shameful, but, unfortunately, necessary.

(2) "Enlightened asceticism" holds that society has always had to maintain a delicate balance between freedom and responsibility in human relationships.

(3) "Humanistic liberalism" contends that the negative fear approach to sexual morality must be replaced by a positive approach concerned, broadly speaking, with the fulfillment of human potentialities.

(4) "Humanistic radicalism" proposes that society should incline in the direction of making it possible for children to have biologically a completely natural sex life.

(5) "Fun morality" upholds the viewpoint that "sex is fun" and the more sex fun a human being has, the better and psychologically sounder he or she is likely to be.

(6) "Sexual anarchy" is based upon the Freudian notion that "sex" repression creates neuroses and that, therefore, all repression is harmful and should be done away with."

It is reported that the consensus of the Work Conference participants was in favor of "enlightened asceticism" or "humanistic liberalism."

Education and guidance.—The final aspect of social policy to be considered here is that finding expression through education and guidance in matters of sex. As the source of suggestion and recommendation, the treatment here capitalizes once more the position taken by the eight textbooks

*"Student Sex Standards Stir Controversy among Educators," *College and University Bulletin,* 16 (Dec. 1, 1963), 2.

on adolescence. Most of these, as previously observed, have the limitation of primary focus on early and middle adolescence; nevertheless, they are the best recurrent source of advice in this area and most of them discuss proposals applicable to the age-level that is our main concern. Two of the books contain no entries on sex education and guidance in their indexes and no such treatments in the text. Consideration in the remaining books ranges from meager to all but comprehensive. Identifiable directives emerging from the digest are as follows:

(1) All the authors admit or imply a *need* for education and guidance with respect to sex. This need is posited on conclusions from investigations of the sources of information as reported by children and by adults from their experiences in childhood. These investigations have found age-mates and companions as predominant sources, which too often mean misinformation and distortion; parents as a much less frequent source; and the school as an infrequent source. Girls receive more of their information from parents (mothers) than boys and there is some evidence that information from parents is on the increase, especially in the population with more education.

(2) A consensus also contends that the education should *begin with the home and parents* and be continued there through childhood and youth. However, all likewise assign an important role in sex education to the *school,* this term being inclusive of elementary school, secondary school, and college.

(3) Two of the books list only physical aspects of sex as appropriate. It is contended by the others that sex education should *not be restricted to physical and physiological facts,* as is sometimes done, but should *extend to the psychological, emotional, social, and ethical aspects* of sex and sex behavior.

(4) As might be expected, some of the authors refer to the obvious necessity of *gearing sex education to the age-level* of youth. Mention is made of the appropriateness of bringing up physical aspects for younger children and reserving emphasis on psychological, social, and ethical aspects for later high school and early college years.

(5) As may be inferred from the third point, the *scope of content* suggested for school instruction in matters relating to sex varies widely. At one extreme, a few authors list only a few topics. At the other extreme another author lists all the topics outlined for the purpose by the American Social Hygiene Association. These, somewhat abbreviated, include: (1) the family in a democracy; (2) problems of the adolescent as a member of the family; (3) boy-girl relations (respect for the opposite sex, normality of sex yearnings, dating, petting, going steady, reproduction); (4) marriage (courting, marriage customs, divorce); (5) problems of homemaking

(place of family in community, economics of the home, culture of the home, management of the home, child care); (6) social problems involving individual, family, and community; (7) governmental and international problems for the betterment of mankind (better housing; reduction of maternal and infant mortality; care and correction of defectives, delinquents, dependents; recreational facilities for youth; medical science and human beings; international phases of social hygiene). This author discusses also the preferability of distributing these topics where appropriate to existing courses like physiology and hygiene, biology, social science, and home economics, or concentrating them in inclusive courses. Because of the risk of missing some of the significant areas, he leans toward the integrated treatment in composite courses.

(6) Two authors distinguished between the *roles of sex education and sex guidance*. They would have sex education concerned only with general topics and problems in sexual development and expression and leave to guidance and counseling exclusively the responsibility of dealing with the special problems of individual youth.

(7) Half the treatments discuss the *competence of teachers and counselors*. Among characteristics specified are: being adequately prepared, being well adjusted, and having high rapport with young people. Two writers add the suggestion that these persons be married, but do not rule out the possibility that single persons could meet the necessary qualifications.

(8) One writer urges the *segregation of the sexes for sex instruction*. It is his opinion that "verbal exploration of even the most matter-of-factly accepted and understood aspects of sex in the presence of both sexes tends to produce or promote an attitude of social tolerance which accepts or encourages physical exploration" (56, 327).

Summary

Illustrations of evidence concerning the sexual behavior of later adolescents with a focus on the college-going population began by citing from the Kinsey reports. The total sexual outlet, in frequency of orgasm, for males is much greater than for females and declines somewhat from early adolescence into adulthood. The total outlet for females increases in some degree and is somewhat greater for subjects of the college-going level than for the total sample, although it rises to little more than one-fifth of that for males in any age-group. Almost all the measures of accumulative incidence by the ages of 15, 20, and 25 for the several types of sexual experience, both for the total samples and for the college-going population, are much larger for males than females. There are also notable shifts with successive age-groups for both sexes in some of the experiences, for example, downward for masturbation and upward for coitus.

Wide individual differences were found for both sexes, but somewhat wider for females than for males. The differences were both in total outlet and in patterns of sources of outlet.

Of the hypothetical influences on sexuality, age at adolescence, parental occupation, rural or urban residence, religious background, and generation or decade of birth, of which all but the first are mainly environmental, only age at adolescence, rural or urban residence, and religious background were found to affect total outlet. Total outlet declines appreciably for males with increasing age at adolescence, but not for females. The outlet is somewhat but not markedly larger for males of urban as compared with rural residence. Median outlets of subjects of both sexes were larger for inactive than for active Protestants, Catholics, and Jews. Males were found to be more often subject to sexual arousal by all but three of a long list of "psychological factors." For these three (moving pictures, reading romantic literature, and being bitten) the percentage of females was larger than for males.

Findings from evidence in the Kinsey report, made by interview, are corroborated by those obtained by questionnaire with a male population of comparable age-groups. In the main, the findings of other investigations into sexual behavior presented bear out the conclusions from the Kinsey project. A study by Pullias found that college freshmen believed that masturbation works serious physical, mental, or moral damage. This is now held to be contrary to the fact, except, as Pullias indicates, that the superstition may produce feelings of guilt and fear, which can give rise to problems of adjustment.

The term "dating" has come to be applied to all premarital paired association of the sexes, although it also includes courtship which is that aspect of dating aimed at finding a mate for marriage. The folkways of youth have expanded premarital association of the sexes far beyond the function of courtship and it currently serves many other purposes, among other things, giving youth broader experience, ability in adjusting to others, and enrichment and development of personality.

Investigation finds that dating has already begun for almost half of both sexes as freshmen in high school and that it involves about four-fifths of the boys and a somewhat larger proportion of girls as seniors. The expectation that the age of beginning of dating is influenced by the age of onset of adolescence and that girls, because of their earlier maturing than boys, begin dating at younger ages, is hardly borne out by the facts; this induces the belief that the beginnings of dating behavior are, rather than being solely biologically determined, in large part products of the culture.

An investigation by questionnaire and interview by Ehrmann of dating behavior at the college level ascertained the stages to which it was being carried. Males tended to go to more advanced stages than females, and this was explained in part by the high ratio at the time of males to females in the institution represented and the resort of the males to off-campus companions, some of whom were of lower social classes than the males. Behavior during dating was reported as primarily, although not generally, initiated by the male and it "went no further" most often because "neither tried" and next most often because the "girl would not." Ehrmann concluded from his study that sexual expression in the female is "profoundly related to being in love and to going steady" while "male sexuality is more indirectly and less exclusively associated with romanticism and intimacy relationships."

An inquiry into sentimental attitudes of college girls supports this conclusion by Ehrmann by finding that very large proportions reported that when they were in love, being loved by the male they love is "the most important thing in the world" or "very important." Another investigation found the most recurrent reasons given by college girls for petting, almost all of whom had reported engaging in it, were infatuation, curiosity, and "because others did it." Two investigations which were digested reported rather high frequencies of male aggression in dating offensive to the female and still another resulted in a refinement in classification which distinguished "commitment" and "noncommitment" steadies, with the former having plans for marriage and the latter not contemplating marriage but being only for convenience in college life.

In an intercultural comparison it was found that Danish (representing Scandinavian) university students approved earliest intimacy in the courtship process, students in a midwestern university next, and students in an intermountain institution with many Mormon students latest. Differences in other attitudes were for the most part analogous. Standards of behavior likewise differed in the same directions, except for petting, for which the proportions tended to increase from Danish to midwestern to intermountain, the explanation being the more frequent resort in the more conservative cultures to petting as a coital substitute.

Certain studies reporting the rating of preferred and objectionable characteristics in dating companions were digested. Attempts to summarize them are hindered by the long lists of characteristics appraised, but it may be said that the rankings by the two sexes are more alike than different. One investigation found the preferences for characteristics to progress rather rapidly toward stabilization during early college years.

A large-scale investigation of courtships among college students found a smaller proportion "endogamous" by denominational affiliation for Catholic than Protestant or Jewish. Reasons for inadequacy of opportunity to meet members of the opposite sex were varied and differed somewhat for the two sexes. Payment of dating expenses almost always followed the conventions. Observance of convention was in large part true for initiative in courtship as indicated by responses to the question "Did the girl take initiative in telephoning, visiting, etc.?" although the investigators indicated their feeling that the women in the sample liked "to present themselves in a conventional, respectable, and sought-after role."

The large number of second, third, and fourth courtships reported in this investigation means that large proportions—almost three-fourths—had been broken off. The breakoffs were attributed in about equal proportions to the subject's or the partner's interest in another person and to mutual loss of interest. Emotional reactions because of breakoffs found the proportions of bitter-to-crushed, of indifferent-to-happy, and of mixed regret and relief for the two sexes not far from equal, but with a partial predominance of bitter-to-crushed for females and of indifferent-to-happy for males. This partial difference is reflected in a limited difference toward longer periods of adjustment for females.

The issue of social policy touching sexual behavior and attitudes, because the area is so heavily emotional, is highly controversial. Discussion of it above was chiefly in relation to positions taken or implied in representative textbooks on adolescence, eight in number. The general positions of these books vary. Some advocate continence and respect for conventional mores; others, while not openly advocating such respect, appear to do so by implication; still another, which seems slanted neither toward conformity nor toward permissiveness, appears mainly to be concerned with the individual's achieving an adjusted personality. The remaining book places emphasis on the necessity of sex education and counseling leading toward a "psycho-affectional concept of sexuality presuming a high degree of ego-involvement which disallows a casual attitude toward sex activity" and strives toward the goal of "the monogamous type of marital relationship which we have already adopted in our society" (2, 431).

The writer just quoted hinted at the helpfulness in preventing sex turmoil of marriage "at a reasonably early age," but does not indicate what this age may be. Facts presented show the proportions marrying at younger ages in the United States to be on the increase, especially from 1940 to 1960, and the lower age is being reflected in the proportions of married students attending college. The issue turns on the particular age, and the relative incidence of divorce and other considerations suggest it should not be during high school years.

The pros and cons of steady dating were reviewed. Although society sees the dependence of successful courtship on "going steady," it is inclined to deplore the practice in early and middle adolescence and prior to marriageable age.

Most of the textbooks mentioned above as having been examined for their positions on sexual behavior and attitudes acknowledge the high percentages of autoeroticism in youth, with almost all boys and a smaller proportion of girls indulging in it at some time in their lives. The concern they express does not relate to mental or physical damage, which is now discredited, but to possibilities of feelings of guilt and withdrawal from normal and wholesome associations. The discussions of homosexuality direct attention to its deep roots and the need for reliance on expert help for remediation of what is regarded as a pathological condition. Recommendations for prevention point to multiplication of wholesome opportunities for heterosexual social activities.

Writers disagree on the rate at which behavior reflecting premarital sexual permissiveness is now increasing, one describing it as slow and another, at the other extreme, as "revolutionary." They agree, however, that the rate of change has been more rapid with females than with males. Whatever the rate of change, the studies of behavior also show that large proportions of youth operate restraint on the stages to which dating behavior is carried, the females more than the males, but both sexes in large proportions. This is the more remarkable, as Ehrmann was quoted above as emphasizing, because our society is almost alone in expecting youth to mix freely males with females and at the same time to exercise sexual restraint. The treatment above reviewed two formulations of current standards, one by Reiss who identified four which he labeled as abstinence, double standard, permissiveness without affection, and permissiveness with affection, and of which he believes the last is probably the emerging standard. However, he believes, because of the variation of standards from group to group, that it can hardly be more than the dominant standard. The other formulation was presented by Rubin at a Work Conference on Current Sex Mores and listed six standards ranging from "traditional repressive asceticism" to "sexual anarchy." The consensus of participants in the conference was in favor of the second or third categories in this gradation, namely, "enlightened asceticism" and "humanistic liberalism."

Six of the eight textbooks on adolescence examined for their positions on social policy concerning sexual behavior contain discussions of the problems of education and guidance in this area. All agree on the need for it, this need arising in large part from the misinformation received from companions. They contend that it should begin with the home and parents but should also involve the school. A few of the books mention only physical facts of sex as appropriate but others would extend the instruction to the psychological, emotional, social, and ethical aspects. This wide range of content would require that it be geared to the age-level of the student. One writer urges that the instruction be given in inclusive courses rather than distributed where appropriate to courses like physiology, biology, or social science. Two authors distinguish education and guidance and urge that only general aspects be taught in the courses and personal aspects be left to individual guidance. Other recommendations mention the characteristics of teachers and counselors, who should be adequately prepared, well adjusted, and have high rapport with young people. One writer urges segregation of the sexes for instruction.

References and Bibliography

1. *Adolescent Girls*: A Nation-wide Study of Girls between 11 and 18 Years of Age Made for Girl Scouts of the U.S.A. by Survey Research Center, Institute for Social Research, University of Michigan (no date).
2. Ausubel, David P. *Theory and Problems of Adolescent Development*. New York: Grune and Stratton, 1954.
3. Bernard, Harold W. *Adolescent Development in American Culture*. Yonkers-on-Hudson, N.Y.: World Book Co., 1957.
4. Bromley, Dorothy D., and Britten, Florence H. *Youth and Sex: A Study of 1300 College Students*. New York: Harper & Bros., 1938.
5. Burchinal, L. G. "How Successful are School-Age Marriages?" *Iowa Farm Science*, 13, no. 9 (March, 1959), 7–10.
6. Burgess, Ernest W., and Wallin, Paul. *Engagement and Marriage*. Philadelphia: J. B. Lippincott Co., 1953.
7. Butterfield, Oliver M. *Love Problems of Adolescence*. New York: Teachers College, Columbia University, 1939.
8. Christensen, Harold T. "Courtship Conduct as Viewed by Youth." *Journal of Home Economics*, 40 (April, 1948), 187–88.
9. Christensen, Harold T. "Dating Behavior as Evaluated by High School Students." *American Journal of Sociology*, 57 (May, 1951–52), 580–86.
10. Christensen, Harold T. *Marriage Analysis: Foundations for Successful Family Life*. New York: Ronald Press, 1950.
11. Christensen, Harold T. "Premarital Sex Norms in America and Scandinavia." *Journal of the NAWDC*, 26 (Jan., 1963), 16–21.
12. Cochran, William G., et al. *Statistical Problems of the Kinsey Report on Sexual Behavior in the Human Male*. Washington: American Statistical Association, 1954.
13. Deutsch, Albert. *Sex Habits of American Men: A Symposium on the Kinsey Report*. New York: Prentice-Hall, 1948.
14. Dickinson, R. L., and Bean, Lura. *The Single Woman: A Medical Study in Sex Education*. Baltimore: Williams & Wilkins Co., 1934.
15. Doshay, Lewis J. *The Boy Sex Offender and His Later Career*. New York: Greene & Stratton, 1943.
16. Ehrmann, Winston W. *Premarital Dating Behavior*. New York: Henry Holt & Co., 1959.
17. Ehrmann, Winston W. "Student Cooperation in the Study of Dating Behavior." *Marriage and Family Living*, 14 (Nov., 1952), 322–26.
18. Ehrmann, Winston W. "The Variety and Meaning of Premarital Hetero-sexual Experiences for the College Student." *Journal of the NAWDC*, 26 (Jan., 1963), 22–28.
19. Ellis, Albert. "Love and Family Relationships of American College Girls." *American Journal of Sociology*, 55 (May, 1950), 550–58.
20. Ellis, Albert, and Abarbanel, Albert. *The Encyclopedia of Sexual Behavior*. 2 vols. New York: Hawthorne Books, Inc., 1961.

21. Ernst, Morris L., and Loth, David. *American Sexual Behavior and the Kinsey Report.* New York: Greystone Press, 1948.
22. Finger, Frank W. "Sex Beliefs and Practices Among Male College Students." *Journal of Abnormal and Social Psychology,* 42 (Jan., 1947), 57–67.
23. Folsom, Joseph Kirk. *The Family and Democratic Society.* New York: John Wiley & Sons, Inc., 1943.
24. Ford, Clellan S., and Beach, Frank A. *Patterns of Sexual Behavior.* New York: Harper & Bros., 1951.
25. Geddes, Donald Porter, and Curie, Enid, eds. *About the Kinsey Report: Observations by 11 Experts on Sexual Behavior in the Human Male.* New York: New American Library, 1948.
26. Giedt, F. Harold. "Changes in Sexual Behavior and Attitudes Following Class Study of the Kinsey Report." *Journal of Social Psychology,* 33 (Feb., 1951), 131–41.
27. Ginzberg, Eli, ed. *Values and Ideals of American Youth.* New York: Columbia University Press, 1961.
28. Glick, Paul C., and Landau, Emanuel. "Age as a Factor in Marriage." *American Sociological Review,* 15 (Aug., 1950), 517–29.
29. Himelhoch, Jerome, and Fava, Sylvia F., eds. *Sexual Behavior in American Society: An Appraisal of the First Two Kinsey Reports.* New York: W. W. Norton, 1955.
30. Hohman, Leslie B., and Schaffner, Bertram. "The Sex Lives of Unmarried Men." *American Journal of Sociology,* 52 (May, 1947), 501–8.
31. Hutson, P. W. "Limited Contract for Steadies." *School Activities,* 26 (Oct., 1954), 47–48.
32. Jersild, Arthur T. *The Psychology of Adolescence.* 2d ed. New York: The Macmillan Co., 1963.
33. Kanin, Eugene J. "Male Aggression in Dating-Courtship Relations." *American Journal of Sociology,* 63 (Sept., 1957), 197–204.
34. Kinsey, Alfred C.; Pomeroy, Wardell B.; and Martin, Clyde E. *Sexual Behavior in the Human Male.* Philadelphia: W. B. Saunders Co., 1948.
35. Kinsey, Alfred C.; Pomeroy, Wardell B.; Martin, Clyde E.; and Gebhard, Paul H. *Sexual Behavior in the Human Female.* Philadelphia: W. B. Saunders Co., 1953.
36. Kirkendall, Lester A. "College Youth and Sexual Confusion." *Journal of the NAWDC,* 26 (Jan., 1963), 6–15.
37. Kirkpatrick, Clifford, and Caplow, Theodore. "Courtship in a Group of Minnesota Students." *American Journal of Sociology,* 51 (Sept., 1945), 114–25.
38. Kirkpatrick, Clifford, and Kanin, Eugene, Jr. "Male Sex Aggression on a University Campus." *American Sociological Review,* 22 (Feb., 1957), 52–58.
39. Kuhlen, Raymond G. *The Psychology of Adolescent Development.* New York: Harper & Bros., 1952.
40. Landis, Paul H. "Marriage Preparation in Two Generations." *Marriage and Family Living,* 13 (Fall, 1951), 155–56.
41. Lowrie, Samuel H. "Dating, A Neglected Field of Study." *Marriage and Family Living,* 10 (Fall, 1948), 90–91, 95.
42. Lowrie, Samuel H. "Sex Differences and Age of Initial Dating." *Social Forces,* 30 (May, 1952), 456–61.
43. Mather, W. G. "The Courtship Ideals of High School Youth." *Sociology and Social Research,* 19 (Nov.–Dec., 1934), 166–72.
44. Packard, Vance. *The Sexual Wilderness.* New York: David McKay Co., Inc., 1968.
45. Pullias, E. V. "Masturbation as a Mental Hygiene Problem—A Study of the Beliefs of 75 Young Men." *Journal of Abnormal Psychology,* 32 (July–Sept., 1937), 216–22.
46. Punké, Harold H. "Attitudes and Ideas of High School Youth in Regard to Marriage." *School and Society,* 56 (Sept. 12, 1942), 221–24.

47. Punké, Harold H. "Dating Practices of High School Youth." *NASSP Bulletin*, 28 (Jan., 1944), 47–54.
48. Ramsey, Glenn V. "The Sexual Development of Boys." *American Journal of Psychology*, 56 (April, 1943), 217–33.
49. Reevy, W. R. "Adolescent Sexuality." In *Encyclopedia of Sexual Behavior*, pp. 52–68. New York: Hawthorne Books, 1961.
50. Reiss, Ira L. *Premarital Sex Standards in America*. Glencoe, Ill.: Free Press, 1960.
51. Ross, Robert T. "Measures of Sex Behavior in College Males. Compared with Kinsey's Results." *Journal of Abnormal and Social Psychology*, 45 (1950), 753–55.
52. Rubin, Isadore. "Sex and the College Student: A Bibliography of New Findings and Insights." *Journal of the NAWDC*, 26 (Jan., 1963), 34–42.
53. Seidman, Jerome M. *The Adolescent—A Book of Readings*. Rev. ed. New York: Holt, Rinehart and Winston, 1960.
54. Smith, Ernest A. "Dating and Courtship at Pioneer College." *Sociology and Social Research*, 40 (Nov.–Dec., 1955), 92–98.
55. Smith, Geraldine F. "Certain Aspects of the Sex Life of the Adolescent Girl." *Journal of Applied Psychology*, 8 (1924), 347–49.
56. Staton, Thomas F. *Dynamics of Adolescent Development*. New York: The Macmillan Co., 1963.
57. Terman, Lewis M. "Kinsey's Sexual Behavior in the Human Male: Some Comments and Criticisms." *Psychological Bulletin*, 45 (Sept., 1948), 443–59.
58. Waller, Willard. "The Rating and Dating Complex." *American Sociological Review*, 2 (Oct., 1937), 727–34.
59. Wattenberg, William W. *The Adolescent Years*. New York: Harcourt, Brace, & World, 1955.
60. Willoughby, Raymond R. *Sexuality in the Second Decade*. Monographs of the Society for Research in Child Development, vol. 2, no. 3 (1937).

5
Occupational Interests

THIS CHAPTER consists of two main divisions, the first dealing with occupational preferences and plans, and the second with vocational interests as disclosed by blanks and inventories devised for the purpose of identifying these interests. The first division is outlined here and the second just before describing the instruments and reporting the outcomes of applications.

Occupational Preferences and Plans

Areas of inquiry.—Numerous studies of occupational preferences and plans of youth have been made over a long period of years and the literature reporting them is extensive. Most of these studies are far from definitive, but at the same time they contribute something to our understanding of the vocational expectations and aspirations of young people. Findings of a number of these studies will be drawn upon in such a way as to answer, at least in part, important questions pertaining to vocational interests from childhood through to young adulthood, with some focus on meaning for the predominant age-group in the community college.

Here are some of the questions to which answers will be sought in the evidence from these studies. What may be said of the reality and stability of occupational preferences and plans, and how are reality and stability influenced by the age of the respondent, or by his ability? Does the manner of inquiry influence the response? What are the sex differences in preferences and plans? And what motives are ascribed by youth for their preferences and plans? Does advent of puberty have a bearing on change in occupational interest? Other questions considered are the prestige of occupations and the important issue of the relation of occupational preference to social mobility.

Stages in occupational choice.—Consideration here of the characteristics of occupational choice may well begin with a categorization designated by Ginzberg and others (23) derived from case studies of subjects ranging in age from childhood to adulthood. Procedures used were neither statistical and factorial nor longitudinal. From this investigation three distinct periods, or stages, in the determination of choice were identified: (1) the period of "fantasy" choices (characteristic between the ages of six and eleven, approximately); (2) the period of "tentative" choices (during early and late adolescence); and (3) that of "realistic" choices (in early adulthood) (60). Concerning the second stage, these authors say that not all adolescents indicate that their choices are tentative, and it sometimes requires a little probing to discover doubts about these choices or about the possibility of realizing them (67). The authors must have found considerable departure from the stages in the respective age-groups, for they also say, "To some degree, the way in which a young person deals with his occupational choice is indicative of his general maturity and, conversely, in assessing the latter, consideration must be given to the way in which he is handling his occupational choice problem" (60).

Although this project by Ginzberg and collaborators does not yield measures of the proportions of subjects at different ages with their choices at the various stages, it does provide a terminology useful in considering occupational preferences and plans of youth. The term "realism," or phrase "reality of choice," emerges with prominence, together with its contrasting term "fantasy." The designation of a "tentative" stage suggests variation in "stability" of choice. Reality and stability of choice, as conditioned by certain influences, or "factors," are criteria of major concern in much of the following consideration of occupational choices of young people, a consideration which is based largely on statistical inquiries, some of them also longitudinal.

Projects involving ninth-grade populations.—In order to better understand the status, or stage of development, of occupational interests in the ages of later adolescence or early adulthood, it will be helpful to begin with studies involving younger adolescents and then to proceed with consideration of studies, either cross-sectional or longitudinal, involving youth into and through later adolescence. Among the best of the projects concerned with occupational choices in early adolescence is one reported by Super and Overstreet (60), who investigated the "vocational maturity" of boys in grade 9. The value of this study is enhanced by the fact that it was made against "hypothetical constructs" in a theory of occupational development. These constructs and theory serve as guidelines for a comprehensive Career Planning Study which will carry the inquiry on the same subjects into adulthood. The population studied consisted of 105 boys in the high school at Middletown, New York. Extensive evidence was collected about the subjects from records, testing, and interviews in order to ascertain their maturity for making a choice of vocation. Twenty "indices" of this maturity were postulated and five of these (examples being "Specificity of Information about the Preferred Occupation" and "Specificity of Planning for Preferred Occupation") were found to have "a sufficient number of significant positive intercorrelations to be considered adequate as measures of vocational maturity at the ninth-grade level" (143). A major inference from the evidence is that "apparently the typical ninth-grade boy has not yet reached a stage at which wisdom of vocational preference can be expected, according to the measures of wisdom used in this study" (149). Bearing on the question of factors or influences on the preferences is the statement that "vocational maturity in the ninth-grade boys studied was associated with (1) living in an intellectually and culturally stimulating environment, (2) having the mental ability essential to respond to that environment, (3) responding to these stimuli by aspiring to occupations at higher rather than lower socio-economic levels, and (4) achieving in one's activities" (147). Concerning the intellectual adequacy of the boys for their vocational preferences, the investigators report that for almost half of the boys intelligence was appropriate but "slightly more than half of them wished to enter occupations that seemed inappropriate in terms of the intelligence required" (149).

Another investigation of occupational interests involving a ninth-grade population, highly informative in several important relationships, has been reported by Stephenson (52). The population included both boys and girls—a total of 443—attending two junior high schools, the majority of whose graduates enter the same senior high school. The ninth grade was selected because it is at this point in the student's educational experience that he must make a choice of his high school curriculum, a choice that is "instrumental in sorting out college from non-college aspirants and in focusing the student's attention upon occupational considerations."

A commendable feature of this investigation lies in the manner of inquiry after the subject's occupational choice. He was asked what kind of work he *planned to do* after completing his schooling and what kind of work he *would like to do*, if he could do anything he wanted. Thus, the questions were devised to distinguish between "occupational plans" and "occupational aspirations," thereby avoiding the weakness of many studies which ask only for the first occupational choice and in consequence may fail to record the actual occupational plans of students. The choices indicated were classified in seven levels, following Alba Edwards' socio-economic grouping of the nation's labor force: (1) professional; (2) owners, managers, and officials; (3) clerks and kindred workers; (4) skilled workers and foremen; (5) semiskilled workers; (6) unskilled workers. In the typical study which inquires only after the student's preference, or first choice, a heavy concentration is found in the first group. Such a concentration was found in Stephenson's tabulation of *aspirations,* as more than half (51.5 per cent) were classified there, with the proportion for boys and girls not differing widely. The proportion of occupational *plans* classifiable in this group, while still large (27.8 per cent), is only about half that for aspirations, indicating that the manner of inquiry bears significantly on the degree of realism of choice.

Stephenson's study compares, as have many other investigations, the percentage distribution of students' choices in these socioeconomic groupings with those of the nation's labor force. The usual striking contrast is found between the distributions of occupations aspired to by students and the actual distributions in the labor force. For example, the percentage of aspirations in group 1, as just reported, is 51.5, whereas in the nation's labor force it is only 6.5. At the other extreme, the students' aspirations for occupations in group 6 (unskilled labor) are almost nonexistent, whereas in the labor force they make up more than a fourth (25.9 per cent). The proportion of *plans* in group 1, already reported here as 27.8 per cent, is also far out of line with the labor force. The partially realistic shift in this decline for group 1 is into groups 3, 4, and 5 for boys and mainly into group 3 for girls. The proportions in group 6 increase slightly but remain small.

This investigation by Stephenson included comparison of the distributions of students' choices with those of fathers' occupations. The latter did not depart widely from the distribution of the nation's labor force, from which one may infer that both the students' aspirations and their plans far exceed in socioeconomic level their fathers' occupations, albeit the plans depart less so than the aspirations. Also included is a comparison of the students' educational plans with the extent of schooling of the fathers. The evidence indicates that fewer than 2 per cent of the students planned to leave school before graduating from high school, and about a third planned college attendance. By contrast, fewer than a fifth of the fathers were high school graduates, a difference which prompts the investigator to say that the occupational plans of these students may not be as unrealistic as they first appear. He comments also that the difference in educational plans of the students and the education of fathers has some bearing on the issue of social stratification.

Trends of choice through high school years.—It is appropriate next to note trends of occupational choice at an age level above grade 9 as has just been reported. This will be done by drawing briefly on two studies of occupational preference through most or all of the high school span. One of these is cross-sectional, the other longitudinal. Each yields something of understanding of vocational interests of youths.

The cross-sectional inquiry was made by Roeber and Garfield (*43*) and concerns the occupational preferences of 912 boys and 1,083 girls in 22 high schools in communities ranging in population from 2,500 to 15,000. Percentages of preferences for each occupation are reported separately for the two sexes and for each of the four high school years. The authors note that the range of occupational preference is considerably wider for boys than for girls; that is, the choices spread through a greater number of different occupations for boys than for girls. A finding of considerable importance is that, although the most favored choices are generally similar for the various grades, the proportions tend to vary from grade to grade and to some extent in the direction of smaller percentages in the upper grade levels for the higher level occupations and larger percentages for non-professional occupations in these grades. Thus, there is a trend, as the authors put it, for "upper-class students [to] choose some of the commonplace occupations more frequently than students in the lower grades." They infer that this trend is "evidence of a more mature and realistic point of view."

The longitudinal study, by Holden (26), is based on a smaller population than that by Roeber and Garfield, using as subjects 109 students in grades 8 and 11 in a suburban community of "relatively high socio-economic level" in western New York. The author investigated the relation of scholastic aptitude as measured by the intelligence quotient (ranging from 84 to 139) to stability of occupational choice. The occupational preferences were rated according to length of the periods of education required for entrance to them, from "no post high school education" to "four or more years of college." When the study group was in grade 8, more than three-fifths (61.5 per cent) of all were considering occupations requiring four or more years of college. By the time these youth had reached grade 11, the proportion had dropped by almost a half (to about 33 per cent). When the shift was considered in relation to scholastic aptitude, it was found that none of the subjects with IQs of 125 and up who had indicated preferences for occupations requiring four or more years of college had shifted their preferences to occupations requiring less preparation; the proportion of those with IQs of 110 to 124 with preferences at this level fell off only slightly (from 60.5 to 55 per cent), whereas those with IQs of 95 to 109 and 85 to 94 had shifted to lower-level occupations in striking proportions, the 95-to-109 group from 59.6 to 11.5 per cent and the 85-to-94 group from 78 to 11 per cent. In his "implications of the study" the investigator comments on the prevalent belief that little faith can be placed in the occupational aspirations of young people on the threshold of secondary education and observes that his evidence "seems to support the hypothesis that the aspirations of the high IQ students are reasonably real. . . . It is helpful to know that the tremendous change in the level of occupational choice is not necessarily distributed evenly through all ability levels but probably concentrated largely in the low IQ group."

Choices of high school seniors and graduates.—Next in order in advancing from one age-group to the next in considering the question of occupational choices at the college level are students in or at the end of their last high school years, that is, when many are near or on the threshold of college. From among the studies bearing on the problem at this level are those by Jones (*29*) and Lockwood (*38*).

The first of these is concerned with high school seniors in Buffalo, New York, and vicinity. These students were asked what occupations they "preferred" and also those which they felt they were "most likely to enter." In addition to the responses to these questions, the investigator had also the "Regents' grades" for all seniors in the sample, which he indicates are a good index of college ability (r of .61 for boys and .65 for girls) and correlate even more closely with achievement and intelligence tests (.70 to .80). As might be expected, the manner of questioning yielded a high percentage of the subjects *preferring* the professions compared with the percentages who thought they would *probably enter* such occupations: the average differences throughout the various communities was about 10 per cent. Coefficients of correlation were computed between the Regents' grades and the level of the occupations preferred and probable. Most of the coefficients were higher for the probable than the preferred occupations, indicative of a nearer approach to realism of the former than of the latter. Most of the coefficients were nevertheless low and the differences far from striking. The relationships were found to be considerably higher for boys than for girls, a difference the investigator attributed to the greater difficulty involved in some of the fields occupied by men such as medicine and law and the less exacting requirements for entrance to some of the professions occupied primarily by women. Jones concluded that the picture of occupational orientation in the area at the time did not look favorable, since ability levels of the seniors were not closely related to anticipated occupational levels. He found considerable variation among the high schools in their concern for occupational and curriculum guidance, and also concluded that schools which showed the greatest interest in guidance excelled to some degree in their correlations.

The study by Lockwood (*38*) concerned graduates of the high schools of Baltimore. The subjects included a stratified sample of 508 of the June, 1954, and February, 1955, graduating classes of the nine academic senior high schools of the city. Equal numbers of boys and girls made up the sample. Two of the schools were "Negro" and the other seven were "white" schools. Desegregation had been in effect only since May, 1954, so was not yet reflected in the graduating classes. Graduates in the sample represented various socioeconomic-cultural levels, diverse residential districts, and several religious faiths.

Realism of occupational choice, in the context of this project, involved the degree of personal fitness of an individual graduate for his vocational preference "as judged by two experienced, professionally trained guidance and placement counselors." A realism rating scale was devised with ratings from 1 to 10, 1 signifying "highly unrealistic" and 10 "highly realistic." Intercorrelations of the ratings of the two judges were very high, not dropping below 0.95.

The average realism score was 5.5 which the report characterizes as "equivalent to a highly realistic vocational preference and a predicted excellent, or better, chance of vocational success." Well over a third (37 per cent) of the realism scores were at 6 or above and were adjudged "super-scores," indicating that the subjects were "under-shooting" in the choices. On the assumption that ratings of 1 through 3 represent unrealistic preferences, only 5 per cent were unrealistic and 95 per cent were judged realistic "in varying degrees."

Inquiry into the relationships of rental district of residence, race, sex, and school attended to the students' realism of vocational preference found all to be insignificant. A single datum at hand concerning the subjects that was found to influence the realism score was intelligence (with IQ groupings of –89, 90–99, 100–109, and 110+). Lockwood says, "The factor of intelligence seems directly related to the level of a student's realism of vocational preference. On an average, the higher the student's IQ level, the higher is his realism index, and the lower the IQ level, the lower the realism score appears to be."

It deserves mentioning that for some years prior to the making of this investigation in Baltimore, students had been subjected to the work of a system-wide Department of Guidance and Placement, and it is likely that the impact of this service had had some influence toward realism of preference. This observation is in harmony with the comment made by Jones in explaining the difference in correlations between ability and level of occupational choice in schools in Buffalo and vicinity with differing degrees of interest in occupational and curriculum guidance.

Inquiries at the college level.—Three studies will be drawn upon to represent the evidence on occupational preferences or plans of the population at the collegiate level. Two of these were made in four-year colleges and universities and the third in junior colleges.

One of the studies, a rather old one by Crathorne (*13*), involved a population of over 2,000 freshmen in a number of colleges and universities widely distributed over the country. Its findings bear mainly on (1) the proportions of freshmen who recalled having had definite leanings toward some particular occupation on entering high school but had made "radical" changes before entering college, and (2) the proportions who reported having, as freshmen, definite plans as to life work. Of the proportion who recalled having definite preferences as high school freshmen, almost exactly half had made radical changes before entering college, indicating considerable instability over the high school span. However, of these college freshmen 85 per cent reported having definite decisions as to life work at the time of Crathorne's inquiry.

The second of these studies (67) was made almost three decades after the first and involves a much smaller number of students, 241, in two universities, one in the South and the other in the Midwest. The students were enrolled in courses in general psychology and about three-fifths were already juniors or seniors. In striking contrast with the findings of the Crathorne study, 55 per cent of the students had made no choice of vocation or were uncertain of the appropriateness of their choices. Inquiry concerning those who had received some counseling disclosed that a larger proportion of them than of the whole group had chosen vocations "satisfactory to them at the moment." As one might expect, the investigator emphasized the need for professional counseling. Speculation over the wide difference in the proportions of the students in these two studies with definite occupational plans suggests that it may be explained in part by the small population in the second study, but there is also the certainty of considerable variation from one study to another in such investigations.

The investigation involving junior college students is that by Wrenn (70) reported in 1935, using data from tests administered to junior college students in 1929. The total population represented was about 10,000 enrolled in junior colleges in California. In addition to the scores on the Psychological Examination the investigator had information concerning the occupational choices of the students.

The comparison in the investigation which yields the crucial findings is that of the top 15 per cent with the lowest 15 per cent of the men as measured by their scores on the Psychological Examination. The average score of the top group was 250.6, equivalent to the 97 percentile for the year, with an "estimate placing the IQ at 140"; whereas the average score for the low group was 62.9, placing them at the 8.0 percentile, with a probable IQ between 90 and 100. The vocational choices of these two groups of men when three-fourths of them were freshmen did not reflect the wide differences in scores, as 51 per cent of the low-score group chose the professions compared with 68 per cent of the top group. The investigator regarded as "somewhat startling" the fact that over half the students representing the lowest 15 per cent in intelligence test scores chose the professions. Almost exactly the same proportion of this same low group chose the professions in 1931, "in the face of the fact that no single one of the group made a 'B' average during his junior college work (as compared with 44 per cent of the high-score group with 'B' averages) and that 49 per cent of them had withdrawn from or had failed in junior college at the time this statement of vocational choice was made."

An obvious conclusion from this study is one of a serious lack of realism in the vocational choices of these students of lower ability. In extenuation of the situation, mention may be made of the fact that the investigation was made something like a generation ago in an earlier period of junior college history, before these institutions had gone far in the development of programs of guidance and counseling. In many institutions today, the current status of these programs doubtless serves to foster a nearer approach to realism in occupational choice.

TABLE 5.1
PERCENTAGE DISTRIBUTION IN ORDER OF FREQUENCY OF OCCUPATIONAL CHOICES OF 258 BOYS IN GRADE 12

Occupation	Per Cent	Occupation	Per Cent
Farmer	11.6	Army-Navy	2.7
Engineer	10.1	Store clerk	2.7
Factory worker	5.4	Designer	2.7
Tool and die maker	5.4	Chemist	1.9
Aviator	4.3	Medicine-surgeon	1.9
Salesman	4.0	Carpenter	1.6
Mechanic	3.9	Lawyer	1.6
Machinist	3.9	Teacher	1.6
Draftsman	3.9	Electrician	1.2
Accountant	3.5	Commercial artist	1.2
Office clerk	3.1	Journalism	0.8

SOURCE: Roeber and Garfield (43).

The specific occupations chosen.—Up to this point our consideration of occupational choices of students has been almost exclusively in respect to socioeconomic classifications of the occupations with little attention to the specific occupations. An adequate treatment of these interests of youth must include consideration of specific occupations which they have in mind. This aspect of the area will now be approached by drawing on the list of specific occupations reported as the preferences of students included in one of the investigations drawn upon previously in this chapter, that by Roeber and Garfield (43). In this instance focus will be on the preferences of students in grade 12 only, since they are all in later adolescence and of ages just younger than those of college freshmen. These choices are reported for boys in Table 5.1 and for girls in Table 5.2. The occupations listed in these tables are only those named most often by these students: the 22 occupations in the boys' table include about four-fifths of all choices named by the 258 boys and the 14 in the girls' table more than nine-tenths of all 285 subjects.

Tables of this kind can be regarded as nothing more than illustrative and certainly not representative or comprehensive. The occupations chosen by any such group are influenced to a considerable degree by time and place. For instance, the large proportion of boys choosing farming arises from the fact that the high schools were in communities ranging in size from 2,500 upward, with some of them adjacent to prosperous agricultural areas, and the large proportion choosing skilled mechanical occupations may have been influenced by publicity for war production in the early forties. The large proportion of girls choosing nursing was presumably influenced also by the war effort.

TABLE 5.2
PERCENTAGE DISTRIBUTION IN ORDER OF FREQUENCY OF OCCUPATIONAL CHOICES OF 285 GIRLS IN GRADE 12

Occupation	Per Cent	Occupation	Per Cent
Stenographer–office worker	36.1	Commercial artist	2.8
		Designer	2.5
Nurse	15.8	Telephone operator	2.5
Teacher	12.3	Housework	2.1
Factory worker	4.2	Musician	2.1
Store clerk	4.2	Journalism	1.8
Beautician	3.2	Actress	0.7
Waitress	3.2		

SOURCE: Roeber and Garfield (*43*).

An important observation on the lists in the two tables concerns the small number of occupational choices common to boys and girls. Only five appear with identical names: store clerk, designer, commercial artist, teacher, and journalism, although there must also be some overlapping in the "office clerk" category for boys and "stenographer-office worker" category for girls. Another important observation relates to the longer list, or greater diversity, of choices of boys than of girls. The authors report that, for all four high school years, only 14 occupations were selected by more than 1 per cent of the girls as contrasted with 23 occupations selected by more than 1 per cent of the boys.

Sex differences in occupational preferences.—The divergence of preferences of the sexes as just reported makes relevant reference to the most extensive inquiry into differences in occupational choices of boys and girls that has been reported in print, that by Lehman and Witty (*36*), made some years before the study by Roeber and Garfield. The Lehman and Witty investigation involved the preferences in a list of about 200 occupations submitted to more than 25,000 boys and girls in Kansas and Missouri ranging in age from 8½ to 18½. The elaborate tables derived by these authors are not reproduced here. Instead, the main conclusions from the study will be presented by a combination of quotation and paraphrase of their "summary of differences."

(1) Fully 90 per cent of the occupations girls would more willingly enter are of "a somewhat sedentary type," although the authors warn that this concept of "type" should be applied with "extreme care." (2) By contrast, almost half the occupations on the boys' list appear to "require movement over a relatively wide geographical area," whereas fewer than 15 per cent of the occupations in the girls' list are of this nature. (3) More than half the occupations in the girls' list require to some extent aesthetic appreciation or interest, whereas fewer than 15 per cent of the occupations in the boys' list involve such appreciation. (4) About a sixth of the occupations on the boys' list demand vigorous physical activity and some even physical danger. (5) Some of the occupations in the girls' list require personal and often even menial service. These are housewife, nurse, beauty parlor specialist, waitress, maid or servant, and social service worker. Only a single occupation in the boys' list, doctor, calls for personal service, and this is a profession. (6) Four occupations in the girls' list involve school teaching, whereas the boys' list includes no occupation associated with teaching. (7) The boys' list often includes occupations which involve the giving of orders or commands—naval or army officer, contractor, doctor, etc.—whereas the girls' list includes more often occupations involving the taking of orders—private secretary, stenographer, typist, etc.

Quoted here is one further observation by Lehman and Witty which relates to changes in occupational preferences with advancing age, from childhood to later adolescence: "There is another important reason why boys change their occupational choices with increase in maturity. With the advance of civilization man's work has become more diversified and more mechanized. . . . Such primitive types of work as those carried on by the cowboy, the fisherman, the hunter, and the trapper are today impossible as means of procuring livelihood for many. Woman's primitive occupation—that of childbearing or rearing—has continued to be a most important one. With all the freedom and independence which she has won, woman has not freed herself from the responsibilities which nature and tradition have placed on her. . . . Woman's function in life seems to have undergone less change than man's."

In the absence of more recent evidence from extensive inquiries into trends in occupations preferred and actually entered by the two sexes, we are left largely to conjecture on the nature of the changes. Such evidence as is available indicates that women have been choosing and entering many occupations formerly entered only by men and that, in consequence, the lists of occupations are somewhat more alike than formerly.

It is in place to mention in connection with a consideration of differences in occupational preferences of the two sexes that a demonstrable relationship exists between these preferences and occupations actually engaged in and measures of masculinity and femininity. This relationship was affirmed in the first large-scale investigation of masculinity-femininity by Terman and Miles (62). For instance, from their evidence they observed, "Engineers . . . tend to score highly masculine; artists, theologians, and musicians to score highly feminine" (469). The figure of average scores for males shows a rapid incline in masculinity from grade 8 to grade 11 and a decline thereafter and, for females, a rapid incline to lower minus (femininity) scores from grade 8 to college sophomores and then rather rapid decline (that is, to higher femininity) to 30 years of age and a moderate decline thereafter (123). It is the opinion of the writers that both nature and nurture have an influence on these measures, but they were not in a position to indicate whether or not one or the other of these factors is predominant. On the basis of a factor analysis of the items of the Terman-Miles test applied to boys and girls in grade 9, Ford and Tyler (20) concluded that psychological masculinity-femininity is not a unitary trait but has at least two dimensions for both sexes, representing emotional characteristics and interests, respectively. They concluded also that there is "another possible third dimension for females having to do with acceptance of a feminine role." This was discussed in Chapter 3.*

Occupational preference and puberty.—A question often arising in considering vocational preferences of youth concerns the relations of these preferences or changes in them to puberty. Lehman and Witty (37) canvassed this relationship as an aspect of their investigation of occupational choices of more than 25,000 boys and girls ranging in age from 8½ to 18½, on which we have drawn above to note sex differences in occupational preferences. In the aspect being epitomized here they presented in chart form comparisons of the percentages of their subjects indicating certain choices with the average percentages of youth prepubescent, pubescent, etc. For example, they present a chart comparing the proportions of boys pubescent at various ages with the percentages at these ages indicating a desire to be "cowboys." The proportion with this desire, high at younger ages, drops to 20 per cent at 14½ and to practically "total disappearance" by 17½. Again, they report "rough correspondence" of the curves for onset of pubescence in girls and the dropoff of interest in becoming movie actresses. Lehman and Witty concluded from their comparisons that "one fundamental fact" disclosed by their study is that "children's vocational attitudes mature relatively rapidly after the onset of pubescence."

*See pp. 94–95.

It deserves mention that this project was a cross-sectional study and that it compared the proportions of youth at the various ages having certain occupational preferences with the proportions of other populations of youth of corresponding ages found by earlier investigators to be at the various stages of maturity, such as prepubescent, pubescent, etc. In view of the rather wide variation in ages at which puberty arrives, as has been reported in Chapter 1, such a cross-sectional study could not be expected to find anything better than an approximate relationship between age and change of occupational preferences. If it exists, a close relationship, re-

TABLE 5.3
FREQUENCY OF REASONS GIVEN BY BOYS AND GIRLS OF HIGH SCHOOL AGE FOR THEIR CHOICE OF OCCUPATIONS

Reason	Boys		Girls	
	Number	Order of Frequency	Number	Order of Frequency
Like it	183	1	409	1
Money	92	2	68	4
Fitted for it	58	3	143	2
Assured of position	31	4	3	9
Offers advancement	24	5	15	6
Travel and adventure	22	6	11	7
Do good	22	7	79	3
Choice of parent	9	8	3	9
Member of family in same work	6	9	5	8
No reason given	0	10	18	5

SOURCE: Based on Hurlock and Jansing (27).

flected in something like saltatory change in occupational interests with the changes of puberty, could only be found in a longitudinal study in which changes in interests of individuals are accurately keyed to the stages of sexual development of the same persons. The literature seems to report no substantial investigation following such a procedure, so we are left with the conclusion that the advent of puberty has its influence on occupational interest, but that we do not know in what degree. That it has an influence is supported also by the postulation of an important developmental task of adolescence.*

Motivation of occupational choice.—Up to this point this treatment has said nothing directly about the motivation of occupational choices. The investigations in this area are almost universally cast in terms of the reasons the subjects give for their choices. Many such studies have been reported and, for purposes of illustration, two are drawn upon here. The first is by Hurlock and Jansing (27) and reports the reasons given by 447 boys and 685 girls 14 to 16 years of age. As may be noted in Table 5.3,

*See p. 80.

the reasons have been succinctly generalized. In addition to reporting the frequency of each reason, for each sex, the table indicates the order of frequency. It may be seen that the most frequent reason given by both boys and girls is "Like it." Other reasons with high frequency are "Money" and "Fitted for it," although the order of emphasis differs somewhat for the two sexes. One of the largest differences of frequency for the sexes is for "Do good," which the girls mention more often than the boys.

The second study is by Hutson (28), which was based on responses of students in high schools of western Pennsylvania. While Hutson reports the reasons given by students in junior and senior high schools, columns for senior high school students only are given in Table 5.4, as these are for later adolescents only. The classification of reasons differs from that made by Hurlock and Jansing in that they are not so tersely generalized and also that the reasons that focus on self have been assembled together. It may be noted that the reasons given by boys outnumber those given by girls, and also that the proportion of girls expressing a liking for or interest in the occupation named is larger than for boys.

Variability and consistency of vocational choices.—Up to this point little has been said or reported here concerning the permanence of occupational choice for individual youth. Few studies of consistency and variability of choice are to be found in print. One of the best of these is by Schmidt and Rothney (46), who reported on the compilation of results of counseling 347 students in high schools in Wisconsin. The term "vocational choice" as used in the study refers to expressions during interviews of intent to enter an occupation. During this study the counselors were working in a face-to-face relationship with the students, as distinguished from questionnaires, and were able to probe when it was necessary to determine the occupation each student actually had in mind. The choices were indicated in each high school year. The degree of consistency of choices during the last three high school years is seen in the following figures:

	PER CENT
Consistent all three years	34.9
Consistent junior and senior years only	13.8
Consistent sophomore and junior years only	17.7
Inconsistent (no choices same over three-year period)	33.6

The authors point out that almost two-thirds (65.1 per cent) changed their vocational plans at least once during the high school period.

The study also included a follow-up of these students from five to seven months after graduation to ascertain whether or not the counseled subjects had entered the post-high-school occupations, or were training for them, which they had chosen during high school years, with affirmative results as follows: choice as sophomores, 46.4 per cent; choice as juniors, 49.3 per cent; choice as seniors, 53.6 per cent. These results for the same 347 students, while still indicating variability of choice, hint at a steady even if small increase from year to year in relationship of choice to occupation or training entered and also show that a full majority were in the occupations which they had chosen as seniors or were in training for them. One notes that there is substantial approach to stability of choice in later high school years and perhaps this is all that can be ex-

TABLE 5.4
PERCENTAGE DISTRIBUTIONS OF REASONS GIVEN BY SENIOR HIGH SCHOOL
BOYS AND GIRLS FOR THEIR OCCUPATIONAL CHOICES

Reasons	Boys	Girls
Self-advantages:		
A. Financial rewards	13.0	9.6
B. Possibilities of advancement	8.0	8.0
C. Promising future of the industry	6.1	.3
D. Easy work	.8	.7
E. Affords steady employment	3.0	2.1
F. Field not crowded	5.3	3.4
G. Others, as health, social status, opportunity for travel, ease of learning	10.0	6.6
Subtotal	46.2	30.7
Expressing liking for, or interest in the occupation (unanalyzed)	35.3	46.2
Expressed liking for, or interested in, some aspect of the work, as "I like mathematics"	1.3	2.1
To help my family	–	.6
Influence of parents or other members of the family, through advice, dictation, or example	2.4	2.6
Having some qualifications for the work	8.4	8.0
The occupation is socially serviceable	2.3	3.9
Mention of source of knowledge of the occupation, as "Learned about it from reading"	1.6	2.4
Restrictions or obstacles forcing the choice	.5	1.6
Affording outlet for, or challenge to, one's powers	1.5	1.5
Having opportunity to enter the vocation	.5	.5
Total	100.0	100.1

SOURCE: Hutson (28, 138, Table 24).

pected with the extent of counseling given. The authors' observation that "planning can not be a one-shot process" must be fully acceptable, as well as their comment that, "since a method of early identification of the consistent ones is not yet available, planning services, continuous and personalized, appear to be needed over the whole high school period."

The prestige of occupations.—While the reasons given by youth for their preferences for occupations shed some light on motivation in this area of human interest, many of the responses are vague and leave one with a wish to get nearer the bases or origins of the interests expressed. An important clue to some of these origins is the social prestige of occupations.

This prestige has been rather extensively investigated. Among the first of the investigations, which was used as a point of departure for others, was one reported by Counts (*12*) in 1925. Counts' study arrived at a ranking of the prestige of occupations by obtaining the ranking of 45 occupations which his respondents were asked to arrange in the order of their social standing, placing the number 1 after the occupation most looked up to; after that which occupies second place in this respect, 2; and so on. He used as respondents teachers, freshmen in college, and seniors in trade schools and in academic high schools. Deeg and Paterson (*17*) 21 years later made up a list of 25 occupations by taking every other occupation in Counts' list, adding others from it, and following the same procedure,

TABLE 5.5
COMPARISON OF THE SOCIAL STATUS RANKS OF 25 OCCUPATIONS IN 1925 AND 1946

Occupation	Rank Order 1925	Rank Order 1946	Occupation	Rank Order 1925	Rank Order 1946
Banker	1	2.5	Insurance agent	14	10
Physician	2	1	Mail carrier	15	14
Lawyer	3	2.5	Carpenter	16	15
Supt. of schools	4	4	Soldier	17	19
Civil engineer	5	5	Plumber	18	17
Army captain	6	6	Motorman	19	18
Foreign missionary	7	7	Barber	20	20
Elem. sch. teacher	8	8	Truck driver	21	21.5
Farmer	9	12	Coalminer	22	21.5
Machinist	10	9	Janitor	23	23
Traveling salesman	11	16	Hodcarrier	24	24
Grocer	12	13	Ditchdigger	25	25
Electrician	13	11			

SOURCE: Deeg and Paterson (*17*, Table 1).

using also Counts' descriptions of the work involved in each occupation, with four groups of respondents making the ratings: 169 students in the General College of the University of Minnesota (freshmen and sophomores), 75 juniors, seniors, and graduate students in a class in vocational and occupational psychology, 31 seniors in a vocational high school, and 200 seniors in an academic high school. The final rankings of the 25 occupations obtained in the two investigations are shown in Table 5.5. A glance at the rankings in the table shows them to be very similar, an impression borne out by the coefficient of correlation of $+0.97$ reported by Deeg and Paterson. This suggests a notable stability of relative prestige of occupations during the 21-year period. They pointed out that there are only three displacements of more than two ranks: farmer dropped three ranks, traveling salesman dropped five ranks, and insurance agent gained four ranks. Two of these were in the sales field. The enhanced prestige of the insurance agent is ascribed to the increasing importance of insurance during the depression and World War II, coupled with marked improvement in the standards of selection and training for this work introduced by insurance companies. Hardly less remarkable than the similarity of rankings over the time span is that, of the rankings by the four groups in the Deeg and Paterson investigation, the coefficients of correlation between them were very high and ranged only from +0.93 to +0.99.

The most extensive evidence extant on the social status of occupations was brought together by Reiss (*41*) in 1961. It relies mainly on a personal poll of a sample population of 2,920 respondents to interviews sponsored by the National Opinions Research Center. The interviewees were representative of geographical regions, size of city (including also rural-farm), age, sex, socioeconomic status, and race. The procedure in interview included ratings of ninety occupations as "Excellent," "Good," "Fair," or "Poor," with the rankings obtained by placing the occupations in the declining order of percentages of the sum of "Excellent" and "Good" ratings. The whole treatment also inquires into income and extent of education of persons engaged in the occupations as correlates of prestige, and compares the ratings on social prestige with the interviewees' ratings of the same occupations on "pays well" and "service to humanity."

Our special interest is more with influence of age and sex on the ratings than with other representations in the population sample. A small number of occupations, for example, officials in international or local labor unions and night-club singers, were found to have higher ratings with younger than older persons, and it is suggested that these are mainly newer occupations; and a somewhat larger number of other occupations are indicated as having lower ratings, although the explanation is not readily apparent. However, the generalization is that "both age and sex produce only very small differences in occupational-prestige ratings . . ." (*41*, 187).

Some clue as to what helps to determine these relative rankings of occupations is provided in comparison of the rankings on prestige scores with the rankings on median income level and median level of educational attainment of persons engaged in the occupations. The rank correlation of income level with prestige is reported as +0.85, and of educational attainment with prestige as +0.83. This means that roughly 72 per cent of the variance on prestige scores is accounted for by income, and 69 per cent of the variance is accounted for by educational attainment. The conclusion is that "either income level or educational attainment is a surprisingly good predictor of the 'general standing' of an occupation" (*41*, 84).

The two other rankings compared with that of the social prestige of occupations in another chapter in *Occupations and Social Status*, that is, rankings on "Pays well" and "Service to humanity," should be nearer to the bases of motivation in occupational preferences than those just considered, because they emerge from attitudes rather than resulting from objective measures like median income and median educational attainments. They were derived in the same manner as the rankings in social prestige, by percentages of ratings of "Excellent" and "Good." These ratings and those on social prestige were obtained from three independent

TABLE 5.6
COMPARISON OF RANKINGS OF CERTAIN OCCUPATIONS ACCORDING TO RATINGS BY INTERVIEWEES ON "PAYS WELL," "SERVICE TO HUMANITY," AND "SOCIAL PRESTIGE"

Occupation	Pays Well	Service to Humanity	Social Prestige
Physician	1	1	1
Architect	2	3	6
Banker	3	6	2
Dentist	3	4	7
Lawyer	5	7	4
College professor	6	2	5
Chemist	7	4	9
Civil engineer	8	9	7
Airline pilot	9	10	12
Factory owner	10	11	10
Restaurant cook	35	35	36
Truck driver	37	37	33
Bartender	38	43	44
Taxi driver	39	40	39
Restaurant waiter	39	40	41
Filling station attendant	41	39	39
Night watchman	41	37	39
Janitor	43	42	43
Soda fountain clerk	44	43	41
Shoeshiner	45	44	44

SOURCE: Reiss (*41*, 193, from Table VIII–5).

groups of respondents on forty-five of the ninety occupations. The product-moment correlations among the three sets of rankings are as follows: "pays well" with "service to humanity," +0.99; "pays well" with "social prestige," +0.96; "service to humanity" with "social prestige," +0.98. These coefficients prompt the observation that *"There is a remarkable consensus on the occupational prestige-status structure of American society"* (*41*, 193). Table 5.6 is introduced here to provide illustration both of the degrees of similarity and of divergence in the rankings: it contains the ten occupations with the top rankings (upper section) and the ten with the lowest rankings (lower section) on "pays well" and the rankings of these same occupations on "service to humanity" and "social prestige." One may note, for instance, that the college professor ranks higher on "service to humanity" than on "pays well" or "social prestige" and that the bartender ranks higher on "pays well" than on "service to humanity" or "social prestige."

In large part, the foregoing consideration of the prestige of occupations and the influences on that prestige has been an excursion into the psychology of occupations and of occupational choice. This makes pertinent a quotation from Roe's *Psychology of Occupations* (42) in which she generalizes on the influences on occupational prestige and preference. This is done at a point following her discussion of the six "levels" under which the National Opinion Research Center has grouped the ninety occupations. She says (307), "It is clear . . . that these prestige ratings are quite closely related to Level. Now Level is determined by several things, of which the most important is the degree of responsibility involved. Training and skill are also important, and intelligence has some relation to Level, but the basic factor is responsibility, or, to put it another way, position in a pecking order. This agrees with Caplow's belief that the most important determinant of prestige is the subject's degree of control of other people's behavior and the degree to which his behavior is controlled by others. . . ." In light of this generalization it is not out of place to quote also two sentences from the preface to Roe's treatise (v–vi): "I have become more and more convinced that the role of occupation in the life of the individual has much broader psychological importance than is generally appreciated. . . . Within limits, occupational choice can be taken as a self-categorization, as an indication of at least some aspects of the self-image."

Vocational preferences and social mobility.—At an earlier point in this chapter reference was made to a study by Stephenson (52) of the occupational plans and aspirations of ninth-grade students, and it was reported that much larger proportions of these plans and aspirations were in higher socioeconomic classifications and much smaller proportions in lower occupational groups than in the distribution of occupations of the fathers of these students, as well as in the total work force of the nation. Stephenson also included comparison of the educational plans of the students with the education of fathers, this comparison yielding a striking contrast, in which the students' plans far exceed the educational attainments of the fathers. Mention was made of Stephenson's comment that the difference had a bearing on the issue of social stratification. Rather than proceeding to consider this issue with further attention to Stephenson's evidence, which, as stated, deals with data relating to both boys and girls in grade 9, it is more appropriate to rely on data for boys only in grade 12 in comparison with data on their fathers: this plan eliminates the factor of sex differences in occupations and in occupational preferences. Such data are provided in an investigation by Kroger and Louttit (33) who obtained from the boys in four high schools of Indianapolis their first, second, and third occupational choices and the facts concerning their fathers' occupations. The percentage distribution of fathers' occupations and of sons' first choices, together with that of the census distribution in Indianapolis in 1930, are reported in Table 5.7. The first and second columns of this table disclose the expected contrast between sons' choices and fathers' occupations. The percentages in the column reporting the distribution in the census do not

TABLE 5.7
DISTRIBUTIONS OF FATHERS' OCCUPATIONS, SONS' CHOICES, AND CENSUS FIGURES BY MAJOR OCCUPATIONAL GROUP

Occupational Groups	Fathers	Sons' First Choice	Census Distribution in 1930
Professional	7.8	46.8	4.4
Semiprofessional and business	40.4	21.8	32.3
Skilled	27.6	19.9	33.6
Labor	11.4	1.3	29.8
Deceased	5.4	–	–
Unemployed	7.1	–	–
No choice	–	10.1	–

SOURCE: Kroger and Louttit (33, Table 1).

depart widely from those for the fathers, although there is some selection upward for the fathers as compared with all workers in the city. Another table in this report indicates that 65.3 per cent (almost two-thirds) of the sons' choices are higher than the fathers' occupations, 19.1 per cent at the same level, and 15.6 per cent lower.

Computation of coefficients of correlation between levels of these choices for sons and the occupations of fathers discloses some tendency, although not striking and not always consistent, for the correlations to rise with the class level (from freshmen to seniors) and with the second and third choices as compared with the first. Both these tendencies suggest some movement toward realism.

Although this contrast of occupational preferences of youth with the occupational distribution of fathers is often deplored as unrealistic, it is also often defended as essential to an open society which allows for vertical movement of individuals from one socioeconomic level to another. Consideration of this mobility, especially as to its extent and the likelihood of its being influenced by education, is germane to an adequate consideration of the occupational interests of youth. This consideration begins here by report of a generalization of its extent by an authority on the issue and is elaborated by citation of evidence from investigations in point.

In the latter portions of his synthesis on *The American Class Structure* (*30*), after having canvassed carefully the evidence in this area of social mobility, Kahl concludes, "The American class structure is not a completely closed one, for between one half and three quarters of the men who are in professional, business, clerical, or skilled jobs have climbed relative to their fathers. No wonder they feel that our society is open, for if they look around them they find that most of their colleagues have moved up in the occupational (and thus the class) hierarchy" (272). However, he admits that "a small decline in over-all mobility has probably been taking place" and that "the American class structure is not completely open." He observes that particularly at the extremes of professional and top businesses and of unskilled workers there is "much more succession or inheritance of position than would be the case under random placement."

For illustrative evidence of the extent and direction of the mobility we may rely on a pair of articles by Centers (*10*, *11*), a staff member of the Office of Public Opinion Research. These articles are based on interviews with a national sample of adult males during which information was obtained concerning the occupations and educational attainments of the interviewees and of their fathers. The occupations were classified according to a hierarchy of seven levels ranging from "large business" through professional to unskilled. The average of the algebraic sum derived from the upward and downward differences of the sons' as compared with the fathers' occupations was +.35 (*11*), which, Centers says, shows that the sons have occupations only .35 of a step away from and above the occupational stratum of the fathers. His opinion is that the "over-all net mobility" is small in amount, a conclusion that seems not to concur fully with that quoted above from Kahl.

For his second article (*10*) Centers analyzed his evidence in such a way as to educe the influence of the extent of schooling on mobility. The conclusion here was more decisive. One compilation he reported is shown in Table 5.8. It shows that, of sons whose education is better than the fathers', almost half have positions better than the fathers', as compared with only about a sixth of the sons whose occupational station is superior to their parents'. Centers points out that the relationship appears "rather striking, considering that education is only one of several factors in, or means of, social elevation." He indicates that striking also is the "almost perfect balance in the percentage distribution of cases where fathers' and sons' educations are equal. . . ." In full appraisal of the influence of education on mobility it should not be overlooked that in this total sample of 416 comparisons, the sons' educations exceed those of the fathers in the great majority—almost 70 per cent—of the cases. The prevalence of these differentials in favor of sons' educations and the expectation that they will continue into the future afford support to a belief in a considerable mobility in our society.

Having found education to bear such an important relationship to social mobility, we should probe somewhat further to ascertain the factors that encourage or discourage continuation in school. Our first approach is to rely on the statistical findings of a study, cited by Kahl (*31*) but credited by him to Samuel A. Stauffer, Talcott Parsons, and Florence R. Kluckhohn, of more than 3,000 sophomore and junior high school boys in cities surrounding Boston. For all these boys data were at hand concerning their IQs and their fathers' occupations. The boys were divided into quintiles by IQs and into the following five classes according to fathers' occupations: (1) major white collar, (2) middle white collar, (3) minor white collar, (4)

TABLE 5.8
OCCUPATIONAL POSITIONS OF FATHERS AND SONS OF VARIOUS RELATIVE EDUCATIONS

Education of Sons in Relation to That of Fathers	Number	Per Cent of Sons' Positions Better Than Fathers'	Per Cent of Sons' Positions Same as Fathers'	Per Cent of Sons' Positions Poorer Than Fathers'
Sons' education better	291	46	33	21
Sons' education same	80	29	41	30
Sons' education poorer	45	16	35	49

SOURCE: Centers (*10*, Table 1).

skilled labor and service, and (5) other labor and service. In answer to the question of whether they expected to go to college the following percentages of boys in the five quintiles gave affirmative answers: first (lowest), 11; second, 17; third, 24; fourth, 30; and fifth (highest), 52. This increasing proportion with increasing aptitude is a matter of rather common knowledge. The percentages for the five occupational groups for the boys in the highest quintile were: (1) 89, (2) 76, (3) 55, (4) 40, and (5) 29, with the proportion for the lowest occupational group being only an approximate third of that for the highest.

Kahl has reported on his effort to find why some "common man boys" with adequate ability for college plan to continue their education in college and some do not. For this purpose he identified in the larger study by Stauffer, Parsons, and Kluckhohn just cited a sample of 24 boys, all within the top three deciles of ability and all with fathers of the "common man" class, who were petty white-collar, skilled, or semiskilled workers. Twelve of these boys had indicated that they expected to go to college and were in college-preparatory courses, while the other twelve had indicated that their plans did not include college attendance and were in non-college-preparatory courses. Extensive interviews were conducted with all the boys and in all the homes. Following is an excerpt from Kahl's observations (*31*): "The interviews disclosed that, although there was a general way of life which identified the common man class, some members were content with that way of life while others were not. Parents who were discontented tended to train their sons from the earliest years of grammar school to take school seriously and use education as a means to climb into the

TABLE 5.9
RELATION BETWEEN PARENTAL PRESSURE
AND SONS' ASPIRATIONS: 24 BOYS

Sons' Aspirations	Parental Pressure Toward College	
	No	Yes
College	4	8
No college	11	1

SOURCE: Kahl (*31*, Table 3).

middle class. Only sons who internalized such values were sufficiently motivated to overcome the obstacles which faced the common man boys in school; only they saw a reason for good school performance and college aspirations." The direction of parental pressure and its influence on their sons' aspirations toward college are seen in Table 5.9.

An investigation which reaffirms the influence of economic status on college attendance has been reported by Sexton (*48*), who found the percentages of seniors in "Big City" who were "requesting transcripts" to be sent to college admissions offices to be as follows:

Class 1	($5,000–)	22.8
Class 2	($6,000–)	34.0
Class 3	($7,000–)	46.3
Class 4	($8,000–)	60.6
Class 5	($9,000–)	81.0

Presentation of this evidence is followed by reference, as substantial corroboration, to that portion of the investigation by Stauffer, Parsons, and Kluckhohn mentioned above, finding the sharp decline, with each step down on the occupational class of fathers, in the proportions of boys of superior ability expecting to go on to college.

It thus appears that our will to maintain an open society providing upward mobility for children of middle- and lower-class families must be served in the main by efforts to surmount economic and attitudinal barriers to college attendance. Persons aware of this have long been urging various measures to this end, among them scholarships, loans, programs of individual guidance, and the community college. While all available measures should be used, proliferation of the community college is a natural for the purpose. The community college lowers the cost of this level of education, thereby removing most or all of the economic barrier, and it is changing the attitudes toward education at the collegiate level through bringing it within commuting distance and broadening the program, just as the multiplication of the high school and enrichment of its program have made attendance at the secondary level almost universal. The nature and extent of this influence is demonstrated in Chapter 7.

Vocational Interests as Disclosed by Blanks and Inventories

Another approach to vocational interests.—The foregoing consideration of occupational preferences and plans of youth has found them often to be dictated by fantasy or otherwise unrealistic. Awareness of the degree of unreliability has over a long period prompted efforts to replace or to supplement these choices by more dependable indications of vocational interests. One approach in efforts at more reliable identification of these interests has been by what are called "blanks" or "inventories" in which respondents indicate their preferences. The purpose of this section is to describe two of the best known and most used of these instruments, and to appraise them by reliance on reported investigations. While some reference will be made to vocations and vocational groups, emphasis will be placed less on potential occupational distributions of youth in any comprehensive list of occupations in our society than on the stability of the interests as disclosed by the instruments and the relationships of these measured interests to vocational preferences as conventionally ascertained as well as to several other kinds of evidence concerning the respondents. It is manifestly impossible to canvass the meaning of these instruments and of their relationships to other evidence without trespassing on the issues of their potential in guidance and counseling. To the extent of this overlapping we are here laying the foundations for recommendations in Chapter 12 concerning their use in the counseling program.

Description of the instruments.—The instrument of earlier development to be considered here is the Strong Vocational Interest Blank, published in its first edition in 1927 and undergoing subsequent revision. In its present form it consists of 400 items grouped in parts according to type of content. The groupings are as follows: (1) occupations, 100 items; (2) school subjects, 36; (3) amusements, 49; (4) activities (hobbies, etc.), 48; (5) peculiarities of people, 47; (6) preference of occupational activities, 40; (7) comparison of interest in pairs of items, 40; and (8) rating of personal abilities and characteristics, 40. There is also a women's form with a total of 400 items, of which it has 263 in common with the men's form. In the first five parts the respondent marks each item *L*, *I*, or *D* to indicate whether he likes, is indifferent to, or dislikes it, while for the remaining parts the manner of response differs from this. Scoring the blank is such a time-consuming task that it is done at certain centers with appropriate equipment, and for the work a charge is made, which has operated somewhat to restrict the use of the blank as compared with the Kuder Inventory next to be described. Nevertheless, the blank has been widely used and an extensive body of investigative literature has been published concerning it.

The Strong Blank has been scored for something like 40 occupations, which may seem a small portion of the almost 30,000 jobs listed in the *Dictionary of Occupational Titles,* a fact which means that, even after all possible grouping of related occupations, interest in the great majority of occupations cannot be scored on it. Norms for the occupations are arrived at by comparing the responses of persons engaged in the given occupation with those of "men-in-general," in order to note the distinctive differences for that occupation.

The other instrument to be described and considered is the Kuder Preference Record: Occupational. It consists of 168 items assessing the following categories of interest: outdoor, mechanical, computational, scientific, persuasive, artistic, literary, musical, social service, and clerical. The method of response called for is to indicate which of three activities—all activities are presented in triads—is liked most and which is liked least. For example, one of the triads requires the examinee to rate in this way: "Visit an exhibit of famous paintings," "Visit an exhibit of various means of transportation," and "Visit an exhibit of laboratory equipment," which indicate, respectively, artistic, mechanical, and scientific preferences. As implied above, the Preference Record is more easily scored than the Strong Blank. It may even be scored, with appropriate direction, by respondents themselves. The smaller expense of using the Preference Record as compared with that of the Strong Blank is an important factor in its widespread use in schools and colleges. Like the Strong Blank, it has been extensively investigated, and thus has been subjected to evaluation in various relationships.

The reading difficulty, as indicated by grade level, on the Lewerenz formula as found by Stefflre (*51*) for the Strong Blank is 10.4 and for the Kuder Record is 8.4. Thus, in this respect both are usable at both high school and college levels, although there is some question of the suitability of the Strong Blank at lower high school levels or with less competent students.

Stability of measured interests.—The widespread use of vocational interest inventories is proof of considerable confidence in them. This is not to say that they are without their severely negative critics. Some of these go so far as virtually to deny that the inventories in their present state of development have *any* utility in guidance and counseling. Lalegar (*35, 93*), near the end of an elaborate report on the application of the Strong and Manson Blanks to more than 700 eleventh-grade girls, sums up by saying that "on the basis of all available data regarding [these inventories], there exists insufficient evidence of their validity and practicability to render them of significant value in vocational counseling." Two other writers, Rothney and Schmidt (*45*), identify, among a number of other reasons, why these devices as counseling tools "should be limited to a few very exceptional uses": the ease of faking responses; the absence of predictive validity when a follow-up is made of subjects who have taken the inventory previously; the student interpretation that these inventory outcomes are scores of aptitude; and the lack of evidence in them on the intensity of interest. These and other strictures on the usefulness of these instruments prompt citation of inquiries that afford at least partial appraisal in significant aspects.

One of these areas of appraisal must be the degree of stability of the interests as indicated by these inventories. Another area is the age of arrival of stability. This area is of particular importance to a canvass, like the present one, of the characteristics of the later adolescent who is of later high school and early college age.

The published evidence bearing on the two issues of stability of measured interests and at what age it arrives is more extensive on the Strong Blank than on the Kuder, so more will be cited about the Strong but without neglect of the latter. The essence of Strong's earlier work was inquiry into the degree of commonalty of interest of younger men (college seniors) and men engaged in certain occupations. The procedures were later extended downwards to include 15-year-olds. The coefficients of correlation between the "likes" of three different age-groups have been reported by him to be as follows:

	r
15 vs. 25 years of age	.82
15 vs. 55 years of age	.73
25 vs. 55 years of age	.88

Strong says, "These coefficients mean that the rank-order of liking the 400 items on the blank is quite similar for all ages from 15 years on" (*56, 91*). The coefficients for the different parts of the blank are reported in Table 5.10. It may be noted that for only three of the parts is the correlation at or below .75 and that for four it is at .86 or higher. In further analysis by age Strong reports that approximately a third of the change in interests takes place between 15.5 and 16.5 years, another third between 16.5 and 18.5 years, and the remaining third during the 6½ years between 18.5 and

25 years. A justifiable interpretation seems to be that, so far as these evidences from the blank are concerned, interests are rather well, even though not fully, stabilized by early college years. Strong's conclusion is that by and large there are some changes in the number of items liked and disliked, particularly between 15 and 25 years of age, but that the changes are "surprisingly small" (288).

As a practical consideration, the assurance of consistency or stability of interests at given school levels, that is, at given high school or college years, is more useful than at given age levels, like 15 or 25. On this account at this point focus is on findings of investigations inquiring into consistency in students at various school levels. The procedures in all investigations

TABLE 5.10
COEFFICIENTS OF RANK ORDERS OF ITEMS IN THE
STRONG BLANK FOR 15- AND 25-YEAR-OLDS

Parts of Blank	Coefficient
Occupations (100 items)	.75
School subjects (36)	.66
Amusements (49)	.83
Activities (48)	.67
Kinds of people (47)	.92
Order of preference of activities (40)	.90
Comparison between two items (40)	.86
Present abilities (40)	.86
Entire blank (400)	.82

SOURCE: Adopted from Strong (56, 98, Table 16).

cited are longitudinal in that the same respondents are represented in all retests. Van Dusen (66) administered the Strong Blank to freshmen at the University of Florida and again to the same men as seniors. The vocations chosen as representative were engineer, lawyer, teacher, office clerk, and certified public accountant. Consistency was studied directly from the freshmen-senior correlations. Van Dusen concluded that "predictions may be successfully based upon the relationships found to exist between freshman and senior scores." Another application of the Strong Blank was made by Burnham (6) on Yale freshmen, who were retested three years later. He found that occupational interest scores revealed a higher stability than psychological test scores, which are known to reveal substantial consistency on retest. In further interpretation of his evidence, Burnham observed that a student's tendency to change his responses between first and second testings was not a chance affair but probably an indication of a real change of interests.

Among investigations of populations at the high school level is one by Canning, Taylor, and Carter (7). This involved boys in an Oakland, California, high school, who were tested, using the Strong Blank for men, as sophomores, juniors, and seniors. The interest scales used were: chemist, lawyer, life insurance salesman, teacher, YMCA secretary, office worker, and certified public accountant. The coefficients of correlation for the scores on test and retest separated by a two-year span ranged from .48 to .66, which is lower than those reported by Strong for college seniors retested five years later—those ranged from .59 to .84. However, the correlations and the stability inferred from them were as high as found in the Van Dusen and Burnham studies. Another investigation, by Finch (*18*), involving students of both sexes, some groups tested and retested at varying intervals in high school and other groups tested in high school and again in college, obtained an "index of permanence." This was done for twenty occupations. He reported that this index was "in general found to be extremely high" and that the sex differences in permanence, while favoring the boys, were much smaller than anticipated, since the scoring was done with keys designed for men. The length of time intervals between test and retest appeared to have little influence on the index. In every group, however, "there occurred occasional cases with zero or negative resemblance between successive sets of scores."

In a project restricted to girls, reported by Taylor and Carter (*61*), 58 students in an Oakland, California, public high school were tested twice with the Strong Vocational Interest Blank for Women, first in grade 11 and the second time a year later in grade 12. These girls had no vocational courses and no systematic vocational guidance during the year. Each test blank was scored for twelve occupational groups: librarian, physician, nurse, social worker, teacher of mathematics, teacher of social sciences, artist, lawyer, saleswoman of life insurance, office worker, stenographer-secretary, and housewife. In addition, the blanks were scored to secure measures of femininity of interests by a procedure devised by Strong. From available files data were obtained for each girl concerning intelligence and socioeconomic status. From these fifteen variables profiles were plotted for each girl in the group, with the results from both tests, for ready comparison, recorded on the same form. In addition, the rank order of scores on the twelve scales from the first testing was correlated with that from the second testing. These *rho* coefficients ranged from −.65 to +.99, with a median of +.74. This rather high positive average suggests that the pairs of profiles indicate at least substantial consistency for most of the girls. This inference is supported by the paired profiles reproduced in the article for eight presumably representative girls, the coefficients for whom were reported as .86, .11, .97, .96, .85, .84, .88, and .01, with two of them indicating negligible resemblance of the paired profiles and the other six high to very high degrees of similarity. The facts prompt the following observation by the authors: "Such results suggest that constancy of pattern of interests varies greatly among individuals, but that in many cases it is sufficient to permit prediction of subsequent interest patterns. Since it is difficult or impossible to select in advance the cases showing stability of pattern, it seems advisable to have retest results as a basis for counseling work wherever possible." They say further, "The data are consistent with the hypothesis that the Strong Vocational Blank for Women provides significant and valuable information about the interests of high school girls."

An investigation by Mallinson and Crumrine (40) concerned administration of the Kuder Preference Record: Vocational to students in grade 9

TABLE 5.11
PERCENTAGES OF CASES IN WHICH THE RANKINGS OF THE THREE HIGHEST AREAS REMAINED CONSTANT

Ninth-grade Interest Area Rankings Compared With Twelfth-grade Rankings	School			
	X	Y	Z	Total
Highest that remained highest	48	63	75	52
Second highest that remained second highest	30	36	70	34
Third highest that remained third highest	27	17	60	28

SOURCE: Mallinson and Crumrine (40, Table II).

and to the same students again in grade 12, that is, three years apart, in three high schools in Michigan. For each student, the nine areas of interest (mechanical, computational, scientific, persuasive, artistic, literary, musical, social service, and clerical) were ranked for each student and the two rankings compared. The method of comparing rankings differed from those previously reported here: it did not involve either computing the coefficients of correlation or preparing profiles, but instead dealt with ascertaining the percentages of students with identical rankings of the interests. An illustrative outcome of this comparison is seen in Table 5.11, which is to be read as follows: In School X, for 48 per cent of the students, the area with the highest ranking in grade 9 remained highest in grade 12, for 30 per cent of the students the second highest ranking in grade 9 remained second highest in grade 12, etc. It may be noted that for more than half the students in all three schools the area with highest ranking in grade 9 remained highest in grade 12. These figures indicate a substantial degree of consistency of interest even as early as the first high school year. At the same time there is enough deviation in the rankings to warn against relying on any single measure of interest on such an instrument for encouraging a student to enter a given occupation.

The conclusion from the evidence of the investigations looking into permanence of interests in relation to age and school level as indicated on the Strong Blank has been well stated by Super and Crites (59, 453), who summarize that the development of interests is "well under way by adolescence, for by age 14 or 15 the interest patterns of boys and girls have begun to take forms similar to those of adults" and that "by the time [they] are from 19 to 20 years of age their interests are fairly well crystalized, and in most cases change very little thereafter." The upshot of analogous studies on the Kuder Record appears to be about the same.

Relation to self-estimates and vocational choices.—A critical issue with respect to vocational interest inventories concerns their usefulness in comparison with self-estimates and with simple expressions of vocational preferences. This usefulness can to a degree be evaluated by statistical comparison of the scores derived from the inventories with self-ratings and occupational choices of the same individuals. Several investigations of this kind have been reported.

An investigation comparing self-ratings with both Strong and Kuder scores was made by Berdie (4) on 500 men who came to the Student Counseling Bureau of the University of Minnesota. These subjects ranged from 14 through 37 years of age, with the median age of 20.6 years; only 7 were under 16 and only 11 were 30 or older. The population consisted of precollege men and students enrolled in several different colleges of the university. The self-rating device provided for the following nine areas of interest: (1) biological sciences, (2) artistic creation and appreciation, (3) physical sciences, (4) technical occupations, (5) social service, (6) musical occupations, (7) business detail, (8) selling, and (9) verbal or literary. The form provided for a continuum of five gradations from very low to very high on each of the areas, the gradations reading as follows: "My interests are very much unlike interests of people in this area"; "Somewhat dissimilar"; "No marked similarity or dissimilarity"; "Somewhat similar"; "My interests strongly resemble the interests of people in this area." The contingency coefficients obtained for each of the areas are reported in Table 5.12. Berdie pointed out that in three areas the Strong scores are more closely related to the self-ratings than are the Kuder scores and that in six areas the Kuder scores are more closely related. He mentions also that the subjects seemed to find it more difficult to estimate their own scientific interests and were more able to estimate their sales and persuasive interests. He said that the results are in general agreement with those obtained by other investigators and that the correlation between the self-estimates and the measured interests approximates .50. The closer relationship for the Kuder is explained by the difference in subtlety of the Strong and Kuder instruments. Berdie concluded that for no occupational area was there close enough agreement between measured interests and self-estimates to suggest that counseling can be done on the basis of one or the other alone.

A somewhat earlier comparison of estimates was made by Crosby and Winsor (14) on students in classes in psychology at Cornell University. This comparison included both men and women and used scores from the Kuder Record only and with respect to seven occupational areas. The average r found was .54, which the authors report is only about 15 per cent better than a guess. They expressed the opinion that the difference shows that students do have a "reasonable idea" of what their interests are,

TABLE 5.12
CONTINGENCY COEFFICIENTS SHOWING RELATIONSHIPS BETWEEN SELF-RATINGS AND SCORES ON THE STRONG VOCATIONAL INTEREST BLANK AND THE KUDER PREFERENCE RECORD

Occupational Area	Self-rating with Strong	Self-rating with Kuder
Technical	.55	.47
Computational	.61	.34
Physical sciences	.32	.46
Social service	.43	.52
Musical	.39	.60
Sales	.58	.58
Biological sciences	.27	.30
Verbal-literary	.51	.61
Artistic	.33	.58
Clerical	.61*	.52

SOURCE: Berdie (4, Table 2).
*This is the same statistic as for "Computational."

although, "as a measure of validity, it is not large enough to warrant any decrease in the use of interest inventories in college guidance work. In fact, it should be interpreted as an indication of the actual need for such well validated devices in aiding the student."

In an inquiry in this investigation into differences between the sexes, only one of the seven parts yielded a significant difference in ability to estimate their own interests. This was in the social service division, in which women seem to be able to evaluate the amount of their interest much more accurately than men. This is explained as being in harmony with the theory that women at this age are more mature in their interests than men.

The expectation would be, because of what may be termed the "transparency" of the ratings in the self-estimates, that is, their apparent relationship to occupations, that the degree of relationship bears out this expectation. Darley (15, 21–25) found a contingency coefficient of .43 between the claimed vocational choices and inventoried interests on the Strong Blank for men at the University of Minnesota. Kopp and Tussing

(*32*) obtained coefficients of .59 and .50, respectively, for high school boys and girls for expressed interests compared with scores on the Kuder Record. The expressed interests were obtained on a questionnaire listing the nine occupational areas represented in the Kuder, with representative occupations enumerated under each, asking the student to number the areas in the order of preference. The coefficients were calculated from the rankings of areas on the Kuder for individual students and their rankings on the questionnaire. The coefficients, while somewhat higher than that just reported from Darley, nonetheless indicate a relationship low enough to reaffirm an admonition analogous to those cited above on the use of

TABLE 5.13
COEFFICIENTS OF CORRELATION BETWEEN SCORES ON THE KUDER PREFERENCE RECORD AND THE AMERICAN COUNCIL ON EDUCATION PSYCHOLOGICAL EXAMINATION

Kuder Record	Men			Women		
	Total Score	Q	L	Total Score	Q	L
Mechanical	−.073	−.065	−.087	−.047	−.069	−.069
Computational	.105	.252	−.038	.124	.371	−.183
Scientific	.041	.059	.026	.112	.027	.020
Persuasive	.010	−.011	.035	.332	.103	.208
Artistic	−.030	−.126	.054	.286	.026	.189
Literary	.273	.106	.383	.415	.009	.437
Musical	.069	.042	.085	−.079	−.104	−.084
Social Science	−.258	−.188	−.289	−.010	−.078	−.213
Clerical	.030	.147	−.081	−.010	−.062	−.269

SOURCE: Triggs (*63*).

self-estimates and scores from measured interests, that counseling should not be done on the basis of either vocational preference or measured interests alone.

Other relationships of interest scores.—Usefulness of the scores from vocational interest blanks must in large part be determined by their relationships to other measures or kinds of evidence concerning the respondents. A number of investigations of such relationships have been made, among them those with measures of intelligence or aptitude and with achievement as measured by standardized tests or by marks assigned for course work. Also, usefulness should to some extent be observable in a comparison of measures for individuals on two or more of these instruments, for example, occupational keys on the Strong Blank with scores on the Kuder Preference Record.

Among the more nearly comprehensive investigations of such relationships is one reported by Triggs (*63, 64, 65*), who utilized Kuder scores and test evidence obtained for 166 men and 101 women, a total of 267, of whom 205, or a full three-fourths, were underclassmen in various colleges at the University of Illinois. The test of aptitude used was the American Council on Education Psychological Examination. Coefficients of correlation were calculated between the nine scores on the Kuder and the total ACE score and the sections of the examination yielding the Q (Quantitative) and L (Linguistic) scores. The coefficients are presented in Table 5.13. It may be noted that the coefficients tend to run higher for women than men. Focusing attention on the coefficients for the Q and L columns only and assuming significance for coefficients larger than .20, either positive or negative, three such coefficients for men may be identified and five

TABLE 5.14
CORRELATION BETWEEN CERTAIN STRONG VOCATIONAL INTERESTS BLANK SCORES AND SCORES ON FOUR IOWA HIGH SCHOOL CONTENT SCORES AND THE PSYCHOLOGICAL EXAMINATION

Iowa High School Content	Strong					
	Engineering	Medicine	Law	Life Insurance	Personnel Managemt.	Purchasing Agent
English Language	−.10	−.11	.09	−.04	.10	−.43
Mathematics	.49	.28	−.03	−.27	−.15	.04
Science	.36	.29	−.01	−.29	−.17	−.26
History and Social Studies	−.16	−.05	.09	.08	.04	−.26
Psychological Examination	.10	−.02	.00	−.12	−.08	−.32

SOURCE: Segel and Brintle (47, Table II).

for women. Of the three for men, the .252 for Computational on the Kuder and Q and the .383 for Literary and L are plausible, although explanation for the negative coefficient for Social Science is not so readily apparent. Again, for the women, the .371 between Computational scores for women and Q, the .208 between Persuasive scores and L, the .437 between Literary and L, are plausible, while explanations of the two negative correlations for Social Science and L and Clerical and L are not at once apparent. It should be noted further that in no instance does a coefficient point to a high degree of relationship.

For evidence on the relationship of vocational interest scores to school achievement as measured by tests and by school marks Triggs relies on a study by Segel and Brintle (47) involving 100 junior college freshmen. Specifically, these investigators reported, as in Table 5.14, the coefficients of correlation between Strong scores for certain occupations and scores on parts of the Iowa High School Content Examinations and the American Council on Education Examination. Nine of the 24 coefficients, both positive and negative, involving the Iowa High School Content scores are greater than .20. The two positive coefficients each for engineering and medicine of this magnitude are in expected directions. The remaining five, with life insurance and purchasing agent, are all negative and less readily explicable. Again, none is high. The only significant coefficient for the psychological examination is −.32 for purchasing agent.

Segel and Brintle (47) also calculated coefficients between the same keys for the Strong Blank and first year college marks in English, languages, mathematics and science, and history. These are not reproduced here, but it may be reported that only five emerged to the level of significance, four of them barely, and a single one rising to −.47 for history and engineering. The authors generalize that the relationship of the scores with college marks is "quite low," their explanation being the "lack of reliability" of marks and "other factors taken into account by teachers in marking."

The urgent need in guidance and counseling for improvement in predictions of competence in school subjects in relation to interests has stimulated a number of investigations relying on refinements of method. Among investigators who have devised advances in method are Frandsen and Sessions, in collaboration (22), working with records of high school seniors, and Frandsen (21), alone, with records obtained for college underclassmen. In the investigation at the high school level the students involved were 137 seniors in their eighth semester in the Logan, Utah, High School. The measures of achievement used were grade-point ratios computed from all their marks in subjects, taken during seven semesters, classified into the nine interest categories of the Kuder Record. For example, under scientific were classified the subjects chemistry, physics, geology, sociology, psychology, genetics, physiology, and cooking. Interest was indicated by (a) percentile scores on the nine parts of the Kuder record and (b) student self-rating for preferences into rank-orders of all different subjects taken by each student. The ratings were then all classified according to Kuder categories, ranks were averaged, and reranked from 1 to 9. The grade-point ratios were also ranked, thus giving for each student three different measures ranked from 1 to 9.

For each individual rank-difference correlations were computed between his rank order of achievement and each of his two rank-ordered measures of interest. The distribution of coefficients and the median and first and third quartile coefficients are presented in tabular form in the full report. Table 5.15 presents only the medians and quartiles, as these, with brief interpretative comments, will yield most of the significance of the study. The median correlation between rank-order of Kuder interests and rank-order of grades is .27, which means that for half of these high school students the correlations between Kuder interest patterns are .27

or higher. The authors say, "This probably means that for some students intrinsic interests as measured by the *Kuder Preference Record* are significantly related to their patterns of school achievement." They point out that for a fourth of these students the rank-difference correlations between interest and achievement patterns are "very high," ranging between .73 and 1.00, but they point out also that for other students the relation between interest and achievement patterns is absent or inverted: for 31.7 per cent the coefficients are zero or lower, and for a fourth, they are between $-.16$ and -1.00. The relations between the self-rated interest

TABLE 5.15
MEDIANS AND FIRST AND THIRD QUARTILES OF INTRA-INDIVIDUAL CORRELATIONS BETWEEN INTERESTS AND ACHIEVEMENT AND BETWEEN MEASURED AND SELF-RATED INTERESTS

Rho	Kuder Interest Rank and Rank-Order of Achievement	Self-rated Interest and Rank-Order of Achievement	Kuder Interest Rank and Self-rating Rank
N	137	109	109
Median	.27	.51	.48
Q_1	−.16	.18	.12
Q_3	.73	.82	.82

SOURCE: Frandsen and Sessions (*22*, adapted from Table 1).

and the rank-order of achievement and between the Kuder interest and self-rating ranks, as seen in the last two columns of the table, run higher and do not differ widely.

The investigation at the underclassman college level by Frandsen (*21*) utilized for 81 students at Utah State Agricultural College (now Utah State University) Kuder measures of interests and scores on the USAFI (College Level) Tests of General Educational Development which had been devised during World War II to measure the competence in general education subject areas of members of the Armed Forces who wished to avail themselves of GI benefits. The scores on Kuder were the usual nine. The achievement tests were those in natural sciences, social studies, and "Correctness and Effectiveness of Expression." This study took into account a hypothesis quoted from Strong that interests may correlate significantly with achievement when achievement involves performance over a considerable time, the assumption being that coefficients formerly found between interests and course marks have been low because performance has extended through single courses only. The manner of assuring conditions conforming to the hypothesis was to administer the tests to students who had had extended contact through courses in the three subject areas named.

The correlations reported by Frandsen are to be found in Table 5.16.

His interpretation is that, contrary to the zero or low correlations usually found between interest and achievement in single courses, some significant and logically consistent correlations between interest and long-time achievement may be observed. He directs attention especially to the coefficient of .50 between scientific interest and achievement in natural science. He mentions that the scatter-diagram for these measures shows further that every person above average in science achieved a relatively high score on this test. He expresses the opinion that "the correlations with natural science achievement of .31 for computational interest, of −.33 for persuasive interest, and of −.30 for social service interest are also signifi-

TABLE 5.16
CORRELATIONS BETWEEN KUDER INTERESTS AND USAFI (COLLEGE LEVEL) TESTS OF GENERAL EDUCATIONAL DEVELOPMENT FOR 81 SOPHOMORES*

Achievement Tests	Kuder Interests								
	Mechanical	Computational	Scientific	Persuasive	Artistic	Literary	Musical	Social Service	Clerical
Natural Science	.14	.31	.50	−.33	−.02	.17	−.10	−.30	−.16
Social Studies	.02	.05	.34	−.12	−.14	.31	−.09	−.37	−.21
C and E† of Expression	−.03	−.02	.15	−.19	.06	.16	.15	−.37	−.51

SOURCE: Frandsen (*21*, Table 1).
*71 women and 10 men.
†Correctness and effectiveness.

cant and suggest plausible interpretations." He mentions also that the correlation of .31 of achievement in the social studies with literary interests is "consistent" but that the negative correlation of −.37 between achievement in social studies and social service is "surprising." He concludes that the general trend of results of this study and the findings from related investigations seem to justify the use of vocational interest inventories in guidance and also to support the otherwise well-established belief in the effectiveness of appeal to interest in teaching.

Another investigation of the relationship of measured interest to ability aiming at an improvement of procedure is one by Wesley, Corey, and Stewart (*68*). The measures of interest were obtained by administering the Kuder Preference Record, although the Persuasive and Social Service categories were omitted because of the lack of adequate tests of ability in these areas. The measures of ability selected to correspond to the interest categories were: Survey of Mechanical Insight; Stanford Arithmetic Test; Iowa High School Content Examination, Section 3, Science; The Meier Art Judgment Test; Iowa High School Content Examination, English and Literature; Seashore Measures of Musical Talent, Series A; and Minnesota Vocational Test for Clerical Workers. Because some of these tests are known as tests of aptitude, in some degree this study may be regarded as an inquiry into the relationship of interest and aptitude. The subjects were 156 male college students enrolled in an introductory course in psychology, of whom the total number varied from day to day during the period over which the different tests were being administered.

The refinement of procedure in this investigation as compared with older ones bearing on the issue of the relation of measured interests to ability is that of obtaining correlations based on scores representing deviations from the *individual's own mean* rather than that of the group. The authors refer to the outcome as the "intra-individual relationship between interest and

TABLE 5.17
CORRELATION BETWEEN INTEREST AND ABILITY BASED ON DEVIATIONS FROM GROUP AND INDIVIDUAL MEANS

Vocational Area	Group Means		Individual Means	
	N	r	N	r
Mechanical	131	.44	126	.50
Computational	115	.24	112	.47
Scientific	126	.33	126	.35
Artistic	131	.29	127	.31
Literary	125	.47	125	.68
Musical	122	.21	118	.23
Clerical	132	.07	125	.33
Mean		.30		.42

SOURCE: Wesley, Corey, and Stewart (*68*, Table 1).

ability." The mean ability score for each subject was computed, in terms of standard score units. The differences between his separate ability scores and his own mean level of ability were next determined. These differences became the measures of relative ability to be correlated with the corresponding measures of interest. Because the Kuder Record is so constructed that every item is chosen at the expense of another, it was assumed that the resulting interest scores were approximately relative to the individual mean and that further manipulation of these data was not necessary. Pearson coefficients between *relative* interests and *relative* ability were computed. For ready comparison, to note the influence of the change in procedure, both the coefficients between interests and ability based on (1) group means and (2) individual means are reproduced in Table 5.17. All coefficients are seen to increase by the change, some only slightly but others substantially. The rise in the mean coefficient is from .30 to .42, which the authors report is significant above the 1 per cent level of confidence.

However, these mean measures conceal the wide variation in correlations for individuals, which are not reported. Rank-order correlations ranged from −.57 to +1.00. The authors sought explanation by comparing the top and bottom fourths in the distribution on (1) age, (2) Army Alpha scores, and (3) scores on the MMPI (Minnesota Multiphasic Personality Inventory). No significant differences were found for age and intelligence, and the meaning of a statistically significant difference found on one scale of the Personality Inventory was problematic. Such a wide range in congruency must raise doubts concerning the adequacy even of the refinement in procedure used to find dependable relationships and shows strongly the need for corroborating evidence from other sources of interest-ability congruency.

Reference to the MMPI in the preceding paragraph suggests the question of the relationship between scores on measured interests and personality. Some decades ago there was considerable interest in nonprojective measures of personality, but in recent years it has subsided almost to extinction, mainly because of the lack of validity of the instruments and the greater promise of projective measures now being developed and in process of appraisal. In consequence, studies of the relationships of measured interests to scores from nonprojective instruments to measure personality traits will not be canvassed here. Neither will investigations of relationships of the measured interests to measures on these subtler instruments be reviewed, in most part because of the dearth of evidence from them bearing on the age-group with which we are mainly concerned.

The single remaining relationship to be considered here is that between the interest blanks or inventories themselves. Triggs (63) has reported the correlations between occupational scores obtained from the Strong Blank and scores on the Kuder scales for the same men and women represented in earlier citations from her investigations in this section. In interpreting such correlations it is important to bear in mind that the Strong scores purport to measure the interests of people in occupations, whereas the Kuder scores measure what may be regarded as more nearly pure interest factors. Triggs correlated the scores for seven groups of occupations classified into areas, the correlations being reported for each group in a separate table: Creative-Scientific, Scientific, Subprofessional, Social Service, Business Detail, Business Contact, and Linguistic. Several of the higher coefficients found are cited here. Relatively high positive correlations with Kuder scientific interest were found for Strong scores for physician (.50) and dentist (.45), and between Kuder artistic scores for interest and Strong scores for artist (.56), architect (.67), and dentist (.45). A few illustrations of relatively high correlations in other tables are: in the Subprofessional table, Carpenter on Strong with Mechanical on Kuder, .67; in the Business Detail table, Accountant on Strong with

Clerical on Kuder, .55; and in the Business Contact table, Life Insurance Sales on Strong with Persuasive on Kuder, .58. A number of significant negative correlations also emerged from the calculations. Thus, the administration of two such inventories as compared with a single one provides needed corroboration. In Triggs' words, "On the whole this study has confirmed relationships which one who was familiar with these instruments might expect to find. A careful study of these data will help counselors to understand and utilize interest measurement more meaningfully . . ." (544). At the same time she says that "a great deal more evidence of this kind is needed before the interpretation of these measures will become the asset it should be in the guidance program."

Usefulness of the instruments.—Stabilization of vocational interests, as measured by the instruments being considered in this section, appears to be in progress in early high school years and well along by later high school and early college years. Whatever the instruments may measure, this stabilization comes at about the same time as realism in vocational choice, which was reported earlier in this chapter to crystallize in later adolescent years. Some degree of congruence is found between these measures and both self-estimates of interest and occupational preference, but the correlation is far from high enough, in counseling students, for reliance on the measurements of interests alone. Reports of investigations of the relationship of measured interests to intelligence and general aptitude have been made and the correlations have usually been found to be low, although they emerge to partial significance when scores on certain interests are correlated with scores on quantitative or linguistic portions of aptitude tests.

The earlier investigations of the relationship of measured interests to course marks or to scores on tests of achievement produced mainly low and few significant correlations, but refinements of method in later investigations have yielded substantially larger coefficients. However, they are still far from large enough to afford a basis for prediction of performance on the basis of scores on interests. Intercorrelations between scores from two different instruments for measuring vocational interest are large enough to afford some degree of reciprocal corroboration, but far from high or consistent enough to warrant accepting the score from one instrument for the score on the other.

Usefulness of the vocational interest blanks and inventories is conditioned not only by relationships like the foregoing, but also by, among others, such factors as the reading ability required to answer them and the scope or range of occupations to which they can be made to apply. Mention was made above of the grade levels of reading difficulty of the Strong Blank and the Kuder Inventory, and it appears that the latter can be administered successfully at lower grade levels and with youth of somewhat less ability than the former. However, experimental efforts have demonstrated that vocabulary study in advance of administration of the instruments increases their intelligibility for respondents.

The Strong Blank has been scored for only forty occupations, and most of these are at the professional, semiprofessional, and other higher levels. The Kuder operates under a somewhat analogous limitation. However, this stricture is moderated to a degree by two considerations, one being the resemblance of specific occupations that permits some grouping into areas and the other that youth, as was reported earlier in the chapter, tend to concentrate their choices in the higher socioeconomic groupings.

It should be clear enough from what has been reported here that we do not have in these blanks and inventories a "quickie" for determining the vocations for individual youth. The most that can be expected of them in their present state of development will be derived from their use in conjunction with other measurements and types of information. After all, the guidance and counseling of the individual concerning his occupational choice and destination, since it is now accepted as being deeply involved with his self-image and personality, should in most, if not all, cases be a protracted process utilizing evidence from many sources, which may well include such instruments aimed at measuring interests.

Summary

The two foregoing divisions of this chapter are concerned with (a) expressed occupational preferences and plans of youth and (b) vocational interests as disclosed by instruments devised to ascertain these interests. The first division presents digests of a selected succession of investigations of preferences and plans, the subjects in the first projects being of junior high school age and those in projects subsequently summarized reaching into later high school years and later adolescence, with the aim of noting the degree of realism of choice or plan of youth near or on the threshold of college. Although the findings of the studies are hardly in full agreement and disclose varying degrees of realism, it is found that youth who have had experience in programs of counseling indicate realistic preferences in larger proportions. The distribution of occupations is found to be influenced by the manner of inquiry, as the responses tend to be more realistic if the request is for occupational plans rather than preferences or aspirations.

The distributions of occupations obtained from these inquiries show a heavy preponderance of preferences and plans in the higher occupational levels, with much larger proportions at these levels than in the distribution of occupations of the fathers of the respondents and of the occupational distribution of adults in the population. These discrepant distributions are often considered as indicative of unrealistic choices, but discrepancy is in substantial part offset by the fact that educational plans of the students typically outreach the educational attainments of fathers and of adults in the population. Realism of choice is somewhat influenced by general aptitude, or intelligence, and the stages of sexual maturity appear to have a significant bearing on choices, although we have need of longitudinal investigations of this relationship.

Specific occupations in the preferences and plans are so diverse as to preclude brief summarization. Specific titles and groups, except in the area of the business and clerical, show very little overlap for the two sexes.

Findings of two inquiries into occupational plans at the college level were in conflict, but the more substantial investigation gave evidence of the great majority having made decisions as to life work. Review of the large-scale study of plans of junior college students (in California) shows those for a major proportion of students of lower ability to be unrealistic, but it must be said that the project antedates the development in junior colleges of extensive programs of guidance and counseling.

Inquiry into motivation as expressed in the "reasons for" choice of occupations finds them to be diverse but more often than otherwise ascribable to monetary return, "liking" the occupation, or belief in fitness for it. Choices of girls, somewhat more than boys, go to socially serviceable occupations.

An investigation in Wisconsin into the variability and consistency of vocational choices by high school students reporting in interview found rather low consistency over a three-year span. However, a follow-up of the students five to seven months after graduation, to ascertain whether or not the counseled subjects had entered post-high-school occupations or were training for those which had been chosen during high school years, found increase by small percentages for choices as seniors as compared with choices as sophomores and juniors. The proportion of consistency of choices as seniors reached a full majority of the subjects, which seems substantial in view of the small extent of counseling given.

Studies of the prestige of occupations over the years have shown a remarkable approach to similarity in rankings, and comparison of the rankings by age of respondents discloses only minor differences, chiefly in higher ratings for newer occupations by younger people. This prestige must be exceedingly influential in the occupational plans and preferences of youth. Objective inquiry finds income level and educational attainment to be good predictors of the general standing of occupations, while rankings on "pays well" and "service to humanity" have been found to be highly correlated with each other and with "social prestige." Because these inquiries are in a sense in the realm of the psychology of occupations and of occupational choice, it is appropriate to bear in mind the observation of an authority in this field, Roe, who said that occupational choice can be taken, within limits, as a self-categorization, "as an indication of at least some aspects of the self-image."

The discrepancies found between the distributions of occupational preferences and plans of youth and of their fathers' occupations (as well as the occupational distribution in the population) is involved in the question of social mobility which is regarded as essential to an open society, since in such a society vertical movement of individuals should be possible from one socioeconomic level to another. The investigations of mobility abstracted above may show disagreement as to its extent but they were in agreement on its existence, and it appears that a significant factor of it is the extent of education. The issue thus turns on the obstacles to continuance of the individual's schooling.

The conclusion is well established that college attendance is encouraged by high aptitude and high socioeconomic status as indicated by the occupational level of the father, and discouraged by low aptitude and low status. In the operation of these forces a large proportion of youth of high aptitude and of low status do not aspire to college attendance, but it appears that this is not merely on account of the economic factor alone, as many youth are also negatively influenced by contentment with the general way of life of families of lower status. Thus, our will to maintain an open society providing upward mobility for children of middle- and lower-class families must be served by efforts to surmount both economic and attitudinal barriers to college attendance. Of great importance in these efforts is the establishment and maintenance of the community college, which is a natural for the purpose; it lowers the cost of this level of education and is changing the attitudes toward education at the collegiate level through bringing it within commuting distance and broadening the program, just as the spread of the high school and the enrichment of its program have made attendance at the secondary level almost universal.

The inadequacy of expressed preferences and plans as indicative of vocational interests has led to the development and application of tests of interests known as "blanks" and "inventories," the two most used of which, the Strong Vocational Interest Blank and the Kuder Preference Record: Occupational, are described in the second main section of the chapter, and their usefulness appraised by summarizing investigations making use of them. The reading ability required is such as to make both instruments usable at both high school and college levels.

The usefulness of the Strong and the Kuder instruments is still controversial. However, from the evidence of a number of studies of the stability of interests as measured by them, the conclusion is drawn that development of interests is well under way by adolescence and that by later adolescence interests are fairly well established. This finding is in accord with the extent of approach to realism in occupational choice inferred for those ages from the investigations of preferences and plans.

Investigators have inquired into the relationship of scores on these instruments to a number of other types of evidence, among them self-estimates of occupational interests and measures of intelligence or aptitude, achievement, and personality. The relationship to each other of measures on the different instruments themselves has also been explored. The relationship of self-estimates of occupational interests and scores on the instruments, while found to be appreciable, is nonetheless low enough that counseling should hardly be done on the basis of measured interests alone. Again, some relationship has been found between measures of interest and those of aptitude, but no correlation is high and many are low even where the expectation would betoken statistical significance. Computed relationships of measured interests to achievement as indicated by marks in courses have been mainly low, the explanation being the unreliability of these marks and factors other than achievement taken into account by teachers. Resort to refinements of investigative procedure, however, such as the use of standardized tests of achievement administered to students who had had extended contact in the disciplines represented, has yielded some significant and logically consistent correlations, although still not sufficiently large and consistent to obviate the need for corroborative evidence from other sources.

A relationship between interests and personality is readily postulated, but the discrediting of nonprojective instruments for rating personality has eliminated from serious consideration conclusions from projects utilizing them. For light on these relationships we must await more investigations applying to the later adolescents the more promising subtler projective instruments for appraising personality.

Inquiry into the interrelationship of measures of interest on instruments like the Strong Blank and the Kuder Preference Record is hampered by the fact that one purports to measure the interests of people in occupations, whereas scores on the other measure what may be regarded as more nearly pure interest factors. The relationships found are high enough to conclude that the administration of two such instruments as compared with a single one provides needed corroboration, but a great deal more evidence is needed before the interpretation of such measures will be the asset it should be in the guidance program.

Examination of the investigative literature on these instruments devised to discover the occupational interests of youth finds that most of it is concerned with the usefulness in guidance and counseling rather than with discovering the distribution of occupational interests among young people. On this account the foregoing treatment may be regarded as a sort of foreword to the consideration of the student personnel program in Chapter 12. The upshot concerning usefulness of the instruments is that they are hardly at a stage of development to permit use of them as the sole means of identifying occupational interests or of determining vocations for individual youth, but they may be used as *one* of the means of establishing these interests, to be corroborated by other means and methods in what should be in most cases a protracted process.

References and Bibliography

1. Adkins, Dorothy C., and Kuder, G. Frederic. "The Relation between Primary Mental Abilities and Activity Preferences." *Psychometrica*, 5 (Dec., 1940), 251–62.
2. Anderson, Rose G. "Do Aptitudes Support Interests?" *Personnel and Guidance Journal*, 32 (Sept., 1953), 14–17.
3. Berdie, Ralph F. "Factors Associated with Vocational Interests." *Journal of Educational Psychology*, 34 (May, 1943), 257–77.
4. Berdie, Ralph F. "Scores on the Strong Vocational Interest Blank and the Kuder Preference Record in Relation to Self-Ratings." *Journal of Applied Psychology*, 34 (Feb., 1950), 42–49.
5. Brink, William G. "Reading Interests of High School Pupils." *School Review*, 47 (Oct., 1939), 113–21.
6. Burnham, Paul S. "Stability of Interests." *School and Society*, 55 (March 21, 1942), 332–35.
7. Canning, Leslie; Taylor, Katherine V. F.; and Carter, Harold D. "Permanence of Interests of High School Boys." *Journal of Educational Psychology*, 32 (Oct., 1941), 481–94.
8. Carter, Harold D. "The Development of Vocational Interests." *Journal of Consulting Psychology*, 4 (1940), 185–99.
9. Carter, Harold D.; Pyles, M. K.; and Bretnall, E. P. "A Comparative Study of Factors in Vocational Interest Scores of High School Boys." *Journal of Educational Psychology*, 26 (Feb., 1935), 81–98.
10. Centers, Richard. "Education and Occupational Mobility." *American Sociological Review*, 14 (Feb., 1949), 143–44.
11. Centers, Richard. "Occupational Mobility of Urban Occupational Strata." *American Sociological Review*, 13 (April, 1948), 197–203.
12. Counts, George S. "Social Status of Occupations." *School Review*, 33 (Sept., 1925), 16–27.
13. Crathorne, A. R. "Change of Mind Between High School and College as to Life Work." *School and Society*, 11 (1920), 28–30.
14. Crosby, R. C., and Winsor, A. L. "The Validity of Students' Estimates of Their Interests." *Journal of Applied Psychology*, 25 (Aug., 1941), 408–14.
15. Darley, John G. *Clinical Aspects and Interpretation of the Strong Vocational Interest Blank*. New York: Psychological Corporation, 1941.
16. Darley, John G., and Hagenak, Theda. *Vocational Interest Measurement: Theory and Practice*. Minneapolis: University of Minnesota, 1955.
17. Deeg, M. E., and Paterson, Donald G. "Change in Social Status of Occupations." *Occupations*, 25 (Jan., 1947), 205–8.
18. Finch, F. H. "The Permanence of Vocational Interests." *Psychological Bulletin*, 33 (Nov., 1935), 682.

19. Fleege, Urban H., and Malone, Helen. "Motivation in Occupational Choice among Junior-Senior High School Students." *Journal of Educational Psychology,* 37 (Feb., 1946), 77–86.
20. Ford, C. Fenton, Jr., and Tyler, Leona E. "Factor Analysis of Terman and Miles M-F Test." *Journal of Applied Psychology,* 36 (Aug., 1952), 251–53.
21. Frandsen, Arden N. "Interests and General Educational Development." *Journal of Applied Psychology,* 31 (Feb., 1947), 57–66.
22. Frandsen, Arden N., and Sessions, Alwyn D. "Interests and School Achievement." *Educational and Psychological Measurement,* 13 (Spring, 1953), 94–101.
23. Ginzberg, E., et al. *Occupational Choice.* New York: Columbia University Press, 1951.
24. Harrison, E. C. "Vocational Choices and Reality One Year Later." *Personnel and Guidance Journal,* 32 (Nov., 1953), 144–46.
25. Hartson, L. D. "Vocational Choices—Before and After College." *Occupations,* 16 (Nov., 1937), 138–42.
26. Holden, G. S. "Scholastic Aptitude and the Relative Persistence of Vocational Choice." *Personnel and Guidance Journal,* 40 (Sept., 1961), 36–41.
27. Hurlock, E. B., and Jansing, C. "The Vocational Attitudes of Boys and Girls of High School Age." *Journal of Genetic Psychology,* 44 (1934), 175–90.
28. Hutson, P. W. *The Guidance Function in Education.* Rev. ed. New York: Appleton-Century-Crofts, Inc., 1968.
29. Jones, Edward S. "Relation of Ability to Preferred and Probable Occupations." *Educational Administration and Supervision,* 26 (March, 1940), 220–26.
30. Kahl, Joseph A. *The American Class Structure.* New York: Rinehart Co., 1957.
31. Kahl, Joseph A. "Educational and Occupational Aspirations of Common Man Boys." *Harvard Educational Review,* 23 (Summer, 1953), 186–203.
32. Kopp, T., and Tussing, L. "The Vocational Choices of High School Students as Related to Scores on Vocational Interest Inventories." *Occupations,* 25 (March, 1947), 334–39.
33. Kroger, Robert, and Louttit, C. M. "The Influence of Fathers' Occupations on the Vocational Choices of High School Boys." *Journal of Applied Psychology,* 19 (1935), 203–12.
34. Kuder, G. Frederick. *Manual, Kuder Preference Record Occupational.* Chicago: Science Research Associates, 1959.
35. Lalegar, Grace E. *Vocational Interests of High School Girls.* New York: Bureau of Publications, Teachers College, Columbia University, 1942.
36. Lehman, Harvey C., and Witty, Paul A. "Sex Differences in Vocational Attitude." *Journal of Applied Psychology,* 20 (1936), 576–85.
37. Lehman, Harvey C., and Witty, Paul A. "A Study of Vocational Attitudes in Relation to Puberty." *American Journal of Psychology,* 43 (1931), 93–101.
38. Lockwood, William V. "Realism of Vocational Choice." *Personnel and Guidance Journal,* 37 (Oct., 1958), 98–106.
39. Longstaff, Howard P. "Fakability of the Strong Interest Blank and the Kuder Preference Record." *Journal of Applied Psychology,* 32 (Aug., 1948), 360–69.
40. Mallinson, George G., and Crumrine, William M. "An Investigation of the Stability of Interests of High School Students." *Journal of Educational Research,* 45 (Jan., 1952), 369–83.
41. Reiss, Albert J., Jr. *Occupations and Social Status.* New York: The Macmillan Co., 1961.
42. Roe, Anne. *The Psychology of Occupations.* New York: John Wiley & Sons, 1956.
43. Roeber, Edward, and Garfield, Sol. "A Study of Occupational Interests of High School Students in Terms of Grade Placement." *Journal of Educational Psychology,* 34 (Sept., 1943), 355–62.
44. Rogoff, Natalie. *Recent Trends in Occupational Mobility.* Glencoe, Ill.: Glencoe Free Press, 1953.

45. Rothney, John W. M., and Schmidt, Louis G. "Some Limitations of Interest Inventories." *Personnel and Guidance Journal,* 33 (Dec., 1954), 199–205.
46. Schmidt, John L., and Rothney, John W. M. "Variability of Vocational Choices of High School Students." *Personnel and Guidance Journal,* 34 (Nov., 1955), 142–46.
47. Segel, David, and Brintle, G. L. "The Relation of Occupational Interest Scores as Measured by the Strong Vocational Interest Blank to Achievement Test Results and College Marks in Certain College Subject Groups." *Journal of Educational Research,* 27 (Feb., 1934), 442–45.
48. Sexton, Patricia C. *Education and Income: Inequalities of Opportunity in Our Public Schools.* New York: Viking Press, 1961.
49. Small, Leonard. *Personality Determinants of Vocational Choice.* Psychological Monographs, vol. 67, no. 1, whole no. 351 (1953).
50. Smith, Mapheus. "An Empirical Scale of Prestige Status of Occupations." *American Sociological Review,* 8 (April, 1943), 185–92.
51. Stefflre, Buford L. "The Reading Difficulty in Interest Inventories." *Occupations,* 26 (Nov., 1947), 95–96.
52. Stephenson, Richard M. "Occupational Aspirations and Plans of 443 Ninth Graders." *Journal of Educational Research,* 49 (Sept., 1955), 27–35.
53. Stordahl, Kalmer E. "Permanence of Strong Vocational Interest Blank Scores." *Journal of Applied Psychology,* 38 (Dec., 1954), 423–27.
54. Strong, Edward K., Jr. *Change of Interests with Age.* Stanford, Cal.: Stanford University Press, 1931.
55. Strong, Edward K., Jr. *Manual for Strong Vocational Interest Blanks for Men and Women.* Palo Alto, Cal.: Consulting Psychologists Press, Inc., 1959.
56. Strong, Edward K., Jr. *Vocational Interests of Men and Women.* Stanford, Cal.: Stanford University Press, 1943.
57. Super, Donald E. "A Theory of Vocational Development." *American Psychologist,* 8 (May, 1953), 185–90.
58. Super, Donald E. "Vocational Interests and Vocational Choice: Present Knowledge and Future Research in Their Relationships." *Educational and Psychological Measurement,* 7 (Autumn, 1947), 375–83.
59. Super, Donald E., and Crites, John O. *Appraising Vocational Fitness.* New York: Harper & Row, 1962.
60. Super, Donald E., and Overstreet, Phoebe L. *The Vocational Maturity of Ninth-Grade Boys.* New York: Bureau of Publications, Teachers College, Columbia University, 1960.
61. Taylor, Katherine V. F., and Carter, Harold D. "Retest Consistency of Vocational Interest Patterns." *Journal of Consulting Psychology,* 6 (1942), 95–101.
62. Terman, Lewis M., and Miles, Catherine C. *Sex and Personality: Studies in Masculinity and Femininity.* New York: McGraw-Hill, 1936.
63. Triggs, Frances O. "A Further Comparison of Interest Measurement by the Kuder Preference Record and the Strong Vocational Interest Blank for Men." *Journal of Educational Research,* 37 (March, 1944), 538–44.
64. Triggs, Frances O. "Further Comparison of Interest Measurement by the Kuder Preference Record and the Strong Vocational Interest Blank for Women." *Journal of Educational Research,* 38 (Nov., 1944), 193–200.
65. Triggs, Frances O. "A Study of the Relation of the Kuder Preference Record Scores to Other Various Measures." *Educational and Psychological Measurement,* 3 (Spring, 1943), 341–54.
66. Van Dusen, Albert C. "Permanence of Vocational Interests." *Journal of Educational Psychology,* 31 (Sept., 1940), 401–24.
67. Webb, Wilse B. "Occupational Indecision among College Students." *Occupations,* 27 (Feb., 1949), 331–32.
68. Wesley, S. M.; Corey, D. Q.; and Stewart, B. M. "The Intra-individual Relationship between Interest and Ability." *Journal of Applied Psychology,* 34 (June, 1950), 193–97.

69. Wittenborn, J. R.; Triggs, Frances O.; and Feder, Daniel D. "A Comparison of Interest Measurement by the Kuder Preference Record and the Strong Vocational Interest Blank for Men and Women." *Educational and Psychological Measurement,* 3 (1943), 239–57.
70. Wrenn, C. Gilbert. "Intelligence and the Vocational Choices of College Students." *Educational Record,* 16 (April, 1935), 217–19.

6
Recreational Interests

THE DESIRABILITY of concern over the occupational preferences and interests of youth should hardly be questioned. Our society takes for granted an occupational role for every adult, and the screening of choices and interests so as to assure the individual's achieving an appropriate vocational destination is generally accepted as imperative. Notwithstanding the urgency of an understanding of the recreational, or avocational, activities and interests of youth, we know far less about these than of vocational preferences and interests. The urgency arises not only from the need for a balanced and wholesome manner of life for youth for the present but certainly no less so as a basis on which to establish appropriate recreational pursuits for adulthood. In support of this urgency for adulthood, we are being frequently reminded of the effects of automation that are shortening the hours of work and thereby creating a situation affording increased leisure available for the pursuit of recreations.

The relative lack of information on avocational as compared with vocational interests must be in large part owing to our puritanical mores which are more favorable to empirical inquiries concerning work than concerning play. Nevertheless, a number of studies have been reported and the main import of these will be reviewed. Certain studies revert to an older day and others do not apply fully to the age-group that is our primary concern. However, some of them pertain to a wide range of ages in which the later adolescent is included; several apply to high school years and yield an understanding of interests that youth bring with them as first-year college students. A few lesser studies tell about recreational interests of college students. Several studies have looked more intensively into major interests like voluntary reading and the use in leisure time of other mass media, namely, movies, radio, and television. Some of the studies shed light on relationships of these interests to pubescence, intelligence, achievement, and social class. And one investigator has made significant inquiry into the relationships of vocational and avocational interests.

Overview of Play and Recreation

Activities and interests by age.—One of the most extensive investigations into recreational activities was reported by Lehman and Witty (20) in 1927. It was made by interviews in certain cities in Kansas and in Kansas City, Missouri, with some 6,000 subjects ranging in age from 6 into the early twenties and against a long list of 200 play activities. From

TABLE 6.1
RANK IN FREQUENCY OF GAMES AND OTHER PLAY ACTIVITIES
MOST COMMONLY ENGAGED IN BY MALES

Activity	Age		
	16	18	20
Reading the newspapers	1	1	1
Looking at the Sunday "funny" papers	2	2	2
Riding in an automobile	3	3	4
Going to the movies	4	4	2
Watching athletic sports	5	5	5
Just playing catch	5	6	6
Chewing gum	6	8	7
Reading books	8	13	12
Baseball	7	12	18
Reading short stories	9	10	10

SOURCE: Adapted from Lehman and Witty (20, 52, Table Vb).

TABLE 6.2
RANK IN FREQUENCY OF GAMES AND OTHER PLAY ACTIVITIES
MOST COMMONLY ENGAGED IN BY FEMALES

Activity	Age		
	16	18	20
Reading the newspapers	1	1	2
Riding in an automobile	3	2	4
Reading short stories	4	7	10
Writing letters	7	3	1
Going to the movies	5	5	6
Looking at the Sunday "funny" papers	2	4	9
Reading books	5	13	21
Playing the piano for fun	6	11	9
Visiting or entertaining company	7	6	3
Reading jokes or funny sayings	6	8	11
Listening to the victrola	9	9	8

SOURCE: Adapted from Lehman and Witty (20, 52, Table Vb).

the total body of evidence presented, Tables 6.1, 6.2, 6.3, and 6.4 have been extracted showing some of the activities "most commonly engaged in" and "liked best" by boys and girls 16, 18, and 20 years of age. In attempting to interpret activities and rankings in these tables, it will be well to remember that the period during which the evidence was assembled antedates the advent and/or the spread of mass media now in wide use, namely, radio and TV. It will be well also, in interpreting Tables 6.1 and 6.2, to bear in mind that all the rankings are relatively high, signifying that all the activities were engaged in by large proportions of the subjects.

Examining the rankings in Table 6.1, one may note that, whatever the changes in activities most commonly engaged in over a long stretch of years, that is, from early childhood through later adolescence, few if any of those listed made notable changes in prominence during the span represented in the table. One change nearest to significance seems to be baseball which dropped from seventh to eighteenth. The rankings for girls in

TABLE 6.3
RANK IN FREQUENCY OF ACTIVITIES "LIKED BEST" BY MALES

Activity	Age		
	16	18	20
Basketball (November and February)	1	1	3
Football (November)	2	2	2
Baseball	3	8	9
Driving an automobile	4	3	6
Going to the movies	6	8	4
Tennis (April)	5	6	7
Having dates	6	5	1
Hunting (November)	7	7	12
Watching athletic sports	8	4	1
Reading books	9	9	9
Social dancing	11	11	10

SOURCE: Adapted from Lehman and Witty (20, 56, Table VIIb).

Table 6.2 disclose somewhat more notable shifts, among these, some decline in reading short stories and reading books, and some rise in rank for writing letters and visiting or entertaining company. However, in interpreting such shifts one should keep in mind the observation previously made, that all the rankings in the table are near the top of a long list of activities and that, therefore, all are prominent throughout the period.

Comparison of the two lists in Tables 6.1 and 6.2 shows the following activities distinctive of the boys' high rankings: watching athletic sports, just playing catch, chewing gum, and baseball, of which all but chewing gum are related to physical activity, although the first does not require it. The activities distinctive of the girls' list are writing letters, playing the piano for fun, visiting or entertaining company, reading jokes or funny sayings, and listening to the victrola. These, in contrast to the activities distinctive with boys, suggest sedentary pursuits and sociability.

Looking for changes in rankings or activities "liked best" by boys in Table 6.3, one sees again relatively few notable shifts in the four-year span. Nearest to significance are the decline for baseball and some elevation for having dates and watching athletic sports. For girls, as seen in

Table 6.4, the rankings remain roughly consistent, with the exception of reading books.

However, comparison of the rankings for activities most commonly engaged in and liked best for the two sexes reveals some rather striking and significant shifts of position. For boys (comparing Tables 6.1 and 6.3) the rise of active participation in sports for all ages represented is apparent: basketball, football, baseball, tennis, and hunting all have high rankings. Analogous comparison for girls (Tables 6.2 and 6.4) finds social dancing, reading books, and having dates rising in rank. Marked plunges

TABLE 6.4
RANK IN FREQUENCY OF ACTIVITIES "LIKED BEST" BY FEMALES

Activity	Age		
	16	18	20
Social dancing	3	1	1
Reading books	1	4	7
Going to the movies	2	3	6
Playing the piano for fun	4	6	2
Having dates	5	2	3
Riding in an automobile	6	5	8
Watching athletic sports	7	6	7
Going to parties or picnics	8	8	9
Driving an automobile	9	7	10
Reading short stories	10	9	8
Visiting or entertaining company	11	10	10

SOURCE: Adapted from Lehman and Witty (*20*, 57, Table VIIIb).

in rankings also may be noted. For example, reading the newspapers drops out of these highest rankings of "liked best" for both sexes, although the authors' complete tables show this activity still a prominent one.

Speculating over the causes of such differences in ranking for activities most commonly engaged in and best liked, one may say that, to a considerable extent, the explanation must be the availability of opportunities for participation and social pressures from various sources like parents and peers.

The impression gained from the evidence just reviewed is of participation by youth in a great variety of special kinds of play activities. Understanding of play-life will, however, be aided by a grouping or classification of the activities. A writer who undertook such a classification is Dimock in his *Rediscovering the Adolescent* (*11*). In his inquiry, restricted to boys mostly younger than those represented in Tables 6.1 and 6.3, he grouped their play interests under five headings, as follows: reading activities (29 per cent participating), including Sunday "funnies," newspapers, books, comic strips, magazines, jokes, short stories; physical interests (19 per cent), including basketball, football, gym work, swimming, bicycle riding, wrestling, volleyball, boxing, races; passive-spectator interests (18 per cent), including radio, car-riding, movies, watching sports, listening to stories; constructive activities (8 per cent), including drawing, making something, fixing something, collecting stamps, etc., playing piano, playing other musical instruments; miscellaneous interests (26 per cent), including Sunday School, whistling, card games, church, writing letters, driving car, excursions, checkers, playing pool, etc. No strictly comparable classification has been reported for girls, but it may be inferred from the rankings

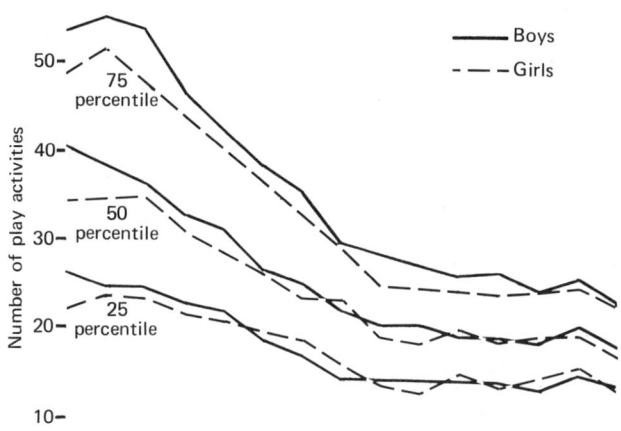

FIG. 6.1
TWENTY-FIFTH, FIFTIETH, AND SEVENTY-FIFTH PERCENTILES OF NUMBERS OF PLAY ACTIVITIES ENGAGED IN BY BOYS AND GIRLS DURING WEEK PRIOR TO QUESTIONING

SOURCE: Frank K. Shuttleworth, *The Adolescent Period: A Graphic Analysis.* Monograph of the Society for Research in Child Development, vol. 4, no. 1 (1949), Fig. 323. From data reported by Lehman and Witty (20, 48).

reported in Tables 6.2 and 6.4 that an important difference would be smaller proportionate participation in physical interests and larger percentages in passive and constructive interests, although the specific activities within the groups would also differ.

Another important consideration concerning recreational activities in respect to age is the number of different activities carried on by the individual, together with whether or not there is any trend in number with increasing age. Lehman and Witty compiled the evidence in answer to these questions from the same sources used for Tables 6.1–6.4, which includes information concerning the numbers of different play activities engaged in by all their boys and girls from 8½ to 22½ years of age. The median and twenty-fifth and seventy-fifth percentile numbers of activities engaged in (during the week prior to questioning) for this full range of ages and for both males and females are shown in Figure 6.1. All the curves show that the numbers are highest at 9½ years, that they decline rapidly until about 16½ years, and then hold almost steady until 20½ years. Thus, the number appears to be almost stabilized by later adolescence. The measures for boys run only slightly higher than for girls. The partial irregularity for the last two years in the figure is probably explained by the smaller number of subjects for those years.

TABLE 6.5
PERCENTAGES OF BOYS AND GIRLS ENGAGING IN ACTIVITIES
OUTSIDE OF SCHOOL

Activity	Boys	Girls	Activity	Boys	Girls
Studying	87	94	Loafing alone	43	61
Radio listening	92	93	Unsupervised sports	57	27
Loafing with friends	85	90	Religious activities	43	58
Jobs and housework	73	86	Chaperoned parties	24	42
Reading	82	91	Parties, unchaperoned	29	37
Movies	67	72	Club activities	40	52
Musical activities	23	43	Supervised sports	50	27
Games	66	60	Concerts, plays, lectures	27	38
Watching sports	68	47	School activities	29	32
Hobbies	33	42	Scout activities	15	5

SOURCE: Olds (26, Table 2).

Activities and interests during high school years.—To provide a picture of the recreational interests youth are likely to bring with them to college, evidence will be drawn from two studies made at the high school level. The first of these is by Olds (26) who reported on all activities engaged in by more than 800 boys and girls in the second, third, and fourth years of a high school in a suburb of St. Louis. The activities reported on are listed in Table 6.5, where it may be noted that a few—studying and jobs and homework—are not strictly recreational. The activities are listed roughly in order of declining percentage. Almost every activity listed has a prominent place in playtime of both boys and girls. Using a 10 per cent differential as significant, activities that interest the two sexes about equally are radio listening (the period represented antedated TV), loafing with friends, reading, movies, games, hobbies, unchaperoned parties, and school activities. Activities more prominent with boys were watching sports, unsupervised sports, supervised sports, and scout activities. Those more prominent with girls were musical activities, loafing alone, religious activities, chaperoned parties, club activities, and concerts, plays, and lectures.

When asked in which activities they would prefer to spend more time, boys emphasized sports both supervised and unsupervised and more time for watching sports, while the girls named concerts, plays, and lectures, reading, musical activities, and movies.

The second source of evidence for the high school level is Coleman's *The Adolescent Society* (*10*) which was drawn upon in Chapter 3 for light on attitudes of this age-level.* Our interest in recreational concerns of youth prompts reproducing the materials in Table 6.6, which is based on responses of about 8,000 youths in nine public high schools, and quoting as follows from the author's interpretation (*13*): "Girls' leisure-time activi-

TABLE 6.6
PERCENTAGES OF BOYS AND GIRLS IN NINE PUBLIC HIGH SCHOOLS
ENGAGING IN CERTAIN LEISURE ACTIVITIES

Activity	Boys	Girls
1. Organized outdoor sports, including football, basketball, tennis, etc.	22.0	6.9
2. Unorganized outdoor activities, including hunting, fishing, swimming, boating, etc.	14.7	11.3
3. "Being with the group," riding around, going uptown, etc.	17.2	32.5
4. Attending movies and spectator events—athletic games, etc.	8.5	10.4
5. Dating or being out with the opposite sex	13.6	11.6
6. Going dancing (girls only)	–	12.0
7. Hobby—working on cars, bicycles, radio, musical instruments, etc.	22.5	20.1
8. Indoor group activities—bowling, cards, roller-skating, etc.	8.0	8.1
9. Watching television	19.4	23.6
10. Listening to records or radio	11.2	31.7
11. Reading	13.7	35.5
12. Other, for example, talking on telephone	7.1	9.3
13. No answer	8.1	3.7

SOURCE: Coleman (*10*, 13, Table 5).

ties show a sharp contrast [with those of boys] in some categories. Girls' favorite leisure activities less often include the active outdoor pursuits of boys. More frequent are activities like 'just being with their friends,' watching television and movies, attending games, reading, and listening to records. Their more active pursuits include one that never exists for boys—dancing among themselves. Perhaps this is an activity that substitutes for the sports at which boys spend their time; in part, it is certainly preparation for dancing with boys. In any case, it suggests the oft-heard quip that boys are interested in sports and girls are interested in boys.

"The general pattern of these leisure pursuits, showing considerably more activity among the boys, is indicative of a situation that seems to be quite general in the adolescent community: boys have far more to *do* than

*See pp. 84–88.

girls. Whether it is athletics, or cars, or hunting, or model-building, our society seems to provide a much fuller set of activities to engage the interest of boys. Thus, when girls are together, they are more often 'just with the group' than are the boys. . . ."

In response to a special inquiry into favorite types of music of these same students, about half of both sexes indicated "rock and roll." Most of the remainder were scattered to calypso, jazz, country and western, and other popular music, with only 6.5 and 9.4 per cent of the boys and girls, respectively, preferring the classical.

TABLE 6.7
Principal Leisure-Time Activities of Out-of-School Youth According to the School Grades Completed

Activity	Percentages of Youth in Each Grade Group		
	9th, 10th, 11th	11th or 12th graduate	1, 2, or 3 years beyond*
Reading	23.3	32.2	42.6
Individual sports	15.9	15.6	15.9
Dancing, dating	15.5	14.0	10.4
Movies	13.4	10.2	8.2
Loafing	7.5	5.9	3.9
Hobbies	8.4	10.4	10.7
Team games	8.7	5.4	4.0
Listening to radio	2.3	1.8	0.9
Quiet games	1.0	0.7	0.9
Other activities	4.0	3.8	3.2
Total	100.0	100.0	100.0

Source: Bell (*3*, 166, Table 67).
*Beyond high school graduation.

While examining the tables displaying the activities of high school students, the reader may have noted the large proportion of preferred interests that involve association with other persons. The majority of preferred activities are of this kind. In reference to this it is appropriate to quote from a conclusion of an older study of leisure-time activities of some thousands of high school students in 22 high schools in Georgia and Illinois by Punké (*27*), where he said, "The fact that students in both states prefer to be with others during their leisure time indicates that play and recreational activities are largely group activities." The evidence from the Olds and Coleman projects supports this conclusion if the word "largely" is used in a sense allowing for a considerable proportion of activities enjoyed on an individual basis.

Activities of college-age youth.—From an investigation by interview of out-of-school youth in Maryland reported by Bell, at times referred to as a "classic" in the field, Table 6.7 contains the columns showing the principal leisure-time activities of three groups of subjects: (1) those who had completed the ninth, tenth, and eleventh grades; (2) those who were eleventh- and twelfth-grade graduates;* and (3) those who had had one to three years of college. These columns permit a focus of attention on the age-group of our major interest at the same time that they disclose any trends with durations of education. Comments in interpretation may well include reference to the rather steady increase in leisure reading with rise in grade

TABLE 6.8
NUMBER OF 100 FRESHMEN MEN REPORTING PARTICIPATION IN AVOCATIONAL PURSUITS

Activity and Rank	Number	Activity and Rank	Number
1. Movies	96	23. Lectures	29
2. Magazine reading	79	24. Musicals	27
3. Social conversation (own sex)	77	25. Playing musical instruments	26
4. Dates	70	26. Checkers	26
5. Card playing	69	27. Radio	21
6. Basketball (attendance)	66	28. Church parties	18
7. Hikes	63	29. Indoor ball (played)	13
8. Walks	63	30. Tennis	10
9. Recitals	62	31. Track	10
10. Auto rides	62	32. Volleyball (played)	8
11. Pool and billiards	60	33. Boxing	7
12. Book reading	58	34. Bowling	7
13. Plays	56	35. Volleyball (attended)	6
14. Dances	50	36. Indoor ball (attended)	6
15. Church meetings	47	37. Chess	6
16. Basketball (played)	42	38. Field-glass observing	6
17. Wrestling	40	39. Horseback riding	4
18. Kodaking	37	40. Wood carving	3
19. Individual hobbies	36	41. Swimming	3
20. Social conversation (other sex)	35	42. Dominoes	2
21. Gymnastic stunts	35	43. Baseball	2
22. House parties	30	44. Skating	2
		45. Golf	1

SOURCE: Stoke and Clive (30).

level, an increase making reading by far the activity most engaged in; the maintenance of the level for individual sports, at the same time that participation in team games is dropping off to some extent; the partial decline in dancing and dating, movies, and loafing. Bell observes concerning the figures for the item last named, "The progressive decline in the amount of loafing as youth have gone from the lower to the higher educational levels suggests that one of the desirable effects of schooling is to substitute definite recreational activities for sheer aimlessness" (3, 166). The period represented was still ante-TV and it may be mentioned that resort to radio was much less than found in contemporary studies.

*There were still some 11-grade school systems in operation at the time.

In another investigation by interview, Stoke and Clive (30) tallied the number of freshmen men in a public higher institution in Ohio reporting participation in avocational pursuits during one month. This is another ante-TV study. The activities and frequencies are given in Table 6.8 in the rank order from greatest frequency downward. The authors mention that they collected the information in February and March and that this explains the relatively low place of summer sports. They point out "two striking facts" to be noted in examining the list: (1) the "almost universal appeal of the movies" and (2) the "marked preference for sedentary forms of recreation." The six highest forms of entertainment in the list are sedentary and no "really strenuous game" is reached until the sixteenth item.

In an effort to arrive at something approaching generalizations and to identify any trends with age, the writer has subjected the frequencies in Table 6.8 to classification of interests of younger adolescents devised by Dimock as described above with the following outcome:

ACTIVITIES OR INTERESTS	DIMOCK'S BOYS, 12 TO 15	STOKE AND CLIVE'S FRESHMEN MEN
Reading	29%	9%
Physical	19	21
Passive-spectator	18	34
Constructive	8	7
Miscellaneous	26	29

A glance at the percentages finds those for three categories, physical, constructive, and miscellaneous, approximately equal for the two levels. The sharp reduction for reading would afford ground for concern, except that Stoke and Clive's list of specifics includes only books and magazines, whereas Dimock's included newspapers, Sunday "funnies," etc., which could easily make up most or all the difference. It may be that the Ohio freshmen under pressure of reading for courses might have reduced their recreational reading, but hardly in such proportions. Including their newspaper and "funnies" reading would have lowered the other percentages, so that the measure for physical interests would show the decline to be expected for boys between early and later adolescence, a less startling increase for passive-spectator interests, and some decline for miscellaneous interests. One is moved to point out, further, that the specifics under the classification last named are not so much of a conglomerate as the designation implies, since they include social conversation, dates, dances, club meetings, and house and church parties. These specifics are clearly social activities and the percentage indicates that the social character of activities and interests found for high school students by Olds and Coleman, as reported above, persists in large proportions into college years.

Another investigation involving students at the college level has been reported by Kaplan (*17*), who submitted a list of recreational activities to the men and women in his classes at the University of Illinois. One of his directions was to "check one or more activities you enjoy doing." The numbers in his total of 104 students who checked the 33 activities are indicated in Table 6.9. This investigation was made recently enough to include television and it is to be noted that enjoyment of this mass medium is among the three recreations checked with a frequency of 90 or more,

TABLE 6.9
NUMBER AMONG 104 STUDENTS REPORTING ENJOYMENT OF CERTAIN RECREATIONAL ACTIVITIES

Activity	Number	Activity	Number
1. Television	90	18. Go to concerts	68
2. Radio	74	19. Walk	60
3. Phonograph	99	20. Sew or knit	26
4. Read a book	87	21. Loaf, sleep	70
5. Read a magazine	84	22. Church activity	33
6. Watch sports	76	23. Make things, wood	24
7. Play in sports	75	24. Make things, clay	19
8. Fish	41	25. Photography	39
9. Hunt	27	26. Conversation	93
10. Play cards	61	27. Work puzzles	30
11. Other indoor games	45	28. Just sit	31
12. Gamble	25	29. Visit friends	79
13. Dance	82	30. Club meetings	42
14. Parties	86	31. Go on trips	85
15. Ride car	68	32. Shopping trips	44
16. Ride airplane	46	33. Sing, play music	47
17. Be with family	80		

SOURCE: Kaplan (*17*, 249, Table 17).

the other two being the phonograph and conversation. Kaplan undertook a classification of the activities and calculation from his compilation yields the following percentages: sociability, 21.6; associations (only church activity and club meetings), 3.9; games, sports, 19.7; art, 16.6; mobility, 15.6; and immobility, 22.7. He makes special mention of the large proportion falling under the classification last named, as if he deplores it in contrast with more active interests.

Kaplan's classifications, while of significance in themselves, do not make for ready comparison with results of groupings made in earlier studies of interests reviewed in this section so that similarities, differences, or trends may be identified. Besides, certain differences of procedure make it unwise to rely on a comparison following Dimock's grouping, as was done with data from the study by Stoke and Clive. One of these differences is combining the responses of men and women into a single tabulation: we are well aware that the interests of the two sexes differ in so many respects that to combine the responses is certain to conceal or distort the actual situation. Other differences in procedure are omitting newspaper reading and combining all active participation in the separate sports into a single category of "play in sports," a method that reduces the computed percentage found to engage in active sports. Tabular analysis of the frequencies in Table 6.9 was made according to the Dimock classification, and the only inferences that can be drawn with at least partial assurance that they are justifiable are (1) that physical interests are still declining with students of this age, (2) that passive-spectator interests are still on the increase, and (3) that the social activities which make up the bulk of the miscellaneous interests are at least holding their own.

Voluntary Reading

The full range of voluntary reading.—The prominence of the mass media in the leisure-time activities of young people makes it desirable in any exposition on recreations to give some special attention to detailed aspects of their utilization. The exposition will begin with the media involving the printed page and this will be followed by consideration of movies, radio, and television, with some attention to the influence of the advent of television on resort to the older media.

Dependence on reading for recreation will be described by drawing in most part on a single investigation by B. Lamar Johnson (*16*), the reason for this being that his is one of the few investigations that undertook to inventory the full range of voluntary reading, in books, magazines, and newspapers. The project was done in Duluth, Minnesota. His investigation included the reading of adults in the community, but the evidence from this phase of the project is not a matter of concern here. Two partial limitations of the project for present purposes should be mentioned. One of these is the fact that it concerns reading activities around 1930, which makes the evidence not quite timely as to specific items read, although inferences drawn from it are hardly invalidated. Its chief inadequacy for present purposes is that students in grade 12 were not included and that the number of students queried in grade 11 was relatively small: this lack of representation in upper high school grades interferes in some degree with identifying trends into the years of later adolescence. However, in the interpretation here this limitation is offset by citation of evidence and conclusions from another study that carried the inventory into grade 12. While Johnson used three groups, grades 5–6, grades 7–8, and grades 9–11, comparisons here for identification of trends will include only the two highest groups.

(a) *In books.* Generalization from the compilation of books read as reported in Johnson's study is easily done without tabular presentation. No nonfiction books appear on the list of most recurrent titles: all those most frequently reported are fiction. This generalization applies to both sexes and to both grades 7–8 and 9–11. Most frequent titles for the younger group of boys included such classics as *Treasure Island, Kidnapped, Robinson Crusoe, Tom Sawyer,* and *Huckleberry Finn,* plus an occasional mystery story like *The Green Murder Case* and a Tarzan story popularized by a movie. By grades 9–11 boys, while holding to some of those just named, had shifted in large part to westerns like *Riders of the Purple Sage, Lone Star Ranger, U P Trail,* and *Bar-20 Days.* Girls' most recurrent items in grades 7–8 included such standard juveniles as Alcott's *Little Women, Little Men,* and *Old-Fashioned Girl,* Gene Stratton Porter's *Girl of the Limberlost,* and other more recent titles liked by pre- and early adolescents. Recurrent titles for girls in grades 9–11 included some of the books found for grades 7–8, such as the books by Porter, but also books of romance and adventure, among them *The Harvester, The Virginian,* and *Oliver Twist.* The difference between the sexes in tastes for fiction, even as early as grades 7–8, is emphasized by the fact that no title in either list of the most frequent appears in the other. The same is true for the two lists for grades 9–11.

Instead of relying on Johnson's study for evidence concerning the reading of nonfiction books, it will be preferable to transfer attention to an investigation that carries the subjects somewhat nearer college age and to the threshold of college. This is done in a study by Eberhart (*12*) which takes into account all books read voluntarily from grade 7 through grade 12 by 112 students of the Bronxville, New York, High School. This study has the additional advantage of being longitudinal, involving the same subjects throughout the period. The evidence was tabulated for two grade-groups, grades 7–8 and 10–12.

The percentages of books of fiction among the thousands of books reported to have been read voluntarily within these two spans of grades declined from approximately 88 to 55. If one adds the percentages of the books read that were dramas (2.4 per cent in grades 7–8 and 17.4 per cent in grades 10–12), the total percentage of books of the "story" type drops from around 90 to about 72. This means an increase in nonfiction books of from about 10 per cent to about 28 per cent—almost a trebling in the proportion for nonfiction. These books were spread to a wide variety of materials, each of which experienced increases: biography and autobiography; history; science and natural history; travel and exploration; hobbies and practical arts; political, social, and economic problems; sports; essays, humor, and criticism; fine arts; and philosophy and religion. This trend is substantial evidence of progress toward variety and maturity in recreational reading. An interesting corroboratory datum is the fact that the median number of books of fiction read dropped from 31 in grade 7 to 7 in grade 12, while the median for nonfiction rose, by somewhat irregular steps, from 2.5 to 6, moving the author to conclude that students in the highest grade were reading "almost as much nonfiction as fiction."

(b) *In magazines.* On the basis of Johnson's report on the magazines most often read by boys and girls in both grades 7–8 and grades 9–11, the percentages in Tables 6.10 and 6.11 were computed. What seems most

TABLE 6.10
PERCENTAGES OF BOYS IN GRADES 7–8 AND 9–11
READING CERTAIN MAGAZINES

Magazine	7–8	9–11
American Boy	28	39
Popular Mechanics	28	26
Liberty	27	44
Saturday Evening Post	27	39
Boys' Life	24	30
Collier's	13	25
American Magazine	12	13
Popular Science Monthly	9	24

SOURCE: Adapted from Johnson (*16*, Table VIII).

TABLE 6.11
PERCENTAGES OF GIRLS IN GRADES 7–8 AND 9–11
READING CERTAIN MAGAZINES

Magazines	7–8	9–11
Saturday Evening Post	34	39
Ladies Home Journal	32	37
Liberty	29	36
Pictorial Review	22	34
Collier's	16	22
American Girl	16	22
Good Housekeeping	14	24
Woman's Home Companion	11	19
American Magazine	11	22

SOURCE: Adapted from Johnson (*16*, Table IX).

significant here is the increase (except for *Popular Mechanics* with boys, which hardly held its own while *Popular Science Monthly* experienced a marked gain) for all magazines in both lists. Thus, the increment for boys applies both to boys' periodicals as well as to the more general weeklies and a monthly magazine. The two tables reflect typical differences in interest of the sexes: the interests of boys in mechanical and scientific concerns and of girls those most characteristically recognized in the women's periodicals.

Percentage frequencies for the reading of various sections of magazines, as reported by Johnson and presented in Table 6.12, disclose increases for

TABLE 6.12
PERCENTAGES OF BOYS AND GIRLS IN GRADES 7–8 AND 9–11
WHO USUALLY READ VARIOUS SECTIONS OF MAGAZINES

Sections	Boys		Girls	
	7–8	9–11	7–8	9–11
Short stories	87	91	90	100
Humorous sections	76	82	93	86
Continued stories	52	65	59	86
Scientific articles	49	72	13	34
Travel articles	25	40	29	46
Advertisements	24	38	22	31
News articles	20	38	24	36
Editorials	9	17	9	27
Articles about politics	5	18	4	15
Articles about successful people	5	8	9	4

SOURCE: Johnson (*16*, Table X).

almost all sections for both sexes. This means both more magazine reading totally and increases not only for fictional portions but also for the nonfictional, among them scientific articles, travel articles, editorials, and articles about politics. Chief difference between the sexes was a greater interest of boys than girls in scientific articles.

(c) *In newspapers.* Voluntary reading of newspapers by boys and girls in the same grade-groups as found by Johnson is reported in Table 6.13. Except for juvenilia like the children's page and puzzles, almost all sections, including such sections as news of your city, foreign news, national

TABLE 6.13
PERCENTAGES OF BOYS AND GIRLS IN GRADES 7–8 AND 9–11
WHO USUALLY READ VARIOUS SECTIONS OF NEWSPAPERS

Section	Boys		Girls	
	7–8	9–11	7–8	9–11
Comic section	92	97	100	100
Front page	72	95	72	91
Sports page	73	87	36	47
Children's page	23	4	55	18
Accident news	37	40	40	44
News of your city	38	50	43	53
Crime news	47	40	21	34
Foreign news	24	32	28	33
News inside paper	27	42	25	52
Puzzles	23	17	31	27
National news	25	36	15	33
Society news	2	8	28	31
Advertisements	9	12	10	30
Editorials	11	27	10	26
Home page	1	1	7	10

SOURCE: Johnson (*16*, Table XI).

news, and editorials, show substantial increases. Chief differences in increments for the sexes were the sports page for boys and society news for girls.

Johnson's evidence concerning the reading of magazines and newspapers shows a considerable trend toward variety and maturity in the reading interests of youth, even though his representation of grade 11 is deficient and absent for grade 12. It would be a logical expectation that, if the inquiry had included adequate representation of the last two high school years, this trend would have been found to be accentuated and analogous in breadth and depth to that found in the Eberhart study of books voluntarily read. The whole body of trends in reading that have been disclosed in this review suggest the acceptability of Ausubel's conclusion, after having summarized all comparable materials: "All of these changes reflect (a) increased intellectual maturity, (b) expanding interest in the wider cultural environment embracing real persons and social problems, and (c) growing concern with self-improvement as an instrument for acquiring primary status."*

Movies, Radio, and Television

Movies and radio.—It is a commonplace that the three mass media of movies, radio, and television have during the current century successively taken over huge sectors of the leisure time of our population, including both children and adults. In an effort to ascertain to what extent and how they affect the playtime of youth, the interests of young people in the three media will be reviewed. Interest in the first two, movies and radio, will be briefly considered through citation from studies made while these media were at their peak of popularity, and interest in television, because the advent of this latest medium is said to be having far-reaching effects on other recreational participations, at somewhat greater length.

The classic study by interview reported by Bell (*3*), previously cited to provide a general description of recreations of youth, contained also the proportionate frequency of movies preferred. The four types found to be preferred by all youth in this study (*3*, 172) were musical comedy (21.4 per cent), historical (21.0), action and western (16.2), and love story (13.5). Other types with smaller frequencies were gangster and G-men, comedy of manners, news, and education. The percentages for males and females for many of these categories were not far apart, but there were rather striking differences for action and western (males, 23.3 per cent; females, 4.8 per cent). Unfortunately for purposes here, the frequencies are not reported by age, so that it is impossible to identify the preferences of later adolescents or the trends with age.

*David P. Ausubel, *Theory and Problems of Adolescent Development* (New York: Gruine and Stratton, 1954), p. 300.

An investigation that is somewhat more helpful in ascertaining preference by age of subject and trends with increasing age is one by Mitchell (24), who ascertained the proportions of each sex attending movies of various types in grade school and high school. These percentages are reported in Table 6.14. A prominent category for both sexes at both school levels is seen to be comedy. A category making notable gains for both sexes between levels is historical and one experiencing notable losses is the western. Differences between the sexes are the high percentages of boys for adventure and of girls for romance, the percentage

TABLE 6.14
PERCENTAGES OF GRADE SCHOOL AND HIGH SCHOOL BOYS AND GIRLS
REPORTING ATTENDANCE AT VARIOUS TYPES OF MOTION PICTURES

	Boys		Girls	
Types	Grade School	High School	Grade School	High School
Adventure	13.7	13.7	7.2	6.1
Comedy	11.4	13.0	16.5	10.3
Educational	1.3	2.8	1.4	2.1
Historical	2.0	12.9	4.6	10.6
Mystery	6.3	8.9	6.8	8.8
Romance	4.7	7.0	13.3	22.8
Sports	5.3	11.9	3.7	8.0
Tragedy	2.1	5.6	7.7	9.9
War	5.1	3.8	2.2	2.2
Western	34.0	7.5	20.2	6.5

SOURCE: Mitchell (24, 167, Table XXII).

for the last named type increasing strikingly, and the larger increase for boys in sports. While the percentages disclose major interests as to types of movies, the wide ranges of ages within each of the two school levels conceal trends within the high school age, so that we are at a loss to know more precisely the distribution of interests at the threshold of college years.

For information about dependence of youth on radio programs for recreation before this medium was competing with television, reliance may be placed on an investigation by Brown who ascertained the proportions of boys and girls in grades 6, 8, 10, and 12 reporting enjoyment in the different types of programs. The percentages for students in grades 8, 10, and 12 are reported in Table 6.15. Interest in mystery plays was found to be almost universal for both sexes in grade 8 but waned noticeably by grade 12, more for girls than for boys. Comic dialogues and skits also experienced a partial decline. Dramatic plays dropped off some with boys, but held their own with girls. Popular dance music and song hits increased in interest, while semiclassical and classical music declined. News, including sports, and political speeches engaged and held the interests of about half the boys through all three grade levels, but lost some ground with the girls. Educational talks interested slightly but not notably higher percentages of both sexes in grade 12 than in grade 8.

Another investigation of radio listening of the same vintage as the one by Brown was made by Clark (8) on youth in the schools of Washington, D.C. This was at a time when 95 per cent of the homes had one or more radios. The evidence applies to three age-groups, 9–12, 12–15, and 15–18, but does not report separately for the sexes. The evidence reported shows large proportionate interest and increases by age for dance, popular and

TABLE 6.15
PERCENTAGES OF BOYS AND GIRLS IN GRADES 8, 10, AND 12 REPORTING ENJOYING DIFFERENT TYPES OF RADIO PROGRAMS

Type of Program	Boys			Girls		
	8	10	12	8	10	12
Mystery plays	94.3	84.9	66.7	95.1	76.0	39.4
Comic dialogue and skits	92.0	87.9	76.8	98.5	93.0	78.3
Dramatic plays	82.8	67.1	55.0	84.7	86.2	89.8
Popular dance music	63.4	83.5	94.2	81.3	95.2	98.7
Popular song hits	52.4	78.1	70.5	60.2	81.3	82.4
Semiclassical music: orchestra and band	78.3	60.8	17.2	81.4	57.2	32.4
News, including sports	47.5	55.3	54.8	31.3	52.6	26.1
Political speeches	46.4	51.2	45.2	19.6	33.0	18.0
Classical music, including opera	16.4	12.3	10.8	25.0	23.1	20.2
Educational talks	11.5	22.0	13.4	8.1	12.2	13.4

SOURCE: Brown (6, 328, Table X).

novelty type, while classical and semiclassical music show small initial interest and only minor gains. The type called comedy and variety has a large initial following which increases with age, while drama has a similarly large initial following but declines. Programs with relatively small initial appeal and with small increments with age are religion; national, public and civic affairs; news; and sports. It is probable that the failure to report for the sexes separately has concealed some significant trends.

The impact of television.—Before reporting on preferences of youth for types of television programs it is desirable to review briefly the facts concerning the rapidity and inclusiveness of the spread of this medium, the time spent in viewing by youth of different age-groups, and the impact of television on other activities, more especially the other recreations. A portrayal of the setting in which the medium operates should contribute to a comprehension of its significance in the life of youth. In their book on *Leisure and Recreation* the Neumeyers say (25, 324), "It took motion pictures nearly three decades to reach the high water mark, and radio about fifteen years; but television became a great giant in the entertainment field in a half dozen years!"

The fact that television has become truly a "mass medium" is established by evidence concerning the growth of family ownership of sets. Meyersohn* refers to an annual survey of ownership of television sets in New Brunswick, New Jersey, which showed an increase from 1.4 owners per 100 families in 1948 to 85.5 in 1955. This survey classified the families into income groups at three levels, and the proportions in 1955 for upper, middle, and lower incomes were, respectively, 90.1, 90.6, and 62.7. Today's estimates place the proportions at all economic levels above 90 per cent, which makes TV available to virtually all youth.

TABLE 6.16
AVERAGE NUMBER OF HOURS SPENT WEEKLY WITH TELEVISION BY ELEMENTARY SCHOOL AND HIGH SCHOOL PUPILS

School Level	1951	1953	1955	1957	1959	1960
Elementary school	19	23	24	22	21	21
High school	14	17	14	12	12	14

SOURCE: Witty (36, Table 1).

Investigations of time spent in televiewing show that it consumes a large part of the day or week, whichever basis of calculation is used. Witty (36) made annual studies of televiewing and found the average hours weekly for children and youth in elementary and high school as shown in Table 6.16. For the years listed the average hours for children in the lower school ranged from 19 to 24, while for high school students it ranged from 12 to 17 hours, or roughly three-fifths to three-fourths of that for elementary school pupils. The averages for parents were about the same as for elementary school pupils, while teachers averaged somewhat less than high school students.

Witty's figures disclose no marked tendency toward a decline in amount of televiewing over the years. However, another investigator, Lewis (21), found some decline in his study involving students in the South Shore High School of Chicago; his average dropped from 23½ to 16¼ hours from May, 1949, to January, 1951. He ascribes the earlier higher averages to recency of purchase, and supports his inference by the following figures:

MONTHS OF OWNERSHIP	AVERAGE VIEWING HOURS PER WEEK
1–12	17.25
13–24	16.25
25–36	15.80
37–48	13.50

*Rolf Meyersohn in Bernard Rosenberg and David M. White, eds., *Mass Culture* (Glencoe, Ill.; The Free Press, 1957), p. 355.

In his interpretation reference is made to English-TV classes in the school where criteria for appraising programs were developed, and it is more than likely that this instruction induced more discriminating and, therefore, less televiewing.

Lewis also computed average viewing hours per week for each age and both sexes, with the following results:

AGE	13	14	15	16	17	18
Boys	18.7	15.2	15.9	14.9	13.8	14.0
Girls	25.3	23.0	16.5	14.1	14.1	13.7

These figures reveal a decline from age 13 to age 16, and near stability of the averages thereafter. In this study the younger girls did more televiewing than boys of the same age, but for the later years the averages were about equal for the two sexes. Other investigators have found a decline with grade or age in high school. Besco (4), reporting on televiewing by students in a Columbus, Ohio, high school, found those in

TABLE 6.17
CHANGES IN TIME SPENT "YESTERDAY" (IN MINUTES PER PERSON) ON DIFFERENT MEDIA AFTER PURCHASE OF A TELEVISION SET*

Medium	Before TV	After TV
Magazines	17	10
Newspapers	39	32
Radio	122	52
Television	12†	173
Total time	190	267

*Derived from a panel study conducted in Ft. Wayne, Indiana, and quoted by Rolf Meyersohn in Rosenberg and White, p. 356.
†From "guest viewing."

grade 10 spending more time at it than those in grades 11 and 12, although in this study girls in these higher grades were spending more time than boys in televiewing. Balogh (1), in an investigation involving boys only, found the average for grade 10 at 20 hours, that for grade 12 at 10 hours, and the average for grade 11 about midway between these figures, at 15½ hours.

It would be expected that spending so much time on a new medium would affect by reduction the amount of time spent on other activities, including the other recreational. The extent of this change as it affects adults is shown in Table 6.17 in which is reported the average number of minutes spent "yesterday" on each of four mass media including television, as found in a panel in Ft. Wayne, Indiana. Reading of magazines and newspapers is seen to have been somewhat influenced toward reduction, but the big differences are the large shift from listening to radio and the even greater time expenditure in televiewing than is represented by this shift in time spent in listening to radio.

The conclusions from investigations of the impact of television's spread are in some instances conflicting, but mainly on the question of influence on the amount of time in reading. An investigation by Maccoby (22), by interview with mothers to obtain activity records on 622 children for a weekday before the interview and for a Sunday, done at a time when it was still possible to compare families with and without TV sets, yielded the conclusion, among others, that "the average amount of viewing is similar at all age levels." Maccoby also concluded that the widely reported shrinkage in reading, movie-going, and radio-listening by adults is true also of children. She mentions that a shift "from active and perhaps more 'creative' play is also involved—on the whole an hour and a half a day" has been shifted from activity of this sort to televiewing. Balogh (1), from his inquiry into televiewing habits of high school boys previously cited, concluded that nothing has been displaced so much as hobbies and creative pursuits. By "creative" activity is meant playing musical instruments, singing, acting or working in theater arts, painting, photographing, writing, working on periodicals, debating and engaging in forensics and other speech arts. It is understandable that attendance at movies has also been lessened, but, in Balogh's study, this shrinkage was less for boys in grades 11 and 12 than below. His explanation is that, as students get older, they achieve a better proportion between viewing and movie attendance, and their movie attendance also shows the influence of more frequent dating.

Several investigators have looked into influence of the advent of television on the amount of time spent in reading. In the study by Besco (4) previously cited, a majority of the girls reported that they did less reading of books, and more of them than of the boys believed they were doing less magazine reading. However, students expressed the opinion that their newspaper reading had been influenced less than any other interest. A study by McDonagh (23) comparing TV and non-TV families showed the former reporting that they were reading less. To the contrary, Lazarus (18), following completion of a project supported by the Ford Foundation to investigate pupils' TV habits, said, "Whether because of TV or in spite of it, youngsters (both elementary and secondary) are reading more than ever...." Against the conclusion of the negative influence of televiewing on hobbies, Battin is quoted by Witty (36) as reporting that

57 per cent of the boys and 59 per cent of the girls followed the same hobbies as before TV; 38 per cent and 34 per cent, respectively, cultivated new hobbies; and only 5 per cent and 9 per cent indicated less hobby interest. It is apparent that the need for investigation of such issues has not been exhausted.

It is not out of place to remind the readers in passing, in view of the huge shift away from radio listening to televiewing, that radio programs themselves have been changed drastically during the rise of television. The Sunday night comedians are gone and most of the network programs are gone, and these features have been displaced in most of the independent stations by popular music, frequent repetitive newscasts, occasional sports announcing, and more frequent interruptions by advertising.

TABLE 6.18
Types of Television Programs Weighted and Ranked in the Order of Preference and Frequency of Choice by Boys and Girls 13 and 17 Years of Age

Program Type	Boys				Girls			
	Age 13		Age 17		Age 13		Age 17	
	Weighting	Rank	Weighting	Rank	Weighting	Rank	Weighting	Rank
Variety	340	1	434	1	402	1	379	1
Drama	313	3	274	3	383	2	374	2
Sports	326	2	370	2	180	4	158	4
News	128	4	114	5	68	5	116	5
Music	112	5	180	4	276	3	239	3
Education	47	6	26	6	11	6	62	6

Source: Lewis (*21*).

With the foregoing overview of the impact of the latest mass medium on other activities portrayed, attention may be directed to preferences for the different types of programs as reported by youth. This is made possible through the adaptation, in Table 6.18, of evidence reported by Lewis (*21*). The table carries weightings based on order of preference and frequency of choice arrived at by a procedure not explained by the author, and ranks determined by these weightings. Variety is in highest esteem at both ages represented and for both sexes. Sports ranks next for boys and drama for girls, while drama stands third with boys and sports fourth with girls. Music ranks higher with girls than with boys, with only a moderate discernible change in weighting and rank for boys during the age-span. Educational programs rank last for both sexes at both ages. While the weightings and ranks disclose differences in predominant interests for the sexes, they show no clear pattern of trends, as was seen for books and the other printed media, and also, in some degree, for movies and radio. It is altogether likely that a more refined classification of types of television programs would reveal trends toward maturity and variety analogous to those found in preferences in voluntary reading previously considered.

Inquiries for Significant Relationships

Relationships of pubescence.—In the foregoing exposition much attention has been given to recreational activities and interests as influenced by age, but discussion has not been addressed directly to the issue of influence of pubescence, the beginning point of adolescence. In this connection reference may be made to a controversy that emerged at the time Lehman and Witty were reporting their extensive studies of play activities. The controversy began with an article by Lehman and Witty called "Periodicity and Play Behavior" (*19*) in which they concluded from evidence presented, "The play trends which characterize a given age group seem to be the result of gradual changes occurring during the growth period. These changes are not sudden and characterized by periodicity but are gradual and contingent." This conclusion was later challenged by Furfey (*13*) who, after presenting some facts from a study of modest proportions that indicated a decline of interest in certain activities with the advent of adolescence, said the trends "certainly suggest that the sudden loss of interest in these activities is due to pubescence." The challenge appears to have prompted Lehman and Witty to recanvass their evidence against the curves of onset of puberty reported by other investigators on other populations of boys and girls of the ages under consideration, with the result that they reversed their opinion on the influence of periodicity. Among the illustrations of interests that they found to wane with girls at this period is playing with dolls, for which they reported percentages of participation as follows: at 10½, 100; 11½, 77; 12½, 44; 13½, 14; etc.; with boys, playing cowboy: at 11½, 100; 12½, 72; 13½, 42; 14½, 17; etc. They do not report on inquiry concerning the *rise* of certain interests with the incidence of pubescence. If one may judge from evidence previously reported in this chapter, among these would be activities associated with dating and dancing for members of both sexes, and reading about romance for girls and adventure for boys.

The situation with respect to recreational interests is in all probability akin to that for vocational interests as postulated in considering the analogous issue in Chapter 5. No extensive inquiries into the relationship of the incidence of pubescence and of recreational interests and activities in identical populations and on a longitudinal basis have been reported, so that inferences must be drawn from comparing the curves for pubescence for one population with the activities and interests of another population. In view of the variations in the ages of pubescence, no conclusion can be drawn on how closely changes in interests are keyed to this momentous physical change and how much variation there may be from individual to individual in the proximity of changes in the two areas of physique and interests. However, whatever the degree of proximity, available evidence assures us of significant relationships over the age-span from early to late adolescence.

Relationships of intelligence, achievement, and social status.—Evidence concerning the relationship to activities and interests of intelligence, achievement, and social status is fragmentary and far from adequate for definitive conclusions, but is at least suggestive. An investigation by Boynton (5) in which he had intelligence quotients and information concerning the hobbies under 22 classifications of 4,779 boys and girls in grade 6 yielded inferences that may to some extent be applicable to later adolescents. Among these conclusions are that "very superior children appear to have a greater diversification of hobby interests than very inferior ones"; that hobbies of collecting, playing musical instruments, and reading of history, science, and biography are more likely to be participated in by those of superior intellectual ability; and that the child without a hobby is more likely to be below average in intelligence than the child with hobbies. A large-scale inquiry by Sterner (29) into interests in seven media (radio, books, comic strips, funny books, magazines, newspapers, and motion pictures—the study antedates widespread TV) of high school students of both sexes, against a variety of hypothetical factors including intelligence, found that "intelligence shows little relationship to the selection of interests, media, and specific titles within media..." (66). This investigator found that "only on the basis of sex is there any real diversity, girls being more apt to seek romance and to read romantic magazines than boys" (65). Evidence from studies of the extent of participation in recreation or use of media in relation to achievement in school is even more meager. A study by Scott (28) who compared scores on standardized tests in arithmetic and reading for children in grades 6 and 7 showed differences in children with higher achievement scores in the somewhat lower portions of the distribution of televiewing time.

The evidence concerning the relationship of social status and activities is rather better than that concerning other hypothetical factors. For elementary school pupils, Lazarus, in a study already cited (18), found televiewing time ranging from a low of 13 hours a week in "homes of high cultural levels" to a high of 24 hours in "homes of the lowest socioeconomic areas." Maccoby (22) found a "tendency," in a study by interview with mothers of children from 4 to 17, inclusive, "for children of the people in the highest socioeconomic level to spend less time viewing TV" than those at lower levels. In still another investigation, White

(*35*), who gathered his data by interviews with mothers in a random sample of families in Cuyahoga County, Ohio, calculated the mean numbers of hours spent in the following groups of activities: (a) church, reading, and school homework; (b) radio, TV, movies, and sports; and (c) remunerative work and home duty. The time spent in these activities by junior high school students was compared, with the families of which the students were members being classified as upper-middle and upper-lower. The procedure used was by matched pairs, with sex, age, IQ, and grade as the basis of matching. The average total number of hours for each sex was found to be almost the same for the two social classes, but the children of the upper-lower class had about three hours more leisure during the four-day period than did those of the upper-middle class, and they devoted almost twice as many hours to radio, television, movies, and sports as did the upper-middle class and correspondingly less to each of the other groups of activities. A somewhat surprising finding was the fact that the upper-middle class spent more time on remunerative work and home duties, but the large difference in use of time was in recreation.

It is apparent that relationships like those being considered offer a fertile field for further inquiry.

The relation of vocational and avocational interests.—An observation warranted by reconsideration of trends with age in occupational interests in Chapter 5 and of recreational interests as disclosed in this chapter is that both are moving toward stabilization during later adolescence. These concurrent trends bring up the question of whether these interests may not often, for given individuals, have a great deal in common. It may be mentioned in this connection that two contrasting theories have some popular acceptance in regard to the role of avocations, one being that occupational and recreational interests for the individual are basically the same, the recreational being in a way an extension of the occupational, or vice versa, and the other that recreational interests are compensatory in that, by being dissimilar from the vocational, they make for a "balance" of interests.

The investigator who has contributed most to resolving this issue is Super, who has reported two investigations, one of them comparing men's occupations with their hobbies and the other involving administering the Strong Vocational Interest Blank to men with known occupations and hobbies and to high school boys.

In the study first described (*33*) Super obtained information from 273 men employed at the time of the study and ranging in age from 20 to 68, who were members of hobby groups devoted to (1) model engineering, (2) music, (3) photography, and (4) stamp collecting. One line of inquiry concerns the men's satisfaction with their jobs, and it was found that the proportions for those with vocations similar to their avocations were: satisfied, 76 per cent, and dissatisfied, 24 per cent; the corresponding proportions for those with vocations unrelated to avocations were: satisfied, 41 per cent, and dissatisfied, 59 per cent. The author's interpretation of this evidence is the obvious one, "that more than three-fourths of those in vocations which resembled their avocations by virtue of the nature of the activities involved in each were satisfied with their jobs, whereas less than half of those engaged in vocations unrelated to their major avocations were satisfied with their work." The outcomes of an inquiry concerning whether or not the men desired to change their occupations were roughly comparable, as almost two-thirds of the men employed in vocations which resembled their major avocations desired to make no change, whereas two-thirds of those in unrelated occupations would have liked to change their occupations.

Another line of inquiry concerned preference for vocation or avocation in relation to the level of the occupations, which were classified in a gradation from professional at the top to unskilled at the bottom. The finding here was a trend of "decrease in the percentage of men deriving more pleasure from their major avocation than from their vocation as one goes up the occupational scale." Super concluded that there is "a rough positive relationship between occupational level and interest in one's work rather than one's hobby." His general conclusion from this study is that avocations are the manifestations of dominant interests which express themselves, if the situation permits, in vocations of the same type. "If the situation is unfavorable, the dominant interest may cause the avocation to compete with the vocation . . . making it the major source of satisfaction."

In the other study Super, as stated, explored the relationship of avocation to vocation with men and the avocational interests of high school boys by use of the Strong Vocational Interest Blank. His analysis of the 420 items in the blank found 143 of them, or about a third, "vocational"; 72, or about a sixth, "avocational"; and 205, or almost half, "either" (*32*, 31). His inference was that it could be used to study avocational interests, and he proceeded to set up patterns of interest by use of the blank for the four hobbies of model engineering, music, photography, and stamp collecting by the method followed by Strong in setting up patterns for occupations.

Concerning the adults represented in the project Super found that men with interest patterns similar to those of their vocations tended to make higher scores in their avocations than did the men in unrelated vocations. This finding suggested that "some vocations and avocations are basically the same but that certain non-vocational interest patterns might be best measured by strictly non-vocational inventories" (125). Adolescent hobbyists were found to be distinguished by their scores on the avocational keys in the same manner as the adults but were "less clear cut." This fact was attributed to "extraneous and maturational factors like the multiplicity of adolescent interests" (126).

Super discussed the psychological role of avocations in light of the evidence from this investigation. He considered the validity of the theories of "balance" and "contribution," corresponding to those of "balance" and "extension" mentioned above, with the conclusion that neither was found adequately to describe his findings. He proposed, instead, an "individualized" theory: "Avocations are chosen according to present needs of an individual in a given situation, and on the basis of the possible ways in which that individual can meet those needs in that situation" (*32,* 128).

From this project Super derived important implications for guidance, among them that avocations are of value in vocational diagnosis, that they have potential value in the vocational orientation of adolescents, and the recommendation that "vocational interest inventories and scoring keys, because of their correlations with avocations, be used in avocational and leisure-time guidance, in the choice of suitable hobbies" (*32,* 128-29).

Summary

Notwithstanding the urgency of an understanding of the avocational interests of youth, we know far less about these than of vocational preferences and interests. The urgency emerges from the need for a balanced life and from the effects of automation which is rapidly shortening the hours of work and creating a situation affording increased leisure available for the pursuit of recreations.

Findings from investigations of recreations of youth are diverse and sometimes in conflict, making generalization difficult. Recreations engaged in by the two sexes have been found to differ widely. Among important differences are the emphasis on participation in and viewing sports by boys and more sedentary pursuits and activities involving sociability by girls. Among the more notable shifts in activities "liked best" during later adolescence for boys are the rise of active participation in sports and dating and, for girls, reading books, social dancing, and having dates. The number of different activities engaged in by the individual was found to drop and become somewhat stabilized by later adolescence.

Findings of compilations of out-of-school activities of high school youth, of interest to this treatment because the subjects were approaching or were on the threshold of college, again show great diversity as well as marked differences for the sexes, although almost every activity listed had a prominent place in playtime of both boys and girls. Activities more prominent with boys were sports and outdoor activities, while those for girls were musical activities, religious activities, chaperoned parties, club activities, and concerts, plays, and the like. When asked in which activities they would prefer to spend more time, boys emphasized participating in and viewing sports, while girls emphasized concerts, plays, lectures, reading, musical activities, and movies. One conclusion from the arrays of participation is that boys have far more to *do* than girls. Special inquiry into favorite types of music found interest ranging across the full spectrum from "rock-and-roll" through other popular music to the classical, but with rapidly declining proportions in the order named. Interpretations laid stress on the large proportion of interests that involve association with other persons.

Studies of recreational activities of populations of college age have been of more limited scope. The evidence is somewhat equivocal, but one infers that more schooling makes for more recreational reading; that, under broad groupings, for men in the first college year, the proportion of physical activities still has prominence, that "passive-spectator" interests increase; that the proportion for "constructive" activities, although not large, holds its own; and that the large category of "miscellaneous" is not so much a conglomerate as a catchall for such activities as social conversation, dates, dances, club meetings, and house and church parties. Thus, they all involve activities in association with others, a factor which was found prominent with youth of high school age.

Inquiry into the books read voluntarily by youth of precollege age shows them to be very predominantly fictional. For boys the books read show a shift from early to later high school years in considerable degree from the classic adventure stories to westerns and for girls during the same period from standard juveniles to books of romance and adventure. A longitudinal research that carried through the last high school year found a considerable increment for nonfiction books in wide variety, indicative of maturing diversity of reading interests.

Trends in voluntary reading of magazines during high school years by both boys and girls are toward wider use of both the general weeklies and the monthly magazines, with emphasis by boys on mechanical and technical concerns and by girls on matter characteristically dealt with in the women's periodicals. There are increases for the various sections of the magazines, disclosing increasing diversity of reading interests. Almost all sections of newspapers experience increases in reading by both sexes, with chief differences in increments for sports pages for boys and society news for girls. Thus, the reading of both types of periodicals shows a trend toward variety and maturity.

Owing to extensive detail, inadequate procedures of investigation, and conflicting findings, generalizations concerning the use for recreation by youth are even more difficult for the three media which have emerged and been developed to date in the present century, namely, the movie, radio, and television, than for reading the printed page. Inquiries concerning movies made before the advent of TV showed musical comedy, historical, adventure, westerns, and love stories preferred, with the chief difference for the sexes being adventure and westerns for males and love stories for females. Comedy was found to be preferred throughout adolescence. It is well known that the advent of radio brought about widespread listening by young people as well as adults, with comedy a prominent category of preference for both sexes at both elementary and high school levels. Interest in historical events was found to increase with age, but interest in westerns declined, while the differences in trends for the sexes were more interest for boys in sports and for girls in romance. Interest in popular music was found to gain with age at the expense of classical. Areas like news, politics, and religion engaged much less interest than those previously named but made appreciable gains through adolescent years.

The impact of television, as measured by time spent with it by young people, has been spectacular. Televiewing soon came to occupy many hours per week for young and old. Repeated surveys have found the average amount of viewing to be stabilized at somewhat in excess of 20 hours for elementary school children and at about two-thirds of this for high school youth, with the averages for the sexes in later adolescence about equal. Viewing appears to decline to some extent with length of ownership.

The advent of TV has had a profound influence on the character of radio programs and has reduced the time spent in listening to them. Inferences from inquiries into influence on time spent in reading are in conflict as one investigator reported a reduction, another an increase. Time spent in hobbies, however, has decreased. The type of program most popular with boys and girls throughout the age-spans studied is variety, next in prominence being sports for boys and drama for girls.

Canvass of the literature encourages belief in the probability of influence of the changes of adolescence on recreational pursuits, but assurance of this influence and knowledge of its nature and timing must await longitudinal inquiries on the behavior of individuals undergoing the attendant physical changes. As concerns the influence of intelligence, brighter youth appear to have a greater diversification of hobby interests than inferior ones, and one investigator reported finding little relationship of intelligence to the selection of specific interests and media, and specific titles within media. The meager evidence on the relationship of achievement scores to televiewing time shows more time for subjects with lower scores. Televiewing time appears to be decreased appreciably by higher social status. However, the entire area of the influence of such hypothetical factors as pubescence, intelligence, achievement, and social status is greatly in need of further research, especially, for understanding the community college student, during the years of later adolescence.

Because both vocational and avocational interests appear to move toward stabilization during later adolescence, the question may be raised of the extent to which, for given individuals, they may often have much in common. In this connection it is appropriate to mention two theories extant concerning the role of avocations, one being that occupational and recreational interests for the individual are basically the same, the recreational being an extension of the occupational, or vice versa, and the other that recreational interests are compensatory in that, by being dissimilar from the vocational, they make for a balance of interests.

The investigator who has contributed most to resolving this issue is Super who conducted two researches: in one he inquired into the difference in satisfaction with their occupations of men (a) whose vocations were similar to their avocations and (b) whose vocations and avocations were unrelated; in the other, after analyzing the Strong Blank to identify its vocational, avocational, and "either" items, he administered it to men and high school boys. In light of his evidence he considered the validity of the theories of balance and extension (which he called "contribution") with the conclusion that neither was found adequately to explain his findings. He proposed, instead, an "individualized" theory to the effect that "avocations are chosen according to present needs of an individual in a given situation, and on the basis of the possible ways that individual can meet those needs in that situation." On the basis of his findings Super deduced as implications for guidance that avocations are of value in vocational diagnosis and that vocational interest inventories and scoring keys may well be used in avocational and leisure-time guidance, in the choice of hobbies.

References and Bibliography

1. Balogh, Joseph K. "Television-Viewing Habits of High School Boys." *Educational Research Bulletin,* 38 (March 11, 1959), 66–71.
2. Battin, T. C. *Television and Youth.* Report published by TV Information Committee, National Association of Radio and TV Broadcasters. Washington, 1954.
3. Bell, Howard M. *Youth Tell Their Story.* Washington: American Council on Education, 1938.
4. Besco, Galen S. "Television and Its Effects on Other Related Interests of High School Pupils." *English Journal,* 41 (March, 1952), 151–52.
5. Boynton, Paul L. "The Relationship between Children's Tested Intelligence and Their Hobby Participations." *Journal of Genetic Psychology,* 58 (1941), 353–62.
6. Brown, Francis J. *The Sociology of Childhood.* New York: Prentice-Hall, Inc., 1939.
7. Cavanaugh, Jean O. "The Relation of Recreation to Personality Adjustment." *Journal of Social Psychology,* 15 (Feb., 1942), 63–74.

8. Clark, Weston R. "Radio Listening Habits of Children." *Journal of Social Psychology,* 12 (1940), 131–49.
9. Coffin, Thomas. "Television's Effects on Leisure-Time Activities." *Journal of Applied Psychology,* 32 (Nov., 1948), 550–58.
10. Coleman, James S. *The Adolescent Society.* New York: The Macmillan Co., 1961.
11. Dimock, Hedley S. *Rediscovering the Adolescent.* New York: The Association Press, 1938.
12. Eberhart, Wilfred. "Evaluating the Leisure Reading of High School Pupils." *School Review,* 47 (April, 1939), 257–69.
13. Furfey, Paul H. "Pubescence and Play Behavior." *American Journal of Psychology,* 41 (Jan., 1929), 109–11.
14. Hileman, Donald G. "The Young Radio Audience: A Study of Listening Habits." *Journalism Quarterly,* 30 (Winter, 1953), 37–43.
15. Hutson, P. W., and Kovar, Dan R. "Some Problems of Senior High School Pupils in Their Social Recreation." *Educational Administration and Supervision,* 28 (Oct., 1942), 503–19.
16. Johnson, B. Lamar. "Children's Reading Interests as Related to Sex and Grade in School." *School Review,* 40 (April, 1932), 257–72.
17. Kaplan, Max. *Leisure in America: A Social Inquiry.* New York: John Wiley & Sons, 1960.
18. Lazarus, Arnold L. "Pupils' TV Habits." *Educational Leadership,* 13 (Jan., 1956), 241–42.
19. Lehman, Harvey C., and Witty, Paul A. "Periodicity and Play Behavior." *Journal of Educational Psychology,* 18 (Feb., 1927), 115–18.
20. Lehman, Harvey C., and Witty, Paul A. *The Psychology of Play Activities.* New York: A. S. Barnes & Co., 1927.
21. Lewis, Philip. "Teenagers Tame TV." *Educational Screen,* 30 (May, 1951), 174–75, 190.
22. Maccoby, Eleanor E. "Television: Its Impact on School Children." *Public Opinion Quarterly,* 15 (Fall, 1951), 421–44.
23. McDonagh, Edward C., et al. "Television and the Family." *Sociology and Social Research,* 35 (Nov.–Dec., 1950), 113–22.
24. Mitchell, Alice M. *Children and Movies.* Chicago: University of Chicago Press, 1929.
25. Neumeyer, Martin H. and Esther S. *Leisure and Recreation: A Study of Leisure and Recreation in Their Sociological Aspects.* 3d ed. New York: Ronald Press Co., 1958.
26. Olds, E. B. "How Do Young People Use Their Leisure Time?" *Recreation,* 42 (Jan., 1949), 458–63.
27. Punké, H. H. "Leisure Time Attitudes and Activities of High School Students." *School and Society,* 43 (June 27, 1936), 884–88.
28. Scott, Lloyd F. "Television and School Achievement." *Phi Delta Kappan,* 38 (Oct., 1956), 25–28.
29. Sterner, Alice. *Radio, Motion Picture, and Reading Interests: A Study of High School Pupils.* Teachers College Contributions to Education, no. 932. New York, 1947.
30. Stoke, Stuart M., and Clive, W. F. "The Avocations of One Hundred College Freshmen." *Journal of Applied Psychology,* 13 (1929), 257–63.
31. Stone, Calvin P., and Barker, Roger S. "The Attitudes and Interests of Pre-menarcheal and Post-menarcheal Girls." *Journal of Genetic Psychology,* 54 (1939), 27–71.
32. Super, Donald E. *Avocational Interest Patterns.* Stanford, Cal.: Stanford University Press, 1940.
33. Super, Donald E. "Avocations and Vocational Adjustment." *Character and Personality,* 10 (Sept., 1940), 51–61.

34. "What TV Is Doing to America." *U.S. News and World Report*, 39, no. 10 (Sept. 2, 1955), 36–50.
35. White, R. Clyde. "Social Class Differences in the Use of Leisure." *American Journal of Sociology*, 61 (Sept., 1955), 145–50.
36. Witty, Paul A. "Televiewing by Children and Youth." *Elementary English*, 38 (Jan., 1961), 103–13.
37. Wrenn, C. Gilbert, and Darley, John G. *Time on Their Hands: A Report on Leisure, Recreation, and Young People.* Washington: American Council on Education, 1941.

Part II

Focus on the Student

7
Aptitude, Social Status, and Academic Competence

IN HIS interpretative summary in 1958 of what is known about college students, *They Come for the Best of Reasons,* Wise said (*96, 3*), "A broad knowledge of college students is needed for fuller understanding and more effective teaching. This deeper understanding of students can be gained by exploring their backgrounds, their homes, their age, ability, sex, race, religion—all these are significant. Their purpose in college and in life, their attitudes and motivation, are keys to understanding."

It is the concern of this chapter and the one following to review what is known about community college students, to the extent that this has not been done in Part I.* It will be recalled that the first section of Chapter 1 presented evidence concerning the distribution by age and sex of these students. The remaining sections of the chapter and Chapters 2–6 have presented evidence bearing successively on physical, mental, and personal and social development, sexual and dating behavior, and vocational and avocational interests of later adolescents—evidence which, while not often dealing directly with community college students themselves, is nevertheless aimed at contributing to understanding that student population. This and the following chapter focus for the most part on community college (or junior college) students themselves, although it is necessary at times, because of a lack of information about them, to draw on evidence concerning related student bodies. Treatment in these chapters will be primarily of students of normal age for these college years, as special consideration to adults is given in Chapter 10.

After a prefatory review of published proposals of who will and should attend community colleges, a main portion of this chapter will be the presentation of evidence on the aptitude and socioeconomic status of the community college student. This treatment will be followed by information

---

*The summary of this chapter and appropriate references and bibliography are combined with those for Chapter 8 and will be found following that chapter.

bearing on the success of these students after transfer to four-year colleges and universities, and their academic deficiencies as they come to the community college. Chapter 8 will continue consideration of the community college student, but will be concerned with evidence bearing on personal characteristics, attitudes, and interests in certain important areas.

The Issue of Clientele of the Community College

The issue of proportions who should attend.—Crucial to an understanding of the community college student, certainly in its dynamic aspects, is the question of who will and should attend the institution, and salient in this connection is the *proportion of the population* who will and should attend. Widely divergent opinions have been put forward on this score. A recent pronouncement by the Educational Policies Commission of the National Education Association, if carried into effect, would virtually universalize attendance during the first two post-high-school years, that is, the community college level (*89*). The foreword to the statement says that the commission "proposes that the nation now raise its sights to make available at least two years of further education, aimed primarily at intellectual growth for all high school graduates." In the body of the statement the argument runs that freedom is essential to our American society and that intelligence and understanding are essential to freedom. The commission indicates that "the goal of universal secondary education is now more than two-thirds of the way toward achievement in the United States" and that "there is reason to expect that most persons capable of completing the studies of an American high school are also capable of further growth toward a free mind" (4). "Therefore, the nation's goal of universal opportunity must be expanded to include at least two further years of education, open to any high school graduate, and designed to move each student toward intellectual freedom" (6). The report urges that "non-selective colleges should exist in every population center" (25) "under controls which ensure that they truly are non-selective," that they be mostly public institutions, and that they be tuition-free.

The commission, as reported above, was aware of the near approach to universalization of high school education that has already been attained and must have been conversant with the reports of recent rapid popularization of education at the college level. In some states the proportion of youth of the population of high school age in school has exceeded 90 per cent. Facts and predictions concerning popularization at the collegiate level were being widely publicized, and under captions like that used by Thompson, namely, *The Impending Tidal Wave of Students* (*80*). Excerpted figures from one of these predictions are presented for certain states in Table 7.1. These percentages are projected, as indicated in the table title, as proportions of the populations of ages 18 through 21, the normal ages for college attendance, and on the basis of a formula that takes account of birth rates during years preceding those represented in the table and the rate of acceleration in college attendance. The states included in this table for illustration are in all regions of the country except the South, where the proportions tend to be lower. While the proportions even for 1970 and 1975 are far from approximating universalization, they are unquestionably high enough to have caused concern as to how the influx of students is to be accommodated. It is worth noting that among a number

TABLE 7.1
Projected Percentages of the Population of Ages 18, 19, 20, and 21 Enrolled in Higher Institutions in Certain States for 1960, 1965, 1970, and 1975

Year	California	Illinois	Kansas	Massachusetts	Utah
1960	60.3	38.5	49.5	54.5	64.3
1965	61.8	41.0	52.0	57.0	65.8
1970	63.3	43.5	54.5	59.5	70.3
1975	64.8	46.0	57.0	62.0	71.8

Source: Adapted from Thompson (*81*).

of "educational alternatives" Thompson lists for meeting this "tidal wave" is to "establish community colleges." In the list of alternatives he includes also "raise tuition fees" and "limit enrollment" which would run counter to the proposals of the Educational Policies Commission.

Readers who have kept in touch with educational discussion in public print will know that this pronouncement by the Educational Policies Commission was preceded fifteen years earlier by a statement by another quasi-official group that took the community college into account in recommending the further popularization of education at the collegiate level. This group was the President's Commission on Higher Education whose report, *Higher Education for American Democracy* (*30*), was issued in 1947 and has been widely influential in developing public policy. On the basis of evidence supplied to it this commission stated that "at least 49 per cent of the population has the mental ability to complete 14 years of schooling with a curriculum of general and vocational studies that should lead either to gainful employment or to further study at a more advanced level" and that "at least 32 per cent has the mental ability to complete an advanced liberal or specialized professional education" (*41*). Toward implementing this degree of popularization the commission recommended the widespread establishment of local publicly controlled tuition-free community colleges. One may note that the 49 per cent mentioned is about half the "universalization" urged by the Educational Policies Commission and was presumably based on the proportions of the population that had been successful in current programs in the first two college years. The latter commission, to have urged universalization, must have contemplated adaptation of programs to meet the needs of the wider range of abilities that would be represented.

A wide gap is apparent between virtual universalization of early college years as advocated by the Educational Policies Commission in 1964 and making this level of schooling available to about half the population of the first two years of post-high-school age as proposed by the President's Commission. However, even the more modest goal of the President's Commission was called into question by Havighurst (25) soon after its report appeared in print. In commenting on the "feasibility" of the commission's proposal, Havighurst elaborated three "principal obstacles," which are the problem of financing, the "ability level of the youth of the country," and the problem of "motivation." Of the last named obstacle Havighurst made a great deal, predicting that even if economic barriers are removed, the proportion of the college-age group going to college might be raised to 35 per cent, nearer a third than a half of all. To get more young people to want to go to college he said that two things are necessary: convincing working-class people and the lower levels of white-collar workers that general education at the college level is worth more for their children than the money they could otherwise be earning, and improving the guidance processes. This more conservative estimate may have been based on studies of college-going of youth in families in the different social classes in places like "Elmtown" and "Prairie City," neither of which could boast a local public community college. Notwithstanding this position, Havighurst, in collaboration with another writer, in a chapter in Hollinshead's *Who Should Go to College?* (34, 165), observed that motivation for college is "related in some degree to propinquity" and that "extension of colleges in the form of the community college . . . would have some motivational value." This citation of position in the 1940s held by one of our eminent students of society is in no way made with an implication of censure, but rather with the intent of reporting an opinion held at a point in history now twenty years ago. We have experienced many striking social changes during this interval.

Comparisons of Aptitude

Earlier comparisons.—Two important respects in which one may judge the degree of approach to universalization or whatever other degree of popularization has been or is being achieved by the junior college must be those of (a) the ability and (b) the socioeconomic status of the clientele. Attention will therefore be directed, first, to evidence derived from meas-

APTITUDE, SOCIAL STATUS, AND ACADEMIC COMPETENCE 273

ures of aptitude, and, following this, to information concerning occupational status of parents. The comparisons will hardly provide fully reliable measures of the actual degree of democratization achieved, but they will nevertheless indicate something of the trend of influence of the community college in this direction.

So far as is known, the first published results of administering tests of aptitude to any considerable number of junior college students and of comparisons with test results for students in four-year colleges and universities were those of the present writer (46, 87–122) in which he used the Army Alpha Test and the Thurstone Test for college freshmen. Following World

TABLE 7.2
MEDIAN AND FIRST AND THIRD QUARTILE SCORES ON THE ARMY ALPHA TEST
FOR FRESHMEN IN CERTAIN HIGHER INSTITUTIONS

Institutions	Median	First Quartile	Third Quartile
Public junior colleges (8–332)*	138.4	118.2	153.9
Private junior colleges (2–259)	126.5	110.5	144.6
Colleges and universities (6–4,479)	136.7	115.7	155.5
University of Minnesota (463)	130.4	108.9	147.1
Ohio State University (2,545)	130.3	116.7	149.0
Oberlin (330)	148.4	132.4	161.5
Yale (400)	159.5	145.0	172.6

SOURCE: Derived from Koos (46, 95, Table 33; 102, Table 36).
*First of two numbers in parentheses, where there are two numbers, is the number of institutions represented; other numbers are all numbers of students.

War I the Army Alpha Test was administered to students in many colleges, and those conversant with the history of aptitude testing know that this use was the impetus for the development of the better tests of aptitude now generally in use in higher institutions. The fact that reports of the results of the Army Alpha on students in higher institutions were available prompted the writer to use it with junior college students, in order to make comparisons. Before he had completed the testing with the Army Alpha, reports from the application of the Thurstone Test, one of the first of the tests of aptitude developed especially to be applied to college freshmen, became available in print, so it was practicable to administer this as well as Army Alpha to freshmen in some of the junior colleges represented in the project. Some of the results of administering the Army Alpha and the Thurstone are reported, respectively, in Tables 7.2 and 7.3.

The measures used for comparison are the median and the first and third quartiles which indicate the range of the middle 50 per cent. If the reader wonders at the small total number of persons represented in the junior colleges, he is reminded that most of these institutions in the early 1920s had relatively small enrollments. The numbers included all freshmen students in attendance on the day of testing and no advance notice was given that the test was to be administered: the aim was to secure complete representation, and it is the writer's belief that this aim was achieved without exception. By examining the first and third rows of measures it may be noted that freshmen in public junior colleges were about on a par with those in six colleges and universities, with medians and first and third quartiles not far apart. These measures for private junior colleges, reported in the second row, are all somewhat lower than for public junior colleges and for colleges and universities, but this may be owing to the fact that only two institutions are represented, and is more likely to be because of

TABLE 7.3
MEDIAN AND FIRST AND THIRD QUARTILE SCORES ON THE THURSTONE TEST FOR COLLEGE FRESHMEN IN 5 PUBLIC JUNIOR COLLEGES AND IN 34 COLLEGES

Group of Freshmen	Median	First Quartile	Third Quartile
Junior college men (122)*	86.8	69.6	99.6
Junior college women (84)	86.5	70.0	97.7
Junior college men and women (206)	86.5	69.8	98.6
College men and women (5,495)	86.6	69.0	102.7

SOURCE: Derived from Koos (46, 104, Table 37).
*Number of students.

the acknowledged unfairness of Army Alpha to women (it was devised for selecting men) who outnumbered the men in these particular institutions.

The remaining rows of measures in Table 7.2 make possible comparisons with individual institutions, namely, two public universities and two private colleges. The measures for the two state universities run somewhat lower than for the public junior colleges. For the University of Minnesota, freshmen in the College of Science, Literature, and Arts only were represented, whereas for the Ohio State University all freshmen were included. It should be said, whatever the present basis of selection, that during the period here involved, practically all midwestern state universities were admitting almost all high school graduates, which is also the practice in public junior colleges. The measures in the two lowest rows, for the two private institutions, are notably higher than those in all other rows, reflecting more selective practices. The measures for Yale are higher even than those for Oberlin, but the difference may be in considerable part owing to a large proportion of freshmen women in Oberlin, who, as explained above, would be disadvantaged by the Army Alpha.

The rather remarkable finding emerging from the comparisons afforded in Table 7.3 is the near equivalence of all the measures for all four groups of students, which include junior college freshmen men and women separate and combined and college men and women combined. This is true not only for the medians but also for the interquartile ranges, except for the slightly higher third quartile measure for the freshmen in the four-year colleges.

Another comparison of ability of freshmen in junior colleges and in other higher institutions was reported by the writer in 1928. This compari-

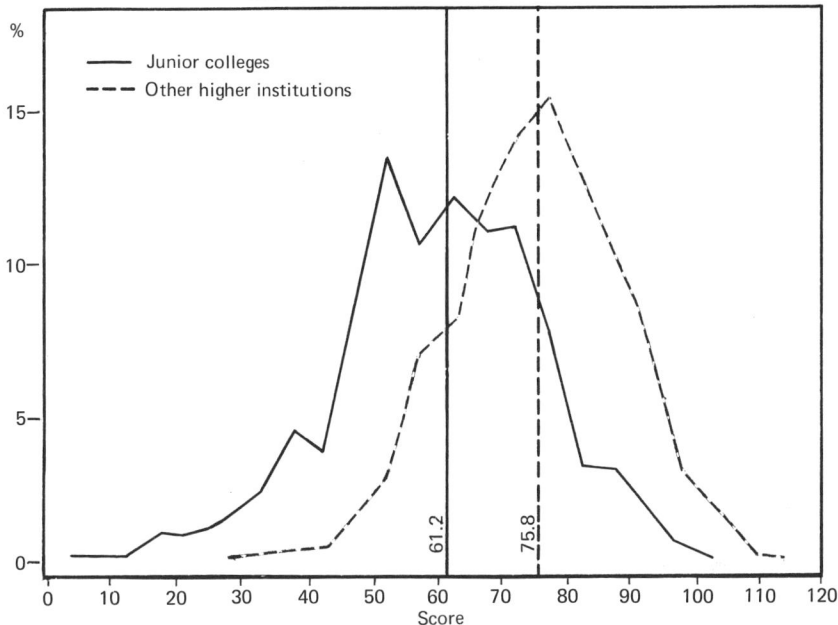

FIG. 7.1

COMPARISON OF THE DISTRIBUTION OF SCORES OF FRESHMEN ON THE THORNDIKE COLLEGE APTITUDE TEST AT FOUR JUNIOR COLLEGES AND THREE OTHER HIGHER INSTITUTIONS IN CALIFORNIA

SOURCE: Leonard V. Koos, *Secondary Education in California—A Preliminary Survey* (Sacramento: California State Department of Education, 1929), p. 71.

son involves freshmen in four local public junior colleges and in two private four-year colleges and a private university in California. The four-year colleges and the university were admitting freshmen on selective bases. The evidence was supplied by authorities in these institutions, where the Thorndike College Aptitude Test had been administered some time previously and independently of the survey project for which the distributions of scores were solicited. The institutions represented include almost all those in the state that were at the time making use of the Thorndike Test on their freshmen.

Graphical representations of the two distributions are reproduced in

Figure 7.1. Similarities and differences of the distributions are readily discernible. Looking first at the upper portions of the distributions, one may note that some students in the junior colleges made scores almost as high as those in the selective private institutions, but that scores for the junior colleges reach into lower ranges than for the other institutions, with considerable proportions of scores in these lower ranges. In consequence, the vertical lines in the figure, which locate the median scores for the two groups, show the median somewhat lower for the junior colleges than for the other higher institutions: the difference in median scores was 14.6 points in favor of the selective private institutions. The obvious conclusion

TABLE 7.4
MEDIAN AND FIRST AND THIRD QUARTILE SCORES ON CERTAIN TESTS OF FRESHMEN IN IOWA JUNIOR COLLEGES AND IN THE UNIVERSITY OF IOWA

Test and Institution	Median	First Quartile	Third Quartile
Iowa Comprehension Test			
Junior college	23	18	28
University of Iowa	22	17	27
Iowa Placement Examination, English			
Junior college	89	66	116
University of Iowa	85	62	113
Iowa Placement Examination, Mathematics			
Junior college	22	14	30
University of Iowa	18	12	26
Iowa High School Content Examination			
Junior college	113	92	138
University of Iowa	112	87	138
Weighted composite scores on four tests			
Junior college	359	291	432
University of Iowa	340	268	424

SOURCE: Compiled from tables in Stoddard (75).

from this comparison is that the junior colleges enrolled some students with almost as high aptitude, as measured by this test, as the three selective higher institutions but that they enrolled a considerably larger proportion of less capable students, at the same time that, by inspection, one notes that a proportion approaching a half of students in the two types of institutions were on a par.

For the further understanding of possible influences on measures of aptitude of junior college students, the findings of two earlier comparisons of aptitude, or ability, of students in junior colleges and in other higher institutions will be drawn upon here. One of these is a comparison by Stoddard (75) of freshmen in public junior colleges of Iowa and in the University of Iowa and the other by Eells (16) of students in California junior colleges with students in higher institutions throughout the country. Outcomes of the Stoddard comparison are presented in Table 7.4 as medians and first and third quartile measures on comprehension, placement, and high school content tests, as well as on composite scores from all these tests. On all the fifteen measures reported, except one, in which the scores are identical, those for junior college freshmen are higher than for University of Iowa freshmen. Stoddard concluded, "While the difference between the groups is slight, it is significantly in favor of the junior college group." Without reporting the evidence to support his statement Stoddard said that there was a wide difference in the scores for individual junior colleges.

TABLE 7.5
MEDIAN SCORES ON THE THURSTONE TEST OF
FRESHMEN IN CALIFORNIA JUNIOR COLLEGES
AND IN NATIONAL COLLEGES AND
UNIVERSITIES

Institutions	Median
National four-year colleges	
Public	129
Private	145
California junior colleges	
District	137
High school	129

SOURCE: Eells (16).

Speculation over the difference between the main findings for the California and the Iowa comparisons suggests several factors of influence. One of these is the selective procedures of the private higher institutions in California as contrasted with a procedure of admission at the University of Iowa, not differing widely from those of other state universities of the Middle West at this period. Another factor must have been the restricted offering in the Iowa junior colleges, limited mainly to transfer curriculums. This would be imposed by the small enrollments of the junior colleges: the total number of freshmen tested was 378, with a range in number from 15 to 59 in the 16 junior colleges involved, and an average of fewer than 30. In addition, these junior colleges were all tuition-charging, whereas the California units were uniformly tuition-free. The significance of a charge for tuition on attendance in a public junior college is canvassed below in reporting on the socioeconomic status of parents of students.

The investigation by Eells (16) was a large-scale undertaking involving comparison of performance by 11,000 junior college students, more than two-thirds of all in California at the time, on the American Council on Education Psychological Examination, referred to by him as the "Thurstone Test," with that of upwards of 30,000 students in more than a hundred public and private colleges and universities. Because of the inferences emerging from the early investigations already cited, it is necessary to report and comment on only a few of the medians, which are presented in Table 7.5. The median for private four-year colleges is seen to reflect the

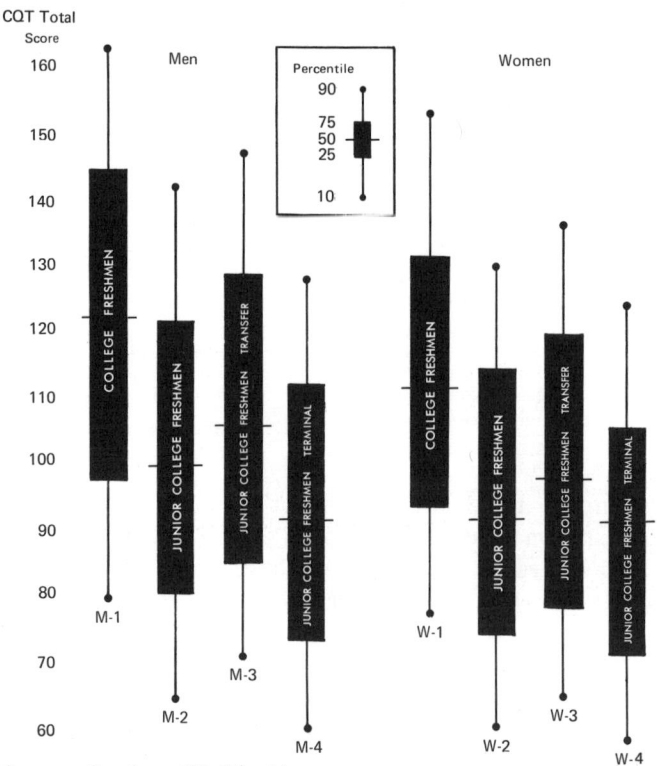

FIG. 7.2
COMPARISON OF THE DISTRIBUTION OF CQT TOTAL SCORES FOR VARIOUS NORMATIVE GROUPS

SOURCE: Seashore (*71*, Fig. 1).

trend of difference in their favor as compared with public institutions and the trend toward superiority over public junior colleges already noted above. The higher median for "district" as compared with "high school" junior colleges calls for a word of explanation. The former group of junior colleges in California was maintained by separate districts superimposed on elementary and high school districts and characteristically separated from high schools below. The junior colleges designated by Eells as "high school" junior colleges were maintained by high school districts under the same boards as high schools. They often used some of the same facilities as the high school and sometimes teachers who worked at both high school and college levels. This means that the factor of proximity in encouraging continuation from high school to college was likely to be at a maximum, and this may well be an important influence in inducing more students of lesser ability to enter junior college.

More recent comparisons.—Results of the relatively recent administration of the College Qualifications Test to junior college freshmen, after establishing norms for the test on approximately 24,000 admitted freshmen in 37 colleges and universities across the country, have been reported by Seashore (*71*). The data used apply to twenty junior colleges, seven of them in California and the remainder scattered in thirteen other states in various sections of the country, one institution in each state. The total number of junior college freshmen included was 7,837. A minor weakness of the comparison for the purpose of studying the aptitude of community college students is that four of the institutions were under private rather than public auspices. However, the presence of scores for these four institutions can influence the measures reported in a limited way only, since the total enrollment in them in a recent school year accounted for only about 8 per cent of the total for the 20 junior colleges: one can assume that the measures for local public units would be approximately the same as for the entire group. The scores used in all the junior colleges are for freshmen carrying programs of at least 12 semester hours in the fall of 1957.

Certain measures from the comparison are presented in Figures 7.2 and 7.3. In the first of these figures, medians, interquartile ranges, and tenth and ninetieth percentile scores are shown for (a) all freshmen men and (b) all freshmen women separately in the four-year colleges, and for three categories of junior college freshmen of each sex, (c) all freshmen, and freshmen in (d) transfer and (e) terminal programs.

The reader should find it informative to ponder the various measures depicted in Figure 7.2. Instead of attempting an original interpretation from these measures, dependence is placed here on Seashore's "statements" concerning them, which to him "seem reasonable":

"The median score for junior college freshmen is near the 25th percentile for senior college freshmen.

"About 24 per cent of junior college men and 20 per cent of junior college women are above the respective medians for freshmen in four-year colleges.

"There is considerable overlap of scores. These distributions tell us that there are many junior college students whose scores would be considered superior in senior colleges, and many low-scoring senior college freshmen would also rate low in junior colleges.

"The difference in favor of the four-year student is slightly greater for women than for men."

The figure displays also the same measures for students reported to be enrolled in transfer and in terminal curriculums. For both sexes the measures are higher for transfer than for terminal students, with larger proportions of the former than the latter being in the upper ranges of four-year

FIG. 7.3
DISTRIBUTION OF MEAN CQT TOTAL SCORES OF JUNIOR COLLEGES

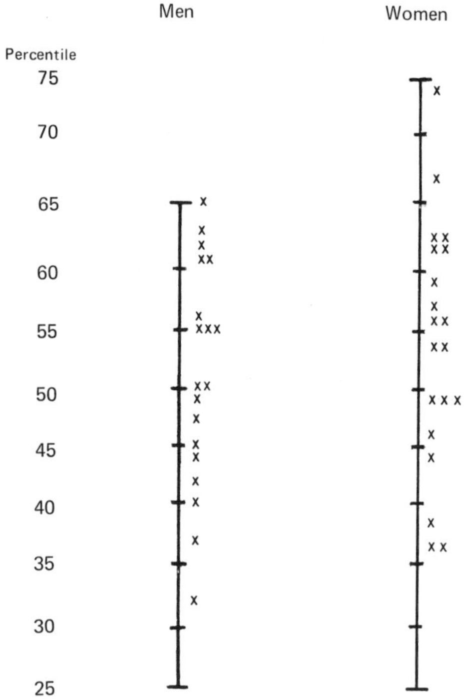

	Men	Women
Percentile 75		x
70		x
65	x	
60	x / x / xx	xx / xx / x
55	x / xxx	x / xx / xx
50	xx / x / x	xxx
45	x / x	x / x
40	x	x
35	x	x / xx
30	x	
25		

SOURCE: Seashore (*71*, Fig. 2).
Note: Each X is the mean score of all freshmen in one junior college, plotted in terms of junior college norms. The number of junior colleges for which means are marked by crosses in the presentation for men is 19 instead of 20 because one institution enrolled only women.

college freshmen and larger proportions of terminal students being below the lower ranges.

For the most part, the measures in Figure 7.2 corroborate the main findings from the evidence in Figure 7.1, which compared the Thorndike College Aptitude Test scores of freshmen in local public junior colleges in California with those of freshmen in three selective higher institutions in that state. Seashore's figure, however, goes further by supporting the observation that more of the terminal than of the transfer students contribute to the larger proportion of students with lower aptitude scores found in the distribution for junior colleges.

The second figure from Seashore's study shows the wide range of mean measures of aptitude from junior college to junior college. This range is hardly wider than known to be characteristic of such means for four-year colleges, except that there is, as may be inferred from the higher measures for such colleges in Figure 7.2, a tendency for the distribution of means to run higher in four-year colleges. As is well known, different units within individual universities sometimes vary widely in standards of admission and, therefore, in the aptitude of their students.

The project by Seashore utilizes test scores of college freshmen obtained before 1960. In order to check on the acceptability of the main conclusions from his investigation and press related inquiry somewhat further, brief summary will be made of limited portions of another and more recent comparison of aptitude of junior college and four-year college freshmen by Seibel (72). This project suffers under the same limitation as the one by Seashore for our primary interest in community college students by including a representation of students in nonlocal nonpublic junior colleges, but hardly enough of them to invalidate the main inferences as applicable to public units. The measures of aptitude used were the Preliminary Scholastic Aptitude Test (PSAT), Verbal and Mathematical scores, and a rank-in-class index with a normalized scale score having a range of 0–26, with the largest figure being the highest index and with a mean of 13. The index is based on information concerning the end-of-senior-year "rank in class" and "size of graduating class" supplied by the high schools. The mean PSAT-Verbal scores for the two-year and four-year freshmen were, respectively, 38.4 and 45.9, and the corresponding PSAT-Mathematical scores were 41.3 and 49.9, indicating that the four-year colleges and universities are more selective in their admission policies than most junior colleges. However, Seibel notes that there are many high-ability students attending junior colleges and "considerable overlap in the distributions of scores for students attending the two types of institutions" (23). The situation with respect to the rank-in-class index is closely analogous, as the means for two-year and four-year institutions are, respectively, 13.3 and 15.8, with high scores in both groups and extensive overlap of the distributions. Means and distributions for the two sexes in the junior colleges are not strikingly different. On the whole, main conclusions from the Seashore and Seibel projects corroborate each other.

What progress toward universalization on aptitude?—Because the Seibel project reports measures for the high school graduates in his sample who did not attend college as well as those who attended two-year and four-year institutions, it is possible to obtain from these measures a partial clue to, even if no exact measure of, progress toward aptitudinal universalization of post-high-school education through influence of the two-year units. Certain of these measures drawn from Seibel's tabulations are presented in Table 7.6. The means for graduates not attending college are all seen to be lower than those attending two-year colleges; the percentages with scores 40 or lower on PSAT-Verbal and Mathematical and with rank 10 or lower are all larger. The measures for those not attending and attending two-year institutions are nearer alike than are those for graduates attending two-year and four-year institutions, which leads to the inference that

TABLE 7.6
CERTAIN MEASURES INDICATING APTITUDE OF HIGH SCHOOL GRADUATES WHO DID NOT ATTEND COLLEGE, ATTENDED 2-YEAR INSTITUTIONS, AND ATTENDED 4-YEAR INSTITUTIONS

Measure	Did Not Attend College	Attended 2-Year Institutions	Attended 4-year Institutions
PSAT-verbal mean	31.9	38.4	45.9
Per cent with scores of 40 or lower	84	40	18
PSAT-mathematical mean	36.2	41.3	49.9
Per cent with scores of 40 or lower	49	51	18
Mean rank-in-class index	12.2	13.3	15.8
Per cent with rank 10 or lower	23	19	3

SOURCE: Based on Seibel (72, 24–29, Tables 6–11).

progress is being achieved by the junior college toward the universalization advocated by the Educational Policies Commission, while the fact that the differences between graduates not attending and those attending two-year colleges are substantial suggests that we still have far to go to attain universalization for high school graduates.

As far as measures of progress toward universalization of the post-high-school level for our total population of appropriate ages, and not merely high school graduates, are concerned, we have little better information than the illustrative percentages cited above from Thompson. As concerns universalization in relation to general ability or aptitude, it would be instructive to have evidence of recent origins along lines assembled in the early twenties by the present writer, which compared the distributions of scores on the Army Alpha test of junior college freshmen and freshmen in state universities with those for the army draft for the country as a whole. In this comparison it was found that *no* score on Army Alpha for any student in the junior colleges or universities dipped down as far as the median for the white army draft. While universalizing post-high-school education for all high school graduates may be seen to be a "larger order," it seems to be a much more realistic proximate goal than trying to do so for the total population of the appropriate age-level, unless during the last four or five decades there has been a marked upward trend in general ability.

Comparisons of Socioeconomic Status

In junior colleges and other institutions.—The socioeconomic status of students, as indicated by the occupation of fathers, has been investigated rather extensively since the early 1920s. A procedure first used by Counts* on high school students has been applied by this writer and others to students in junior colleges and in other higher institutions, thus making possible comparisons of socioeconomic status of students at this educational level in individual or groups of institutions. The classification of occupations of students' fathers used is an adaptation of the occupational grouping of the federal census. To refresh the reader's memory, Counts' classifications are reproduced here:

1. Proprietors
2. Professional service
3. Managerial service
4. Commercial service
5. Clerical service
6. Agricultural service
7. Artisan-proprietors
8. Building and related trades
9. Machine and related trades
10. Printing trades
11. Miscellaneous trades in manufacturing and mechanical industries
12. Transportation service
13. Public service
14. Personal service
15. Miners, lumber workers, and fishermen
16. Common labor
17. Occupation unknown

The information used for classifying the fathers was supplied on forms filled out by the students in such a way, inclusive of answers to supplementary questions, that rather precise categorization is assured. Previous applications of the socioeconomic classification have pointed to the feasibility of focusing attention on the higher and the lower groups in differentiating institutions with respect to their service in democratization. Specifically, the larger grouping found advantageous for this purpose includes in one "higher group" the first three classes (proprietors, professional service, and managerial service), and in another "lower group" classifications 8–16, inclusive.

The first comparisons here are of the proportions of fathers, in these two large groupings, of freshmen in colleges and universities and in junior

---

*George Sylvester Counts, *The Selective Character of American Secondary Education*, Supplementary Education Monographs, no. 19 (Chicago: Dept. of Education, University of Chicago, 1922).

colleges. The investigations represented are among the earlier ones using the Counts classification and range from 1922 to 1934. These comparisons are provided in Table 7.7. The first impression given by a glance down the two columns of percentages is of the relatively larger proportions in the higher and the relatively small proportions in the lower groups. Closer examination shows larger proportions at the higher level in private colleges and universities and in private junior colleges than in state universities, about the same proportion in state universities and in public junior colleges in 1922, and the smallest proportion in public junior colleges in 1934.

TABLE 7.7
PERCENTAGES OF FRESHMEN IN VARIOUS TYPES OF INSTITUTIONS WHOSE FATHERS WERE MEMBERS OF CERTAIN HIGHER AND LOWER SOCIOECONOMIC GROUPS

Type of Institution	Socioeconomic Level	
	Higher	Lower
Private colleges and universities, 1926*	55.9	10.9
State universities, 1926*	50.4	11.3
Private junior colleges, 1934†	63.2	8.9
Public junior colleges, 1922‡	49.4	15.6
Public junior colleges, 1934†	36.8	22.9

*Reynolds (66, 16).
†Anderson (1).
‡Koos (46, 138).

Smallest proportions at the lower level are to be seen for the first three groups of institutions, with somewhat larger proportions for the two groups of public junior colleges, with that for public junior colleges in 1934 being appreciably larger than that for public junior colleges in 1922. The writer hastens to mention that the differences between the figures for the two groups of public junior colleges is less likely to be owing to difference in the period represented than to the factor of tuition charge, which will be seen below to be highly influential. The study involving junior colleges in 1922 was made without regard to tuition, some of them levying such a charge and others not doing so, whereas the junior colleges in 1934 were all in California and were uniformly tuition-free.

The influence of proximity and tuition.—The comparisons just afforded in Table 7.7 suggest that both proximity of opportunity and the practice of imposing a charge for tuition are influential in the proportions of students of different socioeconomic levels who attend. An investigation made by the writer during the early 1940s establishes these influences more unequivocally. This investigation was a follow-up of 11,932—almost twelve thousand—high school graduates in 57 school systems. Of this total number, 2,528 were graduates in systems without junior colleges (and also without other higher institutions in the vicinity), 3,156 were graduates in systems with tuition-charging public junior colleges, and 6,248 were graduates in systems with tuition-free junior colleges. In all but a small proportion of schools a full count of graduates was included and in a few an acceptable method of generous sampling was used. Data for socioeconomic classification were gathered for all seniors in the high schools represented in the second semester. For the second step in October, an alphabetical list was sent to the principal to report for each student on whether or not he had graduated, whether or not he had continued in college, and, if he had continued, the name of the institution he was attend-

TABLE 7.8
MEDIAN PERCENTAGES, FOR CERTAIN GROUPS OF SCHOOL SYSTEMS, OF ALL 1941 HIGH SCHOOL GRADUATES, GRADUATES IN HIGHER SOCIOECONOMIC GROUPS, AND GRADUATES IN LOWER SOCIOECONOMIC GROUPS ENTERING COLLEGE

Group of Systems	All High School Graduates	Graduates in Higher Socioeconomic Groups	Graduates in Lower Socioeconomic Groups
Without junior colleges (12)*	19.7	38.7	10.8
With junior colleges (45)	48.4	60.7	39.1
With tuition-charging junior colleges (15)	31.8	48.9	19.7
With tuition-free junior colleges (30)	53.5	67.5	46.7

SOURCE: Leonard V. Koos, *Integrating High School and College* (New York: Harper and Bros., 1946), p. 124, Table 30.
*Number of systems represented.

ing. Of 63 high schools in the 57 systems whose principals were invited to do so, data were supplied for all but two. The classification and grouping used are the same as in Table 7.7 and certain results of the follow-up are presented in Table 7.8. In interpreting the results, it should be kept in mind that the percentages of all graduates continuing are reported, irrespective of institution entered, as this procedure is intended to reflect the influence of proximity and tuition policy.

The first column of figures in the table reports the median percentages of all graduates continuing. The influence of proximity is seen in the fact that the median percentage of graduates in systems with local junior colleges is about two and one-half times that in systems without junior colleges. When the systems with junior colleges are separated into those in which the junior colleges are tuition-charging and those in which they are tuition-free, the median proportion for the latter is found to be one and two-thirds times the former.

Analogous comparisons for graduates in the higher and lower socioeconomic groups afforded by the second and third columns of figures likewise show differences in the same direction but not of equal magnitude. However, the medians in the second column show that the presence of a junior college added more than half to the proportion in the higher socioeconomic level who enter college from high schools in systems without junior colleges and that tuition-free junior colleges added a third or more to the proportion in this level as compared with tuition-charging junior colleges. The contrasts for the lower socioeconomic group are much more striking, as the proportion at this level in systems with junior colleges was almost four times that in systems without, and the proportion in systems with tuition-free junior colleges was much more than doubled as compared with tuition-charging junior colleges. From evidence in this table the inference is obvious that proximity is a potent influence on college attendance of young people and a tuition-free policy is not far from equally influential. The two influences operating together give great promise of bringing about a popularization at the lower collegiate level that has been already attained at the high school level immediately below, with a promise at the same time of fostering social mobility in our society.

To underline the potency of a free-tuition policy in promoting popularization of attendance at the lower college level, another investigation made by the writer may be cited. The purpose of this inquiry was not so much to study degree of popularization as to provide a basis for projecting junior college enrollments in school systems not having junior colleges but in which establishing them was under consideration. The procedure was to compute the ratio of the high school enrollments and the junior college enrollments in systems with these units, and to compare these proportions in (a) systems in which tuition was being charged for attendance with (b) systems in which attendance was tuition-free. A total of 110 systems is represented in this study, 52 with tuition charges of $50 or more per year and 58 with no or low tuition. These systems included about half of those in the country maintaining local public junior colleges at the time the study was made. The annual charges made in the tuition-charging junior colleges ranged from $50 per year upward, with an average around $90 per year. Only a few of the other group levied a tuition charge, none over $25 per year, and the average for this group was between two and three dollars. In essence, therefore, this is a comparison of the percentages of high school enrollments in junior colleges which charge tuition and junior colleges which are tuition-free.

Significant measures from this investigation are presented in Table 7.9. They are given as median and first and third quartile percentages. The median reported for the no- or low-tuition group is almost 2.4 times that for the tuition-charging group. The ratios for the first and third quartiles are not notably different. It is not assumed that all the students in the junior college advanced from the local high schools. It has been found, however, that the great bulk of students in local junior colleges come from the local constituency, and the appropriate inference is that a free tuition policy is a potent influence toward democratization of the lower college level.

More on the influence of proximity and free tuition.—In published investigative literature there may be found much evidence, some of it direct but most of it less direct, bearing on the influence of proximity and tuition policy in encouraging or discouraging college attendance. Some of this evidence will be cited at this point, with the order of presentation being

TABLE 7.9
PERCENTAGES WHICH JUNIOR COLLEGE ENROLLMENTS ARE OF HIGH SCHOOL ENROLLMENTS IN 52 SCHOOL SYSTEMS WITH TUITION OF $50 OR MORE A YEAR AND IN 58 SYSTEMS WITH LOW- OR NO-TUITION JUNIOR COLLEGES

Measure	Tuition of $50 or More	No or Low Tuition
Median	14.10	33.37
First quartile	10.44	24.74
Third quartile	22.31	44.12

SOURCE: Koos (*45*, Table 5).

(a) reasons given for attending local public junior colleges, (b) report on tuition charges being made in such institutions, (c) the cost of college education away from home, and (d) the lack of motivation toward college attendance, especially of superior youth.

(a) In a study made by the writer forty or more years ago he distributed to a sampling of students in seven widely scattered local public junior colleges a simple form; students were requested to take the form home, ask a parent to fill it out, and send it in an accompanying stamped, self-addressed envelope to the writer's place of work. The form directed the parent simply to state in space provided the reason or reasons why the son or daughter was "attending the junior college rather than a college or university elsewhere." Returns were received from 199 parents, and they gave a total of 423 reasons, the most recurrent of which were generalized as follows: attendance at junior college less expensive, 33.8 per cent; home influence extended, 27.9 per cent; training received as good or better, 14.9 per cent; more attention to the individual student, 11.1 per cent. These four reasons account for seven-eighths of all those given and no other reason was mentioned more than six times.

The reason of special interest here is the first, "Attendance at junior college less expensive," and this reason accounted for a third of all reasons given. This was not always an admission of inability to finance education away from home, although the reason was often so stated. The lower cost, of course, arises from proximity, low or no tuition, or both.

(b) The significance for socioeconomic democratization of a tuition charge has been indicated above. Interest at this point is in the proportion of public junior colleges making no such charge and information on the distribution and trends in charges for those that do. The evidence is available in two studies of practice, one by Hackett (22) in 1954 on these annual charges for 267 public junior colleges for which the evidence was available in published sources, and the other by D'Amico and Iffert (12) for 281 similar institutions with the data applicable to the academic year 1963–64. The tuition charges considered here are those for resident students and do not take account of increased charges made of nonresidents. The measures reported here are presented as rounded figures. Hackett's study found the percentage of tuition-free institutions to be 38, while for the second study, the proportion following this practice had shrunk to 15 per cent. The computed median tuition increased from $61 to about $130; the first quartile, from $0 to a little under $50; and the third quartile from $116 to about $200. To arrive at an estimate of total costs, one would need to add such fees as were being charged and the cost of living at home, which is usually less than living away from home.

Concerning the practice of making a tuition charge for attending a local public junior college, one may say, in relation to the evidence reported on its effect as reported earlier in this section, that it tends to obstruct the very democratization which it is a major function of an open-door institution to achieve, and to continue to increase the charges is merely to raise the barrier to attendance, especially for students in less fortunate situations.

To the criticism that may be alleged by some that conclusions based on evidence gathered a quarter century ago can no longer be valid for a society which has in the meantime grown increasingly affluent, recent evidence may be cited that demonstrates that the obstructive influences are still operative. In connection with the contemporary controversy in California where attendance in public junior colleges, colleges, and universities has been tuition-free and while pressure was being applied to bring about abandonment of this policy, an editorial writer for the San Francisco *Examiner and Chronicle* quoted at length from a nationwide investigation of the relationship of family income and college attendance which had been sponsored by the National Association of State Universities and Land Grant Colleges. A single illustration from the materials of the study will suffice to establish persistence of the relationship: although 40 per cent of families have incomes of less than $6,000, only 19.5 per cent of freshmen in two-year and four-year public and private institutions come from this group.*

(c) By contrast with the tuition situation in the public junior college as just reviewed and attendance as affected by proximity, the cost of attendance in higher institutions away from the home base is much higher. As illustrations of these costs one may cite the estimates of annual costs including tuition, fees, books, and board and room, quoted in a Research Bulletin of the National Education Association† and indicated as having been supplied by the American School Counselor Association.‡ These estimates are as follows:

State college or teachers college	$ 900 to $1,200
State university	$1,300 to $1,500
Private coeducational college	$1,500 to $1,800
Private women's college	$1,700 to $2,200
Private men's college	$1,800 to $2,200
Institute of technology	$1,900 to $2,400
Junior college	$1,700 to $2,000

With continued inflation since 1961, these estimates would be substantially higher by now. The estimate given above for junior college must be for private institutions most of which have less endowment than many of the private four-year colleges and are, therefore, maintained in larger part from tuition income. One meaning of this contrast with costs for junior colleges is the smaller proportion of youth from lower socio-economic levels who can attend without subsidization in the form of scholarships scaled to the needs of the individual student.

The expectation that the costs of attendance in colleges and universities as just exemplified operate as a stricture on attending college is corroborated by follow-up studies of high school graduates, a number of which have been reported and two of which will be drawn upon briefly at this point. One of these is by Barber (2) and concerns graduates of superior ability of the three academic high schools in Erie, Pennsylvania, in 1948. Superiority was determined by their having intelligence quotients of 115 or higher, assumed to indicate ability to do college work. There were 183 with this ability in the total of 763 graduates. Of the whole group 56 had entered college by the following year, "approximately three out of ten of these good college risks." Omitting those of the remainder who had entered the armed forces or moved out of the city,

*Alan Cline, "Effect of Rising Tuition Costs," San Francisco *Examiner and Chronicle*, Feb. 5, 1967, section 1, p. 11.
†National Education Association, *Research Bulletin*, 39, 3 (Oct., 1961), Ch. 6.
‡American Personnel and Guidance Association, *How About College?* Washington, 1959.

Barber conducted interviews with 111 of the graduates, with about twice as many girls as boys.

The reasons given by these graduates for not having attended college are reported in Table 7.10, which includes only the eight reasons most frequently mentioned. The reasons are reported in the table as "chief reason," which is the first reason given, and as the "total of first, second, and third reasons." It may be noted that "lack of finances" is the reason of highest frequency in both pairs of columns. This finding accords with expectation based on the influence of proximity and cost. In this connection it should be mentioned that in the fall of 1949, the year in which

TABLE 7.10
CHIEF REASONS AND TOTAL OF FIRST, SECOND, AND THIRD REASONS GIVEN BY SUPERIOR HIGH SCHOOL GRADUATES FOR NOT ATTENDING COLLEGE

Reasons	Chief Reasons		Total of First, Second, and Third Reasons	
	Number	Per Cent	Number	Per Cent
1. Lack of finances	38	34	56	50
2. Lack of academic interests	22	20	42	38
3. Lack of serious purpose	14	12	20	18
4. Preference for work experience	16	13	27	24
5. Preference for more challenging work	4	4	6	5
6. Preference for engagement or marriage	4	4	10	9
7. Preference for freedom from parental control	–	–	8	7
8. Indecision	3	3	7	6

SOURCE: Barber (2, Table 1).

these interviews were made, a branch of Pennsylvania State University was established at Erie, and it would be interesting to know what influence this has had on college attendance of superior high school graduates there under the influence of proximity and, to some extent, of cost of attendance. However, it should be noted as to the cost factor that the annual tuition charge of $525 at the branch is in the highest reaches of the distribution of tuition charges for public junior colleges reported above from Hackett's and D'Amico and Iffert's studies. Some of the other reasons in the table are appropriate for consideration below in dealing with motivation to attend college.

The other investigation with its main conclusion in a similar vein is by Wright and Jung and concerns college attendance of high school graduates in Indiana (*100*, 29–32). They reported that of the top 10 per cent of the Indiana graduates of 1955 who were not continuing beyond high school, 28.1 per cent said that the cost of further education prevented them from continuing; the parents of 80.2 per cent said that they had discussed the cost of further education with their children; 11.2 per cent said they needed to stay at home and help their families financially; and 34.7 per cent of the parents said that the cost of continuing education was a factor in the decision not to continue school

A definitive inquiry in one state.— A study by Windham (95), somewhat disconcerting from the standpoint of democratization of the post-high-school years by means of the junior college, has been reported for Florida, a state which has since 1956 and 1957 experienced spectacular development of community colleges. The development was initiated by and carried out in accordance with a statewide survey that identified the locations of these institutions so that only a small percentage of prospective students (high school graduates) were beyond commuting distance from them. Implementation of the plans for the system was expedited by competent leadership in the State Department of Education, so that practically all units in the system were in operation at the time to which lines of evidence used by Windham apply.

In advance of drawing from the study itself it is desirable to report briefly on the charges for tuition made in the public universities and junior colleges of the state. At this writing the charge for students from Florida for its state universities, as fixed by the legislature, is $150 per quarter including student activity fees, or $450 for the academic year of three quarters. The legislature has allowed the junior colleges some flexibility in the amounts of their charges which are usually referred to as "matriculation fees." For the 1969–70 school year these fees, including the activity fee, for "in-district" students ranged from $150 to $250, with the median at $200 and the arithmetic mean not much greater. The charges for "out-of-district" students were somewhat larger, with the median at $270, and the median for "out-of-state" students was $450. The charges as here reported, reflecting the trend toward increasing them, had been somewhat lower for the year for which Windham made his investigation. For 34 states other than Florida for which information on the annual tuition charge in public junior colleges is available to the writer, the median was $255 and the range was from lows of no charge (California) and $40 (Hawaii) to the two highest of $580 and $682.

The study by Windham is concerned with all public higher education in the state, and comparisons are included for the universities and the junior colleges. The most significant comparison for purposes here is that of the percentage distribution by family income classes of freshmen and transfer students in these institutions; these are reported as follows (95, 62, Table 9):

Percentage in Each Income Class

	$0–2,999	$3,000–4,999	$5,000–6,999	$7,000–9,999	$10,000–14,000	$15,000–20,000	$20,000–above
All Universities	6.3	12.0	17.7	23.0	23.6	10.1	7.3
All Junior Colleges	6.3	12.7	21.2	24.3	22.8	7.8	4.9

In interpreting the figures, Windham says they "suggest that the junior colleges are slightly more equalitarian [than the universities] but that this is really only for the income groups between $5,000 and $10,000." Point is given to the small proportions from the lowest family income levels by the much larger percentages of 1965 income tax reports at these levels—35.9 for $0–2,999, 19.6 for $3,000–4,999—whereas the three income groups at $10,000 and above included only 10.5 per cent of all for the state in that year.

Windham calculated from results of a Board of Regents survey that "of all university students in the state in the Fall of 1967, 52.5 per cent were white males, 39.6 per cent were white females, 4.2 per cent were Negro males, and 3.7 per cent were Negro females" (95, 77). Opposition to a question on race in the junior college questionnaire (36.2 per cent refused to answer the question) made it impossible to estimate the white-Negro ratio in the junior colleges and, therefore, in the entire system of higher education including them. It may be assumed that, owing to the combination of appreciably lower tuition charges, proximity, and less selective procedures of admission, the proportion of blacks would almost certainly be somewhat larger in the junior colleges than in the universities, because of the known greater proportion of low family incomes than for whites. However, the percentage of them in attendance must still have been smaller than their proportion of the total population.

Before leaving the question of the proportions of students from the different family income groups, mention should be made of the facts that these proportions vary from institution to institution, and that some of the junior colleges enroll larger proportions at lower income and smaller proportions at higher income levels than others. For example (95, 93–96, Table 14), adding the figures for students in the two lowest income classes for one junior college near the top of the list in alphabetical order yields 31.2 per cent, and for this junior college only 6.9 per cent came from families with incomes of $15,000 and above. By contrast, for another junior college in this list, the respective percentages were 12.4 and

22.2. Such differences may reflect either or both differing degrees of egalitarianism or of distributions of family incomes in the districts.

Another important aspect of Windham's research has to do with the incidence of Florida's tax structure. Tax income at the state level is predominantly from levies on consumption, and Windham shows that this makes for disproportionate payments in relation to benefits (with proportions of payments exceeding those of benefits, as in the case of higher education) for lower as compared with higher incomes (*95*, 57, Table 6; 59, Table 7; 60, Table 8). This inference of a regressive bias may be said to have ironic overtones in relation to public polity.

Windham's opinion of the influence of the charges for tuition is as follows (*95*, 86–87): "State financed higher education is usually subsidized to such an extent that the tuition costs alone do not constitute an important barrier to entry. This is not to say that the fees and charges incurred by students do not cause a hardship which is inverse to the student's income level. The fees and charges are, for the average low-income student, only one of several barriers which may deter his entry to or hasten his departure from the system." In discussing scholarships he advocates restricting them to needy students, thereby making possible more substantial grants to those who need them. He contends that "foregone earnings" are a more potent factor than tuition charge in keeping prospective students out of the community colleges and this can be true of the more employable. This factor is involved with and in large part synonymous with motivation for continuance of one's education, consideration of which is expanded below. In advance of this further reflection on motivation it should not be out of place to urge that, important as they are, proximity, no or low tuition charges, and the open-door policy will be hardly enough to assure anything approaching universalization of post-high-school education. What will be needed in addition are curriculum offerings that appeal as "relevant" (to use a currently overworked word) to the presently unmotivated and a concerned and protracted counseling and guidance contact with individual youths. Some indication of what these programs can and should be is afforded in Chapters 11 and 12.

On the issue of motivation.—In an earlier chapter* dealing with occupational plans of later adolescents something was made of the conclusions from a study by Kahl looking into the sources of motivation of "common man" sons of superior ability who were expecting to go to college in comparison with those of the same ability not intending to continue their education. The difference in motivation of the boys was found to be in differences in the aspirations and drives of the families, some of which were content with the way of life in the common-man class while others

*Ch. 5, pp. 208–9.

were not but were striving for elevation in social status. Reverting to the follow-up study of high school graduates by Barber in Erie, which was drawn upon above, and looking again at reasons in Table 7.10 for not having continued into college other than the first one already considered, we may note that among them are "lack of academic interests," "lack of serious purpose," "preference for work experience," and others that have much in common with this lack of motivation of sons in families of lower socioeconomic levels. It is logical to assume, moreover, that many or most of the graduates among Barber's interviewees proffering such reasons were from families of lower socioeconomic levels, although we may assume also that these spread to some extent to youth from higher levels.

It is apropos to mention, in connection with this consideration of the unmotivated in our youth population, that those in lower socioeconomic levels surpass in *gross numbers* the youth of superior ability in the higher socioeconomic levels. Evidence in support of this assertion was provided long ago by Byrns and Henmon in their article on "Parental Occupation and Mental Ability" (7). These authors compiled the results of administering aptitude tests to more than 100,000 seniors in Wisconsin high schools over a five-year period. In the information available on these students was that concerning occupations of fathers. The scores on the tests were transmuted into percentiles, and one of the conclusions from the compilation of these percentiles by occupations is that "more than half of the superior children in the high schools of Wisconsin come from the occupational groups that rank the lowest," this fact arising from the much larger proportion of the population employed in these lower level occupations and their larger numbers of offspring. One may judge from the evidence in the early portions of this section that it must be in considerable part the youth from homes in these lower categories who account for the larger differences of proportionate attendance at college of seniors where the institution is close at hand in a community college that is tuition-free. At the same time, the popularization spreads to youth of lower ability, as we know from the comparisons of aptitude in community colleges and in other institutions.

If one were to quarrel with the anthropologists and others who have noted the non-college-going traditions in the behavior of lower-class families, it would be on the point that they may overlook the practical certainty that motivation, or lack of it, can be modified by proximity and low cost of attendance. This surely has proved true in the case of high school education, which is now free of cost near most homes and has in consequence been almost universalized. There is no reason to believe that the same influences will not be effective at the next higher level, although we cannot know without more experience how near to complete universalization we can come.

Readers will be generally aware of another method often advocated and applied to encourage superior youth to attend college, that is, subsidization by means of scholarships. In recent years scholarship plans have been developed on statewide and even nationwide bases, and they have increasingly been scaled to the economic status of the family. From the evidence cited above, it should be manifest that the provision of the tuition-free community college is at once both a more economical and more effective method of encouraging college attendance. Moreover, in addition to encouraging only superior youth to attend, as do the scholarship plans, the community college alternative, through proximity and low cost, encourages attendance through something like the full range of ability of high school graduates. The only subsidization needed in states with comprehensive community college systems would be subsistence allowances for youth in areas of sparse population remote from community colleges. With well-developed community college systems, scholarship plans could well be reserved for and concentrated on students at the upper collegiate and university levels.

Without doubt, some persons will take exception to the opinion just expressed as to the preferability of community college development to scholarship programs. An illustration in point is that expressed by Jencks, while reviewing impending changes in education at the federal level of encouragement (*37*). While advocating a shift from plans of aid to institutions to those of aid to students, he said, "By shifting the emphasis from the support of institutions to the support of individuals, it might give somewhat higher priority to the need of many undergraduates for subsistence stipends. By failing to provide such support, even to the very needy, the present system encourages all but the affluent to attend commuter colleges which enable them to live 'on the cheap' at home. But for many such students getting away from home is the *sine qua non* of intellectual growth. A nation as rich as America ought to aim at providing every student who can benefit from it enough money to attend a residential college if he wants to. A scholarship program seems to me the most politically promising way to move in this direction." It is apparent that, in advocating scholarships, Jencks is emphasizing advantages differing from and/or beyond those of equalizing educational opportunity usually in the minds of those who favor them.

Two Comparisons Involving Both Ability and Environmental Factors

A project comparing noncollege, junior college, and college populations.—An investigation that has thrown light on both the ability and social status of junior college students is Project TALENT, which began in 1960 with extensive testing of 440,000 high school students who attended schools in a 5 per cent probability sample of the population of high schools in the United States (9). The results reported are based on test data and additional information obtained from original eleventh graders on their college status one year out of high school. Additional understanding of the ability and social status of the junior college student arises from the fact that comparisons are made not only of junior college and four-year college students, but also of these groups with the non-college-going students. Considerable assurance for the acceptability of the findings is afforded by the total numbers presented in the three criterion groups which included over 16,000 males and 18,000 females.

TABLE 7.11
MEANS OF ABILITY SCORES OF NONCOLLEGE, JUNIOR COLLEGE, AND COLLEGE MEN AND WOMEN

Variable	Men			Women		
	Non-college	Junior College	College	Non-college	Junior College	College
Vocabulary information	12.7	14.3	16.0	11.6	13.3	15.2
Social studies information	15.4	17.7	19.6	13.7	15.7	18.0
Mathematics information	8.7	11.7	15.4	6.7	9.2	13.0
Physical sciences information	9.0	10.8	12.7	6.5	7.5	9.9
Creativity	9.1	10.4	11.7	8.5	9.5	10.8
Abstract reasoning	8.9	9.9	10.7	8.8	9.7	10.5

SOURCE: Measures quoted from Cooley and Becker (9, Tables 1 and 2).

Comparison of ability.—The battery of tests of ability and achievement extended through fourteen variables, as follows: Vocabulary Information, Literature Information, Social Studies Information, Mathematics Information, Physical Science Information, Biological Science Information, Memory for Sentences, Disguised Words, English Total, Reading Comprehension, Creativity, Abstract Reasoning, Mathematics Total, and Arithmetic Computation. To give an impression of the comparative outcomes, it is necessary only to illustrate by reporting the means of the measures on six of the variables, as is done in Table 7.11. These means disclose a rather consistent progression upward for both sexes from the noncollege, through the junior college, and to the college groups. At the same time, the evidence concerning these variables, as reported in Table 7.12, shows extensive overlapping of the distribution of scores for the three groups. The figures disclose, as the authors state, that about a third of the junior college students fall below the noncollege mean, and a third fall above the college mean.

The remaining third of the junior college population falls between the average noncollege student and the average college student.

Comparison on environmental factors.—The following socioeconomic cultural items supplied on a Student Information Blank were used in comparing the three criterion groups: mother's and father's education; father's job; number of books in the home; whether or not the student had a room, desk, and typewriter of his own at home; and two items on the extent to which luxury appliances and electronic equipment (TV, etc.) were present

TABLE 7.12
PERCENTAGES OF JUNIOR COLLEGE STUDENTS BELOW NONCOLLEGE MEANS AND ABOVE COLLEGE MEANS ON CERTAIN VARIABLES

Variable	Per Cent Below Noncollege Mean		Per Cent Above College Mean	
	Men	Women	Men	Women
Vocabulary	31	31	28	28
Social studies	29	33	32	29
Mathematics	27	30	23	21
Physical sciences	31	39	30	28
Creativity	36	39	36	36
Abstract reasoning	35	37	37	37

SOURCE: Cooley and Becker (9, Table 3).

TABLE 7.13
RELATIVE PREDICTIVE POWER OF THE SOCIOECONOMIC VARIABLES

SIB Item	Discriminant Function
Number of books	.32
Number of appliances	.14
Number of electrical appliances	.20
Own room	.58
Father's job	.48
Father's education	.30
Mother's education	.43

SOURCE: Cooley and Becker (9, Table 9).

in the home. The authors say that the means have no absolute interpretation in terms of socioeconomic status, but that they can be viewed relatively across the three groups. Instead, therefore, of focusing on the averages, recourse is taken to the "discriminant functions" for each of the seven variables, which are reported in Table 7.13. In interpreting these measures the authors point out that the largest group differences are for the item on the extent to which the student has his own room, his own study desk, and typewriter. Next in importance are the father's job and the mother's education. They regard it as interesting that the mother's education is more related to group membership than the father's, which follows closely the number of books in the home.

The authors state that it is "extremely difficult to make reasonable comparisons between the relative nature of the group differences" in ability and in environment, the main reason being that much more is known about measures of ability than measures of environment. They believe that measures in both areas are much involved in determining whether a student goes to college, to a junior college, or to no college at all, and that they see a tendency for junior college students to be more like noncollege students in terms of ability and slightly more like college students in terms of socioeconomic factors. The sexes seem not to differ in these respects. Unfortunately for our primary interest in the community college student, Project TALENT did not distinguish between local public and other types of junior colleges, including private units, and we are left to speculate over the differences for these two groups.

A project comparing influence of types of institutions.—Another major project looking into the influence of both ability and socioeconomic and other environmental factors on college attendance is one by Medsker and Trent (*60*) done at the Center for Research and Development in Higher Education of the University of California at Berkeley, which has been the source of much enlightenment of issues relating to student personnel at the collegiate level. This project differs in approach from Project TALENT which distinguished only, as concerns post-high-school education, junior college and college attendance. The Medsker-Trent project was set up to ascertain the influence on attendance at the collegiate level of institutions of different types located in the communities studied. Specifically, the investigation reported was a follow-up study in October, 1959, of about 10,000 June graduates of 37 high schools in 16 communities, 14 in the Midwest and 2 in California. The communities in the Midwest were of comparable demographic and industrial make-up and ranked in population from about 25,000 to 100,000. Four of these had public junior colleges only, four had extension centers, four had state colleges, and two were without collegiate-level provisions of any kind. One of the California communities had a public junior college and was not unlike those in the Midwest, and the other was a metropolitan community with a "variety of colleges," including a junior college and a state college. Information in considerable variety was assembled concerning each graduate, although in the treatment here use is made only of ability quintiles (obtained from aptitude test scores), quintile ranks in class, father's occupational classification, and father's education.

The first measures, reported here in Table 7.14, are the percentages of these graduating classes who had by October entered college, special schools, or no college. The percentages of attendance included all types of collegiate institutions, wherever located, and not merely in the home community. It is to be noted that the highest percentage who continued was in the communities with junior colleges, next highest in those with state colleges and the one with multiple colleges. Lowest percentages were those with extension centers and without colleges. Figures for the two sexes, not shown, have all the proportions somewhat larger for men than for women.

TABLE 7.14
EDUCATION OF HIGH SCHOOL GRADUATES BY TYPE OF LOCAL COLLEGE IN COMMUNITY (REPORTED IN PERCENTAGES)

Further Education	Type of College in Community				
	Junior College	Extension Center	State College	Multiple Colleges	No College
College	53	34	47	44	33
Special school	5	9	5	4	11
None	42	57	48	52	56
Total	100	100	100	100	100

SOURCE: Medsker and Trent (*60*, 61, from Table 43).

TABLE 7.15
GRADUATES' ABILITY QUINTILES AND QUINTILE RANKS IN HIGH SCHOOL BY TYPE OF COLLEGE ENTERED (REPORTED IN PERCENTAGES)

Type of College	Ability Quintiles		Quintile Ranks in Class	
	I–II	IV–V	I–II	IV–V
Private 2-year	54	31	49	26
Private 4- or 5-year	69	14	72	13
Private university	82	5	84	3
Public 2-year	44	33	42	26
Extension center	58	18	62	19
Public 4- or 5-year	54	23	56	20
Public university	69	12	72	11

SOURCE: Medsker and Trent (*60*, 71–72, from Tables 49 and 50).

In an effort to distill the main significance of the Medsker-Trent project without reproducing its content at full length, four measures only, bearing on continuation at the collegiate level of the high school graduates, will be used: two of ability—ability quintile and quintile rank-in-class—and two of environment—father's occupational classification and father's extent of education. Even for these, comparisons will be made of combined percentages of highest and lowest measures for each type of evidence, since it appears that these comparisons will yield clues to the main conclusions. These percentages are presented in Tables 7.15 and 7.16. Interpretation of the evidence in these tables may be illustrated by saying, in reference to the first row of figures in Table 7.15, that, of graduates entering private two-year colleges, whatever the location of these institutions, 54 per cent were in the two highest quintiles of their classes and 31 per cent from the two lowest quintiles. A glance at the pair of columns of percentages relating to ability finds the proportions for test ability quintiles and quintile ranks in class very much alike, suggesting that these two measures are almost on a par as predictors of attendance. When attention is directed to differences for types of institutions, it is noted that the proportions from the upper groups for private colleges and universities and public universities are much larger and from the lower groups are much smaller than for the other institutions, reflecting their selective policies. It may be seen that substantial proportions of the more able graduates enter the other types of institutions, including the public two-year colleges, and that the

TABLE 7.16
FATHER'S OCCUPATIONAL CLASSIFICATION AND EXTENT OF EDUCATION BY TYPE OF COLLEGE GRADUATES ENTERED (REPORTED IN PERCENTAGES)

Type of College	Father's Occupational Classification		Father's Education	
	Professional and Managerial	Semiskilled and Unskilled	Graduate School or Finished College	Elementary School or Some High School
Private 2-year	20	14	20	34
Private 4- or 5-year	32	11	27	28
Private university	49	4	42	17
Public 2-year	16	21	14	37
Extension center	13	19	7	39
Public 4- or 5-year	19	14	17	30
Public university	35	9	31	23

SOURCE: Medsker and Trent (*60*, 71, 73, from Tables 52 and 54).

proportions from the lower quintiles in these public two-year institutions are largest. The proportions in the two pairs of quintiles entering the public four- or five-year colleges are between those for the more selective and less selective institutions. Extension centers are more selective with respect to ability than the public two-year colleges.

On the environmental measures in Table 7.16, private universities appear to be most highly selective, being followed rather closely by public universities and private four- or five-year colleges, with the public two-year institutions again being less selective and, thus, more conducive to social mobility. Public four- or five-year colleges are again found in the main between the four- or five-year private colleges and the private and public universities on one hand and the public two-year colleges on the other, and the extension centers, while serving relatively large proportions of graduates from homes of fathers with low level occupations and less education, enroll far fewer at upper levels.

It was the evidence telescoped in Tables 7.14, 7.15, and 7.16 and other kindred data on which Medsker and Trent based the following conclusion in their final chapter (60, 100): "A factor which clearly had a bearing on whether certain graduates went immediately to college was the type of public college, if any, in the community. As had been hypothesized, graduates in communities with public junior colleges were the most likely to continue their education and the communities with state colleges were next in order. The relative impact of the junior college on men and on young people from low socioeconomic homes, particularly with high ability, was striking."

It is regrettable that in this project the number of communities with public junior colleges was not large enough, though it included several with tuition-charging and tuition-free institutions, to allow for inquiry into the influence of variation in this practice on socioeconomic democratization.

Follow-up Inquiries of Junior College Graduates

Comparisons of community college transfers and "native" students.— Another important area of characterization of student bodies in community colleges is with respect to their ability and achievements as transfers to four-year colleges and universities. Interest in the ability and performance of community college students, including graduates, who have continued their education in these senior institutions has over a long period prompted the making of numerous studies; many of the studies were minor and local, but some of them involved more institutions and probed into more presumptive influences on measures of success.

A recent and extensive inquiry of the success of transfers will be drawn upon at considerable length below, but it should afford some background for the evidence reported from it to epitomize recurrent findings from the earlier local and mainly minor studies. Outcomes of these studies, as might be expected, vary rather widely, some of them indicating greater success of transfers than others and identifying some junior colleges with a higher proportion of successful transfers than others. Marks earned by the students before transfer average appreciably higher than those of the native students below their junior years, the explanation usually given being the fact, illustrated in the treatment of aptitude of students above, that junior college students are in competition with a larger proportion of less able students than are the native students with whose records they are being compared: in the distribution of grades in junior colleges these students fared better than they would have fared in the first two years of the institutions to which they transferred. Success of the transfers as measured by grades received manifests a tendency to slump for the first term or semester after transfer, this decline usually being attributed in the interpretations to the pressures of readjustment to a new and usually more complex environment for education and living. The extent of recovery from this decline seems to depend in considerable part on the degree of selection at time of transfer. With less selection, recovery is less complete, somewhat smaller proportions of transfers attain degrees, and others are delayed in attaining them. On the other hand, with higher selection, recovery in grades is favored, larger proportions attain degrees on schedule, and match or exceed these and other records of native students. It will be interesting to note to what extent these findings are corroborated, refined, or extended in the investigation from which findings will next be reviewed.

The Knoell-Medsker investigation in ten states.—At the same time the most definitive and the most comprehensive investigation of transfer students from two-year to four-year colleges and universities so far reported is one by Dorothy M. Knoell and Leland L. Medsker, another of the highly informative projects concerning collegiate populations carried on by the Center for Research and Development in Higher Education in the University of California at Berkeley. Although appearing as reports of two projects (43, 44), the evidence of the second relates to the same populations as the first and is virtually an extension of it. The investigation concerns junior college transfers in ten widely distributed states having extensive junior college development, two in the East (New York and Pennsylvania), three in the Midwest (Illinois, Kansas, and Michigan), three in the South (Florida, Georgia, and Texas), and two in the West (California and Washington). Represented in the follow-up were 7,243 junior college students who transferred to 44 higher institutional campuses which were classified for the study as (1) major universities, (2) teachers' colleges, (3) other state colleges and universities, (4) private colleges and universities, and (5) technical schools. Comparisons are made in various respects with a total sample of 3,349 "native" students in these institutions.

Unfortunately, in this large-scale inquiry, it appears to have been impossible to follow a procedure involving matched comparisons. The authors say that "ideally a comparison of native and junior college transfer students would involve the selection of matched groups at the freshman level in the two types of institution, with a follow-up over at least a five-year span," but they also state that such a longitudinal study was "not economically feasible" (44, 127). However, efforts were made to compensate for this lack by making comparisons of the two populations in various important respects, including, among others, academic aptitude, socioeconomic status, marital status, grade-point ratios earned at lower and upper college levels, and percentages graduated on schedule. In the report here of findings from the investigations, the order of presentation is not that in the published reports, but instead, for convenience in comparability, in the order of portrayal up to this point in the current chapter. While the order here may not do full justice to this substantial research, it should aid the reader in coordinating the evidence in the chapter from the various sources.

(a) *Comparisons of ability and aptitude.* Being unable to follow a procedure of matched comparisons in respect to ability and aptitude, these investigators resorted to use of evidence from tests already available in the cooperating higher institutions. The evidence was derived from a wide variety of tests administered, as concerns the different institutions, at differing times in the educational careers of the subjects (in grade 12 for natives and transfers, at time of admission as freshmen for natives, and in their second or third college years for transfers). Data for the comparisons were supplied by nine institutions in six states: five major universities, two other state universities, one teachers' college, and one technological institute. These particular comparisons, in contrast with those to follow, are only for students who graduated (presumably with bachelors' degrees). The limitation of relying on comparisons of this population is that it does not allow for the admitted influence of attrition on the measures obtained. However, the findings will be illustrated and the conclusion cited, and it may be stated that in the main these corroborate conclusions drawn from other less extensive studies.

A major inference by the investigators from the tabular presentation is that "the native students tended to earn higher test scores than the transfer students, except in the comparison involving the teachers college. With this one exception, in all comparisons which produced statistically significant differences in means, the higher scores were earned by the native students" (*43*, 53). In further comment on the exception, they say that the evidence suggests that the native and transfer students who graduated from the teachers college did not differ with respect to their ability to do college work (*43*, 55).

With no assumption that the instance is typical, measures may be cited for two universities in a single state, designated in the report as State Universities D and E, in which all twelfth-grade students in the state must take a battery of aptitude and achievement tests before high school graduation. Examination of the table (*43*, 63, Table 24) shows all the 24 means (6 each for men and women—ACE total, English, social studies, natural science, mathematics, and the total of the foregoing five) for graduating natives higher than for graduating transfers. Fifteen of these differences, nine for State University D and six for State University E, were found to be statistically significant. All but two of the standard deviations of the means are larger for transfers than for natives, suggesting a somewhat wider distribution of abilities among transfers than natives.

Corroborative of the conclusion of some tendency to superior ability of natives when compared with transfers are the larger proportions of native graduates classifiable as having "high ability." For all of the six universities for which percentages above the cutting scores set are reported (*43*, *54*, Table 20), they are larger for the natives. Nevertheless, there are always substantial proportions of transfers above the cutting scores, which means that these proportions are on a par in ability with superior natives.

TABLE 7.17
PERCENTAGES OF FATHERS OF NATIVE AND 1960 TRANSFER STUDENTS WITH FATHERS IN (A) HIGHER AND LOWER PROFESSIONAL AND (B) SKILLED, SEMISKILLED, AND UNSKILLED OCCUPATIONS

Sex	Comparison Group	Higher and Lower Professional	Skilled, Semiskilled, and Unskilled
Men	Native	13	29
	Transfer	10	35
Women	Native	16	26
	Transfer	12	32
Total	Native	14	27
	Transfer	11	32

SOURCE: Knoell-Medsker (*44*, 138, Table 54).

TABLE 7.18
PERCENTAGES OF FATHERS AND MOTHERS OF NATIVE AND 1960 TRANSFER STUDENTS WITH FATHERS AND MOTHERS WHOSE EDUCATION WAS (A) LESS THAN HIGH SCHOOL GRADUATION AND (B) WHO HAD ATTENDED COLLEGE

Sex	Comparison Group	Less than High School Graduates		Attended College	
		Father	Mother	Father	Mother
Men	Native	32	24	38	33
	1960 Transfer	43	34	26	25
Women	Native	27	19	44	41
	1960 Transfer	35	30	35	32

SOURCE: Based on Knoell-Medsker (*44*, 140, Table 140).

The comparative competence of native and transfer graduates as indicated by grade-point averages is reported below in discussion of other aspects of their success as students.

(b) *Socioeconomic status.* Among the kinds of information obtained by these investigators concerning their transfers and their sample of native students were occupation of fathers, education of fathers and mothers, the proportion of financial support received from parents, and their years of birth. Condensed adaptations of their tables containing evidence along these lines will next be presented, with running commentary. First of these is Table 7.17, which is based on a much larger table in the Knoell-Medsker report, showing the percentages of fathers in nine occupational categories for natives and 1960 transfer men and women in each of the five types of four-year colleges and for the total of all types of colleges. For purposes here Table 7.17 presents only the percentages for the totals of both sexes whose fathers were in two contrasting occupational groups combining (1) the higher and lower professional and (2) the skilled and semi- or unskilled workers. The percentages in the former group are seen to be consistently larger for the native than for the transfer students and the percentages for the latter group consistently larger for the transfer group, indicating a considerable difference in socioeconomic status in favor of the native group. For only a single type of institution, the teachers' college, is there an exception to this generalization and the exception applies only to women.

TABLE 7.19
PERCENTAGES OF NATIVE AND 1960 TRANSFER STUDENTS (UPPER DIVISION ONLY) RECEIVING (A) FROM ABOUT HALF TO ALL AND (B) NONE OR ALMOST NONE TO LESS THAN HALF OF THEIR FINANCIAL SUPPORT FROM PARENTS

Proportion	Sex	Natives	1960 Transfers
About half to all	Men	51	45
	Women	73	63
None or almost none to less than half	Men	49	55
	Women	27	37

SOURCE: Knoell-Medsker (*44*, 141, Table 56).

(c) *Education of parents.* The Knoell-Medsker comparison of the "highest level of education attained" by fathers and mothers of native and transfer students classifies them into three groups, less than high school graduate, high school graduate, and attended college. Table 7.18 presents the percentages for the lowest and highest levels only. For transfer students of both sexes considerably larger percentages of both fathers and mothers were at the lower level and, correspondingly, for native students of both sexes, considerably larger percentages of both fathers and mothers had attended college. When attention is focused on the percentages for the different types of institutions (not reproduced in Table 7.18), the only exceptions are (a) for women in the teachers' colleges, where the proportions with less than high school graduation are equal for parents of natives and transfers and the proportions who had attended college are slightly higher for parents of transfers than of natives; and (b) for men in the institutes of technology where, although the percentages of both parents with less than high school graduation (especially of fathers) are larger, the percentages who had attended college are also somewhat larger. Thus, it is correctly inferable from the evidence in Tables 7.17 and 7.18 that to a considerable degree native students come from more economically and educationally privileged families than do transfer students.

(d) *Proportion of support from parents.* The evidence concerning proportion of financial support received from parents, presented in Table 7.19, is in harmony with that on socioeconomic status as indicated by father's occupation. Larger percentages of natives than transfers received about half to all their support from parents and, reciprocally, larger proportions of transfers than natives received none to almost none to less than half. Comparison of the percentages of the sexes finds a preponderance of parental support for both native and transfer women.

(e) *Ages of natives and transfers.* From the data on years of birth of native and transfer students in the Knoell-Medsker report, Table 7.20 re-

TABLE 7.20
PERCENTAGES OF NATIVE AND 1960 TRANSFER
STUDENTS WITH YEARS OF BIRTH 1940
OR LATER

Sex	Natives	1960 Transfers
Men	59	48
Women	88	78

SOURCE: Knoell-Medsker (*44*, 135, Table 51).

produces the percentages only of these groups with years of birth 1940 or later, which means the percentages who were 20 years of age or younger at the opening of their third college year. It may be seen that the percentages in this age-group are larger for natives than for transfers. Also, the percentages are larger for women than for men. A factor frequently ascribed as accounting for the latter difference is the earlier maturing of girls. Speculation over the trend of difference in favor of natives suggests influences like those associated with the trends of differences in aptitudes and ability previously reported, more frequent postponement of entrance to the first college year for economic reasons, and lesser motivation on account of socioeconomic and educational factors in the environment.

(f) *Comparative academic success.* The Knoell-Medsker report offers several kinds of evidence bearing on the academic competence of junior college transfers, some of them in comparison with those of native students. Among the measures are the grade-point averages of the same groups of students involved in the comparisons of measures of aptitude and ability on which report was made above. The grade-point averages are reported for "lower division" and "upper division" for each of the five types of four-year college (*43*, 54, Table 20). For the lower division the comparisons are of grade-point averages earned by natives during their first two years with those earned by the transfers while in junior college. Seven of the averages are higher for transfers than for natives, and six of these are indicated as being statistically significant. For instance, these lower division ratios for natives and transfers in major state university A are, respectively, 2.71 and 2.96. The two remaining averages are only slightly, and not significantly, higher for natives than transfers. Explanation has been made above of the higher ratio at this level for transfer students: in the junior college students are in competition in student bodies with typically larger proportions of less capable students. Comparison of the upper-division averages finds all of those for natives higher than for transfers, six of the nine having statistically significant differences. This trend toward superiority in ratios is mainly explainable by such factors as the trend toward superiority in aptitude previously reported and the problem of adjustment

TABLE 7.21
PERCENTAGES OF NATIVE AND TRANSFER STUDENTS WHO EARNED GRADE-POINT AVERAGES BELOW C IN THE UPPER DIVISION IN NO TERM, IN ONE TERM, AND IN NO AND ONE TERM COMBINED

Calendar System	Student Comparison Group	Number of Terms Below C		
		0	1	0 and 1 combined
Semester	Native	82	13	95
	Transfer	72	20	92
Quarter	Native	76	15	91
	Transfer	64	17	81

SOURCE: Adapted from Knoell-Medsker (*44*, 155, Table 65).

in shifting to a new and more complex institutional environment, especially during the first term after transfer.

Some report should be made here on some of the comparisons indicative of the scholarly competence of the total number of graduating transfers with the large sample of graduating natives, not merely those for whom comparable aptitude test data were available. The comparisons to be cited concern (1) the number of terms (semesters or quarters) during which, in the upper division, students earned grade-point averages below C and (2) grade-point averages of the two main groups in the different types of institutions. The findings on the first comparison are given in Table 7.21, which shows somewhat, but not strikingly, smaller percentages of transfers than natives with no terms below C and somewhat, but not strikingly, larger, percentages with one term below C. From other evidence presented in the Knoell-Medsker report and in reports of earlier investigations, it seems likely that a large proportion of transfers earning averages below C does so because of the problems of adjustment encountered, as previously mentioned, in the shift from junior college to the higher institution.

The Knoell-Medsker evidence concerning grade-point averages for the two groups of graduates is illustrated in Table 7.22, which shows the averages for four types of institutions. For only two of the comparisons in this table, namely, for "Lower Division" and "Junior College" under Type 2 and for "Upper Division" and "Upper Division" under Type 4, were the differences not found statistically significant. The rather consistently higher averages for the transfers at the "Lower Division" and "Junior College" levels have been explained above. It may be stated that, while the differences at the upper division level are reported to be statistically significant, the distributions from which the measures have been computed are more alike than different. It should be remembered also that attrition among transfers has been found to be somewhat greater than among natives, and

TABLE 7.22
MEAN GRADE-POINT AVERAGES* EARNED BY NATIVE AND TRANSFER STUDENTS IN DIFFERENT TYPES OF INSTITUTIONS

Institutional Level	Student Comparison Group	Types of Institution			
		1. Major State University	2. Teachers' College	3. Other State University	4. Private Universities and Technical Institutions
Lower division	Native	2.64	2.60	2.54	2.52
Junior college	Transfer	2.92	2.62	2.73	2.98
Upper division	Native	2.88	2.78	2.80	2.71
Upper division	Transfer	2.68	2.70	2.67	2.67

SOURCE: Knoell-Medsker (44, 160–61, Table 67).
*All grades have been converted to C=2.

that more of them than of natives require more than two years to obtain the bachelor's degree.

Without attempting to review further the findings of this dual investigative project by Knoell and Medsker, it may be said that they corroborate with scarcely an important exception those reviewed near the opening of the present section as being generalized from smaller and local studies. Thus, this extensive inquiry, from the fact that it is near national in scope and pursued various refinements in procedure, adds substantial assurance to the acceptability of earlier findings. Quoted here is the first only of a number of conclusions drawn by the authors in the final section of the second report (44, 103): "Junior colleges are making it possible for increasing numbers of high school graduates to begin work for baccalaureate degrees who would not otherwise be able to do so for reasons of academic or economic deficiency, or for lack of family encouragement. The large number of successful teachers, engineers, businessmen, government workers, and other useful citizens who began their degree work in a two-year college is impressive." Such findings and conclusions are certainly by now sufficiently well founded to assure acceptance of the preparatory service of the community college for upper-division programs in four-year colleges and universities. Although a large-scale matched comparison is still desirable and could add assurance and supply precision to the findings, we need not await further inquiry in this direction before accepting as one of its prominent functions the preparatory service of the community college.

A different follow-up with dramatic outcomes.—A follow-up project with significant outcomes, one concerned with a highly selected population (as indicated by academic competence) and departing in important respects from procedures used by Knoell and Medsker, has been reported by Schultz (*70*). In this instance the subjects were admittedly superior, being members of Phi Theta Kappa, a national honor society in junior colleges, eligibility for which usually requires the student to be in the top 10 per cent in scholarship. The data concern alumni members who were initiated into the organization in 1947–48, 1957–58, and 1960–61; thus, members of the oldest group at the time of the study were in their late thirties, the second group in their late twenties, and the youngest group in their mid-twenties and just completing graduate study and/or getting launched in their careers. These alumni represented 72 chapters of the organization located in 27 states, with 51 of the institutions being public and 21 private. Follow-up data were analyzed for a total of 2,758 alumni members, with about two-thirds from public and the other third from private junior colleges.

The proportions of these junior college alumni who transferred to senior college is notably high, 91 per cent of the men and 70 per cent of the women. The proportions of the transfers graduating with bachelors' degrees were even higher, including 98 per cent of the men and 90 per cent of the women. Nearly two-thirds reported having received scholastic honors, a fourth were awarded academic scholarships while in senior college, and as many as two-fifths had held some sort of student office while in senior college. Further proof of their scholarly competence is seen in the fact that they had not been delayed in graduating after transferring to senior college: 6 per cent said they were delayed by a summer term, and only 3 per cent that they had been delayed by a year or more.

Of a sample of 386 men who had received at least bachelors' degrees, a full half majored in science, mathematics, or engineering, and two-fifths had earned graduate or professional degrees. These men were rendering service in a wide variety of esteemed professions, among them teaching, engineering, research science, accounting, medicine, dentistry, veterinary medicine, and pharmacy.

When Schultz directed his attention to the socioeconomic status of these honor students as evidenced by the occupation of the head of the family, he found that two-thirds of the public junior college group came from families where the employment of the head of the household represents what sociologists refer to as "gray" and "blue" collar occupations. Those who attended private junior colleges came from "a considerably higher socio-economic background." As concerns extent of education, over a fourth of the heads of households of alumni who had attended public junior colleges had not continued beyond the eighth grade and 69 per cent had no formal education beyond high school. "Even in the case of those who attended private junior colleges, one-third of the heads of families had not finished high school and over half . . . had not attended college." The author's concluding comments on this aspect of his investigation is that "the study demonstrates again that junior colleges—especially public ones—contribute very significantly to the American dream of a free and open society. A larger proportion of honor students came from humble backgrounds and families of extremely limited financial means."

Academic Deficiencies and Study Habits

Academic deficiencies.—Full consideration of the question of academic competence of students in community colleges should include, in addition to information on their aptitude and their degree of success after transfer to other educational institutions as these have been reviewed in this chapter, some discussion toward comprehension of their abilities in two other areas. One of these is their relative status in respect to "academic deficiencies," or their skills or lack of skills in the "tools of learning," meaning by this term abilities or disabilities in reading, grammatical usage, spelling, and related skills in the area of communication, and in mathematics. The other is in their study habits. Many community colleges have been concerned with these, have investigated them, and have instituted remedial or developmental programs of varying scope. Notwithstanding a sizeable array of experimentation and experience in these areas in junior colleges, the literature dealing with them, especially that reporting distributions of scores on instruments designed to identify strengths and weaknesses, is scant. However, because of the high correlation known to exist between measures of aptitude and the instruments that have been devised for identifying and diagnosing the disabilities, there is no urgency to report at this point the scores and distributions *in extenso,* as the general situation in respect to disabilities may be inferred in large part from foregoing comparisons of aptitude. Many of the tests of aptitude emphasize ability in reading and mathematics.

An informative approach to the question of the incidence of academic deficiencies of students at the lower college level is afforded by drawing on findings in the early work of one of the leaders in this area of inquiry, Guiler, who reported on evidence assembled concerning freshmen at Miami University (Ohio). In an article published a third of a century ago (20), he described as follows the deficiencies disclosed by tests. He introduces these findings with the sweeping generalization that large numbers of college entrants "have never acquired such fundamental adaptations as ability to read rapidly and with understanding, to manage number concepts in their mathematical relationships, and to use clear, accurate, and cogent English." He particularized as follows: "In a survey made at Miami University more than half of a group of 437 college freshmen (55 per cent) were below the standard for high school seniors, when measured by the Shank reading test; one-third could not read as well as the average pupil in the first year of the senior high school; one-fifth were unable to read as well as the average pupil in the last year of the junior high school. They showed a somewhat better mastery of the background essentials in English fundamentals, but practically two in five were below the standard for high school seniors, and one in every five were below the standard for pupils in the beginning year of the senior high school. In computational arithmetic 48 per cent fell below the standard for high school seniors; 45 per cent did not attain the standard for the first year of the junior high school; and 19 per cent did not reach the standard for the sixth grade. . . ." Analogous deficiencies for these freshmen were reported in spelling words frequently used in written discourse.

For some students the deficiencies may be owing to deterioration from disuse over a period of years after having acquired desirable skills in lower school years, while for others the desirable skills needed may never have been acquired. Whatever the cause, many or most of the deficiencies would operate as a serious hindrance to the scholarly competence of college students. Presumably Miami University, in common with many other four-year colleges and universities, now exercises greater selection of its freshmen than it did in the thirties, and in all probability, the incidence of deficiency is lower, although more recent investigations suggest that it persists in varying degrees in all higher institutions. As implied above, reasoning from the high correlations typically found between college aptitude and these academic deficiencies and the larger proportionate measures of students with lower aptitude scores in community colleges than in the more selective colleges and universities, it is safe to conclude that a community college student body will typically manifest more of the deficiencies and in somewhat higher degree. Writers on the community college have recurrently taken cognizance of the problem, as when Kastner speaks of the "dilemma" presented by having to adapt the curriculum to serve both students who have deficiencies and those who do not (40). The fact that workers in the junior college have long been aware of the problem, as have those in other institutions at the collegiate level, may be illustrated by reference to a description by Tyler of remedial efforts in the Sacramento (California) Junior College in the early thirties (87). The deficiencies are prevalent enough to have induced a leader in the community college movement to advocate provision of a program for students with educational deficiencies as one of the purposes of the institution.*

Study habits.—The situation with respect to study habits may be assumed to be analogous to that for academic deficiencies, again with somewhat greater incidence in junior than in four-year colleges because of a

TABLE 7.23
COMPARISON OF CERTAIN PERCENTILE SCORES ON THE BROWN-HOLTZMAN SURVEY OF STUDY HABITS AND ATTITUDES OF NORMS AS PUBLISHED ON COLLEGE FRESHMEN AND FRESHMEN IN JUNIOR COLLEGE X

Percentile Score	Men		Women	
	Norm*	Junior College X	Norm*	Junior College X
Tenth	19	15	19	18
Fiftieth	36	24	33	30
Ninetieth	52	44	46	41

*These norms cited from 5, 8, Table 1.

wider spread of abilities. Several instruments are available for diagnosing disabilities and motivating efforts in the student to ameliorate or remove them, among them the Wrenn Study Habits Inventory (SHI) and the Brown-Holtzman Survey of Study Habits and Attitudes (SSHA) (5). Experimental use of such instruments has shown them to be useful for the purpose. It is sometimes contended that the Brown-Holtzman Survey is more useful because it was developed more recently and emphasizes somewhat less the mechanics of study and somewhat more the motivational attitudes conducive to study. The stated purposes of the SSHA are (1) to identify students whose study habits are different from those of students who earn high grades, (2) to aid in understanding students with academic difficulties, and (3) to provide a basis for helping such students to improve their study habits and attitudes and thus more fully realize their best potentialities.

In the absence of evidence from more extensive application of one of the study habit inventories to junior college students and in comparison with those in other colleges, recourse is here taken to illustrative comparison only of certain measures on the SSHA of freshmen in a Florida community junior college with the corresponding measures drawn from norms

*Leland L. Medsker, *The Junior College: Progress and Prospect* (New York: McGraw-Hill, 1960), pp. 64-68.

for other college freshmen as reported by the authors of the survey. The comparison is made in Table 7.23. The measures reported are the tenth, fiftieth, and ninetieth percentiles for 2,114 men and 1,446 women, all but about 8 per cent of them freshmen in a number of colleges and universities. The comparison shows the measures all lower for the junior college than for the college students. The differences are larger for men than for women. To the extent that a comparison involving such a small population of junior college students can be considered valid, one may say that the total distribution on which these measures are based is again in accord with the differences in aptitude between public junior college and more selective college populations identified earlier in the chapter: while all the measures are lower for the junior college, and, therefore, the average is lower, the measures for a substantial proportion of junior college students in the upper reaches are about as high as for students in more selective institutions.

8
Personal Characteristics, Attitudes, and Interests

AS STATED at the opening of Chapter 7, attention in this chapter is focused mainly on personal characteristics, attitudes, and interests of the community college population. Admittedly, published materials bearing on these aspects of human make-up of this population are scantier than those bearing on aspects dealt with in the foregoing chapter. In part this is owing to greater intangibility, but it is also owing to the recency of community college development. Nevertheless, these aspects are of such moment for the educative process that the materials will be examined both for their current meaning and for their promise of expanded significance following further elaboration of the instruments and procedures they embody or employ. Here again, to some extent, reliance must be placed on evidence collected from students at the same level in parallel institutions.

Perhaps it is unnecessary to remind the reader that the treatment in the chapter provides a sort of focal consideration of the community college student for which many parts of Chapters 3-6 provide the background or setting. These are concerned with components of personality and with attitudes and interests of youth, with emphasis on information concerning those near the threshold of college and during early college years. The reader will do well to relate the findings in the following treatment to this background both in its general and its more particular aspects.

Personal Characteristics

Promising inquiries at the Berkeley Center for the Study of Higher Education.—As may be expected from the discussion of personality in Chapter 3, description and measurement of personality, or personal characteristics, of students are not as far along in objectivity as procedures concerning aptitude or even social status. Among most promising leads in this direction are those being followed at the Center for the Study of Higher Education at the University of California at Berkeley.* Applica-

*Now called Center for Research and Development in Higher Education.

tions of the procedures were first made and reported on students in four-year colleges by McConnell and Heist and subsequently applied in a comparison by Tillery of junior college with university students. In order to facilitate understanding of the procedures and results for the latter comparison, it is desirable to precede by illustration from the McConnell-Heist investigations with students in four-year colleges. These involved, in addition to measures of aptitude, application of Omnibus Personality Inventory (OPI) Scales and of Allport-Vernon-Lindzey (A-V-L) Study of Values Scales. For illustrative purposes here, evidence only from the OPI measures will be reported.

The characteristics presumed to be represented in the OPI Scales may be indicated by their published descriptions, which are as follows (27, 286n):

"Thinking-Introversion-Extroversion: Liking for reflective thought and work with abstractions; interest in ideas as such rather than their practical outcomes.

"Social Introversion-Extroversion: Discriminates between those who tend to withdraw from social contacts and relationships and those seeking them and finding satisfaction therein.

"Responsibility: Identifies persons along a continuum of social responsibility versus social irresponsibility.

"Complexity of Outlook: The tendency to perceive and react to a complexity of environmental patterns versus perception and reaction at a level of greater simplicity.

"Originality: A highly organized mode of responding to experience, associated with independence of judgment, freedom of expression, novelty of construction and insight.

"Social Maturity: Differentiates degrees of general primitiveness of subjects' conceptions of others and of their relationships with them. A more direct, more personality-centered, less ideological measure of authoritarianism.

"Authoritarian Personality (F) Scale: The original fascistic scale. . . . Characteristics of high scorers include conventionality, rigidity, identification with power, emotional coldness and prejudice. Scored in a true-false fashion in this inventory. Low scores denote nonauthoritarianism."

Results for four-year college students.—An informative comparison reported from the McConnell-Heist studies (27) is provided in Table 8.1, which presents the mean standard scores on scales of the OPI for samples of male National Merit Scholarship students attending colleges ranked high and low on a "productivity criterion" developed by Knapp and Greenbaum (41). This criterion is based on the proportions of graduates of these colleges continuing into graduate schools. The first pair of columns present the comparison for the total sample of students represented and the second pair that for samples of fifty students equated on scores on a widely used test of aptitude. Five of the six comparisons in the first pair of columns and four of those in the second pair show differences significant at either the .05 or the .01 level, supporting the inference that "most of these students of superiority in the high group can be described as having a different orientation and very likely a different pattern of motivation than students of the same ability in the less productive institutions" (27, 290). It may be noted that the difference between the two groups on the Authoritarian Scale is opposite in direction from the other scales.

TABLE 8.1
MEAN STANDARD SCORES ON SOME OMNIBUS PERSONALITY INVENTORY SCALES FOR MALE STUDENTS IN THE NATIONAL MERIT SCHOLARSHIP SAMPLE ATTENDING INSTITUTIONS RANKED HIGH OR LOW ON PRODUCTIVITY CRITERION

Scale	Total Sample		Sample Equated For SAT Scores	
	High	Low	High (50)	Low (50)
Thinking introversion-extroversion	71.5	68.5*	70	69
Social introversion-extroversion	45.0	45.0	43.5	46.0*
Complexity of outlook	62.5	55.5*	60.5	55.5†
Originality	64.0	56.5†	63.0	56.5†
Social maturity	67.0	61.0†	66.5	63.0
Authoritarian scale (F)	36.0	43.0†	36.5	42.0*

SOURCE: Heist (27, portion of Table 2).
*Differences significant at the .05 level.
†Differences significant at the .01 level.

A comparison involving junior college and university students.—The application of the OPI involving junior college students was made by Tillery.* His subjects were in a sample pool of students who were among the upper 14.8 per cent of high school graduates (2,319 in number) whose achievement made them eligible to enter the University of California. Of this sample, 26 per cent actually attended a campus of the university upon graduation, while 18 per cent went to a junior college for first collegiate attendance.

In reporting in his paper his findings from application of the OPI to these students, Tillery generalized all but the last two measures on the OPI scale values as measures of "intellectuality." On this basis, he found 31 per cent of the university entrants and 18 per cent of the junior college students to have high intellectuality measures; the proportions indicated as low measures were in reverse order, 16 per cent for the university group

*Dale Tillery, Report to the Conference for Chief Student Personnel Administrators on Implementing the Open Door, January 10, 1964, Pacific Grove, California.

and 25 per cent for junior college students. The contrast was greater for women than for the whole group: 36 per cent high for university women and 19 per cent for junior college women. The investigator reports also the percentages of high and low intellectuality scores for women on the different campuses of the university in comparison with women in junior colleges, and citing these may help to understand the relative position of the junior college group: 45 per cent of Berkeley women had high scores and 35 per cent of UCLA women. Only 4 per cent of the Berkeley women were classified in the low intellectuality group as compared to 23 per cent at UCLA and 27 per cent for the junior colleges.

Tillery gives the measures of social maturity on the OPI special attention. He reports that 40 per cent of the university students in the sample had high social maturity scores and only 7 per cent low scores. The percentage of high scores for the junior college students was only half that of those entering the university, and they had three times the university percentage of low scores.

The paper makes only passing mention of authoritarianism but, in view of the evidence in Table 8.1, one may infer that the junior college students in the sample had a larger proportion of high scores on the Authoritarian Scale than the university group—with the higher scores indicating a greater degree of authoritarianism.

The evidence on the OPI just reviewed was generalized as follows by Collins for the Committee of the American Association of Junior Colleges on Appraisal and Development of Junior College Student Personnel Programs:* ". . . when junior college high ability students are compared with a like group in universities they are found to be significantly lower in social maturity, in autonomy, and, for women, in intellectual disposition, thinking introversion, theoretical orientation, estheticism, and complexity. Junior college men and women are more conventional, less independent and more authoritarian."

Another way of interpreting the findings of this comparison on measures of intellectuality of superior high school graduates who continue their education in junior colleges and in the university is to say that both types of institution enroll students both high and low on these measures, the difference between the institutions being that the junior colleges enroll smaller proportions of the high and larger proportions of the low. This conclusion is somewhat analogous to that drawn from comparisons on aptitude of student bodies in junior colleges and in colleges and universities with selective admission policies, as generalized in early portions of Chapter 7.

*Charles C. Collins, *Junior College Student Personnel Programs: What They Are and What They Should Be* (Washington: American Association of Junior Colleges, 1967), p. 11.

A comparison on the California Psychological Inventory.—Another instrument devised for personality assessment that has been used with junior college students is the California Psychological Inventory (CPI). The application was made by Telford and Plant (*78*) on students in certain junior colleges in California. The problem in the project was to "determine if there are significant changes in selected personality traits, ideologies, and values of students who attend a public junior college" (1). This investigation made use not only of the CPI, but also of certain other personality measures; the latter are not mentioned here because comparisons with student groups at other levels (high school and four-year college) are not available. The comparison here is also restricted to only five of the eighteen characteristics represented in the CPI.

In further description of the CPI it may be said that it is self-administering and that the scales are in four groups, two with six scales and two with three scales. Many of the items were borrowed from the Minnesota Multiphasic Personality Inventory (MMPI) which is a projective instrument. One of the five scales administered in the Telford-Plant project, Sociability, is in Class I, Measures of Poise, Ascendancy, and Self-Assurance; two, designated as Responsibility and Self-Control, are in Class II, Measures of Socialization, Maturity, and Responsibility; and the remaining two are designated as Achievement via Independence and Intellectual Efficiency. The nature of the contrast between high and low scorers on the scales may be seen by quoting from the description for the Responsibility Scale, the purpose of which is "to identify persons of conscientious, responsible, and dependable disposition and temperament" (*78*, 10):

High: "Planful, responsible, thorough, progressive, capable, dignified, and independent; as being conscientious and dependable; resourceful and efficient; and as being alert to ethical and moral issues."

Low: "Immature, moody, lazy, awkward, changeable, and disbelieving; as being influenced by personal bias, spite, and dogmatism; and as undercontrolled and impulsive in behavior."

The purpose here in reporting measures from the CPI is to characterize the personality of junior college students by comparison with those at other levels in other institutions (high school and four-year college). The purpose in the Telford-Plant study, as previously stated, was to inquire into the impact on personality of attendance at a junior college, and clearly differs from the purpose here. However, reporting the measures from the Telford-Plant investigation in comparison with the measures for high school and four-year college students should nevertheless help to an understanding of the personality of junior college students. On this account, certain measures from the Telford-Plant report are presented in Table 8.2.

Interpretation of the evidence in this table may be facilitated by first examining numbered columns 3–8 which report the means on the five scales for junior college males and females who attended junior college (a) 3 or 4 semesters, (b) 1 or 2 semesters, and (c) had not attended junior college but had in 1960 indicated intention of doing so. One finding sup-

TABLE 8.2
Mean Scores on Certain Scale Variables in the California Psychological Inventory (CPI) for High School Males and Females, for Junior College Males and Females Who Had Attended 3 or 4, 1 or 2, and 0 Semesters, and for College Males and Females

Variable	High School		Junior College Males		
	Males	Females	3 or 4 Sems.	1 or 2 Sems.	0 Sems.
	(1)	(2)	(3)	(4)	(5)
Sociability	21.5	21.4	24.42	24.54	24.55
Responsibility	26.7	30.3	30.10	28.94	29.28
Self-control	25.3	27.6	27.30	26.37	25.28
Achievement via independence	22.3	24.1	20.04	18.20	18.81
Intellectual efficiency	33.6	34.4	37.74	36.77	36.38

Variable	Junior College Females			College	
	3 or 4 Sems.	1 or 2 Sems.	0 Sems.	Males	Females
	(6)	(7)	(8)	(9)	(10)
Sociability	24.33	23.78	23.55	25.4	26.0
Responsibility	32.22	31.40	31.45	30.8	33.3
Self-control	28.85	28.66	28.09	27.6	30.8
Achievement via independence	20.63	19.67	19.12	27.6	28.8
Intellectual efficiency	38.47	37.25	36.43	39.8	41.4

Sources: Mean scores for high school and college students from Gough (*18,* 34–35, Tables 3–4); for junior college students from Telford and Plant (*78,* 30–34, Tables 4–9).

ported by comparison of the measures for the corresponding three pairs of groups is that women's mean scores typically exceed in some degree those for men, which is in accord with conclusions in portions of certain chapters of Part I which found females maturing at somewhat earlier ages than males. The only exception is in the measures of Sociability which are all but one slightly higher for males than for females. Another finding is that many of the means decline with decreasing duration of attendance, but there are at the same time several exceptions in the triads of measures of Sociability, Responsibility, and Achievement via Independence for men, and of Responsibility for women. Also, many of the differences are small and these, with the exceptions just noted, are suggestive of the near-equivalence of the measures for the three corresponding groups of each sex.

An important aspect of the investigation from which specific scale measures are not cited here is inquiry into the differences in the mean scale measures for the six groups between 1960 when the subjects were first tested and when they were retested two years later. This inquiry involved 30 comparisons, for 27 of which the differences were found to be statistically significant, and all differences were in the same direction, which was toward higher scores. The author's inference from this evidence is that "there is a general personality development under way *apart from the amount of educational experience* [italics added] of the groups of subjects. The evidence indicates that this change takes place in all sex and educational attainment groups" (*78*, 36). In view of the equivocal nature of the differences for the triads—some positive, some negative, and often small and not statistically significant, at the same time that those for the increments for the three groups of males and females between 1960 and 1962 are all positive and almost all statistically significant—it is not surprising that the authors have called the whole issue of "college impact," which other investigators have reported, into question. They say, "Within the limits of our data and study design, it has been generally concluded that many of the changes attributed to collegiate experience by others may be no more than developmental changes under way in young persons like those who aspire to college whether or not they attend college" (72).

In proceeding with other comparisons afforded by the measures in Table 8.2, it may be noted first that means on the CPI are reported for males and females in high school (Columns 1 and 2) and in college (Columns 9 and 10). These measures are drawn from the CPI Manual for populations referred to as "samples," although there is no statement in the manual concerning the distribution of the subjects by high school grade or college year. Comparison, first, of the mean scores for the sexes finds all but a single measure in the ten pairs, that for Sociability, higher for females than for males, and the two measures in this pair are within a tenth of a scale point of each other. This finding accords with that noted in comparing the respective measures for the three junior college groups, where the speculative explanation was the greater maturity of females than of males in this age-span.

When attention is directed to the measures for students in the three types of institutions, that is, high school, junior college, and college, it may be noted that, with a small number of exceptions, and these for a single variable (Achievement via Independence), all the means for junior college groups of each sex lie between the corresponding means for high school and for college students. For instance, all three means for Sociability for junior college males (24.42, 24.54, and 24.55) lie between those for high school males (21.5) and college males (25.4). Whether the differences in the progressions are statistically significant is not known, although it may be conjectured from their magnitude that some of them are. The upward trend from high school to college is, however, rather consistent. Also, whether the differences are attributable to normal developmental changes without regard to school attendance at this level, as inferred by Telford and Plant for their project involving junior college populations, or to "college impact" cannot be made certain from the evidence at hand.

One further observation seems justifiable from comparison of the measures reported for junior college and college populations. Although the distributions of the scores are not at hand, the means for the two types of institutions are not far apart, which suggests much overlapping of the two populations in the characteristics under consideration. The inference is supported by examination of the standard deviations of the distributions which are not reported here, most of which are smaller for the college men and women than for the junior college students, although not strikingly so. Here again, as on measures of aptitude and of characteristics represented in the OPI, a tendency to superiority of college over junior college students is indicated, but with much overlapping and with many in the junior college on a par with the best in the four-year colleges.

A differing interpretation of research on the student.—In light of the review in the preceding chapter of the evidence concerning aptitude and socioeconomic status, and up to this point in the current chapter on personal traits of junior college students, it is in place to compare the conclusions with those of another recent synthesis of pertinent researches in the same areas, many of them the same projects that are being relied upon for generalization in this treatise. Reference is to *The Junior College Student: A Research Description* by Cross (*11*). Following are two sentences quoted from what may be assumed to be the key inference from the synthesis appearing in one of the concluding paragraphs and regarded as so important as to be presented also, in italics, on the page facing the Introduction (6): "We must conclude that intellectual dimensions sharply differentiate junior college students, as a group, from senior college students. The junior college student is less able—on our present tests; he is less intellectually oriented—on our present measures; and he is less motivated to seek higher education—in our traditional colleges."

In the Introduction the author states that most of the research on which the report is based is published and available at the same time that the interpretation is her own. Illustrations follow of her particular inferences in the several sections of the report, which can be assumed to have induced the sweeping conclusion. One notes the recurrence of phrases like "as a group," "in general," and "quite different," implying the univerality of the differences between populations of two-year and four-year colleges.

"We can state, with considerable confidence, that the mean score for students attending four-year colleges exceeds that of students in two-year colleges, and that two-year college students score higher as a group than high school graduates who do not go to college" (*11*, 11).

". . . as a group [junior college students] showed less interest in intellectual attitudes sampled by the Scale than senior college students . . ." (*11*, 29).

"In general, junior college students are more conventional, less independent, less attracted to reflective thought, and less tolerant than their peers in four-year institutions" (*11*, 32).

"We know that students who choose junior colleges base their selection on a set of variables quite different from those of students entering four-year institutions" (*11*, 34).

"Generally speaking, junior college students have lower educational and occupational aspirations than their peers who begin their education in four-year colleges" (*11*, 41).

One is taken aback while encountering the sweeping generalization and the recurrent inferences of marked differences in the several specialized measures represented in the comparisons to find alongside at many points, both in tables and in the running text, evidence establishing *extensive overlapping* for junior college and four-year college populations. A few of the numerous instances may be cited. The proportion of students entering junior college from the top third of high school graduates is fully half as large as that for students entering the four-year institutions (*11*, 12, Table 1). The percentages of high school graduates in the top third of the distributions of scores on a scale of intellectual predisposition for students entering junior colleges and four-year colleges were found to be, respectively, 36 and 59 (30, Table 6). The percentages of two-year and four-year college populations reporting "Keen competition for grades" in their own institutions were, respectively, 42 and 60 (37, Table 10). Differences in curriculum choice between students in two-year colleges, four-year colleges, or universities are generalized as "not dramatic" (38). For one study of educational aspirations the percentages of junior college and four-year college students aspiring to the Master's degree were reported, respectively, as 17 and 22, while for another they were 22 and 37 (41, Table 11).

Such instances reaffirm the conclusion of overlap in ability and other characteristics for substantial proportions of junior college and four-year college populations previously drawn at several points in this and the foregoing chapter of this treatise: the junior college enrolls just as capable and promising students as the four-year college. Witness also the many investigations establishing the success after transfer of large proportions of junior college graduates and the "dramatic success" record of junior college honor students as reported by Schultz (70). The difference is only in the *proportion* of the more highly selected, and the *proportion is smaller because of the commitment of the community college to universalizing this level of schooling.* As progress toward universalization continues, the proportion of less capable and less motivated will increase and, unless the four-year colleges themselves become less selective, the gap between the measures of central tendency for students in junior and senior colleges will continue to widen, at the same time that the numbers of superior youth in the junior colleges will hardly decline.

If the phrases like "in general" and "as a group," which are encountered recurrently in the Cross synthesis, are being used with their standard implications of inclusiveness, the question may be raised as to whether a sweeping conclusion like the one quoted and the specialized inferences in support of it are not a disservice to the community college movement. They would be so because they violate the concept of a comprehensive institution. However, any stricture on interpretation in the synthesis does not at all gainsay the need which Cross emphasizes for more information about and understanding of junior college students, especially those of lower ability and interest levels about whom much less is known than of the more highly selected who are of the long-standing college-going tradition.

An inquiry bearing both on attitudes and subcultures.—Brief treatment here is warranted of an exploratory project bearing on attitudes of junior college students at the same time that it seeks light on the subcultures among them (57). The procedure followed is a modification of a typology devised by Clark and Trow (69, 17–70) for use with students in residential four-year colleges, which yields the following four types of student cultures: the *academic*, which strongly identifies with the college (through the faculty) and is involved with ideas; the *collegiate* which also identifies with the college (through the fraternities or athletic teams, etc.) but is not involved with ideas; the *nonconformist*, which is concerned with ideas in the classroom but more with issues in the wider society, and does not identify with the college, being critical of the "establishment"; and the *vocational*, which neither identifies with the college nor is involved with ideas. The facts that junior college students, at least in the public units, are almost exclusively commuters and that the institution extends over only two years prompted Mauss to substitute the degree of *identification with the adult community* for the *collegiate* and he labeled the new category *perpetual teenagers*. He submitted his questions looking into (a) "adult" attitudes and (b) commitment to ideas ("intellectuality") to a sample of about 500 students on a suburban junior college campus in the East San Francisco Bay area and collected from them data on their age, sex, religion, social background, plans, grades, habits, use of time, etc.

The percentage distribution of the sample of 462 students to the four types was found to be: academic, 9.5; vocational, 24; incipient rebels, 23; perpetual teenagers, 44. Although something more than half the total sample were male, three-fourths of the academic subculture were girls, an overrepresentation which Mauss conjectures "might be common to junior colleges as a greater parental willingness to send academically talented boys away from home for the freshman year" (57, 8).

Several of the percentage distributions for the variables of the types derived from the questionnaires, such as those in social background, general college information, use of time, and student evaluation of various teaching devices, afford some corroborative validation of the typology. For instance, an appreciably larger proportion of academics among students aspiring to more than bachelor's degrees; more free reading and studying among academics and more talking to friends and dating among vocationals and teenagers; and larger proportions among academics and incipient rebels than of vocationals and teenagers rating special research projects and essay tests as "very helpful." Mauss did not subject the differences between the groups to tests of statistical significance, though inspection suggests that some would have passed muster. At the same time, distributions show much merging together and overlap of the types.

This exploratory project finds over two-thirds of one junior college student population of types (perpetual teenagers plus vocationals) presumably more susceptible than the others to the "cooling out" process of the open-door college (8, Ch. V). If extension and refinement of Mauss' procedure should find the proportion generally anywhere nearly as large, we shall have clues to significant explanations of the severe attrition in junior colleges—attrition that is reported in Chapter 11 to amount, before the beginning of the second year, to about half the first year enrollment. Mauss suggests two ways, either or both of which he deems applicable but the second more "practical," of holding "all kinds of students as long as possible." One is to modify the system to make it "reach" the students who are not of the academic subculture, and the other to modify the students so that they can "reach" the system. He describes the second as an "ungraded pre-college orientation year" of "programs designed largely to build skills and change attitudes."

A Comparison on Socioeconomic Values

The Walker project.—As concerns the attitudes or values of junior college students, as distinguished from characteristics of personality and membership in subcultures as just considered, an informative investigation has been reported by Walker (*90*). This project had as its purpose inquiry into the impact of the program of general studies in the University College of the University of Florida on the socioeconomic beliefs of its students by the opening of their junior year. It yields some understanding of the beliefs of junior college students because the samples of populations studied included representation of transfers to the university as juniors of graduates of public junior colleges which had experienced rapid development in the state by the time the investigation was planned and executed.

Data analyzed in the project were scores on (1) a scale of socioeconomic values and (2) information concerning all students supplied by them on questionnaires filled out at the time of checking the scale. The instrument used is known as the Florida Scale of Civic Beliefs, devised by Ralph B. Kimbrough and Vince A. Hines; it has been used extensively on a variety of investigative projects. It consists of 60 items involving statements of position ranging from very conservative to very liberal. Examples of the statements are: "Free enterprise, with an absolute minimum of governmental control, is the best way to assure full productivity in our country"; "All government spending should be on a pay-as-you-go basis"; "Some races are by nature inferior mentally, emotionally, and physically"; "The government should increase its activity in matters of health, retirement, wages, and old-age benefits." The subjects are asked to respond by indicating that they "strongly agree," "agree," "neither agree nor disagree," "disagree," or "strongly disagree," and each item is scored by giving one point for a strongly conservative response, two points for a conservative response, three points for a moderate or apathetic response, four points for a liberal response, and five points for a strongly liberal response. The total score for each person is the sum of all the scores he makes on the 60 items. The range of possible scores is, thus, 60 to 300. In uses of the scale, scores of 60–120 have been regarded as "strongly conservative" and scores of 240–300 "strongly liberal," with 150–210 being "moderate." The personal questionnaire sought information on the student's sex, social class status, sectional and urban-rural background, political party preference, denominational preference, and field of specialization. Thus, by using this information in conjunction with scores on the Scale of Civic Beliefs, it was possible to relate socioeconomic values to personal characteristics, and to determine what ideological differences exist between men and women; among Democrats, Republicans, and Independents; among Protestants, Catholics, and Jews; and so forth.

When the investigator prepared and examined the frequency distributions of scores for his sample groups he found that, although some approached normal distribution, others were definitely skewed, some badly, making assumption of population normality impossible. This precluded the use of parametric techniques and meant that the t test and F test of significance of differences were not applicable. He therefore adopted the Mann-Whitney U test and the Kruskal-Wallis one-way analysis of variance by ranks as the best alternatives, respectively, to the t and F tests (90, 67–68), and he justified the application by quotation from Siegel.* In the summary of findings of the project to follow, reliance is placed on Walker's interpretation of results from these techniques rather than on the medians reported, although the medians are presented in the accompanying tables (8.3, 8.4, 8.5) as being partial clues to similarities of and differences between the populations. The categories in the tables will at least serve as guides to the interpretation.

TABLE 8.3
MEDIAN SCORES OF CERTAIN GROUPS OF STUDENTS AND FACULTY AT THE UNIVERSITY OF FLORIDA ON THE FLORIDA SCALE OF CIVIC BELIEFS

Sample Group	Median Score
Freshmen	203
All juniors	206
Juniors—university	208.5
Juniors—public junior college	205
University college faculty	231

SOURCE: Walker (90, 87–92, Tables 4, 5, 6, 8, 9).

Findings of the Walker project.—The program of the University College is one of General Studies. The main hypothesis of the Walker project is that the socioeconomic values of students who have completed a two-year general education program differ significantly from the socioeconomic values of entering freshmen (90, 55). He found that "no significant difference exists between the two groups." He reports that, while the juniors scored slightly higher, the difference between them can be attributed to chance variations within a single population. When the juniors were separated into (a) those who had experienced the University College program and (b) those who had had their first two years in public junior colleges—the group of our special interest—there was again no significant difference. However, the faculty of the University College were found to be significantly more liberal as measured by the scale than freshmen, all juniors, and both of these groups of juniors.

When political party preference is taken into account against scores on the scale for all Republicans, Democrats, and Independents, including

*Sidney Siegel, *Nonparametric Statistics for the Behavioral Sciences* (New York: McGraw-Hill, 1956), pp. 19–20, 116, 126, 184, 194.

freshmen, juniors, and faculty members, significant differences were found, with those labeling themselves as Democrats being significantly more liberal than Independents and Republicans, and Independents more liberal than Republicans. When the comparisons were restricted to freshmen of the three preferences, the only significant difference was for that comparing the scores of Democrats and Republicans, with the Democrats significantly more liberal. Of the comparisons for all juniors (bottom of left-hand columns in Table 8.4) those for Republicans and Democrats and for Re-

TABLE 8.4
Median Scores of Certain Groups of Students and Faculty at the University of Florida on the Florida Scale of Civic Beliefs, by Political Preference

Sample Group	Median Score	Sample Group	Median Score
Freshmen, juniors, and faculty, combined		Juniors, Republicans	
Republicans	190	University of Florida	181
Democrats	214	Public junior college	191
Independents	206	Juniors, Democrats	
Freshmen		University of Florida	216.5
Republicans	191	Public junior college	207.5
Democrats	209	Juniors, independents	
Independents	199	University of Florida	209
Juniors		Public junior college	205
Republicans	188	University College faculty	
Democrats	210	Republican	188
Independents	208	Democratic	241
		Independent	215

Source: Walker (*90*, 100–17, Tables 14–15, 21–22, 25–26, 28, 37–39, 41–42).

publicans and Independents show significant differences, with the Democrats more liberal. Of the comparisons of juniors who were Republicans, Democrats, and Independents coming up (a) through the University College and (b) from public junior colleges (see right-hand column in Table 8.4), none showed a significant difference. All comparisons for the three party preferences for the University College faculty (see bottom of right-hand column in Table 8.4) showed the differences between Republicans and Democrats and between Independents and Democrats statistically significant with the Democrats more liberal than either Republicans or Independents. An important inference concerns the greater influence on ideology of preference for party of juniors as compared with freshman classification, or of type of institution (university or public junior college) the student attended during his first two college years.

When religious preference is taken into account against scores on the Florida Scale of Civic Beliefs and for all groups of students and faculty combined (see Table 8.5), comparisons showed significant differences between Jewish and Protestant and between Jewish and Roman Catholic groups, with Jewish groups more liberal, and between Protestant and Other and between Roman Catholic and Other, with the Other group more liberal. When the groups of different Protestant denominations were compared with each other, significant differences were found between scores for Unitarians in comparison with each of the other denominations, with the Unitarians more liberal than the others. Episcopalians also shared in

TABLE 8.5
MEDIAN SCORES OF ALL GROUPS OF STUDENTS AND FACULTY COMBINED AT THE UNIVERSITY OF FLORIDA ON THE FLORIDA SCALE OF CIVIC BELIEFS, BY DENOMINATIONS

Denomination	Median Score
Jewish	212
Protestant	204
Roman Catholic	203
Other	222
Protestant	
Baptist	201
Congregational	205
Episcopal	211.5
Lutheran	203
Methodist	198
Presbyterian	202
Unitarian	253

SOURCE: Walker (*90*, 128–50, Tables 54–56, 61–66, 69–73, 76–79, 82–84, 87–88, 91).

this greater liberalism, but not to as great an extent as did the Unitarians. No significant differences between denominations were found for freshmen considered separately; for juniors the only significant difference was found between Jewish and Protestant, with Jewish juniors more liberal; and no significant difference emerged for the faculty.

The relationship of certain other variables, although not all that were investigated, will be more briefly summarized. The major fields of specialization entered by juniors seem not to be significantly related to ideology as measured by the scale, although the colleges in which they were enrolled were found to be so: examples of significant differences in the direction of liberalism were between Business Administration and Agriculture, between Education and Agriculture, and between Arts and Sciences and Engineering. Walker says of such differences, "All that can legitimately be concluded is that students in certain broad areas of specialization, particularly those with a strong humanistic orientation . . . and those in which interpersonal relations are of primary importance, are likely to be more liberal than students in areas strongly oriented towards technology and production" (*90, 222*). No significant differences were found for sex, class (social) status, and urban-rural or sectional backgrounds of students (*90*, Ch. VII).

Concluding observations on the project.—When essaying major implications from his project, Walker observes that students' measures on the scale, as indicated by their significant relationships to party and religious preferences, are subject to long-time influences of family life and culture and not by their brief two-year exposure to general studies (*90, 221*). This conclusion is not out of accord with Jacob's generalization on the impact of the college on students' values and attitudes.* Walker postulates a longer period, say a four-year college span, or longer, over which to await significant influences, and, in contemplation of further research in the area, recommends substitution of longitudinal for the cross-sectional procedure followed in his investigation.

It may be repeated that the sample of junior college transfers was found not to differ in ideology, as indicated by the scale, from students who had taken their work in University College and from university freshmen. Whether or not this would be true of the nontransfer population in the junior colleges or in what degree these nontransfers would differ from the transfers would be a matter of conjecture, although we know that there would be a substantial degree of selection upward in aptitude and socio-economic status in the transfers. This question is open for investigative inquiry, as is almost the entire area of values and attitudes of junior college students and the impact on them of programs in which they are enrolled.

Interests—Health, Marital, Vocational, and Avocational

The areas of interest canvassed.—It is a truism to state that interests of students can be a useful guide to the make-up of educational programs for them. Among important areas of interest in which inquiries have been made with junior college students are those of health, marriage, and occupation. The concern of this section of the chapter will be a review of the results of these inquiries, with the aim of identifying some of the predominant areas and interests. Other areas of interest are hardly less important but are so meagerly represented in investigative literature that little would be gained by reviewing them. A partial exception is the area of avocations, since a few illuminating studies of reading interests have been reported. Besides digesting these, the brief treatment will re-emphasize the need for more research to fill this serious lacuna.

Health interests.—Lantagne (*48*) investigated the health interests of a thousand students equally divided between men and women attending

*See p. 130.

Pasadena City College and Ventura Junior College in California, using an inventory devised by Oliver E. Byrd, M.D., Director of Health Education at Stanford, and based on analyses of health problems dealt with in leading medical and public health journals. The inventory consisted of 300 health problems and respondents were requested to indicate in which of these problems they were interested. Before application of the inventory to the junior college population, the instrument had been used with high school students and was found to have correlations near .90 between test

TABLE 8.6
HIGHEST 25 IN RANK ORDER OF 300 HEALTH PROBLEMS AS RATED BY 1,000 JUNIOR COLLEGE STUDENTS

Order	Item	Per Cent	Order	Item	Per Cent
1.	Sex instruction	79.0	15.	Can drug addicts be cured?	58.9
2.	Causes of mental illness	78.3	16.	Effects of tea and coffee	58.3
3.	Lifelong care of eyes	76.8	17.	Sweets and dental decay	58.2
4.	Preparation for marriage	71.4	18.	Communicable disease	58.1
5.	Tobacco and human health	71.0	19.	The ability to have children	57.5
6.	Juvenile delinquency	68.0	20.	Mental health and marriage	57.5
7.	Cancer	66.9			
8.	Social diseases	64.6	21.	Health hazards with foods	57.4
9.	Problems of alcohol	64.7			
10.	Jealousy	62.9	22.	How to have good posture	56.9
11.	Conquest of disease	61.9			
12.	Causes of suicide	61.5	23.	Poliomyelitis	56.3
13.	How to report accidents	59.3	24.	Types of mental disorders	55.6
14.	Safest age to have a baby	59.0	25.	Atomic warfare	55.4

SOURCE: Lantagne (48, Table 1).

and retest on three different groups, as well as by the split-half method. A significant finding was that about 80 per cent of the same health problems emerged in the 50 items of greatest interest for both high school and junior college students. An important difference between the compilations for the two populations is that the junior college group showed about a 25 per cent greater interest in health problems.

Some impression of the diversity of the problems prominent in the health 8.6, which names the 25 problems in the inventory emerging with highest interests of these junior college students is afforded by the items in Table percentages of ratings. This list of problems is seen to begin with Sex Instruction and Causes of Mental Illness and to end with Types of Mental Disorders and Atomic Warfare. It may be noted that more than three-fourths of the students indicated interest in the top items, and that the proportion was still well over half for the twenty-fifth in this list. The diversity of items even in this top-rated list is so great as to be somewhat confusing. For the purpose of simplification the author has grouped the indications of interest on all 300 problems into 21 major health areas and presented the percentage distribution in Table 8.7. This distribution affords a better organized analysis of the ratings, although it hardly cancels the conclusion of diversity of the interests.

The author lists separately the 50 items of greatest interest to each of the sexes. Comparison of the lists discloses both similarity and differentia-

TABLE 8.7
Rank Order of Major Health Areas as Determined by the Ratings of 300 Health Problems by 1,000 Junior College Students

Order	Area	Per Cent	Order	Area	Per Cent
1.	Habit forming substances	52.6	11.	Infection and immunity	34.4
2.	Mental health	46.4	12.	Health as a social accomplishment	33.0
3.	Family health	44.2	13.	Nutrition and health	32.2
4.	Health as a social problem	39.8	14.	Heredity and eugenics	30.1
5.	Safety	39.4	15.	Excretion and health	27.8
6.	The care of special organs	37.2	16.	School health	27.7
7.	Exercise and body mechanics	36.2	17.	Community health services	26.2
8.	Chronic and degenerative disorders	35.9	18.	Trends and possibilities	22.8
9.	Health and the physical environment	35.7	19.	Occupational health	21.6
10.	Fatigue and rest	34.6	20.	Health services and facilities	21.5
			21.	International health	17.7

Source: Lantagne (48, Table 2).

tion, but more of similarity. The two lists have 31 items (of the 50 in each) in common. Of the first ten in these two lists, seven were the same: Sex Instruction, Lifelong Care of the Eyes, Tobacco and Human Health, Causes of Mental Illness, Preparation for Marriage, Juvenile Delinquency, and Cancer. The other three highest for men were Problems of Alcohol, Atomic Warfare, the Problems of Tooth Decay, while for women they were Jealousy, Causes of Suicide, and Social Diseases. Other instances of items differentiating the sexes, most of them readily understandable, are: for men, Speed and Accidents, Sunburn, Marijuana, Is There an Athletic Heart?, and How to Use a Gun Properly; for women, Food during Pregnancy, Dangers of Sleeping Pills, Safety in Water, Births in Hospital or at Home, and Socialized Medicine.

Interests relating to marriage and parenthood.—One could predict from the relatively high incidence of interest in items relating to sex and marriage in the project just reviewed that, with a focus on the area, many more problems in it would be rated high by junior college students. This expectation is affirmed by a special investigation of interest in marriage and parenthood made and reported a few years later than the one on health by the same author (*49*). Evidence reported in Chapter 4 also leads to the same expectation. The inventory used by Lantagne in his study was de-

TABLE 8.8
HIGHEST 30 IN RANK ORDER OF 60 ITEMS OF INTEREST IN MARRIAGE AND PARENTHOOD AS RATED BY 2,000 JUNIOR COLLEGE STUDENTS

Order	Item	Per Cent
1.	Normal sex relations	66
2.	Parent-child relationships	65
3.	Happiness with home and family	62
4.	Religion and marriage	60
5.	Juvenile delinquency prevention	59
6.	Demands of the opposite sex	59
7.	A college education	58
8.	Pregnancy—problems	58
9.	Mental adjustments in marriage	58
10.	Living with the opposite sex	58
11.	Responsibilities of parents	57
12.	Causes of divorce	55
13.	Wholesome attitude toward marriage	55
14.	Birth control problems	54
15.	Desirable age for marriage	53
16.	Planning and budgeting	51
17.	Dating	51
18.	Marriage while in college	50
19.	The family as a unit	50
20.	Engagement period	48
21.	Problems of mixed marriages	48
22.	Childbirth	48
23.	Infant care	48
24.	Social life for parents	47
25.	Significance of family backgrounds	45
26.	Job or probable career	45
27.	Health considerations before marriage	44
28.	Protocol, reception, honeymoon	44
29.	How and where to live	44
30.	Advantages of early marriage	43

SOURCE: Lantagne (*49*, Table 1).

vised by him from an analysis of textbooks and other literature on this area and was administered to 1,000 students of each sex in eight California junior colleges. The inventory included 60 items and was administered anonymously. Reliability of the instrument was established by correlations of .83 and .87 between test and retest with two college groups and of .93 by use of the split-half method.

The 30 items of the 60 in the inventory rated highest by the students of both sexes are listed in Table 8.8 in order of highest percentage downward.

The percentages reported are those for ratings of "interested" and "vitally interested." Items at or near the top of this list, "Normal Sex Relations" and "Parent-Child Relationships," are seen to have been so rated by about two-thirds of all students, and even those at the bottom, "How and Where to Live" and "Advantages of Early Marriage," were so rated by more than two-fifths of these students.

Lantagne's report also presents tables listing the 25 items with the highest percentages of ratings by the two sexes considered separately. While the problems emerge in somewhat different rank order in the two tables, the fact that 22 of the items are identical attests the predominant similarity of these interests. The items differentiative of these two lists are, for males, Job or Probable Career, How and Where to Live, and Advantages of Early Marriage, and for females, Childbirth, Infant Care, and Significance of Family Backgrounds. In the main, these reflect sex roles in our society.

Lantagne also presents tables listing the ten items of least interest and states that the four to which there was least response were "practically identical" for both college men and women and pertained to problems of health and welfare which, he says, were "of little concern to the college student."

Tabulations were also made for the denominations represented, Protestant, Catholic, Jewish, and Other, and the conclusion drawn was that there were no "significant trends" between denominations, although Protestant women "seemed to have a greater response than the men," and "the Jewish male had a considerably greater interest than the Jewish college women."

Occupational objectives.—Up to this writing no large-scale investigation of occupational interests involving a widespread sampling of community college students is available in print. The best that can be done in this area is to draw on reports of studies of these interests in individual institutions, which at best can yield only illustrative rather than representative results. One such local study is by Lubick (*52*) inquiring into the occupational objectives of entering students in Long Beach (California) City College in September, 1952. In addition to compiling and classifying these objectives, the investigation included inquiry into the persons who had been of most help to the students in selecting their occupational objectives and the "factors or goals" which had influenced them in selecting the objectives.

A total of 1,226 students—670 boys and 556 girls—were involved in the study. Of this number, 418, or 34.0 per cent, indicated that they were undecided as to their occupational objectives. The proportion undecided is usually large at this educational level, although it varies with the amount of counseling in relation to occupation the students may have had before college entrance. This fact is reported in Table 8.9, with the percentages of objectives found for occupations receiving at least 2.0 per cent of the indications. Teaching is the most frequent objective, more often with girls than boys. A large group designated "clerical" was next in frequency, again with more girls than boys. Engineering and dentistry were objectives exclusively, or almost so, with boys. The three remaining groups in the table, with 2 per cent of all students indicating each, are medicine, dental assistant, and nursing. From this point on in the total distribution the occupations vary widely and range in frequency from a single student to 17 of the total number. The author reports that 23 occupational titles were listed once only and the total array of titles extended to 64.

TABLE 8.9
OCCUPATIONAL OBJECTIVES OF STUDENTS ENTERING
LONG BEACH CITY COLLEGE*

Occupational Objective	Boys	Girls	Total	Per Cent
Undecided	230	188	418	34.0
Teacher	61	116	177	14.5
Clerical (typing, general office, secretary, bookkeeping)	17	107	124	11.0
Engineer	117	–	117	9.5
Dentist	30	2	32	2.6
Medicine (M.D., veterinary, optometrist)	19	9	28	2.0
Dental assistant	–	26	26	2.0
Nurse	1	22	23	2.0

SOURCE: Lubick (52, Table 1).
*Copied here only are the occupations named by 2 per cent or more of the total of 1,226 students.

Lubick classified the objectives as to occupational level from professional and managerial to skilled labor, and found the numbers and percentages to be as shown in Table 8.10. This compilation shows the distribution concentrated toward upper-level occupations, as was found in Chapter 5 in the preferences and choices for later adolescents. Both the large proportion without objectives and the concentration just noted point up the need for more attention to guidance concerning occupation.

The percentages of responses to the question concerning the persons who were of most help in selecting occupations were as follows: parents, 26; counselors, 22; friends, 15; teachers, 14; relatives, 7; and group guidance classes, 5. Eleven per cent made no answer to the question. The author comments that, when school workers are combined, taking counselors, teachers, and group guidance classes as one group, it appears that 41 per cent received most of their help from school workers. He does not make the observation, but it is nonetheless true, that this proportion is larger than has been typical in inquiries of this kind. In view of the large proportions found to be "undecided," this does not gainsay the desirability of increasing the proportion who are so aided.

The percentage distribution of "factors or goals" which the students reported as influencing their selection of vocational objectives is as follows: personal satisfaction, 42; job security, 21; service to others, 16; financial reward, 10; supervise or direct others, 3; high job prestige, 2; and no response, 6. The main difference between the sexes in this response was a much larger proportion of girls than boys indicating service to others as a factor.

TABLE 8.10
MAJOR GROUPINGS OF THE OCCUPATIONAL OBJECTIVES OF ENTERING STUDENTS AT LONG BEACH CITY COLLEGE

Major Occupational Groups	Boys		Girls		Total	
	Number	Per Cent	Number	Per Cent	Number	Per Cent
Professional and managerial	339	51	201	36	540	44
Semiprofessional	31	5	44	8	75	6
Clerical and kindred	17	2	107	19	124	10
Sales and kindred	11	2	5	1	16	1
Agriculture, fisheries, forestry	11	2	–	–	11	1
Personal service	–	–	9	1	9	1
Protective service	14	2	1	–	15	1
Skilled occupations	17	2	1	–	18	1
Undecided	230	34	188	34	418	34
Totals	670	100	556	99	1,226	99

SOURCE: Lubick (52, Table II).

Data are at hand in the way of a tabulation of answers to a question to entering students that is known to be in most cases closely related to occupational choice, the choice of the major undergraduate field of study.* The question was asked of new students entering five new community junior colleges and the state universities of Florida: "Do you have a major undergraduate field of study in mind?" The data relate to totals of 1,858 community college and 6,549 university students, only small percentages of whom made no answer. Of all community college entrants almost 29 per cent answered "no," whereas only 10 per cent of all university entrants answered in the negative. The percentages for men and women considered separately were, respectively, 31 and 25. It is interesting and perhaps significant that the proportion entering the community

*Emerson Tully, *Research Notes*, no. 16 (March 8, 1967), Office of Academic Affairs, Florida Board of Regents.

colleges is not far from that of both sexes in Long Beach City College (see Table 8.9) who indicated they were "undecided" on their occupational objectives. The larger proportion of the junior college than of university entrants answering "no" prompts the investigator to say that "this finding has great significance for counselors in the junior colleges." The report included also the percentages of entrants of different ages, that is 18 and below, 19, 20, 21, etc., who answered "yes" and "no." As might be expected, the proportion answering "no" decreases appreciably with age: it drops from 31 per cent for 18 and below to 23 per cent at 23 years and to 20 for the ages above 24, although the percentage at the older ages is still twice the total for university entrants.

Avocations: an area of interest almost devoid of inquiry.—As indicated near the opening of this section on interests, little evidence concerning recreations from objective inquiries involving the community or junior college student has seen its way into print. A partial exception is in the reading of periodicals, and the treatment of interests here will be concluded with a digest of and interpretative comments on two of these and related items. In the absence of conclusions in this area specifically relevant to a community college student population, the person who seeks understanding in it must rely on materials like those presented in Chapter 6, which to a considerable extent portray the scope and trends in recreational interests (a) up to the college threshold and (b) to a lesser extent of later adolescents by year of age, irrespective of scholastic attainment. Beyond this, such a person should urge and cooperate with efforts at research in the area, which should inquire into recreational participation in relation to age, sex, classification in college, social status, and religious affiliation, and in both intraschool and extraschool life. These researches should also include follow-up studies of students to ascertain the influence of activities and interests while in school on postschool life both in courses and in the extracurriculum. The dearth of inquiry in this area, as suggested in Chapter 6, has much of its origin in our traditional puritanical mores which disparaged play and are no longer fully appropriate for a society whose hours of labor are on the decline and whose margin for leisure is on the increase.

Reading interests of junior college students.—The most extensive report of voluntary reading by junior college students was presented by Eells (*17*) in 1942. It is based on information obtained from 13,498 students in 55 junior colleges in 22 states, and relates only to reading of periodicals. The information was supplied in response to the direction, "Name the magazines or periodicals, including daily newspapers, which you read fairly regularly, and circle the ones which you enjoy and value most." In addition to the naming of the periodicals read, the student supplied information concerning his sex, college classification (freshman or sophomore), and curriculum (transfer or terminal).

Eells reported that the periodicals fell, in frequency of report, into four "quite distinct" groups: the two which were read regularly by more than 25 per cent of the students; the six read by 10 to 25 per cent; the 18 read by 1 to 10 per cent; and the 27 read by fewer than 1 per cent. In the order of frequency, the eight periodicals most frequently reported are *Reader's Digest, Life, Time, Saturday Evening Post, Good Housekeeping, American Magazine, Collier's,* and *Ladies Home Journal.* A remarkable concentration in periodical reading is evidenced by the fact that these eight titles include almost two-thirds of all frequencies reported and that *Reader's Digest* and *Life* alone account for well over a third of all. In addition, almost three-fourths report they are reading one or more daily papers.

Comparison of the twelve periodicals with highest frequencies for freshmen and for sophomores shows eleven identical, although in somewhat different order. The twelfth in the list for freshmen was *Look,* while that for sophomores was *Harpers.* Of the first twelve for men and women, five (*Reader's Digest, Life, Time, Saturday Evening Post,* and *American Magazine*) were identical, almost all those distinctive for the women's list being women's magazines like *Good Housekeeping* and *Ladies Home Journal* and those for the men's list being more varied and not including a women's magazine. Another finding, derived from computation of the averages of numbers of periodicals reported, is that transfer students were reading more, although not strikingly more, than terminal students.

Eells reported that a similar question to that put to junior college students had been asked six years earlier of 17,000 students in 200 secondary schools. He found that of the first twelve periodicals in the two lists, nine were identical with the list for junior college students, with *Reader's Digest* and *Life* being at the top in both, and with only *Vogue, Newsweek,* and *Harpers* being distinctive for junior college students.

An enlightening comparison is afforded by results from a lesser inquiry by Weaver (*91*), at a time not long after the studies by Eells, "gathered not from a special and peculiar source but from a general and fair source," of the "personal reading" done by 246 students in the Division of Arts and Sciences of the University of Michigan. In the order of frequency, the six periodicals most often reported by these students during "the past year" were *Reader's Digest, Life, Time, Saturday Evening Post, National Geographic,* and *Esquire.* Analysis of responses to a request to name the magazines they were *currently* reading showed five of them the same, with only some change in order of frequency and the replacement of the *National Geographic* with the *New Yorker.* While the conclusions from the three sources, namely, Eells' evidence from high school and junior college and this study by Weaver, do not add up to a longitudinal investigation involving the same population at different levels, the persistence of predominant magazine reading interests throughout these studies might encourage the cynic to raise the question of the influence of education toward a higher intellectualism in recreational reading with advancement in school level. The cynicism is supported by the fact that at least two of the periodicals at or near the top of all lists may be thought of as disparaging *reading,* one by minimizing it by condensation and the other by pictorial means in presentation.

The second study concerned specifically with reading by junior college students, while a lesser project than that by Eells, is of a kind to add depth to one's understanding of reading interests of terminal students. This study is reported by Hull (*35*), the teacher of a course in Communication Skills to freshmen in the New York State Agricultural and Technical Institute at Canton, New York, which enrolls many students in terminal programs with many of them from "rural districts." The author refers to them as a "junior college group." The outcomes of the study are in harmony with the finding by Eells that the reading by terminal students is less extensive than that by transfer students. The evidence in this study was derived from analysis of the materials in books and periodicals being read by students for the course named. These students were required to report briefly on their readings but were given practically complete freedom as to what they read; that is, it was virtually free reading. The nonfiction articles read appeared mostly in the *Reader's Digest* and *Coronet,* with the incidence in the former far exceeding that in *Coronet.* The lower incidence in other periodicals was widely scattered. The preferences in fictional reading ran more to biographical or autobiographical than to other types of items, with boys preferring exciting reading in adventure, westerns, and historical romances, while girls preferred quiet romances, stories of family life, and of everyday people. Other concluding observations by the author refer to the "easy items" preferred by the "typical non-reader" found frequently among these students, the persistence of "more juvenile reading" among them "than one would expect," and the almost total disregard by these students of the "so called classics previously encouraged by high schools in required reading lists."

The findings of this study point up a responsibility of community colleges, which, because of their prevailing policies of admitting all high school graduates, are confronted with the problem of raising the level of and broadening the reading interests of many students with similarly restricted reading interests. This they must do while improving interest in the printed page for students with interests more nearly typical of the great body of students in lower college years.

Summary (Chapters 7–8)

Opinions concerning the proportions of youth of appropriate ages who should attend community colleges which, even in the early history of the movement, leaned toward liberality and flexibility have in late years moved toward universalizing the level, at least as applied to high school graduates. This is the position in the recent statement of the Educational Policies Commission of the National Education Association. Another quasi-official group, the President's Commission on Higher Education, about fifteen years earlier had set the proportion at about half (49 per cent) of the population, presumably taking account of the ability required to succeed in the currently operating programs at the level of the first two college years. Some students of the issue and of our society, even after taking account of the rapid popularization of higher levels of schooling, have questioned such high proportions as overly optimistic, citing as obstacles problems of financing, the ability of youth of the country, and the problem of motivation.

Application of measures of aptitude and of socioeconomic status have revealed something of the degree of democratization, or approach to universalization, that has been achieved by existing institutions. Early comparisons on measures of aptitude yielded conflicting conclusions, as some pointed to comparability of ability of students in junior colleges and in four-year colleges and universities, some to superiority of junior college students, and others toward superiority of freshmen in the four-year colleges and universities. As the senior colleges have become more selective, the differences have increasingly favored the freshmen in senior institutions.

Among the more recent definitive comparisons of the aptitude of junior college and college and university freshmen are those by Seashore and Seibel. On their evidence it may be concluded that, while the junior college enrolls some students on a par with superior students in more selective institutions, the proportion of these is typically smaller, the proportion of those with lower aptitude is somewhat larger and, therefore, measures of central tendency run lower in the junior colleges. At the same time, Seashore's study shows that these measures vary from institution to institution, so that those for some junior colleges may tend to be higher than for less selective four-year institutions. His study shows that the typical difference for students in terminal curriculums in junior colleges is even greater than for students in transfer curriculums, and the difference in favor of the four-year college student is slightly greater for women than for men.

Seibel's study uses, besides evidence from a test of aptitude, the rank in graduating class, from which the inferences are not unlike those from the test. It includes also comparisons with high school graduates not attending either two- or four-year colleges and finds that the measures for those not attending and attending two-year institutions are more nearly alike than those for graduates who are attending two-year and four-year institutions. This fact leads to the inference that progress is being achieved through the junior college toward the universalization advocated by the Educational Policies Commission at the same time that we still have far to go. Universalization as concerns the total population of appropriate ages is more remote.

The influence of the community college toward democratizing this level of education is seen also in comparisons of the socioeconomic classification of students in these institutions with those in four-year colleges and universities, with the classification done in relation to the occupations of fathers. Application of this procedure finds smaller proportions of students with fathers who are engaged in upper-level occupations and larger proportions engaged in lower-level occupations in local public junior colleges than in the other types of institution. Influencing factors on these proportions are proximity and tuition policy, since the proportions of high school graduates entering college from lower socioeconomic levels are much larger where local public junior colleges are operative than where they are not and even notably larger where these local institutions are tuition-free than where they are tuition-charging. Expectation of this influence is supported (1) by the reasons given by parents for their children's attendance at local junior colleges since the most frequent reason given is that attendance at a local junior college is "less expensive"; (2) by published estimates of cost of attendance in institutions away from home; and (3) by the prominence of reasons like "lack of finance" given by superior high school graduates for not continuing their education.

An investigation by Windham in a single state, Florida, with community colleges within commuting distance of all but a small percentage of prospective students, found the proportions of the population from low-income groups not markedly greater for the community colleges than for the state universities. He expressed the opinion that "foregone earnings" are a greater factor of deterrence to attendance than the tuition charges imposed which, if true, would call for further efforts toward motivation through curriculum offerings and protracted counseling.

It is apropos to bear in mind that the gross numbers of superior high school seniors from families with fathers of lower socioeconomic status far exceed those from higher status, and it is to be expected that proximity and low cost of junior college education can and will affect the motivation to attend this level, just as they have already done for the high school level.

Two major projects reviewed combine the advantages of applying both measures of aptitude and evidence concerning environmental factors to the same populations. They are Project TALENT and a follow-up of high school graduates by Medsker and Trent. The former compares the measures and evidence not only for junior college and four-year college populations, but includes as another criterion group a population not attending either type of institution. Measures indicative of ability rise rather consistently from the noncollege through the two-year college to the four-year college group, and significant relationships are found between certain of the environmental factors and attendance or nonattendance, prompting the investigators to conclude that both kinds of evidence "are very much involved in determining whether a student goes to college, junior college, or to no college at all." On the basis of internal evidence they conclude also that junior college students are more like noncollege students in terms of ability and more like college students in terms of socioeconomic factors.

The project by Medsker and Trent went further than Project TALENT by inquiring into the influence on attendance of the type of collegiate institution in the community, viz., public junior college, extension center, state college, multiple college, and no college. They found the public junior college attracting the largest proportion of all local graduates and the relative impact of this institution on young people from low socioeconomic homes, particularly those with high ability, was characterized as "striking." State colleges were next in order in the total proportion, but tended to enroll smaller proportions at lower ability levels because of increasing commitment in such institutions to policies of selection.

A number of minor and more or less local studies of the success of transfers from junior colleges to four-year colleges and universities have been made and reported, of which typical findings have been that marks earned by transfers in their junior colleges tend to be higher than those earned in lower college years by native students; that marks for transfers tend in some degree to slump for the period immediately following transfer; there is some tendency to recovery from the slump following this early period, the comparative recovery depending somewhat on the degree of selection of transfers.

The extensive follow-up project by Knoell and Medsker involved 7,243 junior college students who transferred to 44 higher institutions of five types in ten states, and 3,349 native students in these same institutions. Among the findings of this monumental and notable investigation the following are prominent, although the order and manner of presentation here depart from the original.

(1) Excepting only in the teachers colleges, native students tended to have higher scores on tests of aptitude than transfer students.

(2) The social status of transfer students, as indicated by the level of occupations of fathers, tended to be somewhat lower than of native students. An exception here again was the teachers colleges.

(3) The education of parents of native students tended to be higher than that of transfer students.

(4) Transfer students tended to be somewhat older than native students.

(5) While average grade-point ratios earned by transfers in junior colleges were higher than those of native students earned in lower college years, the order of superiority of these ratios was reversed for the upper college years.

(6) The attrition among transfers is somewhat greater than among natives and more of them are delayed beyond two years in meeting requirements for bachelors' degrees.

While the tendencies to difference that have just been recounted are, for the most part, assured by indications of statistical significance, few seem really pronounced, and the distributions of many or most measures overlap extensively and are more alike than they are different. Once again, despite the tendencies to difference, the two populations resemble each other in large degree and justify the general conclusion among others of the investigators that "junior colleges are making it possible for increasing numbers of high school graduates to begin work for baccalaureate degrees who would not otherwise be able to do so for reasons of academic or economic deficiency, or for lack of family encouragement."

Another large-scale follow-up of junior college graduates with what the investigator characterized as "dramatic" outcomes was made by Schultz and concerns the later careers of members of an honor society with chapters in public and private junior colleges in all sections of the country. Notably large proportions of these alumni continued in senior colleges; even larger proportions of these transfers received bachelors' degrees, almost all of them on schedule; a majority pursued the more difficult disciplines; large proportions received honors in process; and large proportions entered esteemed professions. The fact that a majority came from homes of low socioeconomic status with parents of limited education justifies Schultz' observation that "junior colleges contribute very significantly to the American dream of a free and open society."

Although there is proof from the evidence concerning the success of junior college transfers in senior colleges that high competence is characteristic of many junior college students, it may also be assumed from comparisons on measures of aptitude that larger proportions than in senior colleges will have academic deficiencies—lack of skills in the "tools of learning," that is in reading, grammatical usage, and other skills in communication and mathematics. The larger proportions have also often been established by direct testing for these skills, and many junior colleges have set up programs toward remedying the deficiencies. An analogous situation exists with study habits, and efforts are being made to improve these.

Because they are less tangible for measurement even than characteristics so far considered, much less is known about personal traits of students generally than of their aptitude, social status, and scholarly competence. However, because of the importance of understandings in this area and of the promise of certain explorations in it, the evidence from a few of the best of these is reviewed in the first main section of Chapter 8. The instrument used in one of these studies is the Omnibus Personality Inventory (OPI) which is designed to test for characteristics like Thinking-Introversion-Extroversion, Complexity of Outlook, Social Maturity, and Authoritarianism. From comparison of results from administering this instrument (previously applied by McConnell and Heist of the Center for the Study of Higher Education at the University of California at Berkeley to four-year college students) to superior seniors in California high schools, some of whom entered the University of California and others the junior colleges in the state, Tillery generalized that 31 per cent of the university entrants and 18 per cent of the junior college students had high intellectuality measures, while 16 and 25 per cent, respectively, of these two groups of entrants had low intellectuality measures. The contrast for women was higher than for the whole group. Tillery's paper gives special attention to results on the Scale of Social Maturity: 40 per cent of the university entrants had high scores and only 7 per cent had low scores, whereas for junior college entrants the proportion of high scores was only half that for university entrants and of low scores three times the university proportion.

From application of certain scales in the California Psychological Inventory (CPI) to populations of students who subsequently attended junior college 3–4, 1–2, or 0 semesters, it was concluded that there is a "general personality development apart from the amount of educational experience," thus raising the question of the impact of education on the traits measured. Comparison of the means for these populations with those for samples of high school and four-year college students finds rather consistent progressions with the level of the institutions. The corresponding measures for the two sexes show those for females almost always higher than for males, which appears to be in accord with evidence in Chapter 1 suggesting the earlier maturing of females.

Once again, in the comparisons of junior college with four-year college students on traits of personality, we note a situation analogous to those found in comparisons on aptitude, social status, and scholarly competence: the measures run appreciably lower for the junior college than for the four-year college populations, and smaller proportions have high scores and larger proportions low scores. At the same time, once again, the proximity of the corresponding measures and the extensive overlapping of the distributions of score values from which they are derived reflect trends of difference rather than distinct populations.

A recent synthesis (*11*) of researches comparing junior college and four-year college populations (many of them the same as those drawn upon in this treatise), by focusing on differences in measures of central tendency and the like, derives a key conclusion that "intellectual dimensions sharply differentiate junior college students, as a group, from senior college students." This conclusion is drawn even though extensive overlapping of distributions is presented alongside. It is pertinent to inquire whether this inference is not a disservice to the movement, in view of the fact that the junior colleges always enroll substantial proportions of superior youth at the same time that their commitment to comprehensive service requires them to serve increasing numbers of the less competent.

The relative paucity of significant reports on attitudes and values of junior college students has restricted further consideration in Chapter 8 to two inquiries. The first of these is an exploratory study bearing both on attitudes and subcultures, and is an attempt to identify types of students by adaptation of a typology devised by Clark and Trow for residential four-year institutions. This was a study of types of students attending a suburban junior college; it showed a relatively small proportion of the "academic" type, with larger proportions of the "perpetual teenager" and "vocational" types more susceptible to attrition which is known to be severe in junior colleges.

The other inquiry compares the socioeconomic beliefs, as measured by a scale devised for the purpose, of a number of student groups: juniors, some of whom had come up through the University College of the University of Florida and another group who had transferred to the University after two years in junior colleges; freshmen in the University College; and faculty of the University College. No significant differences were found in the scores for the two groups of juniors and between the scores of all juniors and freshmen, although members of the faculty were significantly more liberal than the groups of students. However, significant differences emerged for students when they were grouped by political party or denominational preferences. The obvious inference is that the socioeconomic values held by the students were not influenced by the program in general studies required in University College—an influence accompanied by the implication that such values are determined by long-time influences of family life and culture. We cannot know, of course, how different the measures would be for the less-selected freshmen and other nontransfer students in junior colleges.

Areas of interest of community college students on which published reports are available are health, marriage and parenthood, and vocational objectives. Despite the large and mounting importance of recreation in our society, inquiry into the interests related to it has been almost negligible, so that little is at hand beyond reports on limited aspects of reading interests of junior college students. A rather large number of problems of health engage the interests of a majority and more of these students; among the problems most prominent with them are sex instruction, causes of mental illness, lifelong care of the eyes, and preparation for marriage. Categorization of this great variety of problems finds them rather well distributed to a full range of rationally organized aspects of the field. Most of the items of greatest interest are common to both sexes. The prominence of sex instruction and preparation for marriage among the health problems leads to the expectation, corroborated by the evidence of a second inquiry, that many problems of marriage and parenthood loom large with these students: a full half of 60 items submitted were assigned high ratings by from two-fifths to two-thirds of the students represented. Again, as with health, most of the items of greatest interest are common to both sexes. Differences by denominational affiliation of the students were mainly negligible.

An illustrative study of the occupational objectives of junior college freshmen found full a third "undecided," while for those who had made decisions there was concentration on teaching, clerical, engineering, and a cluster of health and medical occupations. The objectives also showed the usual concentration in upper-level occupations, and a larger proportion of the students than usual in such studies reported the influence of educational personnel on their choices. Closely related to the problem of not having an occupational choice on entering college is that of having no major undergraduate field in mind. It has been found that the proportion of students who answer "no" to the question "Do you have a major undergraduate field in mind?" is almost three times that for university entrants. This should be a fact of special concern to junior college counselors.

The only substantial study of reading interests of junior college students concerns the reading of periodicals, which was found to be concentrated in a relatively small number of popular magazines, with *Reader's Digest* and *Life* heading the list and alone accounting for a third of all frequencies reported. All but one of the twelve periodicals most frequently read were the same for sophomores as for freshmen. The lists of highest frequencies for the two sexes differed mainly in the presence of magazines for women in the women's list. Students in terminal programs read somewhat less than those in transfer programs. Another study of free reading done by students in terminal programs found periodical reading restricted mainly to a few of the popular magazines. Comparisons with voluntary periodical reading done by high school students and students of a Division of Arts and Sciences in a university raises the question of the influence of education toward a higher intellectualism in recreational reading with advancement in school level.

References and Bibliography (Chapters 7–8)

1. Anderson, H. Dewey. "Whose Children Attend Junior College?" *Junior College Journal,* 4 (Jan., 1934), 165–72.
2. Barber, Leroy E. "Why Some Able High School Graduates Do Not Go to College." *School Review,* 59 (Feb., 1951), 93–96.
3. Blakeman, Edward W. "Spiritual Values in Community Colleges." *Religious Education,* 50 (Sept., 1955), 312–21.
4. Brown, Donald R., ed. *Social Changes and the College Student.* Washington: American Council on Education, 1960.
5. Brown, W. F., and Holtzman, W. H. *Manual for the Survey of Study Habits and Attitudes.* Rev. ed. New York: Psychological Corporation, 1956.
6. Bugelski, Richard, and Lester, Oliver P. "Changes in Attitude in a Group of College Students During Their College Course and After Graduation." *Journal of Social Psychology,* 12 (1940), 319–32.
7. Byrns, Ruth, and Henmon, V. A. C. "Parental Occupation and Mental Ability." *Journal of Educational Psychology,* 27 (April, 1936), 284–91.
8. Clark, Burton R. *The Open-Door College—A Case Study.* New York: McGraw-Hill Book Co., 1960.
9. Cooley, William W., and Becker, Susan J. "The Junior College Student." *Personnel and Guidance Journal,* 44 (Jan., 1966), 464–69.
10. Cooper, Leland R. "The Difficulty of Identifying the Real Transfer Student." *Junior College Journal,* 38 (Dec.–Jan., 1967–68), 38–40.
11. Cross, K. Patricia. *The Junior College Student: A Research Description.* Princeton, N.J.: Educational Testing Service, 1968.
12. D'Amico, Louis A., and Iffert, Robert E. "Tuition and Fees in Public Junior Colleges." *College and University,* 40 (Spring, 1965), 334–38.
13. Davenport, F. J. *Adolescent Interests, A Selected Study of Sexual Interests and Knowledge of Young Women.* Archives of Psychology, no. 66 (1923).
14. Davie, James G. "Social Class Factors and School Attendance." *Harvard Educational Review,* 23 (Summer, 1953), 175–85.
15. Duncan, Carl P.; Bell, Graham; Bradt, Kenneth H.; and Newman, Slater E. "How the Poorer Student Studies: A Research Report." *Journal of Educational Research,* 45 (Dec., 1951), 287–92.
16. Eells, Walter Crosby. "California Junior College Mental-Educational Survey." *Educational Record,* 11 (Oct., 1930), 281–91.
17. Eells, Walter Crosby. "Periodicals Read by Junior College Students." *Library Quarterly,* 12 (July, 1942), 474–85.
18. Gough, Harrison G. *Manual for the California Psychological Inventory.* Palo Alto, Cal.: Consulting Psychologists Press, 1964.
19. Gray, William S. "Reading Difficulties in College." *Journal of Higher Education,* 7 (Oct., 1936), 356–62.
20. Guiler, Walter S. "Background Deficiencies." *Journal of Higher Education,* 3 (Oct., 1932), 369–72.
21. Guiler, Walter S., and Coleman, J. H. "Reading at the College Level." *American Association of Collegiate Registrars Journal,* 17 (Oct., 1941), 16–27.
22. Hackett, Roger C. "Tuition Rates in Public Junior Colleges." *Junior College Journal,* 25 (Dec., 1954), 229–30.
23. Hagemeyer, Richard H. "Socio-Economic Background of Full-Time Male Stu-

dents in Henry Ford Community College." *Junior College Journal,* 29 (Feb., 1959), 313–21.
24. Havighurst, Robert J. *American Higher Education in the 1960s.* Columbus: Ohio State University Press, 1960.
25. Havighurst, Robert J. "Social Implications of the Report of the President's Commission on Higher Education." *School and Society,* 67 (April 3, 1948), 257–61.
26. Havighurst, Robert J., and Newgarten, Bernice L. *Society and Education.* Boston: Allyn & Bacon, 1957.
27. Heist, Paul A. "Diversity in College Student Characteristics." *Journal of Educational Sociology,* 33 (Feb., 1960), 279–91.
28. Heist, Paul A. "The Entering College Student: Background and Characteristics." *Review of Educational Research,* 30 (Oct., 1960), 285–97.
29. Heist, Paul A. "Implications from Recent Research on College Students." *Journal of NAWDC,* 22 (April, 1959), 116–24.
30. *Higher Education for American Democracy.* A Report for the President's Commission on Higher Education. Vol. 1. New York: Harper & Bros., 1947.
31. Hill, George E. "College Proneness as a Guidance Problem." *Personnel Guidance Journal,* 33 (Oct., 1954), 70–73.
32. Hills, John R. "Transfer Shock: The Academic Performance of the Junior College Transfer." *Journal of Experimental Education,* 33 (Spring, 1965), 201–15.
33. Holland, J. L. "Parental Expectations and Attitudes about Colleges." *College and University,* 34 (Winter, 1959), 164–70.
34. Hollinshead, Byron S. *Who Should Go to College?* New York: Columbia University Press, 1952.
35. Hull, Ramona E. "Reading Interests of Technical Institute Freshmen." *Junior College Journal,* 21 (Jan., 1951), 292–97.
36. Iffert, Robert E. *Retention and Withdrawal of College Students.* U.S. Office of Education Bulletin, no. 1. Washington, 1958.
37. Jencks, Christopher. "Education: What Next?" *New Republic,* 153 (Oct. 16, 1965), 21–23.
38. Johnson, Elizabeth S., and Legg, Caroline C. "Why Young People Leave School." *Bulletin of NASSP,* 32 (Nov., 1948), 14–24.
39. Jones, Vernon. "Attitudes of College Students and the Changes in Such Attitudes During Four Years in College." *Journal of Educational Psychology,* 29 (Jan.–Feb., 1938), 14–25, 114–34.
40. Kastner, Harold H., Jr. "Student Deficiencies and the Community College Dilemma." *Junior College Journal,* 30 (Nov., 1959), 140–42.
41. Knapp, R. H., and Greenbaum, J. J. *The Young American Scholar: His Collegiate Origins.* Chicago: University of Chicago Press, 1952.
42. Knoell, Dorothy M. *Toward Educational Opportunity for All.* Albany: State University of New York, 1966.
43. Knoell, Dorothy M., and Medsker, Leland L. *Articulation Between Two-Year and Four-Year Colleges.* Berkeley: University of California, 1964.
44. Knoell, Dorothy M., and Medsker, Leland L. *Factors Affecting Performance of Transfer Students from Two-Year to Four-Year Colleges: With Implications for Coordination and Articulation.* Berkeley: University of California, 1964.
45. Koos, Leonard V. "How to Democratize the Junior College Level." *School Review,* 52 (May, 1944), 271–84.
46. Koos, Leonard V. *The Junior College.* Minneapolis: University of Minnesota Press, 1924.
47. Koos, Leonard V. "Who Should Go to College?" *Junior College Journal,* 18 (Jan., 1948), 229–30.
48. Lantagne, Joseph E. "An Analysis of Health Interests of 1,000 Junior College Students in California." *Junior College Journal,* 21 (April, 1951), 429–33.
49. Lantagne, Joseph E. "Items of Interest in Marriage and Parenthood of 2,000 Junior College Students." *Junior College Journal,* 26 (Dec., 1955), 210–18.

50. Levi, Albert William. "Social Beliefs of College Students." *Journal of Higher Education,* 15 (March, 1944), 127–34.
51. Lide, Edwin S. "Social Composition of the CWES Junior College in Chicago." *School Review,* 43 (Jan., 1935), 28–33.
52. Lubick, Emil E. "Vocational Objectives of Entering College Students." *Junior College Journal,* 25 (Feb., 1955), 319–26.
53. McConnell, T. R., and Heist, Paul. "Do Students Make the College?" *College and University,* 34 (Summer, 1949), 442–52.
54. McConnell, T. R. (with Paul Heist). "The Diverse College Student Population." In *The American College,* edited by Sanford Nevett, ch. 5. New York: John Wiley & Sons, 1962.
55. McConnell, T. R. "Student Personality Characteristics Associated with Groups of Colleges and Fields of Study." *College and University,* 37 (Spring, 1962), 229–41.
56. Maguire, Ruth E. "Syracuse University Looks at Its Junior College Transfers." *Junior College Journal,* 20 (Oct., 1949), 95–98.
57. Mauss, Armand L. *Toward an Empirical Typology of Junior College Subcultures.* Abstract no. ED013076 in *Research in Education,* 3:2 (Feb., 1968). ERIC Clearinghouse for Junior College Information.
58. Maxwell, Walter K. "Do Junior College Students Study?" *Junior College Journal,* 5 (March, 1935), 304–9.
59. Means, Marie Hackl. "Fears of One Thousand College Women." *Journal of Abnormal and Social Psychology,* 31 (Oct.–Dec., 1936), 291–311.
60. Medsker, Leland L., and Trent, James W. *The Influence of Different Types of Higher Institutions on College Attendance from Varying Socio-Economic and Ability Levels.* Cooperative Research Project no. 438, Center for Research and Development in Higher Education. Berkeley: University of California, 1965.
61. Metgang, Herbert. "What College Youth is Thinking." *Survey,* 87 (Feb., 1951), 58–59.
62. Nelson, Erland. *Radicalism-Conservatism in Student Attitudes.* Psychological Monograph, vol. 50, no. 4. Washington: American Psychological Association, 1938.
63. Newcomb, Theodore M., and Wilson, Everett K., eds. *College Peer Groups.* Chicago: Aldine Publishing Co., 1966.
64. Panos, R. J. *Some Characteristics of Junior College Students.* Washington: American Council on Education, 1966.
65. *The Performance of Junior College Transfer Students and Native Students in the University System of Florida.* Tallahassee, Fla.: Board of Control, 1964.
66. Reynolds, Edgar. *The Social and Economic Status of College Students.* Teachers College Contributions to Education, no. 272. New York: Columbia University, 1927.
67. Richards, James M., Jr., and Braskamp, Larry A. *Who Goes Where to Junior College?* Iowa City, Iowa: American College Testing Program, 1967.
68. Roper, Elmo. *Factors Affecting the Admission of High School Seniors to College.* Washington: American Council on Education, 1949.
69. Sanford, Nevitt. *The American College,* pp. 811–46. New York: John Wiley & Sons, 1962.
70. Schultz, Raymond E. "A Follow-Up on Honor Students." *Junior College Journal,* 38 (Dec., 1967), 9–15.
71. Seashore, Harold. "Academic Abilities of Junior College Students." *Junior College Journal,* 29 (Oct., 1958), 74–80.
72. Seibel, Dean W. *A Study of the Academic Ability and Performance of Junior College Students.* Princeton, N.J.: Educational Testing Service, 1965.
73. Sherman, Arthur W., Jr. "Emancipation Status of College Students." *Journal of Genetic Psychology,* 68 (June, 1946), 171–80.
74. Smith, Herbert A., and Penny, Lawrence L. "Educational Opportunity as a Function of Socio-Economic Status." *School and Society,* 87 (Sept. 12, 1959), 342–44.
75. Stoddard, George D. "A Mental-Educational Survey of Iowa Junior Colleges." *School Review,* 36 (May, 1928), 346–49.

76. Stoke, Stuart M., and Clive, W. F. "The Avocations of One Hundred College Freshmen." *Journal of Applied Psychology,* 13 (March, 1929), 257–63.
77. Strang, Ruth. "Reading Interests, 1946." *English Journal,* 35 (Nov., 1946), 477–82.
78. Telford, Charles W., and Plant, Walter T. *The Psychological Impact of the Public Two-Year College on Certain Non-Intellectual Functions.* Cooperative Research Project 914, U.S. Office of Education. Washington, 1963.
79. Thompson, Ronald B. "College-Age Population Trends, 1940 to 1970." *College and University,* 29 (Jan., 1954), 215–24.
80. Thompson, Ronald B. *The Impending Tidal Wave of Students.* Washington: American Association of Collegiate Registrars and Admissions Officers, 1954.
81. Thompson, Ronald B. "Numbers of College-Age Youth and College Enrollments Projected to 1975." In *The College Bluebook,* 9th ed., pp. 921–32. Baltimore: C. E. Burckel, 1959.
82. Tillery, Harry D. "Differential Characteristics of Entering Freshmen at the University of California and Their Peers at California Junior Colleges." Ph.D. dissertation, University of California (Berkeley), 1964.
83. Traxler, Arthur E. "Spelling in College." *Journal of Higher Education,* 19 (May, 1948), 256–59.
84. Traxler, Arthur E. "What Is a Satisfactory IQ for Admission to College?" *School and Society,* 51 (April 6, 1940), 462–64.
85. Trent, James W., and Medsker, Leland L. *Beyond High School.* San Francisco: Jossey-Bass, Inc., 1968.
86. *The Two-Year College and Its Students: An Empirical Report.* Iowa City, Iowa: American College Testing Program, Inc., 1969.
87. Tyler, Henry T. "Remedial Reading in the Junior College." *Junior College Journal,* 4 (Oct., 1933), 28–31.
88. Uhrbrock, Richard S. "The Freshman's Use of Time." *Journal of Higher Education,* 2 (March, 1931), 137–43.
89. *Universal Opportunity for Education Beyond the High School.* Educational Policies Commission of the National Education Association. Washington: National Education Association, 1964.
90. Walker, John E. "Liberal-Conservative Differences among Selected College Groups." Ph.D. dissertation, University of Florida, 1967.
91. Weaver, Bennett. "What Do Students Read?" *College English,* 10 (April, 1949), 411–13.
92. Webb, Paul E. "The Holding Power of Junior Colleges." *Junior College Journal,* 3 (Jan., 1933), 179–84.
93. Webster, Harold. "Changes in Attitudes During College." *Journal of Educational Psychology,* 49 (June, 1958), 109–17.
94. Williams, Cornelia T. *These We Teach: A Study of General College Students.* Minneapolis: University of Minnesota Press, 1943.
95. Windham, Douglas M. "State-Financed Higher Education and the Distribution of Income in Florida." Ph.D. dissertation, Florida State University, 1969.
96. Wise, W. Max. *They Come for the Best of Reasons—College Students Today.* Washington: American Council on Education, 1958.
97. Wolfle, Dael L. *America's Resources of Specialized Talent: A Current Appraisal and a Look Ahead.* New York: Harper & Bros., 1959.
98. Wrenn, C. Gilbert, and Humber, Wilbur. "Study Habits Associated with High and Low Scholarship." *Journal of Educational Psychology,* 32 (Nov., 1941), 611–16.
99. Wrenn, C. Gilbert, and Larsen, Robert P. *Studying Effectively.* 2d ed. Stanford, Cal.: Stanford University Press, 1955.
100. Wright, Wendell W., and Jung, Christian W. "Why Capable High School Students Do Not Continue Their Schooling." *Bulletin of the School of Education,* 35, 1 (1959), 29–32. Bloomington: Indiana University.

9
Personal Problems

To UNDERSTAND youth it is important to know their problems as they see them. Numerous efforts have been made to identify these problems. In this chapter procedures used in various inquiries will be reviewed and evaluated.

Identifying the Problems

Earlier identification of problems.—Among the efforts, one of the best known is that by Bell (*1*), made by interview of a large sampling of youth in Maryland during the period of the depression of the thirties. The sampling included subjects of both sexes ranging rather widely in age and representative of both those in and those out of school. From one of the compilations of the report, Table 9.1 has been extracted. This table makes possible a comparison of the percentage distributions of the opinions of young people of two age-groups, 16-year-olds and 20-year-olds, on "what constitutes the youth problem." These age-groups are used here because they make possible some identification of trends of opinion within the dominant age-span of the community college.

The trends seen in the table reflect, as might be expected, the influence of a period of recession. The most prominent area of problems is the economic, which included more than half the problems in both age-groups and which, as could be expected from the high incidence of unemployment of the period and the problems of financing education for those in school, increased from the younger to the older group. Other areas showing significant changes, and these are in the direction of decrease, are education and vocational choice and recreation. The proportions for the two remaining special areas are not far from identical for both age-groups.

Among earlier published discussions of problems of college students, as distinguished from youth in the general population, is one by Pressey (*23*) who described forty "cases" distributed in six chapters corresponding to as many types of problems: "Study Problems," "Health Problems," "Family Problems," "Social Problems," "Moral Problems," and "Vocational Problems." Among other writings antedating recent investigations of the problems of college students is one by Lunger and Page (*18*), which reports some of the results of administering a "Worry Inventory" to a hundred college freshmen of each sex. Each item on the inventory was answerable in one of three ways: items worried about "very much," "some," or "not at all." About half the subjects expressed some concern over such items as general religious problems, physical defects, being late for appoint-

TABLE 9.1
PERCENTAGE DISTRIBUTION OF OPINIONS OF YOUTH ON WHAT CONSTITUTES THE YOUTH PROBLEM

Areas	16-Year-Olds	20-Year-Olds
Economic	53.5	58.6
Conduct or morals	10.4	10.1
Education and vocational choice	13.1	10.3
Home	7.6	7.4
Recreation	7.9	4.0
Other	7.5	9.6
Total	100.0	100.0

SOURCE: Bell (*1*, 250, Table 99).

ments, familial obligations, inability to make friends, and vocational success. About a third were concerned about personal defects, losing their friends, and not being as happy as one felt one should be; a fifth to a fourth worried about social obligations, mental inferiority, being nervous, inability to get along with other people, what happens after death, and insufficient funds; and a tenth to a fifth about developing some disease or being injured, familial difficulty, and social success. Contrary to the conclusions of studies to be reviewed below, no relationship was found between the sexes in either incidence or intensity of worries and none between incidence and scores on the ACE Intelligence Test.

As the reader will note in the following treatment, the types of problems and the particular worries in these two older writings foreshadow the areas and items in such an instrument as the Mooney Problem Check List next to be described, as if the earlier analyses may have in some way served as prototypes.

The Mooney Problem Check List.—The bulk of the present chapter will be given over to report on problems of a sample of community college students as identified by the Mooney Problem Check List, one of two rather similar instruments frequently used in such studies. The other instrument is the SRA Youth Inventory. In addition, the total treatment will include some comparison of the findings of this report with those of other studies using the same checklist in other types of institutions at the collegiate level, and observations concerning the usefulness of such a list.

The specific form of the Mooney List used with this sample of students is the college form (C), 1950 revision. As with the high school form, it consists mainly of a total of 330 specific problems, or "items," with 30 problems in each of the following "areas":

     I. Health and Physical Development (HPD)
    II. Finances, Living Conditions, and Employment (FLE)
   III. Social and Recreational Activities (SRA)
   IV. Social-Psychological Relations (SPR)
    V. Personal-Psychological Relations (PPR)
   VI. Courtship, Sex, and Marriage (CSM)
  VII. Home and Family (HF)
 VIII. Morals and Religion (MR)
   IX. Adjustment to College Work (ACW)
    X. The Future: Vocational and Educational (FVE)
   XI. Curriculum and Teaching Procedure (CTP)

The nature of the individual items in the checklist will become apparent in the treatment of the evidence to follow, although, because of the space required, the full list will not be presented. The items were derived from extensive compilations of problems supplied by students, from observation, and from related literature, and the list is the outgrowth of experimentation and revision. In the form the items are all numbered from 1 to 330 downward in 11 columns, with 55 items in each column, grouped with 5 items in each area in the order of areas as named above. Special investigation has found that very few subjects on whom the list is used identify the grouping of the problems (*8*), a situation desirable in preventing subjects from skipping whole areas that seem inappropriate to them, without bothering to read the items, or which they may wish to conceal.

The Problem Check List is self-administering. After supplying information concerning his age, sex, classification, marital status, the date of answering, etc., the subject is directed, as a first step, to "read the list slowly, pause at each item, and if it suggests something which is troubling you, underline it. . . . Go through the whole list, underlining the items which suggest troubles (difficulties, worries) of concern to you." As a second step, the subject is asked to "look back over the items you have underlined and *circle the numbers* in front of the items that are of *most concern* to you. . . ." In the special project reported here, chief reliance is placed on responses in this second step, the identification of what seem to the subjects their more serious problems. A third step, answers to which were not requested and used in the project, asks the student to answer some "summarizing questions" designed to enhance the value of the list as an instrument of individual guidance. Another detail of the procedure followed in this project, which differs from a situation in which the responses are to be used in personal guidance, is that the students were not asked to supply their names. It was assumed that anonymity in such an inquiry encourages candor in response.

Before reporting the evidence from the special project, it is desirable to indicate that the instrument used is designed to identify the subject's problems *as he sees them*. It is important to know what he thinks his problems are or is willing to admit them to be. The maker of the checklist emphasizes that it is not a test, but rather that its usefulness "lies in its economy for appraising the major concerns of the group and for bringing into the open the problems of each student in the group" (22, 3). A collaborator on the checklist admits that it "reveals only those problems that the individual is willing to admit and discuss, and is not intended to be a depth technique for determining 'real problems' or 'unconscious conflicts' of the individual" (7, 790).

The institutions and students involved.—The sample of students used in the administration of the Mooney Check List for the illustrative study reported here was in attendance at five community junior colleges, two in Illinois, one in Michigan, and two in Florida. Cooperation in administering the checklists was solicited by the writer in connection with visits made to the institutions for other purposes. The dates of the visits ranged from late 1958 to the spring of 1960. Sampling was done in such a way as to assure rather substantial representation of both freshmen and sophomore classes, of both sexes, and of three age-groups, namely 18 and under, 19 through 21, and 22 and over. For some of these groups, however, the numbers of students are too small to assure reliability of differences found. The total number of students filling out usable forms was 623, including 312 freshmen and 311 sophomores. The division by sex is 395 men and 228 women, which reflects a typical preponderance of men in public community colleges. The numbers in subgroupings by age in the sample will be found in the tables to be presented.

Comparison of numbers of problems underlined and circled.—First presentation of evidence from this special project concerns the numbers of items underlined and circled. This is done in Table 9.2. The evidence is given for each sex in each of the junior college classes. The measures reported are the median and first and third quartile numbers, with the thought that these will give the reader some impression of the typical numbers of problems reported as "troubling" and "of most concern" to the students. Thus, the median number of problems underlined by men in the freshmen group is 37, with the range for the middle 50 per cent being from 19 to 58. The respective measures for freshmen women are seen not to be notably different, being 35, 20, and 52. The measures decrease somewhat for sophomore men, while those for sophomore women are somewhat higher than for men. The full range of items underlined, not reported in the table, is also a matter of interest, but we do not know of how much significance: for freshmen men it was from only one item to 179 (more than half the 330 items), while for freshmen women it was from a single item to 113 (more than a third of all). The ranges for sophomore men and women were almost equally wide.

TABLE 9.2
MEDIAN AND FIRST AND THIRD QUARTILE NUMBERS OF PROBLEMS UNDERLINED AND CIRCLED BY STUDENTS IN FIVE JUNIOR COLLEGES

Class and Sex	Underlined			Circled		
	Median	First Quartile	Third Quartile	Median	First Quartile	Third Quartile
Freshmen						
Men (196)*	37	19	58	7	3	13
Women (116)	35	20	52	7	3	13
Sophomores						
Men (199)	29	16	48	5	2	11
Women (112)	31	21	52	7	3	12

*Number of students represented.

The numbers of problems circled ("most concern") are seen in Table 9.2 to have been *much* smaller. The three measures for freshmen men and women were identical, with 7 as the median and the interquartile range being from 3 to 13. The measures for sophomore men, 5, 2, and 11, ran somewhat smaller than for freshmen, while those for sophomore women remained almost at the freshman figures, being 7, 3, and 12. The full range of problems circled was correspondingly much smaller than for problems underlined and for all four groups began at none or very near it to 65 to 75 as a maximum.

The striking differences between the numbers of problems underlined and circled have just been noted. In the project being drawn upon here extensive compilation and analysis were made of both types of response to the checklist. However, from this point forward, report will be based solely on the response purporting to indicate problems of most concern, for the reasons that these will yield, since the items survived reselection by the subjects, much of the significance of the whole project and that it can be accomplished within practicable limits of space.

Distribution of circled problems to the areas.—From a mere count of the number of problems circled the report shows next their distribution in the eleven areas into which the problems are classified. This distribution for all students is presented in Table 9.3, which gives the total numbers of times problems in each area were circled by all the 623 subjects involved in the investigation. By way of interpretation of the table, one may say, for example, that problems in the first area, that of Health and Physical Development, were circled 394 times by the 623 students. The total of all circlings of the 330 problems is reported at the foot of the table, and was 6,592. The third column of the table reports the percentages which each of the numbers of circlings in each area is of this total: e.g., again, the 394

TABLE 9.3
NUMERICAL AND PERCENTAGE DISTRIBUTION OF THE PROBLEMS CIRCLED BY 623 JUNIOR COLLEGE STUDENTS IN AREAS OF THE MOONEY PROBLEM CHECK LIST AND RANK ORDER OF FREQUENCY ACCORDING TO DISTRIBUTION

Area	Number	Per Cent	Rank Order*
I. (HPD)	394	6.0	10
II. (FLE)	683	10.4	2
III. (SRA)	538	8.2	7
IV. (SPR)	544	8.3	6
V. (PPR)	641	9.7	3
VI. (CSM)	617	9.4	4
VII. (HF)	496	7.5	9
VIII. (MR)	500	7.5	8
IX. (ACW)	1,250	19.0	1
X. (FVE)	549	8.3	5
XI. (CTP)	380	5.8	11
Total	6,592	100.1	—

*Based on actual number, not on per cent.

circlings represent 6.0 per cent of all circlings by all subjects. The last column indicates the rank order, from largest number downward, for the eleven areas.

It may be seen that the area of Adjustment to College Work (IX) includes almost a fifth of all the circlings made. The number of circlings of problems in this area, 1,250, means an average of about two problems in this area per student. The next larger number, making up something more than half the proportion for ACW, is Finances, Living Conditions, and Employment (II). Other relatively high numbers and proportions are those for Personal-Psychological Relations (V) and Courtship, Sex, and Marriage (VI). Among the areas with lower numbers and proportions are Curriculum and Teaching Procedure (XI) and Health and Physical Development (I). However, it is apparent that the number and proportion for *no* area is small, and one may assume that large proportions of all students felt problems of "most concern" in all areas. The fact deserves mention that the total of 6,592 circled problems signifies an average of between 10 and 11 per student.

The influence of class, sex, and age.—By means of Table 9.2 partial answer was given to the question of the influence of classification and sex on the number of problems underlined or circled by students. It remains to look for the influence of these two possible factors as well as age on the incidence of problems in each of the areas as reported by these students. This is made possible by Table 9.4, which shows the percentage of students

TABLE 9.4
PERCENTAGES OF STUDENTS IN FIVE JUNIOR COLLEGES GROUPED BY CLASS, SEX, AND AGE CIRCLING PROBLEMS IN THE 11 AREAS ON THE MOONEY PROBLEM CHECK LIST

Area	Class		Sex		Age-Group		
	Freshman (312)*	Sophomore (311)	Men (395)	Women (228)	18 and Under (270)	19–21 (244)	22 and Over (109)
I. HPD	36.5	34.7	30.6	44.3	37.4	33.6	35.8
II. FLE	45.5	39.9	44.6	39.5	43.0	42.2	43.1
III. SRA	39.1	37.0	37.2	39.5	40.4	38.5	31.2
IV. SPR	39.1	35.0	32.7	44.7	41.1	35.2	32.1
V. PPR	56.7	39.5	45.3	53.1	48.9	41.0	34.9
VI. CSM	38.5	37.6	36.5	40.8	39.6	45.5	17.4
VII. HF	37.5	32.5	29.4	44.7	39.3	33.6	27.5
VIII. MR	34.6	33.1	29.4	37.2	34.1	34.8	22.0
IX. ACW	53.2	59.0	53.9	60.5	50.0	63.5	56.0
X. FVE	41.7	38.9	41.5	38.6	44.4	41.0	29.4
XI. CTP	29.5	25.7	27.9	27.2	26.3	30.3	24.8
Average Per Cent Per Area	38.9	35.4	37.2	42.7	44.4	43.9	35.4

*Number of students.

circling problems in each area and not, as reported in Table 9.3, the percentage of *all problems* circled which are represented by those circled in each area. Table 9.4 is interpreted by running commentary on notable differences.

(a) *By classification.* The most notable difference between the classes is the larger proportion of freshmen with problems in Personal-Psychological Relations (v), a difference readily attributable to feelings of insecurity of newcomers to an institution. There is a small difference in the same direction, and probably for the same cause, in Social-Psychological Relations (IV). The difference in the opposite direction in Adjustment to College Work (IX) is not readily explicable, as one might expect sophomores to have worked out a better adjustment than freshmen. Finances, Living Conditions, and Employment (II) seems to be a somewhat more frequent problem for freshmen than for sophomores; the latter have had a longer period in which to solve such problems.

(b) *By sex.* The only areas in which men more often have problems than women appear to be Finances, Living Conditions, and Employment (II) (a difference of 5 per cent) and The Future: Vocational and Educational (X) (only about 3 per cent). The former difference is perhaps somewhat accounted for by the male's usually carrying the costs of dating. Notably larger proportions of women than men circled problems in Health and Physical Development (I), Social-Psychological Relations (IV), Personal-Psychological Relations (V), Home and Family (VII), Morals and Religion (VIII), and Adjustment to College Work (IX). There were smaller differences in the same direction in Social and Recreational Activities (III) and Courtship, Sex, and Marriage (VI).

(c) *By age.* A glance down the columns for the three age-groups discloses roughly equal percentages across the columns for Health and Physical Development (I) and Finances, Living Conditions, and Employment (II). A somewhat similar condition applies to Curriculum and Teaching Procedure (XI). For most of the remaining areas there is something approaching a consistent decline through the three groups: this is true of Social and Recreational Activities (III), Social-Psychological Relations (IV), Personal-Psychological Relations (V), Home and Family (VII), and The Future: Vocational and Educational (X). There is some decline between the 19–21 and the 22-and-over groups in the incidence for Morals and Religion (VIII). Exceptions appear to be Courtship, Sex, and Marriage (VI), for which the proportion rises for the 19–21 group to drop off sharply for those 22 and over, and Adjustment to College Work (IX), in which the proportion is highest for the 19–21 group, but is still high for those 22 and over, as it is for all groups in the table. An appropriate observation concerning the evidence on the declining proportions by age is that these students seem to be making progress toward achieving their development tasks of adolescence with which most of the problems have much in common.

Before leaving consideration of the percentages in this table, it seems desirable to call attention once more to the large proportions in all areas for all groups of students. For three areas only, and in these only for students 22 years of age or older, does the proportion fall below a fourth of all members of the group. Problems of most concern are widely prevalent and in great variety.

Comparison of the proportions for two community colleges.—The percentages of students with problems of most concern were ascertained for each of the five community colleges represented in the project and the institutions were compared with each other to note the similarities and dissimilarities. The similarities were more frequent than the dissimilarities. For no one of the institutions were the percentages astonishingly different than those for the others. It is more than likely, to be sure, that with more institutions in the sample, the variation in percentages would have been wider.

The percentages for two institutions with about as wide differences as those between any other two community colleges in the group of five represented are reported in Table 9.5. College A is in Illinois and has been in operation for at least twenty years. College B is in Florida and, when checklists were administered, was in its third year of operation. The average percentages per area (at foot of table) are not far apart—including

TABLE 9.5
COMPARISON OF TWO JUNIOR COLLEGES IN THE PERCENTAGES OF THEIR STUDENTS CIRCLING PROBLEMS IN EACH OF THE 11 AREAS ON THE MOONEY PROBLEM CHECK LIST

Area	College A (185)*	College B (140)*
I. HPD	33.5	35.7
II. FLE	41.6	44.3
III. SRA	40.0	38.6
IV. SPR	30.8	35.7
V. PPR	57.8	48.6
VI. CSM	39.5	40.7
VII. HF	38.9	35.7
VIII. MR	28.6	32.9
IX. ACW	46.6	68.6
X. FVE	41.6	32.9
XI. CTP	28.6	34.3
Average Per Cent Per Area	38.3	40.7

*Number of students.

about two-fifths of all students. For six of the areas, the percentages are not far from being on a par; for two (Areas V and X), they are appreciably smaller for College B, and for three (Areas IV, IX, and XI) appreciably larger. No explanations for these differences are readily apparent, except to some extent for the largest, which is that for the area of Adjustment to College Work (IX). The checklist was administered in mid-semester in College A, whereas it was administered near the end of the semester in College B. It is more than probable that the concerns of marks and scholarship were more prominently in the mind of students in College B, to account in considerable part for this large difference, which suggests that time and circumstances can to a degree influence the proportions. Nevertheless, this comparison reaffirms the conclusion above that large proportions of students report problems that seem serious to them in all the areas of the checklist.

The specific problems of highest and lowest frequency.—Up to this point in reporting on the special project on the problems of community college students, the focus, as already intimated, has been on the areas in which the problems lie, and little or nothing has been disclosed concerning the specific problems included within the respective areas or the extent to which they were underlined or circled by the sample of students. Unless the reader has had prior acquaintance with the checklist, his comprehension of the significance of the project must remain inadequate until the nature of these detailed items is brought to his attention.

To reproduce the entire list of 330 items in this treatise, in order to remedy the deficiency, is not practicable. Nor is it feasible to cite illustrations of problem patterns of individual students extensively enough to give the reader a well-ordered view of the incidence of specific problems for individual subjects. The confusion resulting from such a presentation may be hinted at by citing the patterns of problems circled by two freshman students in one of the two community colleges in Illinois, one being a boy of sixteen and the other a man of thirty. It happens that these two students, without request, supplied additional information concerning their situations in the portions of the form following the list of items, where certain general questions are asked, aimed at obtaining a summary in the students' own words. The boy summarized that his "main problem" was "no steady income." He reported that he lived on a farm and got "part of the crops" and also "did farm work for neighbors during vacations, but not enough for school." He disliked "to keep asking parents for money." He had circled 8 problems and underlined 27. Among the circled problems were "Needing a part-time job now" (FLE), "Transportation or commuting difficulty" (FLE), "Not spending enough time in study" (ACW), "Unable to enter desired vocation" (FVE), and "Unable to take the courses I want" (CTP). The man of thirty summarized as follows: "Being a church pastor, having a wife and five children and managing my farm, gives me too many outside interests for excellent college work. I am gradually lessening my farm work until this, my greatest problem, will be taken care of." He had circled only a single problem, "Having too many outside interests" (ACW).

A curtailed method of illustrating the nature of the detailed items that at the same time gives a partial overview of their incidence is to report the frequencies for those items in each area most often circled and also the frequencies for those least often circled. The most frequently circled are listed by area in Table 9.6 which cites the top four in frequency in each area, except for Area VI which has five because the last two were circled by equal numbers of students. In scanning the table the reader may be helped to an appreciation of the relative extent of concern by bearing in mind that the total number of students was 623 and also by noting the

TABLE 9.6
SPECIFIC PROBLEMS MOST FREQUENTLY CIRCLED IN EACH AREA
COMPARED WITH THE AVERAGE NUMBER OF STUDENTS
CIRCLING THE PROBLEMS IN THESE AREAS

	Frequency
I. HPD (13.1)	
Not getting enough sleep	55
Feeling tired much of the time	41
Being overweight	38*
Frequent headaches	22
II. FLE (22.8)	
Needing a part-time job now	75*
Needing a job during vacations	57
Too many financial problems	51*
Disliking financial dependence on others	40
III. SRA (17.9)	
Wanting to improve my mind	39
Wanting very much to travel	35
Wanting to improve my appearance	28*
Too little social life	28
IV. SPR (18.1)	
Wanting a more pleasing personality	47*
Being timid or shy	37
Feeling inferior	37*
Worrying how I impress people	34
V. PPR (21.4)	
Lacking self-confidence	61
Nervousness	56
Worrying about unimportant things	53*
Taking things too seriously	46*
VI. CSM (20.8)	
Wondering if I'll ever find a suitable mate	42*
Sexual needs unsatisfied	41*
Too few dates	38
Deciding whether I'm in love	32
Thinking too much about sex matters	32*
VII. HF (16.5)	
Wanting love and affection	36
Irritated by habits of a member of my family	30
Not getting along with a member of my family	29
Family quarrels	28
VIII. MR (16.7)	
Wanting to feel close to God	66*
Not going to church often enough	47
Can't forget some mistakes I've made	29*
Wanting to understand more about the Bible	28
IX. ACW (41.7)	
Not knowing how to study effectively	107
Not spending enough time in study	93
Easily distracted from my work	80
Having a poor background for some subjects	80

TABLE 9.6—Continued

X. FVE (18.3)	
Wondering if I'll be successful in life	59
Not knowing what I really want	59
Needing to decide on an occupation	34
Restless at delay in starting life work	32
XI. CTP (12.7)	
Hard to study in living quarters	53
Campus lacking in recreational facilities	28
Too much work required in some courses	25
Forced to take courses I don't like	23

*Problems with relatively large difference of incidence for the two sexes.

average numbers of students circling the items in each of these areas. These averages are given in parentheses in the table following the key letters of the areas. These averages were obtained by dividing all the circlings of items in each area by 30, which is, as already reported, the number of items in each area. The average number of students circling each of the 330 problems in the entire checklist was just a shade below an even 20, being 19.98.

To acquaint himself with the nature of the detailed items in the checklist the reader may wish to examine Table 9.6 with care. Attention will be directed here only to some of those of greatest frequency, and to differences of incidence for men and women. The four most frequent in the list of 45 items are those in the area of Adjustment to College Work, which have to do with effective study, time in study, distraction from work, and poor background for some subjects. The prominence of these items is in harmony with that of this area as reported in Tables 9.3, 9.4, and 9.5. The next highest frequency is for "Needing a part-time job now" in the area of Finances, Living Conditions, and Employment, and this item is seen to be associated with other rather similar items circled with high frequency in this area and combining to lift the area into prominence. Other instances of relatively high recurrence of circling among the 45 items of this long table are "Not getting enough sleep" (I, HPD), "Wanting a more pleasing personality" (IV, SPR), "Wanting to feel close to God" (VIII, MR), "Wondering if I'll be successful in life" and "Not knowing what I really want" (both in X, FVE), and "Hard to study in living quarters" (XI, CTP).

In dealing with the differences in incidence for men and women in their circling of items of "most concern," it is essential to have at hand the percentages for each sex on each item. These percentages were computed but are not reported in Table 9.6 because of problems of space. However, the chief significance can be made apparent by generalizing from the evidence and by citing the items on which the proportions of men and women students differed most widely. Of the 45 items listed in the table, larger percentages of women than men circled 30, or two-thirds, and larger percentages of men circled the remaining 15, or a third of all. This is accordant with the evidence in Table 9.4, in which the percentages for 8 of the 11 areas and the total average at the bottom are larger for women than for men. For 13 of the items, the differences between the sexes were 4 per cent or larger, and 4 of these differences apply to men and 9 to women. These items were marked with an asterisk (*) in the table. The four items for men are: "Needing a part-time job now" (II), with a percentage difference of 6.5; "Too many financial problems" (II), 5.3; "Sexual needs unsatisfied" (VI), 9.1; and "Thinking too much about sex matters" (VI), 4.0. The items for women are: "Being overweight" (I), 6.7; "Wanting to improve my appearance" (III), 5.4; "Wanting a more pleasing personality" (IV), 4.0; "Feeling inferior" (IV), 4.5; "Worrying about unimportant things" (V), 8.7; "Taking things too seriously" (V), 4.3; "Wondering if I'll ever find a suitable mate" (VI), 8.0; "Wanting to feel close to God" (VIII), 4.9; "Can't forget some mistakes I've made" (VIII), 4.5.

Something may be added to understanding the problem situation of community college students by brief illustration of the items least frequently circled. The illustration may be prefaced by stating that not a single item in the total array of 330 in the checklist failed to receive indication of being of "most concern" to at least one student, and that 41 different items circled one to five times, accounting for 2.1 per cent of all circlings. The items are listed here in the order of area, with the least frequency for items in the area reported in parentheses. For areas where two or more items were circled with identical frequency, the first item in the check list with this frequency is cited: (HPD) "Sometimes feeling faint or dizzy" (1); (FLE) "Tiring of the same meals all the time" (2); (SRA) "Nothing interesting to do in vacations" (3); (SPR) "Losing friends" (2); (PPR) "Feeling life has given me a raw deal" (5); (CSM) "Embarrassed by talk about sex" (4); (HF) "Relatives interfering with family affairs" (4); (MR) "Failing to see the relation of religion to life" (1); (ACW) "Needing a vacation from school" (8); (FVE) "Family opposing my choice of vocation" (3); (CTP) "Classes too large" (2). The illustrations manifest a diversity hardly less obvious than shown by the items found among the most frequent. Some seem to suggest serious problems, while others are vague but may conceal problems of real concern.

Problems of married students.—One phase of this study of problems of community college students with noteworthy findings is that involving a comparison of the incidence of the problems of married students with those of the entire sample. Before taking up this comparison it is necessary to make a brief report on the number and proportion who reported they were married and on their ages. The total of married students in the sample of 623 was 77, 48 of them men and 29 women. The percentage of the total sample married was 12.4—very near one-eighth of all. The percentages for men and women married were almost identical, being respectively, 12.2 and 12.7. These numbers are not large, but large enough to justify the comparisons made.

A remarkable contrast emerges in comparing the distributions of ages of the married men and women. Tabulation disclosed that, while both groups ranged widely in age (from 17 to 40 for men and from 18 to 47 for women), the men were mainly in the younger age-groups and the women were mainly in the older groups. This may be seen in the facts that while

TABLE 9.7
MEDIAN AND FIRST AND THIRD QUARTILE NUMBERS OF PROBLEMS UNDERLINED
AND CIRCLED BY MARRIED STUDENTS IN FIVE JUNIOR COLLEGES

Sex	Underlined			Circled		
	Median	First Quartile	Third Quartile	Median	First Quartile	Third Quartile
Men (48)*	18	11	33	4	1	8
Women (29)*	18	9	30	2	1	5

*Number of students represented.

39, or over four-fifths of the 48 men, were 26 years of age and under, 22, or over three-fourths of the women, were 27 and over. If anything approaching these differing proportions holds true for most community colleges, as may well be, it indicates a different type of function for the two sexes: for most men the community college is laying the foundation for their first and presumably their permanent careers, while for many, perhaps even most, women it may be providing preparation for a second career.

The evidence on problems checked finds a striking difference between the married students and the total sample in incidence both (1) in the numbers of problems and (2) in some of the areas most frequently checked. The median numbers and interquartile ranges underlined and circled by the married men and women students are shown in Table 9.7. These measures are seen to be not far from equal for the two sexes, although they tend to be slightly higher for men than for women, a difference that may be explicable by the contrasting age distributions already reported. The strikingness of the differences between total incidence of problems for married students and the total sample emerges from comparison of the measures in this table with those in Table 9.2, in which the corresponding measures far exceed those for the married students in the total sample. This large difference in incidence is given emphasis by the mean numbers of problems circled by the married students and the total sample, respectively, 5.7 and 10.6. The indisputable inference is that married students report far fewer problems than the total sample, which is seven-eighths single students.

The percentage distributions by areas of problems circled for married students of the two sexes are shown in Table 9.8. This table also indicates the ranks of the areas according to these percentages from the largest percentage downward. It may be seen that, as for all groups in earlier interpretations in this chapter, the area of Adjustment to College Work also looms largest for these students. A glance down the columns finds the area of Courtship, Sex, and Marriage with almost negligible percentages and in the lowest rank for both sexes. This is much lower than the

TABLE 9.8
PERCENTAGE DISTRIBUTIONS OF PROBLEMS CIRCLED BY MARRIED STUDENTS* IN FIVE JUNIOR COLLEGES ON THE MOONEY PROBLEM CHECK LIST AND RANK ORDERS OF FREQUENCY ACCORDING TO DISTRIBUTION

Area	Men		Women	
	Per Cent	Rank	Per Cent	Rank
I. HPD	8.9	5½	9.5	5
II. FLE	15.1	2	8.8	6
III. SRA	9.2	4	7.3	8
IV. SPR	4.6	8½	11.7	3½
V. PPR	8.9	5½	14.6	2
VI. CSM	1.6	11	1.5	11
VII. HF	4.6	8½	11.7	3½
VIII. MR	6.9	6	8.0	7
IX. ACW	24.6	1	20.4	1
X. FVE	12.1	3	2.2	10
XI. CTP	3.6	10	3.6	9

*48 men and 29 women.

rank of this area for the total sample shown in Table 9.3, where it is ranked 4 with 9.4 per cent of all problems. Further comparison of the rankings in the two tables prompts the following observations: the first area, Health and Physical Development, has higher ranks for married students than for the total sample: the area of Finances, Living Conditions, and Employment is ranked 2 for the married men, which is the same rank it has in Table 9.3, although its rank is lower for married women; the area of Personal-Psychological Relations ranks second for married women and within one point of the same rank for the total sample; the area of Home and Family ranks higher for married women than for the total sample; and the area of The Future: Vocational and Educational ranks considerably higher for married men than for both married women and the total sample.

Relatively little is added, beyond what has already been reported, to the understanding of problems of married students from inquiring into the frequency of circling of specific items on the checklist, as was done for the total sample. This may be in part owing to the small number of married students and the consequently much smaller incidence of circling. Only 39 of the total of 330 items were circled by 4 (5.2 per cent) or more students, and 10 by 6 (7.8 per cent) or more students. Of these 10, 4 are in the area of Adjustment to College Work, which we already know to be an area of major concern, 2 are in Health and Physical Development, and the remaining 4 scattered singly to as many other areas. Among these 10 items, the incidences for 5 show some predominance for one sex or the other: (1) "Not getting enough sleep" has a higher proportionate incidence for women than men; (2) "Too many financial problems," more for men than women; (3) "Carrying heavy home responsibilities," more for women than men; (4) "Weak in spelling and grammar," more for men than women; and (5) "Slow in reading," more for women than men. Predominance for the second and third items seems more rational than for the others.

The upshot of this comparison of the problems of married students and the total sample is that marriage reduces markedly the aggregate of problems of "most concern" and also reduces the incidence of these problems in all the areas and in varying degrees. Thus, those persons who have been advocating permissiveness of marriage for college students have another argument, or at least a variant of their argument, for previous support of their position.

Other Studies with the Mooney List

Variation among the studies.—Resort to the Mooney Check List in the project just reported makes possible some comparison of the findings with those of investigations that have been reported following its use in other institutions at the collegiate level. A number of such studies are in print in educational and psychological periodicals, as may be noted in the References and Bibliography at the end of this chapter. Unfortunately, from the standpoint of making comparisons, they are made and reported variously, some emphasizing the outcomes of underlining by students, others the outcomes of combining counts of underlining and circling, and a few only being based mainly, as in the project above, on the evidence from the circling of items of most concern. The results of this smaller number of reports are used at this point for comparison with the statistical findings of the study just reported, and further conclusions pertinent to community colleges will be drawn from others in this group of investigations in which the checklist was administered to students in universities.

Comparison of the findings.—Three of these previously published studies made on students at the collegiate level reported average numbers of circled problems. The investigations, with these averages, are as follows: Bennett (2) on 1,000 freshmen at the Ohio State University, 4.5; Houston and Marzolf (10) on 404 entering freshmen of both sexes at Illinois State Normal University, 5.8; Stone (26) on 352 freshmen and 126 sophomore men and women at River Falls (Wisconsin) State Teachers College, respectively, 6.3 and 7.3. The average for both men and women for the community college sample is 10.6, while those for men and women separately are, respectively, 10.2 and 11.2, with the average for women one item larger than that for men. Thus, the averages for the community college sample are much larger than those for the other student populations. Nothing in the studies affords a clue to this wide difference, although speculation over differences in the average numbers for the areas or for individual items may be suggestive in this direction.

For purposes of further comparison, rankings have been assigned, in the order from largest downward, to the average numbers of problems in each of the 11 areas, for all studies for which these averages of circled problems are readily available. This has been done for the sample of community college students and for three investigations in other types of institutions, namely, the investigations by Bennett and by Stone from which total averages have just been cited, and an investigation by Klohr (16), involving 117 women, mostly freshmen but including a small number of transfer students, enrolled in an introductory course in home economics at the University of Illinois. The rankings have been assembled in Table 9.9. For convenience in considering similarities and differences the first column presents the rank order for both sexes combined in the community colleges. Before turning to the comparisons of these rankings with those for the three other institutions, running commentary is made, in part by repetition, on the differences in rank orders for the two sexes in the community college. This is done the better to speculate over the reasons for differences between the rankings for students in the community colleges and the other institutions. The more frequent concern of men than women with problems of Finance, Living Conditions, and Employment has been previously noted. The higher frequencies for women in Personal-Psychological and Social-Psychological Relations are probably explained by their stronger personal-social interests. The higher position for men of the area of The Future: Vocational and Educational probably is induced by the traditionally greater concern in our culture for careers for men. The higher ranking for women of Home and Family emerges from their closer association with or dependence on the institution of the family.

The most conspicuous fact disclosed by the comparison of the rankings across the table is the uniformity with which the area of Adjustment to

College Work takes first place in students' problems. Among other approximations to equivalence of rankings, although they are not identical as for this first one, are those for Personal-Psychological Relations, which are relatively high, and for Morals and Religion, which are relatively low. For Home and Family the rankings are lower, as already pointed out, for women in other colleges than for community college women: this can be an area of somewhat less concern for students living away from home. The relatively lower ranking of the area of Courtship, Sex, and Marriage for

TABLE 9.9
RANK ORDERS OF PROBLEM AREAS ACCORDING TO AVERAGE NUMBERS OF PROBLEMS CIRCLED IN EACH OF THE 11 AREAS BY A SAMPLE OF COMMUNITY COLLEGE STUDENTS AND BY STUDENTS IN THREE OTHER STUDIES

Area	Community College Sample			Bennett (2)*	Klohr (16)*	Stone (26)*
	Men and Women (623)†	Men (395)	Women (228)	Men (1,000)	Women (117)	Men and Women (478)
IX. (ACW)	1	1	1	1	1	1
II. (FLE)	2	2	8	5	10½	4
V. (PPR)	3	5	2	4	2	3
VI. (CSM)	4	3	5	6	8	8
X. (FVE)	5	4	10	2	6	2
IV. (SPR)	6	8	3	9	7	9
III. (SRA)	7	6	6	3	3	6
VII. (HF)	8½	9	4	10	9	10
VIII. (MR)	8½	7	7	11	10½	11
I. (HPD)	10	11	9	7	4	7
XI. (TCP)	11	10	11	8	5	5

*Number in list of References and Bibliography at end of chapter.
†Number of students included.

students in the last three columns may be explained by their being in a new environment with new associates, whereas the community college students are attending an institution with most of the same associates they have had for many years. The high ranking of The Future: Vocational and Educational for freshmen in a large state university (see Bennett column) is explicable by the uncertainty of many concerning careers at this age-level and classification, while the somewhat lower ranking of this area for women in a home economics course (Klohr column) may be because women are somewhat less often career conscious.

It is probably not profitable to speculate over the smaller differences in ranking for student groups like those represented in Table 9.9. The difference between the highest and lowest averages for individual areas that determined the rankings for community college men and women combined in Table 9.9 is only from 2.0 to .6, and the differences in averages for other groups are comparable. It is clear from this that a ranking of the areas from 1 to 11, as has here been reported, is not in proportion to the averages, and that the method of ranking, while helping to an understanding of the differences, exaggerates them. This is no less true for the other types of institutions, for which the total averages of problems were reported above to be much smaller than for the community colleges. The unequivocal conclusion from the whole comparison is that, while the area of Adjustment to College Work looms larger than others in all the types of institutions represented, large proportions of students in all the types of institutions also identify problems of most concern in all the areas.

Comparability of the evidence concerning the sample of community college students with that concerning students in other colleges and universities with respect to detailed items checked (within the areas) is seriously impeded, first, by the lack of information in most of the reports on frequency of checking of these items, and, second, by the lack of uniformity in reporting the frequencies. When supplied, the frequencies are based on underlining or on underlining and circling combined, and not on circling alone, as are those that were mentioned for illustration above for the community college sample.

The only studies available that allow for even inadequate comparison are two involving women only, one by Klohr (*16*) already represented in Table 9.9, and the other by Mooney (*21*) concerned with 171 freshmen women in the Ohio State University. In the comparison of problems of community college women with those of Klohr's women in the University of Illinois, the 18 most frequent items as circled by the former group were checked against the 18 most frequent items underlined by the Illinois group. Ten of the items were identical, with concentrations in the areas of Personal-Psychological Relations and Adjustment to College Work. Thus eight of the items were different for each of the two groups. However, there was a further partial concentration for each of the two groups in the area of Adjustment to College Work, although the concentration was on different items. Remaining items were somewhat more widely distributed among the areas for the community college than for the Illinois women. It is impracticable to do more than illustrate these remaining items: for the community college women, examples are "Being overweight" (HPD), "Wondering if I'll ever find a suitable mate" (CSM), and "Not knowing what I really want" (FVE), while for the Illinois women examples are "Daydreaming" (PPR) and "Not enough time to myself" (SRA).

The only area for which frequency is reported for detailed items in the Bennett study is Adjustment to College Work, and comparison here must be made with most frequent items circled by community college women with those "marked" by the freshman women at the Ohio State

University. Comparing the top 13 items in these two lists of frequencies finds 9 of them identical, with only 4 in each of the lists different.

While the evidence on similarities and differences on checking specific items is too meager to warrant an assured conclusion, it may nevertheless be ventured that there is nothing in it that points to problem patterns any different from those suggested by the rankings of the areas as previously interpreted.

Two other articles which report on applications of the Mooney Problem Check List in state universities should have meaning for the community college, and in diverse directions. One is by Horrall (9) and was made at Purdue University; in the other, Williams (28) discusses the uses made of the checklist in the General College at the University of Minnesota. The study at Purdue was concerned with freshmen and involved administration of several measuring instruments, those with results of most concern to issues here being the ACE Psychological Examination, English and Mathematics Examinations, and, as mentioned, the Mooney Problem Check List. An experimental group of students was identified with percentile ranks at or below the tenth percentile on the ACE Psychological Examination and below the thirtieth percentile on the English and Mathematics Examinations. These were matched with two control groups as to sex, academic school in the university, membership in a social fraternity ("organized" or "unorganized"), and financial status (that is, whether earning money or being family-supported). Subjects in the control groups were chosen from (1) the middle range in the Psychological Examination Scores, fortieth to sixtieth percentiles, and the thirtieth to seventieth percentiles on the English and Mathematics tests, and (2) from the ninetieth percentile upward on the Psychological Examination and at or above the seventieth percentile on the English and Mathematics tests. The numbers of subjects in the three groups were, respectively, 70, 68, and 69. The mean percentile ranks of the three groups were reported, respectively, at 4.80, 47.07, and 87.59. Administration to these students of the Mooney Check List found the lowest group to have the greatest number of problems, the middle group to have the next highest number, and the high group to mark the smallest number of problems in the areas of Personal-Psychological Relations, Adjustment to College Work, and Curriculum and Teaching Procedures. The same progression from low to middle to high appeared in the three types of total scores obtained: total number of underlined problems, total number of circled problems, and total number of underlined problems that were also circled. Computation of critical ratios for the differences in numbers of problems in the area of Adjustment to College Work found that between the low and middle groups to be 3.4, that between the middle and high groups to be 4.3, and that between the low and high groups to be 7.6, all these ratios indicating statistical significance.

The findings of higher incidence of problems with students of lower college aptitude is to be expected, especially in the area of Adjustment to College Work, and is significant for the community college which, as an "open-door" institution, typically admits and endeavors to serve the needs of all high school graduates. It is interesting in this connection that Horrall concludes that "those students who are low in intelligence as measured by the ACE Psychological Examination appear to constitute a radically different group from those who are in the middle or at the top of the distribution." Under "Recommendations" the investigator "strongly suggests that the University should raise entrance barriers, making it impossible for those of low college aptitude to enter a situation in which from the outset they are bound to face discouragement, defeat, and eventually a doubt as to their own ability and worth." Another recommendation is that until the university can bring itself to adopt the recommendation of exclusion, it should set up a one-year curriculum for these students of low college aptitude, and then "guide them into jobs commensurate with their abilities. . . ." An appropriate observation at this point is that development of the community college has been discouraged rather than encouraged in Indiana, the location of Purdue University, and that the nearest approach to it is the extension centers of the universities, which are hardly up to the full range of community college service.

The article by Williams (28) bears mainly on the problems in a single area of the Mooney Check List, that of Home and Family, and affords a perceptive discussion of these problems in the University of Minnesota's General College, which she refers to as a "community college," since two-thirds of its students came from the Twin Cities and the immediate vicinity. As with all community colleges, most students in the General College are commuters, prevailingly living at home. From analysis of the results of administering the checklist to the students, she found, to use her designations, that "problems of educational and vocational adjustment" (ACW) were most frequent, "problems of personal-social-emotional adjustment" (presumably PPR and SPR) next most frequent, and "problems of family adjustment" (HF) third on the list. This appears to be the rank order of top areas reported for community college women in Table 9.9. Williams says that "a slightly higher percentage of women than men admit family problems," from which it may be assumed that this proportion was relatively greater than for the sample of community college men, for whom the rank reported in Table 9.9 is low, and for whom we have already noted that the ranking is different from that for women. Illustrations of detailed problems named in the report are "being unjustly criticized by parents, being treated like a child at home, not getting along with siblings, general family quarrels, and severe illness of one parent."

In assessing the results of administering the checklist, Williams points out what has already been intimated in first describing it earlier in the chapter, that there is "nothing subtle or devious" about it, and that any student who chooses to conceal his real worries may easily do so. She regards it as obvious that the frequency of problems revealed is "a minimum estimate of their true frequency," and this opinion should apply no less to problems in the area of home and family than to others. She penetrates the issue further by asserting that "some kinds of behavior defined as maladjustive by a clinician may not be a cause of worry to the student—a notable example being the student completely satisfied with a state of overdependence."

Williams' analysis and observations are of peculiar significance to the community college, which, by contrast with the residential college, has a more serious responsibility in aiding its students to achieve in wholesome ways the developmental task of emancipation from home and parents. While admitting that only a minority of students in a typical college population are suffering from serious family adjustment problems, Williams urges that this minority is a source of proper concern for the college. Her recommendations of ways of helping these students include (a) alerting staff members to the possibility of family troubles in any student, (b) "including within the curriculum a generous number of courses open to all students in which a student can acquire understandings and attitudes which have immediate, practical, and specific bearing upon his personal and family adjustments, present and future," and (c) providing staff members "(counselor, dean, specially trained instructor) whose time and skill can be made available . . . to students most seriously troubled by and eager to find solutions to their family problems."

Further Studies of Problems

In junior college.—Among other published studies of student problems that appear to be of enough significance to be briefly reviewed in this chapter are one reported by Douglas and Rack (5) in two parts and based on evidence coming from junior colleges and another by Stratton and Schleman (27) having to do with problems in social usage as these were reported by students in a number of colleges and universities. The evidence for the first of these investigations was obtained by questionnaire from 1,956 students in 20 junior colleges in Texas which the authors assure us "represented a well-scattered geographic distribution." The 64 problems, chosen after preliminary experiment, were assigned, 8 each, to 8 categories as follows: (1) Social Relations, (2) Home and Family, (3) Adjustment to School Work, (4) Preparation for the Future, (5) Religion and Morals, (6) Recreation and Use of Leisure, (7) Health and Physical Development, and (8) Finances. These are seen to correspond, except for the number of categories, to areas in the Mooney Check List. This correspondence is true also for many of the specific statements, except for total number, as may be seen in these statements as they are cited for illustration below. The procedure used in obtaining indication of the relative seriousness of the problems to the student was to ask him to rank the specific statements under each category from 1 through 8 "in the order of importance to him as a junior college student," with the statement ranked first as a major source of distress and that ranked eighth as least important. Unlike the procedure used for the Mooney Check List, the results yielded measures of relative importance of problems within each category, but without comparison of the categories with each other. A detail of procedure for the tables for each category was to compute and compare the sums of first and second rankings and of the seventh and eighth rankings for each statement.

The first of the two articles compares the percentages for private and public junior colleges. Examination of the percentages finds wide differences for the individual statements in each category. As an example of the range, it may be reported that the percentage of first and second rankings by students in public junior colleges of "Inability to concentrate" in the category of "Adjustment to College Work" is shown as 40.07, while that for "Do not get enough personal attention in college" is 12.63. However, the differences between percentages for the two groups of institutions, private and public, are not large: for "Inability to concentrate" it is only that between 45.07 and 40.07 per cent. The final rankings of the eight statements within this category are identical for the two groups of institutions. In summary of the article the authors say that the students seem able to indicate the relative importance of the problems but that the two groups of students are "very much alike with respect to the problems about which they are most and least concerned."

In the second part of the study by Douglas and Rack (5) the students were grouped by size of enrollment of the junior colleges. The institutions were placed in three divisions as follows: Group A, 300 students or fewer; Group B, 300 to 1,000; Group C, over 1,000. Otherwise, the evidence is treated in the same way as in the first part of the investigation. Outcomes of this compilation do not differ markedly from, as just illustrated, those derived from grouping by type of control, as public or private. The rankings disclose the ability of students within each size group to differentiate the problems. For example, the percentages of first and second rankings combined finds the highest item under the category Adjustment to College Work to be "Inability to Concentrate," at 45.26, 42.93, and 36.09, respectively, and the percentages of these rankings to be lowest for all three groups for "Do not get enough personal attention in college," at 5.77, 12.25, and 13.02. The rankings of the remaining six problems in this category do not correspond for all three groups, but it is impossible to discern any consistent tendency by size of enrollment in the rank order of problems in this or the other seven categories. The conclusions of the authors are, therefore, that "there is much greater agreement than difference between groups," and "no dependable relationships between the sizes of the schools . . . and the problems with which the students are concerned."

Thus, the outcomes of this investigation are negative as concerns the hypotheses implied for it, namely, that auspices of organization, public or private, under which they operate or size of enrollment might be factors of differentiation with respect to the incidence of students' problems, at least with respect to incidence within the categories, although it does not answer the question of differences between the total categories of Social Relations, Home and Family, etc. What may be assumed to be significant factors between categories, referred to as "areas," were, however, found in investigations reviewed above. These are mainly classification (freshmen or sophomore), sex, age, and ability as measured by a test of general aptitude.

Problems of etiquette.—The study by Stratton and Schleman (27) is different from those previously reported or reviewed in this chapter in that it does not deal with problems in any comprehensive sense, but only with problems of social usage or etiquette. It was made from replies of students in nine widely distributed institutions, mainly universities, but including a few teachers colleges, by means of a sort of "open-end" questionnaire directing students to "jot down specific detailed questions of social usage or etiquette which have puzzled you as a college student. Let your questions concern any areas of social behavior which come to your mind. . . ." A total of 6,200 questions were turned in. Tabulations reported are by individual institutions and for the entire group of institutions, without regard to classification or sex, which might have yielded some interesting and significant differences. The topics into which the twenty most frequent questions fell for the entire body of questions, from the highest frequency downward, were: Introductions, Table Manners, Conduct in Public Places, Dates, Clothes, Dances, Smoking and Drinking, Receptions and Teas, Restaurants, "Petting," "Co-ed bids," Conversation, Cars, "Dutch treats," Flowers, Correspondence, Addressing faculty, Theater, Courtesy to elders (including chaperones), and Telephone calls.

The authors, who were, respectively, a dean of women and a director of residence halls for women, observe that the questions cover most of the areas traditionally dealt with in books on etiquette and also "many aspects of campus life in which practice has not yet been standardized." They point out that "questions of the latter kind cannot be found in manuals of etiquette." They say further that the significance which may be attached to such a study will depend largely on the reader's philosophy of education: "If he believes that the sole responsibility of the colleges is to encourage and develop mental abilities and intellectual interests of their students, he will consider this study irrelevant and of no significance. . . . If, on the other hand, he believes with the writers that the colleges have a responsibility for encouraging and assisting their students to become socially adequate, well-poised individuals, as well as for encouraging their intellectual development, he may find this study concerning the problems in social usage which puzzle college students of interest to him." The place in the program suggested by these authors for recognition of the need they believe they see is in the freshman orientation course.

Uses of Data on Student Problems

Where the data have been put to use.—Before summarizing this chapter on student problems report will be made on the uses to which the information supplied by the checklists has been or may be put. Some of these uses are identified or implicit in the foregoing treatment, and the manuals on the instruments, from which quotation might be made, suggest possible applications, but it seems preferable to draw mainly on reports of experience in applications of the data in actual school practice. This will be accomplished by an effort to illustrate and generalize from published reports on such uses. Reliance for this digest on use will be placed on eight articles which are among the more pragmatic available. Half of these have already been cited in the foregoing review of the incidence of problems. The presentation will be by paraphrase and quotation.

The features of educational practice in which the uses reviewed are reported fall into three main aspects, namely (1) guidance and counseling, (2) research, and (3) the broad area of curriculum and instruction, and also the extracurriculum. This canvass of uses may be regarded as both rounding out the treatment in the current chapter and as anticipatory to consideration of the serviceability of instruments like the problem checklists in connection with the curriculum and student services dealt with in Part III.

Use in guidance and counseling.—The eight writings are unanimous in ascribing value in guidance and counseling to use of the problem checklists. Limitations of the checklists in the respect that they can only spot the problems the subjects are willing and themselves able to identify have been touched on earlier in the chapter, and one of the writers (*28*) has previously been cited as saying of the Mooney Check List that there "is nothing subtle or devious" about it, while still another (6) admits that it is "not a depth technique. . . . It is not useful for the systematic study of the unconscious." Nevertheless, both these authors report on helpful experience with the list, and this second author elaborates by saying that it may be used to facilitate counseling by "preparing the counselee for an interview by giving him an opportunity to review and summarize his own problems and to see the full range of items he may wish to discuss, providing the counselor with a quick review of the various problems which are of express concern to the counselee, [and] establishing rapport by furnishing something concrete and, in a sense, impersonal about which to talk."

From among these reports of actual use of data from the checklists in guidance and counseling three more will be briefly abstracted. In one college (4) the checklist was administered twice, first in October and again in December, to freshmen in an orientation course, which is looked upon as an agency for guidance. Comparison of the results for the two applications found a decrease of 24 per cent during the interval in the average number of problems checked. The six areas of the checklist with the greatest declines were: Adjustment to College Work, 36 per cent; Social and Recreational Activities, 34 per cent; Morals and Religion, 30 per cent; Home and Family, 27 per cent; Health and Physical Development, 23 per cent; and Personal-Psychological Relations, 23 per cent. The author gives credit to the orientation course for the notable reduction in incidence.

In a pilot study (21) in a state university, the checklist was administered to a sample of freshmen women living in dormitories. Compilations of frequencies of marking items and in areas were made and those of highest frequency identified. One line of activities in guidance included publicizing widely in the dormitory the particular services on the campus to help students having problems with academic work, setting aside space in the dormitory where students could go at specified times for help on study problems, checking more closely on the conditions for study and sleep in the dormitories, and providing in the dormitories a circulating library of good books on emotional development. A second line was the more specific one of selecting on the basis of the checklists students to whom particular services could be directed. For example, 51 students were identified who marked more items in Adjustment to College Work than in any other area and these were considered as a group for whom problems in academic work should have special appeal. There were comparable groups in other areas. While community colleges do not typically operate dormitories, analogous activities are readily conceivable for populations of community college students.

The most extensive use in guidance of information from administering a checklist encountered in the group of eight articles appears to have been made on more than four hundred freshmen in a state university in the Midwest (*10*). Following tabulation from the lists the Student Personnel Committee of the institution agreed that the results were of such importance that they should be brought to the attention of the entire faculty. This committee, aware that totals and averages obscure individual cases, identified forty students who seemed to be in need of immediate help; it conferred with them, concerning their problems, with the goal of consulting faculty members of their choice. The presentation before the faculty "resulted in many profitable generalizations," with the result that the students' copies of the checklists were filed, for faculty reference, in the registrar's office with admission blanks, scholarship reports, and class schedules—all commonly used in counseling. Faculty members availed themselves of this access for a considerable proportion of students. Analysis of the lists led to the conclusion that certain problems were so prevalent and of such a nature that they could be handled by group approach, and the president of the university discussed briefly in freshman assembly such matters as budgeting one's time and choice of student activities. The Committee on Remedial Instruction canvassed the lists to identify the students who thought they had weak backgrounds in grammar, spelling, writing, and mathematics and who were not already enrolled in noncredit courses in these areas. The students were "told of the benefits which might accrue to them . . . from instruction of this type." A large faculty committee, appointed to determine steps to be taken to effect maximum personal development in the students, began with the area Social and Recreational Activities, but soon spread its inquiry and efforts to most of the categories of the checklist. One member of the Student Personnel Committee became so interested in problems marked in the area of Health that he made a list of students who had underlined or circled them and submitted it to the university physician who checked the health problems which the students thought they had against the records from physical examinations.

The authors generalize from the experience by saying that the use of the checklist "served as a means of sensitizing the faculty to the specific problems of the individual students." They close their report, however, with observations not in conflict with the limitations on the usefulness of the lists that were mentioned earlier in the chapter: "Frequency of expressed concern and of expressed serious concern is not a valid index of genuine seriousness of the problem; it may represent common rationalizations, superstitions, or misinformation. . . . The problem does not mean the same for all who are concerned about it. . . . "

Use in research.—As judged by the content of the eight articles being reviewed, the implications of the possibilities in research by use of the checklists are much less promising than they are for guidance and counseling. Only a half of the articles contain such implications, and in at least one or two, they are hardly more than intimations. One article, merely in passing, hints at the desirability of comparing the incidence of problems of students in a midwestern state university, from which he was reporting data from the checklists, with those of students in a small liberal arts college. A second article (4), the main finding of which was reported in the foregoing section on uses in guidance and counseling, reports on the changes in frequency of marking problems by the same students between two administrations of the checklists, which suggests the possibilities of investigating the effect of experimental programs on frequency of marking by students. A third article (9) is the one abstracted above in reporting on studies involving the use of the Mooney Problem Check List which was administered in conjunction with tests of scholastic aptitude and in English and mathematics and which showed students scoring low on these tests marking larger numbers of problems. The fourth article (24) reports a sort of pilot study on veterans of correlation between "indexes of concern" derived from administering the Mooney Check List and scores on a temperament test. Of course, almost all the articles report the results of administering the checklists to groups of students, that is, from inquiries of the "survey" type, but, notwithstanding their usefulness, critics are not inclined to regard these as qualifying on the canons of genuine research.

The hindrance to more extensive use of the checklist in research may be that it is not strictly objective. The authors of the Mooney Problem Check Lists themselves (22, 3) urge that it "is not a test" and they warn against the temptation to treat the number of items checked as a score. Nevertheless, they list research on the problems of youth as one of the broad classes of reasons for administering the instrument and identify the purposes of this research as follows: (1) to show changes and differences in problems in relation to age, sex, social background, school ability, interest patterns, and the like; (2) to discover clusters of associated problems; and (3) to measure changes brought about by a planned problem-reduction program (22, 3). A conservative observation would be that such instruments lend themselves to more and better research which uses the checklists than has typically been reported in print.

Use in curriculum and instruction.—The frequency of utilizing the results of administering a problem checklist in relation to curriculum and instruction as reflected in the eight articles is scarcely greater than for research, since it emerges only five times. One propitious instance is supplied in an application of results of administering the Mooney Check List to freshmen men in a large midwestern state university and reorganizing the results of the required course in hygiene around problems of high recurrence (2). Because problems in the area of Adjustment to College Work loomed largest in the tabulations, the first unit of the new outline was entitled "Adjustment to College Life and Mental Health." The second unit, called "Some Common Health Problems of College Men," was developed in relation to problems of high frequency marked in the area of Health and Physical Development, like "being underweight," visual defects, and poor teeth, and a third unit, called "Looking Ahead to Marriage," was developed around the problems checked in the area of Courtship, Sex, and Marriage. The instance previously cited of administering the same checklist twice in the same course in orientation to note changes in frequencies (4) suggests the feasibility of utilizing such results in appraising and deciding on units or other elements of such a course. Mention has already been made of the article (28) recommending the inclusion within the offering of a number of "courses in which the student can acquire understandings and attitudes which have immediate, practical, and specific bearing upon his personal and family adjustments. . . ." This article and two others speak of the service of the information from checklists in sensitizing the teaching faculty to the specific problems of students, which can be expected to lead to personalizing and individualizing teaching procedures. Two articles mention the services of the information in suggesting extension and other improvement of the program of student activities.

These instances of use of information from checklists in providing directives for curriculum and instruction fall far short of potentialities, as a further glance at the problem areas represented could confirm: merely to rename most of these areas in the Mooney Check List can prompt suggestions of new emphases or new units in existing courses, courses in addition to those in typical offerings, improved approaches in teaching, and diversification and re-invigoration of the extracurriculum. A look at the specific items that recur with greatest frequency in the student's returns within these areas will bolster the suggestion. A check of these areas and items against a list of the developmental tasks of later adolescence* brings additional confirmation.

The contention here is not at all that these problems are to be regarded as the sole source of direction for the curriculum and other portions of the educational program. Even when combined with a knowledge of the characteristics of students which the materials of Chapters 7 and 8 supply, they do not offer anything approaching a well-rounded basis for program-making. They afford suggestions only on the personal or individual aspects. The community college, no less than any other school, has the obligation

*See pp. 79–80.

also to serve society, as distinguished from serving the individual only, and to this end it has worked out some rather generally accepted social purposes. A formulation of these purposes is presented near the opening of Chapter 11 and they may be seen to bear mainly on this social function of the institution. Having a regard for these purposes at the same time that the characteristics and recurrent problems of the students are used as directives should achieve for the program a commendable individual-social balance.

Summary

Efforts have been made over a considerable period of years to ascertain the recurring problems of students and other young people. Procedures used in the inquiry have involved interviews, case study, and questionnaires. Earlier experiences have led to development and frequent resort to a variant of the questionnaire, the checklist. Two such instruments in recent use are the Mooney Problem Check List and the SRA Youth Inventory. The former was employed in the special study of problems of community college students, the results of which were reported above and compared with those obtained in other studies employing the instrument in colleges and in universities.

The Mooney Check List consists of 330 numbered "items," or problems, which the student underlines if they "suggest something which is troubling" him. He circles the numbers of the items that are "of most concern" to him. The items are distributed in 11 areas, with 30 items in each area. Special inquiry has found that few students identify the grouping. The areas are: I, Health and Physical Development; II, Finances, Living Conditions, and Employment; III, Social and Recreational Activities; IV, Social-Psychological Relations; V, Personal-Psychological Relations; VI, Courtship, Sex, and Marriage; VII, Home and Family; VIII, Morals and Religion; IX, Adjustment to College Work; X, The Future: Vocational and Educational; XI, Curriculum and Teaching Procedure. The instrument is not a test from which a score is derived and it is not intended to be a depth technique. Its value lies mainly in identifying the student's problems as he sees them and is willing to admit and discuss them. The originator says that its usefulness "lies in its economy for appraising the major concerns of the group and for bringing into the open the problems of each student in the group."

In the special community college study reported in this chapter the checklist was administered to a sampling of 623 community college students in five institutions in three states, two midwestern and one southern. The analysis of responses grouped the students by class (freshman and sophomore), sex, age (in three groups, 18 and under, 19 through 21, and

22 and over), and marital state. The typical numbers of problems underlined and circled, as indicated by the medians and interquartile ranges, do not differ strikingly for the sexes and for the two classes, although sophomore women tend to underline and circle more problems than sophomore men.

The proportionate distribution of circled problems for the total sample found by far the largest percentage—almost a fifth of all—in Adjustment to College Work. The next largest proportion, about a tenth of all, was that for Finance, Living Conditions, and Employment. Other relatively high proportions were in Personal-Psychological Relations and Courtship, Sex, and Marriage. Lowest proportions were in Health and Physical Development and Curriculum and Teaching Procedures. However, the proportions in these areas are considerable, and it is correct to conclude that large proportions of students have problems "of most concern" in all the areas.

Inquiry into the influence of class on the incidence of problems in the areas finds freshmen circling many more problems than sophomores in Personal-Psychological Relations and appreciably more in Social-Psychological Relations, both differences explainable by feelings of insecurity of newcomers in an institution. Other appreciable differences between the two classes are a higher frequency for sophomores in Adjustment to College Work and for freshmen in Finances, Living Conditions, and Employment. The only areas in which men circled more problems than women are Finances, Living Conditions, and Employment, whereas women circled items with notably greater frequency in all but a few of the remaining nine areas. While the proportions in a few of the areas show little change through the three age-groups, more of them show something approaching a consistent decline. Exceptions are Courtship, Sex, and Marriage, for which the proportion rises for the 19–21 group, to drop off sharply for those 22 and over; and Adjustment to College Work, for which the proportion is highest for the 19–21 group, but is still high for those 22 and over. In the main, the proportions by age suggest that these students are making progress toward achieving developmental tasks of adolescence.

Differences in incidence reported for individual community colleges were not found to be striking, although it is probable that, with more institutions in the sample, greater variation would have been found. The greatest difference found for two institutions compared was for Adjustment to College Work, and a plausible explanation for this is the time of administering the checklist which, for the community college with the greater incidence, was shortly before the period of examinations.

The nature of the specific items, or problems, may be indicated by quoting some of those circled with greatest frequency: the four most frequent are in the area of Adjustment to College Work and have to do with effective study, time in study, distraction from work, and poor background for some subjects. The prominence of these is in accord with that of this area as previously reported. The next highest frequency is for "Needing a part-time job now" in the area of Finances, Living Conditions, and Employment. Other instances of relatively high recurrence of circling are "Not getting enough sleep" in Health and Physical Development and "Wanting a more pleasing personality" in Social-Psychological Relationships. For the 45 items with highest frequency in the areas, the percentages for 30 were higher for women, and 15 higher for men.

Comparison of the incidences of problems for married students and for the total sample of community college students shows that the average total number of problems of "most concern" for the former group is much smaller—approximately half—than for the latter group. This inference applies equally to both sexes. For married students the incidence is highest for the area of Adjustment to College Work and lowest for Courtship, Sex, and Marriage. Understandable differences in incidence for the two sexes of married students are (a) a higher percentage for men than women in the area of Finances, Living Conditions, and Employment, and (b) a higher percentage for women than men in the area of Home and Family. The findings of this particular comparison afford ammunition for those who have been contending for permissiveness toward early marriage for college students.

Comparison of findings of studies using the Mooney Check List in other colleges and in universities is hindered by the varying procedures in compiling the responses. The most conspicuous conclusion from comparing the evidence for the community college sample with that from other institutions is that the area of Adjustment to College Work ranks highest in *all* the studies. Another area with a high ranking in all studies is Personal-Psychological Relations. The area of Morals and Religion tends to rank low in all. It should be said that the rankings exaggerate the differences between the types of institutions, and tend to obscure the fact that large proportions of students in all the institutions circle as serious many problems in all the eleven areas. An investigation at Purdue University involving the use, among other instruments, of the ACE Psychological Examination and the Mooney Check List, found a group with lowest ability marking the greatest number of problems, a middle group marking the next highest number, and a high group marking the smallest number of problems in the areas of Personal-Psychological Relations, Adjustment to College Work, and Curriculum and Teaching Procedures. A report of the application of the Mooney Check List in the study of problems of students in the University of Minnesota's General College, most of the students of which are commuters, has peculiar significance for community colleges by emphasizing the need for attention to problems of home and family of students who attend school while still living at home.

Two further studies of students' problems deserve mention. One study made in junior colleges in Texas secured the rankings by students of problems in eight areas rather similar to those in the Mooney Check List, and was aimed at comparing the responses from students in (a) private and public junior colleges and (b) junior colleges grouped by size of enrollment. The findings were essentially negative as to the influence of auspices under which the institution was operating, that is, private or public, and as to the influence of size. Thus, this investigation added no factor of influence on incidence of problems to those previously identified, which are classification of students, sex, age, marital status, and ability as measured by a psychological examination.

Still another study dealt with problems of social usage and etiquette of students in a number of higher institutions. A large number of such problems were identified, some being of sorts traditionally dealt with in manuals of etiquette and others peculiar to college campuses and not yet standardized. The investigators were of the opinion that such problems should have attention in freshman orientation courses.

The uses in educational practice of data on problems of students reported on checklists, as these uses turn up in reports and articles dealing with the lists, range through (1) guidance and counseling, (2) research, and (3) curriculum and instruction (with occasional reference to the extra-curriculum). On usefulness in guidance and counseling the reports are unanimous. While some of the articles point out that the instrument is not a depth technique, they nevertheless report or advocate use of the lists in preparing counselees for interviews and providing counselors with a quick review of express concerns of counselees. Other actual uses in guidance involved repeated administration to the same subjects to note changes in frequency of problems, and administration to identify students to be directed to various special services available in an institution. Uses in research are less often reported but include references to comparison of incidence for different types of higher institutions and comparison for students of varying abilities. A hindrance to more extensive application in research may be the fact that the checklists are not strictly objective. Instances of use of the returns from checklists as a source of directives in curriculum and instruction include the organization of units in a course in hygiene for freshmen, suggestions for "courses in which the student can acquire understandings and attitudes which have immediate, practical, and specific bearing upon his personal and family adjustments," and extensive utilization in sensitizing a teaching faculty to the specific problems of students, which can lead to personalized and individualized teaching.

The proportion of instances of use of checklist results as directives for improving curriculum and instruction fall far short of potentialities. However, the contention is not that these problems are to be regarded as the sole source of direction for the curriculum and other parts of the education program. Joined with knowledge of the characteristics of students canvassed in Chapters 7 and 8 they afford suggestions only on the personal and individual aspects. The directives for services to society are provided by the generally accepted social purposes of the community college. The recognition of students' characteristics and problems on one side and of socially oriented purposes on the other can provide an educational program of commendable individual-social balance.

References and Bibliography

1. Bell, Howard M. *Youth Tell Their Story: A Study of the Conditions and Attitudes of Young People between the Ages of 16 and 24.* Pp. 249–53. Washington: American Council on Education, 1938.
2. Bennett, Bruce L. "The Use of the Mooney Problem Check List for a College Hygiene Course." *Educational Research Bulletin,* 31 (Dec. 10, 1952), 231–40, 244.
3. Byrne, John T. *A Study of Student Problems in Catholic Men's Colleges.* Catholic University of America Educational Research Monographs xx. Washington: Catholic University Press, 1957.
4. Congdon, Nora A. "The Perplexities of College Freshmen." *Educational and Psychological Measurement,* 3 (Winter, 1943), 367–75.
5. Douglas, O. B., and Rack, Lucile. "Problems of Junior College Students." *Junior College Journal,* 20 (March–April, 1950), 377–89, 437–52.
6. Fick, Revel L. "Problem Check List: A Valuable Approach to Counseling." *Occupations,* 30 (March, 1952), 410–12.
7. Gordon, Leonard V. "The Reflection of Problem Changes by the Mooney Problem Check List." *Educational and Psychological Measurement,* 9 (Winter, 1949), 749–52.
8. Gordon, Leonard V., and Mooney, Ross L. "A Note on the Organization of the Mooney Problem Check List." *Educational Research Bulletin,* 28 (Nov. 9, 1949), 212–14.
9. Horrall, Bernice M. "Relationships between College Aptitude and Discouragement—Buoyancy Among College Freshmen." *Journal of Genetic Psychology,* 74 (June, 1949), 185–243.
10. Houston, V. M., and Marzolf, Stanley S. "Faculty Use of the Problem Check List." *Journal of Higher Education,* 15 (June, 1944), 325–28.
11. Hunter, Ruth A., and Morgan, David H. "Problems of College Students." *Journal of Educational Psychology,* 40 (Feb., 1949), 79–92.
12. Jameson, Samuel Haig. "Adjustment Problems of University Girls from the Urge for Recognition and New Experience." *Journal of Social Psychology,* 14 (August, 1941), 129–44.
13. Jameson, Samuel Haig. "Adjustment Problems of University Girls because of Parental Patterns." *Sociology and Social Research,* 24 (Jan.–Feb., 1940), 262–71.
14. Jameson, Samuel Haig. "Adjustment Problems of University Girls in Collective Living." *Social Forces,* 17 (May, 1940), 502–8.
15. Jameson, Samuel Haig. "Certain Adjustment Problems of University Girls." *Journal of Higher Education,* 10 (May, 1939), 249–55, 290.
16. Klohr, Mildred C. "Personal Problems of College Students." *Journal of Home Economics,* 40 (1948), 447–48.

17. Koile, Earle A., and Bird, Dorothy J. "Preferences for Counselor Help on Freshman Problems." *Journal of Counseling Psychology,* 3 (Summer, 1956), 97–106.
18. Lunger, Ruth, and Page, James D. "Worries of College Freshmen." *Journal of Genetic Psychology,* 54 (1939), 457–60.
19. McClusky, Howard Y. "The Changing Needs of Young Adults." In *Trends in Student Personnel Work,* edited by E. G. Williamson, pp. 40–51. Minneapolis: University of Minnesota Press, 1949.
20. McIntyre, Charles J. "The Validity of the Mooney Problem Check List." *Journal of Applied Psychology,* 37 (August, 1953), 270–72.
21. Mooney, Ross L. "Personal Problems of Freshman Girls." *Journal of Higher Education,* 14 (February, 1943), 84–90.
22. Mooney, Ross L., and Gordon, Leonard V. *The Mooney Problem Check List—Manual.* 1950 rev. New York: The Psychological Corporation, 1950.
23. Pressey, Luella C. *Some College Students and Their Problems.* Columbus: Ohio State University Press, 1929.
24. Singer, Stanley L., and Stefflre, Buford. "Concurrent Validity of the Mooney Problem Check List." *Personnel and Guidance Journal,* 35 (Jan., 1957), 298–301.
25. Smeltzer, C. H. "A Method of Determining What College Students Consider Their Own Difficulties." *School and Society,* 32 (Nov. 22, 1930), 709–10.
26. Stone, L. Gordon. "Student Problems in a Teachers College." *Journal of Educational Psychology,* 39 (Nov., 1948), 404–16.
27. Stratton, Dorothy C., and Schleman, H. B. "Problems in Social Usage Which Puzzle College Students." *Harvard Educational Review,* 8 (October, 1938), 485–94.
28. Williams, Cornelia D. "College Students' Family Problems." *Journal of Home Economics,* 42 (March, 1950), 179–81.

10
Adult Education and the Adult Student

THE EVIDENCE on the ages of junior college students reported in the opening section of Chapter 1 shows that substantial proportions of the full-time enrollments are adults. Many of these institutions also enroll adults in part-time and evening programs. Thus, a treatise on the community college student must also give consideration to the adult, and this is the concern of the current chapter. However, before proceeding to a digest of the evidence on the abilities and other characteristics of adults and of adult students, the status and growth of adult education generally and in junior colleges will be briefly reviewed, and the rationale of adult education will be canvassed. The treatment of ability of adults will proceed from consideration of their intelligence and the question of its decline or increase during the adult life-span, to their skill in reading, and to their competence in class performance in comparison with younger students. This chapter is concluded with a section on the characteristics and motives in attendance of adult students, and a summary.

Growth and Status of Adult Education

The phenomenal growth of adult education.—Among the most remarkable developments in the whole realm of schooling in our American society since the beginning of the century has been the spread of adult education. The proliferation of enrollments and offerings and programs for adults under various auspices has been on a scale somewhere nearly comparable to the growth of junior high schools and junior colleges, although one's impression is that these two movements may have got under way somewhat sooner. In important respects, as in the influence on educational democratization toward universalization, adult education may be considered as having been stimulated by similar social influences.

While it would be desirable to substantiate this assertion concerning the rapid growth generally in adult education over a half century or more, this cannot be adequately done because of the lack of evidence gathered on similar bases at year-points a few to several decades apart. The best that can be done is to cite evidence from a study of the status of adult education programs in the country for some recent period. Such a study has been reported by Woodward (66) for the year 1958–59. A repetition of this study for a later year has been promised and this, when made, will yield the evidence needed for a close-up measure of growth, at least in the sector of the field covered by this investigation. This sector is that of adult education programs offered by public school systems, but not including junior colleges and other public institutions at the higher levels. The universe specified for this survey included local public school systems enrolling 150 pupils or more in elementary and secondary full-time schools. In a first step of the procedure used in getting at the full extent of the programs the districts were classified in three groups according to the size of total elementary and secondary school enrollment, and requests for data on adult education went to a total count of the two groups of largest districts (with enrollments of 25,000 and over and 12,000 to 24,999, respectively) and to a sample only of the districts with smaller enrollments. For this third group, the estimate of the adult enrollment in all was projected on the basis of replies received from the sample. Reliability of the evidence is assured by the almost full count of responses received.

The total enrollment in adult education programs for the year estimated from this careful procedure was 3,428,000, of whom all were in classes except for about 7,000 in correspondence courses and in private lessons or other individual activities. The "unduplicated count" of persons participating in these programs was found to be only about a half million less than the total count.

Evidence from the Woodward survey indicates the diversity in the offerings in adult education and, therefore, something of the scope of interests of the adults enrolled. Some of this evidence is reproduced in Table 10.1, which shows the percentage distribution of the total enrollments in classes in the various fields of instruction. The categories are seen to reflect extremely wide ranges of interest, touching most or all main aspects of life and living, among them: preparation in Americanization and citizenship for the foreign-born; education for literacy; completion or continuation of elementary, high school, or advanced academic education; civic, political, and social concerns; family life and homemaking; vocational preparation in various areas (farming, business, and industry); recreation and esthetics in the fine and practical arts; and concern for health and physique (including safety).

The Woodward survey also included inquiry into the extent of provision of "informal group activities" for adults, not in classes, but identified as "activities whose primary purposes are recreation or the pursuit of hobbies" and "cultural or leisure-time activities which are not planned for attendance by the same group of persons at every meeting in a series." These included (1) activity groups, such as workshops, camps, excursions, and tours; (2) programs for audiences, such as lectures, concerts, plays, films, and radio or television instructional programs (except correspondence courses); (3) recreational activities, such as sports or folk-dancing conducted primarily

TABLE 10.1
PERCENTAGE DISTRIBUTION BY FIELD OF INSTRUCTION OF
ENROLLMENT IN ADULT EDUCATION CLASSES OFFERED
BY LOCAL PUBLIC SCHOOL SYSTEMS IN THE
UNITED STATES, 1958–59

Field of Instruction	Per Cent
Americanization and citizenship	5.0
Literacy education	1.4
Elementary education	1.1
High school academic education	12.0
Advanced academic education	1.5
Civic and public affairs	2.1
Personal development and group relationships	2.1
Family relationships	3.9
Homemaking and consumer education	13.4
Agricultural courses	3.1
Distributive education	2.6
Trade, industrial and technical courses	16.4
Business education	10.9
Fine arts	4.9
Techniques in practical arts and crafts	8.2
Health and physical education	5.5
Safety and driver education	3.4
Remedial education	.3
In-service training for professional persons	1.9
Other	.3

SOURCE: Woodward (66, 15, Table 12).

without instruction; and (4) other group activities where no instruction is provided. Manifestly, compilation of numbers of participants in such activities would be difficult. Instead, data were obtained that permitted ascertaining the proportions of school systems promoting such activities. About a fifth of all school districts studied provided them, with a somewhat greater proportion of the larger than of the smaller doing so.

The comprehensive view of growth and status of adult education must include reference to these developments in or by several other institutions and organizations. Focus on this growth and status in junior colleges follows immediately. Part-time programs for adults got under way in connection with other colleges and universities, public and private, before they were characteristic of junior colleges, and these programs now constitute an important avenue of adult education, especially for programs at the higher levels. Among other institutions and organizations that are contributing to the expanding opportunities in adult education are libraries, churches and other religious organizations, workers' groups, business and industry, the Armed Forces, and health and welfare agencies. While the number and diversity of agencies contributing to adult education make it difficult to arrive at a full count of participants in the population, two such summations have been made in recent years, one by the United States Office of Education in cooperation with the Bureau of the Census in 1957, and the other by the National Opinion Research Center for 1961–62. The first of these (*62*) contained an estimate of over 9 million participants, or 8.6 per cent of the age-groups canvassed, and the second (*33, 22*) over 17 million. The difference between the two would be explainable only in part by the difference in time and more by differences in procedure and in the agencies of adult activity represented in the canvass. These totals are impressive for their magnitude, especially in view of what Clark (*12*) has characterized as the "marginality" of adult education, by which he means the financial and a tangle of kindred limitations under which it operates, as compared with full-time schools. The rapid growth and status in spite of the marginality attests the vitality of the movement.

Growth and status in junior colleges.—In advance of considering the adult education development in junior colleges, usually regarded as for part-time students, it may be helpful to take note of the proportions of adults among full-time students in these institutions. This is facilitated by referring once more to distributions of students by age-groups reported in the first section of Chapter 1. While the groupings in Table 1.4* do not follow the conventional separation of those who have reached or passed their majority (21) from younger students, it may be noted that in this author's sample, 12.4 per cent were 20–22 and 13.3 per cent were 23 and over. The proportion of students represented in Medsker's study in the older grouping was much larger, but it was suggested in the interpretation that it was larger than is usual for community colleges. The appropriate observation is that full-time enrollments in these institutions include considerable proportions which by convention are classified as adult.

The literature on junior colleges contains two articles reporting on the extent of adult education in these institutions on a nationwide basis. Regrettably, neither brings the status down to date, although both afford some impression of the dynamics of development. The earlier of these articles is by Eells (*22*), and the essential evidence from it is to be found in Table 10.2. The compilations reported were made from annual reports from the junior colleges to Eells as Executive Secretary of the American

*See p. 7.

Association of Junior Colleges. In actuality, these reports designate the enrollees here counted as adults as "special" students and they are presumably all part-time. Eells' interpretative expression on this point is "special students, largely adults." In view of his long experience with the institutions and these reports, this interpretation may be assumed to be substantially correct, although one must admit that some counted here may not have reached the age of maturity as set by law or convention. The signifi-

TABLE 10.2
TOTAL ENROLLMENTS, IN JUNIOR COLLEGES FOR CERTAIN SCHOOL YEARS, ENROLLMENTS OF ADULTS, AND PERCENTAGES WHICH ADULTS WERE OF TOTAL ENROLLMENTS

School Year	Total Enrollment	Adults	Per Cent of Adults
1936–37	136,323	20,750	15.2
1937–38	155,588	33,204	21.3
1938–39	196,710	52,849	26.9
1939–40	236,162	73,371	31.1
1940–41	267,406	102,369	38.3
1941–42	314,349	158,425	50.4
1942–43	325,151	193,360	59.5
1943–44	249,788	161,791	64.8

SOURCE: Eells (22).

cant fact is the notably and steadily mounting proportion of these special students from 1936–37 to 1943–44: the proportion increased during seven years from less than a sixth to almost two-thirds. In answer to his own question of "Why this surprising increase?" Eells responded, "[It] is found in the fact that the junior college, particularly the local, publicly-controlled junior college, increasingly is being thought by its progressive leaders and supporters as a community institution with the opportunity and obligation to meet the educational needs, at the collegiate level, of all the community's citizens."

Another effort to measure the status of junior college adult education throughout the country was made for the school year 1947–48 by Martorana (39). This study was made at the request of one of the commissions of the American Association of Junior Colleges and, therefore, enjoyed the almost complete cooperation of the membership. It ascertained not only the numbers and proportions of students enrolled in the programs, but also the numbers and proportions of junior colleges offering the programs and the proportionate distribution of the areas of instruction or of curriculums being offered. The study had also the presumptive advantage over the Eells compilation of asking for the enrollment of "adults" (however, without defining the term), instead of depending on reports on "special" students.

This special inquiry (see Table 10.3) showed about a half of the smaller junior colleges (with enrollments of fewer than 300) and about two-thirds of the larger units (300 and over) offering adult programs. The proportion for private units was a little over a fourth. The proportions of the total student bodies who were reported in the adult education programs (see Table 10.4) were, respectively, about two-fifths and a half, while the proportion for private units averaged something over a fourth. Martorana's evidence found more men than women enrolled.

TABLE 10.3
NUMBERS OF PUBLIC AND PRIVATE JUNIOR COLLEGES ANSWERING AND THE NUMBERS AND PERCENTAGES WITH ADULT PROGRAMS

Type of Institution	Number Answering	Number with Adult Programs	Per Cent with Adult Programs
Small public	84	43	51.2
Large public	86	57	66.3
Total public	170	100	58.3
Private	167	44	26.3
All junior colleges	337	144	42.7

SOURCE: Martorana (39, Table 1).

TABLE 10.4
NUMBERS OF REGULAR AND ADULT STUDENTS ENROLLED IN PUBLIC AND PRIVATE JUNIOR COLLEGES AND PERCENTAGES ADULT ENROLLMENTS WERE OF TOTALS

Type of Institution	Enrollments			Per Cent Adult of Total
	Regular	Adult	Total	
Small public	6,720	4,496	11,216	40.1
Large public	53,049	52,347	105,396	49.7
Total public	59,769	56,843	116,612	48.7
Private	12,311	4,931	17,242	28.6
All junior colleges	72,080	61,774	133,854	46.2

SOURCE: Martorana (39, Table 3).

Inquiry concerning the offerings in these programs (see Table 10.5) found half of them providing instruction in courses preparatory for higher education, while almost all reported nonpreparatory offerings, the latter ranging through wide variety and reflecting a diversity of interests spreading over occupational areas, citizenship, homemaking, and recreation.

Because the manner of reporting enrollments for the *Junior College Directory* has been modified since the years for which Eells prepared his report on the extent of adult education, only an estimate can be made of the growth of adult education in junior colleges in the meantime and of the recent comparative status of adults and minors. Recent issues of the directory have reported enrollments of "full-time" and "part-time" students, with the total in all junior colleges for October, 1966, at almost a million and a half. The actual count was 1,456,263, with 792,006 full-time and

664,157 part-time students. Of these, the independent (private) junior colleges enrolled 138,751 (less than 10 per cent of the total) of whom 113,950 were full-time and 24,801 part-time. The numbers of full-time and part-time students in the public units were more nearly equal, being, respectively, 678,056 and 639,356. Although one cannot be certain of the exact proportions, he can be sure from the distributions of ages in the early portions of Chapter 1 that a small proportion of the full-time students were 21 and over and, therefore, classifiable as adults. Conversely, it seems

TABLE 10.5
PERCENTAGES OF PUBLIC AND PRIVATE JUNIOR COLLEGES OFFERING
ADULT EDUCATION COURSES IN VARIOUS AREAS OR CURRICULUMS

Area of Curriculum	Public	Private	All
Preparatory to higher education	56.0	36.4	50.0
Nonpreparatory	98.0	93.2	96.5
Vocational	90.0	65.9	82.6
Commercial	80.0	52.3	71.5
Technical	61.0	25.0	50.0
Agricultural	34.0	6.8	25.7
Cultural and Citizenship	71.0	54.6	66.0
Homemaking	45.0	11.4	34.7
Recreation	41.0	15.9	33.3

SOURCE: Martorana (*39*, Table 6).

plausible to conjecture that a somewhat comparable minority of part-time students were under 21, so that the total numbers and proportions of minors and of adults in public units were each not far from 600,000 to 700,000 and likewise not far from a half of the total enrollment for that year. Compared with the figures for the early 1940's in Table 10.2, this means spectacular growth in the interim in numbers both of minors and of adults, the latter being at this point our special concern.

Two diverse examples of development.—Treatment of the growth of adult education in the local junior college will be concluded by describing two situations in which the development took place in widely different forms. The descriptions here are based on articles written by administrative officers connected with the developments and published in the *Junior College Journal* while Eells was editor and about the time he was emphasizing attention to the suitability of the community college as an agency of adult education. The two expositions are among a number of such articles published during the period of his editorship of the journal.

One of these descriptions, by Hackman (*27*), concerns the development of tuition-free evening junior colleges in Chicago. Three such junior colleges were established during September, 1938, in high school plants in three different sections of the city. They were housed separately from the daytime junior colleges which were primarily for full-time students, and they operated under administrators separate from those in charge of the daytime units. The evening junior colleges looked to the day units for guidance in developing their curriculums. They took over with varying extent of change the survey courses in the humanities, the social, physical, and biological sciences, and the course in English composition that had been developed for the day units, including the syllabi. Other courses, such as literature, chemistry, mathematics, economics, sociology, psychology, accounting, business organization, business law, marketing, statistics, secretarial training, architectural and engineering drawing, etc., were patterned after those in the day units and were usable either for transfer to four-year colleges or professional schools in universities, or for improving skills and understandings in occupations in which the students were already engaged.

The enrollment in the evening junior colleges, beginning with 1,870 students, more than trebled in two years. The ratio of men to women among these students was about two to one. Most were young adults, reflected in the fact that over three-fourths were 25 years of age and under, and about the same proportion had been out of high school five years or less. All but a small proportion (13 per cent of the men and 9 per cent of the women) were still unmarried. The reasons given for attendance were primarily economic: the great majority said that they could not afford to attend a daytime college and were attending the evening college in order to be able to change to better occupations or to obtain promotions in their present work. A much smaller proportion were attending for "general cultural reasons." More than half planned to continue to bachelors' degrees, most of them in evening colleges. The ability of these students to carry this work is attested by the fact that, on the American Council on Education Psychological Examination, 60 per cent received scores above the thirty-third national all-college percentile.

Description of these evening junior colleges in Chicago may be capsulized as follows: they were institutions offering programs paralleling closely those of daytime units and serving primarily single young men and women of college-level ability who were not long out of high school, could not afford to attend daytime institutions, and were seeking vocational advancement.

The other description is by Morris (43) and concerns the adult education development during the early 1940s at San Mateo, California. Beginnings of an adult program in this junior college were not unlike many others, consisting of a "sprinkling" of adults with full-time students in regular junior college classes and the giving of evening lecture series "in the various fields of liberal arts and discussions of national and international problems." However, the great development followed the appointment of a full-time director, the public announcement of establishment of the Adult

Center, and the invitation to residents of post-high-school age to ask for activities along the lines of their interests. This resulted in "immediate expansion" of the typical night school classes in English, language, citizenship for aliens, history, mathematics, philosophy, psychology, economics, handicrafts, art, music, secretarial training, bookkeeping, etc. Individuals requested courses in consumer buying, homemaking, news writing, short story writing, and other subjects. Organizations of "self-propelling" adult units were encouraged to develop and sponsor special classes: for example, parent-teacher associations asked for courses in child care and adolescence; police and firemen's associations requested in-service training; labor unions asked for courses in the theoretical aspects of their trades; the Peninsula Forum, a discussion group, solicited help in carrying on its program; the Toastmasters Club asked to have the leadership of a qualified instructor of public speaking; the Peninsula Little Theater affiliated itself with the college, as did various choral and other organizations. The total program was also augmented by activities carried on in cooperation with prosecution at the time of World War II. The policy, as expressed in the description, was to encourage learning by people "through participation in vital activities, selected in large part by themselves, but planned and conducted by the technically qualified experts provided through the Adult Center." Following is the philosophy guiding the whole development: "San Mateo Junior College is dedicated to the thought that the preservation of democracy depends largely on the services rendered by locally controlled educational institutions and that these services are due both to youth and the adults of the community. It is believed to be the business of the junior college to make available to all residents of post high-school age the opportunity to acquire a wider realization of essential values and a more complete understanding of and participation in democratic society."

During the process of development the expanded program under the Adult Center spread to forty different buildings and locations in the district. Another indication of its magnitude is provided in the figures on enrollment reported by this junior college for the *Junior College Directory* for 1941–42, the year preceding the time Morris was preparing the description: the enrollment of "regular" (full-time) students in that year was reported as 990, while that of "special" students was 4,794, the latter being almost five times the former.

The two programs described here present a striking contrast. One is restricted to paralleling the offering in the daytime unit, the sole difference between the two Chicago programs being the time at which they were scheduled. The other goes far beyond this and aims at serving the active and wholesome interests of the entire population of post-high-school age. Between these extremes of policy are many or most of the adult programs administered by community colleges. It may be said that in some situations comprehensiveness is achieved by cooperation or coordination of various local agencies providing adult education at different levels or in different areas, with the community college serving as the coordinating agency. The community college shares with all local schools the advantage of affording a natural focus for adult interests, and it possesses the additional advantage over the lower schools of the prestige of educational level.

The Rationale of Adult Education

Our rapidly changing society.—Although this chapter is committed primarily to the portrayal of the characteristics of adults, some attention must be given to the rationale of adult education. The most recurrent reason given for developing programs of education for adults is the rapidity of change in our society. It is sometimes contended that in a static society schooling can be planned and operated solely for young people who, once equipped in youth with the understandings and skills needed for successful living, can go to the end of life without "retooling the mind," to use a phrase coined by a recent contributor to the *Atlantic (10)*. But we are reminded over and over again by advocates of adult education that, in a society like ours, with all the complex of transformations continuously taking place, the educative process must also be continuous. This accelerating pace of social change is the theme developed by the Commission of the Professors of Adult Education in its statement of *A New Imperative for Our Times (13)*.

Because these changes have been repeatedly reviewed in popular literature, it is unnecessary to do more here than enumerate some of them without elaboration. Among those usually mentioned first are the scientific and technological changes of the last century, and, more especially, since these changes seem to be following a geometrically accelerating curve, of the last half century or so. Spectacular advances have been and are being made in such areas as transportation, communication, and automation in industry. The changes have been accompanied and followed by profound adjustments in our economic, social, and political worlds. To mention one aspect of the economic area only, that of occupations, the writers often remind their readers that these are undergoing constant and rapid modification and replacement, so that they are seldom now life-time employments. The problems precipitated in this area are augmented by the processes of automation, which are reducing the need for manpower and thereby compelling attention to the need for education for the use of expanding leisure. The ramifications of influence for change in a host of other aspects of economic, social, and political institutions and behavior are no less profound and pervasive.

Social change not the sole origin of need.—Notwithstanding the obviously important impact of social change in creating a need for adult education, at least one authority in the field has entered a demurrer to accepting it as the sole factor of need (*16*). Cotton categorizes the "major themes" that explain the need under five captions: our free society, the world we live in, the educational process, the Good Life, and adult needs and responsibilities. The reader can note that, as developed by Cotton, who identified these as themes, some are anchored in social change while others may be more or less independent of it.

In discussing the first of these themes Cotton indicates the assumption to be that a democratic society makes special demands on the individual which are of three types, each of which has implications for adult education: adults who can exercise their responsibilities of citizenship in an enlightened manner, who have an understanding and appreciation of freedom, and who can exercise effective leadership. The world we live in is a "rapidly changing world," a "revolutionary world," and a "world in crisis." The educational process he favors utilizes the *functional* (as contrasted with the *formalistic*) approach which aims at influencing behavior, is a continuing process (goes on "whether school keeps or not"), emphasizes "life-long learning," is the outcome of meaningful experience, and involves the active role of the learner in the process. The "overall concept" of the Good Life is that of achieving emotional, intellectual, and aesthetic growth. The adult responsibilities identified comprehend achieving competence in vocation, married life, as parent, consumer, citizen, and member of the community.

The needs of adults as seen in developmental tasks.—The five adult responsibilities just cited as having been identified by Cotton may suggest to the reader that they are areas or strands of life and living pointing to "developmental tasks" of adulthood. In considering personal and social development of youth in Chapter 3, this concept is introduced as having been applied by Havighurst and the tasks as seen by him for adolescents were listed.* At that point Havighurst's definition of a developmental task was quoted as one "which arises at or about a certain period in the life of an individual, successful achievement of which leads to his happiness and to success in later tasks, while failure leads to unhappiness in the individual, disapproval of society, and difficulty with later tasks" (*29*, 2). Havighurst applied this serviceable concept to all main periods of the life span, including early adulthood, middle age, and later maturity, which are the concern of this discussion. His formulation for these three age-spans is assembled in Figure 10.1 in such a way as to permit comparison of the tasks in each area or strand of living and to note the continuity of each

*See pp. 79–80.

area and the changes within it from stage to stage of adulthood. With the thought that the key words used by Havighurst and Orr (*31*, 32) to identify the areas for tabulation will be helpful in tracing the tasks across the diagram, these are introduced in parentheses after the statement of each task of early adulthood. The tasks as listed in the column for middle age include two subsequently added in a reformulation by Havighurst and Orr (*31*, 9). Some running commentary on the display of tasks in Figure 10.1 may not be out of place. It is apparent that almost all the tasks of early

FIG. 10.1
Developmental Tasks of Early Adulthood,
Middle Age, and Later Maturity

Early Adulthood Ages 18–30	Middle Age Ages 30–55	Later Maturity Ages 55 and over
1. Selecting a mate (Spouse)*		
2. Learning to live with a marriage partner (Spouse)	5. Relating oneself to one's spouse as a person	3. Adjusting to death of spouse
3. Starting a family (Parent)		
4. Rearing children (Parent)	3. Assisting teen-age children to become responsible and happy adults	
5. Managing a home (Homemaker)	2. Establishing and maintaining an economic standard of living	6. Establishing satisfactory physical living arrangements
6. Getting started on an occupation (Worker)	Reaching the peak in one's work career†	2. Adjustment to retirement and reduced income
7. Taking civic responsibility (Citizen)	1. Achieving adult civic and social responsibility	5. Meeting social and civic obligations
8. Finding a congenial social group (Friend)	Making an art of friendship†	4. Establishing an explicit affiliation with one's age group
	4. Developing adult leisure-time activities	
	6. Accepting and adjusting to the physiological changes of middle life	1. Adjusting to decreasing physical strength and health
	7. Adjusting to aging parents	

Source: Formulated by Havighurst (*29*, Chs. 16–18).
*Key words follow the designations in Havighurst and Orr (*31*, 32, Table 1).
†Havighurst and Orr, p. 9.

adulthood have their counterparts for middle age and later maturity. Justification of this observation on continuity is strengthened by merely cursory consideration of two tasks postulated for middle age, one of which, developing adult leisure-time activities, has no corresponding entry for early adulthood or for later maturity, and the other, accepting and adjusting to the physiological changes of middle life, has no entry for early adulthood. These omissions may be in the nature of inadvertencies, as it is difficult to believe that younger adults have no special problems in respect to recreational pursuits and in the area of physique and health, and that older persons approaching or entering retirement have none in respect to leisure.

The problem of leisure time throughout adulthood is being increasingly emphasized in public discussion because of (1) the notable reduction during a half century and more in daily and weekly hours of labor and (2) the marked trend toward earlier retirement ages. There was a time when 60 to 70 hours of labor per week were common. These have been rapidly and rather steadily shrinking so that the 40-hour week is now typical, and there is frequent advocacy of a maximum of 30 and 35 hours. Students of cybernetics predict an even lower workload. This reduction operates through early adulthood and middle age while early retirement makes for a sudden increment of leisure time for later maturity.

The tasks as formulated in Figure 10.1 are not particularized for the sexes. A little speculation while considering the tasks will prompt the observation that for certain of the areas, more especially those of homemaker and of worker, the developmental tasks of men and of women will in considerable measure be different. The differences reflect divergences in sex role in our society. Even in these tasks, the sexes must cooperate, and cooperation will call for an understanding by the members of each sex of the problems and responsibilities of the other.

It may not have escaped the reader that, as has been pointed out, while most of the areas or strands extend through all three portions of the period of adulthood, the tasks change character from stage to stage, often signally. Thus, although as a young adult one is concerned with selecting a mate and learning to live with her (him), during middle age one must relate oneself to her (him) and, in later maturity, must adjust to the death of the spouse. Again, the individual as a young adult, especially the male, but often also, in our current economy and culture, the female, must get started in an occupation, reach his peak in work career in middle age, and adjust to retirement and reduced income in the period of later maturity. To be sure, all the tasks postulated for early adulthood represent substantial deviations in need from those seen for the adolescent as quoted from Havighurst in Chapter 3.*

*See pp. 79–80.

Beyond all the variation in developmental tasks from adolescence to young adulthood and through the stages of adulthood are the far-reaching social changes in our society which are touched on above. These changes operate to compound the complexities of accomplishing the developmental tasks, and they do so by effecting modifications in the tasks themselves even while the person involved is trying to negotiate them. The maze of tasks is, in consequence, so large and so shifting that the individual is in need of maximal understanding for accomplishing them, and a process of life-long education, either institutional or self-directed or both, is essential to success. Contemplating the complexity of problems endlessly faced by the adult, a recent writer (26) has referred to continuous education as "a way of life," and one must concede that it is at least an important part of the effective way.

The focus on later adulthood.—Of late years, we have seen a focus of attention on later adulthood. The attention has moved toward comprehensiveness, including concern for, among other areas, physical and mental health, economic security, personal and social relationships, and use of leisure time. To a considerable extent, the concern has been prompted by a popular belief that the proportion in the population in the older age groups, especially persons over 65, is rapidly increasing and will continue to mount. Before considering the appropriateness of and implications for education for this older group, it is desirable to draw from authoritative sources evidence and opinion calling for correction of this popular belief. Wattenberg and Scammon, in a section on "The Demography of Age Distribution" in *This U.S.A.* (63, 26–29), supply the following figures compiled from the census:

YEAR	NUMBER OF PERSONS OVER AGE 65	PER CENT OF TOTAL POPULATION
1850	.6 million	2.5
1950	12.3 million	8.2
1960	16.6 million	9.2
1964	17.9 million	9.3

These figures show that, during the century from 1850 to 1950, the proportion over 65 did rise at a startling rate and that the rapid increase continued to 1960. These writers refer to the numbers as "staggering, especially if projected into the future: should the 1950–60 rate of increase have continued to the year 2000, close to 15 per cent of our population would be aged sixty-five and over." They point out, as may be seen in the figures cited for 1964 as compared with 1960, that the acceleration has already slowed down, and they assure us, moreover, that further important acceleration will not come about, because the tide of immigrants who account for much of the increase has long since subsided. This tide took place mostly between 1902 and 1914, and was made up mostly of young adults who now go to explain much of the "boom in Senior Citizens." The immigrant tide receded and has not risen again in such large dimensions. This is no denial that these elder citizens are now a large and important sector of the population and will remain so. Continuance of our concern for their welfare is called for, which means that they are in need of help throughout the rest of life in understanding and solving problems emerging in their tasks.

That certain problems may emerge and others become accentuated in later adulthood is to be inferred from evidence on the proportions of males and females found to be in the labor force by census figures. These are presented in Table 10.6. All but a small proportion of males are seen to

TABLE 10.6
PERCENTAGES OF MALES AND FEMALES IN THE
LABOR FORCE IN THE UNITED STATES IN 1960

Age	Male	Female
30–34	95.8	35.5
35–39	95.8	40.3
40–44	95.4	45.3
45–49	94.4	47.4
50–54	92.2	45.8
55–59	87.7	39.7
60–64	77.6	29.5
65–69	43.8	16.6
70–74	28.7	9.6
75 and over	11.1	4.2

SOURCE: *1960 Census of Population*, Vol. 1, Pt. 1, p. 487, Table 194.

have been in the labor force in 1960 up through the 45–49 age-group, although a decline is seen to begin during this age span. From this point on the decline is increasingly rapid, dropping to 77.6 per cent for the 60–64 age-group and to 43.8 per cent, or less than half, for ages 65–69. The proportions for women in the labor force are, of course, much smaller, as most are classified as housewives. These proportions increase substantially for the early age-groups, as responsibilities of childbearing and rearing ease off, but begin to drop off again for the 50–54 age span and decline rapidly thereafter.

This dropping off is now on the increase, as may be illustrated by comparisons with corresponding figures for the 1950 census: the percentages of males in the labor force for the 60–64 age-group dropped during the intervening decade from 79.4 to 77.6 and that for the 65–69 group from 59.7 to 43.8. For females there were, on the other hand, some increases in proportions in the labor force in these older age-groups, although only a small minority was counted here.

That one of the tasks of adulthood, especially of later maturity, that of finding suitable recreations, is accentuated by these marked trends in the labor force is reflected in studies of leisure, which show the older population with "more time on their hands." Pressey and Kuhlen (*50*, 390) refer to evidence, for a national sample of college graduates, that "increased participation in leisure activities appeared to accompany increased amounts of leisure in old age, earlier in the case of women than men because (apparently) increased time becomes available earlier for them as children leave home and family unit size shrinks."

This focus on the needs of later adulthood will be concluded by brief description of some "experiments" in education for members of this age-group to help them meet these needs. The descriptions are of programs initiated as early as 1948 through the University of Michigan's Extension Service and are based on reports of the experiments by Donahue (*21*), a leader in developments in the field of gerontology.

The first course concerning the problems of later adulthood consisted of twelve two-hour sessions given over to lectures by various specialists from the university faculty. It was a noncredit course and was open to all interested persons. At its conclusion the students evaluated the course and recommended its continuance. The lectures identified as being of most value dealt with psychological aspects of aging, biology of aging, mental health, physical health, and living arrangements, while those of least value dealt with creative activities, such as gardening, silver work, and recreational and cultural pursuits. An expressed criticism of the course was that there was not enough discussion, although the opinion was also voiced that the lack of discussion was owing to the diffidence of the students towards expressing themselves in public rather than from an absence of opportunity. The Extension Service has continued to offer courses patterned after this one. Students in the courses have ranged in age from the late teens to the eighties, with a mean age of sixty-one. Their educational backgrounds have ranged from fourth grade through years of graduate work.

A subsequent course development of the Extension Service, as described by Donahue (*21*), combined educational experience with social and recreational activities "to provide knowledge and practice in the art of mature living." The first hour of the class convened at 5:30 P.M. and was devoted to a discussion of such topics as health, nutrition, psychological change, mental hygiene, financing the later years, employment opportunities, and retirement. This discussion was followed by the group's having lunch together, after which an hour was devoted to practice in social living. The social-recreational activities included games, group singing, square dancing, instrumental music, dramatics, hobby shows, and a party. These activities were carried out by the students, but they were studied with reference to their meaning for the total pattern of living.

Still another course fostered by the service was done over television. This course was called "Living in the Later Years: Hobbies Put to Work"; it ran through seven weeks, and stressed hobbies with twenty-minute demonstrations of book-binding, sculpture, pottery-making, cake-decorating, spice-blending, gardening, stenciling and other crafts for shut-ins, gem-cutting, woodworking, toy craft, painting, silversmithing, and music. Faculty guests were utilized for the demonstrations. The viewing audience at times rose to 100,000. A total of 252 students was enrolled in the course, roughly divided between men and women, and ranging in age from 15 to 68.

Abilities of Adults

Earlier inquiries.—Provision of programs of adult education can hardly be justified unless adults are able to profit from them. It is less than a half century since the belief was commonly held that adults cannot learn and that the time for education is limited to childhood and youth. Researches reported over the period of the last several decades have done much to dispel this stereotype of adult inability to learn. Although this change of mind concerning the adult's ability was not mentioned above in reviewing the influences making for the rapid growth of the programs for adults, it must have been at least a contributing and accelerating factor.

One of the early investigators whose findings did much to discredit the stereotype was Thorndike, who, with his associates, reported procedures and findings in 1928 (*60*). Instead of describing the procedures and drawing on the detailed evidence from this battery of studies, dependence on the project will be restricted to brief quotation from the conclusion (177–78): "In general, nobody under forty-five should restrain himself from trying to learn anything because of a belief or fear that he is too old to be able to learn it. Nor should he use that fear as an excuse for not learning anything he ought to learn. If he fails in learning it, inability due directly to age will rarely, if ever, be the reason. . . . In general, teachers of adults of age 25 to 45 should expect them to learn at nearly the same rate and in nearly the same manner as they would have learned the same thing at fifteen to twenty."

Among recurrent exceptions taken by critics of the Thorndike projects are the upper age limit of his subject population, which seldom went beyond the forties, and the too great reliance on tests of memory.

The other earlier investigation to be drawn upon, in this instance by citing certain measures as well as interpretative comments, is the Stanford Later Maturity Study made from 1930 to 1932, subsidized by the Carnegie

Corporation, and reported by Miles (*40*). This project had the advantages over Thorndike's of covering a much longer age-range and comprehending tests through a wide array of mental functions. It included inquiry also into affective aspects, but with the focus here on intellectual elements, the findings concerning these will not be touched upon.

The age-grouping used and the number of subjects in each group in this project were as follows: B, 10 to 17 (90); C, 18 to 29 (90); D, 30 to 49 (180); E, 50 to 69 (320); F, 70 to 89 (130). Each subject was tested individually in a single two-hour period broken into four half-hour sessions each of which took place in a different room. The percentages reported below were computed with the highest mean as base, which was with few exceptions the mean for early adulthood.

(a) *Visual efficiency*: B, 100; C, 95; D, 93; E, 76; F, 46.

(b) *Perceptual span*: "The results show a curve for performance that rises in the adolescent period B, declines then slightly but continuously to age 60, to fall rapidly from this point onwards."

(c) *Motility and skill*: (1) rotary motility, B, 90; C, 100; D, 97; E, 89; F, 70; (2) reach and grasp, B, 92; C, 100; D, 98; E, 88; F, 70. "The smallness of the decline in reaction speed in middle maturity and to persistence in later maturity and in old age in rotary motility and in reach and grasp is very striking."

(d) *Memory*: relative amounts of learning in a maze, B, 95; C, 100; D, 92; E, 83; F, 55. "The age decrement in learning ability here is as great as the decline in sensory capacity."

(e) *Imagination*: C, 100; D, 99; E, 97; F, 94. Tested with a Kinephantom. "Results for a single measure of imagination challenge further investigation, for they show extremely slight age change. . . . Apparently spontaneous imagination measured here has the quality of true agelessness."

(f) *Comparison and judgment*: B, 72; C, 100; D, 100; E, 87; F, 69. "The maximal performance persists from young adulthood through early maturity, decline is first evident in later maturity, and old age scores little lower than the adolescent mean. Speed is not a factor here and memory is scarcely called upon."

(g) *Combination and abstraction*: "Intelligence test results contain partial measures of combination and abstraction. . . . The age-score curve from a standard intelligence test . . . shows a top mean of 15 or 16 years mental age at life-age 18, persistence at practically this same mental level through two decades, then gradual decline to old age. . . . Stated in another way, the test ability gain of the last three years in the period of mental age growth is gradually lost in the next three score years. . . . Further examination of the separate items which make up the Otis Omnibus Test used shows that verbal associations, generalizations, interpretations of meaning, and recognition of relations show marked resistance to the influence of age. Speed, organization and recall of unfamiliar material, and difficult logical procedures involving a relatively wide immediate memory span show speedier decline. Perhaps I should call the decline registered in our curve not one in intelligence as such but rather a diminution in reaction speed and sum of energy available for new work types. This would mean that the decline correlates with physiological rather than psychological deterioration."

(h) *Individual differences*: one other finding of this Stanford Later Maturity Study of considerable significance concerns the individual differences disclosed. In the most adequately discriminative tests the measures of dispersion were found to be consistently large from decade to decade. For instance, in reaction time, a fourth of the subjects over 70 were as quick as the average for the total group, and in intelligence, the standard deviation varied little from decade to decade, and here also, even when speed was a factor, about a fourth of the older subjects equaled or exceeded the mean for all adults.

Later studies of general intelligence and change in abilities with age.— Over the intervening decades since the investigations by Thorndike and Miles a rather impressive array of reports bearing on the intelligence and ability in learning of adults has been published. Some of them corroborate findings of the earlier studies, some represent a challenge to previous conclusions, and still others are in areas significant for adult education but not represented in investigations summarized up to this point. Evidence or inferences from certain of these later studies will be reviewed next, so that the reader may note any important modifications in major conclusions, especially as they bear on educability of the adult population. The studies concern mainly general intelligence, reading ability, and aptitude and performance of adults enrolled in extension and other courses.

Among conclusions previously presented here that have been questioned because of findings in later studies is the earlier one by Wechsler* indicating a gradual decline in general intelligence from early to later adulthood, a decline from which negative correlations between age and intelligence are computable. One of the studies with this conflicting conclusion is by Corsini and Fassett (*14*) who administered the Wechsler-Bellevue Test and analyzed the performances on it by 1,072 inmates of the San Quentin prison, 372 of whom were above the age of 49.

Analysis by the authors included separate consideration of the subjects' records on the Performance and Verbal portions of the Wechsler test. They found that the items most resistant to drop are Information, Arithmetic, and Comprehension, all of which they regard as verbal and of which only

*See pp. 46–47.

Arithmetic was timed. The items most susceptible to drop with age are Block Design, Picture Arrangement, and Digit Symbol, each of which is timed, and each calling for visual acuity and motor performance. It has already been noted above that visual acuity and performance under timing are subject to rather marked decline during adult years. It is these authors' opinion that the decline in performance ability is, therefore, a function of age, and not necessarily of intelligence. They found that the San Quentin population showed in terms of the verbal material an increase of 9 per cent, and, in consequence, their conclusions are: "1. General intelligence does not decline from early to late maturity"; "2. Test ability will vary in a downward direction if the subtests contain visual and motor factors, and will vary in an upward direction if the subtests contain material which depends on continued learning."

All the projects investigating the ability of adults so far reviewed here were cross-sectional. Attention will now be turned to two longitudinal studies, one based on retesting college students and the second on test and retest of a population referred to as "gifted adults." The first of these comparisons was made by Owens (47). The subjects were 127 former Iowa State College male students to whom the Army Alpha was administered both in college and after thirty years. The investigator reported the "shifts" in median scores on all subtests and in the total score. These shifts were positive for all subtests except Arithmetical Problems, for which the negative change was small and without statistical significance. Significance at the 1 per cent level was found for the changes in Practical Judgment, Synonym-Antonym, Information, and for the change in total score, and at the 5 per cent level for Analogies. The author comments that "if the effect [of increased maturity] can be detected in such a homogeneous sample as the present one, it seems reasonable to assume that it would be magnified in a sample from the 'general population.'"

The other longitudinal project, by Bayley and Oden (2), involved application of a special Concept Mastery Scale. It was administered twice, 12 years apart, to 1,103 adults, of whom 768 were selected as children by Terman for inclusion in his Stanford Study of Gifted Children. The other 335 were spouses of the subjects in the Terman study. The main finding of the investigation pointed to "a highly significant increase in scores at the second testing both by the subjects of the gifted study and by their husbands and wives." The increases occurred in all occupational and educational levels and at all levels of ability tested, except where the test ceiling prevented, and at all ages from 20 to 50 years. Variability of the scores was less for the subjects of the gifted study and decreased at the second testing with increasing age, while variability of the spouses' scores was greater and increased on retest.

These longitudinal studies afford assurance that, for populations of the kind investigated, there is continuance of growth in intelligence as measured and of ability to learn. Their limitations, from the standpoint of the projection of comprehensive plans of adult education, are mainly in two directions. In the first place, they are restricted in age-span, not following subjects into later adulthood of 60 years and beyond. In the second place, they are concerned only with intellectually selected subjects—the Owens project with the considerable degree of selection represented in a college-going population and the Bayley-Oden project concerned only with those identified as gifted and their spouses. It hardly needs saying that investigations of mental ability should reach into the years of senility and across the full range of ability in the population. They should also at the same time look intensively into the contributions to intelligence and learning of the various components of mentality.

Duration of schooling as a factor.—The impact of one other influence should be considered before acceptance of the conclusion of gradual decline of intelligence during the period of adulthood, certainly to the degree that might be assumed from the curves drawn from the early investigations made by Jones and Conrad, Miles and Miles, and Wechsler which are cited in the section on "Mental Change Through the Life Span" in Chapter 2.* The reference here is to the relation of reading ability to extent of schooling, or, to apply the phrase used by the census, to "years of schooling completed." It will be established below that the median of these years of schooling has been rising over a long period. This is reflected in the medians for the 1960 census, which showed, for the country as a whole, a median of 12.3 years for the age-span 25 to 29 years, whereas that for the age-span 75 years and over was 8.2. The difference between the two medians is roughly equivalent to that between completing high school and completing the eight-year elementary school. It will also be established, as is to be expected, that reading skills rise with the rise in last school grade attended. When one couples with these facts the dependence of performance on most intelligence tests of ability to read, a dependence so great that these tests have often been criticized for being too largely dependent on reading skills, one has a basis for qualifying any conclusion attributing significant decline of intelligence to advancing age, as some interpretations have done from measures in investigations like those cited in Chapter 2. To arrive at such a conclusion, it would be necessary first to control the factor of extent of schooling for the successive age-groups being investigated. It is doubtful that, except in the years of senility or in cases of debilitating illness, the curve of average intelligence declines to any large extent or at all from early adulthood onward.

*See pp. 41–47.

One authority's opinion.—In the absence of conclusions from an all-inclusive investigation of adult intelligence, resort may be taken to quotation from the summary of a chapter on the learning ability of adults by an authority who has investigated and written extensively in the field of gerontology. The quotation is from Birren's *Psychology of Aging* (*4*, 169): "The evidence that has been accumulating on both animal and human learning suggests that changes with age in the primary ability to learn are small under most circumstances. When differences do appear, they seem to be more readily attributed to processes of perception, set, attention, motivation, and the physiological state of the organism (including that of disease states) than to a change in the primary capacity to learn. Since Thorndike's studies in 1928, there has been a general tendency to advance the age at which subjects in learning research are regarded as aged. At the present time there is little evidence to suggest that there is an intrinsic age difference in learning capacity over the employed years; that is, up to age sixty. This is not to say that learning of certain psychomotor skills may not show limitations in older persons because of problems of performance, of speed limitations, or of life-long habits that elude laboratory study. Clearly, further studies are needed to indicate the optimum conditions for adult learning over the life span. . . ."

Ability in reading.—Among abilities of adults concerning which some understanding is essential for persons interested in adult education are those in reading. It is important, to be sure, to know about their intelligence, evidence on which was just reviewed, and, because of the well-known high correlation of performance on tests of reading with those of intelligence, the latter afford a considerable clue to the ability in reading. Nevertheless, the dependence of learning in schools on reading is so great that it is desirable here to canvass some of the evidence bearing directly on the adults' capabilities in this field of learning.

The classic study in this particular field is one by Buswell, *How Adults Read* (*8*). Its chief limitation is that, for purposes of the present, it was done about thirty years ago. However, as will be noted below, it is possible in some degree to compensate for this limitation.

Buswell selected the subjects for his investigation with great care. Of the 982 adults identified for it, he was able to obtain all necessary data for 897. For the original 982 the occupational distribution was as follows: professional, 102; office and sales, 504; skilled labor, 104; unskilled labor, 245; and unclassified, 27. This distribution corresponded approximately to that of the urban population. The age-range was 25–45. Among the types of information obtained from the subjects besides those already mentioned were the last school grade attended and the types of reading engaged in. He also administered to these adults a test of reading devised for the project.

The distribution of scores on this test according to the last school grade reported as having been attended by the subjects is shown in Table 10.7. Cursory examination shows the distributions for all columns ranging rather widely. However, it may be noted also that there are relatively heavy concentrations in the lower test-score divisions for subjects whose last school grade was grade 6 or below and, by contrast, somewhat comparable concentrations in higher divisions for subjects whose last school grade was grade 13 or above. Intervening columns have their concentrations largely in the middle divisions. These tendencies of distribution are reflected in the

TABLE 10.7
Scores on Reading Test for Adult Subjects Grouped by Last School Grade Attended

Total Score	Number of Subjects by Last School Grade					All Subjects
	6 or Below	7–8	9–10	11–12	13 or Above	
76–93	0	4	6	9	23	42
57–75	2	38	74	92	101	307
38–56	25	96	88	91	29	329
19–37	53	58	31	7	4	153
0–18	44	16	5	1	0	66
Total	124	212	204	200	157	897
Median Score	25.0	43.8	51.8	56.7	65.1	50.8

Source: Buswell (8, 33, Table 7).

median scores in the bottom row of the table, which rise consistently for the five groups of subjects and yield a full range of 40 points (25.0 to 65.1) on the test from lowest school grade to highest. The evidence warrants an inference of a fairly high correlation between score and last school grade. Other tables in Buswell's report show relatively little difference by age-groups, although the median score for subjects 25 years and under is appreciably smaller than for the older age-groups. As indicated above, there was no group reaching past middle age. His measures also show the test score to be only moderately influenced by the length of the period of years out of school.

To explore for the influence of reading ability on the reading habits of his subjects Buswell asked them to indicate the frequency with which they read newspapers, magazines, and books. The compilation of responses is reproduced in Table 10.8, which facilitates comparison of the 100 with the lowest test scores with the 100 with the highest test scores. One may judge from what has been reported in Table 10.7 that this comparison is in major part also a comparison of subjects with (a) low last school grades and (b) high last school grades attended. Predominant regular reading by the hundred poorest readers is seen to be in newspapers. The hundred readers with highest scores read newspapers hardly less regularly, but most of them also read magazines regularly and many books. This contrast provides food for speculation as to the competence of the poorer readers to profit from programs of adult education without simplification of content, extensive adaptation of procedures, and/or prior efforts at improving reading skills.

Had Buswell administered to his subjects a reading test previously standardized by application to school populations instead of using one espe-

TABLE 10.8
READING HABITS OF 100 ADULT SUBJECTS WITH LOWEST READING TEST SCORES COMPARED WITH HABITS OF 100 ADULT SUBJECTS WITH HIGHEST READING TEST SCORES

Type of Material Read	Numbers of Subjects	
	100 Lowest	100 Highest
Newspapers		
Regularly	88	96
Occasionally	11	4
Never	1	0
Magazines		
Regularly	22	74
Occasionally	69	26
Never	9	0
Books		
Many	12	70
Few	40	28
None	48	2
Median Score	21.7	74.5

SOURCE: Buswell (8, 39, Table 12).

cially devised for his project, it would have been possible to report adult reading abilities in comparison with those of children and youth in school grades. The absence of such a possibility made it necessary for Gray, writing on the reading ability of adults for a yearbook of the National Society for the Study of Education in 1956 (32, Ch. II) to resort to a circuitous procedure to arrive at some estimate of this ability. The procedure involved compilation of scores on the Iowa Silent Reading Test, gathered from many schools, of school populations grade by grade from grade 4 through grade 12 and relating these to the median number of grades completed in the adult population. With this evidence before him Gray gave it as his considered opinion (51–52) that at least half the adult population was able to read at the ninth grade level or above, which enables them to read with ease and understanding the more popular types of newspapers, magazines, and books." Looking at the other side of the shield, he observed that somewhat less than half our adult population were reading below the ninth grade level, and a third were "functionally illiterate," that is, were unable to read at the fifth grade level. Many of the remainder, he said, could not read easily and with understanding much of the popular materials prepared for adults today nor would they be able "to use reading effectively in the study of personal and social problems."

Relating the reading ability of the adult population to the number of school grades completed suggests inquiring into any trend in this measure as found in successive census data. The median numbers of years completed

TABLE 10.9
MEDIAN NUMBER OF SCHOOL YEARS COMPLETED IN THE TOTAL POPULATION 25 YEARS AND OVER IN THE UNITED STATES IN 1940, 1950, AND 1960

Year of Census	Population		
	Total	Men	Women
1960*	10.5	10.3	10.7
1950*	9.3	9.0	9.6
1940†	8.4	8.3	8.5

SOURCES:
*1960 Census of Population, Vol. 1, Pt. 1, *Characteristics of the Population* (Bureau of the Census, Department of Commerce).
†1940 Census of Population, Vol. 1, Pt. 1, *Characteristics of the Population* (Bureau of the Census, Department of Commerce).

by the population of the United States as found in the censuses for 1940, 1950, and 1960 are reported in Table 10.9. It is seen that the median for the total population rose approximately a year for each of the two intervals represented, and that the increases for each of the sexes rose at about the same amount, although the measures for women are fractionally higher than for men. Thus, in view of the correlation between reading ability and years of schooling, we may be assured that the level of this ability has already risen considerably above Gray's estimate and, what is even more reassuring, will continue to rise and bring larger proportions of the population into levels where effective adult education is feasible.

The prospect of feasibility is enhanced by the possibilities of improving the reading efficiency of adults with special programs for this purpose, as may be indicated by summarizing the description and results of an illustrative experiment carried on by Broxson in extension courses of the University of Florida and reported by him as long ago as 1943 (7). The experiment consisted of conducting off-campus classes enrolling 180 adults in many different walks of life, all of whom were high school graduates, many of whom had attended college, and some of whom were college graduates. The author did not report the ages of the students. The course extended through twelve weeks, with four-hour sessions one day each week, the first two hours of which were used for lectures, discussions, assigned readings, and quizzes, and the second two hours, after an hour of intermission, for demonstration, laboratory work, and exercises. Tests for visual defects showed 24 in need of lens correction or medication or both. Of the 180 students, 175 completed the course.

The significant finding of the experiment concerns the gains made in reading ability as seen in a comparison of the results of administering alternate forms of the Iowa Silent Reading Test, Advanced, near the opening of the course and after eight weeks of class sessions. These gains may be illustrated as follows: the proportion of students with rates of reading at the high school and college levels combined increased from about 37 per cent to about 66 per cent, or from less than two-fifths to two-thirds of all, and the proportion with percentile scores in comprehension of 80 and above increased from 52 per cent to about 76 per cent, or from about a half to three-fourths of all. These figures suggest that remedial efforts can increase substantially the proportion of adults who can profit from instruction addressed to consideration of their needs.

Abilities of adults in class and in courses.—Having canvassed successively the questions of the intelligence and the reading ability of adults, the treatment now turns to the even more immediate issue of the abilities of adult students in the classroom, that is, their aptitudes and their performance in courses. Over the years since the early thirties a number of inquiries have been made and reported, in most cases in comparison with younger students. Eight of these studies, in considerable variety, are here briefly reviewed—enough of them to afford a basis for a working judgment on the question of the relative competence of adults as students, and at the same time to provide some supplementary insights on similarities and differences.

(1) The first two of these studies were made by Sorenson, a pioneer in research on adult students. The first of these (55) concerned students in three classes in the Extension Division of the University of Minnesota made up primarily of elementary school teachers, with an age range of 36 years (20–56) to whom Sorenson had administered the Miller Analogies Test and, at the end of the course, a comprehensive objective examination on course content. Subjects were divided into two groups, one of which had been in more nearly continuous contact with study activity, as indicated by taking extension courses, than the other. Hypotheses of the research appear to have been (1) that age might be a factor in learning and (2) that the lapse of years since carrying on active study (influence of disuse) might affect competence in the extension course. Sorenson concluded that the students for whom the extension classes had been preceded by attending several to many courses showed no age handicap. For this group, at least up to the age of fifty, there was no decline in ability with

age. For the other group there was a "slight disability, which can be overcome by the resumption of study."

(2) The other research by Sorenson (*56*) appears to have been done to answer the question of whether the conclusion of decline in intelligence with age through adulthood which was inferred in investigations like those of Jones and Conrad and Miles and Miles, as cited in Chapter 2, applies also to students in extension courses. In making this investigation Sorenson administered to his subjects tests of vocabulary and of paragraph reading which were currently being used with full-time students at the University of Minnesota. The age-range of the subjects, 641 in number, was from 16 to 70. They were selected from a total population of between 5,000 and 6,000 part-time students in such a way as to set up five-year groupings with years of schooling and occupational distribution held constant throughout the total age-range. He found that under these conditions the age curve for vocabulary ability went up while that for paragraph-reading ability "went neither up nor down."

(3) Another among the earlier studies to be cited here is one by McGrath and Froman (*37*). These authors administered to all subjects a 10-minute test which was an adaptation of a similar section of the Thurstone American Council on Education Test and was composed of 54 sets of five words, one of which is the "cue" word. The subject is directed to underline the one word of the remaining four which is the same as, or the opposite of, the cue word. The subjects included 1,296 extension course students, in the Evening Session of the University of Buffalo, 213 freshmen and 53 seniors in the College of Arts, and 523 high school seniors. The mean scores for these four groups were, respectively, 31.81, 30.85, 36.35, and 26.18. The conclusion drawn by the authors is that, "considering the college student body as a whole, there is not a great difference in college aptitude between these [college] students and those who come to the evening session."

(4) In an investigation representative of the more recent period, Farnum (*24*) administered the ACE Psychological Examination and the Cooperative Reading Comprehension Test to freshmen in the College of Business Administration of the University of Rhode Island and to students taking an extension course corresponding to a requirement in that college. Four pairs of mean scores were reported for the two groups of students. For two of these pairs of scores, on the ACE Psychological Examination and on speed in reading, the difference between the two groups was found not statistically significant. For the other two scores, those on vocabulary and on comprehension on the Cooperative Reading Test, the differences were in favor of the extension students, and were found to be statistically significant, the former at the 1 per cent and the latter at the 5 per cent

level. The mean ages of the two groups were 19.6 for campus students and 29.6 for extension students. The investigator concluded that the "extension students who were enrolled in a program leading to a college degree were capable of doing college work...."

(5) An investigation comparing both the verbal ability and the performance of campus and extension students at the University of Illinois in a course in introductory psychology has been reported by Costin and Johnston (15). The mean ages of the two groups of students were 20.3 and 27.7 and their mean scores on the Verbal Ability section of SCAT were, respectively, 21.8 and 18.9. This investigation followed a matched-pairs

TABLE 10.10
CAMPUS AND EXTENSION STUDENTS' ACHIEVEMENT IN AN INTRODUCTORY
PSYCHOLOGY COURSE (MATCHED COMPARISON)

Course Examination	Number of Items	Campus (70)		Extension (70)		Differences in Means	t
		Mean	SD	Mean	SD		
Topic I	65	50.8	5.9	49.4	7.2	1.4	1.43
Topic II	65	50.4	5.8	48.5	7.2	1.9	1.73
Topic III	65	52.8	8.1	48.7	6.8	4.1	3.44*
Topic IV	65	53.8	7.6	48.3	7.4	5.5	4.49†
Topic V	90	68.8	8.1	64.9	11.0	3.9	2.62†

SOURCE: Costin and Johnston (15).
*$P < .01$.
†$P < .05$.

procedure, with 70 of the campus students (in a total of 104) matched on verbal score with the same number (in a total of 115) extension students, and with the mean verbal score at 21.2 for both groups. Comparison was made of the performance scores of these students on course examinations on five topics, with results as shown in Table 10.10. All the mean measures are seen to be lower for the extension than for the campus students, although the differences are not large. For three of the comparisons, those for the examinations on Topics III, IV, and V, the differences were found to be statistically significant. In concluding their report, however, the authors say, "All in all, the results of this study indicate that it is reasonable to expect extension students taking an introductory psychology course to achieve as well as campus students taking the same course. Those differences in achievement which did favor the campus students were small enough... to justify such a conclusion."

(6) An invesigation reported by Halfter (28) differs from those so far reviewed in that it shows comparison of the achievement of older with younger students enrolled in courses given on campus only, not by comparing campus with extension students. It differs also in being restricted to

women, the comparison relating to women 18–25 and women over 40 enrolled in courses leading to degrees. The report contains no distribution of ages nor indication of the average ages of the two groups. The population studied were attending De Paul University and Roosevelt University in Chicago during the academic year 1959–60. The final sample included 133 older and 384 younger women completing work in 215 courses in De Paul University and 76 older and 552 younger women completing 164 courses in Roosevelt University.

The measure of comparison used is derived from the relative percentile ranks of the marks assigned to students in individual courses. A mean score of 50.00 or better by older women indicated that they were performing at least as well as the younger women. The percentile rank for the older women in the 254 courses in De Paul University was found to be 57.40 and for those in the 164 courses in Roosevelt University 63.93. The means were computed also for all "fields of study," for example, Business, Communications, Humanities, Modern Languages, Science and Mathematics, Nursing, etc.—eight divisions for each institution. The mean percentile for only a single division, Natural Science and Mathematics at De Paul, was reported to fall below 50, and this was 49.41. The superiority in achievement for older women emerged both for culturally and for vocationally oriented courses.

One aspect of this research considered separately the achievement records of women who had had (a) better-than-average and (b) average achievement records in high school. The older women with above-average high school achievement were found to contribute disproportionately to the better-than-young average total performance and to the better-than-young average performance in each of the fields of study. Older women with average high school achievement gave an average relative performance in college work. Disuse, in the sense of the length of time since these older women had previously been in school, had "no discernible effect" on their performance.

(7) Still another of the researches on adult students to be abstracted here differs from the others in that it was avowedly experimental and made use of television (23). It was conducted under the auspices of the Chicago City Junior College and compared ability and achievement of regular students as control groups and students utilizing TV as experimental subjects. In excess of four-fifths of the regular students were under 21 years of age, whereas the average age of the experimentals was 36. Regular courses of the City Junior College were presented to the experimental groups, using study guides, in-person review sessions, and examinations. A second control group received the telecasts plus 20 minutes of classroom teaching at each session.

In all subjects taught, namely English, Biology, Social Science, and Mathematics, the resulting measures were higher for experimental than for the control groups, but only for Biology was the difference large enough for statistical significance (at the 5 per cent level in this instance). Because Otis Intelligence Test and ACE Critical Thinking Test scores for experimental groups ran somewhat higher than for control groups, this factor was controlled by using matched pairs. No significant differences emerged from this second comparison, although the measures for the experimental groups tended to be somewhat higher.

(8) Latest among the investigations to be reviewed is an experimental project by Schultz and Ulmer which was confined to a single junior college where such variables as facilities, teachers, course material, methods, course objectives, and student ability could be carefully controlled (51). Six day and six evening classes (five courses) were used for the study: World Literature, Inorganic Chemistry, Plane Trigonometry, Accounting Principles, and two sections of freshman English. The same teacher instructed the day and evening section of a given course, with two teachers having one day and one evening section each of English. There were thus six paired classes in which each teacher used, for both sections of the matched classes, the same course objectives, methods, materials, assignments, and examinations. The only difference was that the day sections met for three 55-minute periods weekly whereas the evening sections met once a week for 2 hours and 45 minutes. Students were not told that they were involved in the study.

A pre-test consisting of the final examination in previous presentations of the courses was administered by each teacher, except for English where the Cooperative English Test was used. In addition, three six-weeks tests were administered in each course. These yielded three residual gain scores on each student during the semester. Achievement comparisons were thus available (a) between day and evening classes and (b) between age classifications. Scores from the California Mental Maturity Test were available on each student.

The primary question in the experiment concerned day and evening achievements with a secondary question of the influence of age. In the interests of brevity the particularized findings of the project are here briefly generalized, with some inevitable loss of inclusiveness. On the whole, the advantage was clearly with the evening classes, as "in no case did a day class have as high a mean score as did the matched evening class." Also, "high ability students under 21 years of age . . . achieved at approximately the same level in the day as in the evening classes, while the low ability students in that age group achieved at a higher level in the evening classes than they did in the day classes." In respect to the age variable, the conclusion is that students of the older age group achieved at a higher level than did young students and, irrespective of ability, were the high scorers in the study: for every test period, an evening age group scored at a higher level than did a day age group.

The findings of these eight projects which spread over the span of a third of a century warrant a general conclusion that the ability of adults enrolled in college-credit courses is usually at least on a par with that of students of normal age for these courses and that the adults' performance in courses is likewise typically at least as good and sometimes better. These findings go far to dispel the myth often given credence, even by some teachers of adults, that they must be carried along by a "soft pedagogy." They are evidence that at least that segment of the adult population who venture into college-credit courses can succeed with them. Moreover, there is promise of the growth of that segment in the steady and rapid rise in the school level being attained by the total population and the accompanying improvement in reading and other abilities and the maintenance of these abilities through most of the life-span. The same rise will also influence the expansion of noncredit offerings for adults—offerings comprehending all major concerns in the adult's developmental tasks as these were reviewed earlier in the chapter.

Characteristics and Interests of Adult Students

The concern of this section.—The final section of this chapter, in advance of the summary, is given over to portrayal of the characteristics of adult students to the extent this can be done through dependence on the literature, which is far from extensive, although in some part enlightening. This portrayal has to a degree been accomplished in the foregoing section, at least with respect to abilities and ages, but little has been reported on socioeconomic status, motivation, and interests, and these will now be emphasized, at the same time that further data concerning age and ability will be presented.

The reports of projects to be reviewed are (1) a limited study of students in a junior college evening program, (2) a study of the opinions concerning adult education of participants and nonparticipants in an adult program, (3) a comparison of clients of three diverse types of adult offerings, (4) a study of motivation for attendance in a large adult student population, and (5) a near-comprehensive comparison of adult students in programs of institutions at three institutional levels that permits a focus of attention on the special function in adult education of the junior college.

An evening junior college student body.—This study (*17*) was reported from Flint, Michigan, and depended on returns from a questionnaire which had been filled out by 353 male and 186 female students, a total of 539.

The median age of these students, both males and females, was 24.5, from which one infers that they were primarily young adults. The percentage distribution of student purposes in the "college-credit" courses, as indicated by enrollments, was as follows:

	PRE-PROFESSIONAL	TERMINAL	TEACHER PREPARATION	LIBERAL ARTS	UNDECIDED
Men	68	7	5	3	17
Women	32	9	24	3	32

The goals of the two sexes are seen to differ strikingly, as indicated by the much larger proportion of men than women headed toward the professions, and a larger proportion of women toward teaching and undecided on goals. The median numbers of hours per week worked by these students was 43 (not including housewives and unemployed), a fact suggesting that they were primarily full-time employees. The four main classes of occupations engaged in by the males were service, unskilled, skilled, and clerical and sales; of the females, clerical and sales, housewife, service, and professional and managerial. Asked to indicate their degrees of job satisfaction, 57 per cent responded that they were "very satisfied" with their jobs, 30 per cent that they were "somewhat satisfied," and 13 per cent "very dissatisfied." This predominantly favorable response appears to be belied by the fact that 85 per cent also said that their purpose in attending evening classes was to improve their work situations. A large proportion expressed interest in educational advisement and a vocational guidance clinic, which likewise leans toward belying the report of a high degree of satisfaction with the students' current employments.

A comparison of the opinions of participants and nonparticipants.— This comparison (42) of opinions and of social status was made in Cortland, New York, by interviews with a careful sampling of 618 persons in the adult population. Following are salient excerpts from the summary of findings: (1) The kinds of courses most preferred by participants were arts and crafts, general academic, commercial and distributive, and homemaking. (2) Participants thought the primary purpose of the adult education program should be: (a) intellectual growth as an end in itself, 57 per cent; (b) enjoyment of leisure time excluding intellectual growth, 15 per cent; (c) family-life education, 5 per cent; (d) "how-to" home improvement education, 3 per cent. Approximately 43 per cent of the nonparticipants favored intellectual growth as a primary purpose. (3) Approximately 40 per cent of the participants were classified in lower occupational groups, such as skilled manual employees, machine operators and semiskilled employees, and unskilled workers, while 53 per cent of the nonparticipants were so classified. (4) Approximately 51 per cent of the participants and 66 per cent of the nonparticipants engaged in no voluntary activity, such as Red Cross, Boy Scouts, political campaigning, and Community Chest work. (5) Approximately 40 per cent of the participants and 50 per cent of the nonparticipants had read no book during the preceding six months. (6) Forty-two per cent of the participants were in Classes I, II, and III according to Hollingshead's two-factor index of social position, while 73 per cent of the nonparticipants were in the lowest classes IV and V, as compared with 54 per cent of the participants. (7) The distribution of participants by age ranged widely, with substantial proportions in all age-groups from under 30 through 61 and over, but with some concentration in the 31–40 span. (8) Thirty-two per cent of the participants were male and 68 per cent female, and approximately 83 per cent were married.

Clients of three diverse offerings.—This investigation (*18*) was made by interviews with a carefully controlled sample of students attending three different types of courses. The courses represented were (a) college-credit courses in the College of Special and Continuing Studies of the University of Maryland (with a modest tuition charge); (b) Great Books Reading and Discussion Groups in Washington, D.C., Public Libraries (tuition free); and (c) noncredit evening school group in the Baltimore high schools (also tuition free). The classification by age of the participants was as follows:

PROGRAM	UNDER 30	30–39	40–49	50–59	60 AND ABOVE
College Credits	34	53	22	17	0
Great Books	12	43	24	16	5
Noncredit Public	51	34	10	4	1

Quotation and paraphrase of the descriptions of the students will indicate differences in motivation and characteristics of the three groups. The college-credit group, who were clustered in the 30–39 age-span, with fewer in the spans above and below, included a large number of respondents who were urged by their employers to attend, with attendance often even made a requirement for promotion. They were characterized by an attitude and interest pattern very different from the other two groups. They were interested in the practical aspects of the course material and often mentioned ways in which they had been able to use it in their regular work. They often professed to taking more pleasure in their work than in any other activity.

The age distribution of the Great Books group ran considerably higher than those of the other two groups. The motivation of the participants was most often ascribed to a desire for cultural broadening and they had few if any vocational interests to prompt enrollment. They mentioned altruistic aims four times as often as the other population samples, and they also differed in the frequency with which they described other persons of higher social and economic status whom they admired and accepted as ego ideals.

The noncredit evening high school students were typically much younger than members of the other two groups. About a third of those interviewed had not finished high school and very few claimed college degrees.

The drop-out rate in voluntary adult education programs is usually high and this is true for two of the groups in the present comparison. Within the Great Books group it was 40 per cent; within the evening school noncredit group it was 43 per cent; within the college-credit group it was 14 per cent. In a classification by occupation and social position with the top 10 per cent designated A, the next 30 per cent B, the middle 40 per cent C, and the bottom 20 per cent D, the ratings for students who dropped out were most frequently C or D, for the completers most often A or B.

An inquiry with focus on motivation.—Reasons for attendance were solicited from a total of more than 5,000 men and women "in different sections of the United States" (46) whose average age was 24, the majority of whom were single, although about a third were married. Three-fourths of the men and two-thirds of the women were employed. Most men were employed in mechanical pursuits, with the second largest number in "persuasive" occupations. Almost half the women were engaged in clerical occupations, with the second largest proportion in social services.

The procedure of investigation was that of requesting the respondents to indicate which of a number of special "reasons" in three different "areas" influenced them to attend. The areas of motive were classified as Economic-Occupational, Intellectual-Cultural, and Personal-Social. Thirty special reasons were included, about equally divided among the three areas.

The average percentages of indication of special reasons under each of the areas of motive and the percentages of indication for certain representative special reasons under each main category of motive are shown in Table 10.11. It must be said that the variety of special reasons under each of the areas and the inevitable overlapping of special reasons on each other is such as to blunt the differences in percentages. Nevertheless, the differences are sufficiently apparent to signify variation in motive from area to area and also from special reason to special reason. The two first areas named reflected a high incidence of motive for both sexes, but with a higher incidence for men for the area Economic-Occupational and the two special reasons under it and a higher incidence for women for the Intellectual-Cultural area and both its subcategories. The Personal-Social area was indicated with about half the proportionate frequency of the first two, but with the women indicating it more often than the men and, likewise, indicating the first two subcategories more often.

A near-comprehensive inquiry.—One of the most enlightening investigative reports on part-time adult students in respect to their characteristics, interests, and motivation, has been reported by Chapman (*11*). It is especially useful for the treatment here because it permits a focus on the adult-education service of the community college by affording a com-

TABLE 10.11
PERCENTAGES OF MEN, WOMEN, AND ALL ADULT STUDENTS INDICATING CERTAIN AREAS OF MOTIVE AND SPECIFIC REASONS FOR SCHOOL ATTENDANCE

Area of Motive and Specific Reason for Attendance	Men	Women	Total
I. Economic-Occupational	63.4	51.2	58.3
a. Will help to earn more	86.8	65.0	77.7
b. Preparing for a position in which not now employed	56.5	46.9	52.5
II. Intellectual-Cultural	60.0	64.0	62.2
a. Wish to become familiar with fine arts, humanities, sciences, and broader aspects of education	64.9	79.6	71.1
b. Desire to learn more about local, national, and world affairs	54.0	64.0	58.2
III. Personal-Social	27.6	35.0	30.7
a. Desire to become better fitted to parenthood	46.1	55.0	49.6
b. Wish to learn certain social skills such as public speaking, singing, playing an instrument, dancing, or making friends	29.9	38.2	33.4
c. Wish to improve my health	21.9	20.1	21.4

SOURCE: Nicholson (*46*, 9–11, Tables II, III, and IV).

parison of the characteristics, interests, and motivation of students attending programs made available at three institutional levels, namely, high school, junior college, and the extension divisions of higher institutions. Its highly informative nature prompts making extensive extracts from it here. The particular situation involved is Contra Costa County in California and the institutions in connection with which the programs were being carried forward were six high schools, two junior colleges, and the extension divisions of the University of California and of San Francisco State College. The students involved totaled 6,610 who were attending adult education classes in October, 1957, with the following distribution to the three subgroups: high school, 3,499; junior college, 2,533; extension divisions, 578.

The project included demographic comparison of the adult students with the total adult population of the county, from which certain differences emerged. Some of these are that the study population as a group were in a better socioeconomic position than the average adult of the county, their educational level was considerably higher, their income higher by hundreds of dollars a year, and their occupational classifications more prestigious. Differences in age distribution were mainly that the younger

TABLE 10.12
PERCENTAGES IN CERTAIN CLASSIFICATIONS OF ADULT STUDENTS IN HIGH SCHOOL AND JUNIOR COLLEGE EVENING PROGRAMS AND IN EXTENSION DIVISIONS

Item	High School	Junior College	Extension Division
Age			
Under 26	17.0	29.7	9.1
Over 45	16.5	9.5	25.0
Sex			
Male	72.4	32.9	70.8
Female	25.9	66.5	27.7
Educational attainment			
Less than high school graduation	29.6	11.3	.6
High school graduation	30.6	35.3	1.6
College graduation	14.5	10.7	81.6
Degree aspiration			
Associate in Arts	1.7	21.0	.4
Bachelor's	2.7	18.0	11.1
Master's and beyond	1.6	7.0	24.7

SOURCE: Chapman (*11*, Tables 3, 4, 5, and 6).

age-group and the age category "over 60" were less well represented than the age-spans between. Specifically, for this older group, only 1.7 per cent were enrolled, although they made up 7 per cent of the population of the county. Although adult males in the county outnumber the females, females far outnumber the males as adult students.

Certain percentages bearing on the age, sex, educational attainment, and degree aspiration are shown in Table 10.12. While the percentages of younger and of older adults were about equal in the high school subgroup, younger adults predominate in the junior college subgroup, and older adults in the classes of the extension divisions. Males made up almost three-fourths of the students in the high school subgroup and again in the classes of the extension divisions, but females predominate in almost the same proportion in the junior college subgroup.

The table carries three measures of educational attainment of the adult students—less than high school graduation, high school graduation, and college graduation. Large proportions of the high school subgroup reported attainment at the first two measures, with, as might be expected in a situation with offerings at all three levels, a smaller proportion at the level of college graduation. In excess of four-fifths of those in the extension classes were college graduates. Of the junior college subgroup only a small minority were not high school graduates, with the largest proportion high school graduates, about a tenth college graduates, and, presumably, although not reported, a considerable proportion with some college work.

As concerns degree aspiration, as may be seen in the lower portion of Table 10.12, only a relatively few in the high school subgroup reported aspiring to any of the degrees, almost a fourth of the extension students

TABLE 10.13
PERCENTAGES OF ADULT STUDENTS IN CERTAIN OCCUPATIONAL CLASSIFICATIONS WHO WERE ATTENDING HIGH SCHOOL AND JUNIOR COLLEGE EVENING CLASSES AND EXTENSION DIVISIONS

Occupational Classification	High Schools	Junior Colleges	Extension Division
Craftsman, foreman, and similar types	10.5	25.6	.3
Homemaker	51.0	14.2	5.0
Professional and technical worker	9.5	19.6	85.0

SOURCE: Chapman (*11*, Table 8).

had aspirations toward graduate degrees, whereas almost a half of the junior college subgroup were aspiring to degrees at one or another of the three levels.

The proportions of adults in three groups of occupations are reported in Table 10.13. The proportion of craftsmen, foremen, and similar types of workers was about a tenth in the high school subgroup, a full fourth of all in the junior college subgroup, and was negligible in the extension classes. Homemakers made up a majority of all in the high school subgroup, receded to a seventh in junior college adult classes, and made up an even smaller proportion of extension students. Professional and technical workers made up about a tenth of the high school adult classes, rose to about a fifth of the junior college subgroup, and accounted for 85 per cent of the extension students.

Chapman included in his investigation administering to a 12 per cent sampling of high school and junior college subgroups a 20-item scholastic aptitude test which had a few years before been produced by the Educational Testing Service and standardized on a national sampling of high school seniors. This test had been found to have a high correlation with ACE and SCAT. It was administered also to a sampling of freshmen in one of the Contra Costa junior colleges. The mean scores for these different populations are reported in Table 10.14. That for the adult junior college subgroup is seen to compare favorably with those of the college-going national sample and of the full-time junior college sample. It may be noted also that the mean for the adult high school subgroup is higher than that for the national norm sample.

The question of motive for attending adult education classes was given extensive consideration in this investigation and dealt with in a major section of the report called "Why Adults Return to School." The data used for this section were collected from interviews, an open-end questionnaire, and a checklist. Although 80 per cent of the students gave multiple

TABLE 10.14
MEAN TEST SCORES OF NATIONAL NORM GROUP OF HIGH SCHOOL SENIORS, ADULT PART-TIME STUDENTS, AND FULL-TIME DAY JUNIOR COLLEGE STUDENTS

Group	Mean Score
National norm sample	9.04
Non-college-going	7.75
College-going	11.69
Adult part-time students	11.12
High schools	9.86
Junior colleges	12.50
Full-time day junior college	
Freshman junior college students	11.80

SOURCE: Chapman (*11*, Table 7).

reasons, an equal proportion said there was a single most important reason. These single reasons clustered around five "major families" which the investigator converted into the same number of categories: (1) persons interested in "leisure-time skills," 14 per cent; (2) persons interested in "social skills" (dancing, singing, speaking, "improving my personality," etc.), 7 per cent; (3) persons with "cultural-intellectual" interests, 14 per cent; (4) persons interested in "economic enhancement," 33 per cent; and (5) those interested in "educational advancement," 14 per cent. The last-named category included adults interested to a much larger degree than were those in other categories in formal educational goals involving diplomas and degrees.

Economic enhancement is thus seen to be the most frequent single reason for attendance, although it does not rise to predominance. It is, of course, intimately involved with occupation. A finding of the investigation is that the lower a person is on the occupational ladder, the more desirous he is to change. Chapman reports, as example, that 75 per cent of the males who were employed as unskilled workers aspired to jobs higher on the ladder, and 40 per cent of those employed as skilled workers aspired to higher job classifications.

Partial appreciation of any peculiar role of adult education in the junior college may be derived from the following differences among the three subgroups of the study: (a) over 63 per cent of the students in the extension divisions were motivated by economic reasons, whereas 45 per cent and 20 per cent, respectively, were so motivated in the junior college and high school subgroups; (b) a desire to learn "leisure-time skills" was the primary reason of one in four in the high schools, but it was fewer than one in twenty in the junior colleges and extension divisions; (c) 10 per cent of the students in the high school subgroup listed a desire to learn "social skills" as their primary reason, while only 4 per cent in the junior colleges and none in the extension divisions did so. Adults whose interests lay in the area of cultural-intellectual pursuits were numerous in all subgroups. The largest proportion (17 per cent) was in the junior colleges, with 12 per cent in each of the other subgroups.

In rounding out his report Chapman applied a useful generalizing concept for the reasons why adults return to school as part-time students. He says that this return is "not a chance event in their lives but is determined by the individual's dissatisfactions" and that adults "look to education as a means of resolving their dissatisfactions and as an aid to realizing their aspirations." In amplification of the concept, he says, "The source of these dissatisfactions extends over a large area of man's experiences. They include: (1) a feeling of insecurity at home, on the job, or in one's social relationships; (2) changes in one's position in life, as for example, marriage and parenthood with their involvement of greater responsibility and need for knowledge of family life education; (3) the sobering effect of age which is frequently accompanied by a realization of the importance of education that one either "passed up" or that was unattainable earlier in life; (4) a feeling of uneasiness about world affairs and a desire to understand more about human behavior; (5) the increase in leisure time through the shortened workday and work-week, for which there is a lack of preparation for its constructive use; (6) a desire for material gain, which is a significant facet of our culture and which is exemplified by the concept of competition; (7) the dissatisfactions that stem from realizing we live in an expanding and rapidly changing local and world environment and the realization that one cannot cope adequately with the problems attendant upon constant change unless they are viewed in light of the experience of others."

While at first thought it may seem parenthetical, it is, in fact, germane to speculate at this point over the relationship of these (a) expressed interests and dissatisfactions deduced from them by Chapman and (b) the needs as represented in the developmental tasks of adulthood as proposed by Havighurst and listed above in considering the rationale of adult education. Speculation shows a considerable degree of coincidence of the interests and dissatisfactions with the task areas. To the extent there is discrepancy, it may be largely owing to unawareness of adults of their true needs. A plausible case can be made for the responsibility of the program of adult education to assist them to an awareness of what these needs are.

In view of the variation in motive for attendance and the variations also in age, sex, education, educational goal, occupation, and occupational objective, it should be no surprise that Chapman concluded that generalizations can hardly be drawn as to who the typical adult part-time student is. He does identify a few "types" with common characteristics, such as homemaker, semiprofessional, office worker, and cultural enthusiast, but he also found many whose identifying characteristics are "so varied as to preclude typing." With all the variation, it should be no surprise, furthermore, that he expressed the opinion that "no single public institution or type of public institution can meet the educational needs of adults in our culture today."

Although it is hardly in the province of this treatise to deal at length with problems of administrative set-up for adult education, the comment may not be out of place that the role of the junior college in respect to the full scope of adult education may in some degree be subject to factors like size and organization of the operating district, the size of the full-time junior college, the location and size of schools at other levels, and agencies other than the junior college at work on adult programs. For instance, in a small district with a small full-time junior college enrollment, it may be desirable for the institution to administer the total adult program at all levels. This is sometimes done in larger districts: witness the program of San Mateo Junior College as described earlier in this chapter. Even when other agencies operate adult programs at other than junior college levels, such as at elementary school, high school, or upper collegiate levels, it may be desirable for the junior college to serve as the coordinating agency for all the adult offerings.

Summary

Programs of adult education and enrollments in them since the turn of the century represent one of the most remarkable developments in the whole realm of schooling. The rapid development has spread to a number of agencies and is reflected in junior colleges, especially in public units. Eells found that the proportion of adults in the total junior college student body increased from less than 21,000 to more than 193,000 during the brief period 1936–37 to 1942–43. Because the method of reporting enrollments for these institutions was subsequently changed, it is impossible to report a correct comparative figure for a recent year, but it may be assumed that the number and proportion of part-time adults has increased. The programs typically range through a variety of preparatory and nonpreparatory offerings, although in some instances they are limited to courses intentionally identical with those available in day-time programs, while, at the other extreme, they aim at recognizing the full range of interests of adults in the community.

The rationale of adult education may be said to stem mainly from our changing society and the needs of adults as seen in their developmental tasks. Portrayal of the changes usually begins with the scientific and technological revolutions of this century, as in transportation, communication, and automation, which have been accompanied and followed by profound adjustments in our economic, social, and political worlds. The developmental tasks, ranging through strands of life and living related to selecting and adjusting to one's spouse, responsibilities as parent, function as homemaker and as worker, responsibilities as citizen and as friend in a social group, participation in leisure-time activities, and adjustment to physiological changes, also change with age from early adulthood, through middle age, and into later maturity. The social changes compound the difficulties of accomplishing the developmental tasks, and together they make education as a way of life imperative. The process of education can not be restricted, as has often been assumed, to the years of childhood and youth.

Recent years have seen an emphasis on attention to the problems of later maturity. This has been stimulated in some part by a startling increase in the proportion of older people in the population, an increase which some have assumed will continue, but which is slowing down, although older people will remain a large segment of the population. Their numerical prominence has brought about a focus on their problems. Important among these is their use of leisure time, especially as they drop out of the labor force at earlier ages than formerly. The concerns have spread also to include physical and psychological aspects of aging, physical living arrangements, reduced income, and congenial association with members of their own age group. These problems have begun to be recognized in courses for later adulthood.

There could have been no rationale for adult education if the myth of the adult's inability to learn commonly accepted a generation or more ago had not been dispelled by contradictory evidence. Thorndike was first to muster evidence, although his inquiries did not reach into later maturity and were limited in the abilities explored. Subsequent investigation established retention of learning abilities over a much longer age-range, although they also found that adults do not fare so well as younger persons in tests involving speed and motility.

Conclusions from earlier cross-sectional applications of intelligence tests to total populations, which seemed to show a rather steady average decline in score through adulthood after the steep gradient in childhood and youth, were later discredited by longitudinal and other studies which found abilities maintained and even increasing with advance in age. Such findings are supported by the indirect evidence of the longer periods of schooling in our society of younger as compared with older persons and the well-known high degree of relationship of ability in reading with years of schooling completed and, in turn, the correspondingly high correlation of ability in reading and scores on intelligence tests. Most of the recent evidence and deliberation over it suggests the conclusion that there is little change in primary ability to learn through the adult years up to senility.

With the rapid rise in years of schooling completed, increasing proportions of adults are found capable of using reading to advance their education, and there is experimental evidence that skills in reading of adults can be improved. Evidence is also at hand through a number of investigations that adults in credit courses, in some instances in extension as compared with campus students and in others in full-time programs, are at least on a par in aptitude with younger students and perform as well or better on course requirements.

The demographic comparisons of participants and nonparticipants in the studies of part-time adult education programs show that the participants tend in considerable degree to come more from homes of higher social status, higher socioeconomic and occupational classifications, with somewhat higher incomes, than nonparticipants, so that there is some justification for the assertion that those who need the programs most are less inclined to benefit from them. The age-group in later adulthood appears to be less well represented than younger adults. Women are better represented than men, although there is variation in this regard from program to program.

Although the motives for attendance in the programs vary widely in any large adult student group, the most recurrent interest has been identified as economic-occupational. Other frequent interests inferred from one or more of the investigations summarized are in the development of leisure-time and social skills, concerns relating to home and family, and political, economic, and social questions in the broad area of intellectual-cultural interests. The prominence of the economic-occupational suggests an unfortunately minimized representation of the several nonoccupational areas of the developmental tasks.

The only report of research on characteristics and interests of part-time adult students reviewed above that compares the subgroups served by high schools, junior colleges, and extension divisions of higher institutions showed the following differences for the junior college subgroup: younger adults and females predominated; smaller proportions than of the high school subgroup were not high school graduates; a much larger proportion had aspirations for degrees; more middle-level occupations and fewer homemakers were represented than in the high school subgroup. On motives for attendance, almost half attended for economic reasons, which was a much smaller proportion than for the extension subgroup and larger than for the high school subgroup; the proportions attending to develop leisure-time and social skills were relatively low, but there was a higher proportion with cultural-intellectual motivation. Such differentiations might disappear for situations in which the junior college undertakes to develop a program in the absence of programs sponsored by high schools and higher institutions.

References and Bibliography

1. Anastasi, Anne. "Age Changes in Adult Test Performance." *Psychological Reports,* 2 (Dec., 1956), 509.
2. Bayley, Nancy, and Oden, Melita H. "The Maintenance of Intellectual Ability in Gifted Adults." *Journal of Gerontology,* 10 (Jan., 1955), 91–107.
3. Birren, James E., ed. *Handbook of Aging and the Individual.* Chicago: University of Chicago Press, 1959.
4. Birren, James E. *The Psychology of Aging.* Englewood Cliffs, N.J.: Prentice-Hall, Inc., 1964.
5. Birren, James E., et al. *Human Aging: A Biological and Behavioral Study.* Washington: U.S. Department of Health, Education and Welfare, 1964.
6. Bromley, Dennis B. "Some Effects of Age on the Quality of Intellectual Output." *Journal of Gerontology,* 12 (July, 1957), 318–23.
7. Broxson, John A. "Improving Reading Ability of Adults." *Adult Education Journal,* 2 (April, 1943), 95–100.
8. Buswell, Guy T. *How Adults Read.* Supplementary Educational Monographs, no. 45. Chicago: University of Chicago Press, 1937.
9. Carey, James T. *Why Students Drop Out: A Study of Evening College Student Motivations.* Chicago: Center for the Study of Liberal Education for Adults, 1953.
10. Chamberlain, Neil W. "Retooling the Mind." *Atlantic,* 214 (Sept., 1964), 48–50.
11. Chapman, Charles E. "Some Characteristics of Adult Part-Time Students." *Adult Education,* 10 (Autumn, 1959), 27–41.
12. Clark, Burton R. *The Marginality of Adult Education.* Notes and Essays, no. 20. Chicago: Center for the Study of Liberal Education for Adults, 1958.
13. Commission of the Professors of Adult Education. *Adult Education: A New Imperative for Our Times.* Chicago: Adult Education Association of the U.S.A., 1961.
14. Corsini, Raymond J., and Fassett, Katherine K. "Intelligence and Aging." *Journal of Genetic Psychology,* 83 (Dec., 1953), 249–64.
15. Costin, Frank, and Johnston, Robert L. "A Study of Achievement in an Introductory Psychology Course." *Adult Education,* 12 (Winter, 1962), 120–26.
16. Cotton, Webster. "The Need for Adult Education—Some Major Themes." *Adult Education,* 13 (Autumn, 1962), 3–12.
17. D'Amico, Louis A. "Flint Junior College Study." *Adult Education,* 9 (Winter, 1959), 98–99.
18. Deane, Stephen R. "Who Seeks Adult Education and Why—A Description of Adult Education Participants." *Adult Education,* 1 (Autumn, 1950), 18–25.

19. DeGrow, Roger. *Ability and Achievement of Evening College Students.* Chicago: Center for the Study of Liberal Education for Adults, 1963.
20. Donahue, Wilma T. *Education for Later Maturity: A Handbook.* New York: Whiteside, Inc., and W. Morrow, 1955.
21. Donahue, Wilma T. "Experiments in the Education of Older Adults." *Adult Education,* 2 (Winter, 1951), 49–59.
22. Eells, Walter C. "The Community's College." *Adult Education Journal,* 4 (Jan., 1945), 13–17.
23. Erickson, Clifford G., and Chausow, Hymen M. *The Chicago City Junior College Experiment in Offering College Courses for Credit via Open Circuit Television.* Chicago: Chicago City Junior College, 1958.
24. Farnum, Hollis B. "A Comparison of Academic Aptitude of University Extension Degree Students and Campus Students." *Journal of Applied Psychology,* 41 (1951), 63–65.
25. Fox, Charlotte. "Vocabulary Ability in Later Maturity." *Journal of Educational Psychology,* 38 (Dec., 1947), 482–92.
26. Goldberg, Maxwell H. "Continuous Education as a Way of Life." *Adult Education,* 16 (Autumn, 1965), 3–9.
27. Hackman, Joseph. "Chicago Evening Junior Colleges." *Junior College Journal,* 11 (Feb., 1941), 305–10.
28. Halfter, Irma T. "Aging and Learning: An Achievement Study." *School Review,* 70 (April, 1962), 287–302.
29. Havighurst, Robert J. *Human Development and Education.* New York: David McKay, Inc., 1953.
30. Havighurst, Robert J. "Life Begins Again at Sixty-Five." *Nation's Schools,* 46 (July, 1950), 23–25.
31. Havighurst, Robert J., and Orr, Betty. *Adult Education and Adult Needs.* Chicago: Center for the Study of Liberal Education for Adults, 1956.
32. Henry, Nelson B., ed. *Adult Reading.* Fifty-fifth Yearbook of the National Society for the Study of Education. Chicago: University of Chicago Press, 1956.
33. Johnstone, John W. C., and Rivera, Ramon J. *Volunteers for Learning: A Study of the Educational Pursuits of American Adults.* Chicago: Aldine Publishing Co., 1965.
34. Kempfer, Homer. "Identifying Educational Needs and Interests of Adults—A Summary of an Evaluative Study." *Adult Education,* 2 (Autumn, 1951), 32–36.
35. Knowles, Malcolm S. *The Adult Education Movement in the United States.* New York: Holt, Rinehart & Winston, Inc., 1962.
36. Korchin, Sheldon J., and Basowitz, Harold. "Age Differences in Verbal Learning." *Journal of Abnormal and Social Psychology,* 54 (Jan., 1957), 64–69.
37. McGrath, Earl J., and Froman, Lewis A. "College Aptitude of Adult Students." *School & Society,* 45 (Jan. 16, 1937), 102–4.
38. Martorana, S. V. "Problems in Adult Education in the Junior College." *Junior College Journal,* 18 (Nov., 1947), 115–23.
39. Martorana, S. V. "Status of Adult Education in Junior Colleges." *Junior College Journal,* 18 (Feb., 1948), 322–31.
40. Miles, Walter R. "Age and Human Ability." *Psychological Review,* 40 (March, 1933), 99–123.
41. Miner, John B. *Intelligence in the United States.* New York: Springer Publishing Co., 1957.
42. Mizruchi, Ephraim H., and Vanaria, Louis M. "Who Participates in Adult Education?" *Adult Education,* 10 (Spring, 1960), 141–43.
43. Morris, Charles S. "The People's College at San Mateo." *Junior College Journal,* 14 (Dec., 1943), 148–52.
44. Mosley, John W. "Adult Education in the Community College." *Junior College Journal,* 20 (Oct., 1949), 75–81.

45. Murphy, Gardner, and Kuhlen, Raymond. *Psychological Needs of Adults*. Chicago: Center for the Study of Liberal Education for Adults, 1955.
46. Nicholson, David H. *Why Adults Attend School: An Analysis of Motivating Factors*. Bulletin 56, no. 30. Columbia: University of Missouri College of Education, 1955.
47. Owens, William A., Jr. *Age and Mental Abilities: A Longitudinal Study*. Genetic Psychology Monographs, 48 (1953), 3–54.
48. Phifer, Bryan M. "Change of Interest between Young Adulthood and Early Middle Age among Participants in Adult Education Programs." Ph.D. dissertation, University of Chicago, 1964.
49. Pollak, Otto. "Conservatism in Later Maturity and Old Age." *American Sociological Review*, 8 (April, 1943), 175–79.
50. Pressey, Sidney L., and Kuhlen, Raymond G. *Psychological Development Through the Life Span*. New York: Harper & Bros., 1957.
51. Schultz, Raymond E., and Ulmer, R. Curtis. "How Do Day and Evening Students Compare?" *Junior College Journal*, 37 (Sept., 1966), 34–36.
52. Sheats, Paul H. "The Junior College and the Educative Community." *Adult Education*, 9 (Winter, 1959), 94–97.
53. Sheldon, Henry D. *The Older Population in the United States*. New York: John Wiley & Sons, 1958.
54. Sorenson, Herbert. *Adult Abilities in Extension Classes; A Psychological Study*. Minneapolis: University of Minnesota Press, 1933.
55. Sorenson, Herbert. "Adult Ages as a Factor in Learning." *Journal of Educational Psychology*, 21 (Sept., 1930), 451–59.
56. Sorenson, Herbert. "Mental Ability over a Wide Range of Adult Ages." *Journal of Applied Psychology*, 17 (1933), 729–41.
57. Strong, Edward K. "Permanence of Interest Scores after Twenty-Two Years." *Journal of Applied Psychology*, 35 (April, 1951), 89–91.
58. Sward, Keeth. "Age and Mental Ability in Superior Men." *American Journal of Psychology*, 58 (Oct., 1945), 443–79.
59. Thorndike, Edward L. *Adult Interests*. New York: The Macmillan Co., 1935.
60. Thorndike, Edward L., et al. *Adult Learning*. New York: The Macmillan Co., 1928.
61. Ulmer, R. Curtis, and Verner, Coolie. "Factors Affecting Attendance in a Junior College Adult Program." *Adult Education*, 13 (Spring, 1963), 153–61.
62. Wann, Marie D., and Woodward, Marthene V. *Participation in Adult Education*. Circular No. 539. Washington: U.S. Office of Education, 1959.
63. Wattenberg, Ben J., and Scammon, Richard M. *This U.S.A.* Garden City, N.Y.: Doubleday & Co., 1965.
64. Wechsler, David. *The Measurement and Appraisal of Adult Intelligence*. 4th ed. Baltimore: Williams and Wilkins Co., 1958.
65. Wheeler, D. K., and Anderson, A. W. "Increasing Adult Reading Speed." *Adult Education*, 9 (Autumn, 1958), 25–30.
66. Woodward, Marthene V. *Statistics of Public School Adult Education, 1958–59*. Washington: Department of Health, Education and Welfare, 1961.

Part III

Implications for the Program

11
Implications for the Curriculum

THE TWO FOREGOING parts of this volume have been given over to exposition, as well as can be done with the materials extant, of the characteristics of the population to be served by the community college. The chapters of Part I do so by reviewing the investigative literature bearing on physical, mental, personal, and social development, sexual and dating behavior, and the vocational and avocational interests of later adolescence, which is the age-group making up the bulk of the full-time student body of the institution. The first three chapters of Part II focus on the students themselves and on related student populations, looking into their aptitude, socioeconomic status, academic competence, personal traits, attitudes, interests, and personal problems. The concern now turns to the implications of evidence and conclusions along these many lines for the program of education for community college students. The procedure followed is to describe the major elements of the program, and in connection with the description, in instances where the relationships may not be obvious, to indicate at appropriate points the characteristics, interests, or problems that call for the particular elements. The exposition can hardly follow the order of treatment in the foregoing sequence of chapters, but will involve presentation of the elements in something approaching a rational pattern and mentioning the implications when this seems necessary and wherever they are deemed to be applicable.

The treatment extends through two chapters, the first, and more extensive one, on curriculum and the second, and final chapter in the treatise, on guidance and counseling, including consideration of related student services and student activities. Significant relationships of curriculum and extracurriculum suggest some appropriateness of considering the two in immediate juxtaposition, but the fact that specialists in the field of student personnel and guidance regard leadership in the extracurriculum as within the province of student personnel and because important reports and literature deal with them in this way, it is practicable to consider the several aspects under the latter organization. In some ways, in view of the diversities among students served by community colleges, together with their diverse needs and goals, a case could be made for dealing first with student personnel services and afterwards with curriculum arrangements. The order here will nevertheless follow tradition in which consideration of curriculum precedes the other major element of the total program.

In the consideration here of the two main components of the program there is no assumption that it can be either comprehensive or conclusive. The aim of the presentation is rather to set forth in brief what has been or is being done in these areas in order to serve the purposes of the community college and through these programs to meet the needs of the students and of the society of which they are members. In describing the many adaptations of the program it should be admitted that few if any of them are cut from whole new cloth; all have been previously made in some junior college or other related school situation. The nearest to novelty involved in the presentation is their being reviewed against the needs of community college students as seen in a review of their nature and development. Admission should be made also that the need of brevity of treatment here makes at times for what may seem like sketchiness. Fortunately, book-length treatment of the total program has recently come to hand, by an author whose interest in problems in this field began as administrator and graduate student and has continued in the university as teacher, researcher, and consultant.*

At the point of summarizing the implications for the curriculum of personal problems of community college students,† it was stated that the institution has the obligation of serving through its curriculum both the needs of the individual and of the society of which he is a member. In the treatment which follows there is recognition of both aspects of need. This is true both in the consideration of purposes and in the presentation and discussion of elements of the curriculum itself. However, no special effort is made to signify just where the interests of the individual, his society, or both would be fostered, because in most respects the contributions of the elements to individual-social balance in the curriculum are obvious, and also because in many instances an element may be expected to serve both the student himself and the members of our society.

Because purposes of an institution are main guidelines for curriculum-making, consideration here begins with brief presentation of these. Following this are sections on general education; health and physical education;

---

*James W. Reynolds, *The Comprehensive Junior College Curriculum* (Berkeley, Cal.: McCutchan Publishing Corp.. 1969).
†See pp. 378–79.

communication and the humanities; social studies, including history; instruction on marriage and family; home economics; science and mathematics; terminal occupational curriculums; transfer curriculums; and remedial and developmental programs. Treatment of curriculum bears mainly on full-time students, as main features of the program for part-time students, both adult and younger, may be inferred from Chapter 10.

Purposes of the Community College

The consensus on purposes of the community college.—Because the stated purposes of the community college indicate most or all major aspects of its program, it is in point to present these purposes early in this treatment. A remarkable fact about them is the near approach to consensus on them to be found when comparison is made of formulations by different authorities and from different sources. This approach to unanimity will be demonstrated here by first abstracting them from a formulation by a committee of distinguished authorities and then comparing with this formulation those drawn from the writings of three individual specialists in the field. It may be stated in advance of the comparison that such differences as are found among them are mainly in the organization of the presentations rather than in the body of concepts into which they may be generalized.

The formulation by committee to be first abstracted is that made for the yearbook on *The Public Junior College* of the National Society for the Study of Education, in its chapter on "The Role of the Public Junior College" (*36*, Ch. IV). It should be pointed out that this chapter is credited to the "Yearbook Committee," and not to an individual author, as are most other chapters in the yearbook, thus foretokening the fact of consensus. This formulation puts forward four "major purposes," namely, (a) preparation for advanced study, usually referred to as the "transfer function," (b) vocational education, typically designated as "terminal vocational education," (c) general education, and (d) community service. Prefatorily to listing these purposes, the statement urges programs serving the needs of youth *and of adults* for post-high-school education, on both full- and part-time bases, and also provision of a variety of public programs and events to assist in "raising the cultural level of the community." In addition to these purposes the formulation names as "unique functions" of the institution "providing low-cost post-high-school education in proximity to the homes of students" and "providing guidance and counseling."

The three specialists whose formulations are summarized for comparison are Medsker, Reynolds, and Thornton, the sources from which they are abstracted all having appeared in print since publication of the yearbook. In the report of his near comprehensive survey of the junior college movement in the country, published in 1960, Medsker has a chapter entitled

"An Educational Program of Many Purposes" in which these are identified under sections headed "Transfer Programs," "Terminal Programs" (with occupational emphasis), "Meeting the Objectives of General Education," "A Program for Students with Educational Deficiencies," "A Program for Adults," and "A Program of Community Service" (*52*, Ch. 3). His particularizations for serving students with deficiencies, which he groups under a "salvaging function," include "providing opportunity . . . for the student to take subjects which he may not have completed in high school and which are required for admission to a senior college or for admission to a sequence of courses in a junior college, providing the student who lacks skills necessary for successful pursuit of certain college subjects an opportunity to improve his skills after entering the junior college, and providing for students whose high school grade-point average is not sufficiently high to admit them to a four-year college an opportunity to improve their scholastic record and thus become eligible for admission to such a college" (64). Although this chapter does not specifically mention the services of guidance and democratization, there can be no doubt of his commitment to them. On the score of his support of guidance, one may mention that he devotes an entire chapter (Ch. 6) to "Student Personnel Services" in the two-year institutions and that he has emphasized its importance in other significant writings. His unequivocal support of the democratizing service may be inferred from his advocacy of the "salvaging" purpose already quoted and from his treatment of "The Junior College as a Democratizing Agency" under the heading of "The Contribution of the Two-Year College" in Chapter 1 (20).

Reynolds (*63*, Ch. II) addresses the question of formulation of purposes by noting their historical emergence. Of purposes of earlier identification classified as "educational" he subscribes to "service to transfer and to terminal students," the terminal service to be rendered through programs of "general education" and "occupational training of junior college grade." From a later analysis of literature dealing with purposes of the junior college by Campbell he adds provision of "opportunity for adult education," and he accepts also Medsker's "salvaging" function. He adds also Clark's concept of the "open-door college," which he relates to the community services of the institution, and one cannot question, both from his manner of reference to it and from the substantial contribution he has made to the exposition of these services, that Reynolds includes it in his formulation. To the present writer "open door" is no less than a happy substitute for the concept of "democratization" in its full ramification. Reynolds does not include guidance in his list of purposes, although the treatment in his chapter on "Students and Student-Personnel Programs" affords assurance of his conviction concerning its importance.

The observation concerning consensus on purposes is illustrated again in the following citation from Thornton, author of an oft-quoted treatise on the community college (77, Ch. 5, 58–70): "1. Occupational education of post-high-school level, 2. General education for all categories of students, 3. Transfer or preprofessional education, 4. Part-time education, 5. Community service, 6. The counseling and guidance of students." No specific reference is seen in this formulation to the democratizing, or popularizing, service of the community college, but from the broad scope of the purposes listed and from the author's recurring reference to a "welcoming admissions policy" one may infer agreement on this score.

The impression of consensus on purposes could be easily reinforced by noting the frequency of their presence in the statements of purpose as presented in the annual catalogs of large proportions of these institutions, as may be readily observed by any one who takes the trouble to leaf through a number of these documents. A notable fact concerning the purposes and one which adds some assurance of their acceptability is, as may be inferred from Reynolds' reference to their historical origins, that almost all of them are to be found in the literature dealing with the junior college as long ago as 1920. The only two that were not clearly enunciated in that early period are guidance and adult education, but it may be said that these also were at least foreshadowed in certain of the purposes occasionally mentioned: guidance as an important aspect in the concept of "allowing for exploration" and adult education by implication in such stated purposes as "offering work meeting local needs" and "affecting the cultural level of the community" (44, 20, Fig. 4).

Two observations concerning the relation of purposes to programs are justifiable from this review that gives such a near approach to complete consensus on purposes and to their stability from the early years of the community college movement to date. One concerns the high degree of confidence that may be placed in them as guides in mapping out the programs. The other observation concerns their direct identification of major elements of the program: it contains no abstruse concepts—only readily intelligible indicants of major areas of instruction and services.

General Education

The goals of general education.—The main order of treatment of the community college curriculum here is that of (1) general education, (2) terminal occupational programs, (3) programs for transfer, and (4) education for correcting deficiencies. However, for expediency in consideration, the working order departs from this dominant order by following discussion of certain preliminary issues in general education and by dealing separately with certain areas of the total curriculum contributing in differing degrees both to general education and to specialization. These areas are communication and the humanities; the social studies, including history; marriage and the family; science and mathematics; home economics; and health and physical education. General education is held in focus first because it contains the portions of the total program usually regarded as essential for all full-time students.

The nature of this general education portion of the program may be approached through consideration of its purposes, or goals. Many formulations of these goals are extant but the most influential appears to be one proposed in *A Design for General Education* (*16*) for the Armed Forces during World War II and still regarded with respect in current discussions. The formulation was made by a committee consisting largely of administrative officers of colleges and universities who had the help of faculty members in these institutions. The committee had been asked "(1) to prepare a design for general education in the form of appropriate outcomes and (2) to outline a series of courses that might be devised to contribute directly to these objectives." The objectives of this general education, in the opinion of the committee, as stated in the final published report (*16*, 14–15), should be for the individual:*

"1. To improve and maintain his own health and take his share of responsibility for protecting the health of others.

"2. To communicate through his own language in writing and speaking at the level of expression adequate to the needs of educated people.

"3. To attain a sound emotional and social adjustment through the enjoyment of a wide range of social relationships and the experience of working cooperatively with others.

"4. To think through the problems and to gain the basic orientation that will better enable him to make a satisfactory family and marital adjustment.

"5. To do his part as an active and intelligent citizen in dealing with the interrelated social, economic, and political problems of American Life and in solving the problems of post-war international reconstruction.

"6. To act in the light of an understanding of the natural phenomena in his environment in its implications for human society and human welfare, to use scientific methods in the solution of his problems, and to employ useful nonverbal methods of thought and communication.

"7. To find self-expression in literature and to share through literature man's experience and his motivating ideas and ideals.

"8. To find a means of self-expression in music and in the visual arts

---

*A formulation with much in common with this one was subsequently put forward by the President's Commission on Higher Education in its report submitted in 1947. See Ch. III, pp. 47–58, in *Higher Education for American Democracy* (New York: Harper & Bros., 1947).

and crafts, and to understand and appreciate art and music as reflections both of individual experience and of social patterns and movements.

"9. To practice clear and integrated thinking about the meaning and value of life.

"10. To choose a vocation that will make optimum use of his talents and enable him to make an appropriate contribution to the needs of society."

Similarities and differences among formulations of goals of general education may be illustrated by a cursory comparison of that just cited with one arrived at by the General Education Workshop held in connection with the California Study of General Education in the Junior College in 1950 (*32*, 21–22). This formulation was adopted for use in the study after considerable inquiry involving students and adults in communities with junior colleges and similar institutions and analysis of other formulations. The majority of the goals derived were similar to those put forward by the war-time committee, with minor differences in phraseology. For example, where the war-time committee said "To think through the problems and to gain a basic orientation that will better enable [the individual] to make a satisfactory family and marital adjustment," the California formulation spoke of "Sharing in the development of a satisfactory home and family life." On the other hand there were differences: where the older formulation spoke of "self-expression in literature," the California formulation did not contain this particular goal; and the latter, as it had twelve statements, included two not directly represented in the earlier—"Using the basic mathematical and mechanical skills necessary in everyday life" and "Understanding his cultural heritage so that he may gain a perspective of his time and place in the world."

As means of implementing the goals it had formulated, the earlier committee recommended the introduction of courses as follows (*16*, 16):

  Personal and Community Health
  Oral and Written Composition
  Problems of Social Adjustment
  Marriage and Family Adjustment
  Development of American Thought and Institutions
  Problems of American Life
  America in International Affairs
  Science: Biological and Physical
  Literature: American Life and Ideals in Literature; Readings in
    the Short Story, Drama, Biography, Poetry, and the Novel
  Form and Function of Art in Society
  Music in Relation to Human Experience
  Philosophy and Religion: The Meaning and Value of Life
  Vocational Orientation

The Executive Committee for the California Study made no recommendation of "a set pattern of general education courses," but it did urge that "the junior college curriculum should provide and ensure vital student experiences in the following fields and areas" (*32*, 50):

Communication Skills	Citizenship
Personal Adjustment	Health
Vocational Orientation	Literature and Creative Arts
Family Life Education	Natural Sciences

The patterns of general education.—Consciousness of the need for general education was followed by the development of a great variety of courses intended to achieve the goals. This variety will be illustrated below, but, before doing so, it will help to an understanding of issues involved if the several patterns of organization of programs through which general education is approached are briefly described. This may be conveniently done by citing the categories of patterns as these have been identified by Johnson (*32*, Ch. III). They are the "great books," "liberal arts," "survey of fields of knowledge," "functional courses," "infusion," and a "composite of approaches."

As Johnson explains the "great books" plan, proponents of it "hold that by studying the greatest books of ages past, students will become acquainted with the processes and results of man's best thinking and will then be able to apply the resultant learning to current and future problems of day-to-day living." Johnson mentions the widespread agreement that this approach is most nearly successful with students of superior scholastic, abstract, and verbal abilities, and reported that none of the California junior colleges were using it as *the single* approach.

Under the "liberal arts" approach students are expected to take a course in English composition and at least one course in each of the major fields of learning, namely, science, history and the social sciences, and the humanities. This is the approach most commonly used in junior and senior colleges. The stricture on it is the tendency to teach each beginning course as though every student is planning to take subsequent courses in the same field.

In the approach designated as the "survey of fields of knowledge" subject matter content is selected to afford a survey of one or several broad fields and under the plan "students are expected to take several survey courses plus selected electives in the field of their choice."

The approach through "functional courses" deals directly with "problems and areas of living derived from and identified by studies of the characteristics and the needs of students and of the society in which they live and of which they are a part." The pattern of courses based on such studies differs widely in title and organization and content from those under the liberal arts plan.

Under the "infusion" approach, which is claimed to be followed in many junior colleges, general education objectives are achieved through courses and activities the primary purpose of which may not be general education. Says Johnson, "Under this plan it is held that outcomes in such areas as human relations, personal adjustment, citizenship, and communication skills can be taught as opportunity arises in any area of the college program."

Finally, there is the "composite of approaches" utilized in many junior colleges that does not consistently follow any single pattern.

An overview of new-type general courses.—In the absence of evidence from a survey of new-type general education courses for a more recent period, recourse is taken to that from a study of the situation in junior colleges around 1950. This study was reported by Putnam (59) who made a count of these courses as they were listed and described in the catalogs of 425 public and private junior colleges, which he refers to as a "sample" but which must have included a majority of these institutions operative at the time. He described the courses which he identified as "(1) general, covering a broad scope of subject matter or . . . of interests and activities of the individual person or of society's major institutions, and (2) of a new type, not the traditional established courses." He states that he did not include among the courses counted broad introductory courses in sociology "that are likely to be very general in nature . . . because they represent a traditional specialty in name," nor "general mathematics courses which are far more numerous than Health or any other title included. . . ." The total count of the frequencies reported in Table 11.1 is 1,673, which was not far from four courses per institution. Putnam found that the average is somewhat larger for public than for private junior colleges.

Some who glance down the column of course titles may be disposed to question whether a few of the categories like "Introduction to Business" or "Work Experience" belong in the list, and some of the titles are unruly enough to resist classification under the three main areas of the curriculum of (1) Natural Science, (2) Social Science, including History, and (3) Humanities and Communication. However, for those more readily classifiable, almost a fourth are in Natural Science, about 40 per cent in Social Science, and something more than a fourth in Humanities and Communication.

Several observations are prompted by speculation over the courses represented by the recurrence of titles in the table, but only two will be made here. One of these concerns the numbers and proportions of courses of the survey type. Although some are found, they are greatly outnumbered by those with more directly functional implications. This corroborates the belief that the early movement toward survey courses has given way to more developments of the functional type. Another observation concerns the small number of "great books" courses found. From these observations the conclusion seems appropriate that the brunt of the current issue con-

TABLE 11.1
NUMBERS, IN A TOTAL OF 425 JUNIOR COLLEGES, OFFERING CERTAIN NEW-TYPE GENERAL EDUCATION COURSES

Title of Course	Number
Health	188
Music Appreciation	146
Social Problems, World Today	112
History of World	101
Art Appreciation	98
Orientation	94
Physical Science Survey	76
History of World Civilization	73
History of World Literature	66
Current Affairs, World	63
Problems of the Individual	61
Communication	53
Comparative Government	47
Introduction to Business	41
Psychology of Adjustment	41
First Aid	35
Survey of Natural Sciences	32
Mental Hygiene	29
Survey of Social Sciences	28
Nature Study	27
Survey of Biological Sciences	26
Recent World History	26
Contemporary World Literature	26
Preparation for Marriage	25
American Institutions	23
Humanities Survey	22
Work Experience and Student Activities	19
Social Problems of the U.S.	18
State or Regional Problems	18
Appreciation of Literature	15
Choosing a Vocation	14
Masterpieces of Literature	10
Comparative Religion	10
Great Books	10

SOURCE: Putnam (59, Tables VI–VII).

cerning the agency of general education is whether it is preferable to provide it through the traditional liberal arts with or without "infusion," or through functional courses.

Liberal arts versus functional courses.—In approaching a review of the issues involved in the controversy over liberal arts as compared with functional courses as general education, it will be well to have in mind concrete instances of these two types of programs at the junior college level. For the former, quotation is made from a circular at hand used to publicize a recently organized community college:

GENERAL EDUCATION REQUIREMENTS

FIRST YEAR

SUBJECT	QUARTER HOUR CREDITS
English	9
Humanities (Literature, Art, Music)	6
Natural Science (Physics, Chemistry, Biology)	8
Mathematics	6
Social Science (History, Economics, Political Science, Sociology)	6
Physical Education	3
Electives	10
	48

SECOND YEAR

SUBJECT	QUARTER HOUR CREDITS
Humanities (Literature, Art, Music)	6
Natural Science (Physics, Chemistry, Biology)	4
Mathematics	3
Social Science (History, Economics, Political Science, Sociology)	6
Physical Education	3
Electives	26
	48

It is probably unnecessary to call attention to the distinctive feature of permitting the meeting of requirements by selecting from the options within parentheses. The battery of functional courses required in one institution, cited as illustrative rather than as exemplary, is as follows:

COURSE TITLE	SEMESTER HOURS
Man and His Institutions: Social, Economic, Political	6
Mathematics and Modern Life	2
Ways of Knowing	2
Effective Communication	6
Family Living	2
Man and His Natural Environment	6
Ideas of Man and His World in Literature	5
Ideas and Social Change in Western Civilization	3
	32

A recent defense of the liberal arts program for general education in the junior college has been made by Rapp (*61*). The main line of his argument may be presented by brief quotation and paraphrase. He points out that, because the liberal arts program has persisted over such a long period, it has had a constancy which is itself a recommendation. General education as a concept is relatively new and "in attempting subject-matter integration of various fields, many of these courses brought a kind of adulteration to the liberal arts. . . . Because the subject matter required to cover vast areas moved so swiftly that the student often saw little and remembered less, shallowness rather than depth seemed to result."

Rapp states that when faculty are given a "free and open choice" they "invariably" take sections of liberal arts rather than the new courses, and that this fact alone "says a great deal": "The word discipline has long been associated with the liberal arts because [they] represent an ordered and rigorous, creative, and critical experience that builds a scholarly attitude toward given sets of material. . . . Yet the liberal arts persist because they deal with the intellectual, the creative, the critical, the sensitive, the human aspects of man's development individually and in relation to the world according to time-tested rules of learning, teaching, and writing. The disciplines also relate to certain sets and divisions of material in the organization and presentation of knowledge. The nature of liberal arts seems to have fitted well the nature of man and his needs. . . . This is where the liberal arts offer a firm foundation for learning. The educational fads will pass in time. The liberal arts will remain."

Rapp next quotes the "goals of general education" and indicates that they can be achieved through the liberal arts: "By taking what he has learned well and deeply in the disciplines and relating it to himself, to his experiences, and to the new knowledge which growth and development bring him, the individual student, not the curriculum, nor the courses, becomes the catalyst and the generalist. Independent study outside the classroom can provide a wealth of general education. Educators should place more responsibility on the individual to seek his own general education." He says further that the home, libraries, the corner store, television, and radio can provide the student's general education.

The differences between the liberal arts program and the functional course approach to general education may be brought home by recourse to two writers, Mayhew and Morse, who have shown discerning concern for the junior college program. Mayhew (*50*), in reviewing the influences toward the revolt against the traditional curriculum finding expression in the new approaches that have been reviewed above, associates it with forces bringing education to larger proportions of the total population. He sees this movement as encouraged by the same influences as those spreading the growth of junior colleges. "General education is collegiate education with non-vocational and non-specialized goals or objectives. It starts from the premise that much of man's life is devoted to being an adequate person, a creative being, a member of groups, and a solver of problems. It assumes that it can contribute to the degree of success individuals achieve in these activities outside their vocation. It therefore concentrates on subjects, skills, abilities, attitudes, and interests which are especially relevant to the person's life as a family member, a consumer, a citizen, a leisure-enjoying person, and an organism in search of satisfactions. . . . General education typically adopts as substantive content of its courses broader segments of knowledge than single disciplines. One of its purposes is to awaken in students an awareness of the scope of human knowledge."

He also emphasizes that, while general education is nonvocational in orientation, this does not suggest that it has no application in preparation for work, since various data "suggest that vocational success is as much the product of an individual's personal adjustment, his ability to deal with people, his facility with symbolic communication, and his depth of interest as it is of sheer technical competency."

In Morse's paper, relied on here to help in an understanding of general education, the emphasis is on the differences between it and the liberal arts. The differences he has in mind are those between the traditional liberal education and the "newer eclectic or instrumentalist [functional] programs of general education." The first difference between them as seen by Morse may best be presented by direct quotation (54, 8–9): "Liberal education is concerned first with a body of subject matter content, drawn largely from the cultural heritage of the Western world. General education of the less conservative type is concerned first with the learner as a human being, who has certain needs and desires that make him distinct from his fellows. The 'unity' of liberal education is Western culture; that of general education is the individual student. Consequently, the predominant method of liberal education might be classified as logical, wherein subject matter is encountered and learned in terms of its systematic organization within somewhat compartmentalized fields of knowledge. General education subscribes, however, to a psychological approach, wherein motivating drives in addition to the desire to learn are capitalized upon, and where a different and less traditional form of content organization may be used, often crossing departmental or even divisional lines."

Another difference, according to Morse, is that liberal education has a content that is relatively fixed, while general education "has a varying content drawn from many sources, suited to the individual, and adjusted to the times." The goals of liberal education are imparting the cultural heritage and stimulating or developing the powers of creative thought, while general education, "not decrying these aims and adopting them in part," is "more concerned with development of the individual on a broader scale—intellectual, emotional, and personal development. . . ." It is this emphasis on individual development that has brought an accompanying emphasis on student counseling services in many institutions. Furthermore, liberal education is considered as "divorced from any pragmatic intent," while general education "keeps the workaday world" in constant view. The clientele for general education is far broader than that for liberal education, consisting of all persons with sufficient aptitude to benefit; thus liberal education is "essentially aristocratic in concept and operation," whereas general education is democratic. Liberal education "implies a concentration in depth" to a greater degree than general education, whereas general education "limits its scope to more selective aspects of culture or of the environment." Still another difference as seen by Morse is with respect to extracurricular activities, which he says liberal arts "allows . . . begrudgingly and in sufferance," whereas in general education the extracurriculum is "welcomed, encouraged, and shaped with a view to its supplementing, reinforcing, and vitalizing the learning drawn from the curriculum."

Morse concludes his comparison by the observation that there need be no war between liberal arts and general education. The differences are those of degree rather than of kind and the two approaches still complement one another, and "each can serve its particular functions in such a manner as to enlarge and enrich the other. They are not partisans but partners."

Obstacles to the spread of the functional approach.—The conclusion favored by the foregoing comparison is one of the appropriateness of the functional, or instrumental, approach for the nonspecialized portions of the community college program, in all-pervasive or, at least, in substantial portion. Appropriateness is apparent from the wide range of abilities, social status, and interests of community college students, as evidence along these lines is reviewed in Chapters 7 and 8. It may seem inexplicable that, although this type of program has made some gains in junior colleges over a period of several decades, it has not spread as rapidly as its advocates might expect and wish. The moderate rate of growth of the movement in junior colleges is the more surprising in view of the earlier development and greater prevalence of general education programs in the four-year colleges and universities, which tend to be selective, some of them with these general programs being much more selective than the junior colleges.

The major obstacle to proliferation of these general education programs in junior colleges seems to be the threat of nonacceptance of the new courses for transfer to the four-year colleges and universities. This is the opinion of Reynolds *(62)* and Dressel *(18)*, both of whom have been friendly to the promotion of functional general education. This stricture would be peculiarly operative for junior colleges most of whose graduates seek transfer, and this condition still applies to many of these institutions. It may come as a surprise that there would be resistance to acceptance of these courses in the higher institutions, since more of them than of the junior colleges operate such programs, but it must be remembered that the higher institutions with these programs are still a minority of all, and the junior college graduate seeking acceptance of general courses can have difficulty in establishing that those he had taken in his first two college years match up in content with those of the institution to which he aspires to transfer. Among the stigmata conducive to denial of credit, according to Dressel, would be the titles of some of these new courses, the variation in content of courses in such broad fields as the humanities, and the absence of laboratory experience in some of the general courses in science.

To this obstacle of the threat to acceptance of the credit in transfer, Reynolds adds the "lack of sympathy of administrators and faculty . . . that may be ascribed to a background of training which has produced a disproportional respect for specialized subject matter programs."

This stricture on transfer credit should in time be in large part removable by a procedure analogous to that encouraged by evidence making for flexibility of admission of high school graduates to college. It has been found that the particular pattern of courses pursued in high school is a relatively negligible factor of success in college as compared with rank in class or position in a distribution of scores of college aptitude. Such a procedure will be touched on again in Chapter 12.

Importance of evaluation.—It is a cliché to urge that all programs of education, especially those involving an innovating approach like the functional courses, should be subjected to evaluation to ascertain whether and in what degree they are effecting the changes in students in their skills, abilities, understandings, attitudes, interests, and behavior for which they have been set up. Several institutions have organized and carried on extensive efforts at evaluation, and a variety of reports and appraisals of these efforts are available in print. Most of these concern the programs in the four-year colleges and universities and so few pertain to junior colleges that it is difficult if not impossible to generalize from the findings, in the main because of the wide variation in the programs and procedures. No attempt will be made at generalization here, although partial digest is made of evaluation by students who have pursued one of the best known programs of general education in universities, one which occupied about 50 per cent of the student's scheduled time during the first two years.

The procedure used in the project (*41*) was the rating by students, mostly "last-term sophomores," of 26 objectives, some general and some special, as to their appropriateness for and achievement in the first two college years. The objectives included some, with modification, from the President's Commission on Higher Education, and others obtained by interview with students and through solicitation of faculty members. The ratings were made on a 5-point scale in relation to (1) the importance of achieving and (2) the degree of achieving them during the first two college years. One sample of students was asked to rate the objectives as to their applicability to and achievement in the general education core while another sample was asked similarly to rate applicability and experiences in all other courses. Conclusions from the study are indicated in the following quotation: ". . . it appears . . . that the Michigan State students questioned are chiefly concerned during their first two years of work with such objectives as developing skill in thinking and communication; understanding the physical, social, and individual aspects of the environment; improving health, emotional and social adjustment, and the ability to get along with others; and securing help in making wise vocational choices. There is evidence for the samples involved that a required core of general education may meet with student approval. The ratings indicate that the students not only recognized the nature of the objectives in the general education program as distinct from many of the objectives in other courses but agreed that the general education core was achieving its objectives about as well as other courses were achieving theirs."

Health and Physical Education

Two-part nature of the offering.—The first in the list of goals proposed in *A Design for General Education* quoted earlier in the chapter is for the individual "to improve and maintain his own health and take his share of responsibility for protecting the health of others." The design also listed first among the courses to be aimed at implementing the goals as one in "Personal and Community Health." Achievement of this goal, however, requires not only the understandings brought by such a course, but also participation in physical activities. This brief section, thus, is given over to exposition and consideration of this two-part program as it operates in a representation of public junior colleges. The institutions whose offerings were examined through their catalogs were twenty-six distributed to thirteen states in all sections of the country—not a strict sampling but nevertheless affording illustration of the scope and variety of the programs.

Many of the departments of health and physical education, like others in the junior college, serve not only the purpose of general education, but also to a degree the specialized purposes of preprofessional and semiprofessional education. The portrayal here includes attention to both general and occupational aspects.

The course in health.—Only nine of the twenty-six junior colleges represented require the course in health, although a somewhat larger number —up to more than half the institutions—offer it. One cannot know, without relying on a more carefully drawn or larger sample, whether the proportion of these institutions in the country not requiring or offering the course is larger or smaller, but it is clear enough that students in many institutions do not have systematized opportunities for studying health problems. The situation may be a reflection of the trend in four-year colleges and universities, as reported by Means (*51*). He states that, although courses in health were increasingly offered and required up through a portion of the twentieth century, the requirement and even the offering have dropped off sharply in recent decades. Among possible factors of the defection Means mentions teachers, methods of teaching, curriculum, etc. He deplores the trend, and mentions as evidence of the need the studies that show students as having many misconceptions concerning matters of health that should be corrected.

The lack of knowledge on the part of junior college freshmen on important problems of health was demonstrated not long ago in California, where a course in health is required for graduation from junior college, by means of a test administered in 34 institutions (*14*). In this project the College Health Knowledge Test, consisting of 100 multiple-choice items grouped into 11 sections, was administered near the opening of school years to more than 5,000 students. The same students were retested near the end of the school year. From the results one may infer both inadequate health knowledge and substantial gain from instruction, as the score on the pretest was 46.6 per cent (of the 100 items) and on the retest 58.5 per cent. The results for schools and classes varied widely and were reported to demonstrate "tremendous differences in the possession of specific health information."

The titles of the courses found in the catalogs examined are almost all simple designations and seldom vary from "Personal Health," "Personal Hygiene," "Personal and Community Health," and "Fundamentals of Health." Most of the catalog descriptions are too brief to indicate even the main divisions of content, although one finds recurrently broad categories like "personal health," "community health," "physical health," and "mental health," and less often narrower ones like "first aid," "safety," "nutrition," "effects of alcohol," "communicable and degenerative diseases," "posture," and "sanitary measures."

A better impression of the scope of content of these courses can be gained by reading chapter headings of standard textbooks of which several in the field are available for use with college freshmen or sophomores and are suitable for junior college students. These headings are not listed here, but it may be said that any check of the topics treated against the health problems rated highest by students in the investigation by Lantagne drawn upon in Chapter 8* shows a large degree of correspondence. This is true when the twenty-five problems of highest rating are considered, and the coverage is even more nearly complete when all fifty problems rated highest by students are considered. The degree of correspondence is such

TABLE 11.2

Sports and Activities Offered for Men, for Women, and Coeducationally in More Than 15 Per Cent of 26 Representative Junior Colleges

Subject	For Men	For Women	Coeducational
Archery	x	x	x
Badminton	x	x	x
Baseball	x	x	
Basketball	x	x	x
Body Building	x	x	x
Bowling	x	x	x
Fencing	x	x	x
Field Hockey		x	x
First Aid	x	x	x
Football	x	x	
Golf	x	x	x
Gymnastics	x	x	x
Handball	x	x	
Horsemanship	x	x	x
Ice Skating	x	x	x
Self-Defense (Combatives)	x	x	
Softball	x	x	x
Special Physical Education	x	x	x
Swimming	x	x	x
Tennis	x	x	x
Track and Field	x	x	
Trampoline	x	x	x
Volleyball	x	x	x
Water Safety	x	x	x
Weight Lifting	x	x	
Wrestling	x	x	
Folk and Square Dancing	x	x	x
Modern Dance	x	x	x
Social Dancing	x	x	x

as to warrant a course requirement in the field of health, unless the students demonstrate by test that they have the understanding needed when admitted to the junior college or they are given this understanding in other courses which they take, as in marriage and family, orientation, etc.

Physical education.—The other main element of programs in departments of health and physical education consists of activities aimed at physical development and recreation. These activities are maintained in

*See pp. 329–31.

great variety, as may be seen in Table 11.2. This table includes those most frequently listed in the catalogs and, except for the kinds of dancing at the bottom of the table, are listed in alphabetical order. Among the categories less frequently offered are Cross Country, Decathlon, Diving, Fly and Bait Casting, Speedball, and Water Polo. Examination of more catalogs would have lengthened the list.

All catalogs indicated a requirement in physical education, most of them of four hours. Exemptions often allowed were of older students, although the ages varied from college to college, ranging in this group from 21 to

TABLE 11.3
Physical Education Subjects Offered for Men, for Women, and Coeducationally in More than 15 Per Cent of 26 Representative Public Junior Colleges

Subject	For Men	For Women	Coeducational
Community Recreation			x
Introduction to Physical Education			x
Life Saving	x	x	x
Sports Officiating	x	x	x
Team Sports	x	x	x
Training and Conditioning Athletes		x	x

29. The specific requirements again differ widely, from a composite of "gym" to freedom of choice from among a number of individual and team sports. In several institutions encouragement seems to be toward activities promising "carryover" into after-college and adult life.

Preprofessional offering.—As will be reported below, a number of the catalogs of this representation of junior colleges display or list transfer curriculums in physical education (including coaching) and recreational leadership. In point of fact, more than three-fourths of the twenty-six institutions offer transfer curriculums in physical education. This is reflected in Table 11.3 which lists courses given in more than 15 per cent of these junior colleges, some of which certainly would not be appropriate as general requirements for all students. In most instances these courses lean more toward theory and less toward physical activity. Among more specialized courses applicable to preprofessional curriculums found less frequently than those in the table are Dance Production, Playground Theory and Practice, and Sports Fundamentals. It goes almost without saying that most or all the sports and activities listed in Tables 11.2 and 11.3 would be applicable for credit in transfer curriculums in physical education and related professions.

A justifiable observation is that most of the offerings in Tables 11.2 and 11.3 would be about equally applicable to semiprofessional as to preprofessional programs in the area of physical education (including coaching) and recreational leadership.

Communications and the Humanities

Communications.—With a commitment to reviewing curriculum innovations from the standpoint of their promise for the community college, when the consideration turns to the field of English, attention must be directed to courses called "Communication" or "Communications." And, because of the long traditional association of English composition and literature, it is appropriate to follow or accompany the consideration of Communications with developments in the Humanities. The report above on new-type general education courses (see Table 11.1) showed courses under this category available in 53 of the 425 institutions represented in Putnam's study. Such courses, while not among those like Health and Music Appreciation at the top of the list in frequency, are well above the middle of the tabulation. There has been a similar development in the four-year colleges, as is indicated by Thomas in reviewing the English requirements in well-known general education programs. He reports that in several of these programs the "one required course which gives instruction in writing is called 'Communication Skills,' 'Basic Language Skills,' or some similar term which may embrace reading, speech, and other related exercises" (76, 307).

The courses in Communications in the junior colleges are not restricted to instruction in written composition, and have taken their departure from surveys, some systematic and others less objective, that find the use of language among educated people ranging through a wide variety of activities, on the "out-put" side, including letter-writing, conversation, group discussion, making speeches, making reports, giving directions or explanations, and story-telling. On the "in-put" side, it involves reading, of various types and for various purposes, and listening, as well as observation. The abilities aimed at in the courses thus comprehend (1) writing clearly and correctly, (2) speaking clearly and correctly, with pleasing and acceptable quality of voice, (3) assimilating ideas effectively through reading, and (4) assimilating ideas effectively through listening and observation.

Besides comprehending more kinds of use of language the new courses have typically striven at better motivation for the expressional activities by developing them in association with reading activities within the potential scope of student interest. The procedure results in intermotivation of expressional and of reading and listening activities. The procedure has also induced the conviction among some who have watched development of these new courses that training in the various phases of expression may well be separated from teaching for literary appreciation.

Often emerging in the institutions in which the courses in communication are going forward is the policy of college-wide attention to development and maintenance of language skills, and this policy has sometimes been put into effect by systematizing the cooperation of departments and teachers in the other disciplines.

From evidence like that in Chapters 7 and 8 it is well known that students come into the community colleges in great heterogeneity as to ability, socioeconomic status, and motivation. We can be certain that their heterogeneity is no less in respect to skills represented in the wide areas of communications, and each individual's degree of competence in these skills must be identified in order best to improve them. This calls for programs of testing for diagnosis, for example, in vocabulary recognition, and rate, comprehension, and interpretation of reading, and this in turn calls for ability of the teachers or others to administer the tests and interpret the results. Thus, courses like Communications require a wide competence of staff members and an accompanying development of arrangements for diagnosis and for developmental or remedial treatments. These arrangements are often coordinated by a department or bureau of testing. A related issue concerns class and course organization for students of the widely varying abilities and interests disclosed by the tests. Some argue for separate classes and even different courses for groups of students with divergent abilities, while others urge heterogeneous classes with efforts at individualization of instruction within them. Such arrangements are described in a later section of the chapter.

The distinguishing features of these innovating courses in Communications can be made more readily apparent by comparing them with the description of the courses in English Composition required of freshmen in most junior colleges. The details of practice have been made available in a report based on information recently supplied from 187 widely distributed institutions, most of them public but some private (*85*), and the following is a partial running description. The typical requirement for graduation is a year of "freshman English," although some institutions—far from a majority—require also a course in literature and/or, in an occasional institution, speech (*85*, 17). In overwhelming proportions the teachers of these courses "feel that the content of the college transfer English course ... resembles that of a course in a four-year liberal arts college" (*85*, 29). It is reported that imaginative literature is not studied as much in the first semester as it is in the second; nevertheless, three-fifths use "some," "much," or "considerable" literature in the first half of the course and a full three-fourths of them do so in the second half. Four-fifths report little or no speech in either semester: "Obviously speech is not a major part of the content..." (*85*, 36). Report is made on the amount of theme-writing, and it is found to range widely; thus the investigators conclude that "some kind of training in either library research or the organization of a long formal paper is almost universal..." (*85*, 40).

The nature and variation in content of these courses in freshman English is suggested by the proportionate frequencies of "types of textbooks" used in them. Reproduced here are the eight types most often reported in the two semesters (*85*, 42):

FIRST SEMESTER	PER CENT	SECOND SEMESTER	PER CENT
Reader (essays, etc.)	73.8	Reader (essays, etc.)	42.0
Literature anthology	11.8	Literature anthology	21.3
Grammar textbook	56.7	Grammar textbook	30.0
Rhetoric	56.2	Rhetoric	35.0
Novel	12.8	Poetry	19.0
Dictionary	19.8	Short story	14.0
Workbooks	11.2	Novel	31.0
Supplementary material	19.3	Drama	22.5

Smaller frequencies are reported for such categories of materials as "Book length essays," "Language-linguistics," "Speech text," and "Controlled research" for the first semester and "Dictionary," magazines like *Harper's*, *Atlantic Monthly*, and *Saturday Review*, "Language-linguistics," "Workbooks," "Speech text," "Controlled research," "Biography," and "Supplementary glossaries and guides" for the second. One may note reflected in the categories and percentages a considerable shift of emphasis from one semester to the next from attention to the mechanics of written composition to imaginative literature.

The typical method of teaching is reported as mixed lecture and discussion (*85*, 38). A full majority of the junior colleges report remedial courses in English. Almost all the department chairmen reporting them regard grammar as of prime importance (*85*, 51–52) notwithstanding the findings of studies that raise the question of the efficacy of instruction in grammar in improving expression. About half those offering remedial English also have courses in remedial reading. Superior students are typically enrolled in the regular English program, although a "substantial number" of institutions provide "honors," "accelerated," or "enriched" courses for them (*85*, 57).

This partial précis of practices in junior colleges should not be left without mention of the proceedings of the conference on research and development of English programs in junior colleges which was in the nature of a follow-up of the Weingarten report of status (*1*). The conference was addressed by leaders in junior college education and others, and participants considered recommendations and research proposals made by six study groups, which were endorsed wholly or in part by the conference as a whole. In the main the addresses and summary report manifest awareness of the pervasive implications of the open-door policy for adapting programs to student bodies of widely differing abilities, with proposals of provisions for both transfer and terminal groups. The concept "communication" emerges more often in these proceedings than in the report of status of English. With cognizance of the dependence of improvement on the education of the teachers, the recommendations include designation of the elements of the preparation in (a) subject matter: an undergraduate program in breadth; undergraduate and graduate concentration in English, including literature, language, composition, and speech ("public speaking and oral interpretation"). Under (b) "professional education," the recommendation is for "methods of teaching English, including analysis of problems and materials in language, literature, composition, and reading"; "background in the functions and problems of the junior college"; and "supervised teaching in the junior college." Beyond this the recommendations say, "Every junior college department of English needs, in addition to the generally trained teachers of English, specialists in reading, in writing, including remedial and developmental phases, and in speech" (*1*, 119).

It must not be inferred from this citation of recommendations that all participants in the proceedings were in agreement with them, as witness the last of six proposals put forward by one of the speakers. Teachers of English, he said, should "Refuse to be a catchall for low-grade service assignments: spelling, elementary grammar, letter writing, how to use the library, so-called research papers, and various kinds of social work. We must devote ourselves to our own crucial task, which is interpreting and teaching literature with skill and enthusiasm. It is irresponsible to allow ourselves to be distracted and to become unfit for our job" (*1*, 32).

The Humanities and the Creative Arts.—Such consideration as is accorded the humanities and the creative arts in this treatment of the community college curriculum is given at this point because language and literature are often linked in discussion and because of the usual association of the other arts with literature. As with other main areas of the curriculum, some of the courses serve purposes mainly of general education, and others either the purposes of general education or those of the specializing student. The purposes of general education in the formulation quoted above to which they chiefly apply are "to find self-expression in literature and to share through literature man's experience and his motivating ideas and ideals," "to find a means of self-expression in music and in the visual arts and crafts, and to understand and appreciate art and music as reflections both of individual experience and of social patterns and movements," and "to practice clear and integrated thinking about the meaning and value of life." In many instances, through allowing for exploration, they are helpful in the choice of vocations.

As currently defined, the area of humanities (inclusive of the creative arts) is an exceedingly broad and diverse one and any list comprehending courses in it in any large number of institutions must be long. This is true of the following list compiled from junior college catalogs, although it could easily have been extended by including more institutions. It is at least illustrative. No brief is held for the classification and, inevitably, courses under the categories overlap. Before proceeding to brief running commentary on the list, it should be mentioned that titles like "Western Civilization" or the "History of Western Civilization," often classified with Humanities, have rather arbitrarily been listed under History and the Social Studies dealt with in another section of the chapter. Among the titles listed are nine identified by Putnam as "new-type general education courses" and included by him in his tabulation of frequencies (see Table 11.1). These are marked with an asterisk in the list. The names of some of the offerings are not as given in the catalogs at the points of description; in some cases where a glamorous title is not sufficiently indicative of content, a more prosaic one has been substituted.

The list is seen to be distributed to seven divisions beginning with integrated courses aimed at overviews of major aspects of the broad field of humanities. One of the pioneers among these courses was developed in the thirties at Stephens College and was referred to as the "Basic Course in the Humanities" (*37*, Ch. III). It sought integration of treatment and appreciative understanding by considering examples of works in music, literature, drama, sculpture, painting, and architecture in respect to background (subject and function), medium, elements, organization, and style and judgment. Other integrated courses have been built around different unifying principles. Still other courses in appreciation in the list are seen to be limited to single areas, as literature, art, architecture, and music. The last category under Music, "Various musical organizations for course credit," represents an arrangement under which an activity which is carried on in some junior colleges as extracurricular is somewhat more formalized in other institutions by allowing credit for regular attendance and participation. The arrangement applies to such organizations as band, orchestra, choir, etc. While many of the courses under all the main groups may be expected to contribute to attaining the general goals of sharing "man's experience and his motivating ideas and ideals" and of practicing "clear and integrated thinking about the meaning and value of life," courses like those under the last one, Philosophy and Religion, are assumed to have some pre-eminence for these purposes.

Courses in the Humanities and the Creative Arts

Integrated Courses
 *Humanities Survey
English Language and Literature
 *Appreciation of Literature
  (Reading for Enjoyment)
 American Literature
 English Literature (courses dealing with various periods or groups)
 Shakespeare
 American Literature
 *History of World Literature
 *Contemporary World Literature
 Bible as Literature
 Masterpieces of Literature
 Short Story
 Contemporary Novel
 Introduction to Poetry
 Modern Drama
 English Review
 Vocabulary Building
 Advanced Composition
 Creative Writing
 English Honors
Speech and Dramatics
 Fundamentals of Public Speaking
 Oral Interpretation
 Voice and Diction
 Introduction to the Drama
 Play Production
 Dramatics
 Technique of Acting
 Technique of Television Acting
Foreign Language
 French
 German
 Spanish
 Italian
 Russian
 Other Languages
Arts and Crafts
 *Art Appreciation
 Appreciation of Architecture
 History of Art
 Drawing and Composition
 Pottery, Ceramics
 Jewelry Design
 Fashion Design
 Photography
 Weaving
 Water Colors
 Painting in Oils
 Sculpture
Music
 *Music Appreciation
 Music Fundamentals
 Harmony and Composition
 Instrumental Instruction
  (individual or group)
 Vocal Instruction
  (individual or group)
 Accompanying
 Conducting
 Opera Workshop
 Various musical organizations for course credit
Philosophy and Religion
 History of Philosophy
 Introduction to Philosophy
 Ethics
 Logic
 *Comparative Religions
 *Great Books

The breadth and variety of content and experiences that the Humanities afford, as here illustrated, likewise make them appropriate for inclusion on a generous scale in curriculum arrangements adapted to the needs of the widely ranging abilities and interests of a community college population. At the same time, only in colleges of the largest enrollment would it be feasible to make such an extended offering as is represented in the list.

The Social Studies, Including History

Scope and role of the social studies.—The area of the curriculum comprehending the social studies under any definition is wide, but much wider under some usages than others. An alternative designation for much of the area often preferred by some is "social science," which is typically applied to subjects like political science, economics, anthropology, sociology, and history, and less often extended to include the disciplines of geography and psychology. For the sake of simplification of treatment, while admitting some inappropriateness, the wider designation of "social studies" is used here.

Of the goals of general education cited earlier in the chapter* as criteria for curriculum content, the pre-eminent one to be attained through the social studies obviously relates to citizenship: this goal urges the individual "to do his part as an active and intelligent citizen in dealing with the interrelated social, economic, and political problems of American Life" and it goes on to call for comparable behavior touching international affairs. It should be apparent that they should also conduce, no less than the humanities, to his practicing "clear and integrated thinking about the meaning and value of life," especially as this relates to social interaction.

The list of courses offered.—As no published complete compilation of courses in the social studies offered in community colleges is at hand, the following list has been assembled from three sources: the "new-type general education" courses readily identified in the table from Putnam's study (Table 11.1), courses identified by Gross and Maynard (26), and additional titles found in recent catalogs of a number of junior colleges in several widely scattered states. Putnam's table supplied nine of the titles (identified by an asterisk) in the following list, telescoped, because of doubts concerning the distinctiveness of content of some of them, from thirteen titles. The courses from Gross and Maynard's analysis, a relatively recent one of the offerings of 140 widely distributed junior colleges, did not extend over the whole area of the social studies as considered here because his concern was primarily with the issue of sequence in courses in history; nevertheless, it supplied many titles for the list to follow. The method used for the third source was to add course names from catalogs until no further titles were encountered. The total list follows and may be considered illustrative, even if not fully representative or complete.

*See pp. 437–39.

Courses in the Social Studies

Integrated Courses
    Introduction to Social Science
        (Social Institutions)
    *Social Science Survey
    *Social Problems
        (American Social Problems)
    *State or Regional Problems
    *Current Affairs
        (Contemporary Affairs,
        World Today)
    *History of World Civilization
    History of Western Civilization
History
    American or United States
        History
    European History
    History of England
    History of Latin America
    History of Russia
    History of the Far East
    Pacific History
    Local History (State, Regional)
    Economic History of the
        United States
Political Science and
    International Relations
    *American Institutions
        (American Political
        Institutions)
    Introduction to Political
        Science (Government)
    *Comparative Government
        (Foreign Governments,
        Modern World Governments)
    Parliamentary Procedure
    Student Government
        (Leadership Course)
    International Relations
        (Contemporary World
        Affairs)
Economics
    Principles of Economics
    Economic Institutions and
        Problems
    Consumer Economics
Anthropology and Sociology
    Physical Anthropology
    Cultural Anthropology
    Introduction to Archaeology
    Introduction to Sociology
Geography
    Economic Geography
    Cultural Geography
    Local and/or Regional
        Geography
    Principles of Human
        Geography
    Geography of Europe
Psychology
    *Problems of the Individual
    General Psychology
        (Principles of Psychology)
    Psychology of Everyday Life
    Child Psychology
        (Child Development)
    Applied Psychology
    Human Behavior
    Psychology of Personality
    Personal and Social Adjustment
    *Psychology of Adjustment
        (Mental Hygiene)

Integrated courses.—It may be noted that five of the nine titles credited as "new-type general education" courses by Putnam have been listed as integrated courses. The thirteen titles from which all nine were condensed account for almost two-fifths of all such courses Putnam found, which must be some indication of the importance ascribed to these courses and to the purposes they are set up to serve. Except for the courses in Current Affairs for which the motivation is mainly in the timeliness of the subject matter, the courses fall into two groups, the broad-field courses and the courses in history, each with its own type of integration.

The broad-field type undertakes integration by some procedure involving content or method in two to several of the social sciences—political science, economics, sociology, etc. These began with the Social Science Survey which typically undertakes to provide an overview of the area and introduction to the several disciplines represented. Such courses have given way over the years to a considerable extent to those concerned with problems consideration of which involves content and procedures characteristic of two or more of the disciplines. Gross and Maynard (26) reported in 1965 that fewer than 3 per cent of the junior colleges represented in their study included such integrated courses in their offerings.

The courses in history, in this list, History of World Civilization and History of Western Civilization, achieve integration by comprehending longer periods and broader cultural regions and/or trends. Gross and Maynard (26) report that, excluding the offerings in United States History, these courses in general history are by far the most common offered in the social studies in junior colleges today. Scrutiny of the list of requirements in the general education programs in the college and university curriculums which were studied by Thomas in his *Search for a Common Learning* shows the course Western Civilization to be prescribed much more often than any other (76, 309–10). The fact of greater frequency in the senior colleges and universities may be a factor of its relative popularity in junior colleges, since the problem of transfer of credit would less often arise. The incidence of offering and requiring the broad-field type of integrated course might well be increased with more centers of experimentation with it in both junior and four-year colleges.

Running commentary on certain other courses.—Two other courses frequently offered in junior colleges and having general education impact could well have been included in the foregoing list—Marriage and Family, and Orientation. They are accorded consideration elsewhere, the former in the section following and the latter in Chapter 12 where services in guidance are considered. The reader may note that four more courses—two each in the titles under Political Science and Psychology—were classed as "new-type general education" by Putnam. Special mention may be made of the course in Student Government (Leadership Course) sometimes required of student officers in junior colleges and administered to enhance student activities and student participation in school government. Almost all the remaining courses are standard liberal arts offerings serving the usual purposes of such courses. In the catalogs these are often assigned numbers corresponding with those they carry in institutions to which junior college graduates are likely to transfer.

The age of students and civic motivation.—Recurrently and persistently educators and others who have observed the behavior of youth who have completed high school and are now "out in the world" have deplored their neglect of the responsibilities of citizenship and their limited civic and constructive social participation. These strictures apply notwithstanding extensive requirements of and generous attention to the social studies in the secondary school curriculum. To cite a single instance of this type of observation, one may draw on Spaulding's conclusions from the Regents Inquiry, where he said that "most boys and girls on the point of leaving school are ready to give at least verbal allegiance to the principles of democratic living and democratic government," but that "once he is out of school, the ordinary boy or girl does practically nothing to add to his readiness for citizenship, nor does he even keep alive the knowledge of civic affairs or the interest in social problems which he may have had when he finished his schooling" (74, 11). The contention seems warranted that in considerable part this deficiency obtains because of the time gap between high school graduation and the voting age. The combination of popularizing college years by means of the community college and making the social studies a prominent element of the program will eliminate most of the gap, and thus confront the prospective voter almost at once with the issues on which he must base his decisions on civic concerns. The impact of the courses on his participation will be more vital if the courses are concerned with real problems of our society and involve, while being taken, some direct experience in citizenship.

Instruction in Marriage and Family

Rationale of the course.—The fourth in the formulation of goals proposed in *A Design for General Education* quoted earlier in the chapter is "to think through the problems and to gain a basic orientation that will better enable him to make a satisfactory family and marital adjustment." The evidence concerning sexual and dating behavior reviewed in Chapter 4 is ample evidence of the need for wholesome and systematic consideration by the students of the problems involved, what with the obvious inferences both that the sex drive is at its peak at the ages represented and that the students are at marriageable age. This need has further support in Chapter 9 which shows personal problems of courtship, sex, and marriage among those of highest incidence, although they appear to be in some degree moderated for the minority of married students.

The need as established in the behavior of youth and in the problems of students is re-inforced by inquiries for their opinions and by conviction derived from mere mention of some of the questions of concern. As an example of the former, it may be reported that almost unanimously junior college students, responding anonymously to questions by Ross (*68*), indicated the belief that parents and the home do not meet the need for adequate education in matters of sex which, it need hardly be argued, are inextricably involved in many matters relating to marriage. Conviction of the need is re-inforced also by mere mention of some of the problems deserving attention: the urge to marry; special problems of the single person; combining career and marriage (for women); wise choice of marriage partner; best age for marriage; courtship, engagement, and wedding; petting and premarital relations; fears of sex, marriage, and childbirth; reproduction; pregnancy; heredity; incidence of divorce.

The courses as given.—The movement for giving courses on marriage and the family appears to have got under real headway during the early thirties. The status of these courses in colleges, universities, and junior colleges in the late forties was ascertained by Bowman and reported in 1949 (6). Made under the joint auspices of the National Council of Family Relationships and the American Social Hygiene Association, his study received the cooperation of 93 per cent of all institutions approached, of which almost exactly half reported having at least one course, more than a third of which had been introduced during the preceding five years. Most recurrent titles of the courses were Marriage and the Family, The Family, and Family Relationships. These courses were almost always characterized as "functional" and not to be confused with the standard historical courses on the family often made available in departments of sociology. Bowman also listed in the order of frequency the textbooks used in the courses, of which a number were available in print at the time of his investigation.

Bowman reported the frequency of offering the course on Marriage and the Family only in the total number of institutions represented and not in the institutions of different types, that is, in colleges, universities, and junior colleges. However, Martorana (*48*), at about the same time, reported evidence from an analysis of the descriptions of these courses which he identified in more than 400 catalogs, all that were available to him at the time of his investigation. As might be expected, they were met with more often in the catalogs of large coeducational institutions than of smaller units. Evidence concerning the more recent status of these courses is not generally available, but they have continued to increase, if one may judge from the frequency of publication of new textbooks and revisions of textbooks intended for use in them.

Martorana recorded the frequency of occurrence of topics named in the course descriptions with results as shown in Table 11.4. He noted that only two of the topics, Psychological Factors in Family Life and Modern Family Problems, were found in more than half of the descriptions, and that topics like the Biological Bases of the Family ("Sex, reproduction, and heredity") and Conserving Family Values ("ideals of family life, standards of family living, and the ethical values involved") were found in smaller proportions of the descriptions. He reported the median number of topics per course at 3.5.

Typical practice makes the course a two- or three-hour elective. There is hesitancy to make it a requirement, despite the widely held belief that all students could profit from it. It is most often made available to sophomores, although many would contend that the freshman year is none too soon, and some argue for offering its analog in later high school years. It is usually taught to classes including both sexes. Martorana found departmental allocation of 40 per cent of the courses to be in Home

TABLE 11.4
SUBJECT-MATTER CONTENT IN 115 COURSES IN MARRIAGE AND FAMILY LIFE

Topic	Number	Per Cent
Psychological Factors in Family Life	92	80.0
Modern Family Problems	67	58.3
Sociological Factors in Family Life	51	44.3
History and Evolution of the Family	46	40.0
Home Development and Management	42	36.5
Preparation for Marriage	34	29.6
Premarital Relationships	31	27.0
Biological Basis of the Family	24	20.9
Parenthood	19	16.5
Child Care and Training	18	15.7
Conserving Family Values	15	13.0
No Content Specified	5	4.3

SOURCE: Martorana (48, Table 4).

Economics (or Homemaking), with fully as large a total proportion in Sociology and Social Science when the numbers in departments with these two designations are combined. As can be expected, the concern over finding teachers suitable in competence and personality is as great for these courses as indicated for sex education in Chapter 4.

Evaluating the course.—Appraisal by means of records of behavior on the part of persons who have experienced instruction in courses in Marriage and the Family has yet to be reported although there are compilations of opinions of this instruction by such persons. Some results are reported here from two studies of the latter type, one by Ellzey (22) of responses to a questionnaire by graduates of a junior college for women who had taken such a course and the other by Landis (45) of responses by students in a university following a term's experience on the subject.

Ellzey's questionnaire was sent out to 3,700 persons who had been enrolled in the course. Replies were received from 1,587, somewhat fewer than half. We can only guess at the opinions of the nonrespondents and perhaps they were less favorable than those of the respondents. The lines of inquiry ranged widely, but the report here is concerned only with general appraisal, and this was rather overwhelmingly favorable. Thus, when asked whether the course had included most problems vital to success in marriage, only a small minority reported feeling that it had not, while almost half felt "much better prepared." When asked to compare the course in value with other courses, about 95 per cent rated it in one of the following ways: "more valuable than any other course in college" (12 per cent); "more valuable than other courses except occupational courses" (23 per cent); "one of the three most valuable courses" (40 per cent); "equally valuable" with other courses (20 per cent). Fewer than 5 per cent rated the course as less or least valuable.

TABLE 11.5
STUDENT AND STAFF RATINGS OF LECTURES

Lecture	Staff	Single Students	Married Students
A. Why Preparation for Marriage	6	8	5
B. Contemporary Religious Views of Marriage	2	10	9
C. Society's Stake in Marriage	10	5	6
D. Students' Marriages at MSC	2	4	4
E. Lengths of Time After Marriage for Adjustment	4	3	3
F. Adjustment in Marriage	8	2	1
G. Sex Education for Children	4	1	2
H. Family Relationships and Child Guidance	9	6	8
I. Your Insurance Program	6	8	10
J. Family Buying	–	–	–
K. The Family Adjustment Life Cycle	1	7	7

SOURCE: Landis (45, Table 1).

The evaluation as reported by Landis is not general but of portions represented by the topics included. The appraisal was concerned with one term of "marriage education" in a full year's course called "Effective Living" which at the time of the investigation was a requirement of the Basic College at Michigan State University. The instruction consisted of weekly lectures throughout the term, three hours of class discussion per week bearing on the subjects of the lectures, and readings on these subjects. About three-fourths of the students in the classes were single, and a fourth married. The list of lectures at the time evaluation was undertaken was as presented in Table 11.5. At the end of the term the students were given an anonymous form evaluating the lectures, discussions, and readings. From the ratings of the lectures were derived the rankings in the two right-hand columns of the table. The table is seen to include also ratings by the staff responsible for instruction.

Comparison of the rankings by single and married students finds them to be much alike. The opinions of the instructors differed notably from those of students. Highest for students were "Adjustment in Marriage" and "Sex Education for Children." Low ratings for Lecture B induced subsequent replacement of it by a lecture on "Mixed Religions Marriages," and, out of regard for the large proportion of single students, a lecture was added on "The Engagement Period." Both changes were found acceptable. Student ratings of the readings placed two books treating the sex phases of marriage at the top, and Landis explains this by mentioning that a fourth of the students were in the early years of marriage and that most of the remainder were men over 20 years of age. In response to a question, 90 per cent of the students said they would recommend the work in the course to another interested student, and a very common comment was that it should be required of all students.

Home Economics

The need for a generous offering.—Instruction and an offering in home economics is a natural for the community college. While it has significance for both sexes, it is traditionally regarded as pre-eminently a field for women. Argument of appropriateness of a generous offering is supported by the ages of students, which, as indicated by census data, are now rapidly moving into the time of life for marriage. Education for homemaking, whether for wives or for others sharing these responsibilities, is usually regarded as general education, although there may be some justification for designating it as vocational for the housewife. Categorizing homemaking education as "general" has the advantage of distinguishing it from preparation for occupations that are open to community college students who take work in this field. There are many such subprofessional occupations: among those listed in the literature and catalogs are food-service occupations, including management; school lunch management; motel and hotel management; low-rent project management; food and appliance demonstration; laboratory testing of textiles and foods; child-care center assistance; and the more traditional employments of domestic and waitress. LeBaron (46), who identifies several of the more recently emerging of these occupations, attributes their development to the rapid urbanization of our society, and she mentions certain of the courses in homemaking as being appropriate as preparation for some of the subprofessional occupations. After identifying these two areas of need for home economics in the community college so far described, that is, general homemaking and terminal occupational, LeBaron speaks of the need for "college parallel" courses usable for transfer as "prerequisites" for students specializing in home economics with the intent of teaching or other professional careers in home economics.

The offerings.—In light of the manifest and extensive need, one who inquires into the status of home economics in community colleges is certain to be disappointed at the large proportion of institutions without offerings in the field. Of the sample of 31 institutions in 13 widely distributed states whose catalogs were examined, fewer than half were found to list such offerings, and, as may be expected, fewer of the smaller than of the larger schools list them. However, some community colleges make available extensive offerings. The courses offered in about 15 per cent or more are those in the following list, with rather wide array of additional titles foretokening significance listed only in an occasional catalog.

Courses in Home Economics and Homemaking

Introduction to Home Economics	Household Marketing (Food Economy)
Clothing Construction	Home Decoration
Dress Design and Construction	Interior Design
Clothing Selection and Design	Home Furnishings
Costume Analysis	House Planning
Tailoring	Home Management
Textiles	Marriage and Family Living
Foods (Food Selection and Cookery)	Consumer Education
Meal Planning and Preparation	Personal and Family Finance
Nutrition	Child Development
Nutrition and Diet Therapy	Pre-School Child

The list supports the contention that this field of home economics is an exceedingly broad one. Broken into main groups, these courses (after the first one listed, which is inclusive) are seen to be concerned with clothing; foods and nutrition; the home in various aspects, such as decoration, design, furnishings, and management; and the child and child care. Also sometimes included, as reported above while indicating the departmental allocation of instruction on Marriage and the Family, are courses in that area. The breadth of the whole field is suggested by the wide variety of disciplines in which it has its ramifying roots, including the physical and biological sciences, the behavioral sciences in wide array, and, in aesthetic aspects of housing and clothing, the humanities. The procedure of selection from such a wide area is suggestive of its high degree of functionalism.

With manifest need and with assurance of function, conjecture turns on why so many community colleges are without offerings in the field. Small units must often, of course, forego extending their offerings, but larger ones should be able to include them, and all should do so. One deterrent factor may be the fact that men students usually outnumber women and the needs of courses for men thus exert a greater pressure. Another factor may be the fact that many women have had courses in later high school years and still another may be the belief that dual-level offerings must be made, some for terminal students and others for transfer, even though procedures of instruction in the field offer opportunity for differentiation and individualization within the same class groups.

Perhaps the greatest obstacle to an adequate offering in home economics is the preparation for teaching at the collegiate level which usually requires specialization in only one of the major aspects of the field of home economics such as clothing or nutrition or home management, so that the junior college, say a small one, looking forward to offering courses in the field, is faced with the problem of employing two or more teachers to cover the special fields offered, when the total offering could not require this much teaching time. To ask a teacher who has specialized in foods and nutrition to give instruction in clothing as well as in her specialty might be as unthinkable as asking one who had specialized in chemistry to teach both chemistry and physics. To require teaching in the two or more aspects of the broad field of home economics would be somewhat analogous to assignments in teaching integrated courses in physical or in biological science. Some teachers equipped to handle the integrated courses in science have been found, which may lead to the hope that broadly equipped teachers in home economics may also be found and thus increase the feasibility of including offerings in home economics in community colleges. Feasibility might also be increased by assigning loads to specialists for both full-time and evening classes.

Science and Mathematics

Integrated courses.—For the individual student the goal of general education in the formulation quoted earlier in the chapter which is pre-eminently served by science and mathematics is "to act in the light of an understanding of the natural phenomena in his environment in its implications for human society and human welfare, to use scientific methods in the solution of his problems, and to employ useful non-verbal methods of thought and communication." Certain of the areas of the broad field represented would also help him "to improve and maintain his own health and take his share of responsibility for protecting the health of others" and "to practice clear and integrated thinking about the meaning and value of life."

While it is possible that all the courses in this broad area of the curriculum can be assumed to serve these purposes in some degree, certain integrated courses have been organized especially to serve the first of the purposes cited. The titles of such courses are as given in the first section of the list to follow, all of which are encountered in the catalogs of 10 per cent or more of a sampling of local public junior colleges in 13 states. One cannot be sure that the integrated courses have increased in number since

Putnam made his study of new-type offerings about 1950, but the course in Introduction to Physical Science emerged in well over a majority of the sample, and the one called Life Science or the Living World far less often. The courses including content from both physical and biological science are even less common. If judgment is based on the titles reported by Putnam in Table 11.1 (marked * in the list below) and on analysis of the more recent course descriptions, these integrated courses have departed from providing a mere overview of the several disciplines represented. The integrated courses in physical science continue to draw content typically from the several disciplines, namely, chemistry, physics, astronomy, geology, and meteorology, but they do so by being concerned with basic principles and concepts and their application to modern living. A prevalently stated purpose is to develop some appreciation and understanding of scientific methodology. The general courses in life science appear to be analogously concerned with concepts and principles, and topics often mentioned are the cell in its operational aspects, evolution, heredity and genetics, organisms in their relation to environment, biology of disease, body defenses, and body structure. In view of the manifestly pervasive impact of the findings of science on modern life and living and the potential of understanding these implications in influencing behavior, it is unfortunate that there is not more widespread experimentation with these courses, and especially, because of the greater lag, in the biological area.

It is altogether likely that the effort to develop interdisciplinary courses in science encounters more and greater obstacles, whatever these may be, than in other curriculum divisions. Thomas, in reviewing the status of such courses in the programs in general education in colleges and universities under scrutiny in his *Search for a Common Learning*, observes that "the history of the general courses in the sciences has been very spotty," and that "as a rule they have been less successful, at least in the judgment of those responsible for their planning than courses in the humanities and the social sciences." He goes on to say that the record of success has been greater in the biological than in the physical sciences (76, 117), which is contrary to the situation in the junior colleges, if we may judge from the relative frequency with which they are offered. In the absence of such courses, most of the institutions represented in Thomas' study resort for their requirements in science to "options from among courses in the separate sciences" (Table v, 310–13).

Besides the courses in General Mathematics, the two integrated courses in addition to those so far considered are the Survey of Botany, identified in several catalogs, and Nature Study, which is made available mainly for students preparing for elementary school teaching. Content of the courses in General Mathematics, like Survey of Botany and Nature Study not among the more frequent offerings, varies so from institution to institution that it is difficult to characterize. In some instances these courses are made available as condensed preparation for more advanced courses in mathematics, but more often they are concerned with developing mathematical understandings and skills that will make the student's other courses and quantitative aspects of his life and environment more intelligible. To do this they deal with mathematics as language, equations and other algebraic expressions, comparative numbers, arithmetic of measurement, exponents, ratio, variation, proportion, and the like.

COURSES IN SCIENCE AND MATHEMATICS

Integrated Courses
  *Life Science (Living World)
  *Introduction to Physical
    Science
  *Basic Science (General
    Science, Biological and
    Physical)
  Survey of Botany
  *Nature Study
  General Mathematics
    (Basic Mathematics)
Biological Science
  General (College) Botany
  General (College) Zoology
  General (College) Biology
  Human Anatomy
  Human Physiology
  Human Anatomy and
    Physiology
  Comparative Anatomy
  Vertebrate Anatomy
  Invertebrate Anatomy
  Microbiology (Bacteriology)
  Microtechnique
  Taxonomy
  Genetics, Heredity
  Field Biology
  Marine Biology
  Entomology
Physical Science
  Beginning (Introductory)
    Chemistry
  General Chemistry
  General Inorganic Chemistry
  Qualitative Analysis
  Inorganic Chemistry and
    Qualitative Analysis

  Quantitative Analysis
  Organic Chemistry
  Physical Geography
  Physical Geology
  Historical Geology
  General Geology
  Paleontology
  Minerology
  Field Geology
  General (College) Physics
  Mechanics
  Electricity and Magnetism
  Optics and Wave Motion
  Electronics
  Astronomy
  Meteorology
Mathematics
  Basic Arithmetic
  Elementary Algebra
  Intermediate Algebra
  Plane Geometry
  Solid Geometry
  College Algebra
  Plane Trigonometry
    (or Trigonometry)
  Analytic Geometry
  Trigonometry and
    Analytic Geometry
  Analytic Geometry and Calculus
  Linear Algebra
  Calculus
  Differential Equations
  Theory of Equations
  Probability and Statistics
  Slide Rule
  Computer Mathematics

Other courses.—The full list of courses in science and mathematics, including the integrated offerings just mentioned but excluding those met with in fewer than 10 per cent of the catalogs, is as above. Only brief running commentary will be necessary in explanation. Titles in the catalogs do not always coincide with those in the list, as there is some variation from college to college, but most of them are seen to be titles of standard liberal arts courses in the disciplines represented. They would thus serve the purpose of transfer and the list appears to be long enough to be not far from ample for this purpose, at the same time that most or all should yield some values in general education. The list in chemistry is lengthened to some extent by the differing patterns of sequence and organization of courses. This is true also in mathematics, where this particular list is further extended by the addition of high school courses to make these available to students who come up to the junior college without them and find, with change in plans, that they now need them.

Terminal Occupational Education

Justification of occupational programs.—A main line of justification for semiprofessional offerings in the community college is to be found in the attrition in its student body, since such a large proportion of this student body neither completes the two-year program nor transfers to the senior college. As long ago as 1941 Eells reported results of a follow-up of more than 57,000 students who entered 392 public and private junior colleges as freshmen in 1937. His finding, put in nearest round numbers, for that student generation was that "of 100 junior college freshmen, 75 continued as sophomores, 50 graduated, and 25 continued in other institutions. In other words, *the junior college is terminal, as far as full-time formal education is concerned, for three quarters of its students who enter as freshmen*" (*20*, 61, original italics).

In answer to the question of whether attrition in junior colleges is currently as serious as reported a quarter century ago by Eells, it may be said that, although no large-scale follow-up for a recent period has been reported, related evidence suggests that marked improvement in retention in the interim has not taken place. The analogous reasoning follows. During the years 1937–38, the academic year for which Eells studied the entering freshmen, the full-time enrollment in junior colleges of the country was 80,398 freshmen and 41,986 sophomores. The number of sophomores was thus 52.1 per cent of the number of freshmen. For 1965, the corresponding percentage was 41.4. Even after allowance is made for the rapid addition to the number of junior colleges in some of which only first-year work might be given during the initial year of operation, it is impossible to read into the declining percentage improved retention since 1940. Doubtless individual institutions have effected improvement, but for the country as a whole the situation now is almost certainly no better than as reported by Eells.

It is a truism that the obligation for occupational competence rests on all or almost all members of our society. Preparation for occupation usually comes last in one's education and, judging from the evidence just cited, the time for it for the majority of community college students is in early college years. While many junior colleges have instituted occupational offerings in varying amounts, it is repeatedly acknowledged that development of these programs has lagged behind the need, and also that, even where they have been provided, students have been reluctant to enroll in them. In the absence of adequate offerings and of willingness of students to avail themselves of them, we have a situation in which large numbers of young people leave school having been exposed only to truncated portions of four-year college curriculums and without understandings and skills applicable to earning their livelihoods.

A two-pronged need for semiprofessional programs.—Reference was made near the opening of the chapter to the frequent advocacy, even in the early stages of the junior college movement, of one purpose of the institution as semiprofessional education. The purpose was posited, by some of the writers whose opinions are represented in the analyses, as a two-pronged need. One of these prongs is the need just canvassed, that of the students, and this is seen to be urgent. The other is the need of society for the services of semiprofessional workers, that is, of workers whose duration of training lies between what can be completed in high school and that requiring a four-year college degree or more and classifying the occupations among the bonafide professions. The existence of such middle-level occupations, pitched at two years of post-high-school education, was affirmed in the early twenties by what was solicited as the "expert opinion" of deans and directors of colleges of business or commerce, engineering, and agriculture. Because better procedures have since been used to identify semiprofessional employments, space can be saved by restricting further report from this inquiry to a single major conclusion, which is to the effect that each of the three fields named contains a number of occupations classifiable as semiprofessions. Less systematic inquiry in other areas disclosed other possibilities in employments at the semiprofessional level (*44*, 135–42).

The opinions concerning the need of and place for preparation for mid-level positions, especially in technical fields, were corroborated in the forties by results of investigation and deliberation of a Consulting Committee on Vocational-Technical Training working under auspices of the United States Commissioner of Education. Consideration of the problem was prompted by shortages of trained manpower in technical fields in wartime. What appears to have been the working hypothesis of the committee was that the shortages might be in considerable part alleviated by assignment of major responsibilities to more highly trained personnel who were graduates of four-year institutions and that workers with education obtained in two-year post-high-school institutions, that is, technical institutes and junior colleges, might be upgraded for technical positions above the craftsman but below the strictly professional level. The method of investigation used was to ascertain for a wide variety of technical pursuits the average

TABLE 11.6
RATIOS OF TECHNICIANS TO ENGINEERS FOR 16 INDUSTRIES, AS REPORTED IN 1944

Industry	Ratio
Lumbering and Wood Processing	20.0
Shipbuilding	13.6
Pulp and Paper Manufacturing	10.3
Electrical Equipment Manufacturing	10.0
Textile Manufacturing	9.8
Telegraph and Telephone Communications Service	9.7
Rail Transportation	9.1
Metal Products Manufacturing	8.0
Iron and Steel Production	6.0
Machine Tool Manufacturing	5.5
Electric Power Production and Distribution	5.3
Petroleum and Butadene Production	5.3
Metal Mining	5.2
Automobile Manufacturing	4.2
Industrial Chemistry	2.2
Hydroelectric Development	2.0

SOURCE: *82*, 22.

number of technicians per professional engineer. The averages found for 16 country-wide industries are seen in Table 11.6 to range from 2.0 for hydroelectric development to 20.0 for lumbering and wood-processing. The average reported for all industries was 5.2. In the portion of the committee's report which sketched the education suitable for the technical positions, four industries in addition to those listed in Table 11.6 were included, namely, Air Transportation, Aircraft Manufacturing, Building Construction, and Industrial Electronics.

The appropriateness of semiprofessional programs for technicians and other semiprofessions in wide variety was solidly reaffirmed as recently as 1966 from evidence assembled by the Office of Manpower, Automation, and Training of the United States Department of Labor. Rosen, representing the office, said in reviewing the evidence that projections of the nation's manpower requirements for the decade ahead "confirm previous findings that professional, technical and kindred workers will continue to maintain their preeminent position as the fastest growing occupational group." In reviewing the evidence, Rosen stated that the sharpest growth occurred among those in electrical and electronics work, but that the number of engineering and physical science technicians had doubled between 1950 and 1960 and that the variety of other technicians ranged from that of "food tester to stage technician." He expressed assurance that the demand for technicians who are well trained "will far outstrip the supply of these workers."

Rosen's review includes reference to occupations proliferating out of our "service-oriented economy" which he believes has great significance for the junior college. Among the activities mentioned here are those concerned with water supply, air pollution, and waste disposal, as well as with repair and maintenance of increasingly complex automobiles, industrial machinery, office equipment, and household appliances. Rosen sees still other opportunities in the area of public service originating in federal poverty programs, such as those for teacher and counselor aides and library personnel. He calls attention again to the large number of bright youth in poor homes and the challenge to the junior college represented in attracting them to programs in preparation for such service (40, unpaged).

Growth of junior college terminal programs.—It is in point to review in brief the increase in semiprofessional and other terminal curriculums in junior colleges. Such programs were developed in technical institutes before they emerged in junior colleges, and the opinion was expressed in 1931, following an investigation of these institutes, that there was "no basis in experience for expecting the junior college of mixed character to do the work of a technical institute successfully" (75, 6). This opinion is belied by the record of development of the programs in the junior colleges.

Development of terminal curriculums in junior colleges for the period from about 1930 to 1947–48 may be noted by comparing the results of studies made by Christensen (9), Schiferl and Eells (20, 53), and Hillmer (30). Although there is some doubt that the three canvasses were made on strictly comparable bases and sound criteria of what constitutes terminal education, one can hardly question that the measures reported represent rapid growth. The numbers and percentages of full-time students in public junior colleges reported to be enrolled in terminal curriculums were as follows: 1931—3,052, or 20 per cent; 1938-39—30,261, or 35 per cent; 1947-48—57,252, or 47 per cent. Without undertaking to report the distribution to specific curriculums, one may be assured that the evidence indicates that there is a spread also to offerings which are increasingly diversified.

Results of comprehensive canvass of these offerings for a very recent

474 IMPLICATIONS FOR THE PROGRAM

date comparable with the preceding are not available. Richards (65) reported for 1956 a catalog analysis of technical and other professional offerings in all public and private accredited junior colleges. Although he identified all "terminal and semi-professional" curriculums, he gave special attention to those he classified as "technical education" curriculums. He found 85.3 per cent of the junior colleges offering one or more of the former classification and 52.3 per cent offering one or more of the latter. His entire list follows; it is in alphabetical order and the technical education curriculums are indicated by asterisks:

Architecture
Art
*Auto Mechanics
Aviation (Flight)
*Aviation Mechanics
*Building Trades
Business: Salesmanship
Business: Secretarial
*Chemical Technology
Dental Laboratory Technique
*Diesel Mechanics
*Drafting
*Electricity: Radio and TV Technology
Elementary Teaching
Food Trades
Forestry
Garment Trades
General Agriculture
General Business Education
*General Electricity
*General Engineering
*General Mechanics

Home Economics
Industrial Chemistry
Journalism
Library Science
Medical Laboratory Techniques
Medical Secretarial
*Metal Work
*Mining
Music
Nursing
*Oil Technology
Optometry
Physical Education
Piloting
Police Science
Printing
Recreational Leadership
*Refrigeration and Air Conditioning
Religion
Social Service
Travel Hostess
Watchmaking
Woodworking

In the absence of evidence from an inclusive recent survey of terminal occupational programs in the junior colleges, resort is taken here to reporting the titles of curriculums found on brochures submitted to the writer in response to a request sent to fifty representative public junior colleges well distributed over the nation asking for copies of catalogs and of any other printed matter describing program innovations. Among materials most often submitted were these brochures, a fact indicative of the prominence of terminal education in the current working concept of the community college. They were submitted by fifteen of the institutions and the curriculums described ranged from a few to as many as a dozen curriculums per junior college, with an average of five. The list of titles, under four divisions, is as follows:

Agriculture
   Agri-business
   Agriculture
Business
   Bookkeeping and Accounting
   General secretarial
   Medical secretarial
   Legal secretarial
   General office work
   Grocery merchandising
   Retail merchandising
   Mid-management
   Small business management
   Fashion design
Industrial and mechanical
   Architectural drafting
   Architectural specifications
   Technical drafting
   Building construction
   Civil technology
   Mechanical technology
   Automotive technology
   Diesel mechanics
   Machine shop
   Metal trades
   Sheet metal
   Welding
   Electronics technology
   Radiation technology
   Aircraft maintenance technology
   Airframe mechanics
   Power plant technology
   Commercial pilot
   Electronic data processing
   Industrial management technology
   Office machines technology
   Refrigeration and air-conditioning technology
   Printing
Health and security
   Dental assisting
   Medical assisting
   Nursing
   Practical (vocational) nursing
   Police science

From its limited source, it must be understood that the list is not put forward as inclusive of all such curriculums. Additional titles come readily to mind for persons conversant with the field. Among these would be forestry; floriculture and landscaping under agriculture; curriculums in food service, hotel and motel management, and child-care assistance in nursery schools as suggested above in considering the place of home economics; library assistance; and curriculums in preparation for service occupations like those suggested by Rosen in his paper, portions of which were paraphrased above. The dynamic character of developments in this area of the program is reflected in the frequency with which articles are published descriptive of projects initiating new offerings, as, for example, Price and Barnett on computer education (*58*), Earnshaw on a curriculum for library assistants (*19*), and Conklin on programs for preparing registered nurses (*10*).

Careful reading of the list of terminal curriculums above prompts the observation that, while most of them, technical and nontechnical, are semi-professional in level, a minority of them may be at the craftsman or clerical level. Insofar as this observation is correct, it is in harmony with the belief in some quarters that the community college should provide vocational preparation at this level as well as at the semiprofessional, and that this is an implication of the open-door policy.

Recommended directions of development.—It was to be expected that awareness of the need for terminal occupational programs from the standpoint of service to students and to society would eventuate in official attention to the problem by the American Association of Junior Colleges. Consideration was given to the problem through the Association's Curriculum Commission with the help of an Advisory Committee representative of the membership. The published report, called *Technical Education in the Junior College: New Programs for New Jobs* (27), prepared by Harris, a recognized consultant in the field, examines with both brevity and cogency the scope of the need for programs and desirable directions of development.

The report reviews the evidence concerning manpower needs touched on above, showing a mounting demand for workers in mid-level employments, especially for those loosely termed technicians. It distinguishes the preparation for these on the one hand from "transfer courses" which are accepted for full credit by universities and four-year colleges and on the other from "vocational" and "trade and industrial education" which provide training for skilled jobs in the fields of agriculture, business, industry, and home economics. It distinguishes further between "semiprofessional" and "technical" education, with the former representing formal curriculums leading to the associate degree and designed to prepare the student for employment such as engineering technician, medical technician, architectural draftsman, business data processor, and registered nurse, and the other, with no unanimously accepted definition of the term, organized into two-year college-level programs, emphasizing work in science and mathematics, giving much attention to technical knowledge and general education, but also stressing practice and skill in the use of tools and instruments, and leading to competence in one of the technical occupations (27, 21).

Differences in the make-up of curriculums suggested for the two levels of technicians may be noted in the following portrayal of "divisions" and "courses" covering the two years (27, 39–40).

For Semiprofessional (Engineering) Technicians

	CREDIT HOURS
Mathematics (technical) covering algebra, geometry, trigonometry, sliderule, analytic geometry, applied calculus, and advanced topics	10
Science for the technician, covering applied physics, or chemistry, mechanics, thermodynamics, metallurgy, etc.	10
Technical specialty courses basic to the student's major—elementary and advanced; theory and practice	30
Supporting technical courses—graphics, engineering laboratory, technical writing	6

General education courses—English, humanities, social studies, etc.	18
Total	74

For Highly Skilled (Industrial) Technicians

Mathematics—a one-year technical mathematics course covering advanced arithmetic, algebra, geometry, trigonometry, and sliderule	6
Applied science—technical physics or technical chemistry	8
Technical specialty courses basic to the student's major—some theory, but emphasis on practice	36
Supporting technical courses—drafting, general shop, etc.	9
General education courses—English, humanities, social science	15
	74

Harris warns in the report of the inadvisability of overspecialization of curriculums and a preference for preparation for "clusters" or "families" of technical occupations, these being referred to as mechanical, electrical/electronic, civil, and engineering laboratory. Listed and commented upon also are the health-related technicians (among them dental assistant, medical office assistant, registered nurse, x-ray technician, etc.); business-related occupations (bookkeeper, data processing technician, legal secretary, etc.); agriculture-related employments (agricultural engineering technician, sales and service technician, landscape and nursery technician, etc.); and "other semiprofessional occupations" (including scientific research technicians in wide variety and employments in public service as fireman, patrolman, sanitation technician, etc.). The portrayal of occupations listed is referred to as the "*spectrum* of middle-level manpower"—jobs that are predicted to account for almost 30 per cent of the labor force by 1970 (*27, 47*).

Cooperative and work-experience programs.—Since the establishment of the first cooperative work-study plan at the University of Cincinnati in 1906 this type of program has spread to a large number of degree-granting institutions and has enrolled many thousands of students. It has also become popular in non-degree-granting technical institutes both public and private. The plan has also been put into operation in public community or junior colleges, but on a more limited scale. Eells reported a list of 71 public and private junior colleges as operating such programs in 1938–39, but gathered and presented no data concerning the practices in them (*20, 141–43*). When Smith in 1941 (*73*) approached these institutions and two other junior colleges which had been named to him as having cooperative programs for information on their practices and applied the criterion of a reasonable definition of cooperative education, he found it necessary to reduce the number thus qualifying to 34. He had defined cooperative education as follows: "By cooperative education is meant that type of curriculum which is based upon alternation between regularly scheduled instructional periods in school and supervised periods in business or industry, with definite provision for treating work experiences as an integral part of the total education of students."

Most of the programs had been instituted between 1930 and 1940, whereas almost half of those in four-year colleges and universities represented in Armsby's study made for the year 1953–54 (2, 7) had been instituted before 1930. Almost three-fourths of the curriculums in Armsby's project were in engineering and the remainder nonengineering, whereas 29 of the 44 curriculums in Smith's study were in the field of business, with only 7 in engineering.

Cooperative enrollments in the junior colleges were found to be prevailingly small. A majority of the periods of alternation between work and study in the four-year colleges and universities were on the semester or quarter basis, whereas in the junior colleges the most frequent alternation was the half day. Smith's tabulation found that students in well over a majority of the curriculums represented received pay, chiefly at current rates, and in some of them both pay and college credit. In about a third of the curriculums they received credit only.

Smith reported no evaluation of these cooperative programs in junior colleges, although soon after this survey of status he made available an appraisal by alumni opinion of cooperative work programs maintained by one technical institute (72). Rather than to rely on this evidence from a single institution which was not a junior college, it is preferable to cite conclusions and evidence from a large-scale project appraising these programs as operated in four-year colleges and universities. The main body of evidence from the project is presented by Wilson and Lyons (86). The project was subsidized by the Fund for the Advancement of Education and involved 17 institutions representative in variety and distribution of the 61 at the time of the investigation operating cooperative programs, as well as a sample of 10 institutions not operating them.

Values of cooperative work programs as derived from the investigation were effectively expressed in the introduction to the complete report by Tyler (80, 6–8). While compactly stated, these values, or advantages, are given here in even briefer form. (1) By coordinating work experience with the program on campus, "theory and practice are more closely related and students find greater meaning in their studies." (2) "This coordination increases student motivation." (3) "Work experience contributes a greater responsibility for the students' own efforts." (4) "Constructive relationships with colleagues develop greater understanding of other people and greater skills in human relationships." (5) "Cooperative education helps markedly to orient college students to the world of work" and it "furnishes students with opportunities for exploring their own abilities in connection with real jobs." (6) "Cooperative education has an important value in making higher education possible and attractive to many young people who would not otherwise go to college." (7) Members of the faculty are "able to keep in touch with business, industry, and some of the professions." (8) "Because cooperative education is commonly organized so half the student body is at work while the other half is on the campus, the plan permits more efficient utilization of the college plant and other facilities." Additional advantages identified by Tyler but not included among these numbered values are found in the fact that the plan provides business and industrial firms a means of maintaining a "flow of trained personnel," for the student it furnishes contacts useful in later occupational placement, and it provides greater recognition by the community of the services the colleges are rendering to it, an important value in public relations.

The general conclusion from the investigation is that cooperative education should be greatly extended. Other fields to which the plan is suggested as applicable are teaching, social work, and the civil service. Recommended also is a great increase in experimentation with cooperative programs in the education of women.

Disadvantages of the cooperative plan most often mentioned in literature dealing with it relate to the hindrance to participation in the activity program of students during periods of alternation in the work portions of the program; the influence of ups and downs of the business cycle, which in periods of depression reduce or cut off the demand for workers, and, therefore, of stations for students; and the problems in the area of competence and cost of coordination. Without unusual competence of coordinators, the programs languish or fail, and coordination calls for additional faculty members who usually are employed for the calendar year, rather than only through the regular school year.

Another arrangement often made at high school and college levels to provide part-time employment is what is known as "work experience" or "work-experience education." It differs from the usual part-time cooperative plan in not involving the "two-man team," one member of which is in employment while the other is on campus. Another difference is that there is less often concern than in cooperative plans for a functional relationship between the student's course instruction and the work being done on the job. In practice this relationship ranges from high to negligible.

The values to be derived from these programs, judging from their purposes, overlap those for cooperative plans but differ in emphasis, as may be seen in those accepted for work experience in California junior colleges (*80*, 39): "To assist young people toward their chosen occupational goals"; "to give young people exploratory occupational experiences"; "to help young people learn, as part of their general education, what employment entails." Less often put forward as purposes were "to help needy students augment their income" and "to help salvage young people who have school adjustment problems."

TABLE 11.7
PERCENTAGES OF STUDENTS IN COOPERATIVE AND NONCOOPERATIVE PROGRAMS IN HIGH AND LOW SOCIAL STRATA

Class Stratum and Group	Freshman Students	Senior Students
Upper and Upper Middle		
Cooperative	35.8	27.1
Noncooperative	44.2	40.6
Upper-Lower and Lower-Lower		
Cooperative	32.6	37.7
Noncooperative	18.9	26.9

SOURCE: Wilson and Lyons (*86*, 43, from Table 8).

The source from which these purposes are quoted is a report on the status and practices in the administration of the work-experience programs in California junior colleges in 1954–55 (*80*, 38–49). Thirty-four of 60 public junior colleges were found to have such programs. They enrolled 3.15 per cent of all students in the two college years, some of the enrollment being in in-school work experience in libraries, laboratories, cafeterias, and offices of the junior colleges. Pay was usually reported as being at "prevailing rates." There was wide variation as to maximum credit allowed for the work and as to the amount of work required per credit hour. The report made much of the importance of supervision of students enrolled for work experience, which is nearly always done by instructors or by persons designated as coordinators who are frequently also instructors. About half of the junior colleges with these programs reported having lay advisory committees and reports on the usefulness of these committees were said to be "almost uniformly favorable and even enthusiastic."

Before leaving consideration of these plans that arrange for part-time employment while students continue in school, it seems desirable to return for brief further consideration of their value, as put by Tyler, "in making higher education possible and attractive to young people who would not otherwise go to college." This value has a peculiar significance for an institution like the community college, one of whose major purposes, as was indicated near the opening of the chapter, is democratization of college level of education. This democratization, and the encouragement of upward mobility in our society which the purpose implies, is reflected in the percentages in Table 11.7 which are cited from the project by Wilson and Lyons. These percentages afford assurance that the cooperative plan overcomes in substantial degree the obstacles to college attendance which are set up by social status, either because of limited family income or because of lack of motivation in the way of life in many "common man" families.*

It is manifest that the opportunities for part-time employment and the pay received for it are designed to overcome both obstacles.

Identifying employments requiring terminal programs.—As has been indicated above† by quotation from Rosen, the occupations for which programs of terminal preparation at the lower college level are appropriate have been identified on a national scale by inquiry of a federal agency. Application of similar procedures to problems of manpower have also been made at the state level, so that persons concerned with setting up such programs for individual community colleges would have left to them the task of identifying these occupations in the more or less immediate areas. Such inquiries have frequently been reported and, for purposes of illustration, three of these are described briefly as to procedures and findings.

An early inquiry of this nature was made for Rochester, Minnesota, location of a noted medical and surgical center, and on behalf of curriculum improvement in what was at the time a local public junior college. The following description is based on an abridgment of the full report (*24*). The procedure used involved three main steps, of which the first was examination of census data. It was found, as might be expected in such a community, that large proportions of the adult population were in professional and related employments, in wholesale and retail trade, and in personal service (especially in hotels and restaurants). The remaining steps in advance of setting up the programs consisted of interviews with employers to identify positions for which preparation at the early college level appeared appropriate and the activities engaged in for which elements of the curriculum should be provided. The areas first recognized in the program were hotel and restaurant operations, retail sales, manufacturing, construction, and dentistry (for dental assistants). Subsequently, a curriculum in ophthalmic optics was established to prepare workers for an optical company which maintains laboratories and a branch in Rochester. Later catalogs of the institution have listed a curriculum for medical secretaries. In addition to the "specialized elements" the curriculums included a "core" of general education.

*See pp. 208–9.
†See pp. 472–73.

The second illustrative project (56), made on behalf of the Contra Costa County Junior College District in California, differs mainly from that in Rochester (1) by inquiring into all occupational education needs in the district and the question of allocating such programs as were found to be needed to (a) junior high school, (b) senior high school, and (c) junior college levels, and (2) in being more extensive as to employers and other personnel consulted. Projections were made of population and employments not only for Contra Costa County but for the San Francisco Bay area as a whole. Focus here is on employments found suitable for terminal preparation at the junior college level. The recommendations in the field of agriculture included offerings in agriculture arts and urbiculture, agriculture-business, and nursery work. For the field of business, no programs in addition to those already being offered were recommended, although the report urged new courses or course sequences in such activities as key-punch operation, marketing and merchandising, the professional secretaryship, etc. Among offerings recommended for women's occupations were those preparing for homemaker, interior decorator, library assistant, medical office worker, medical record technician, and transportation hostess. Programs preparing for the semiprofessional positions of technicians (automotive, chemistry, drafting, electronics, instrument, mechanical, and x-ray) were recommended, as well as for construction superintendents and engineering aides, and it was indicated that a number of other technician occupations seemed to warrant further study. There was a conclusion of justification also for continuing trade-level programs already going forward in training for carpenter, cook's helper, electrician, motor mechanic, welder, etc., and for apprentice-related training in some of these employments as well as others.

The third study (55), made for the College of Marin in California, added one more approach to those used in Rochester and Contra Costa County: to ascertain the interests in and choices of certain occupational programs of seniors in contributing high schools and of freshmen and extended day and adult education students in the College of Marin. As the college was already offering a number of terminal programs, the point of interest in conducting the inquiry was in terminal programs that should be *added*. The recommendation of the report (55, 8), based on attitudes of students and on occupational opportunities, was that the college seriously consider soon adding programs for law enforcement, dental assistant, registered nurse, and medical secretary. Longer range planning should include further consideration of introducing programs in cosmetology; building technology; banking, saving and loan, stock brokerage; and specialized occupations in business data processing.

A pregnant state-wide inquiry.—Germane to the problem of terminal occupational education at the post-high-school level, but with significance for other vital aspects of community college development, is a recent report by Dorothy Knoell prepared for the State University of New York (*43*). It differs also from the three projects just reviewed by looking for implications for all community colleges in the state of the increasingly accepted assumption that post-high-school education should be universalized. The merits of the project far exceed the brief sketch of its procedures and findings that can be provided here.

The lines of inquiry in this project included (1) a canvass of the manpower situation in the state with a focus on low-level occupations for which preparation is feasible in early post-high-school years; (2) interviews with (a) high school students who had made no plans to attend college by January of their senior year, (b) parents of these students, and (c) recent high school graduates who had not continued their education in college; and (3) questionnaire responses from administrators, trustees, and faculty of the existing community colleges indicating their attitudes toward the introduction of programs adapted to the needs of this less able and/or relatively unmotivated population.

It is no easy task to generalize in brief from the evidence and conclusions of a project of this magnitude. Assurance is provided of the presence of a wide variety of low-level occupations for which some preparation at the post-high-school level could be appropriate. Inferences from responses in the interviews are that while a minority of the youth would avail themselves of the opportunities, if offered, especially if associated with work experience, most do not look forward to extension of their school experience. A further obstacle is that awareness of the existence of the community colleges is not widespread. It is obvious that, if introduced, such programs would be without students unless guidance and counseling of youth who can profit from them is greatly expanded. Furthermore, while some among trustees and staff of the community colleges look with favor on such programs, desirability of their introduction is questioned by many, so that education of trustees and faculties concerning the full scope of function of their institutions would be imperative. Thus, universalized post-high-school education can hardly be expected to come automatically, but will require persistent and intelligent effort.

Transfer Curriculums

Dimensions of the transfer-student service.—In approaching the subject of terminal occupational education in the foregoing section, a finding by Eells of three decades ago was cited indicating that only about 25 per cent of students enrolling as freshmen in public junior colleges ultimately continued their education in senior institutions, and from analogous speculation over related evidence for recent years it was concluded that the proportion continuing beyond the junior college cannot have risen notably in the meantime. To be sure, it varies from institution to institution, being much larger for some at the same time that it is even smaller than a fourth of all for others. This minority of the entering student body is, of course, the group for whom transfer curriculums are planned and appropriate.

A serious problem for the junior college emerges because the population enrolling in the transfer curriculums far exceeds the proportion who continue into the third college year. Many who begin them do not go beyond the first year, and many do not complete that one. As a matter of fact, even in junior colleges with well-developed terminal programs, students enrolled in transfer curriculums typically often far outnumber those in terminal curriculums. The upshot is that large proportions of students are enrolled in what turn out for them to be truncated or aborted curriculums which, although not a total loss, are nevertheless far less functional for these students than they might well be. The outcome is widespread frustration among the students enrolled. The obvious implication is much more effective guidance and counseling for the student population, which is the concern of Chapter 12. However, for a minority of students enrolled in them—a segment of unquestioned potentiality for society and for themselves—the curriculums are in large and major part appropriate. On this account, illustrative evidence bearing on their range in scope and number is presented.

The range of transfer curriculums offered.—The transfer curriculums which are either portrayed or listed in 15 per cent or more of the junior college catalogs used for the representation in earlier sections in this chapter approach half a hundred in number. They are listed alphabetically.

The curriculums are seen to range through the major professional categories and, near the end of the list, through the separate disciplines in arts and sciences, most of which would be selected by students with vocational intentions for teaching or other occupations in wide variety. It is to be taken for granted that for professional schools for which the Bachelor's degree is required for admission, the offering covers only the first two years of work. Among additional curriculums met with less frequently than in 15 per cent of the catalogs are Agricultural Engineering, Horticulture, Ministerial, Mechanical Engineering, and, in the liberal arts and sciences, Anthropology, Criminology, Geography, International Affairs, and Sociology. The total number of different curriculums encountered in the twenty-six catalogs was almost a hundred and the number would have been greater had a larger sampling of institutions been included in the analysis.

The importance of these transfer curriculums in the minds of community college administrators is reflected not only in their wide range and scope

Agriculture and Forestry
  Agriculture
  Forestry
Arts and Architecture
  Architecture
  Art
  Drama (Theater)
  Music
Business
  Business Administration
  General Business
  Secretarial Science
Education and Physical Education
  Education
  Elementary School Teaching
  Secondary School Teaching
  Physical Education
  Recreational Leadership
Engineering
  Engineering
  Chemical Engineering
  Civil Engineering
  Electrical Engineering
Health and Related Professions
  Medicine
  Medical Technology
  Dentistry
  Nursing
  Veterinary Medicine
  Pharmacy
  Optometry
  Occupational Therapy
  Physical Therapy
  Home Economics
Law and Other Government
  Related Professions
  Law
  Police Science
  Social Welfare
Liberal Arts (Arts and Sciences)
Separate Disciplines in
  Arts and Sciences
  Biology
  Chemistry
  Economics
  English
  Foreign Languages (several)
  Geology
  History
  Mathematics
  Philosophy
  Physics
  Political Science
  Psychology
  Science
  Zoology

but also in the total number typically portrayed or listed. The actual range in the catalogs examined is from 3 to 52, with a median of 16, and a mean at 19+. Surprisingly, no significant difference in medians was found when the catalogs were separated into those for larger and smaller institutions.

Comment on this portion of junior college catalogs should not be concluded without reference to its service in counseling and guidance, even though the comment trespasses on the concerns of Chapter 12. This service is signalized in certain of the catalogs by such a designation as "Career Plans." In many instances the section is separated into two parts setting forth the terminal and the transfer curriculums, while in others the curriculums are merged in different groupings, sometimes merely in alphabetical arrangement and sometimes under occupational or disciplinary categories.

The California catalogs in the representation exhibited a variant in presentation seldom if ever encountered in junior colleges in other states, and found on further inquiry to be practically universal in that state: the transfer curriculums are particularized for the individual universities and/or types of higher institutions in the state. The need for doing so may at times add confusion for the students, complexity to the task of counseling them, and magnitude to the problem of administrators in setting up the program. Consideration of the need for such extreme particularization is touched upon in Chapter 12.

The role of the General Curriculum.—Many junior college catalogs, in addition to portraying or listing the many transfer curriculums as just reviewed, make provision also for a General Curriculum, description and consideration of which is appropriate at this point. This designation does not refer to the general education program dealt with in an earlier section of this chapter, but is applied to an *unspecialized* curriculum analogous to the more specialized transfer programs. This curriculum varies widely among junior colleges but usually prescribes a few of the subjects common to all curriculums, namely, English, something in the field of the social studies, and Physical Education, and leaves most of the student's program open for wide election.

This general curriculum serves two main groups of students. Among entering freshmen who register in it are many who are still so uncertain of their occupational plans as to be hesitant to commit themselves to any of the specialized curriculums available. The other group includes many students who at the time of entering college committed themselves to specialized curriculums but who decide later on for various reasons that they do not wish to continue in them and find it inconvenient or prefer not to shift to another specialization. Much of this shift is symptomatic of ill-chosen occupational goals and inadequate guidance. The presence of the General Curriculum in the program of many junior colleges is evidence of the need for the flexibility it affords. Its weaknesses emerge where its requirements are so limited that it does not assure the general education that its title implies and that a student who completes it will have experienced what may be regarded as only a curricular miscellany.

Remedial and Developmental Programs

Acknowledgment of the need.—Among the purposes posited for the community college as reported in the first section of this chapter that derive from the "open-door" policy is serving the needs of (1) high school graduates of lower ability. For such students it is a frequent practice to administer "remedial," or "compensatory," programs of various types. Many junior colleges also admit (2) nongraduates who are 18 years of age or older, and for some of these students programs of remediation may be appropriate. Associated here also are (3) applicants for admission who are high school graduates who first attended four-year colleges and universities but have left these institutions with failing or otherwise unsatisfactory records. For some of the third group also the need for remediation would be indicated, and they are one of the groups identified near the opening of the chapter* to which the "salvage" function applies.

Report of an inquiry into practices in junior colleges and opinions of administrators touching admission of students of lower ability and programs to serve them has been made by Schenz (71). The information was obtained by questionnaires sent to all public and private junior colleges with full-time enrollments of 400 or more, this figure being used because of the investigator's belief that "junior colleges with smaller enrollments would be unlikely to have students with low ability in sufficient numbers to merit special curricular consideration." The proportion of administrators of the public units reporting admission of students of low ability was nine-tenths, of private units less than half. Means of identification of these students were primarily (1) tests, (2) both tests and grades, and (3) tests, grades, and interview, with the second combination more often used than the other criteria. The tests most often used are the standardized instruments for measuring college aptitude, such as SCAT, SAT, etc. Well over half the public junior colleges were reported as providing and either requiring or recommending "special remedial courses" for students of low ability; about a fifth provide and require or recommend a "special program of courses" for them, and another fifth provide only "regular courses" or follow some other practice. Schenz' conclusions from his study refer to the emerging awareness by administrators of junior colleges of the problem of meeting the needs of students of low ability, acceptance of the responsibility of providing courses and curriculums to meet these needs, and acceptance also of the remedial function as legitimate for these institutions.

Scope of the program.—Main aspects of the remedial programs relate to the tools, or skills, needed for successful learning and school progress. As encountered in educational literature dealing with the college level, these skills are primarily in reading, writing, mathematics, and procedures in study. The literature bearing on them is extensive, leading to a temptation to extensive treatment here, which cannot be indulged. Consideration will be brief and restricted to reading, writing, and skills in study, because the needs for them in the student population are often regarded as more nearly universal than in mathematics. Even where one disagrees with the opinion that the need for remediation is less widespread in mathematics, there is another reason for not dealing at length with such corrective efforts, and this is the fact that the remedial courses in this discipline seldom deviate from a telescoped review of one or more of its divisions, namely, arithmetic, algebra, geometry, trigonometry, etc. It will become apparent as consideration of the programs proceeds that the skills and the needs for the three areas of reading, writing, and study skills overlap—a

*See p. 436.

fact of importance for the organization of the remedial program as a whole.

The program in reading.—The literature dealing with remedial programs in reading borders on the voluminous, although most of it is relatively recent, in that the bulk of it has been published since 1950. The earliest efforts in colleges in this area seem to have been made around 1930 or thereabouts. By 1940 the efforts were taking on something of the nature of a movement, although writers of the period were in some disagreement over its magnitude. Witty (*88*) in that year, reporting from an inquiry mainly of institutions known to be operating "corrective reading" programs, concluded that opportunities for college students to improve their reading ability were "regrettably meager." By contrast, Charters (*8*), from a "quick survey" in which he sent out 675 inquiries and received 172 replies, found well over a hundred indicating that they were operating projects in remedial reading. He named 24 institutions, one of them a junior college, which impressed him as having developed "seasoned programs." Rapidity of spread of the programs is seen in figures quoted by Shaw (*29*, 338), who found almost three-fourths of 418 institutions reporting reading programs in progress by 1956.

The programs have been spreading rapidly because testing has shown that the deficiencies are widely prevalent in the student body. Shaw cites Halfter and Douglass as concluding, after eight years of testing, that two-thirds of entering college freshmen lack the ability in reading required for academic success (*29*, 337), and other investigators reporting conclusions bear witness to states of deficiency no less widespread. The institutions operating the programs include many of the most selective on the American collegiate scene. This fact and the reported prevalence of the deficiencies suggest that the programs should be regarded as developmental rather than remedial, although the latter designation has been so long in use as to make it difficult to replace. One may affirm that, if selective institutions find the programs desirable or necessary, the community college, with its typically less selected student body, must find them imperative.

Three patterns of organization of the reading improvement programs are in operation. That most frequently followed is (1) the separate special service, and the others, in the order of decreasing frequency, are (2) as part of the regular language-arts course and (3) as an intrinsic part of instruction in subjects to which the skills apply. In something approaching half the institutions where separate courses are in operation, credit is given. Important reasons for the relative infrequency of the third type, and to some extent also of the second, are the lack of competence and/or the unwillingness of subject specialists to teach the necessary skills.

The instruction is usually concerned first with increasing rate and comprehension in reading and it has been found that rate is more susceptible to improvement than comprehension. Among the more common approaches to improve the latter is to strive for ability to identify and grasp main ideas. Efforts to improve skills are often related to the differing purposes in reading, as in exploration of material, general orientation in an area, seeking specific information, recreation, review, studying details, or thorough understanding, and to different types of reading, as skimming, rapid reading, or careful intensive reading.

A prime consideration of programs of remedial or developmental reading should be the criterion used in evaluating them. Too often this has been nothing more than the extent of improvement in one or more reading skills when it should be nothing less than improvement in measures of academic success, or scholastic improvement, of students in their regular programs. An investigator in reporting the third in a series of controlled experiments with remedial reading courses carried on at Yale during the 1940s (66) observed, after reading the reports of nearly a hundred studies, that the effectiveness of most programs was at that time still "largely suspect," and that among the studies fewer than a dozen made references to their effect on scholastic improvement. He contended that "academic performance is clearly the *sine qua non* for the validation of the remedial courses."

Remedial work in writing.—Earlier in this chapter* it was reported from a study of English programs in junior colleges that a full majority of these institutions were offering remedial courses in them. It was also reported that the study of grammar was given primary emphasis in the remedial courses, despite published researches indicating the lack of correlation between knowledge of formal grammar and competence in writing. These courses typically are concerned with a wide range of skills variously related to writing, including spelling, parts of speech, grammar, punctuation, capitalization, vocabulary improvement, diction, usage, sentence structure, paragraph development, use of dictionary, theme organization and writing, remedial reading, use of library, etc.

Dissatisfaction with outcomes of the typical remedial course has led to a variety of efforts to increase its effectiveness. A few of the more promising innovations reported in the literature are identified here. One of these is to restrict the range of skills attacked, for instance, by leaving improvement in spelling and vocabulary development to instruction in the disciplines to which the vocabularies are peculiar, or leaving improvement in reading to the special course in remedial reading. One innovator following this line emphasized only construction, punctuation, diction, usage, capitalization, and theme-writing. It was his opinion that theme-writing is necessary to keep the course focused on its main objective—critical thinking. His primary emphasis was on the sentence because of its "close relationship to

*See pp. 454–55.

critical thinking" (*13*). Grammar introduced in this innovation was described as "structural" rather than formal. Another important change reported with some frequency is forsaking the traditional lecture-discussion method on behalf of a laboratory procedure geared not so much to logical organization of subject matter in English as to the particular deficiencies of the individual student, these deficiencies being identified by tests of writing and speaking competence in various aspects. Still another departure from customary procedure is through efforts at motivation, which was done by finding subjects or topics for writing that were matters of genuine interest to the students and about which they cared to talk or write. One experiment utilizing motivation of this kind involved gathering extensive information concerning the students, and not merely their intelligence quotients. Included in this information were their occupational plans. Compilation had shown that for 86 per cent their level of language usage was unsuited to these occupational plans and this was brought home to the students. This experiment used the additional motivation of participation, by having the students working in pairs and correcting each other's writing "with the instructor acting as a sort of resource person" (*84*).

Improvement of skills in study.—Instruction in study skills is given in an increasing number of junior colleges (as well as of four-year colleges and universities), either in separate courses or as part of courses in orientation, and is usually, if not always, administered under auspices of the institution's organization for counseling services. The proportion of institutions allowing credit for the separate course has been increasing but has not yet reached a majority. The content of the courses is suggested by the following list of divisions or units included in them, albeit the particular designations and the total number of divisions differ from course to course: adjustment to college, keeping physically and mentally fit, importance of a study schedule, note-taking, preparing assignments and methods of study, use of library and laboratory, preparing for tests and examinations, memorization, reading skills, skill in listening, vocabulary building, preparing papers, and speaking skills. Items in the list suggest overlapping on remedial courses in reading and writing as these have previously been described.

Textbooks are available for use in these courses. A criticism sometimes lodged against the courses is that, as often taught by a method of lecture and discussion and with the use of an accompanying textbook, they remain theoretical and do not result in improved study skills. Efforts at offsetting the criticism include use of a workbook that provides exercises which call for application by the students of procedures looking to improvement and space for records on tests "before and after taking."

Some of the courses include, besides the generic skills applicable to all collegiate fields, consideration of study skills peculiar to particular disciplines, as foreign language, a specific area of science, or mathematics. Critics of this extension insist that instruction in and development of these specialized skills should be the responsibility of the teachers of these disciplines, and that the skills should receive attention at the points where they are needed. The rejoinder of the teachers of the study-skills courses which include attention to the special skills is that the subject specialists are unwilling or unprepared to give such instruction.

Unwillingness is said to have its origin in the belief that all high school graduates should come equipped with all study skills needed at the college level. In line with this belief is the prevalent condemnation of preparation in high school in many other respects. From the fact that the students are all high school graduates, most of them representing some degree of selection, one can infer that the great plurality are equipped with the skills needed for success in high school, although they may need help in attaining the study skills required in disciplines at the college level, and the help can be provided in general study skills courses, in connection with courses in the special disciplines, or, preferably, in both.

An illustrative composite program.—The overlapping on each other that has been noted in the programs in reading, writing, and study skills that have just been described affords at least partial sanction for merging them into something like a single process. Such in effect, although put forward primarily as a program to improve competence in writing, is one described by Cowan, Hawkins, and McPherson as being carried forward in Clark College, a junior college at Vancouver, Washington (*11*). These authors preface their exposition by stating that they had tried without success several plans with students of low competence, such as the usual remedial courses and putting the students in regular freshman composition sections both with and without additional remedial periods. The decision after these experiences was to set up a course which "would not be primarily remedial," but provide these students with enough English to warrant accepting the credit for it toward graduation, although it was not regarded as adequate for transfer credit. Requirements for graduation from this college include nine hours of Communication, six of which can be obtained by taking this three-quarter sequence of two hours each quarter and adding the remaining three hours by an introductory course in speech.

On the assumption that reading and writing skills are inseparable, each student registered for the first quarter of nontransfer English must also register for two hours of reading laboratory per week, during which he works through as much reading as he can at his own level which is determined by test. The class work during the first quarter concentrates on developing fluency in writing. Most of this is done in the first twenty minutes of each period, and on subjects within the range of the student's interests.

In one of the periods each week he writes a summary of a book he has been reading for pleasure. The rest of the class period for the first quarter is spent on discussions on how to study, how to outline, how to underline main points, how to take lecture notes, and how to take tests. Time of the second quarter is taken up with more intensive instruction in writing, with home assignments and emphasis on exposition and argument. The third quarter extends the work of the second quarter, with emphasis on rational argument. While the course, as stated, is not regarded as primarily remedial, a small proportion of the students pass eligibility tests at the end of the first quarter and enter regular composition classes.

Nothing is said in this description of the program concerning efforts at integrating with it the course in speech added by students to complete their requirements in English. If this is being done, it is, together with other elements of the course as described, a long step toward a course in Communication not unlike those identified near the opening of the chapter, while at the same time including elements aimed at making up for inadequacies in reading, writing, and study skills.

An overview of the problem and related research.—The foregoing treatment of efforts at remediation in the junior college is too brief to do more than indicate the need for it and the main lines of current effort to provide it. The reader looking for a more extensive and penetrating review of the rationale of remediation in the institution as well as an interpretative analysis of all related researches should see Roueche's *Salvage, Redirection, or Custody?,* a publication subtitled *Remedial Education in the Community College* (69). A complete bibliography is included.

Innovation in Curriculum

New purposes and a program to implement them.—A generalization that seems warranted by the foregoing review of the special purposes of the junior college and of the trends of change in the several elements of its program is that it is destined to serve as a vehicle of innovation. The pattern of purposes accepted for the institution goes far beyond the traditional preparatory service of this early post-high-school period (with the admission that it may also contribute to general education) by adding the functions of terminal occupational education, remediation, adult education, and community service. To achieve all these purposes effectively, as the chapter to follow emphasizes, it must also greatly expand student personnel and guidance service. This broad pattern of purpose is an implication of commitment to universalization of this school level.

Evidence of innovation is reflected in most of the several sections of the treatment describing elements of the program, as in the emergence of "new-type" general courses (Communications, Western Civilization, Life Science, and the like); the terminal occupational offerings, together with part-time cooperative and work-experience programs; and remedial and developmental programs, including courses in remedial reading, remedial English, and study skills. Here also are Orientation courses (see Chapter 12).

The "paucity" of innovation and an organization to encourage it.—Although the institution's *raison d'être* is to perform services previously unperformed (as well as certain others in the educational tradition), and although in some degree it is performing them, systematic inquiry shows the extent of curriculum innovation in the community college lagging far behind the needs. In point of fact, the dearth of innovation extends at least to all areas pertaining to use of faculty services, and doubtless even beyond. The dearth has been well established by Johnson who made a nationwide inquiry in junior colleges for such innovations with a conclusion of what he terms their "paucity." However, he reports that he found some two-year colleges which, because of institutionwide planning, he called "islands of innovation," certain others in which departments or individual staff members were trying out new ideas, and a "few clusters of colleges" which were "engaging in cooperative curriculum planning and on occasion share the services of faculty members" (*33*, 13).

Johnson's awareness of the "paucity" and the need for innovation must have prompted the recent establishment of the League for Innovation in the Community College of which he has become executive director. Some of the purposes of the league, as stated in its organ *Jottings* (No. 1, Nov. 8, 1969), are "Experiment in teaching, learning, guidance and other aspects of junior college operation," "Share results of experiments," "Exchange instructional materials and procedures designed to enhance learning," and "Evaluate the impact of the institution's practices on its students and community." Members of the league are junior colleges in thirteen districts in eight states. Examples of projects are a systems approach to general education, an experimental college for vocational students with low verbal achievement but with high potential, education for the disadvantaged, and a workshop for teachers of English composition.

A frequent criticism of innovations, not only in junior colleges but in educational institutions generally, is that they are seldom, if ever, evaluated. Inclusion of evaluation among the purposes of the league has already been noted. It is reaffirmed in *Jottings* by an editorial captioned "Evaluation—A Watchword for the League."

Summary

A noteworthy fact about the purposes of the community college is the near approach to consensus on them. Although individuals or groups summarizing them may present them with variation in organization or subordination, current formulations seldom depart from inclusion of general education, terminal occupational education, preparation for further education or the "transfer" function, adult education, and community service. To assure realization of these purposes, the formulations also include reference to guidance and remediation, the latter concept being expanded to a "salvaging" function which includes service to varieties of students who may not previously have achieved up to their potential, qualified for specific programs, or have had unsatisfactory experiences in the first year or two of four-year institutions. The wide scope of service involved by acceptance of such a formulation is sustained further by the universal acceptance of the democratizing or "open-door" policy which requires availability of the programs to all intellectual and social levels in society.

The purposes are noteworthy also because writers on the institution have been in practically full agreement on them since the early years of the movement. A few of them only, like guidance and adult education, were not conspicuous in the earlier statements, but even these were at least foreshadowed by prototypical words or phrases.

An influential formulation of the goals of general education is one proposed by a committee which had been asked to prepare for the Armed Forces in World War II "a design for general education in the form of appropriate outcomes" and to outline "a series of courses devised to contribute directly to these objectives." Key phrases of the ten goals identified call for the individual "to improve his own health" and "take his share of responsibility for protecting the health of others"; "to communicate through his own language in writing and speaking"; "to attain a sound emotional and social adjustment"; to achieve the understandings "to make a satisfactory family and marital adjustment"; "to do his part as an active and intelligent citizen"; "to act in the light of an understanding of natural phenomena" and "to use scientific methods in the solution of his problems"; "to find self-expression in literature and to share through literature man's experience and his motivating ideas and ideals"; "to find a means of self-expression in music and in the visual arts and crafts"; "to practice clear and integrated thinking about the meaning and value of life"; and "to choose a vocation." The committee suggested titles of courses aimed directly at attainment of these goals.

The patterns of general education as identified by B. Lamar Johnson are the "great books," "liberal arts," "survey of fields of knowledge," "functional courses," "infusion," "and a composite of approaches." Of these, the "liberal arts," being traditional, is the most extensively followed in junior and four-year colleges, and the others are variously innovational, most of them with varying degrees of functionalism.

A survey, reported in 1951, of new-type general courses, most of them apparently functional by intention, found them given in many junior colleges, with an average approaching four courses per institution. This seems a rapid development for the short period of the history of the courses but, because no comparable study has been recently reported, one can only venture his opinion, based on recurrent contact with community colleges and their programs, that functionalism has been on the increase.

The relative merits of liberal arts and functional curriculums have been a matter of some controversy. One writer, Rapp, contends that the liberal arts persist "because they deal with the intellectual, the creative, the critical, the sensitive, the human aspects of man's development individually and in relation to the world according to time-tested rules of learning, teaching, and writing," and that "by taking what he has learned well and deeply in the disciplines and relating it to himself, to his experience, and to the new knowledge which growth and development bring him, the individual student, not the curriculum, nor the courses, becomes the catalyst and the generalist." To the contrary, Mayhew, in behalf of the program of general education and reviewing the influences toward revolt against the traditional curriculum, associates it with forces bringing education to larger proportions of the total population. It emerges "from the premise that much of man's life is devoted to being an adequate person, a creative being, a member of groups, and a solver of problems," and it "therefore concentrates on subjects, skills, abilities, attitudes, and interests which are especially relevant to the person's life as a family member, a consumer, a citizen, a leisure-enjoying person, and an organism in search of satisfactions." Among differences between liberal arts and innovating general education programs as seen by Morse, another writer with extensive experience in both, is that liberal education is "concerned first with a body of subject matter content, drawn largely from the cultural heritage of the Western World, while general education of the less conservative type is concerned first with the learner as a human being, who has certain needs and desires that make him distinct from his fellows." He says further, "the predominant method of liberal education might be classified as logical, wherein subject matter is encountered and learned in terms of its systematic organization within somewhat compartmentalized fields of knowledge," whereas general education subscribes to a psychological approach, wherein motivating drives in addition to the desire to learn are capitalized upon, and where a less traditional form of content organization may be used, often crossing departmental or even divisional lines. However, Morse concludes his comparison by the observation that the differences are those of degree rather than of kind, that the two approaches still complement one another, and that "each can serve its particular functions in such a manner as to enlarge and enrich each other. They are not partisans but partners."

Reflection over the obstacles to the more rapid spread of the functional program puts the focus on two circumstances, one being the unreadiness of four-year colleges and universities to accept the courses for transfer credit. This would seem surprising, in view of the more frequent early development of the programs in these institutions than in junior colleges, were it not that the general education movement is still restricted to a minority of them. The other obstacle is the background of preparation of teaching and administrative staffs of the junior colleges which has provided experience only with traditional courses.

The offerings in the field of Health and Physical Education available in a representation of public junior colleges are made up of two main parts, the course in health and the program for physical education. Only a large minority place the course in health among requirements, although a majority or more make it available. It goes by such names as "Personal Health," "Personal and Community Health," and "Fundamentals of Health." Its scope of content is indicated by chapter headings and topics treated in standard textbooks in the field which show a large degree of correspondence with the problems of health rated highest by students. The lack of knowledge in these matters on the part of freshmen has been established by test, as well as substantial gains in understanding from instruction in the subject.

The other part of the program consists of the activities in physical education which range through wide variety. All the institutions indicate a requirement in this part, from a composite of "gym" to freedom of choice from among a number of individual and team sports, with encouragement in several institutions toward activities promising "carry-over" after college and into adult life. Well over a majority of these junior colleges list a transfer curriculum in physical education in which these activities are applicable, as well as certain courses, such as "Community Recreation," "Introduction to Physical Education," and "Sports Officiating," which lean more toward theory and less toward physical activity, and are applicable both in transfer and terminal occupational programs.

One of the more frequent new-type functional courses identified by Putnam (see Table 11.1) is "Communication" or "Communications." These courses are not restricted to instruction in written composition and in their origins were based on surveys, with varying degrees of objectivity, of the use of language among educated people—these uses, on the "output" side, including letter-writing, conversation, group discussion, making speeches, preparing reports, giving directions, and story-telling, and, on the "input" side, involving reading of various types and for various purposes, listening, and observation. The courses aim not only at improvement in more kinds of use of language but strive for better motivation of expression by resorting to reading activities within the scope of student interest, at the same time separating training in expression from teaching for literary appreciation. The approach is sometimes accompanied by college-wide attention to language skills through cooperation of teachers in the other disciplines.

Differences between the courses in Communications and the usual courses in Freshman English as given in junior colleges, as found in an investigation in a large number of junior colleges, are suggested by the fact that most teachers of the latter feel that their college transfer English course "resembles that of a course in the four-year liberal arts college"; that three-fifths of the courses use "some," "much," or "considerable" imaginative literature in the first half of the course and a full three-fourths do so in the second half. The predominant types of textbooks reported for the first half are reader (essays, etc.), grammar textbook, and rhetoric, with less use of other materials, while for the second half these ease off to some extent as the use of poetry, short story, novel, and drama increases. Four-fifths report little or no speech in either semester. Grammar is reported to be of prime importance and the typical method of teaching is mixed lecture and discussion. A majority of the respondents report courses in remedial English and about half of this number report remedial reading.

For overview, the offerings in the Humanities, inclusive of the creative arts, were classified into seven groups, beginning with integrated courses and extending through English Language and Literature, Speech and Dramatics, Foreign Language, Arts and Crafts, Music, and Philosophy and Religion. New-type general courses were identified in most of the groups, and include the Humanities Survey, History of World Literature, Contemporary World Literature, Art Appreciation, Music Appreciation, Comparative Religions, and Great Books. Usually catalogued among the Humanities also are courses in Western Civilization or History of Western Culture which were, rather arbitrarily, left for listing under Social Studies, including History. The scope and variety of both the general and the more specialized courses are seen to be wide and adapted to achieving appropriate general goals of education and serving the special needs and interests of a diverse student body.

In addition to a category of "Integrated Courses" the division of Social Studies in junior colleges includes courses in History, Political Science and International Relations, Economics, Anthropology and Sociology, Geography, and Psychology. Those listed under the integrated category are Introduction to Social Science, Social Science Survey, Social Problems, State and Regional Problems, Current Affairs, and the two courses already identified as usually grouped under the Humanities, History of World Civilization and History of Western Civilization. These titles account for most of the new-type general courses, although a few are also to be found in the lists of offerings under Political Science and Psychology. The broad-field type of course undertakes integration by one of two procedures—one which aims to provide an overview of an area and introduction to two or more disciplines, such as political science, economics, sociology, etc., and the other which deals with problems consideration of which involves content and procedures characteristic of two or more such disciplines. Courses of the latter type have been displacing those of the older survey type. The new-type courses in history achieve integration by comprehending longer periods and broader cultural regions and/or trends.

Almost all the other courses typically offered in the several disciplines of the Social Studies are standard liberal arts offerings serving the purposes of transfer and of general education.

The obvious relationship of preparation for citizenship and courses in many or most of the social studies calls to mind the studies that disclose the prevalent lack of interest and participation in civic affairs of high school graduates after leaving school, notwithstanding their extensive exposure to instruction in the social studies during high school years. The explanation may well be the time-gap between leaving school and voting age, which will be largely removed by the increasing popularization of junior college education, together with exposure to significant instruction in the social studies in these early college years.

The goal of general education of helping the student "to think through the problems and to gain a basic orientation that will better enable him to make a satisfactory family and marital adjustment" and the high incidence of personal problems in courtship, sex, and marriage among students afford a convincing rationale for instruction in marriage and family in the community colleges. It is not surprising to find large proportions of these institutions offering courses variously designated as Marriage and the Family, The Family, and Family Relationships. Departmental allocation of the courses is more often under Home Economics and Sociology (or Social Studies) than elsewhere. The courses are usually elective and taught in classes including both sexes. Recurrent topics treated in order of frequency as reported by Martorana include Psychological Factors in Family Life, Modern Family Problems, Sociological Factors in Family Life, History and Evolution of the Family, Home Development and Management, Preparation for Marriage, Premarital Relationships, Biological Basis of the Family, Child Care and Training, etc. General appraisal of courses by those who have taken them has been highly favorable.

The need for an offering in Home Economics is supported by the ages of the students in the community college, who are rapidly moving into the time of life for marriage. Education for homemaking is usually regarded as general education, although there may be justification for regarding it as vocational for the housewife. Classifying it as "general" has the advantage of distinguishing it from preparation for many subprofessional occupations, such as those in food service (including management), school lunch management, motel and hotel management, low-rent project management, food and appliance demonstration, laboratory testing of textiles and foods, child-care center assistance, and the more. traditional employments of domestic and waitress. In addition to preparation for homemaking and terminal occupations, the community college offering should include "college parallel" courses for students who transfer.

Examination of catalogs of a representation of community colleges showed a large proportion, especially of smaller junior colleges, without offerings in Home Economics. For those providing such an offering, it is wide and includes courses in groups concerned with clothing; foods and nutrition; the home in various aspects, such as decoration, design, furnishings, and management; and the child and child care. Deterrent factors to having such an offering in community colleges are the pressure for offerings for men who outnumber the women, the fact that many women students have had high school courses in the field, and the belief that dual-level offerings must be made, some for terminal students and others for transfer. Perhaps the greatest obstacle to an adequate offering is the preparation for teaching the subject at the collegiate level, which usually requires specialization in one only of the major aspects of the field, as clothing or nutrition or home management, so that the small junior college is faced with the problem of employing two or more teachers to cover the special fields when this much teaching time is not required. The solution would appear to be finding or preparing teachers competent to cope with two or more major aspects.

The offerings in Science, as with other main divisions of the curriculum, include both new-type integrated courses aimed at general education and a long list of more specialized courses in the biological and physical sciences. The new-type courses in Biology are given such names as Life Science or The Living World, and in Physical Science, Introduction to, or Survey of, Physical Science. There is a smaller incidence of general courses drawing on both biological and physical aspects. Appraisal by persons in touch with new-type courses in the field of science shows that their development has been slower and less effective than in other major divisions of the curriculum. Experimental efforts at further development will need to be even more vigorous and persistent than in the other divisions. The long list of more specialized courses in Science ranges through subjects suggestive of adequacy for purposes of transfer, as well as the contribution to general education provided through such courses.

The offerings in Mathematics extend through the courses needed for transfer and often also those in high school mathematics for students who come up without them and find that changes in plans now require competence in them.

The development of terminal occupational curriculums in community colleges emerges from a two-pronged need—the need of students for such programs and that of society for the services for which the programs prepare. The need from the standpoint of the student is highlighted by the extensive attrition in the student body, which shows only a half of entering freshmen graduating and no more than a fourth transferring to four-year institutions after graduation, and by the obligation for occupational competence resting on all members of our society. The need from society's standpoint is emphasized by the presence and recent rapid increase in occupations the extent of preparation for which lies somewhere between that required for craftsmen or clerical workers and the bonafide professions requiring four or more years of college-level training. Although junior colleges were formerly slow in offering terminal occupational programs, the growth has recently been rapidly accelerating, and is being officially encouraged by the American Association of Junior Colleges. Curriculums are being developed and offered leading to a great diversity of pursuits concerned with agriculture, business, industry, health, security, and other areas of activity.

A promising type of program suitable for vocational preparation is the work-study or part-time cooperative plan. It was first introduced in four-year colleges and universities and is now more prevalent there and in technical institutes than in junior colleges. Most of the cooperative programs in four-year colleges and universities are in engineering and the periods of alternation in work and study are on a semester or quarter basis, whereas those in junior colleges are mainly in business and usually have half-day periods of alternation.

Another arrangement often made at high school and college levels to provide part-time employment and frequently operative in junior colleges is for "work experience" or "work-experience education," which differs from the cooperative plan in not involving the two-man team of alternation and in being less concerned with a functional relationship between the student's course and the work being done on the job. In this plan, as in the cooperative programs, there is usually remuneration for the student's work time.

Investigation has disclosed an extended list of values, or advantages, of cooperative and work-experience programs, one of which is that it makes higher education possible and attractive to youth who would not otherwise go to college. This value has a peculiar significance for an

IMPLICATIONS FOR THE CURRICULUM

institution like the community college, one of whose major purposes, as identified near the opening of the chapter, is democratization of college level education. This democratization, and the upward mobility implied are reflected in the larger percentages of students from lower than from upper levels of social status in attendance on such programs.

The occupations for which programs of terminal preparation are appropriate have been identified on a national scale by inquiry of a federal agency and use of similar procedures has been applied to the state level. For the individual community college it would be necessary to identify these occupations in the more immediate area. The procedures that have been followed include analysis of federal census data for the locality, interviews with prospective employers, and ascertaining the interests and choices of occupational programs of seniors in contributing high schools and of freshmen and extended-day and adult education students in the community college.

An extensive array of curriculums is set up in community colleges for students who graduate and transfer to four-year colleges and universities. The proportion of entering freshmen who graduate and transfer found in one large-scale inquiry was about a fourth of all, although, to be sure, the proportion varies widely from institution to institution. A serious problem arises because the population enrolling in the transfer curriculums far exceeds the proportion who continue into the third college year. The upshot is that large proportions of students are enrolled in what for them turn out to be aborted curriculums conducive to confusion and frustration. The implication is a need for more effective guidance and counseling. For a minority of students enrolled in these transfer curriculums—a segment of unquestioned potentiality for society and for themselves—they are in large and major part appropriate.

The transfer curriculums portrayed or listed in the catalogs of a representation of junior colleges were found to provide the first two years of collegiate preparation for all the major categories of professions, as well as specialization in the disciplines of the arts and sciences. The total array of different titles found in 15 per cent or more of the catalogs was almost 50 and with those listed less often added up to almost a hundred. The median number per institution was 16. Mention should be made of the service in guidance and counseling rendered by the section of the catalog that portrays or lists the transfer curriculums. This is signaled in certain of the catalogs by such a designation as "Career Plans."

Many junior colleges make provisions also for a General Curriculum, which is an unspecialized curriculum analogous to the more specialized transfer curriculums. It usually prescribes a few subjects common to all curriculums, namely, English, something in the Social Studies, and Physical Education, and leaves most of the student's program open for election. The curriculum serves two main groups of students, (1) entering freshmen who are undecided as to occupational plans and (2) the many students who at the time of entering college committed themselves to specialized curriculums but who decide later that they do not wish to continue in them and do not wish to shift to another specialization. The presence of the General Curriculum is evidence of the need of the flexibility it affords, but its weaknesses emerge where its requirements are so limited that it does not assure the general education its title implies and that a student who completes it has experienced at best only a curricular miscellany.

The open-door policy of community colleges makes imperative inclusion in its offerings of a program of remediation. Almost all these institutions enrolling 400 or more students have been found to admit students of lower ability, who are identified primarily by tests, both tests and grades, or by tests, grades, and interview; and well over half were found to require for these students special remedial courses, although some of the institutions make other provisions for them.

The main aspects of the program relate to the skills needed for successful learning, primarily in reading, writing, mathematics, and procedures in study. First courses in remedial reading in colleges emerged around 1930 and by the middle 1950s had spread to three-fourths of colleges reporting, this proportion attesting to the prevalence of deficiencies involving, according to some estimates, two-thirds of the student body, and the prevalence suggesting that the programs should be regarded as developmental rather than merely remedial. Among institutions providing these programs are some of the most selective.

The patterns of organization of the reading-improvement programs are (1) the separate special course, (2) as part of regular language-arts courses, and (3) as intrinsic parts of subjects to which the skills apply, with the separate course most common and with credit given for it in something approaching half the institutions. Instruction bears mainly on increasing rate and comprehension, of which rate seems more susceptible to improvement. The criterion of effectiveness should be the influence of the program on improvement in academic performance.

Remedial efforts in writing have traditionally emphasized grammar review, although investigation has found a low correlation between a knowledge of grammar and writing competence. The courses are concerned with a wide range of skills, among them spelling, parts of speech, grammar, capitalization, punctuation, vocabulary improvement, diction, sentence structure, paragraph development, use of library, etc. Dissatisfaction with the remedial courses has led to a number of efforts to increase their effectiveness, such as focus on a smaller range of skills, emphasis on sentence structure, resort to laboratory procedure, attention to particular deficiencies of individual students, and greater motivation of students by utilizing topics of interest and readings within the scope of interests of these students and extensive knowledge of the students, inclusive of their occupational ambitions.

Instruction in study skills is given in an increasing number of junior and other colleges and universities, either in separate courses or in courses in orientation, and credit is often granted for these courses. Topics dealt with in the courses include, among others, adjustment to college, keeping physically and mentally fit, importance of a study schedule, note-taking, preparing assignments and methods of study, use of library and laboratory, preparing for tests and examinations, memorization, reading skills, vocabulary building, etc. Some of the courses include attention not only to the general study skills but also the special skills peculiar to the separate disciplines, and whether or not they should do so is a subject of controversy. Textbooks are available for use in the courses. These and the typical lecture-discussion method of teaching have been criticized as too theoretical an approach that does not result in improved study techniques. To meet the criticisms, workbooks are being used that provide actual practice in and testing of the desired skills.

The overlapping and interrelationships of the abilities involved in reading, writing, and study skills were certain to prompt efforts in some institutions to put into effect a program of improvement that would comprehend most or all of them. An instance of such a composite program, but with its main focus on writing, was described above as operating in a junior college that had tried other approaches unsuccessfully. In this institution the originators of the plan adopted frankly admitted that relatively few of the students of lower ability for whom the plan was devised would be able to qualify for admission to the course in transfer English and administered a developmental sequence adapted to a lower level of ability and motivation. As described, the sequence seemed to resemble in some respects the composite course in Communication.

As a new institution committed to universalizing education in the early post-high-school years, the community college is adding new purposes to the more traditional ones of preparation for higher levels of education and general education, among them terminal occupational education, remediation, adult education, and community services. Thus, it is a vehicle of innovation. However, the frequency of innovation, in curriculum as well as in other areas, lags behind the need for it, although awareness of the need is apparent in the establishment of a league to encourage it.

References and Bibliography

1. Archer, Jerome W., and Ferrell, Wilfred A. *Research and the Development of English Programs in the Junior College.* Champaign, Ill.: National Council of Teachers of English, 1965.
2. Armsby, Henry H. *Cooperative Education in the United States.* United States Office of Education Bulletin, 1954, no. 11. Washington: Government Printing Office, 1954.
3. Bauder, P. D. "Freshman English Experiment: General Education in a Traditional Curriculum." *Junior College Journal*, 22 (Feb., 1952), 337–39.
4. Blake, Walter S., Jr. "Basic Study Skills Program for Colleges and Universities." *Junior College Journal*, 26 (Nov., 1955), 164–67.
5. Bowman, Henry S. "The Content of a Functional Marriage Course." *College & University*, 27 (April, 1952), 355–64.
6. Bowman, Henry S. "Marriage Education in the Colleges." *Journal of Social Hygiene*, 35 (Dec., 1949), 407–17.
7. Carter, John T. "Programs of Agricultural Instruction in Junior Colleges." *Junior College Journal*, 26 (Sept., 1955). 38–40.
8. Charters, W. W. "Remedial Reading in College." *Journal of Higher Education*, 12 (March, 1941), 117–21.
9. Christensen, Alfred. "The Student Body in Public Junior Colleges." *Junior College Journal*, 3 (Oct., 1932), 13–16.
10. Conklin, Shirley. "A Planning Year for Registered Nursing Programs." *Junior College Journal*, 37 (Sept., 1966), 16–18.
11. Cowan, Gregory; Hawkins, Richard; and McPherson, Elizabeth. "Incompetence in Comp: A Realistic Solution." *Junior College Journal*, 35 (Sept., 1964), 24–27.
12. Crane, William J. "Work Experience Programs in Junior College." *Junior College Journal*, 22 (April, 1952), 460–65.
13. Dabbs, Lowell. "Report on Remedial English in the Colleges." *Junior College Journal*, 27 (March, 1957), 381–87.
14. Dearborn, Terry H. "The Junior College Health Knowledge Study in California." *Journal of School Health*, 33 (Feb., 1963), 90–92.
15. Defore, Jesse, Jr. "Profile of an Engineering Technology Student." *Journal of Engineering Education*, 57 (Nov., 1965), 227–28.
16. *A Design for General Education:* For Members of the Armed Forces. American Council on Education Studies. Series I, Reports of Committees and Conferences, no. 18, vol. VIII. Washington: American Council on Education, 1944.
17. Dressel, Paul L., ed. *Evolution in the Basic College at Michigan State University.* New York: Harper & Bros., 1958.
18. Dressel, Paul L. "Transfer of General Education Credit." *Junior College Journal*, 24 (Jan., 1954), 292–97.
19. Earnshaw, Helen. "Starting a Two-Year Curriculum for Library Assistants." *Junior College Journal*, 36 (Oct., 1965), 22–23.
20. Eells, Walter C. *Why Junior College Terminal Education?* Washington: American Association of Junior Colleges, 1941.
21. Eiss, Albert F. *Science Education in the Junior College: Problems and Practices.* Washington: National Science Teachers Association, 1966.
22. Ellzey, W. Clark. "Marriage Questionnaire Report." *Marriage and Family Living*, 11 (Nov., 1949), 133–35.
23. Fisher, Beverly E. "Communications Courses for Junior Colleges." *Junior College Journal*, 21 (Jan., 1951), 289–91.
24. Goddard, Roy W. "A Terminal-Occupational Curriculum Inquiry in One Community." *Junior College Journal*, 17 (Sept., 1946), 3–10.
25. Graney, Maurice R. *The Technical Institute.* New York: Center for Applied Research in Education, Inc., 1964.
26. Gross, Richard E., and Maynard, David M. "Social Science Offerings in Junior

Colleges Reveal Urgent Curricular Problems." *Social Studies*, 56 (April, 1965), 123–27.
27. Harris, Norman C. *Technical Education in the Junior College: New Programs for New Jobs*. Washington: American Association of Junior Colleges, 1964.
28. Henninger, G. Ross. *The Technical Institute in America*. New York: McGraw-Hill Book Co., 1959.
29. Henry, Nelson B., ed. *Development in and Through Reading*. Sixtieth Yearbook of the National Society for the Study of Education, part 1. Chicago: University of Chicago Press, 1961.
30. Hillmer, M. A. "Terminal Curriculums Offered in Public Junior Colleges in the United States." *Junior College Journal*, 20 (Nov., 1949), 128–30.
31. Johnson, B. Lamar, ed. *The Experimental College*. Los Angeles: Junior College Leadership Program, University of California, 1968.
32. Johnson, B. Lamar. *General Education in Action. A Report of the California Study of General Education in the Junior Colleges*. Washington: American Council on Education, 1952.
33. Johnson, B. Lamar. *Islands of Innovation*. Los Angeles: Junior College Leadership Program, University of California, 1964. (Since completion of this list of references, this publication has been enlarged by the author into a book entitled *Islands of Innovation Expanding: Changes in the Community College* [Beverly Hills, Cal.: Glencoe Press, 1969].)
34. Johnson, B. Lamar, ed. *New Directions for Instruction in the Junior College*. Los Angeles: Junior College Leadership Program, University of California, 1965.
35. Johnson, B. Lamar. "Patterns of General Education." *Junior College Journal*, 17 (Oct., 1946), 45–52.
36. Johnson, B. Lamar, chairman. *The Public Junior College*. Fifty-fifth Yearbook of the National Association for the Study of Education, part 1. Chicago: University of Chicago Press, 1956.
37. Johnson, Roy Ivan. *Explorations in General Education*. New York: Harper & Brothers, 1947.
38. Johnson, Roy Ivan, and McCammon, Hugh. "Language Instruction in the Junior College." *College English*, 2 (March, 1941), 584–92.
39. Jorgensen, Vivian. "A Home Economics Survey at the Junior College Level." *Junior College Journal*, 25 (Oct., 1954), 91–95.
40. *Junior College Student Personnel Programs—Appraisal and Development*. Washington: American Association of Junior Colleges, 1965.
41. Kidd, John W.; Warrington, Willard G.; and Jackson, Robert A. "Student Attitudes Toward General Education." *Journal of Higher Education*, 25 (April, 1954), 209–13, 228.
42. Kilby, Richard W. "The Relation of a Remedial Reading Program to Scholastic Success in College." *Journal of Educational Psychology*, 36 (Dec., 1945), 513–34.
43. Knoell, Dorothy M. *Toward Educational Opportunity for All*. Albany: State University of New York, 1966.
44. Koos, Leonard V. *The Junior College Movement*. Boston: Ginn & Co., 1925.
45. Landis, Judson T. "An Evaluation of Marriage Education." *Marriage and Family Living*, 10 (Fall, 1948), 100–101.
46. LeBaron, Helen R. "Home Economics Beyond the High School." *National Association of Secondary School Principals Bulletin*, 48 (Dec., 1964), 73–79.
47. Light, Israel. "Training for Health Occupations." *Junior College Journal*, 22 (March, 1963), 16–21.
48. Martorana, S. V. "Functional Family-Life Education in Junior Colleges." *Junior College Journal*, 19 (Oct., 1948), 79–88.
49. Mayhew, Lewis B., ed. *General Education: An Account and Appraisal*. New York: Harper & Brothers, 1960.
50. Mayhew, Lewis B. "Significance of General Education." *Junior College Journal*, 27 (Jan., 1957), 251–55.

51. Means, Richard K. "Problems and Needs in College Health Education." *Journal of School Health*, 35 (Jan., 1965), 40–44.
52. Medsker, Leland L. *The Junior College: Progress and Prospect.* New York: McGraw-Hill Book Co., 1960.
53. Merson, Thomas B. "A Faculty Study of General Education." *Junior College Journal*, 24 (Jan., 1954), 260–67.
54. Morse, H. T. "Liberal and General Education—Partisans or Partners?" *Junior College Journal*, 24 (March, 1954), 395–99.
55. *Occupational Curriculum Study: College of Marin.* Palo Alto, Cal.: George Ebey Associates, 1962.
56. *Occupational-Vocational Education Study for Contra Costa County: A Progress Report.* Contra Costa County Junior College District, 1957.
57. Parr, F. W. "Teaching Ways of Study." *Journal of Higher Education*, 5 (Oct., 1934), 377–81.
58. Price, Wilson T., and Barnett, Raymond A. "Beginning Computer Education." *Junior College Journal*, 34 (Sept., 1963), 19–23.
59. Putnam, Howard L. "A Survey of New-Type General Courses in American Junior Colleges." *Junior College Journal*, 21 (March, 1951), 402–9.
60. Radnor, Sanford. "Three-track Community College English Program." *Junior College Journal*, 29 (Oct., 1958), 97–100.
61. Rapp, Marvin A. "Liberal Arts and General Education." *Junior College Journal*, 36 (May, 1966), 24–28.
62. Reynolds, James W. "General Education and the Junior College." *Junior College Journal*, 20 (Jan., 1950), 239–40.
63. Reynolds, James W. *The Junior College.* New York: Center for Applied Research in Education, Inc., 1965.
64. Rice, James G. *General Education: Current Ideas and Concerns.* Washington: National Education Association, 1964.
65. Richards, Maxwell J. "An Analysis of the Technical Education Provided by Accredited Junior Colleges." *Junior College Journal*, 28 (Oct., 1957), 105–8.
66. Robinson, H. A. "A Note on the Evaluation of College Remedial Reading Courses." *Journal of Educational Psychology*, 41 (Feb., 1950), 83–96.
67. Rodes, Harold R. "Cooperative Technical Education—Pro and Con." *Junior College Journal*, 24 (Feb., 1954), 362–66.
68. Ross, Robert T. "Some Student Opinions Regarding Sex Education." *California Journal of Educational Research*, 2 (Jan., 1951), 15–17.
69. Roueche, John E. *Salvage, Redirection, or Custody?* Washington: American Association of Junior Colleges, 1968.
70. Scannell, William J. "What Do Teachers Think about English in Junior Colleges?" *Junior College Journal*, 37 (Sept., 1966), 24–29.
71. Schenz, Robert F. "What Is Done for Low Ability Students?" *Junior College Journal*, 34 (March, 1964), 22–27.
72. Smith, Leo F. "A Cooperative Work Program." *Journal of Higher Education*, 15 (March, 1944), 156–57.
73. Smith, Leo F. "Cooperative Work Programs in Junior College." *School and Society*, 56 (Oct. 3, 1942), 305–7.
74. Spaulding, Francis T. *High School and Life.* New York: McGraw-Hill Book Co., 1938.
75. *A Study of Technical Institutes.* [A report to the] Society for the Promotion of Engineering Education. Lancaster, Pa.: Lancaster Press, 1931.
76. Thomas, Russell. *The Search for a Common Learning—General Education 1800–1960.* New York: McGraw-Hill Book Co., 1962.
77. Thornton, James W., Jr. *The Community Junior College.* Rev. ed. New York: John Wiley & Sons, 1966.
78. Triggs, Frances O. "Reading at the College Level." *Journal of Higher Education*, 20 (Feb., 1949), 65–70.

79. Triggs, Frances O. *Remedial Reading: Diagnosis and Correction of Reading Difficulties at the College Level.* Minneapolis: University of Minnesota Press, 1943.
80. Tyler, Henry T. *Report of the Study of Work Experience Programs in California High Schools and Junior Colleges.* Bulletin of the California State Department of Education. Sacramento, Cal., 1956.
81. Van Wagner, R. C. "Business Education Enrollments in California Junior Colleges." *California Schools,* 34 (May, 1963), 155-62.
82. *Vocational-Technical Training for Industrial Occupations.* Bulletin no. 228, Vocational-Technical Training Series No. 1. Washington: U.S. Government Printing Office, 1944.
83. Warrington, Willard G.; Kidd, John W.; and Dahnke, Harold L. "General Education—Its Importance During First Two Years of College." *Junior College Journal,* 26 (Dec., 1958), 228-32.
84. Weber, Cornelius B. "What About Student Deficiencies in Writing?" *Junior College Journal,* 24 (Nov., 1953), 147-51.
85. Weingarten, Samuel, chairman. *English in the Two-Year College.* Champaign, Ill.: National Council of Teachers of English, 1965.
86. Wilson, James W., and Lyons, Edward H. *Work-Study College Programs—Appraisal and Report of a Study of Cooperative Education.* New York: Harper & Bros., 1961.
87. Wittenborn, John R. "Classes in Remedial Reading and Study Habits." *Journal of Educational Research,* 37 (April, 1944), 571-86.
88. Witty, Paul A. "Practices in Corrective Reading in Colleges and Universities." *School and Society,* 52 (Nov. 30, 1940), 564-66.

12
The Student Personnel Program

ATTENTION NOW turns to the second main portion of an adequate community college program, the student personnel program and related services and activities. In reviewing the purposes of the institution in the first main section of Chapter 11, it was indicated that the purpose of guidance was only partially foreshadowed in the early literature dealing with the junior college, but that more recent writings had elevated the purpose to major consideration.

Concept, Need, and Proposals

An expanding concept and the need.—Although the full scope of what is currently comprehended by the concept of student personnel and guidance will become apparent in the review of the areas of activity to follow, it may be well to precede the presentation by a brief definition of guidance that is at least suggestive of the significance of the service renderable—a definition not unlike many that have been put forward by advocates of the purpose (56): "the process of assisting the individual in determining and analyzing his interests, aptitudes, limitations, and problems, and in the light of this knowledge helping him to make wise choices and adjustments in order that he may have a fuller life."

The need for extensive development of personnel and guidance programs in community colleges is recurrently and insistently underwritten by the characteristics and needs of the student population, actual and prospective, as these have been reviewed in the chapters of Parts I and II of this treatise. It should suffice, instead of recapitulating these at length, to identify in retrospect a scattered sampling of the larger areas of need. Among the areas suggestive of need seen in Part I are (in Chapter 1), despite a concentration of full-time students in the later years of adolescence, an actually wide disparity of ages from youngest to oldest because of the presence of a minority from the older population; diversity of attainment of physical maturity within and between the sexes; differences between the sexes in physical strength and in interest in physical activity; (in Chapter 2) increasing differentiation of mental abilities with age and some differences between the sexes; (in Chapter 3) need for help in the growth for maturity in meeting the problems and tasks of later adolescence; (in Chapter 4) the complex problems of sex, dating, and courtship; (in Chapter 5) the large proportions of students without occupational plans or with unrealistic occupational choices, and the desirability of motivation toward upward mobility of youth of higher ability but of lower social status; (in Chapter 6) the increasing need in our society for encouraging participation in wholesome and absorbing avocations.

The review of needs for guidance from Part II, content of which focuses more directly on the student at the junior college level and less on the generality of later adolescents, identifies areas, as is to be expected, overlapping extensively on those found in Part I, but with some of them in comparison more particularized because students do not include all later adolescents. The evidence on aptitude in Chapter 7 finds the student average lower than in most four-year colleges, with some students on a par with the brightest in the four-year institutions, but with a larger proportion in the lower ranges of the distribution. At the same time a large majority aspire to become transfers (looking to the professions), or at least enroll in transfer curriculums, notwithstanding only a minority reach the four-year institutions. A larger proportion of students in community than in four-year colleges have disabilities in skills in reading, language, mathematics, and study. Larger proportions come from families of lower social status and have a higher incidence of economic problems and/or lower motivation for continued attendance. The need for guidance in respect to personal qualities and attitudes, which are reviewed together with interests in Chapter 8, is less apparent because of the relative intangibility and the limited research concerning them, although these restrictions can hardly minimize their importance. To illustrate from the findings, in comparison with students in four-year colleges and universities, junior college students have been found to average significantly lower in social maturity and autonomy or independence, and are more conventional and authoritarian. Assuming that such traits are modifiable, the junior college environment should be such as to bring about improvement. The findings of studies of vocational interests show large proportions of students (as already indicated for later adolescence) without choices or with unrealistic ones. Avocational interests of junior college students, except in part for reading, are still lacking investigation, but it is clear enough that education and guidance toward them are needed. The evidence on reading interests bears on periodicals only and suggests the need for emphasis toward intellectualization. Chapter 9 shows a wide prevalence of personal problems among students on which they can benefit from guidance. These range across virtually all areas of in-school and out-of-school life, including health, finances, recreation, personal and social relationships, courtship, family, academic competence, occupation, and course of study. The incidence is high for both sexes and both freshman and sophomore classes and is only partially mitigated by age. The high incidence for a small proportion of students hints at a need of some students for psychiatric help. The concerns and abilities of adults as reviewed in Chapter 10 indicate that they share in the need for guidance, and inquiry has disclosed that the benefits of student personnel programs are seldom extended to them.

Persons not converted to the need for highly developed student personnel programs may be inclined to direct attention to the automatic service in guidance performed by a curriculum offering of the scope and content that is reviewed in Chapter 11, and it can not be doubted that a rich and flexible offering is notably helpful in this direction. Helpfulness is enhanced when portions of the offering are given over to what is termed "group guidance," as in orientation courses and others providing information on careers. However, the needs for guidance reach beyond the group to the individual, and provision must be made for penetration to him. This is true whatever the size of the institution, although the problem of personalization, or individualization, of guidance grows with increasing enrollment. Time was, in the earlier history of the junior college movement, when individualization may have been less urgent than now, but with the mounting enrollments and proliferation of larger units in larger districts, personnel programs must expand provisions for focus on the individual.

The need for an effective student personnel program is especially critical at this particular age and educational level. It is inherent in the first two college years in any institution, but, by comparison, is greatly augmented for the comprehensive community college which has the most widely diversified offering of institutions operating at this level at the same time that its policy of open-doorness admits students of the most widely ranging abilities, characteristics, and interests.

Proposed student personnel programs.—The broad scope and increasing awareness of the need for guidance in the community college has conduced to the publication in periodicals and elsewhere of numerous proposals for student personnel programs. Quite a flurry of these proposals appeared around the 1950s, at a time when the junior college movement was undergoing one of its most rapid expansions in numbers of institutions and enrollments. Among the more nearly comprehensive and useful of the presentations of that time are those appearing in articles by Brumbaugh (*14*), Humphreys (*42*), and Traxler (*90*). The one by Humphreys may be regarded as in a sense authoritative, as he was at the time serving as chairman of the Committee on Student Personnel Services of the American Association of Junior Colleges, and concurrence of other members of the committee can be assumed. The elements of student personnel work in this proposal are listed under six main "areas" as follows: orientation and high school relationships, admission procedures, guidance services, student life, job placement, and administration. The first area is particularized as high school visitation, orienting students to college life (how to study, college organizations), and orienting students to their own capacities and potentialities. Admission procedures are listed as evaluating high school records, testing (precollege and at opening of freshman year), classification of students in curriculums, health and physical examinations, organization of classes and class schedules, and housing and boarding. Guidance services include work with individuals through counseling, testing, and interviewing. Under the area of student life are listed student government, student activities, intercollegiate activities, cooperative relationships (national, state, and community), and development of ethical and spiritual values. Job placement and follow-up are indicated to include placement service for part-time and full-time workers; student aid, scholarships, and loan funds; on-the-job training; and refresher and up-grading programs for graduates. Among subcategories under administration besides those relating to staff and facilities are cumulative personnel and academic records and research, and evaluation of the program. A check of the needs for guidance against the areas and subdivisions of such a student personnel program finds them so well geared to each other that, if put into effect, the program recommended would serve the plurality of these needs.

Conviction in the American Association of Junior Colleges of the importance of promoting student personnel programs is seen again in the delegation in 1960 by its Commission on Student Personnel to J. W. McDaniel, another leader with experience and understanding in the field, for preparation of a special report descriptive of elements of a desirable program. His recommendations were presented in a publication entitled *Essential Student Personnel Practices for Junior Colleges,* published by the association in 1962 (*52*). The increasing conviction of the centrality of guidance services for the community college led a few years later to the seeking of substantial subsidization for a major project investigating the whole problem of an adequate student personnel program for the institution. The project was mainly underwritten by the Carnegie Corporation, and done with consultation by a National Advisory Committee representative of various interests and related disciplines. It was directed by Max R. Raines, and is frequently referred to as the "Raines project." The published outcomes are presented in an extensive unpaged report, *Junior College Stu-*

dent Personnel Programs: Appraisal and Development (*45*). A commendable brief summary, *Junior College Student Personnel Programs—What They Are and What They Should Be* (*18*), was prepared by Collins, a member of the national committee.

In view of the availability of the published reports in both complete and summarized versions, there is no need here to resummarize. All that need be done at this point is to refer to one main conclusion, which is that "basic student personnel functions are not being adequately performed in the majority of those junior colleges studied" (*18*, 25), and to list, in the groups under which they are classified, the student personnel functions regarded as "basic" (20, Table I). The numerals in parentheses following the functions indicate the rank order, from highest to lowest, of the degree of "adequacy of performance" of the functions (21, Table II) in the junior colleges included in the survey of practice.

Orientation
  1. Precollege Information (1)
  2. Student Induction (15)
  3. Group Orientation (16)
  4. Career Information (19)
Appraisal
  5. Personnel Records (12)
  6. Educational Testing (7)
  7. Applicant Appraisal (8)
Consultation
  8. Student Counseling (14)
  9. Student Advisement (6)
  10. Applicant Consulting (9)
Participation
  11. Co-curricular Activities (5)
  12. Student Self-Government (3)
Regulation
  13. Student Registration (2)
  14. Academic Regulation (4)
  15. Social Regulation (11)
Service
  16. Financial Aids (10)
  17. Placement (18)
Organizational
  18. Program Articulation (13)
  19. In-Service Education (20)
  20. Program Evaluation (21)
  21. Administrative Organization (17)

Comment here on the functions is restricted to mention of the extensive coincidence, notwithstanding the differing organization, of the areas and subdivisions in Humphreys' recommendations quoted above, and the relatively low ranking on adequacy assigned to functions as vital to an effective program as student counseling, group orientation, placement, and career information.

Admission, Appraisal, and Orientation

The pattern of more detailed consideration.—The treatment here of the student personnel program now proceeds to exposition in more, even if not great, detail of its main aspects. It consists of three sections preceding the chapter summary. After brief description of bases of admission to community colleges, the current section deals with (a) means used to assemble information concerning the student (types of tests and inventories and the cumulative record), and (b) provisions for informing the student (orientation and career courses and the student handbook). The section following that deals mainly with services to the student, including counseling, placement in employment and transfer to senior institutions, and guidance in relation to emotional adjustment. The third section is concerned with student organizations and activities.

Bases of admission.—Junior college catalogs without exception include sections explaining their bases and procedures in admission. To throw some light on the bases (less on procedures) analysis was made of those set forth in recent catalogs of 31 public institutions distributed in 15 states— catalogs assembled for study in connection with certain later portions of this chapter rather than for this particular section. While not strictly a sample of public junior colleges, it cannot be far from a representative group. A look at the first bases stated in these catalogs, which can be assumed to be the primary ones, finds them to range rather widely, but at the same time to be heavily concentrated on a single practice. The most flexible of all is found once only and states simply, "All persons applying for study are admitted." Fifteen units of high school credit (without mention of high school graduation) is the specified basis in another catalog. All remaining catalogs (29 of 31) require only graduation from high school (usually indicated as "accredited"), although three of them state that graduates in the lower portions of the ability distributions enter "on probation": two of these indicate the lowest fourth and one in the lowest third of their graduating classes.

Almost all the catalogs specify alternative bases of admission. These and their frequencies are: age (over 18 in 11 catalogs, over 19 in 1, and over 21 in 3); GED certificate of high school equivalency (in 8 catalogs); 15 acceptable units (in 4 catalogs); and a year of active military service (in a single catalog). The average number of bases, including that first stated, is slightly under two.

Besides the indication of probation for low-ranking high school graduates already mentioned in three junior colleges, certain other strictures are specified in a small number of colleges. In one junior college, applicants falling below a designated point on a state-wide test administered to high school seniors are placed in a program devised to correct their weaknesses; in still another, nongraduates may enter only "special and trade courses"; and in eight institutions, admission to certain transfer curriculums is limited to students who present units in specified academic subjects. This is the nearest approach to the prevalent practice followed in many four-year colleges of prescribing specified numbers of units in academic fields like mathematics, foreign languages, science, etc., and setting maxima acceptable in certain others.

The procedures in admission of 13 of the catalogs also specify the applicant's taking a "guidance examination," a battery of "precounseling tests," or an English Placement Test before admission is assumed to be completed. It is clear from the statements of the requirement that these measures are for purposes of advisement and classification, not for exclusion. A few of the catalogs ask for report on health status by the family or other physician; these are for institutions that do not include the physical examination under school authority as a detail of admissions routine.

The manifest conclusion from this evidence on requirements for admission to public junior colleges is one of commitment to "open-doorness," in harmony with accepted stated purposes. It reveals a striking contrast with practices in the typically more selective four-year college or university.

One other practice of considerable moment emerges from the examination of the sections of the catalogs dealing with admission. Eight of the 31 catalogs describe arrangements for superior high school seniors to pursue courses in the junior college. One of these arrangements appears to refer to a full junior college program for highly qualified seniors, with the recommendation of the high school principal. All the others refer to partial programs of one, two, or more courses for superior seniors, again on approval by the high school principal. It is more than likely that other junior colleges in this group make provision for such arrangements without mentioning the practice in their catalogs. Such practices merit commendation for the opportunity for adaptation and acceleration they provide for superior students.

Types of tests and inventories used and usable.—Diverse kinds of information concerning the individual student are needed for the many lines of concern in the student personnel program, which include admissions counseling; placement in appropriate courses; counseling concerning education, vocation, and personal problems; arranging for transfer to another college or university; and placement in employment, part-time or full-time, temporary or permanent. A large amount of this information, although far from all, can be derived from tests in wide variety. Reported here is a summary of the status of testing in public junior colleges, based on a recent survey made by Seibel (*80*) who obtained his information by visits to 63 junior colleges distributed in 18 states, 42 of them public and half this number independent. The institutions were representative of junior colleges of the country, except that the distribution as to size for public junior colleges tended to be toward larger enrollments than the distribution nationally. The inquiry relates to initial testing only, meaning by this the administration of standardized tests to entering freshman students either just before or just after admission (last semester of senior year in high school or first semester of freshman year in college).

The types of initial tests used, those most often used, and the approximate fractions of the public institutions using them are reported in Table 12.1. They are seen to range through seven types, with interest inventories and tests of general ability, broad subject matter, and achievement, with highest frequencies. It should be said that the number of junior colleges with measures of intelligence *available* concerning freshmen must actually be larger than as reported, because this is a type of test very often admin-

TABLE 12.1
Types of Tests Used for Initial Testing in Public Junior Colleges and Approximate Fractional Proportions Using Them

Type of Test	Most Often Used	Proportion Using the Type
1. General Ability	American Council on Education, Psychological Examination (ACE), College Qualification Tests (CQD), Otis Quick-Scoring Mental Ability Tests (OTIS), School and College Ability Tests (SCAT)	Four-fifths
2. Intelligence	Tests yielding Intelligence Quotient (IQ)	One-fourth
3. Broad Subject Matter	American College Testing Program (ACT)	One-half
4. Achievement	English Mathematics Reading	Three-fourths
5. Interest Inventory	Kuder Preference Record (KPR) Strong Vocational Interest Blank (SVIB)	One-half
6. Special Aptitude	Differential Aptitude Test (DAT) General Aptitude Test Battery (GATB)	Two-fifths
7. Personality	(not listed)	One-fourth

Source: Based on Seibel (*80*, 13–39).

istered in high school and IQs for many students will come up with high school transcripts. The achievement tests presumably include instruments like the Cooperative English Test and the Iowa Silent Reading Test that provide a basis for course placement, inclusive of remedial programs. Seibel says that the frequency of use of personality tests in his sample colleges "is surprisingly high, since it is questionable whether this kind of instrument has any general utility in academic situations" (*80*, 33).

Seibel's tables contain also the numbers of institutions and proportionate frequencies with which the instruments are used for selection, guidance and counseling, course placement, or certain other purposes, as well as their use with the entire freshman class or with subgroups of the freshman class only. It is significant that the purposes most often reported are for guidance and counseling and course placement and, in harmony with the open-door policy of the public junior college, seldom for selective admission. The special aptitude test is the only type used in two-fifths or more of the institutions that appears to be used with subgroups of freshmen more often than with the entire freshman class. The number of different *types* of tests used in the public junior colleges in these initial programs ranges from a single one to as many as 6, with about a fourth of them administering as many as 4, and with the median midway between 3 and 4. The number of different *tests* ranges from 1 to 11.

A type of instrument that does not emerge in Seibel's report, presumably because it is not strictly a test or because it was not in use in the junior colleges of his sample, is one that inquires into study habits and skills. One such instrument is the Brown-Holtzman Survey of Study Habits and Attitudes which was described and an application of which was reported in Chapter 7.* Among other such instruments that have often been used in colleges is the Wrenn Study Habits Inventory (SHI). These are sometimes administered to all entering freshmen during the orientation course or to individual students in connection with counseling and advisement, especially with those experiencing academic difficulties.

Another instrument, again not a test, sometimes administered to college students is the Mooney Problem Check List, as may be noted from the content of Chapter 9. The evidence of that chapter suggests that it may well be used as a screening device for identifying students with problems in many areas of in-school and out-of-school life. Like the study habits inventories, it may be administered to all freshmen, as in the orientation course, or to individuals or subgroups in the student body. Still another instrument, the Bown Self-Report Inventory (SRI) has more recently been put forward as a screening device in the area of mental health (*11*). The authors have used it in comparing junior college students with students at the comparable level in the University of Texas and found some statistically significant differences. It takes only about ten minutes to complete and is easily scored, but apparently has projective overtones that require interpretation by counselors and other professionals.

The pre-eminent instrument both for screening and follow-through in respect to personality and mental health for college students appears to be the Minnesota Multiphasic Personality Inventory (MMPI). Reference was made in Chapter 8 to instructive use of an adaptation of portions of it as the Omnibus Personality Inventory (OPI) in comparing students entering the junior colleges and the universities of California. The literature reporting investigations in which it has been administered discloses its usefulness not only in identifying personal characteristics, but also in screening for

*See p. 312.

qualities and inclinations to behavior inimical or conducive to mental health. To cite instances, Gough (*31*) found a significant relationship between measures of an adaptation of portions of the MMPI and social participation of girls in college, and Osborne, Sanders, and Young (*63*) found it to a considerable extent effective in predicting unsocial behavior or identifying potential behavior deviates among freshman college women. The MMPI appears to have had relatively little use in junior colleges—a situation explicable by the time-consuming task entailed for individual administration, the professional competence, because of its projective character, required for interpretation, and the relatively undeveloped state of concern for the mental health in many new institutions.

Before leaving the subject of testing for guidance in the junior college mention should be made of one of the most discerning and comprehensive statements extant in the area of means of appraisal of students in the institution, which includes consideration not only of tests but also of other kinds of information from admission of the student and throughout his connection with the institution and subsequently. The statement is by Dobbin and Turnbull (*45*) and was made before a session of the National Committee for Appraisal and Development of Junior College Student Personnel Programs in November, 1965. It is too extensive to attempt to generalize here, although one can hardly refrain from drawing on a few of its observations and recommendations. These authors note the absence of "any convenient measure of motivation for young people in the college situation," implying that such an instrument would be useful. They urge development of an instrument for use at the end of the sophomore college year analogous at this lower level to the Graduate Record Examination (GRE). They remind us that the "best single prediction of academic success next year is the record of how well [the student] has done this year and last year." They urge the validation of available instruments within and for the given junior college and point out the "gaps" in means of appraisal that should be filled through research at three levels: (a) for the local situation; (b) for groups of institutions in a city or region; (c) on a national scale through the American Association of Junior Colleges.

The cumulative record.—The measures from instruments like those identified in the foregoing section represent, to be sure, only a portion of the kinds of information concerning the student that are needed to afford a basis on which to advise him. A host of other items should be at hand for the person who will do the counseling. It is now the almost universal practice to assemble all these kinds of information for each student, on a form known as the "cumulative record." Some years ago Carlin (*17*) collected these forms from a sampling of 150 junior colleges in 35 states and made a detailed count of the different items called for on them and grouped these under more than a score of categories. From analysis and comparison of items on current record forms with Carlin's categories, this writer has telescoped and restated some of them and arrived at a somewhat shorter but nearly comprehensive list:

1. Personal Identification
2. Family History
3. High School Record
4. Attendance Record
5. Junior College Academic Record
6. Health Data
7. Extracurricular Activities
8. Stated Interests, Hobbies, Recreations
9. Measures from Tests and Inventories
10. Educational Plans
11. Vocational Plans
12. Work Record and Experiences
13. Honors Received
14. Provision for Counselor's Comments
15. Follow-up Information

Running commentary is made here on some of the categories in order to indicate the nature of items under them. Personal identification would include the student's name, address, date and place of birth, and home address. Family history would include father's name, address, occupation, and education; mother's name, occupation, and education. High school record would include name of high school from which graduated and date of graduation, subjects taken and credits earned with marks earned, rank in graduating class and number in class, high school measures of intelligence or aptitude, and extracurriculum activities engaged in. Inclusion of the high school record (and sometimes elementary and junior high school records) is one reason for referring to the college record as "cumulative." Junior college academic record would include courses taken, credits, grades, and honor points. Health data would list height, weight, disabilities, condition of vision, hearing, and teeth. Extracurricular activities record would provide for entries concerning organizations and activities engaged in, by year, and offices held. Stated interests, hobbies, and recreations would include both out-of-school and in-school activities not in the extracurriculum. The measures from tests and inventories would be those identified in the foregoing section as desirable. The nature of the entries under the remaining categories hardly requires elaboration except, perhaps, to state that the honors received would include both scholastic and athletic recognition and follow-up information would include activities after graduation or discontinuation of attendance.

Information from the numerous entries on the cumulative records, suggested by the categories listed and the multifarious items named and unnamed under them, is essential to counseling and guidance of the individual student. It is no less necessary for researches concerning groups of students or the total student body of an institution. To accommodate such extensive information calls for a large record form, and both Carlin's study (17) and this writer's inquiry showed frequent use of 8½x11 double-faced cards and 9½x12 folders. A folder has the advantage of holding both the permanent records and such temporary or supplementary forms and correspondence as may apply to the individual student.

Orientation and career courses.—In Table 11.1,* quoted from Putnam's study of offerings in 425 junior colleges reported in 1950, it may be noted that 94 were found to be giving a course called Orientation. This is between a fifth and a fourth of all institutions represented. The course was sixth in frequency among the new-type offerings. Almost a third of the 31 recent catalogs of public junior colleges examined for the evidence on practices in admission reported above were found to offer and require such courses of all entering freshmen. While the representation in this latter group of institutions is too small to justify a direct comparison, it is safe to infer that large proportions of junior colleges give and require the course. Putnam's table shows that courses in the Psychology of Adjustment and Choosing a Career and their variants were being given in a number of junior colleges, although in far fewer than the course in Orientation. These same courses were found also in the more recent catalogs, the former in almost half and the latter in about a fifth. They go under a variety of titles: Psychology of Adjustment is sometimes called also Personal and Social Adjustment and Personal Psychology, and the course in Vocations given such names as Career Course, Your Occupation, or Vocational Planning. These courses differ also from the Orientation course in that they are almost uniformly elective rather than required.

Analyses of courses in Orientation have been reported in print but, instead of drawing on these analyses, description here will be restricted to a single course in this area worked out in a recently established institution in which those who instituted and organized it are conversant with courses given elsewhere and presumably have incorporated in the course what they regard as the best of past experience and innovations they regard as promising. Use of this course as illustrative has the advantage of its having been appraised by students taking it.

    Unit I. "Where Am I?" Orientation
      Focus 1: Getting Acquainted: The Junior College Picture
      Focus 2: The SFJC Picture, including an Overview of Student Personnel Services
      Focus 3: How to Be a College Student
    Unit II. "The Individual and His Dynamics. What Kind of Person Am I?"
      Focus 1: How Do I seem to Myself?

*See p. 441.

Focus 2: How Do I seem to Others—"The Image"
Focus 3: How Am I Different from Others? "The Individual Differences Which Make Us Unique"
Unit III. "How Did I Get to Be the Way I Am?" The Investigation of Genetic and Environmental Factors
Focus 1: What Are the Wellsprings of My Existence? Investigation of Environmental Factors
Focus 2: What Were the Values I Grew Up With?
Unit IV. "What Problems Will I Confront?" Social Trends and Tensions
Focus 1: Major Influences in Contemporary Society: Anonymity and Mobility
Focus 2: Major Influences in Contemporary Society: Wealth
Focus 3: Major Influences in Contemporary Society: Government
Focus 4: Major Influences in Contemporary Society: The World Next Door
Focus 5: Major Influences in Contemporary Society: Persuaders
Unit V. "Where Do I Go from Here?" Determining the Future
Focus 1: How Will I Spend the Major Part of My Life?—Vocation
Focus 2: What Are the Pure Joys in Life?—Leisure
Focus 3: What Do I Want in Terms of Love, Sex, Marriage?
Focus 4: How Do I Keep Happy and Well?—Mental Health
Unit VI. "Developing Some Perspectives to Help Me Live Effectively."

The course, a three-semester-hour offering of Santa Fe Junior College in Florida, is called "The Individual in a Changing Environment" and is one of six general courses in the "Common Program" required of all students, the others being in Mathematics, Sciences, Humanities, Social Sciences, and English Language.

The course on "The Individual in a Changing Environment," as are other courses in the Common Program, is taught in classes limited to 25 students. It is taught by members of the student personnel staff, assuring involvement of counselors in teaching, curriculum development, and evaluation of instruction. Departure from the predominance of the lecture in instructional procedures and encouragement of participation by the student are reflected in the activities listed in Table 12.2. The appraisal, done on forms not asking for students' signatures, shows large proportions of ratings of "above average" or "excellent" on a five-point scale ranging from "poor" to "excellent." When the percentages in the table are increased by ratings of "average," for only a single activity, Films, does the total percentage drop below the 80s and 90s.

The bearing of the course on numerous relationships is seen in Table 12.3. The percentages reported are the totals for ratings of "Some," "Much," and "Very Much" help, on a five-point scale beginning with

TABLE 12.2
PERCENTAGES OF STUDENTS IN SANTA FE JUNIOR COLLEGE RATING COURSE THE INDIVIDUAL IN A CHANGING ENVIRONMENT ABOVE AVERAGE OR EXCELLENT*

Activities	Per cent
1. The course in general	58
2. Your personal growth	46
3. Course content learned	39
4. Reaction papers	50
5. Small group discussions	60
6. Psychological tests	36
7. Films	22
8. Tape recordings	48
9. Lectures	40
10. Guest speakers	35
11. Individual projects	49
12. Readings in general	48

*Data supplied by Dr. Joseph W. Fordyce, President of the College.

"None" and "Little." The percentages are all high, and suggestive of outcomes in adjustment overlapping generously those expected to be fostered by courses carrying such names as Personal and Social Adjustment, Psychology of Personal Adjustment, etc.

TABLE 12.3
PERCENTAGES OF STUDENTS IN SANTA FE JUNIOR COLLEGE REPORTING HAVING RECEIVED SOME, MUCH, OR VERY MUCH HELP IN VARIOUS RELATIONSHIPS FROM THE COURSE THE INDIVIDUAL IN A CHANGING ENVIRONMENT*

Received help in	Per cent
1. Understanding yourself	89
2. Understanding others	93
3. Examining your values	93
4. Exploring educational plans	79
5. Exploring future career possibilities	70
6. Your self-confidence	78
7. Work habits in other school subjects	61
8. Improving relationships with:	
Family	59
Friends of same sex	63
Your spouse or dates	61
Teachers	74
9. Your freedom to discuss and express feelings on:	
The nature of man	87
Religion	78
Your relation to Santa Fe Junior College	81
Sex	66
Love	70
Marriage	65

*Data supplied by Dr. Joseph W. Fordyce, President of the College.

Ratings were also made of the teachers of this course. They were rated on nine characteristics, such as "Interest in his students," "Preparedness for class," "Knowledge of subject," and "Being comfortable with his students." The average percentage of ratings of "Above Average" and "Excellent" on a five-point basis beginning with "Poor" was a shade above 80—about four-fifths. Asked to evaluate these instructors *as persons,* more than 90 per cent gave them ratings of "Top notch" and "Significant in my life."

The courses variously called "Career Course," "Vocational Planning," and "Your Occupation" may have descriptions like the following: "A course designed primarily for students whose educational-vocational plans are undecided or uncertain. All factors relating to a realistic self-concept, including data from extensive psychological testing, are considered and examined with reference to the problem of occupational choice and adjustment." The courses usually provide an overview of the world of work and, for the individual student, focus on some specific occupation or group of occupations, examining them under such headings as importance and relation to society, nature of the work, qualifications, preparation required, conditions of work, and earnings.

The student handbook.—A practice in orientation sometimes followed in public junior colleges, but much less often than in residential institutions, is "freshman week" or "orientation week," which may be thought of as a telescoped version of aspects of an orientation course. On this account no more than mention need be made of it here. A means of orientation deserving of some special attention is the student handbook or manual which is made available, in such institutions as issue one, to all full-time students. The handbook is often a project of the student body organization, and prepared for that body by a committee of students with the advice of a member of the faculty or administration.

Student handbooks were received from 10 of the 31 junior colleges, admission practices for which were summarized above. The 10 institutions were distributed in 8 widely scattered states. The handbooks were analyzed to identify the items included. The analysis showed that these items fall into six main categories, although other analyses might come up with differing classifications or with differing allocations of specific items. The categories are preliminary matters, regulations, information on offerings, student services, student organizations and activities, and other informative items. In the complete list presented here each item is followed by the initial letters of "high," "medium," and "low" in parentheses to indicate the relative frequency with which it appeared in the tabulation: H in 7 to 10 handbooks, M in 4 to 6, and L in 1 to 3. In all likelihood, analysis of a larger number of these publications would have shown more items as well as some shift in their relative frequency. Following is the full list as found, which can be used as a checklist by persons or committees with the responsibility of assembling content for such a publication:

Preliminary Matter
  District or college board, with or without photos (L)
  Administrative officers, with or without photos (L)
  Greetings from administrative head (H)
  Faculty list (M)
  Directory (M)
  History of institution (L)
  Institutional purposes and/or promotional matter (L)
  Accreditation (M)
Regulations
  Admission and registration (M)
  Scholarship requirements (L)
  Grading and grade points (H)
  Bases of classification (L)
  Graduation requirements and degrees (H)
  Change of registration or program (M)
  Attendance requirements (M)
  Tutoring (L)
  Withdrawal, probation, dismissal (M)
  Transfer and transcripts (M)
Information on Offerings
  Specimen curriculums (L)
  Evening and adult education (M)
  Summer school (L)
Student Services
  Guidance, counseling, and testing (H)
  Placement in employment (H)
  Library (M)
  Student center or lounge (M)
  Bookstore (H)
  Food services (M)
  Health and accident emergencies (H)
  Lockers (L)
  Parking and traffic (H)
  Lost and found (M)
  Bulletin boards (M)
  Telephones (L)
  Arrangements for housing (M)
  Mailboxes (L)
  Scholarships, loan funds, employment assistance (M)
  Honors and awards (M)
Student Organizations and Activities
  General student organization, description (H)
  Constitution and by-laws (M)
  Officers of general student organization, with or without photos (M)
  Budget of student organization (L)
  Activities card (M)
  List of student organizations and activities (H)
Other Advisory and Informative Items
  Blank for student's schedule (M)
  Advice on study (L)
  Work activities and student load (M)
  Calendar (M)
  Schedule of events and activities (M)
  Maps and/or floor plans (M)
  Traditions, social conduct and standards, including attire (H)
  College songs, yells, colors (H)
  Suggested readings (L)
  Information for veterans (L)

Comparison of the list with the content of college catalogs will show much overlapping. At the same time it may be stated that the relative frequency indicated is somewhat influenced by the extent of treatment in the catalogs, with some items given full treatment in the catalogs less often recognized in the handbook, and vice versa. On the whole, the items should be helpful in the orientation and adjustment of many students during early periods of attendance.

Student Services

A generic picture of the services.—In order to provide a general impression of the scope and nature of the services provided in public junior colleges, analysis was made of the descriptions of these services as set forth in the 31 catalogs from which materials are used at other points in this chapter. The descriptions are often meager and sometimes hardly more than enough for identification, but they afford a point of departure for some elaboration below of the several areas of service. Counseling and guidance is usually the first of areas of service named, and closely associated with this, as it should be, is placement. Scholarships, loan funds, and part-time employment comprise another important area. The remaining areas identified with considerable frequency are services in connection with health and housing.

(a) Frequency of mention or description places "counseling and guidance," "counseling," or "guidance" among the most frequent of the services. Referred to in connection with these services in 10 of the catalogs are the kinds of tests used, which need not be named, as all fall within the kinds identified in the earlier consideration of tests in this chapter.

(b) Examination of the catalogs finds mention in two-thirds of them of services in placement provided for students and graduates. Mention is often made of the "employment office," "placement office," or "clearing house" for student employment. All catalogs referring to this service indicate that it applies to part-time employment for current students, half of them to full-time employment for graduates, and only a few specify "placement in higher institutions" for graduates and other students, although other matter in the catalogs indicates that advice for transfer students is universal. Reference should be made here also to the placement service rendered in connection with the work-experience programs which are touched on below in describing the provisions for financial aid under (c).

(c) Various types of financial assistance are specified in the catalogs. Most common are scholarships, which are listed for all but two of the institutions. It appears that vigorous efforts have been made to muster substantial numbers of this type of student subsidy. One prominent type is the scholarship. For some of the institutions the nature of the listing of these is such that the total number available is not apparent, but for the 20 catalogs for which they could be counted, the total number ranged from a few scholarships to well over a hundred. The median number was about 35. A surprising fact is that the median was larger for the tuition-free than for the tuition-charging junior colleges. When specified, the scholarships appear to be available with about equal frequency for high school graduates (entering freshmen), for returning students (sophomores), and for graduates to encourage continuance in senior institutions.

A full two-thirds of these junior colleges administer loan funds, and about half of these were arranging for loans under the National Defense Student Loan Program. The loan funds are available no less often in tuition-free than in tuition-charging institutions. Instances of funds were met with as large as $30,000 and $48,000, and in a few institutions were "incorporated" as "foundations." Mention is made in a few of the catalogs of the "Director of Student Welfare," one of whose responsibilities is administration of assistance under the loan funds.

Six among this representation of catalogs describe work-experience programs like those considered in Chapter 11,* one of the signal merits of which was indicated to be financial facilitation of attendance.

(d) Candidly described, the general picture of health services for students as set forth in our representation of catalogs is not a flattering one. For a small minority of institutions they appear to approach the exemplary, but high commendation must be far from pervasive. The actual situation may be better than as identified, but if it were much better, this would, as with other provisions outlined in the catalogs, be reflected in the descriptions. Only seventeen of the 31 catalogs mention or describe the provisions available. In 14 of the institutions nurses are stated to be available, on schedule, for first aid and advice, and in 8, a "college physician" is available on schedule in a "health center." Eight catalogs specify the requirement of a physical examination at registration, in 5 instances given by the college and in 3 by the family's or student's physician. In 3 instances the only entry under the heading of "Health Services" asserts that health and accident insurance is to be had, and in one of these the recommendation is made that students avail themselves of it.

It is safe to say that a comparison of provisions of health services in residential colleges would find them much more nearly adequate than in these public junior colleges. The explanation of the difference may be assumed to converge on the fact that students in the local junior colleges are living at home and have access to home health care and the family physician. However, the explanation should hardly excuse all junior colleges from developing programs of adequate health service.

One may not doubt that some of the junior colleges represented in this analysis include attention to both physical and mental health, but none of the descriptions mentioned concern for mental health. The partial void in

*See pp. 479-80.

this area is in harmony with Bown and Richek's observation (*11*) that there is "virtually complete absence of references [in educational literature] to the mental health problems of junior college students."

(e) It is hardly to be expected that community colleges, student bodies of which are overwhelmingly commuters, would have more than minor responsibilities in connection with housing. Exceptions would be local public junior colleges in states with a few widely scattered institutions. Nevertheless, almost half the catalogs in the analysis of student services reported here make some reference to student housing. A small proportion require approval of housing for students not living at home, slightly more prepare a list of approved housing that is available, about as many volunteer to provide assistance or advice in locating suitable housing, and a few assert that their institutions provide no on-campus housing; and, again, a few mention opportunities for students to earn board and room. A single catalog (in a state with a few widely scattered junior colleges) states that all out-of-town students are required to live in residence halls. An extreme position is that in one catalog which states that "the college has no housing and assumes no responsibility for assisting or supervising the student in locating suitable housing." One may hope that few, if any, of the institutions whose catalogs make no statement concerning housing assume a similarly negative position.

Counseling, educational and vocational.—Admittedly, the foregoing portrayal of student services in the junior college is hardly adequate in certain areas for understanding possibilities and practices and, on this account, some amplification is in order. The areas are, in function, intimately interrelated: educational and vocational counseling, placement, and advisement bearing on emotional adjustment and mental health.

Cowley and others, in a discussion of occupational orientation of college students, once said, "Ideally, educational counseling and occupational counseling are one and the same" (*19*, 52). This can hardly be denied for later adolescence, the period during which decision-making concerning careers is at its peak. Doubtless, students at this school level can profit also from guidance on elective portions of general education and for recreation, but the concern with vocation is typically predominant. Besides, no matter how effective the group guidance in classes in orientation or on careers has been, supplementation by personalized advisement will usually be useful and often indispensable.

The stages through which the counseling with the individual student must pass will often work back and forth on each other but, if they follow a conventional progression, will include (1) a review of the facts about the occupation or occupations in which the student is interested, with the mustering of any new evidence on them, (2) diagnosing, by reference to test results and other data available in the student's cumulative record, with supplementation from additional tests deemed advisable, and (3) counseling with him in planning his program. The plans should be subjected to periodic review and revised as needed.

Status and importance of placement.—With the distributive service of the public junior college increasingly acknowledged and spiraling, placement of its students is mounting in importance and becoming an indispensable aspect of the personnel program in the institution. Reporting in 1948 on the status of placement for the Commission on Student Personnel of the

TABLE 12.4
PERCENTAGES OF LOCAL AND DISTRICT JUNIOR COLLEGES PROVIDING PLACEMENT SERVICES FOR GRADUATES AND NONGRADUATES

Kind of Service	Large		Small	
	Graduates	Nongrad	Graduates	Nongrad
Finding full-time positions	77.8	76.5	72.2	61.1
Finding part-time positions				
While attending	76.5	91.4	68.1	76.4
After leaving	49.4	45.7	36.1	33.3

SOURCE: Adapted from Meinecke (*54*, Table 2).

American Association of Junior Colleges, Meinecke (*54*) identified three kinds of help being provided: (1) help in selection of colleges, professional schools, and universities (help in transfer); (2) help in finding full-time jobs; and (3) help in finding part-time jobs. Approximately nine-tenths of both large and small public junior colleges were found to be giving help on transfer to graduates; the proportion of large institutions giving this help to nongraduates was about the same, while the proportion of small ones doing so was less than three-fourths. The proportions providing help in finding jobs, as seen in Table 12.4, was generally smaller, with help to nongraduates less frequent than for graduates. The help to drop-outs ("after leaving") is seen to be even less frequent, with the proportion down to a third of the smaller institutions. The investigator stressed the finding that "all groups of colleges were more concerned with placement of students in higher institutions than they were with job placement." From evidence she reports concerning the other duties performed by the placement officers and the time officially assigned for the work, one infers that placement service at the time was not sufficiently prominent in the guidance program nor adequately integrated with it. The Raines report of more recent date showed placement still lagging in development, as it turned up fourth from the bottom in "adequacy of performance" among the "21 basic student personnel functions" (*18*, 21).

The persisting concern of the Commission on Student Personnel for development of placement service led to the publication by the American Association of Junior Colleges of a special booklet on the subject (59). It was prepared by Milton C. Mohs, Dean of Placement over a long period of years for Pasadena City College, with the cooperation of an advisory committee of a dozen persons most of whom were directors of placement in California junior colleges. The three contributing chapters of the publication discuss the need, the organization, and the operation of a junior college placement bureau. The focus is on the service in assisting the following groups in finding suitable employment: the students seeking part-time employment, the terminal graduates, the drop-outs, and the alumni. Comment concerning drop-outs suggests that placing them in employment presents more complexities than do other groups (59, 25-27). Nothing is said about the assignment of students to work-experience programs which are offered in many junior colleges. The list of groups served also overlooks students planning transfer to four-year colleges and universities. Explanation of the omission may be that the assignment from the Commission contemplated recommendations only for placement in employment.

Follow-up studies.—Discussions of placement services recurrently mention the essentiality of follow-up studies. Meinecke implied this in the title ("Placement and Follow-up in Junior Colleges") of her article reporting practices in 1948 (54). Mohs referred to follow-up studies as "a corollary, an integral feature of placement" (59, 46). He has himself periodically directed such studies for Pasadena City College and it should be instructive to report in small part at least his methods and findings. In one of these studies which he called *Employer Evaluations of 1,000 Placements* (58), he reports tabulations and interpretations of the first thousand responses to questionnaires sent out to employers. The population included drop-outs who had been in attendance various numbers of semesters, graduates of terminal courses, and graduates who had followed curriculums leading to junior standing in advanced institutions. For this study the thousand subjects were separated into two groups, Group 1 who had majored in work which prepared for employment with two years or less of college and Group 2 who had majored in transfer curriculums. The percentage distributions of job categories under which all the 500 men, 500 women, and total of 1,000 former students were classified are shown in Table 12.5. Further condensation of categories would show 50.1 per cent of all, or just over half, in business occupations (office and merchandising), 33.0 per cent (about a third) in industrial occupations, and about a sixth in service occupations. To be expected is a notably different distribution for the two sexes, with more men in industrial and more women in business and service jobs. Not shown in the table are the distributions for the two groups identified for the study, which may be generalized by saying that for the group that had pursued terminal occupational curriculums there was a considerable degree of relationship between the curriculums pursued and employments, whereas for the transfer curriculum group, little or no such relationship could be or was apparent.

Other lines of inquiry and kinds of evidence in this study relate to lengths of time on the job, reasons for termination, strengths and weaknesses of employees, and college aptitude scores (ACE) in relation to membership in the two groups, length of stay in college, grades earned, and job-holding. The study also includes report on employers' identifica-

TABLE 12.5
PERCENTAGE DISTRIBUTION TO JOB CATEGORIES OF FORMER STUDENTS OF PASADENA COLLEGE

Occupational Group	Men	Women	Total
Office	12.2	60.2	36.2
Technical	34.8	1.6	18.2
Merchandising	18.4	9.4	13.9
Service	9.2	24.6	16.9
Trades	17.2	3.4	10.3
Manufacturing	8.2	0.8	4.5
Total	100.0	100.0	100.0

SOURCE: Adapted from Mohs (58, 8).

tion of "strengths" and "weaknesses" of the employees, which lead to a conclusion of "very little criticism or praise of the school program *per se*, but great attention to personality traits . . ." (58, 52).

Further mention here of the Placement Bureau of Pasadena City College should include reference to its annual report (57). For 1962 it consists of two parts, the first part reporting on matters like 15 years of placements, the work-study program, and international students. The second part reports a follow-up during the year after graduation of the class of 1961 of the college, and is itself in two sections, one on transfers to higher institutions and the other on terminal graduates. That on transfers indicates the grade-point averages institution by institution and includes differentials for the various types of institutions from grades earned in Pasadena City College. The follow-up of "graduates on the job" who at least temporarily were working on full-time job situations considers them in two groups. Group 1 accounts for the graduates who pursued transfer curriculums while in Pasadena City College but who did not continue with advanced study because of poor grades, disinterest, financial reasons, and the like, and they make up about a fourth of all transfer graduates. Of the terminal graduates almost half were employed. An appropriate generalization about the occupations would be that for Group 2 the work is much more often than with Group 1 related to the curriculums pursued in junior college. Large numbers of the graduates, for diverse reasons, return to Pasadena City College for a third year: the summary places the proportion at "around 20 per cent" (57, 23).

Improving placement of transfers.—The review in Chapter 7 of researches concerning the record of transfers in senior colleges and universities reveals both the success of major proportions of these transfers in later college years and at the same time varying degrees of disappointment and failure for others. The growth of the junior college movement is certain to continue and the number of transfers will mount with this growth, so that, for the country as a whole, the typical route that will be taken by students whose education extends through senior college years will be from elementary school, through high school, through junior college, and into the advanced levels. Transfers will inevitably multiply, and the problems of articulation will persist to the extent they are not ameliorated. Attention here is on whatever may be done, especially through counseling and guidance and other activities by personnel within the individual junior college, to improve articulation and to foster the success of the transferring student. Although important for long-term policy, less attention will be given to what the senior colleges and coordinating agencies working on a statewide or regional basis can and should do.

One of the most obvious directions advice to prospective transfers should take is (1) to brace them for a slump in grades or grade-point average during the first semester or quarter in the senior institution. This slump is characteristic for students at wide levels of ability and arises from problems of adjustment to living away from home for the first time, a differing and often more complex educational and social environment, and instructors and instructional procedures in varying degrees unlike those to whom the student is accustomed. As may be judged from the evidence in Chapter 7, there is subsequent recovery of standings for many or most transfers.

An appropriate direction of counsel that may well be associated with the one concerning the initial slump, certainly for the competent junior college student, is (2) to encourage him to expect recovery in subsequent semesters or quarters in his measures of academic success. Performance is the best predictor of subsequent performance, and competent transfers from junior colleges have been found to stand up well in competition with native students.

In listing additional lines along which counsel and other activity in relation to transfer is desirable, recourse may well be taken to "conclusions and implications" set down in the last chapter of Knoell and Medsker's

From Junior to Senior College (47, 86–102), most of the earlier chapters of which summarize the evidence of their large-scale follow-up projects drawn upon in Chapter 7.* The conclusions and implications have been distilled by the authors not only from deliberation over the large body of evidence of their projects, but also from numerous conferences with administrators and counselors, as individuals and in groups. The implications are, thus, a carefully considered source of recommendations for counsel and other practices and policies pertaining to transfer. The implications cited, which include mainly only those applicable within the junior college, are here in some instances paraphrased, mostly in the interests of brevity, and are presented in an order differing from that in the Knoell-Medsker version.

The facts that abilities and interests of prospective transfers vary and that standards and programs of the senior institutions in a state or region also differ provide leeway for counselors (3) to effect a proper matching of student and institution. The practice of trying to secure admission only to the institutions with greatest selectivity and prestige will turn out to be a disservice both to students and the junior college from which they come. Each junior college should (4) examine periodically "the grade-point differentials with *each* four-year college to which a sizeable number of its students transfer." This could be the core of a systematic follow-up of transfer students. As a part of this follow-up (5) transfers should be permitted and encouraged to return to the junior college to talk through their problems with their counselors and instructors. Another implication points to (6) using caution in placing dependence on "the C grade and the C-grade-point average earned in the junior college as indicators of a student's likelihood of success in four-year institutions," because "a C grade may be given as a reward for compliance with course requirements at only a minimally acceptable level" and because it "may mean many things when given by different instructors to different students for different reasons." Two implications bearing on the length of stay in junior college are that (7) "weak students with both subject-matter and scholarship deficiencies should probably remain in junior college for more than two years" and that (8) "most students should be urged to remain in junior college until they can transfer with full upper division standing, with all lower division requirements met." The problems of C-grade transfers who come from homes that can provide little or no financial help for attendance at the upper-division level away from home and, in consequence, have their school work suffer because of their efforts at self-support prompts an implication of (9) "critical examination both of the current philosophy of financial aid and of the nature of existing programs." Knoell and Med-

*See pp. 302–9.

sker urge also (10) "cautious but deliberate attempts" to "beef up" the instruction of the university-bound transfer students during their second year in the junior college.

Among the implications of the Knoell-Medsker summary is one bearing on the use of test results in admitting transfers to upper divisions. Their assertion on this is (11) "Test results should probably not be used to deny admission to transfer students if their college grades are good and if their occupational goals are reasonable ones," although it is at the same time conceded that some possible uses of test results at the time of transfer include placement in course sequences, demonstration of proficiency, qualification for honors programs, and validation of credit for courses for which transfer credit is not normally awarded. One investigation affording justification for this position reported correlations between the cumulative GPA and the following measures for transfers into the University of California at Berkeley: high school GPA, transfer GPA, first semester GPA in the university, and Verbal, Quantitative, and Total scores on the College Ability Test (CAT) (46). The highest correlation, as expected, was for the first semester GPA. However, that for the Transfer GPA was next highest, this being followed in order by Total CAT score, Verbal CAT, and high school GPA. An implication for counseling was that use of the CAT could provide useful information concerning appropriate choice of a college major.

One further implication of the Knoell-Medsker study, with pervasive import for practice and policy within the junior college in respect to counseling for prospective transfers, should be mentioned: (12) the need for adequate financial support and an appropriately trained staff for the service.

Several of the implications point to recommendations for practice and policy of the senior institutions receiving the transfers or of agencies undertaking coordination of state higher educational systems. One of these concerns the extreme particularization of transfer curriculums to be found in some junior college catalogs—particularization that specifies all subjects in transfer curriculums for individual institutions. Mention is made of these in the section on transfer curriculums in Chapter 11,* with the observation that they often emerged in examination of catalogs of California junior colleges. Knoell and Medsker's conclusion reads: "Junior colleges should not be expected to offer an infinite number of transfer programs to parallel those of all four-year institutions to which their students might transfer." In addition to other objections to such a practice, it may be questioned whether such extreme particularization is needed to insure success after transfer. At the level of admission from high school to college, many and

*See pp. 485–86.

perhaps now most colleges and universities have eased up on the requirement of specific patterns of preparatory subjects, as investigation and experience have shown that the best predictor of college success is the student's rank in class with whatever his pattern of courses in high school has been. It seems likely that the situation for the junior college graduate is in some part analogous, and that higher institutions might well move in the direction of more flexibility of subject matter requirements. A kindred implication concerns capable junior college students who are attracted into terminal curriculums and who the authors of *From Junior to Senior College* think should be permitted to transfer, depending on their achievement, abilities, and changing interests. They also point out that the higher institution, at the same time that it shows concern for the adjustment and welfare of freshmen, usually leaves the transfer student, whose need for both counseling and academic advising is often acute, to make his own adjustment to the new situation.

Concern for emotional adjustment.—The major aspect of student services left for brief consideration is counseling and guidance for emotional adjustment, or mental health. It is certainly no less important than those previously dealt with, that is, counseling about educational program and occupation and placement in occupation or for transfer, but practices and policy in it in junior colleges have been much less extensively investigated and reported, so that not as much that is definitive can be said concerning it. In now considering emotional adjustment somewhat separately from other aspects there is no assumption that satisfying decisions concerning the curriculum one pursues or an occupational choice or placement is not conducive to emotional adjustment: they have much to do with an acceptable self-image and, after all, the several aspects named should be regarded and worked out as an integrated, even though composite, program. Moreover, outcomes of advisement done with the aid of instruments for measuring deficiencies in skills in study, reading, or written composition, which are a part of educational counseling, are known to resolve problems and conduce to wholesome attitudes.

A word is in order in explanation of the lag of service toward emotional adjustment behind educational and vocational counseling and placement. In studies which need not be cited and which inquire as to which functionaries or persons students would seek out for advice on occupational choice, preponderance of preferences indicate the school or college counselor, whereas for advice on personal problems counselors are less often indicated as preferences than parent or pastor. In part this reflects the undeveloped state of counseling over essential but less tangible areas of counseling. In part, also, it arises from what a writer on psychotherapeutic techniques with adolescents has observed, that they are more difficult to deal with than children or adults: they are difficult to approach because of fear and their hesitation to let you in on their daydreams (6).

In deliberating over the method and timing of identifying students with serious problems, the question may arise as to whether to administer at the time of admission and registration and in association with the physical examination a projective instrument like the MMPI or a simpler preliminary screening tool like the Mooney Problem Check List or the Bown SRI. Resort to the former procedure would be prohibitive for all or almost all junior colleges because of the absence of adequately prepared personnel and/or, even more, the cost in time and funds. Much more nearly practicable is administration and interpretation of one of the simpler instruments.

It is in place to review briefly what has been presented in theory, as the source of problems of the later adolescent, and the principal areas in which they are found. One writer, Burman (16), identifies three factors of an emotional nature which must be dealt with by the junior college student, which, he says, evolve from three main areas of living: emancipation from the home, heterosexual development, and attainment of status among peers. Blos, eminent in both thinking and practice in the field, some years ago explained the origin as follows (7): "Among the older adolescent, the college student is in a position peculiarly his own. He has postponed, either willingly or under moral or social pressures, the attainment of adulthood for the sake of educational advantages or social prestige. This protracted adolescence, with its unavoidable effects on the psychic economy of the individual, is still a stepchild of psychiatry and mental hygiene. The problems created by the artificial prolongation of a maturational period affect almost every student at one point of his college career. Most students can cope with this situation, but an appreciable number undergo personal disturbances, some of which are at this time amenable to corrections. . . ."

The types of problems which this specialist at work in a four-year college reported that he met with regularity were (7): "(1) The student who cannot study, who complains of inability to concentrate; (2) the student who is lonely, who cannot make friends; (3) the student who is afraid of examinations, who is unable to speak in class; (4) the student without any purpose or vocational aim; (5) the habitual evader, obstructionist and complainer; (6) the student in acute conflict with his family; (7) the student with a physical defect; (8) special problems of veterans."

One may take comfort in an assertion made by a psychiatrist at work in an eastern college that "mental health does not imply freedom from stress, from conflict or from anxiety. It connotes freedom from crippling amounts of these qualities" (27, 101). When he gets down to serious cases he reports that the usual estimate by those familiar with student problems is that about 10 per cent of the student body will require help each year (*27, 173*). This estimate is made for four-year residential colleges and we can only speculate as to whether it would be true of a community college population, or whether it would be larger or smaller.

Even if the proportion needing professional help for emotional adjustment is much smaller than this estimate, large public junior colleges should have, and some do employ, professional psychologists or psychiatrists for the service. The small junior college will not require a full-time specialist for the work and must make some other provision, for example, a part-time specialist with the rest of his time assigned to other responsibilities, such as teaching courses in psychology, or arrangements with a private practitioner for part-time service.

Personnel services for adults.—The description of various aspects of service provided in the foregoing portions of this section are those for full-time students. When it comes to describing the personnel services for part-time students, more especially adults, little can be said because the services are largely nonexistent. In his summary of practices in junior colleges of the country Raines says that "most junior colleges readily admit that evening students receive little or no attention as far as guidance is concerned" (*45*). Some proponents of the community college have urged that its counseling and guidance services extend also to nonstudents, and even that those in charge serve as coordinators of all local guidance services in the locality. Raines reports that not more than four or five among all the institutions represented in his investigation "were able to extend their guidance services to non-students."

A safe conjecture is that the explanation for this near void of advisement for evening students, whether adults or later adolescents, is the general lag of development of student personnel services behind the need for them for the regular students in many junior colleges, and the expectation is warranted that the service will be increasingly provided as personnel programs become more nearly full-scale. Later adolescents in part-time programs need help in deciding on occupations and in placement, and many adults will need advice on changes in careers as a consequence of automation and other technological changes. From this point the next step is a comprehensive program or cooperation and coordination with other local agencies to provide it.

Further factors of effectiveness.—No exposition of the student personnel program, no matter how brief, should neglect mention of certain additional factors making for effectiveness. They are less aspects of the program than relationships or conditions under which the program operates. Among the more influential of these are the research approach in guidance, professionalization of the service, and its organizational relationships. Permeation of the program with the research approach is implicit in many of the means and methods used in it, as may be noted by merely mentioning the most recurrent: tests and inventories, follow-up studies, evaluation, and statistical procedures. Ability to administer and interpret the results of these procedures, together with the grounding in psychology and the other behavioral sciences to render service through all its aspects, raises the position of the director of guidance and the counselor to the level of professional specialization.

Professionalization has, in turn, implications for organization of the service, which should be set up as a major division of the junior college on a par with instruction. Charts of administrative organization for junior colleges now typically make the director of personnel work coordinate with the dean or director of curriculum and instruction. Participation of teachers on a part-time basis or through cooperation is often indicated on these charts by horizontal lines connecting the teaching and counseling functions, and approaching a consensus is the conviction that, for the sake of effectiveness in the relationships, teachers should have preservice and/or inservice preparation.

However, the need for appropriate internal organization is not enough. Effectiveness is also greatly influenced by the degree of vertical articulation of the guidance services through the various successive units of the school system. In the treatment of placement of transfers above, passing mention was made of certain means of encouraging articulation between junior and senior colleges. The need for articulation with the high school is even more important because it is the source of all junior college freshmen while only a minority of these freshmen continue into the senior college level. The present writer long ago reported the advantage of close association of guidance programs at these two levels (*49*). He had inquired into the influence of degree of cooperation on (1) the percentages of retention into the second college year and on (2) the percentage of students in terminal programs. Both measures were significantly larger for the situations with the nearest approach to unification of guidance programs at the two levels.

Student Organizations and Activities

Values claimed for the extracurriculum.—Following the lead of the Raines project described in the first section of this chapter, which includes the extracurriculum or cocurriculum as a part of the student personnel program, this section deals with student organizations and activities. The values claimed for them are mainly those of general education. This is implied in the title of a chapter, "The Extra-curriculum and General Education," written by Williamson for the yearbook on general education in colleges (*94*). He stated that the purpose of the extracurriculum, as viewed by general education, is its "contribution to the personal development of student participants" (231). He identified several types of activities and, in analyzing the underlying philosophy, said that "the content of the extracurriculum is determined by the nature of its social or group context as principally interpersonal experiences and relationships" and that "it provides rich opportunities for participants to become intimately acquainted with other persons and to learn how to enjoy them and work co-operatively with them on common enterprises" (235–36). Johnson, in a chapter on "The Extra-class Program" in the report of his investigation of general education in California junior colleges, asserted that this program "must be recognized as an integral part of the curriculum and as a highly significant avenue to general education" (*44*, 283).

An objection sometimes raised to the claim that the study of a given subject or participation in some activity contributes to one's general education is that it fails to specify which among many aspects of general education are being fostered. The statement by Williamson just quoted points to at least one major particularization, the aspect of interpersonal experiences conducive to learning how to enjoy others and to work co-operatively with them. Further particularization is provided in an older analysis of values claimed in the literature dealing with the extracurriculum (*48*, 11), which identified, among others, values in civic-social-moral relationships, values related to "socialization," "social co-operation," "actual experience in group life," "ethical living," "citizenship in a democracy," "training for leadership," etc. Among still other values in general education claimed are those relating to recreation and aesthetic participation, health, and exploration. Also, certain values claimed fall outside the area of general education, as vocational preparation in organizations and activities related to the individual student's occupational plans.

The scanty evaluative research.—The claims made for values derived from participation in the extracurriculum far outreach the positive findings of research supporting the claims. The explanation is the actual dearth of evaluative research, although there is a great deal of literature descriptive of practice. Of the limited offering of reports of research related directly or indirectly to appraisal are two with experimental approach pertaining to freshmen in two state universities in North Central states, Minnesota and Wisconsin, and one concerning graduating seniors in high school, location not indicated in the report. (1) The experiment at the University of Minnesota (*1*) was aimed at ascertaining the effect of counseling to encourage social participation and had as subjects girls only. On these girls the following measures were available: high school percentile rank, raw score and percentile rank in the American Council Psychological Examination, Cooperative English Test, Minnesota Inventory of Social Attitudes, Bell Adjustment Inventory, and Rundquist-Sletto Inferiority Scale. Information had also been supplied by the girls on an Individual Record Form concerning the activities in which they engaged frequently. These were separated as group activities, such as team sports, clubs, and church organization, and individual activities, done alone or with a single other individual, like sewing, reading, or tennis. Both experimental and control samples were drawn from girls whose scores on Social Preferences, Social Behavior (Minnesota Inventory of Social Attitudes), and group activities were in the lower half of the distributions. The girls in the control group were handled "in the customary manner," with the usual counseling, which might include some social guidance. The treatment of the experimental group went further in encouraging and giving all its members an opportunity to participate in social activities.

At the end of the freshman year both experimental and control groups were retested on the scales of social attitude, and an activities record during the year was at hand for all subjects. Both groups made gains on most of the scales, but the gains of the experimental group were larger and, while the number of individual activities circled was about equal for the two groups, the experimental group reported participating in more group activities. The experimental group reported more hours per week spent in extracurricular activities and more offices and committees in these activities. A justifiable inference is that the emphasis in counseling resulted in both more social participation and more socialization of the student.

(2) The experiment at the University of Wisconsin (*37*) compared the gains on two tests of social adjustment of two groups of students matched on a total of fifteen measures, among them sex, age, size of home community, size of high school, percentile ranks in high school and on the American Council test, degree of self-support, church affiliation, fraternity affiliation, extent of participation in activities in first semester, and scholastic average for the first semester in college. The students in one of these matched groups were "stimulated" to participate in extracurricular activities, on the assumption that this would result in "improved scholastic achievement and improved social adjustment." The investigator concluded that the staff stimulation improved the social adjustment of the students but had negligible influence on scholastic achievement, from which the inference seems justifiable that in this situation the increased participation took place without negative influence on scholarship.

(3) In the project involving high school graduates (*68*) virtually the same conclusions are arrived at as in the Wisconsin experiment. The hypothesis here was that extracurricular participation influences negatively competence in scholarship. Available were the decile measures on scholar-

ship, and on the Otis Higher Examination, and a leadership score based on extracurricular offices held during high school years. The discrepancies between deciles on scholarship and potential as indicated by the decile on the Otis Examination were compared with leadership scores. The medians of the leadership scores were found to be in very slight degree related to the discrepancies and the investigator noted that, if anything, "students who gained in scholarship rank held more extracurricular offices than did those who, by not participating intensively in such affairs, were able to devote more time to schoolwork." The author concluded her report with the observation, "Whatever the explanation, it is obvious . . . that the often accused participation . . . is not usually an important contributing factor to the low scholarship of intelligent students." However, use of the word "usually" suggests that it may have had this effect in individual instances.

The dearth of objective evaluation of the extracurriculum for which so much is claimed may be regrettable, but it is little different from the situation in the several collegiate disciplines, and even more widely in the educational world. We have long relied mainly on speculative and experiential appraisal of programs rather than on experimental and related procedures, which should be increasingly applied.

The organizations and activities.—To make possible portrayal of the extracurricular offerings in public junior colleges, analysis was made of the content descriptive of them in the college catalogs represented in certain other portions of Chapters 11 and 12. This content usually appears under headings like "Student Organizations," "Student Activities," or "Student Organizations and Activities." Simple tabulations were made of the kinds of organizations and activities named. The results of these compilations are reproduced in Tables 12.6 and 12.7. In most instances it was not difficult to distinguish between organizations and activities, although in practice the two groups merge in varying degrees. It should be stated that the only catalogs used were those that appeared to present each institution's complete list and did not refer to "organizations like the following." Tabulation from the catalogs was continued until few new types of organizations or activities were emerging to be added to the lists. This situation appeared to have been reached after analysis of about 20 catalogs: catalogs of 21 public junior colleges located in 13 states are represented in the tabulations.

One may say that the total array to be found in Table 12.6 can serve as something approaching a complete checklist of kinds of organizations, although some additions from offerings in additional colleges are conceivable. The total number of different interests represented exceeds a hundred, accounting for a total of almost 400 organizations, with an average of about 19 per institution. As expected, when the institutions were grouped

TABLE 12.6
STUDENT ORGANIZATIONS IN 21 JUNIOR COLLEGE CATALOGS*

Subject Interests (32)
  Astronomy, 1
  Biology, 3
  Chemistry, 1
  Earth Sciences, 1
  Geology, 2
  Mathematics, 1
  Physical Science, 1
  Science, 1
  Communication, 1
  Political Science, 1
  Social Science, 1
  French, 7
  German, 5
  Spanish, 5
  Foreign Language, 1
Occupational (76)
  Agriculture, 5
  Architecture, 1
  Aviation, 1
  Business, 8
  Business Administration, 2
  Child Study, Exceptional
    Children, 2
  Cosmotology, 1
  Dental Assisting, 1
  Education, 9
  Electronics, 3
  Engineering, 10
  Forestry, 1
  Home Economics, 10
  Journalism, 6
  Music Education, 2
  Nursing, 7
  Petroleum, 1
  Prelaw, 1
  Premedicine, 2
  Printing, 1
  Secretarial, 2
Music, Art, and Crafts (78)
  Bagpipe Band, 1
  Band, 15
  Brass Ensemble, 1
  Choir, Choral Organization, 15
  Glee Club, 2
  Instrumental Ensemble, 1
  Madrigal Singers, 4
  Orchestra, 5
  Quartet (vocal), 2
  Swing Band, 1
  Women's Chorus, 1
  Art, Fine Arts, 9
  Crafts, 1
  Dance, 1
  Dance-drill Team, 3
  Modern Dance, 2
  Dramatics, 14

Political (17)
  International Relations, 5
  Parliamentary Procedure, 1
  Political, 1
  Student Forum, 2
  United Nations, 2
  Young Democrats, 3
  Young Republicans, 3
Physical (9)
  Bowling, 2
  Hiking, 1
  Jujitsu, 2
  Rodeo, 1
  Skiing, 3
Hobbies (13)
  Birdwatchers, 1
  Bridge, 2
  Camera, Photography, 3
  Chess, 2
  Fishing and Hunting, 1
  Motor Sports, 1
  Radio, 2
  Wild Life, 1
Service (28)
  Circle K, 9
  Collegiate Civitan, 2
  Other Men's Service Groups, 4
  Woman's Service Groups, 6
  Student Assistants, 2
  Booster, Pep, 5
Religious (23)
  Christian Fellowship, 4
  Denominational, 11
  YMCA, 4
  YWCA, 4
Scholastic and Other Honorary (33)
  Scholarship, 17
  Athletic, 10
  Dramatic, 5
  Journalistic, 1
Miscellaneous (18)
  Foreign Students, 1
  Hawaiian Students, 1
  Individualists, 1
  Indian Students, 1
  Latin American Students, 3
  Men Residents, 1
  Women Residents, 1
  Social (men), 1
  Social (women), 2
  Veterans, 6
Student Body and Class
Organizations (63)
  Associated Students, 12
  Associated Men Students, 10
  Associated Women Students, 13
  Student Council or Senate, 10
  Freshman Class, 9
  Sophomore Class, 9

*Numbers following each title are the total found in 21 catalogs.

by size of enrollment, the larger institutions were found to have more organizations than smaller ones. The organizations are seen in the table to be grouped under 11 headings: Subject Interests; Occupational; Music, Art, and Crafts; Political; Physical; Hobbies; Service; Religious; Scholastic and Other Honorary; Miscellaneous; and Student Body and Class Organizations. The obvious comment prompted by the list concerns the extremely wide range of interests represented.

TABLE 12.7
ACTIVITIES LISTED IN 21 JUNIOR COLLEGE CATALOGS*

Intercollegiate Athletics	Baseball, 3, 0
Basketball, 14	Touch football, 3, 0
Track, 14	Handball, 2, 0
Golf, 13	Horseshoes, 1, 1
Football, 12	Swimming, 1, 1
Tennis, 12	Wrestling, 2, 0
Basketball, 11	Croquet, 1, 0
Wrestling, 7	Cross country, 1, 0
Swimming, 4	Horseback riding, 0, 1
Cross country, 2	Rifle, 0, 1
Gymnastics, 1	Sailing, 0, 1
Rifle, 1	Tumbling, 0, 1
Skiing, 1	*Speech and Dramatics*
Water polo, 1	Debate, 4
Intramural Activities†	Forensics, public speaking, 4
Tennis, 5, 5	Oral interpretation, 1
Basketball, 6, 3	Oratory, 1
Softball, 5, 4	Radio broadcasting, 3
Badminton, 4, 3	Dramatics, 6‡
Bowling, 4, 3	*Publications*
Archery, 0, 6	Student paper, 21
Volleyball, 5, 1	Yearbook, 19
Golf, 2, 3	Literary magazine, 8
Field hockey, 0, 4	Student guide or handbook, 2
Table tennis, 3, 1	
Track, 3, 1	

*Numbers following names of activities indicate numbers of junior colleges.
†First number for Intramurals applies to men, the second to women.
‡In addition to 14 junior colleges with Dramatics Clubs.

The compilation of student activities listed in the catalogs is reproduced in Table 12.7. They are seen to fall into four main groups, namely, Intercollegiate Athletics, Intramural Activities, Speech and Dramatics, and Publications. Comparison of the numbers of institutions listing intercollegiate and intramural athletic activities shows the former much larger than the latter, and suggests that some junior colleges may already be stressing intercollegiate sports to the neglect of physical welfare of the general student body. Catalogs usually mention the frequency of publication of the student newspaper, and this frequency varies greatly, ranging from weekly to bimonthly, with the more common practices being weekly, biweekly, and monthly.

Illustrative all-college activities.—As it is out of the question to deal at length with any considerable number of the vast array of organizations and activities which appear to be operative in junior colleges, treatment will be limited to two activities only, and these are for illustration of considered approaches to shaping the activity into an effective educative agency. The two identified for scrutiny are the college newspaper and assembly programs, both of them of the all-college type in the sense that they aim at being meaningful to the total student body. They are at the same time activities concerning which evaluative projects have been reported from which recommendations may be inferred or derived.

The assumption in the project concerning the college newspaper, reported by Harrington (*35*), is that the junior college newspaper should be evaluated by its contribution to the achievement of the institution's objectives which he formulated in terms very similar to the purposes accepted for the public junior college in the early portions of Chapter 11. His version of these objectives included preparation for advanced study, vocational education, general education, community service, and guidance. To a large group of "jurors" consisting of junior college administrators, leaders in journalism education, university faculty members concerned with junior college education, and education editors and school reporters for metropolitan newspapers, he submitted for rating more than a hundred "criteria" specifying various types of content. His published report lists the 38 criteria which received the highest mean ratings and which he suggests might be useful in individual junior colleges as a basis for a "self-evaluation check list." Of the 38 criteria, 14 were related to general education, 8 each to guidance and vocational education, and 4 each to preparation for advanced study and community service, from which one may infer that the college newspaper can be so organized and produced as to foster attainment of all important purposes of the institution. This inference is supported by the content specified in illustrative criteria: announcement and reports of art exhibits, concerts, musicales, and other events held on campus or in the community (general education); descriptions of placement services and procedures for graduates of vocational curriculums (vocational education); descriptions of opportunities for club membership and/or participation in student body activities (guidance); reports of visits by counselors or other representatives of four-year colleges or universities to interview or assist prospective students (preparation for advanced study); announcement or descriptions of special cultural events planned by regular faculty and the student body for parents or other members of the community, such as art exhibits, concerts, lectures, etc. (community service).

The project on assembly programs was done by Rogers (*74*), a sponsor of such programs in a junior college who sought, as a part of the project, the practices and opinions in a number of junior colleges in Colorado, Kansas, Missouri, Nebraska, and Oklahoma. Inquiry for "best programs" brought response in great variety. Among those named were a concert from a visiting college group on tour, senior day assembly for seniors from surrounding high schools, speech by a visiting university dean, French class skit and songs, pep club program, and student senate talent show featuring students of outstanding ability in different entertainment fields. Among recommendations in the interest of improving junior college assembly programs drawn from the project are the following: The committee arranging the programs should include a competent, interested, enthusiastic sponsor and several energetic students. The committee should have a regular meeting time, should set up its aims in the light of school objectives, and plan a schedule of programs early in the school year. A high percentage of student participation should exist. Some audience participation is desirable. Most assemblies should have some good music. Adequate screening and follow-up evaluation should be made. A few good programs from outside the school are advisable but, on the whole, programs should represent accomplishments from within the school. Attendance and good attitudes should be promoted through publicity, worthwhile programs, and teacher and student build-up.

The extracurriculum for adults.—The state of development of extracurriculum programs for adult evening part-time students is not markedly dissimilar from that indicated above for guidance for this group. Despite large enrollments in evening classes, with many junior colleges having more evening than daytime students, most institutions are without extracurriculum programs for adults or operate them on a meager basis. In some part this is explainable by the role that courses taken play in the lives of these adults: while most are known to pursue these courses for occupational advancement, for a large minority they may be regarded as recreational and cultural and, therefore, somewhat analogous to the extracurriculum in the life of the full-time student. Besides, the method of teaching in courses for adults often becomes less authoritarian and involves more student participation than with younger persons in full-time programs. However, it is not difficult to convince oneself of the desirability of greater development of the extracurriculum on behalf of part-time adult students.

Few expositions of such programs have appeared in print. One of the best of these concerns the extracurriculum in the Evening Division of Los Angeles City College and was made by the dean of that division (*28*). When the report was prepared, the program had been in operation for eight years. The student body organization is described as a "federation" of evening student clubs and societies, each group being entitled to two representatives on a Student Executive Board which elects its own officers each year. This may be seen to differ from the student body organization of daytime colleges, which always includes also representatives elected from the freshman and sophomore class organizations.

Several "phases" of the extracurriculum program are identified. Appreciation of the importance of cultural activities as a necessary part of a college student's life finds expression in a lecture and concert fund. Well-known lecturers and artists are brought to the campus, with admission to all performances free. A second phase provides opportunities for artistic expression on the part of students themselves, in musical performances, dance exhibitions, talent shows, etc. Mentioned in this connection is a "Festival of Arts," with a week of special programs, including an art exhibit with prizes for work by students, a theater production, a book exhibit, and a concert. A third phase encourages integration of college and community by allocating funds for student body membership in civic, cultural, and professional organizations active in the community.

Among clubs in operation are the first one, which came into being as the result of requests by evening students and which has become the official service club of the evening college; one which provides a program of activities of special interest to students in the social sciences; a club to provide additional opportunity to practice spoken and written Spanish; a theater arts group; and a psychology club which publishes its own newspaper, sponsors monthly meetings with guest speakers and demonstrations dealing with subjects like group dynamics, hypnosis, etc., and arranges field trips to observe police work, retarded children, and medical facilities for mental health.

The author of the article is convinced that the development he describes "has enriched the academic program by supplementing classroom instruction and making it more meaningful for students" and "has helped the faculty and administration to provide a more effective educational program."

The extracurriculum and student leadership.—In concluding consideration of student organizations and activities it is in point to canvass briefly their relationship to student leadership, even though, being manifestly intimate, it may seem gratuitous to do so. It deserves mention in advance that, in appraising the "participating functions" of student self-government and cocurricular activities, the evaluators in the Raines project, in their attempt to quantify their assessment of the scope and quality of all student personnel functions, arrived at relatively high ratings. Both these functions were rated among the five highest in the full array of 21 functions (*18, 21*). Whatever the causes, whether in administrators' and/or faculty members' convictions of values or in students' enthusiasms or both, these organizations and activities are already at a relatively well-developed status compared with other personnel functions.

The administrators' belief in the potential values is reflected in the introduction of courses in student leadership for officers in student organizations. In his report on general education in the junior colleges of California, Johnson cited evidence to the effect that in 1951 as many as 16 of these institutions were giving such courses. He listed the following topics as being ordinarily included: student government and activities, student association constitution, parliamentary procedures, public speaking, actual group leadership, and actual practice in club leadership (*44, 296*).

Description of one of the earliest of these courses, called "Group Dynamics," a one-hour course in Compton College required of presidents of all student organizations and open to other students, has been provided by Siemens (*82*). He stated his belief that training along the lines provided in the course is valuable and essential not only for the improvement of student government, but also "for the deferred values that these abilities and practices will have for the students in their adult living." The class work of the course was concentrated into the first part of the semester in order that the training should have an early effect on the groups governed by the students. One hour a week was devoted to lectures and assignments concerning parliamentary law, development of leadership qualities, group thinking and action, committee procedures, preparing the agenda, responsibilities of various officers, and similar problems and procedures of a democratic group in action. A second class meeting each week was devoted to a laboratory session in which practice in the various techniques and procedures was entered into by each student. Siemens, in evaluating the course, said that a number of faculty sponsors of student groups reported improved morale in their clubs, more efficient and effective meetings, and a greater feeling of security on the part of the student presidents, and that the student council, which had legislative and executive control of student body activities, conducted its business in a much more effective manner.

Because the educative effectiveness of student organizations and activities is conditioned by the attitudes of faculty and students, it is pertinent to draw on a compilation of opinions of student leaders as to what hindered or hampered them in their efforts at discharging their responsibilities. The compilation was made by Rhoades in late summer by submitting a questionnaire to June graduates of California junior colleges who had served as student leaders (*70*). It is based on responses from something more than a hundred graduates about equally divided between men and women and representing 26 institutions. In answer to the question of what faculty members did that hampered most, recurrent responses referred to the following behavior and attitudes: domination and control of activities; lack of confidence in students' abilities; lack of interest in and cooperation in student activities; and holding to traditional ways of doing things. Concerning what faculty members did to help brought the following more frequent answers: helped with ideas, knowledge, and experience; were understanding, kind, and interested; participated, attended affairs, and worked; encouraged initiative and gave credit. Among hindrances by fellow leaders most often charged were: undependability and inefficiency; interference with other leaders; unwillingness to contribute or cooperate; and desiring glory without working for it. Help from other leaders was indicated to come from: cooperation in each other's activities; giving ideas and making suggestions; being friendly, considerate, and appreciative; doing their share of work; and being dependable and reliable. Suggestions these leaders would be disposed to make to the faculty are: be interested and friendly; participate in activities and attend student affairs; guide rather than control; and teach the techniques of leadership. A general regard for the admonitions expressed and implicit in these opinions should redound to the efficacy of the organizations and activities.

In considering student leadership, comment should be made on the relationship of the cocurricular activities and the provision for student government through the student council, associated students, or whatever it is called in given junior colleges. In almost all situations this central executive and legislative body is the coordinating agency for the clubs and other organizations and activities. It is often referred to as "student self-government," a term which expresses an ideal the degree of attainment of which varies from one institution to another, and is dependent on the willingness of the administration to concede authority and of the ability of the student body to assume responsibility. Control and coordination of the extracurriculum is a good place for the student body organization to begin assumption of responsibility for school affairs.

In summarizing reports on the status of student self-government in large junior colleges, Raines and McDaniel say that it existed in some form on all of the campuses. It took the form in most instances "of a student council serving as the leadership body for a group of student clubs, and also providing the leadership for a limited program of recreational and entertainment activities for the entire student body." They make the further observation that the weakest student personnel programs were about as apt to have favorable cocurricular activities as the strongest programs, but that many more of the stronger programs had what were appraised as favorable implementations of "student self-governing" (45).

In their appraisal of student personnel programs Raines and McDaniel cite two illustrative descriptions presenting contrasting programs of the student self-governing function, one of which refers to how "the student government organizations involve themselves in community problems" and "the Dean of Men spends considerable time in working with students to develop leadership and student involvement in real and valuable community projects." The description of the other, and presumably less commendable, program shows the student council restricted to social and interest needs of students with no involvement with the community. We have in the first of these programs exemplification of one of the several components of community service that make of the local public junior college a *community* college. Other components include adult education programs, part-time cooperative and work-experience programs, and cooperative efforts on problems and in activities of the community through students under the supervision of teachers in regular courses, as in social studies, music and the other arts, health, recreation, and the like.

More than two decades ago Bottrell analyzed the responses of 119 sponsors and supervisors of community services to an inquiry from which he reported a classification of these service activities of students (8). He prefaced his report with a definition of community service as "responsible, directed participation by students in the services and activities of local agencies, organizations, and groups, involving cooperative arrangements between the colleges and the community, organized services in the form of activities and projects, and supervision of student participation." He also summarized the "values" as seen by the sponsors consulted, most of which are quoted: "Student participation in service to the community is valuable in the general education of students. . . . Students enjoy such participation . . . and the personal and social satisfaction associated with it. . . . Participation . . . affords an effective medium for guidance. . . . Participating students show social growth, increased community understanding, and more responsible citizenship. . . . Community service provides realistic student experience through a planned approach to community participation and learning to do by doing. . . . Service activities and student participation in them reduce isolation of the college and withdrawal by the community by acquainting the community with the resources . . . of the college and the potentialities of youth as community workers."

Reported to Bottrell by the sponsors was an impressive array of community service activities which had actually been carried on under their supervision. These he classified under nine areas, with subcategories of individual or group participation under each. The areas are listed here, with illustrations under each for the sake of concreteness. Some of the specific activities must have been strictly extracurricular, others curricular in the sense of being connected with course instruction in the junior colleges, while still others would seem to lend themselves to use in either connection. The reader may care to speculate over where they might be used, that is, whether in curriculum, extracurriculum, or both. The areas and illustrations are as follows: (1) leadership in youth groups (Girl

Scouts, Boy Scouts, Hi-Y, youth center work); (2) assistance in welfare and social agencies(service in community house, carnival to raise funds for underprivileged camp, welfare projects at Christmastime); (3) leadership in church and religious organizations (young people's organizations, church youth work); (4) recreational leadership (playground leaders or supervisors, camp counselors); (5) child-care services (child-care aides, work in nursery and kindergarten schools, work in day nurseries); (6) Red Cross services (nurse's aide, blood bank, fund-raising campaign); (7) tours and excursions (tours to social and welfare agencies, tours to settlement house, orphanage, slum-clearance project); (8) community surveys and field study (survey of recreation needs, survey of population trends, survey of housing conditions, community surveys); (9) projects in cooperation with community (hostesses at USO, music for community clubs and other groups, talks for community clubs and other organizations, entertainment and visitation in hospitals, work with League of Women Voters).

The great diversity of opportunities for community services suggested by these illustrations and the fact that they are applicable variously in the curriculum, in the extracurriculum, or in both makes it essential that in the individual institution a plan of organization, assignment, and coordination be devised for them. Bottrell found that a majority of the junior colleges represented in his study had no plan of coordination and he identified several types of organization (9). In the instance of the large junior college cited above from Raines and McDaniel, the Dean of Men appears to have carried this responsibility through the student governing body. Usually this body would assume responsibilities only for the extracurricular community services, and it is necessary for overall coordination to include both the curricular and the extracurricular, in order that these experiences, which are valuable in preparation for responsibility and leadership of the student and in services to the community, be distributed with optimum effectiveness at both giving and receiving ends.

A galvanizing influence on learning.—The foregoing portrayal and consideration of student organizations and activities, including their manifestations both on campus and in the community, to the extent that claims made for them are at all tenable, appear to have an impressive potential for the education of the later adolescent. This is implicit in the long list of specific activities related to subject matter disciplines, to vocations and the professions, and to recreations and hobbies, as well as in the all-college student organizations like the student council or associated students. The activities and organizations as a whole, therefore, may be assumed to have impact on both general and vocational education, with, perhaps, more on general than vocational. As compared to the curriculum offering, they seem at present to have (a) considerable advantage in the self-propulsion in the initiative of student participants and (b) the fact that, because they almost always involve *groups* of later adolescents, they more often draw on the leverage inherent in the peer culture. In reviewing the merits of these activities and organizations one should not overlook the opportunities they set up for assumption and discharge of responsibilities by the participants, which in turn provide growth toward maturity.

Some may see in the mention of advantages in motivation in student activities and organizations identified above a deprecation of the regular program of instruction. To the contrary, it is reaffirmed that the curriculum is and should be a school's major avenue to learning. There may be, however, an admonition for teachers in the difference noted, to the effect that their procedures relinquish some of the traditional reliance on the lecture and other authoritarian methods and that they resort more often to those which invite student initiative and participation and allow for the play of the peer group culture.

Summary

Guidance as a purpose of the junior college, which was only partially foreshadowed during the institution's earlier years, has become increasingly prominent as the movement has grown. The need for well-developed and comprehensive programs of guidance is sustained by the evidence concerning later adolescents canvassed in the chapters of Part I, which need not be reviewed here, but which concerns physical growth and status, mental development, personal and social development, sexual and dating behavior, and vocational and avocational activities and interests. Many of these needs emerge again in the chapters of Part II and become more particularized because the evidence concerns students in junior college years rather than the generality of adolescents. Among the kinds of evidence are the wide variation in aptitude, as compared with those in more selective higher institutions, the larger proportions from lower socioeconomic status, the larger proportion with academic disabilities, the wider variation in personal attitudes and traits, the need for help in selecting careers and avocational concerns, and the prevalence of problems that spread over the full range of life and living. The need is inherent in the first two college years in any institution but is greatly augmented for the comprehensive community college which has the most widely diversified offering of institutions operating at this level at the same time that its policy of open-doorness admits students of the widest range of abilities, characteristics, and interests.

By the middle of the century leaders in the field were proposing almost comprehensive student personnel programs. The American Association of Junior Colleges through committees has promoted their development, and its efforts in the early 1960s culminated in initiation and prosecution of what is known as the Raines project involving investigation and promotion of personnel programs in junior colleges on a nationwide scale. The report distributed the activities to more than a score of "basic personnel functions" which were grouped under seven areas: orientation, appraisal, consultation, participation, regulation, service, and organizational. The nature of the most of these basic functions is apparent in the following digest based on a large body of pertinent investigation and literature.

The almost universally stated basis for admission to local public junior colleges is high school graduation, with infrequent specification of subjects. A frequent alternative basis is age (usually over 18). A small proportion of variants are to be found, such as placing graduates in lower portions of the distributions on probation and admitting superior high school seniors for part-time work. Procedures of admission in many junior colleges specify the taking of a "guidance examination" and other tests, but it is clear that these are for purposes of advisement and not for selection and exclusion.

In gathering information about students the junior colleges administer tests and inventories. Among those more often used than others are tests of general ability or aptitude and broad subject matter and achievement (English, mathematics, reading), interest inventories, and tests of special aptitude. The colleges often have measures of intelligence which come up with the records from high school. Study habits inventories and instruments for screening for problems related to mental health are less often used. As stated above, in harmony with the open-door policy, the test scores are used chiefly for counseling and placement and seldom for selection of students.

The measures from the tests and inventories are entered on cumulative records for the individual student, which often reach back into secondary school and even elementary school careers and include an extensive array of data concerning such matters as the student's academic record, health information, activities and interests, educational and vocational plans, work experiences, honors received, etc. Chief usefulness of these data is in counseling, placement, and research.

Group guidance is provided by orientation courses and others in the Psychology of Adjustment and on Careers. A large proportion of institutions offer the orientation course and make it a requirement of freshmen. Content in it varies but is concerned with the students' adjustment to college and to life. The course described at some length above and of which student appraisal was reported includes seven "units," each of which consists of two or more "focuses" set up to induce consideration of such matters as the local institution and its student personnel services; being a college student; one's personal image; one's genetic and environmental origins; problems of contemporary society; choice of vocation and recreations;

love, sex, and marriage; and mental health. When offered, the courses on Psychology of Adjustment and Careers are elective.

Another means of orientation is the student handbook, often a project fostered by the student body organization. The information spreads to a wide variety of items classifiable under such headings as preliminary matter, regulations, information on course offerings, student services, student organizations and activities, and other advisory and informative items.

Analyses of junior college catalogs to arrive at a generic picture of student services suggests that the kinds of service include counseling and guidance; placement; financial help through scholarships, loan funds, and part-time employment; and attention to health and housing. It must be said, however, that the references to services respecting health are less reassuring than on others and that provisions relating to housing are scanty because it can hardly be a major concern for institutions with only small proportions of noncommuters attending.

Educational and vocational counseling, which may be regarded in large part as a single guidance service for the junior college age group, appears to have experienced greater development than placement and attention to emotional adjustment. Placement services, however, have been increasing, although the focus has been much more on the student transferring to senior college, with less concern for graduates seeking employment and even less for the drop-out. Follow-up studies are essential to the effectiveness of placement. A cogent array of conclusions and implications concerning placement of transfers was derived from their nationwide follow-up by Knoell and Medsker (findings of which were drawn upon in Chapter 7) which, if respected in practice, would encourage success of transfers and bring on improved articulation of junior and senior colleges.

The relatively undeveloped state of guidance for emotional adjustment is in line with the infrequent resort in junior colleges to screening for problems in mental health. It is perhaps explainable by the greater intangibility of the problems and the reticence of adolescents in this area. Blos, a specialist with long experience in counseling college students, has identified as problem types students who cannot study and complain of inability to concentrate; who are lonely and cannot make friends; who are afraid of examinations or unable to speak in class; who are without purpose or vocational aim; who are habitual evaders and complainers; who are in acute conflict with their families; and who have physical defects.

The values claimed for participation in student organizations and activities—the extracurriculum or cocurriculum—are usually cast in terms of general education, with emphasis on improvement in interpersonal relationships. When attention is turned to particularizations in these broad areas, reference is made to "socialization," experience in "social cooperation," "ethical living," "citizenship in a democracy," "training for leadership," recreational and aesthetic participation, and exploration. In addition, some of the claims fall outside the general area and mention preparation along the lines of one's vocational interests.

Few objective investigations of the attainment of the values claimed have been made. To a degree such as have been reported show increased participation as an outcome of counseling, some increase in socialization of the individual, and participation usually without detriment to academic success. In this failure to substantiate claims by objective inquiry the advocates of student activities differ little from advocates of subjects in the curriculum, who have not often conducted studies to justify their claims.

The organizations and activities found to be operative in junior colleges are wide in variety and large in number. For 21 junior colleges the clubs and related organizations were found to range over ten groups (in addition to student body and class organizations): subject interests; occupational; music, art, and crafts; political; physical; hobbies; service; religious; scholastic and other honorary; and miscellaneous. The total array of different interests exceeded a hundred, with an average of about 19 per institution, and usually with some relationship between size of enrollment and number of organizations.

The student activities going forward in the same junior colleges were classified under four divisions, namely, intercollegiate athletics, intramural activities, speech and dramatics, and publications. The larger numbers of institutions reporting intercollegiate athletics than intramural sports suggest that some junior colleges are already tending to stress the former to the neglect of the physical welfare of the general student body.

For two all-college activities on which reports were available, it appears that it is possible to serve purposes like those generally accepted for the public junior college.

The extracurriculum is much less well developed for adult part-time students than for students in the daytime program. The disparity is almost as great as for student personnel programs. However, a description was found in the literature of a strong activities program in an evening junior college, demonstrating that such development is feasible.

Efforts to increase the effectiveness of student organizations and activities and improve the leadership in them have included courses in leadership which are required of student officers. Inquiry made of student leaders as to the attitudes of faculty members that hampered them most found these to be domination and control, lack of confidence in students' activities, lack of interest and cooperation, and holding to traditional ways of doing things. The things they did that helped most were helping with ideas, knowledge, and experience; being understanding, kind, and interested;

participating; and encouraging initiative and giving credit. Among hindrances by fellow leaders were undependability and inefficiency, interference, unwillingness to cooperate, and desiring glory without working for it; while help from other leaders came through such activities and attitudes as cooperation, supplying ideas, being friendly and considerate, doing their share of work, and being dependable.

Coordination of the organizations and activities is accomplished in the junior colleges through the central organization of the student body, such as the student council or associated students. It is Raines and McDaniel's observation that junior colleges with the weakest student personnel programs were about as apt to have favorable cocurricular activities as the strongest programs, but that many more of the stronger programs have what were appraised as "favorable implementations of student self-governing." One may infer also that these institutions with stronger student government arrange for more services to the community.

Community services may be and are rendered by students not only through the extracurriculum but also through the curriculum, by being incorporated with course instruction. An investigation by Bottrell involving sponsors and supervisors of community services in junior colleges identified a long and diverse list which he grouped under headings like leadership in youth groups, assistance in welfare and social agencies, recreational leadership, child-care services, community surveys and field study, etc. Examination of the specific services shows some of them appropriate for the curriculum, some for the extracurriculum, and still others suitable in either relationship. His summary of the values to students of participation refers to values in general education, enjoyment, and personal and social satisfaction; social growth, increased community understanding, and more responsible citizenship; and realistic experience through a planned approach to community participation.

As a whole, student organizations and activities appear to have an impressive potential for the education of the later adolescent. As compared with the curriculum, they seem at present to have the advantages of (a) self-propulsion in student initiative to participate and (b) the fact that they can draw on the momentum of the peer culture. If this seems in deprecation of the regular program of instruction which is and should be after all the main avenue to an education, it is so because the teachers often place too great reliance on the lecture and other authoritarian methods instead of resorting more often to procedures inviting student initiative and participation and allowing for the play of the peer culture.

References and Bibliography

1. Aldrich, Margaret G. "An Exploratory Study of Social Guidance at the College Level." *Journal of Educational and Psychological Measurements*, 2 (Feb., 1942), 209-16.
2. Anderson, Bert D. "Placement Service for the Drop-Out Student." *Junior College Journal*, 27 (Nov., 1956), 141-44.
3. Aumack, Gordon D. "Experiences of Compton College Guidance Office in Developing a Twenty-Year Educational Follow-up Study." *Junior College Journal*, 22 (Nov., 1951), 158-63.
4. Bennett, Margaret E. "Trends in Junior College Orientation Courses." *Junior College Journal* (April, 1934), 353-57.
5. Berdie, R. F. "Prediction of College Achievement and Satisfaction." *Journal of Applied Psychology*, 28 (1944), 239-45.
6. Berman, Sidney. "Psychotherapeutic Techniques with Adolescents." *American Journal of Orthopsychiatry*, 24 (April, 1954), 238-45.
7. Blos, Peter. "Psychological Counseling of College Students." *American Journal of Orthopsychiatry*, 16 (1946), 571-80.
8. Bottrell, Harold R. "Opportunities for Community Service." *Junior College Journal*, 18 (Sept., 1947), 12-19.
9. Bottrell, Harold R. "Patterns of Organization in Community Service." *Junior College Journal*, 18 (Oct., 1947), 57-63.
10. Bottrell, Harold R. "Techniques in Community Service." *Junior College Journal*, 18 (Nov., 1947), 128-34.
11. Bown, Oliver H., and Richek, Herbert G. "Mental Health of Junior College Students." *Junior College Journal,* 37 (Dec., 1966–Jan., 1967), 18-21.*
12. Brayfield, Arthur H. "Functions of a Student-Counseling Service." *Journal of Higher Education,* 24 (Jan., 1953), 30-34.
13. Brower, Daniel. "The Relation between Intelligence and MMPI Scores." *Journal of Social Psychology*, 25 (May, 1947), 243-45.
14. Brumbaugh, A. J. "Better Student Personnel Services in Junior Colleges." *Junior College Journal*, 21 (Sept., 1950), 37-41.
15. Burke, Ada P. "A Look at Student Government." *Junior College Journal*, 27 (Nov., 1956), 150-53.
16. Burman, Arthur C. "The Emotional Adjustment of Junior College Students." *Junior College Journal*, 24 (April, 1954), 491-96.
17. Carlin, Leslie O. "Present Status of Counseling Records in Public Junior Colleges." *Junior College Journal*, 21 (Dec., 1950), 240-42.
18. Collins, Charles C. *Junior College Student Personnel Programs—What They Are and What They Should Be.* Washington: American Association of Junior Colleges, 1967.
19. Cowley, William H.; Hoppock, Robert; and Williamson, E. G. *Occupational Orientation of College Students.* Washington: American Council on Education, 1939.
20. Curry, E. M. "Sources and Expenditures of Student Activity Fees in the Community-Junior Colleges of Illinois." *Junior College Journal*, 20 (Nov., 1949), 141-45.
21. Darley, John G. *The Use of Tests in College.* Washington: American Council on Education, 1949.
22. DeRidder, Lawrence M. "Comparative Scholastic Achievements of Native and Transfer Students." *Junior College Journal*, 22 (Oct., 1951), 83-85.
23. Dula, Thomas J., and Schultz, Raymond E. "Academic Probation and Suspension Practices in Public Junior Colleges." *Junior College Journal*, 32 (Oct., 1961), 78-83.
24. Durnall, Edward J., Jr. "A Testing Program for a Junior College for Women." *Junior College Journal,* 23 (Jan., 1953), 261-67.

25. Engelhart, Max D. "Examinations to Facilitate Transfer of Junior College Graduates to Senior Colleges." *Junior College Journal*, 20 (Feb., 1950), 332-36.
26. Engelhart, Max D. "Testing for Guidance and Placement in the Junior College." *Junior College Journal*, 18 (Sept., 1947), 3-11.
27. Farnsworth, Dana L., M.D. *Mental Health in College and University*. Cambridge: Harvard University Press, 1957.
28. Fox, Frederick G. "For Adults Only: An Extracurricular Program for Evening Students." *Junior College Journal*, 27 (Oct., 1956), 86-89.
29. Freedman, M. "Some Observations of Students as They Relate to Orientation Procedures in Colleges and Universities." *Journal of College Student Personnel*, 2 (Oct., 1960), 2-10.
30. Fry, Clements C. *Mental Health in College*. New York: Commonwealth Fund, 1942.
31. Gough, Harrison G. "Predicting Social Participation." *Journal of Social Psychology*, 35 (May, 1952), 227-33.
32. Gough, Harrison G. "Factors Relating to the Academic Achievement of High School Students." *Journal of Educational Psychology*, 40 (Feb., 1949), 65-78.
33. Grant, Claud W. "How Students Perceive the Counselor's Role." *Personnel and Guidance Journal*, 32 (March, 1954), 386-88.
34. Harmon, Lindsey R., and Wiener, Daniel N. "Use of the MMPI in Vocational Advisement." *Journal of Applied Psychology*, 29 (April, 1945), 132-41.
35. Harrington, Johns H. "Criteria for Rating Junior College Student Newspapers." *Junior College Journal*, 30 (Jan., 1960), 254-58.
36. Hawkes, G. "Use of the MMPI in Screening College Students for Counseling Purposes." *Journal of Education Psychology*, 41 (March, 1950), 116-21.
37. Hill, Reuben. "An Experimental Study of Social Adjustment." *American Sociological Review*, 9 (1944), 481-94.
38. Hoppock, Robert. "Courses in Careers." *Journal of Higher Education*, 3 (Oct., 1932), 365-68.
39. Hopkins, E. H. "The Essentials of a Student Personnel Program." *Educational and Psychological Measurements*, 8 (Autumn, 1948), 430-50.
40. Hoyt, Donald P. "Predicting Grades in Two-Year Terminal Programs." *Junior College Journal*, 36 (Feb., 1966), 20-23.
41. Hudson, Robert I. "Vocational Guidance in the Junior College." *Junior College Journal*, 78 (Feb., 1957), 343-45.
42. Humphreys, J. Anthony. "Personnel Service in the Junior College." *Junior College Journal*, 8 (Oct., 1937), 26-30.
43. Humphreys, J. Anthony. "Toward Improved Programs of Student Personnel Services." *Junior College Journal*, 22 (March, 1952), 382-92.
44. Johnson, B. Lamar. *General Education in Action*. Washington: American Council on Education, 1952.
45. *Junior College Student Personnel Programs: Appraisal and Development*. Washington: American Association of Junior Colleges, 1965.
46. Kirk, Barbara A.; Cummings, Roger W.; and Goodstein, Leonard D. "The Differential Validity of the College Ability Test for Transfer Students in Six Current Fields." *Junior College Journal*, 33 (Nov., 1962), 131-40.
47. Knoell, Dorothy M., and Medsker, Leland L. *From Junior to Senior College: A National Study of the Transfer Student*. Washington: American Council on Education, 1965.
48. Koos, Leonard V. "Analysis of the General Literature on Extra-Curricular Activities." In Twenty-fifth Yearbook of the National Society for the Study of Education, part 2, *Extra-Curricular Activities*, ch. 2. Bloomington, Ill.: Public School Publishing Co., 1926.
49. Koos, Leonard V. "Some Essentials in Student Personnel Work." *Junior College Journal*, 10 (May, 1940), 602-9.

50. Leuenberger, Harold W. "Occupational Information Needed by Students." *Junior College Journal*, 8 (Oct. 19, 1937), 31-32.
51. Lubick, Emil E. "Vocational Objectives of Entering Junior College Students." *Junior College Journal*, 25 (Feb., 1955), 319-26.
52. McDaniel, J. W. *Essential Student Personnel Practices for Junior Colleges*. Washington: American Association of Junior Colleges, 1962.
53. Matson, Jane. "Statements on Student Rights." *Junior College Journal*, 38 (Nov., 1967), 38.
54. Meinecke, Charlotte D. "Placement and Follow-up in Junior Colleges." *Junior College Journal*, 19 (Oct., 1948), 59-67.
55. Meinecke, Charlotte D. "Student Government and the Honor Code." *Junior College Journal*, 23 (April, 1953), 426-34.
56. Mitchell, Guy C. "Guidance in Higher Education." *Junior College Journal*, 22 (Dec., 1951), 207-15.
57. Mohs, Milton C. *Annual Report of the Placement Bureau, 1962*. Pasadena, Cal.: Pasadena City College, 1962.
58. Mohs, Milton C. *Employer Evaluations of 1,000 Placements*. Pasadena, Cal.: Pasadena City College, 1961.
59. Mohs, Milton C. *Service Through Placement in the Junior College*. Washington: American Association of Junior Colleges, 1962.
60. Mueller, Kate H., et al. *Counseling for Mental Health*. American Council on Education Studies, series VI, Student Personnel Work, no. 8. Washington: American Council on Education, 1947.
61. O'Connor, Thomas J. *Follow-up Studies in Junior Colleges: A Tool for Institutional Improvement*. Washington: American Association of Junior Colleges, 1965.
62. Olsen, Lionel R. "Promoting the Junior College Club Program." *California Journal of Secondary Education*, 34 (May, 1959), 295-99.
63. Osborne, R. T.; Sanders, Wilma; and Young, Florence M. "MMPI Patterns of College Disciplinary Cases." *Journal of Counseling Psychology*, 3 (Spring, 1956), 52-56.
64. *Personnel Services in Education*. 58th Yearbook of the National Society for the Study of Education, part II. Chicago: University of Chicago Press, 1959.
65. Prator, Ralph. "Administering Junior College Athletics." *Junior College Journal*, 24 (Jan., 1954), 278-84.
66. Raines, Max R. "The Student Personnel Situation." *Junior College Journal*, 36 (Feb., 1966), 6-8.
67. Reinhard, Herb F. "The Union Is the Center." *Junior College Journal*, 37 (May, 1967), 29-30.
68. Remmlein, Madaline K. "Scholastic Accomplishments as Affected by Intelligence and Participation in Extra-curricular Activities." *Journal of Applied Psychology*, 23 (Oct., 1939), 602-7.
69. Reynolds, James W. "Community Services." In *The Public Junior College*, 55th Yearbook of the National Society for the Study of Education, part I, ch. 8. Chicago: University of Chicago Press, 1956.
70. Rhoades, Otto. "Student Leaders Speak Up." *Junior College Journal*, 14 (Sept., 1943), 300-304.
71. Rice, Louis A. "A Suggested Student Personnel Philosophy for the Junior College." *Junior College Journal*, 21 (April, 1951), 457-60.
72. Rodes, H. P. "Successful Transfer in Engineering." *Junior College Journal*, 20 (Nov., 1949), 121-27.
73. Rogers, Carl R. "Significant Aspects of Client Centered Therapy." *American Psychologist*, 1 (1946), 415-22.
74. Rogers, Lucille V. "Junior College Assembly Programs Are Important." *Junior College Journal*, 24 (Nov., 1955), 152-55.
75. Rothney, John W. M. *Guidance Practices and Results*. New York: Harper & Brothers, 1958.

76. Schmidt, Hermann O. "Test Profiles as a Diagnostic Aid: The MMPI." *Journal of Applied Psychology,* 29 (April, 1945), 115–31.
77. Schultz, Raymond E. "Impact of Academic Probation and Suspension Practices on Junior College Students." *Junior College Journal,* 32 (June, 1962), 271–75.
78. Seashore, Harold. "Tests as Aids to Administration and Counseling in Junior Colleges." *Junior College Journal,* 26 (May, 1956), 504–8.
79. Seibel, Dean W. "Measurement and Evaluation." *Junior College Journal,* 38 (Nov., 1967), 13–16.
80. Seibel, Dean W. *Testing Practices and Problems in Junior Colleges—A Survey.* Princeton, N.J.: Educational Testing Service, 1966.
81. Sheldon, William D., and Landsman, Theodore. "Investigation of Nondirective Group Therapy with Students in Academic Difficulty." *Journal of Consulting Psychology,* 14 (June, 1950), 210–15.
82. Siemens, Cornelius H. "Group Dynamics in Action." *Junior College Journal,* 19 (Dec., 1948), 208–12.
83. Siemens, Cornelius H. "Predicting Success of Transfer Students." *Junior College Journal,* 14 (Sept., 1943), 24–28.
84. Shepard, Charles E. "Health Programs in California Junior Colleges." *Junior College Journal,* 11 (Oct., 1940), 65–71.
85. Spencer, George M. "A Freshman Orientation Program." *Journal of Higher Education,* 25 (May, 1954), 272–74.
86. Stehr, Bennie W. "The Development of an Adequate Faculty-Advisor Service." *Junior College Journal,* 27 (Dec., 1956), 194–96.
87. Stern, George G.; Stein, Morris I.; and Bloom, Benjamin S. *Methods in Personality Assessment.* Glencoe, Ill.: The Free Press, 1956.
88. Thorndike, Robert L. "The Background of Standardized Tests in Colleges." *Junior College Journal,* 26 (May, 1956), 509–13.
89. Torrance, E. Paul. "Some Practical Uses of a Knowledge of Self-Concepts in Counseling and Guidance." *Educational and Psychological Measurement,* 14 (Spring, 1954), 120–27.
90. Traxler, Arthur E. "Establishing a Functional Guidance Program in a Junior College." *Junior College Journal,* 22 (Feb., 1952), 309–20.
91. Williamson, E. G., and Bordin, E. S. "Evaluating Counseling by Means of a Control-Group Experiment." *School and Society,* 52 (Nov. 2, 1940), 434–40.
92. Williamson, E. G. "An Outsider's View of Junior College Guidance Programs." *Junior College Journal,* 30 (May, 1960), 489–501.
93. Williamson, E. G. *Counseling Adolescents.* New York: McGraw-Hill Book Co., 1950.
94. Williamson, E. G. "The Extra-Curriculum and General Education." In 51st Yearbook of the National Society for the Study of Education, part I, *General Education,* ch. 11. Chicago: University of Chicago Press, 1952.
95. Williamson, E. G., ed. *Trends in Student Personnel Work.* Minneapolis: University of Minnesota Press, 1949.
96. Wrenn, C. Gilbert, and Kamm, Robert B. "A Procedure for Evaluating a Student Personnel Program." *School and Society,* 67 (April 3, 1948), 266–69.

Acknowledgments

As INDICATED in the Preface, *The Community College Student* is in large part a synthesis of published and other materials dealing with the population with which the book is concerned. This fact, joined with the sheer size of the work, has made it advisable to obtain a large number of permissions to quote and in other ways to cite from the many publications drawn upon. Following are the acknowledgments of these permissions which, for the books and monographs, indicate their publishers, authors, titles, and dates of copyright or publication, and for articles, specify the organizations sponsoring the periodicals, the authors, the titles of the articles or other publications, and the dates of issue. Wherever advised by the publishers, permission has been obtained also from the authors. Both publishers and authors have been generous in granting the permissions. In addition to the following acknowledgments, specific citations are made at the points of use to the References and Bibliographies at the ends of the chapters.

Acknowledgments for permissions from publishers to the trade to quote from their books and monographs are as follows:

American Guidance Service, Inc., from Edgar A. Doll, *The Measurement of Social Competence: A Manual for the Vineland Social Maturity Scale*, 1953.

Appleton-Century-Crofts, Inc., from P. W. Hutson, *The Guidance Function in Education*, rev. ed., 1968.

A. S. Barnes & Co., Inc., from Harvey C. Lehman and Paul A. Witty, *The Psychology of Play Activities*, 1927.

Consulting Psychologists Press, from Harrison G. Gough, *Manual for the California Psychological Inventory*, 1964.

Harper & Row, for the Thomas Alvah Edison Foundation, from James W. Wilson and Edward H. Lyons, *Work-Study College Programs*, 1961.

Holt, Rinehart, and Winston, Inc., from Gordon W. Allport, *Pattern and Growth in Personality*, 1961, and Winston W. Ehrmann, *Premarital Dating Behavior*, 1959.

Houghton Mifflin Co., from George G. Thompson, *Child Psychology: Growth Trends in Psychological Adjustment*, 1962.

The Macmillan Co., from Gordon W. Allport, *The Individual and His Religion: A Psychological Interpretation*, 1953; James S. Coleman, *The Adolescent Society: The Social Life of the Teenager and Its Impact on Education*, 1961; and Albert J. Reiss, Jr., *Occupations and Social Status*, 1961.

McGraw-Hill Book Co., from Leland L. Medsker, *The Junior College: Progress and Prospect*, 1960.

David McKay, Inc., from Robert J. Havighurst, *Human Development and Education*, 1953.

Prentice-Hall, Inc., from James E. Birren, *The Psychology of Aging*, 1964, and Francis J. Brown, *The Sociology of Childhood*, 1939.

W. B. Saunders Co., from Alfred C. Kinsey, Wardell B. Pomeroy, and Clyde E. Martin, *Sexual Behavior in the Human Male*, 1948, and Alfred C. Kinsey, Wardell B. Pomeroy, Clyde E. Martin, and Paul H. Gebhard, *Sexual Behavior in the Human Female*, 1953.

John Wiley & Sons, from James W. Thornton, Jr., *The Community Junior College*, rev. ed., 1966.

Williams & Wilkins Co., from David Wechsler, *The Measurement and Appraisal of Adult Intelligence*, 4th ed., 1958.

Acknowledgment for permission to use materials from their publications is made to three university presses, as follows:

University of California Press, for the Board of Regents of the University, from Harold E. Jones, *Motor Performance and Growth: A Developmental Study of Static and Dynamometric Strength*, 1949.

University of Chicago Press, from books: Leona M. Bayer and Nancy Bayley, *Growth Diagnosis: Selected Methods for Interpreting and Predicting Physical Development from One Year to Maturity*, 1959; Guy T. Buswell, *How Adults Read*, 1937; Alice M. Mitchell, *Children and Movies*, 1929. From the *American Journal of Sociology*, Clifford Kirkpatrick and Theodore Caplow, "Courtship in a Group of Minnesota Students," 51 (Sept., 1945), 114–25; and from the *School Review*, George D. Stoddard, "A Mental-Educational Survey of Iowa Junior Colleges," 36 (May, 1928), 346–49; B. Lamar Johnson, "Children's Reading Interests as Related to Sex and Grade in School," 40 (April, 1932), 257–72; LeRoy E. Barber, "Why Some Able High School Graduates Do Not Go to College," 59 (Feb., 1951), 93–96; Dale B. Harris, "Life Problems and Interests of Adolescents in 1936 and 1957," 67, no. 3 (Autumn, 1959), 335–49.

Stanford University Press, from Edward K. Strong, Jr., *Vocational Interests of Men and Women*, 1943.

Educational Testing Service has granted permission to quote from two reports by Dean W. Seibel, *A Study of the Academic Ability and Performance of Junior College Students,* 1965, and *Testing Practices and Problems in Junior Colleges—A Survey,* 1966, and from K. Patricia Cross, *The Junior College Student: A Research Description,* 1968.

Acknowledgments are made for permission to draw on materials appearing in a large number of periodicals (some of them organs), yearbooks, monographs, and other publications of professional societies and organizations. These associations and their publications are:

The Adult Education Association in *Adult Education*: Walter C. Eells, "The Community's College," 4 (Jan., 1945), 13–17; Charles E. Chapman, "Some Characteristics of Adult Part-Time Students," 10 (Autumn, 1959), 27–41; Frank Costin and Robert L. Johnston, "A Study of Achievement in an Introductory Psychology Course," 12 (Winter, 1962), 120-26.

The American Association of Junior Colleges in the *Junior College Journal*: S. V. Martorana, "Status of Adult Education in Junior Colleges," 18 (Feb., 1948), 322–31, and "Functional Family-Life Education in the Junior Colleges," 19 (Oct., 1948), 79–88; Charlotte D. Meinecke, "Placement and Follow-up in Junior Colleges," 19 (Oct., 1948), 59–67; Howard L. Putnam, "A Survey of New-Type General Courses in American Junior Colleges," 21 (March, 1951), 402–9; Joseph E. Lantagne, "An Analysis of Health Interests of 1,000 Junior College Students in California," 21 (April, 1951), 429–33, and "Items of Interest in Marriage and Parenthood of 2,000 Junior College Students," 26 (Dec., 1955), 210–18; Emil E. Lubick, "Vocational Objectives of Entering College Students," 25 (Feb., 1955), 319–26; M. J. Richards, "An Analysis of the Technical Education Provided by Accredited Junior Colleges," 28 (Oct., 1957), 105–8; Harold Seashore, "Academic Abilities of Junior College Students," 29 (Oct., 1958), 74–80. Also, from three other publications, *Junior College Student Personnel Programs: Appraisal and Development,* 1965; Charles C. Collins, *Junior College Student Personnel Programs—What They Are and What They Should Be,* 1967; Norman C. Harris, *Technical Education in the Junior College: New Programs for New Jobs,* 1964.

The American Personnel and Guidance Association in its *Personnel and Guidance Journal*: M. E. Deeg and Donald G. Paterson, "Change in Social Status of Occupations," 25 (Jan., 1947), 205–8; William W. Cooley and Susan J. Becker, "The Junior College Student," 44 (Jan., 1966), 464–69.

The American Psychological Association, from the *Journal of Abnormal Psychology*: E. V. Pullias, "Masturbation as a Mental Hygiene Problem— A Study of the Beliefs of 75 Young Men," 32 (July–Sept., 1937), 216–22;

from the *Journal of Abnormal and Social Psychology*: Robert T. Ross, "Measures of Sex Behavior in College Males Compared with Kinsey's Results," 45 (1950), 753–55; from the *Journal of Applied Psychology*: Ralph F. Berdie, "Scores on the Strong Vocational Interest Blank and the Kuder Preference Record in Relation to Self-Ratings," 34 (May, 1943), 257–77; Stuart M. Stoke and W. F. Clive, "The Avocations of One Hundred College Freshmen," 13 (1929), 257–63; G. J. Dudycha, "Religious Beliefs of College Students," 17 (1933), 585–603; Robert Kroger and C. M. Louttit, "The Influence of Fathers' Occupations on the Vocational Choices of High School Boys," 19 (1935), 203–12; W. L. Valentine, "Common Misconceptions of College Students," 20 (1936), 633–58; S. M. Wesley, D. Q. Corey, and B. M. Stewart, "The Intra-individual Relationship between Interest and Ability," 34 (June, 1950), 193–97; from the *Journal of Educational Psychology*: Herbert S. Conrad, Harold E. Jones, and H. H. Hsaio, "Sex Differences in Mental Growth and Decline," 24 (March, 1933), 161–69; Percival M. Symonds, "Happiness as Related to Problems and Interests," 28 (April, 1937), 290–94; Edward Roeber and Sol Garfield, "A Study of Occupational Interests of High School Students in Terms of Grade Placement," 34 (Sept., 1943), 355–62.

The American Sociological Association from the *Journal of Educational Sociology*: Paul A. Heist, "Diversity in College Student Characteristics," 33 (Feb., 1960), 279–91.

The National Association of Secondary School Principals from its *Bulletin*: Harold H. Punké, "Dating Practices of High School Youth," 28 (Jan., 1944), 47–54.

The National Council of Teachers of English, from Samuel Weingarten, *English in the Two-Year College*, 1965.

The National Council on Family Relations from the *Journal of Marriage and Family*: Judson T. Landis, "An Evaluation of Marriage Education," 10 (Fall, 1948), 100–101; Winston W. Ehrmann, "Student Cooperation in the Study of Dating Behavior," 14 (Nov., 1952), 322–26.

The National Education Association, from James G. Rice, *General Education: Current Ideas and Concerns*, 1964.

The National Recreation and Park Association from *Recreation*: E. B. Olds, "How Do Young People Use Their Leisure Time?" 42 (Jan., 1949), 458–63.

The National Society for the Study of Education from Nelson B. Henry, ed., *Adolescence*, Forty-third Yearbook, Part I, 1944.

The Society for Research in Child Development, from Frank N. Freeman and Charles D. Flory, *Growth in Intellectual Ability as Measured by Repeated Tests*, Monograph No. 2, 1937; Caroline M. Tryon, *Evaluation of Adolescent Personality by Adolescents,* Monograph No. 4, 1938; Frank K.

Shuttleworth, *Physical and Mental Growth of Boys and Girls Six to Nineteen in Relation to Age at Maximum Growth,* Monograph No. 3, 1939; Anna S. Espenshade, *Motor Performance in Adolescence,* No. 1, 1940.

The Society for the Advancement of Education from *School and Society*: Harold H. Punké, "High School Youth and Family Quarrels," 58 (Dec. 25, 1943), 507–11.

Acknowledgments for permission to quote from other professional journals and related publications as follows:

Educational and Psychological Measurement from Arden N. Frandsen and Alwyn D. Sessions, "Interests and School Achievement," 13 (Spring, 1953), 94–101.

Journal of Educational Research (published by Dembar Educational Research Services, Inc.) from David Segel and G. L. Brintle, "The Relation of Occupational Interest Scores as Measured by the Strong Vocational Interest Blank to Achievement Test Results and College Marks in Certain College Subject Groups," 27 (Feb., 1934), 442–45; Frances O. Triggs, "Further Comparison of Interest Measurement by the Kuder Preference Record and the Strong Vocational Interest Blank for Men," 37 (March, 1944), 538–44.

Journal of Psychology (The Journal Press) from Sidney L. Pressey, "Changes from 1923 to 1943 in the Attitudes of Public School and University Students," 21 (1946), 173–88.

Journal of Social Psychology (The Journal Press) from Stuart M. Stoke and Elmer D. West, "Sex Differences in Conversational Interests," 2 (1931), 120–26, and Adam R. Gilliland, "Changes in Religious Beliefs of College Students," 37 (Feb., 1953), 113–16.

Journal of Genetic Psychology (The Journal Press) from E. B. Hurlock and C. Jansing, "The Vocational Attitudes of Boys and Girls of High School Age," 44 (1934), 175–90; Frederick H. Lund, "Adolescent Motivation: Sex Differences," 64 (1944), 99–103; Raymond G. Kuhlen and Martha Arnold, "Age Differences in Religious Beliefs and Problems during Adolescence," 65 (1944), 291–300; S. A. Luchins, "On the Theories and Problems of Adolescence," 85 (1954), 47–63.

Genetic Psychology Monographs (The Journal Press) from Harold E. Jones and Herbert S. Conrad, *The Growth and Decline of Intelligence: A Study of a Homogeneous Group Between Ages of Ten and Sixty,* Vol. 13, No. 3 (April, 1933); Elise H. Campbell, *The Social-Sex Development of Children,* Vol. 21, No. 4 (1939); Erland Nelson, *Student Attitudes Toward Religion,* Vol. 22, No. 3 (1940).

The last group of acknowledgments are those for permissions from authors to draw on their writings—books, reports of research, etc.—not included in the foregoing classifications of sources. They are:

J. W. Getzels and P. N. Jackson, "The Study of Giftedness: A Multidimensional Approach," pp. 1–18 in *The Gifted Student,* Cooperative Research Monograph, no. 2, U.S. Department of Health, Education, and Welfare (Washington: Government Printing Office, 1960).

Dorothy M. Knoell and Leland L. Medsker, *Articulation Between Two-Year and Four-Year Colleges* (Berkeley: University of California, 1964); *Factors Affecting Performance of Transfer Students from Two-Year to Four-Year Colleges: With Implications for Coordination and Articulation* (Berkeley: University of California, 1964); *From Junior to Senior College: A National Study of the Transfer Student* (Washington: American Council on Education, 1965).

Armand L. Mauss, *Toward an Empirical Typology of Junior College Subcultures, Research in Education,* 3:2 (Feb., 1968), ERIC Clearinghouse for Junior College Information.

Leland L. Medsker and James W. Trent, *The Influence of Different Types of Higher Institutions on College Attendance from Varying Socio-Economic and Ability Levels* (Berkeley: Center for Research and Development in Higher Education, University of California, 1965).

W. H. Sheldon, S. S. Stevens, and W. B. Tucker, *The Varieties of Human Physique—An Introduction to Constitutional Psychology* (New York: Harper and Row, 1940).

Dale Tillery, from a paper presented to a Conference for Chief Student Personnel Administrators at Pacific Grove, Cal., Jan. 10, 1964.

The one hundred or so sources listed above are far outnumbered by references in passing and other limited citation not under necessity of acknowledgment, but, nevertheless, contributing to elucidation and comprehension of the issues and other matters considered. These are all, just as with the acknowledged sources, identified by specification of items in the lists of References and Bibliography to be found at the ends of the chapters.

Author Index

ABERNETHY, Ethel M., 53
Adelson, Joseph, 89
Aldrich, Margaret G., 537–38
Allport, Gordon W., 106, 110, 122–24, 130, 134–35
Anastasi, Anne, 58
Anderson, H. Dewey, 285
Archer, Jerome W., 455
Armsby, Henry H., 478
Arnold, Martha, 115–16
Ausubel, David P., 81, 89–90, 113, 172, 174, 249

BALOGH, Joseph K., 254
Barber, Leroy E., 289–90, 294
Barker, Roger G., 17–18, 54, 55
Barnett, Raymond A., 475
Battin, T. C., 254–55
Bayer, Leona M., 12–13
Bayley, Nancy, 12–13, 14, 21–22, 35, 404–5
Becker, Susan J., 295–98
Bell, Howard M., 241–42, 249, 350–51
Benedict, Ruth, 71
Bennett, Bruce L., 366–68, 378
Berdie, Ralph F., 216–17
Berman, Sidney, 534
Bernard, Harold W., 171
Birren, James E., 406
Bloom, Benjamin S., 126, 129
Blos, Peter, 534
Bottrell, Harold R., 547–48
Bown, Oliver H., 516, 526
Boynton, Bernice, 23
Boynton, Paul L., 257
Brintle, G. L., 219–20
Brogan, A. P., 107
Brown, Francis J., 250–51
Brown, W. F., 312–13

Broxson, John A., 409–10
Brumbaugh, A. J., 510
Bryan, A. I., 56
Burchinal, L. G., 173
Burman, Arthur C., 534
Burt, Cyril, 59–60
Buswell, Guy T., 406–8
Byrd, Oliver E., 330
Byrns, Ruth, 294

CALDWELL, Otis W., 103
Campbell, Doak S., 436
Campell, Elise H., 93–94
Canning, Leslie, 213–14
Caplow, Theodore, 167–70
Carlin, Leslie O., 517–19
Carter, Harold D., 213–15
Centers, Richard, 207–8
Chamberlain, Neil W., 394
Chapman, Charles E., 419–24
Charters, W. W., 488
Chassell, Clara F., 112–13
Chausow, Hymen H., 414–15
Chave, E. J., 120
Christensen, Alfred, 473
Christensen, Harold T., 164–67
Clark, Burton R., 323, 344, 388
Clark, Mamie P., 56, 58
Clark, Weston R., 251
Cline, Alan, 288–89
Clive, W. F., 243
Coleman, James S., 84–89, 95, 240–41, 243
Collins, Charles C., 317, 512, 544
Congdon, Nora A., 375, 377
Conklin, E. S., 104
Conklin, Shirley, 475
Conrad, Herbert S., 42–43, 45–46, 405, 411

Cooley, William W., 295–98
Corey, D. Q., 222–24
Corey, Stephen M., 79
Corsini, Raymond J., 403–4
Costin, Frank, 412
Cotton, Webster, 395
Counts, George S., 202, 283–84
Cowan, Gregory, 491
Cowley, William H., 526
Crathorne, A. R., 193–94
Crites, John O., 216
Crosby, R. C., 217
Cross, K. Patricia, 321–23
Crumrine, William M., 215
Cureton, Thomas K., 35

DABBS, Lowell, 489–90
D'Amico, Louis A., 288, 415–16
Darley, John G., 217–18
Deane, Stephen R., 417–18
Dearborn, Terry H., 449
Deeg, M. E., 202–3
Dimock, Hedley S., 31, 90–91, 114–15, 237–38
Dobbin, John E., 517
Doll, Edgar A., 131–32
Donahue, Wilma T., 400–401
Dorr, Mildred, 110–11
Douglas, O. B., 371–73
Douglass, Frances M., 488
Douvan, Elizabeth, 89
Dressel, Paul L., 446–47
Dudycha, G. J., 119–20

EARNSHAW, Helen, 475
Eberhart, J. C., 108–9
Eberhart, Wilfred, 246–47
Eells, Walter C., 276–79, 336–37, 388–89, 390, 470–71, 473, 477, 483
Ehrmann, Winston W., 159–62, 175–76
Elkin, Frederick, 69–70, 81–82, 88
Ellis, Albert, 125, 162–63
Ellzey, W. Clark, 463–64
Epperson, David C., 88–89
Erickson, Clifford G., 413–14
Erikson, Eric, 131
Espenshade, Anna S., 26–28

FARNSWORTH, Dana L., 534–35
Farnum, Hollis B., 411–12
Fassett, Katherine K., 403–4
Ferrell, Wilfred A., 455
Fick, Revel L., 377
Finger, Frank W., 152–54
Fisher, T. R., 101–3

Fleming, Virginia V., 128–29
Flory, Charles D., 39–42, 48–49
Foley, John P., Jr., 58
Ford, C. Fenton, Jr., 198
Fordyce, Joseph W., 521–22
Fox, Frederick G., 543–44
Frandsen, Arden N., 220–22
Freedman, Mervin B., 129–30
Freeman, Frank N., 39–42, 48–49
Froman, Louis A., 411
Furfey, Paul H., 256

GARFIELD, Sol, 190–91, 195–96
Garrett, H. E., 56–58, 101–3
Gebhard, Paul H., 146–52
Getzels, J. W., 62–65
Gillespie, James M., 106, 110, 130
Gilliland, A. R., 121–22
Ginzberg, E., 187
Goddard, Roy W., 481
Goldberg, Maxwell H., 398
Gordon, Leonard V., 352, 353, 377
Gough, Harrison G., 319, 517
Gould, Harley N., 16–17, 18
Gray, William S., 408–9
Greenbaum, J. J., 315
Greulich, Walter W., 15–16, 20–21, 25
Gross, Richard E., 458
Guiler, Walter S., 311
Guilford, J. P., 64–65

HACKETT, Roger C., 288
Hackman, Joseph, 391–92
Halfter, Irma T., 412–13, 488
Hall, Calvin S., 125
Harrington, John H., 542
Harris, Dale B., 73, 74–76
Harris, Norman C., 476–77
Hartshorne, Hugh, 108, 112
Hartson, L., 49, 51–52
Havighurst, Robert J., 79–80, 90, 110–11, 112, 127, 272, 395–97
Hawkins, Richard, 491
Heist, Paul A., 315–16, 343
Henmon, V. A. C., 294
Henry, Nelson B., 20
Hill, Reuben, 538
Hines, Vince A., 325
Hohman, Leslie B., 154–55
Hollingsworth, Leta S., 60
Hollinshead, Byron S., 272
Holtzman, W. H., 312–13
Hoppock, Robert, 526
Horrall, Bernice M., 369, 377
Houston, V. M., 366, 376

Howells, T. H., 108
Hsaio, H. H., 46
Hull, Ramona E., 338
Humphreys, J. Anthony, 510–11
Hurlock, E. B., 199–200
Hutson, P. W., 174, 200

IFFERT, Robert E., 288

JACKSON, C. M., 17, 18–19
Jackson, P. N., 62–65
Jackson, Robert A., 447–48
Jacob, Philip E., 130, 329
Jansing, C., 199–200
Jencks, Christopher, 295
Jensen, Arthur R., 128
Johnson, B. Lamar, 245–49, 439–41, **493**, 537, 545
Johnson, Roy Ivan, 456
Johnston, Robert L., 412
Johnstone, John W. C., 388
Jones, Edward S., 192
Jones, Harold E., 29–30, 42–43, 45–**46**, 405, 411
Jung, Christian W., 290–91

KAHL, Joseph A., 207, 208–9, 293–94
Kanin, Eugene J., 163
Kaplan, Max, 244–45
Kastner, Harold H., Jr., 311
Kidd, John W., 447–48
Kimbrough, Ralph B., 325
Kinsey, Alfred C., 146–52, 179–80
Kirkpatrick, Clifford, 163, 167–70
Klohr, Mildred C., 366–68
Kluckhohn, Florence R., 208
Knapp, R. H., 315
Knoell, Dorothy M., 302–9, 341, **483**, 530–33
Koos, Leonard V., 6, 273–75, 284–87, 536
Kopp, T., 217–18
Kroger, Robert, 206
Kuder, G. Frederick, 211
Kuhlen, Raymond G., 71, 115–16, 400
Kuznetz, G. M., 42

LALEGAR, Grace E., 212
Landis, Judson T., 464–65
Lantagne, Joseph E., 329–33, 450
Laslett, H. R., 133–34
Lazarus, Arnold L., 257
LeBaron, Helen R., 465
Lehman, Harvey C., 196–97, 198, 235–38, 256

Leuba, James H., 117–19
Lewis, Philip, 252–53, 255
Lindzey, Gardner, 125
Livesay, T. M., 49, 51
Lockwood, William V., 192–93
Louttit, C. M., 206
Lowrie, Samuel H., 156–58
Lubick, Emil E., 333–35
Luchins, A. S., 71–72
Lund, Frederick H., 28–29
Lundeen, Gerhard E., 103
Lunger, Ruth, 351
Lyons, Edward H., 478, 480–81

MACCOBY, Eleanor E., 254
McConnell, T. R., 49–50, 315, 343
McDaniel, J. W., 511, 546, 548
McDonagh, Edward C., 254
McGrath, Earl J., 411
McNemar, Olga, 42
McPherson, Elizabeth, 491
Mallinson, George G., 215
Martin, Clyde E., 146–52
Martorana, S. V., 389–91, 462–63
Marzolf, Stanley S., 366, 376
Mather, W. G., 166–67
Mauss, Armand L., 323–24
Mayhew, Lewis B., 444–45, 495
Maynard, David M., 458
Mays, Mark A., 108, 112
Means, Richard K., 449
Medsker, Leland M., 7–8, 298–301, 302–9, 312, 341, 388, 435–36, 530–33
Meinecke, Charlotte D., 527
Meredith, Howard V., 23
Meyersohn, Rolf, 252
Middleton, Warren C., 53
Miles, Catherine C., 44, 60, 198, 405, 411
Miles, Walter R., 44, 401–3, 405, 411
Mitchell, Alice M., 250–51
Mitchell, Guy C., 508
Mizruchi, Ephraim H., 416–17
Moffett, D. C., 53
Mohs, Milton C., 528–30
Mooney, Ross L., 351, 352–53, 368, 375, 377
Morris, Charles S., 392–94
Morse, H. T., 444–46, 495

NEILEN, Patricia, 126–27
Nelson, Erland, 120–21
Neumeyer, Martin H., 251–52
Neumeyer, Esther S., 251–52
Nicholson, David H., 418–19
Nixon, H. K., 101

ODEN, Melita H., 404–5
Olds, E. B., 239, 241, 243
Orr, Betty, 296–97
Osborne, R. T., 517
Overstreet, Phoebe L., 188–89
Owens, William A., Jr., 404

PACKARD, Vance, 176
Page, James D., 351
Parsons, Talcott, 94–95, 208
Paterson, Donald S., 202–3
Peck, Robert F., 127
Perl, R., 56
Plant, Walter T., 318–21
Pomeroy, Wardell B., 146–52
Pope, Charlotte, 72
Powell, Lee, 133–34
Prescott, Daniel A., 79
Pressey, Luella C., 23–24
Pressey, Sidney L., 97–101, 400
Price, Wilson T., 475
Pullias, E. V., 154–55
Punké, H. H., 91–92, 157–58, 241
Putnam, Howard L., 441–42, **452, 456,** 458, 459, 460, 468, 496, 519

RACK, Lucile, 371–73
Raines, Max R., 511, 546, 548
Ramsey, Glenn V., 154
Rapp, Marvin A., 444, 495
Reiss, Albert J., Jr., 203–5
Reiss, Ira L., 177
Remmlein, Madaline K., 538–39
Reuter, E. B., 70–71
Reynolds, Edgar, 285
Reynolds, James W., 434, 435–36, 446–47
Rhoades, Otto, 545
Richards, Maxwell J., 474
Richek, Herbert G., 516, 526
Rivera, Ramon J., 388
Roberts, Katherine E., 128–29
Robinson, H. A., 489
Robinson, Myra Z., 110–11
Roe, Anne, 205
Roeber, Edward, 190–91, 195–96
Rogers, A. L., 49–50
Rogers, Lucille V., 542–43
Rosen, Howard, 472–73, 475, 481
Rosenberg, Bernard, 252
Ross, Robert T., 152–54, 461–62
Rothney, John W. M., 200
Roueche, John E., 492
Rubin, Isadore, 156, 177

SANDERS, Wilma, 517
Sanford, Nevitt, 130, 323

Sargent, Epes W., 112, 133
Scammon, Richard E., 32
Scammon, Richard M., 398–99
Schaffner, Bertram, 154–55
Schenz, Robert F., 487
Schiferl, Max, 473
Schleman, H. B., 371, 373–74
Schmidt, John L., 200
Schmuller, Allen M., 126–27
Schneck, M. R., 57
Schultz, Raymond E., 309–10, 323, 414–15
Scott, Lloyd F., 257
Seashore, Harold, 278–81, 339
Seashore, Robert H., 29–30
Segel, David, 60, 219–20
Seibel, Dean W., 281–82, 339, 514–16
Sessions, Alwyn D., 220–21
Sexton, Patricia C., 209
Shaw, Phillip, 488
Sheldon, W. H., 32–34
Sherman, A. W., Jr., 92
Shock, Nathan W., 25–26
Shuttleworth, Frank K., 10–11, 13, 54
Siegel, Sidney, 326
Siemens, Cornelius H., 545
Simmons, Katherine, 15–16
Singer, Stanley L., 377
Slavens, G. S., 107
Smith, Ernest A., 163
Smith, Leo F., 478
Sorenson, Herbert, 410–11
Spaulding, Francis T., 461
Spranger, Edward, 127
Staton, Thomas F., 180
Stauffer, Samuel A., 208
Stefflre, Buford, 211, 377
Stephenson, Richard M., 189–90, 205
Sterner, Alice, 29
Stewart, B. M., 222–24
Stoddard, George D., 276–77
Stoke, Stuart M., 104–5, 110, 243
Stone, Calvin P., 17–18, 54, 55
Stone, L. Gordon, 366–67
Stott, L. H., 91
Stratton, Dorothy C., 371, 373–74
Stratz, C. H., 20
Strong, Edward K., Jr., 210, 212–13
Super, Donald E., 188–89, 215, 258–60
Swineford, Frances, 59
Symonds, Percival M., 72–79, 128

TABA, Hilda, 112
Taylor, Katherine V., 213–15
Telford, Charles W., 318–21
Terman, Lewis M., 60, 156, 198

Thomas, Russell, 452, 468
Thompson, George G., 95–96, 107–8, 109
Thompson, Ronald B., 270–71, 282
Thorndike, Edward L., 42, 47, **401, 403,** 406
Thornton, James W., Jr., 437
Thorpe, Louis P., 126–27
Thurstone, L. L., 58, 120
Thurstone, T. C., 58
Tillery, Dale, 316, 343
Todd, John Edward, 127–28
Traxler, Arthur E., 510
Trent, James W., 298–301, 341
Triggs, Frances O., 218–19, 224–25
Trow, W. C., 323, 344
Tryon, Caroline M., 82–84
Tuddenham, Read D., 14, 21–22, 35
Tully, Emerson, 325
Turnbull, William W., 517
Tussing, L., 217–18
Tyler, Henry T., 312, 480
Tyler, Leona E., 198
Tyler, Ralph W., 478–79, 480

ULMER, R. Curtis, 414–15

VALENTINE, W. L., 101–2
Vanaria, Louis M., 416–17
Van Dusen, Albert C., 213
Viteles, Morris S., 54–55

WALKER, John E., 325–29
Wann, Marie D., 388
Warrington, Willard G., 447–48
Wattenberg, Ben J., 398–99
Weaver, Bennett, 338
Weber, Cornelius B., 490
Wechsler, David, 46–47, 405
Weingarten, Samuel, 453–55
Wesley, S. M., 222–24
West, Elmer D., 104–5, 110
Westley, William A., 69–70, 81–82, 88
White, David M., 252
White, R. Clyde, 257–58
White, R. H., 130
White, Richard E., 8
Williams, Cornelia D., 369–71, 374, 378
Williams, Lucile H., 72
Williamson, E. G., 526, 536–37
Willoughby, Raymond R., 154, 156
Wilson, James W., 478, 480–81
Windham, Douglas M., 291–93, 340
Winsor, A. L., 217
Wise, W. Max, 269
Witty, Paul, 60, 196–97, 198, 235–38, 252–53, 254–55, 256, 488
Woodward, Marthene V., 386–87, 388
Wrenn, C. Gilbert, 194–95
Wright, Wendell W., 290–91

YOUNG, Florence M., 517

Subject Index

ABILITIES, fine motor and mechanical, 29–30
Abilities of adults. *See* Adults, abilities of
Ability and environmental factors: comparison of noncollege, junior college, and college populations, 295–98; comparison of influence of institutions, 298–301
Academic deficiencies, 310–12; and study habits, 312–13
Academic success, comparison of transfers and "native" students, 306–9
ACE Critical Thinking Test, 414
ACE Psychological Examination, 50, 51, 277, 312, 351, 392, 411, 421, 538
Achievement in school, relation to recreations, 257
Activities: high school years, 239–41; college-age youth, 241–45
Activities, student. *See* Student organizations and activities
Admission, bases of, 513–14
Adolescence: stereotype of, 69; cultural explanation of behavior at, 70–71; problems and interests during, 72–79
Adolescent behavior, explaining, 69–72
Adolescent Growth Study at University of California (Berkeley), 23, 25
Adult education: growth, status, and phenomenal growth in general, 385–88; growth and status in junior colleges, 388–91; enrollments, 389–91; two diverse examples, 391–94; rationale, 394–95; needs as seen in developmental tasks, 395–98; focus on later adulthood, 398–401; extracurriculum for, 543–44
Adults, abilities of: from earlier inquiries, 401–3; later studies and change of abilities with age, 403–5; during schooling as a factor, 405; one authority's opinion, 406; in reading, 406–10; in class and courses, 410–15
Adult students: in an evening junior college student body, 415–16; comparison of participants and nonparticipants, 416–17; clients of three diverse offerings, 417–18; an inquiry with focus on motivation, 418–19; a near-comprehensive inquiry, 419–24; personnel services for, 535
Age, change in mental organization with, 55–60
Ages of community college students: recent sampling, 3–6; comparison with 1921–22, 6; comparison with Medsker's evidence, 6–8; recent, in Minnesota, 8; sex differences, 9
Aggression, male, in heterosexual associations, 163
Agriculture, curriculums in, 475
Allport-Vernon-Lindzey (A-V-L) Study of Values Scales, 315
American Association of Junior Colleges, 389, 476, 500, 511, 517, 528, 549
American School Counselor Association, 289
Amherst College, 19
Aptitude, comparison of students in junior colleges and colleges: earlier, 272–79; more recent, 279–81; in the Knoell-Medsker project, 302–4

570

SUBJECT INDEX

Army Alpha Test, 45, 224, 273, 404
Assembly programs, 542–43
Athletics, body types in relation to, 35
Attitudes and subcultures of junior college students, 323–24
Attitudes and values: studies of wrongs, likes, and worries, 97–101; unfounded beliefs, 101–4; conversational interests, 104–6; social problems of impersonal import, 106; personal attitudes and social values, 106–8; attitudes toward property, 108–9; concerning ascription of social idealism, 109–10
Avocational interests. *See* Play and recreation
Avocations almost devoid of inquiry, 336
Awkwardness in adolescence, 31

BALTIMORE, Md., 192
Beliefs, unfounded, 101–4
Bell Adjustment Inventory, 538
Biological science. *See* Science and mathematics
Blanks and inventories: another approach to vocational interests, 210; description of instruments, 210–11; stability of measured interests, 211–16; relation of measures to self-estimates, 216–18; other relationships, 218–25; usefulness of, 225–26
Blood pressure, changes in, 22–23
Body types: identification of somatotypes, 32–34; in relation to temperament, 34–35; in relation to athletics and health, 35
Bown Self-Report Inventory (SRI), 516, 534
Brace Test, 27
Brigham Young University, 165
Bronxville (New York) High School, 246
Brown-Holtzman Survey of Study Habits and Attitudes, 312, 516
Brown Psychological Examination, 55
Buffalo, N.Y., 192
Buffalo, University of, 411
Bureau of the Census, 388
Business, curriculums in, 475

CALIFORNIA MENTAL MATURITY TEST, 414
California Psychological Inventory (CPI), 318
California Study of General Education, 439–40
California, University of (at Berkeley), 298, 314, 419, 532
Career courses, 519, 522
Career Planning Study, 188
Carnegie Corporation, 401–2
CAVD Test, 57
Center for Research and Development in Higher Education, 6, 7, 298, 302, 314
Characteristics preferred and objectionable in mates, 164–65
Chicago City Junior College, 391–92, 413
Chicago Tests of Primary Abilities, 56
Chicago, University of, 48, 62
Cincinnati, University of, 477
Clark College (Wash.), 491
Cleveland High School, St. Louis, 72
Clientele of the community college, issue of, 270–72
Cocurriculum. *See* Student organizations and activities
College attendance: related to economic status, 209; proportion of population who should attend, 270–72; reasons for attending public junior college, 287–91; reasons for not attending college, 289–91; motivation for, 293–94; scholarship plans and democratization of attendance, 295
College Health Knowledge Test, 449
College of the City of New York, 57

College Qualifications Test, 279
Columbus, Ohio, 253
Commission of the Professors of Adult Education, 394
Commission on Higher Education, President's, 271–72
Committee for Research on Problems of Sex of the National Research Council, 146
Committee on Appraisal and Development of Junior College Student Personnel Programs, 317
Communications and the humanities: communications, 452–55; humanities and the creative arts, 455–58; remedial work in communications, 488–90
Community services, 547–48
Compensatory programs. See Remedial and developmental programs
Compton (Cal.) College, 545
Concept Mastery Scale, 404
Consistency and change in personality, 124–31
Contra Costa County (Cal.), 419, 482
Conversational interests of college students, 104–6
Cooperative and work-experience programs: beginnings and frequency in higher institutions, 477–78; values and purposes, 478–80
Cooperative English Test, 414, 515, 538
Cooperative Reading Comprehension Test, 411
Cornell College (Ia.), 50
Cornell University, 166, 217
Cortland, N.Y., 416
Costs of attendance in higher institutions, estimates of, 289
Counseling: concept of guidance and, 508; educational and vocational, 526–27
Courtship among college students, 167–70
Creative arts. See Communications and the humanities
Creativity, giftedness and, 60–65
Criticisms of parents by adolescents, 91
Cultural explanation of adolescence, 70–71
Cumulative record, 517–19
Curriculum: use of personal problem data in, 377–79; scope and organization, 434–35; innovation in, 492–93
Curriculums, transfer. See Transfer curriculums
Cuyahoga County, O., 258

DATING BEHAVIOR: concept and functions of, 156–57; during early and middle adolescence, 157–59; at the college level, 159–61; investigations of, 162–63; intercultural comparison of attitudes and behavior, 163–64; characteristics preferred and objectionable in mates, 164–67; pros and cons of steady dating, 173–74
Deficiencies, academic, 310–12
Denmark, dating attitudes and behavior in, 163–66
Department of Labor, U. S., 472
DePaul University, 413
Design for General Education, A, 438–39
Developmental programs. See Remedial and developmental programs
Developmental tasks: of adolescence, 79–81; of adults, 395–98, 423–24
DeWitt Clinton High School (New York City), 104
Differential Aptitude Tests (DAT), 60
Duluth, Minn., 245

ECTOMORPHY, 32
Educational and vocational counseling, 526–27
Educational Policies Commission of the National Education Association, 270–72
Educational Testing Service, 421
Egalitarianism in state universities and junior colleges of Florida, 291–93

SUBJECT INDEX

Emancipation from parents: boys by late puberty, 90–91; criticism of parents by adolescents, 91; quarrels with fathers and mothers, 91–92; at the college level, 92–93
Emotional adjustment, concern for, 533–55
Endocrine factors in growth, 23–25
Endomorphy, 32
English, courses in. *See* Communications and the humanities
English Placement Test, 514
Environmental factors. *See* Ability and environmental factors
Etiquette, problems of, 373–74
Evaluation: of general education, 447–48; of instruction in Marriage and Family, 463–65; of extracurriculum, 538–39
Extracurriculum. *See* Student organizations and activities
Extracurriculum for adults, 543–44

FAMILY INCOME CLASSES, in universities and junior colleges in Florida, 291–92
Femininity, 198
Financial assistance, 524–25
Flint, Mich., 415
Florida Scale of Civic Beliefs, 325
Florida, University of, 325, 409
Follow-up inquiries of junior college transfers: comparisons of transfers and "native" students, 301–2; Knoell-Medsker investigation, 303–4; comparisons of ability and aptitude, 303–4; socioeconomic status, 304–5; education of parents, 305–6; proportion of support from parents, 306; ages of natives and transfers, 306; comparative academic success, 306–9; follow-up with "dramatic" outcomes, 309–10; improving placement of transfers, 530–33
Follow-up of employment, 528–30
Ft. Wayne, Ind., 254
Functional courses. *See* General education

GENERAL COLLEGE, University of Minnesota, 202, 369
General courses, overview of new-type, 441–42
General curriculum, role of, 486
General education: goals of, 438–39; formulated by California Study of General Education, 439; courses proposed, 439–40; patterns of, 440–41; new-type general courses, 441–42; liberal arts *vs.* functional courses, 442–46; obstacles to spread of functional approach, 446–47; importance of evaluation, 447–48
General Education Development (GED) Tests: relation to Kuder measures, 221; use of in admission to junior college, 513
General Education Workshop, 439
Giftedness and creativity, 60–65
Girl Scouts of America, 158
Graduate Record Examination (GRE), 517
Great Books course, 417–18, 440
Grover Cleveland High School, New York City, 74
Guidance and counseling: use of personal problem data in, 374–76; concept of, 508

HANDBOOK, student, 522–24
Harvard Growth Study, 13
Harvard University, 32, 123
Hawaii, University of, 51
Health and physical education: two-part nature of the offering, 448; course in health, 449–50; physical education, 450–52
Health: interests of junior college students, 330–31; and security curriculums, 475; services, 525–26
Height and weight, growth in: to later adolescence, 10–11; PMH at successive ages, 12; as related to MG age, 13–14; rates in relation to menarche, 15–16; in college years: women, 16–18; men, 18–19

History. *See* Social studies, including history
Home economics: need for, 465; subprofessional occupations in, 465; offerings in, 466–67; obstacles to adequate offerings, 466–67
Homosexuality, treatises on, 174
Hormones and physiological changes, 24–25
Housing, student services in, 526
Humanities. *See* Communications and the humanities
Hunter College, 57

IDEALISM, ascription of, 109–11
Illinois State Normal University, 366
Illinois, University of, 219, 244, 366
Indiana University, 154
Industrial and mechanical curriculums, 475
Infusion approach in curriculum, 441
Innovation in curriculum. *See* Curriculum, innovation in
Institute for Social Research, University of Michigan, 158
Integrated courses, 459–60
Intelligence: variation among individuals, 40–41; sex differences, 41–42; change during the life span, 43–47; and creativity, 62–65; and morality, 111–13; and recreation, 257
Intercultural comparison of sexual attitudes and behavior, 163–64
Interests: conversational, 104–6; avocational, 234–65
Interests of adolescents. *See* Problems and interests of adolescents
Interests of adults. *See* Characteristics and interests of adults
Interests of junior college students: areas of interest canvassed, 329; health interests, 330–31; relating to marriage and parenthood, 331–33; occupational objectives, 333–36; avocations, 336; reading interests, 336–38
Inventories, vocational blanks and. *See* Blanks and inventories
Iowa High School Content Examination, 219
Iowa Silent Reading Test, 408, 410, 515
Iowa State College, 404
Iowa, University of, 276–77

JOHN DEWEY SOCIETY, 79
Junior college: and university students, comparison on OPI, 315–17; comparison with high school and college students on California Psychological Inventory, 318–21

KANSAS CITY, Mo., 235
Kansas State Teachers College, 77
Kinsey reports; evidence from, 146–52; early reception of, 149–50
Kuder Preference Record: Vocational, 211

LEADERSHIP COURSE, 460, 545
League for Innovation in the Community College, 493
Lehigh University, 19
Liberal arts: approach in curriculum, 440, 444–45; *vs.* functional courses, 442–43
Life span, mental change through, 43–47
Loan funds, 525
Logan (Utah) High School, 220
Long Beach (Cal.) City College, 333
Los Angeles City College, Evening Division, 543

MARIN (Cal.), College of, 482
Marriage: decreasing age of, 172–73; interests of junior college students in, 331–33
Marriage and family, courses in: rationale, 461–62; content, 462–63; evaluation, 463–65

SUBJECT INDEX

Married students, personal problems of, 362–65
Maryland, University of, 417
Masculinity, 198
Masturbation: and beliefs of college freshmen, 155–56; and treatises on adolescence, 174
Mathematics. *See* Science and mathematics
Maturity, criteria of, 131–35
Measurements, cautionary word concerning, 31–32
Mechanical curriculums, industrial and, 475
Meier Art Judgment Test, 222
Mellon Foundation, 130
Mental development: childhood to youth, 39–43; change through the life span, 43–47; growth during college years, 47–53; relation to physical growth and maturation, 53–55
Mental growth: nature of growth curve, 42–43; and puberty, 53–55; relation to physical growth, 53–55
Mental health services, 525–26
Mental organization, change with age, 55–60
Mesomorphy, 32
MG-age, growth in relation to, 13–14
Miami University (O.), 311
Michigan, University of, 158, 337, 400
Middleton, N.Y., 188
Miller Analogies Test, 410
Minnesota, ages of junior college students in, 8–9
Minnesota Inventory of Social Attitudes, 538
Minnesota Multiphasic Personality Inventory (MMPI), 224, 318, 516, 534
Minnesota, University of, 8, 17, 19, 30, 167, 202, 216, 217, 274, 369, 410–11, 537
Minnesota Vocational Tests for Clerical Workers, 223
Misconceptions, 101–4
Mooney Problem Check List, 115, 351, 516, 534
Morality, relation to intelligence, 111–13
Mormon culture, dating attitudes and behavior in, 163–66
Motor performance: growth in, 26–28; in fine and mechanical abilities, 29–30
Movies, radio, and television: movies and radio, 249–51; television, 251–56

NATIONAL ASSOCIATION, State Universities and Land Grant Colleges, 288
National Committee for Appraisal and Development of Junior College Student Personnel Programs, 517
National Defense Student Loan Program, 525
National Education Association, 270, 289
National Opinion Research Center, 203, 205, 388
National Society for the Study of Education, 408, 435
New Brunswick, N. J., 252
Newcomb College, 16, 18
Newspapers, college, 542
New York State Agricultural and Technical Institute, 338
Northwestern University, 122

OAKLAND, Cal., 213–14
Oberlin College, 51, 274
Occupational education, terminal. *See* Terminal occupational education
Occupational objectives of junior college students, 333–36
Occupational preferences and plans: areas of inquiry, 187; stages in occupational choice, 187–88; projects with ninth graders, 188–90; in relation to nation's labor force, 190; trends through high school, 190–91; choices of high school seniors and graduates, 192–93; inquiries at college level, 193–95; specific occupations chosen,

195–96; sex differences in occupational preferences, 196–97; in puberty, 198–99; motivation behind, 199–201; and self-image, 205; and social mobility, 205–9; relation to undergraduate major, 335–36

Occupations, prestige of, 201–5
Office of Education, United States, 388
Office of Public Opinion Research, 207
Ohio State University, 97, 103, 274, 366, 368
Ohio State University Psychological Examination, 51
Omnibus Personality Inventory (OPI), 315–17, 516
Oregon, University of, 104
Organizations and activities. *See* Student organizations and activities
Orientation and career courses, 519–22
Otis Group Intelligence Test, 54
Otis Omnibus Test, 402

PARENTS, emancipation from, 90–91
Pasadena (Cal.) City College, 329, 529
Peace Corps, 110
Peer culture: derivation, 81; an objector to the concept, 81–82; in early adolescence, 82–84; high school years, 84–88; more recent opinions, 88–89; and developmental tasks, 89–90
Pennsylvania, University of, 19
Personal characteristics of junior college students: inquiries at the Center for Research and Development of Higher Education, 314–15; results for four-year college students, 315–16; comparison of junior college and university students, 316–17; comparison on the California Psychological Inventory, 318–21; a differing interpretation, 321–23; an inquiry on attitudes and subcultures, 323–24
Personality and character, consistency and change with age: obstacles to generalization, 125–26; from childhood to adolescence, 126–27; from 10 to 16, 127; from high school to college, 127–28; from adolescence to adulthood, 128; from precollege, through college, to postcollege years, 128–29; generalization, 129; college impact on, 129–31
Personal problems of junior college students: earlier identification, 350–51; Mooney Problem Check List, 351–53; institutions and students involved, 353; comparisons of problems "troubling" and "of most concern," 353; distribution of problems of most concern, 354–56; influence of class, sex, and age, 356–57; comparison for two junior colleges, 357–58; problems of highest and lowest frequency, 358–62; problems of married students, 362–65
Personal problems of students, further studies: in colleges and universities, 365–71; in junior college, 371–72; problems of etiquette, 373–74
Personal problems, uses of data on: where put to use, 374; in guidance and counseling, 374–76; in research, 376–77; in curriculum and instruction, 377–79
Phi Theta Kappa, 309
Physical activity and motivation, 28–29
Physical education. *See* Health and physical education
Physical growth, relation to mental growth, 53–55
Physical science. *See* Science and mathematics
Physiological changes: other than height and weight, 19–22; pulse rates, blood pressure, etc., 22–24; and endocrine factors, 24–25
Placement Bureau of Pasadena (Cal.) City College, 529
Placement of transfers, 530–33
Placement services, 524
Play and recreation, activities and interests: by age, 235–38; in high school years, 239–41; college-age youth, 241–45
Play interests: classification, 237–38; involving association with other persons, 241
Preliminary Scholastic Aptitude Test (PSAT), 281–82

SUBJECT INDEX

Premarital conduct, standards of, 174–77
President's Commission on Higher Education, 271–72
Pressey X-O Test, 97
Prestige of occupations, 201–5
Primary Abilities, Chicago Tests of, 56
Problems and interests of adolescents: rankings by high school students, 74–76; by older adolescents, 77–78; in relation to happiness, 78–79
Project TALENT: comparisons of ability, 296; comparisons on environmental factors, 297–98
Property, attitudes toward, 108–9
Proximity, influence on socioeconomic democratization, 284–88
Psychological Examination of the American Council on Education, 50–51
Puberty and mental growth, 53–55
Pubescence, play and recreations in, 256–57
Pulse rates, changes in, 22–23
Purdue University, 76, 165, 369
Puritanical mores concerning play and recreation, 234
Purposes of the community college: consensus on, 435; as formulated by Yearbook Committee of the NSSSE, 435; as formulated by Medsker, Reynolds, and Thornton, 435–37

QUARRELS, youth with parents, 91–92

RADCLIFFE COLLEGE, 123
Radio. *See* Movies, radio, and television
Reading: of terminal junior college students, 338; ability of adults, 406–10; remedial program, 488–89
Reading, voluntary. *See* Voluntary reading
Realism of occupational choice, 188
Recreational interests. *See* Play and recreation
Recreations: in pubescence, 256–57; related to intelligence, achievement, and social status, 257–58; related to vocational interests, 258–60
Religion, influence on sexuality, 151
Religious attitudes and beliefs: age of conversion, 113; of adolescent boys, 114–15; of boys and girls, 115–16; at the college level, 116–22; Allport on religion in adolescence and among college students, 122–24
Remedial and developmental programs: need for, 486; scope, 497; in reading, 488–89; in writing, 489–90; of study skills, 490–91; illustrative program, 491–92; overview and related research, 492
River Falls (Wis.) State Teachers College, 366
Rochester (Minn.), 481
Roosevelt University, 413
Rorschach Test, 128
Rundquist-Sletto Inferiority Scale, 538

SAN FRANCISCO *Examiner and Chronicle*, 288
San Francisco State College, 419
San Jose State College, 55
San Mateo (Cal.) Junior College Adult Center, 392–93
Santa Fe (Fla.) Junior College, 520
Scale of Civic Beliefs, Florida, 325
Scholarship plans and democratization of college attendance, 295
Scholastic Aptitude Test (SAT), 436
School and College Aptitude Test (SCAT), 412, 421, 436
Schooling, duration as a factor in adult intelligence, 405
Science and mathematics: integrated courses in, 468–69; other courses, 470
Seashore Measures of Musical Talent, 222

Services, community, 547–48
Services, student. *See* Student services
Sex education and guidance: need for, 177–78; scope of content, 178–79; competence of teachers and counselors, 179
Sex hormones, influence on growth, 24–25
Sexual behavior: evidence from Kinsey reports, 146–50; individual variation, 150; influences on sexuality, 150–52; corroboration by questionnaire, 152–54; evidence from other reports, 154–56
Sexuality, influences on: age at adolescence, 151; parental occupation, 151; urban or rural residence, 151; religious background, 151; generation of birth, 151–52; psychological, 152
Social competence scale, 131–34
Social Maturity Scale, 133
Social mobility, relation to vocational preferences, 205–9
Social policy on sexual behavior: controversy, 171; treatise on adolescence, 171–72; decreasing age of marriage, 172–73; steady dating, 173–74; masturbation and homosexuality, 174; standards of premarital conduct, 174–77; education and guidance, 177–79
Social science. *See* Social studies, including history
Social-sex role: from childhood into adolescence, 93–94; seen by a sociologist, 94–95
Social status, relation to televiewing, 257–58
Social studies, including history: scope and role, 458; list of courses, 458–59; integrated courses, 459–60; other courses, 460; ages of students and civic motivation, 461
Society for Research in Child Development, 154
Socioeconomic status of junior college students: investigations of, 284–88; of honor students, 309–10; Knoell-Medsker projects, 364–65
Socioeconomic values, from the Walker project, 324–29
Somatotypes. *See* Body types
South Shore High School, Chicago, 252
SRA Youth Inventory, 351
Stability and change in personality, 124–31
Stanford Arithmetic Test, 222
Stanford Later Maturity Study, 401–3
Stanford Study of Gifted Children, 404
Stanford University, 17, 18, 55
State University of New York, 483
Steady dating, pros and cons of, 173–74
"Storm and stress": in adolescence, 69–70; cultural explanation of, 70–71
Strength and motor performance: tests of strength, 25–26; motor performance, 26–28
Strong Vocational Interest Blank, 210–11, 258, 259
Student activities. *See* Student organizations and activities
Student government organizations, 546–47
Student handbook, 522–24
Student leadership, extracurriculum and, 544–47
Student loans, 525
Student organizations and activities: values claimed for the extracurriculum, 536–37; evaluative research, 537–39; organizations and activities, 539–41; illustrative all-college activities, 542–43; extracurriculum for adults, 543–44; extracurriculum and student leadership, 544–48; influence on learning, 549
Student Personnel, Commission on, 511
Student personnel programs: expanding concept, 508; need for, 508–10; proposed, 510–12; admission, appraisal, and orientation, 512–17; cumulative record, 517–19; orientation and career courses, 519–22; student handbook, 522–24
Student problems. *See* Personal problems
Student services: generic picture, 524–26; educational and vocational counseling, 526–28; follow-up studies, 528–30; placement of transfers, 530–33; concern for

emotional adjustment, 533–35; personnel services for adults, 535; other factors of effectiveness, 536
Study habits or skills: relation to academic deficiencies, 312–13; improvement of, 490–91
Study of Values Test, 127
Subcultures of junior college students, 323–24
"Suburb Town," adolescents in, 70–71
Superstitions, 101–4
Survey of Mechanical Insight, 222
Survey-type courses, 440

TECHNICAL EDUCATION CURRICULUMS, 474
Technicians, suggested curriculums for engineering and industrial, 476–77
Televiewing: time spent in, 252–54; influence on other recreations, 254
Television. *See* Movies, radio, and television
Terminal occupational education: justification of, 470–71; two-pronged need for, 471–72; growth of terminal programs, 473–75; recommended directions of development, 476–77; cooperative and work-experience programs, 477–81; identifying employments requiring terminal programs, 481–82; a state-wide inquiry, 482–83
Tests and inventories, 514–17
Texas, University of, 107
Thorndike College Aptitude Test, 280
Thorndike Intelligence Examination, 49–50
Thurstone Test, 273
Transfer curriculums: dimensions, 483–84; range offered, 484–86
Transfers: success of, 301–2, 306–9; improving placement of, 530–33
Tuition: influence on socioeconomic democratization, 284–88; rates in public junior colleges, 288–89
Tulsa (Okla.) High School, 74

UNFOUNDED BELIEFS, 101–4
United States Department of Labor, 472
Universalization of post-high-school education: advocated by the Educational Policies Commission, 270; progress toward, in aptitude, 281–83; in socioeconomic status, 283–93
University College, University of Florida, 325
USAFI Tests of General Educational Development, 221
Utah State University, 221

VACO TEST, 41–42
Values, attitudes and, 95–113
Values, socioeconomic. *See* Socioeconomic values
Vassar College, 130
Ventura (Cal.) Junior College, 330
VISTA, 110
Vocational choices, variability and consistency of, 200–201
Vocational counseling, relation to educational counseling, 526–27
Vocational education. *See* Terminal occupational education
Vocational interest blanks and inventories: description, 210–11; reading difficulty of, 211; stability of measured interests, 211–16; relation to self-estimates and vocational choices, 216–18; other relationships, 218–24; usefulness, 225–26
Vocational interest scores in relation to: self-estimates and vocational choices, 216–18; ACE Psychological Examination, 218–19; school achievement, 218–22; other measures, 222–24; each other, 224–25
Vocational interests, relation to avocational interests, 258–60

Vocational preferences: and social mobility, 205–9. *See also* Occupational preferences and plans
Vocational-Technical Training, Committee on, 471
Voluntary reading: range of, 245; in books, 245–47; in magazines, 247–49; in newspapers, 249

WASHINGTON, D. C., 251
Washington Irving High School (New York City), 101
Wechsler-Bellevue Intelligence Scale, 47, 58, 403
Weight, increase in. *See* Height and weight
Wisconsin, University of, 538
Work Conference on Current Sex Mores, 177
Work-experience programs, 479–81
Worry Inventory, 351
Wrenn Study Habits Inventory, 312, 514
Writing, remedial programs in, 489

X-O TEST, Pressey, 97

YALE UNIVERSITY, 274, 489